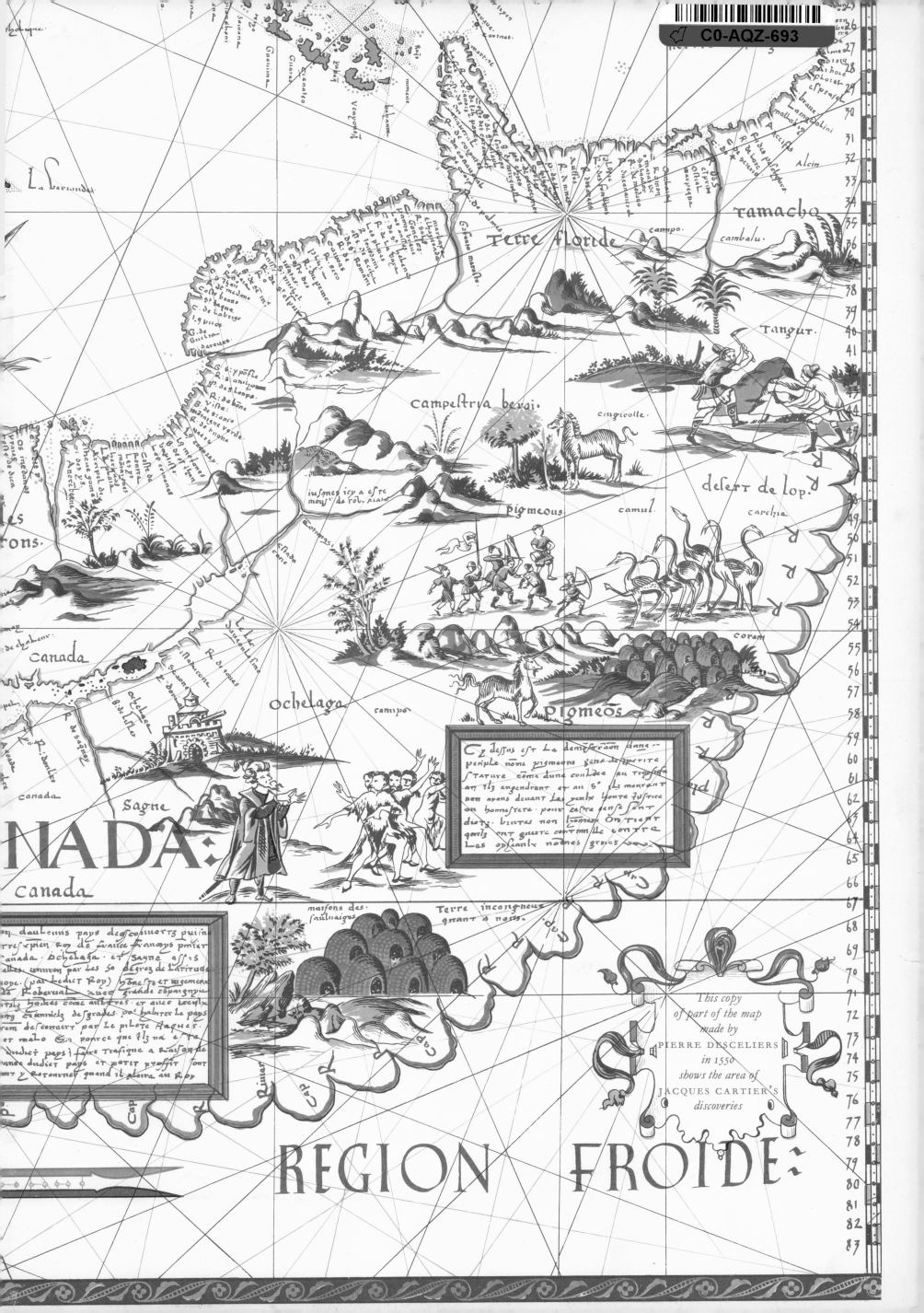

THE READER'S DIGEST

GREAT WORLD ATLAS

THE READER'S DIGEST ASSOCIATION

LONDON · SYDNEY · MONTREAL · CAPE TOWN

THE READER'S DIGEST GREAT WORLD ATLAS

Prepared and Published by The Reader's Digest Association Limited. Planned under the direction of the late

FRANK DEBENHAM

O.B.E., M.A., D.SC. (HON.), EMERITUS PROFESSOR OF GEOGRAPHY, CAMBRIDGE UNIVERSITY

The Reader's Digest expresses its gratitude to the following
who have generously contributed to and advised on the preparation of this Atlas:

Academy of Science of the U.S.S.R.

P. J. Adams, B.SC., PH.D., F.G.S., Institute of Geological Sciences

J. B. Allen, B.SC., PH.D., F.G.S., Institute of Geological Sciences

W. R. Aykroyd, C.B.E., M.D., SC.D.

John Bartholomew & Son Ltd.

Andrew Boyd, M.A.

British and Foreign Bible Society

British Broadcasting Corporation

British Medical Association

Maurice Burton, D.SC.

Canadian Department of Mines and Technical Services

Wm. Collins, Sons & Co. Ltd.

J. G. Cook, PH.D., F.R.I.C.

Department of National Health and Welfare
(Information Services), Ottawa

F. W. Dunning, B.SC., F.G.S., Institute of Geological Sciences

F. V. Emery, B.LITT., M.A.

Food and Agriculture Organization of the United Nations

General Register Office

Geographical Projects Ltd.

Madeleine Glemser, M.A.

Greater London Council

Michael Hart, M.A.

Cdr. H. R. Hatfield, R.N.

Information Service of India

Institute for Strategic Studies

B. Gyrth Jackson, M.SC., School of Agriculture,
University of Cambridge

E. A. Jobbins, B.SC., F.G.S., Institute of Geological Sciences

H. C. King, PH.D., M.SC., F.R.A.S., F.B.O.A.

H. A. G. Lewis, Esq., Directorate of Military Survey
(War Office and Air Ministry)

Lick Observatory

Longmans, Green & Co. Ltd.

N. B. Marshall, M.A., British Museum (Natural History)

R. J. Marston, B.SC., PH.D., F.G.S., Institute of Geological Sciences

Ministry of Agriculture, Fisheries and Food

Ministry of Health

The Rev. Vernon P. Mitchell

Patrick Moore, F.R.A.S., Director, Armagh Planetarium

Mount Wilson and Palomar Observatories

National Institute of Oceanography

B. M. Nichol, O.B.E., M.B., CH.B.,
Nutrition Adviser, Government of Nigeria

K. P. Oakley, D.SC., F.B.A., British Museum (Natural History)

Office of the South African High Commissioner

The Rev. E. G. Parrinder, M.A., PH.D., D.D., London University

E. Penkala, Esq.

The Polar Institute

The Rev. B. M. G. Reardon, M.A.

C. S. Roetter, LL.B.

C. A. Ronan, M.SC., F.R.A.S., Royal Society

Royal Geographical Society

Scientific Liaison Office, Australia, New Zealand, Canada

Scottish Office

Peter Small, Esq.

P. A. Smithson, B.SC., F.R.MET.S.

Robert Spencer, B.A., British Trust for Ornithology

United Nations, London Information Centre

B. B. Waddy, D.M., London School of Hygiene and Tropical Medicine

G. R. Wadsworth, M.D., London School of Hygiene and Tropical Medicine

The Wellcome Foundation Ltd.

The Wellcome Museum of Medical Science

Bernard Workman, M.A.

World Health Organization

Norman C. Wright, C.B., M.A., PH.D., D.SC., F.R.I.C., F.R.S.E., Deputy-
Director-General, Food and Agriculture Organization of the United Nations

Yerkes Observatory

Acknowledgment is also made to the numerous authors
and compilers of technical books and journals to which reference was made
in the preparation of this Atlas

CONTENTS

From the centre of the Earth

to the outermost limits of space

PARADISE IS SOMEWHERE IN THE FAR EAST. JERUSALEM IS THE CENTRE OF ALL NATIONS AND COUNTRIES, AND THE WORLD ITSELF IS A FLAT DISK SURROUNDED BY OCEANS OF WATER. So the monks, map-makers of the Middle Ages, saw the world they lived in.

Today, our knowledge of the world has increased through travel and exploration and scientific discovery. This Atlas has drawn on the sum of that knowledge—knowledge that has been accumulated through many life-times of research.

We look at THE FACE OF THE WORLD, starting with a view of our Earth in space. The following maps made from sculptured models show in relief how our world would appear to an observer at a point some hundred miles above the Earth's surface. The peaks of the great mountain ranges show in sharp contrast to the worn surfaces of older rocks and the flat plains formed by the great rivers. The levels of the ocean floor tell the history of submerged lands and of yet unexplored deeps. Here, a new dimension has been added to standard map-making.

Next come THE COUNTRIES OF THE WORLD. Towns and cities, rivers and railways can all be found easily, for the colouring is subdued and the text clear and definitive. Together with the relief maps they complete a picture of the landscape of our Earth and of the places where we live.

The third section portrays THE WORLD AS WE KNOW IT. Incurably inquisitive, man searches continually for knowledge about our world and about other worlds beyond. He now knows that he is only one of many forms of life on the thin crust of a planet revolving round the Sun—a minor star at the edge of the Milky Way. A multi-million starred galaxy, the Milky Way is itself only one among a million other galaxies moving in the black infinity of space where traditional concepts of north and south are meaningless.

It is a vision that dwarfs the globe on which we live and makes man seem very small; but it also gives him a new importance. For on this tiny planet life has been created and developed, and as yet we do not know whether the delicate balance of conditions which has made evolution possible on this planet has ever been repeated on any other.

The marvel of this creation cannot be told by any single map or chart. Each feature in the third section of this Atlas has been devised to illustrate a facet of it—our place in the universe, the mystery of our neighbours in space, the world beneath our feet, the evolution of life, the creatures around us, the growth and disappearance of civilizations, the beliefs of man, and his migrations. Each subject is linked to another: climate to cultivation, cultivation to food, food to health, for none of the world's problems can be seen in isolation. All are related to and interwoven with one another.

This Atlas, in presenting geographically the facts about Earth and life and space, also offers many pointers towards exploration in the future which lies before us.

THE EDITORS

SECTION ONE

THE FACE
OF
THE WORLD

CONTENTS

Pluto

Neptune

Uranus

Saturn

THE SUN AND ITS PLANETS—AS VIEWED FROM A POINT IN SPACE

THE Sun dominates and dwarfs its solar family of nine major planets and at least a thousand tiny planets called "asteroids". Jupiter, the Sun's largest dependent planet, is but a speck by comparison with it, and the volume of Jupiter is roughly 1,300 times that of Earth. The Sun contains over 99·87 per cent of the entire mass in our Solar System. Yet, despite their comparative smallness and the enormous distances of empty space that separate them from the Sun and from one another, the Sun keeps its planets under strict control.

Revolving round it continuously in elliptical orbits, these planets are held near the Sun by the pull of gravity, and kept from being drawn into it by the speed with which they move through space. The closer they are to the Sun, the faster they move. Mercury—at an average distance of 36 million miles, the planet nearest to the Sun—averages only 88 days to travel right round it, moving at a speed of nearly 30 miles a second. The Earth, whose average distance from the Sun is 93 million miles, needs exactly one year to complete its orbit, travelling at a speed of 18·5 miles per second, or roughly 66,600 miles per hour. Pluto, the most distant known planet, about 3,666 million miles from the Sun, takes just over 248 years at a speed of a mere three miles a second to make one journey round it.

Moving at different speeds, in separate orbits, and at varying distances from the Sun, the planets, as viewed from the Earth

which is itself moving, *appear* to be changing constantly in size and brightness. Venus, well known as the Morning Star or Evening Star, comes as close to the Earth as about 25·5 million miles, and goes as far away as 160 million miles.

Life as we know it cannot exist on any other planet in our Solar System. Mercury is so close to the Sun that the temperature on its sunlit side is estimated to be of the order of 400°C. Venus, about twice as far from the Sun as Mercury is roughly 25 million miles closer to it than the Earth, and probably has a maximum surface temperature of 440°C. Of the planets farther than Earth from the Sun, Jupiter, Saturn (its semi-transparent rings made up of fine particles, dense enough to throw a shadow over the planet's surface), Uranus, Neptune and Pluto are all too cold, and their atmospheres

THE SOLAR SYSTEM

Jupiter

Mars

Earth

Mercury

Venus

SUN

contain high concentrations of poisonous gases—helium, hydrogen, methane and ammonia. Some form of life is thought to exist on Mars, but, to live in the planet's thin, icy air, is probably a form of primitive vegetation.

The Earth is the only member of our Sun's family known to support living creatures. Alone among the planets in the Solar System—though not perhaps among those belonging to the millions of sun-like stars in the Universe—the Earth's composition and distance from the Sun seem to have provided exactly the right conditions in which evolution to an advanced form of life could develop.

The life-giving energy of the Sun, the source of all the heat and light in our Solar System, is generated by nuclear reactions in its interior, which raise the temperature deep inside it to about 14 million degrees Centigrade. So tremendous is the radiation rate of the Sun's energy, that it loses some four million tons in weight every second. Yet, despite this rate of loss, it is estimated that the Sun will survive as a source of energy for at least another 8,000 million years.

DISTANCE OF PLANETS FROM EARTH (IN MILES)

	MOON	MARS	URANUS
Maximum	253,000	247,000,000	1,946,000,000
Minimum	222,000	34,000,000	1,594,000,000
	MERCURY	JUPITER	NEPTUNE
Maximum	136,900,000	597,000,000	2,891,000,000
Minimum	49,100,000	362,000,000	2,654,000,000
	VENUS	SATURN	PLUTO
Maximum	160,900,000	1,023,000,000	4,506,000,000
Minimum	25,700,000	773,000,000	2,605,000,000

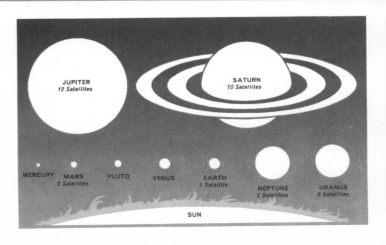

JUPITER
12 Satellites

SATURN
10 Satellites

MERCURY   MARS
2 Satellites

PLUTO   VENUS   EARTH
1 Satellite

NEPTUNE
2 Satellites

URANUS
5 Satellites

SUN

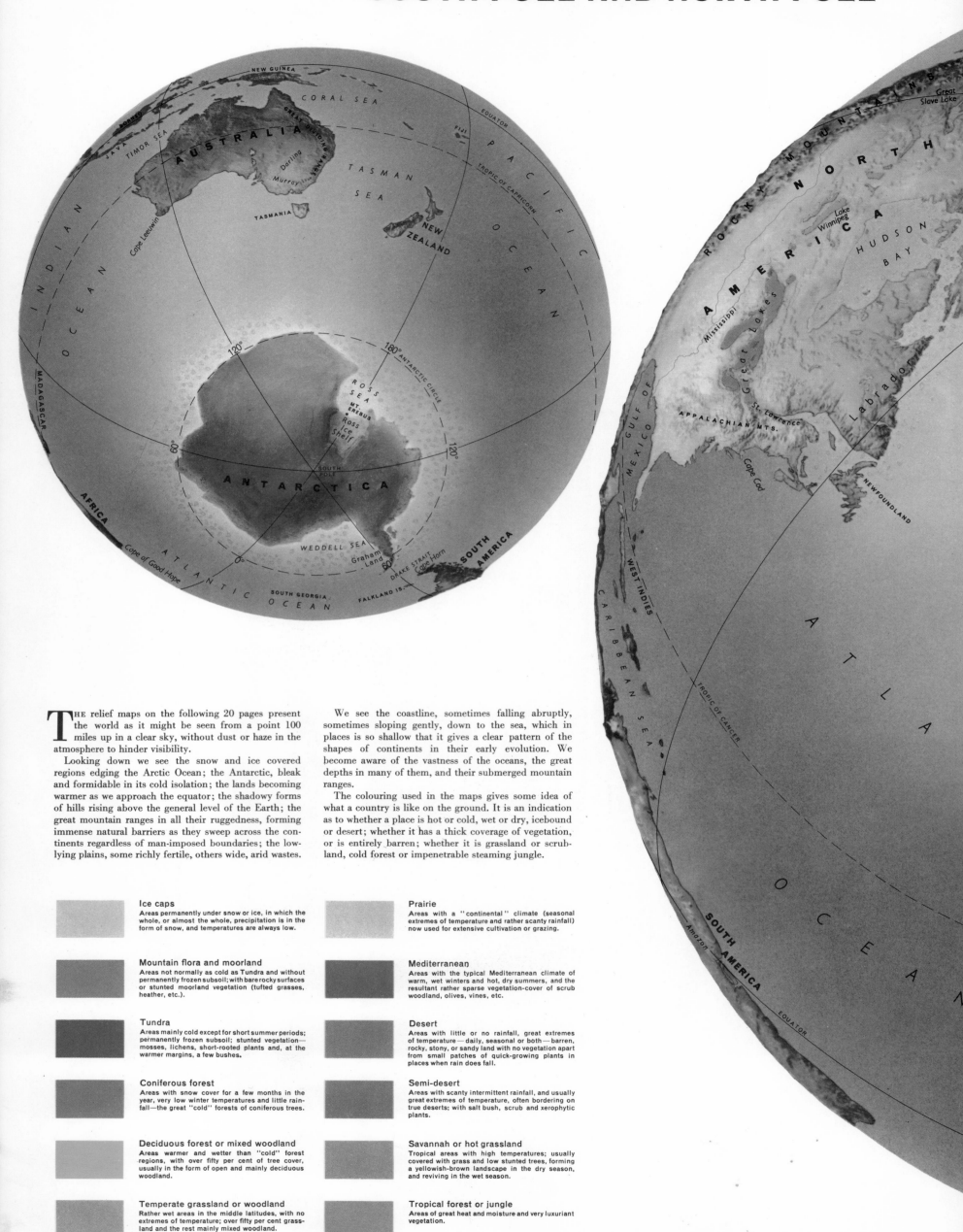

THE relief maps on the following 20 pages present the world as it might be seen from a point 100 miles up in a clear sky, without dust or haze in the atmosphere to hinder visibility.

Looking down we see the snow and ice covered regions edging the Arctic Ocean; the Antarctic, bleak and formidable in its cold isolation; the lands becoming warmer as we approach the equator; the shadowy forms of hills rising above the general level of the Earth; the great mountain ranges in all their ruggedness, forming immense natural barriers as they sweep across the continents regardless of man-imposed boundaries; the low-lying plains, some richly fertile, others wide, arid wastes.

We see the coastline, sometimes falling abruptly, sometimes sloping gently, down to the sea, which in places is so shallow that it gives a clear pattern of the shapes of continents in their early evolution. We become aware of the vastness of the oceans, the great depths in many of them, and their submerged mountain ranges.

The colouring used in the maps gives some idea of what a country is like on the ground. It is an indication as to whether a place is hot or cold, wet or dry, icebound or desert; whether it has a thick coverage of vegetation, or is entirely barren; whether it is grassland or scrubland, cold forest or impenetrable steaming jungle.

Ice caps
Areas permanently under snow or ice, in which the whole, or almost the whole, precipitation is in the form of snow, and temperatures are always low.

Mountain flora and moorland
Areas not normally as cold as Tundra and without permanently frozen subsoil; with bare rocky surfaces or stunted moorland vegetation (tufted grasses, heather, etc.).

Tundra
Areas mainly cold except for short summer periods; permanently frozen subsoil; stunted vegetation—mosses, lichens, short-rooted plants and, at the warmer margins, a few bushes.

Coniferous forest
Areas with snow cover for a few months in the year, very low winter temperatures and little rainfall—the great "cold" forests of coniferous trees.

Deciduous forest or mixed woodland
Areas warmer and wetter than "cold" forest regions, with over fifty per cent of tree cover, usually in the form of open and mainly deciduous woodland.

Temperate grassland or woodland
Rather wet areas in the middle latitudes, with no extremes of temperature; over fifty per cent grassland and the rest mainly mixed woodland.

Prairie
Areas with a "continental" climate (seasonal extremes of temperature and rather scanty rainfall) now used for extensive cultivation or grazing.

Mediterranean
Areas with the typical Mediterranean climate of warm, wet winters and hot, dry summers, and the resultant rather sparse vegetation-cover of scrub woodland, olives, vines, etc.

Desert
Areas with little or no rainfall, great extremes of temperature—daily, seasonal or both—barren, rocky, stony, or sandy land with no vegetation apart from small patches of quick-growing plants in places when rain does fall.

Semi-desert
Areas with scanty intermittent rainfall, and usually great extremes of temperature, often bordering on true deserts; with salt bush, scrub and xerophytic plants.

Savannah or hot grassland
Tropical areas with high temperatures; usually covered with grass and low stunted trees, forming a yellowish-brown landscape in the dry season, and reviving in the wet season.

Tropical forest or jungle
Areas of great heat and moisture and very luxuriant vegetation.

ALEUTIAN ISLANDS

BERING SEA   Kamchatka

BERING
STRAIT   180°   SEA OF OKHOTSK

Mackenzie   BEAUFORT
SEA   A R C T I C

ke   120°   O C E A N   NOVOSIBIRSKIYE
OSTROVA   Lena   120°   Baykal

NORTH POLE   Yenisey

BAFFIN BAY   Zapadno-   Sibirskaya   Ob'

ELLESMERE ISLAND   SVALBARD   NOVAYA   BARENTS   Nizmennost'

ISLAND   GREENLAND   ZEMLYA   SEA   URAL'SKIY KHREBET   Ozero   Tarim
Balkhash   Basin   Tibetan

80°   80°   Onezhskoye   Plateau

DAVIS
STRAIT   ARCTIC CIRCLE   NORWEGIAN   0°   Oz.   ARALSKOYE   PAMIRS

Farewell   ICELAND   SEA   Lodozhskoye   MORE

Oz.   Volga   CASPIAN SEA

BRITISH   NORTH   SEA   Plateau of Iran   Deccan
ISLES   SEA   BALTIC SEA   KAVKAZ

E U R O P E S   Danube   BLACK SEA   A

Cape Finisterre   A L P S   Euphrates   PERSIAN GULF

PYRENEES   Arabian   SEA

T I C   Peninsula

STRAIT OF GIBRALTAR   MEDITERRANEAN SEA   RED   SEA

ATLAS MOUNTAINS   Nile

CANARY
ISLANDS

AHAGGAR   TIBESTI   A

S a h a r a

Cape Verde

Lake Chad

A   Niger   F   R   I   C   Lake
Victoria

Congo

GULF OF GUINEA

9

EURASIA

ARCTIC OCEAN

SEVERNAYA ZEMLYA

Mys Chelyuskin

Poluostrov Taymyr

Gory Byrranga

Ozero Taymyr

NOVOSIBIRSKIYE OSTROVA

LAPTEV SEA

EAST SIBERIAN SEA

O. VRANGELYA

ST. LAWRENCE I. (U.S.A.)

Mys Navarin

60°

CHUKOTSKIY KHREBET

Nordvik

Tiksi

Khatanga

Khsto

•Igarka

Yenisey

Sredne

Sibirskoye

Ploskogor'ye

Nizhnyaya Tunguska

Yana

Verkhoyansk

Sredne Kolymsk

Sylgy Ytar

Kolyma

KHREBET CHERSKOGO

Indigirka

Anadyr

Nizhniye Kresty

ARCTIC CIRCLE

KORYAKSKIY KHREBET

KOMANDORSKIYE OSTROVA

BERING SEA

180°

Vilyuy

Vilyuysk

Yakutsk

VERKHOYANSKIY KHREBET

Lena

Olekminsk

Aldan

Okhotsk

Magadan

Nikolayevsk

KHR. DZHUGDZHUR

SEA OF OKHOTSK

Petropavlovsk Kamchatskiy

Mys Lopatka

160°

Kamchatka

KURIL'SKIYE OSTROVA

•Tomsk

•Krasnoyarsk

vosibirsk

op'yevsk •Novokuznetsk

Barnaul

Ob'

Kyzyl

TANNU OLA

Tulun

Angara

Ozero Baykal

Ulan Ude

Kirensk

SEVERO-BAYKAL'SKOYE NAGORYE

STANOVOY KHREBET

YABLONOVYY KHREBET

Vitim

Chita

Shilka

Amur

SIAO HINGAN LING

TA HINGAN LING

Sungari

Khabarovsk

Amur

TATARSKIY PROLIV

SAKHALIN

LA PEROUSE STRAIT

Otaru Sapporo

HOKKAIDO Kushiro Hakodate

SOCIALIST REPUBLICS

Irkutsk

Kyakhta

Selenga

Kerulen

Manchouli

Hulun Chih

Manchuria

Harbin

Ozero Khanka

Vladivostok

SIKHOTE ALIN

TSUGARU KAIKYO

SEA OF JAPAN

40°

ALTAI

LUKHA 14,784

Ubsa Nor

Jirgalanta

Jibhalanta

Koso Gol

Ulan Bator

MONGOLIA

Gobi

Changchun

Shenyang

Liao

KOREA

An-tung Hungnam

Kwantung Pen. P'yongyang

Seoul

Inch'on

Pusan

Niigata

SADO-SHIMA

Tokyo Yokohama

Kyoto Nagoya

Kobe Osaka

Kochi

SHIKOKU

HONSHU

JAPAN

zungaria

Urumchi

Turfan

SINKIANG

Tarim

Lop Nor

•Ansi

ALTYN TAGH

NAN SHAN

Tsaidam

Ch'ing Hai

Changyeh

Lanchow

Changkiakow

Hwang Ho

Ordos

Paoting

Taiyuan

Peking

Tientsin

PO-HAI WAN

Talien

Tsinan

SHANTUNG PEN.

YELLOW SEA

CHEJU-DO

Fukuoka

Hiroshima

Nagasaki

KYUSHU

Kagoshima

Kobe

RYUKYU RETTO

KUN LUN SHAN

kan

Tibetan

Plateau

Tsaidam

MIN SHAN

Sian

CHINA

Loyang Kaifeng

Suchow

CH'IN LING SHAN

Wuhan

Anking

Nanking

Yangtze Kiang

Shanghai

Hangchow

EAST CHINA SEA

TROPIC OF CANCER

HIMALAYA RANGE

MT. EVEREST 29,028 MT. MAKALU

KANGCHEN JUNGA

SIKKIM

BHUTAN

Darjeeling

Lhasa

Brahmaputra

NAMCHA BARWA

Yangtze Kiang

Kialing

MINYA KONKA 24,900

Paan

Ipin

Red Basin

Chengtu

Ichang

Chungking

Po-yang Hu

Tung-T'ing Hu

Changsha

Nanchang

Hengyang

Changsha

Wenchow

Foochow

Hong Kong (Br.)

PACIFIC OCEAN

Kunming

Patna

Ganga

Shillong

KHASI HILLS

Silchar

Katmandu

NAGA HILLS

BURMA

Myitkyina

Tali

Paoshan

Salween

Mekong

Brahmaputra

NAN LING

Kwelyang

Kanchow

Changting

Amoy

Swatow

Canton

Si-Kiang

Hong Kong (Br.)

TAIWAN

STRAIT OF FORMOSA

Tainan

Taipei

20°

120°

100°

11

THE BRITISH ISLES

REPUBLIC OF IRELAND
NORTHERN IRELAND
ENGLAND
WALES
FRANCE
ATLANTIC OCEAN
ENGLISH CHANNEL
IRISH SEA
NORTH CHANNEL
ST. GEORGE'S CHANNEL
BRISTOL CHANNEL
STRAIT OF DOVER
CARDIGAN BAY
GALWAY BAY
DONEGAL BAY
SLIGO BAY
DINGLE BAY
BANTRY BAY
LYME BAY
THE WASH
SOLWAY FIRTH
ISLE OF MAN
ISLE OF WIGHT
ISLES OF SCILLY
ANGLESEY
ARAN ISLANDS
ACHILL ISLAND
LUNDY
ALDERNEY
Dublin
Belfast
Cork
Limerick
Galway
Waterford
Wexford
Wicklow
Arklow
Dun Laoghaire
Drogheda
Dundalk
Newry
Armagh
Lisburn
Londonderry
Coleraine
Ballymena
Antrim
Larne
Downpatrick
Portadown
Cookstown
Dungannon
Omagh
Strabane
Enniskillen
Donegal
Ballyshannon
Sligo
Boyle
Roscommon
Ballina
Castlebar
Athlone
Longford
Mullingar
Kells
Navan
Cavan
Tullamore
Port Laoighise
Athy
Kildare
Carlow
Kilkenny
Thurles
Nenagh
Tipperary
Clonmel
Dungarvan
Youghal
Lismore
Fermoy
Cobh
Ennis
Listowel
Tralee
Killarney
Bantry
Dingle
Mizen Head
Cape Clear
Fastnet Rock
Dursey Head
Achill Head
Carnsore Pt.
Hook Head
Tuskar Rock
Wicklow Head
London
Birmingham
Manchester
Liverpool
Leeds
Sheffield
Bristol
Newcastle
Gateshead
Sunderland
South Shields
Durham
Hexham
Carlisle
Penrith
Kendal
Lancaster
Preston
Blackpool
Fleetwood
Barrow
Whitehaven
Workington
Keswick
Dumfries
Kirkcudbright
Wigtown
Stranraer
Douglas
Ramsey
Middlesbrough
West Hartlepool
Stockton on Tees
Darlington
Northallerton
Whitby
Scarborough
York
Hull
Goole
Harrogate
Ripon
Bradford
Halifax
Huddersfield
Burnley
Blackburn
Bolton
Wigan
St. Helens
Oldham
Stockport
Doncaster
Rotherham
Chesterfield
Buxton
Derby
Nottingham
Lincoln
Grantham
Newark
Louth
Grimsby
Boston
Skegness
Kings Lynn
Norwich
Great Yarmouth
Lowestoft
Cromer
Bury St. Edmunds
Ipswich
Harwich
Clacton
Colchester
Southend-on-Sea
Cambridge
Ely
Peterborough
Stamford
Leicester
Coventry
Rugby
Warwick
Northampton
Bedford
Buckingham
Luton
St. Albans
Hertford
Aylesbury
Oxford
Reading
Windsor
Swindon
Gloucester
Worcester
Hereford
Kidderminster
Wolverhampton
Stratford on Avon
Shrewsbury
Stoke on Trent
Crewe
Chester
Birkenhead
Oswestry
Wrexham
Welshpool
Rhyl
Denbigh
Colwyn Bay
Conway
Bangor
Beaumaris
Caernarvon
Holyhead
Harlech
Dolgellau
Aberystwyth
Cardigan
Fishguard
St. Davids
Pembroke
Carmarthen
Swansea
Neath
Merthyr Tydfil
Rhondda
Ebbw Vale
Cardiff
Barry
Newport
Monmouth
Bath
Weston super Mare
Bridgwater
Taunton
Yeovil
Dorchester
Weymouth
Poole
Bournemouth
Salisbury
Winchester
Southampton
Portsmouth
Chichester
Brighton
Eastbourne
Hastings
Guildford
Croydon
Greenwich
Tilbury
Chatham
Maidstone
Tunbridge Wells
Canterbury
Margate
Ramsgate
Dover
Folkestone
Barnstaple
Exeter
Torquay
Plymouth
Launceston
Bodmin
Truro
Falmouth
Penzance
Land's End
Lizard Point
Start Point
Hartland Point
Eddystone Rocks
Portland Bill
Selsey Bill
Beachy Head
Dungeness
Spurn Head
Flamborough Head
Boulogne
Dieppe
Cherbourg
C. de la Hague
Cowes
Newport
The Needles
Salisbury Plain
The Weald
Vale of Kent
Vale of Sussex
Fens
Cheshire Plain
Vale of York
Lincoln Wolds
Lincoln Edge
Yorkshire Wolds
Charnwood Forest
Cannock Chase
COTSWOLD HILLS
CHILTERN HILLS
NORTH DOWNS
SOUTH DOWNS
MENDIP HILLS
MALVERN HILLS
CLENT HILLS
PENNINES
THE PEAK
CAMBRIAN MTS.
WICKLOW MTS.
Dartmoor
Exmoor
Bodmin Moors
Bog of Allen
PLYNLIMON
CADER IDRIS
SNOWDON
Thames
Severn
Trent
Ouse
Shannon
Lough Neagh
Lough Derg
Lough Corrib
Lough Mask
Lough Conn
Liffey
Boyne
Barrow
Suir
Nore
Slaney
Blackwater
Lee
Suck
Bann
Foyle
Erne
Avon
Wye
Usk
Tamar
Exe
Parrett
Test
Kennet
Cherwell
Nene
Welland
Witham
Humber
Tees
Tyne
Eden
Mersey
Dee
Ribble
Lune
Aire
Wharfe
Derwent
Stour
Yare
Cam
Lea
2°
0°
2°
4°
6°
8°
10°
50°
52°
54°
Miles

CANADA

ARCTIC OCEAN

BEAUFORT SEA

PACIFIC OCEAN

U.S.S.R.

CHUKOTSKIY ARCTIC CHREBET

O. VRANGELYA

CHUKCHI SEA

Cape Lisburne

Point Barrow

PRINCE PATRICK ISLAND

QUEEN ELIZ

SVERDR

BATHURST ISLAND

PARRY ISLANDS

MELVILLE ISLAND

VISCOUNT MELVILLE SOUND

PRINCE O

WALE

ISLAND

BANKS ISLAND

VICTORIA ISLAND

BERING STRAIT

Mys Dezhneva

KOTZEBUE SOUND

Noorvik

BROOKS RANGE

Cape Bathurst

AMUNDSEN GULF

ST. LAWRENCE I. (U.S.A.)

Nome

Seward Pen.

Yukon

Tanana

Fort Yukon

Aklavik

CORONATION GULF

NORTON SOUND

Holy Cross

Fairbanks

Circle

Eagle

Fort Good Hope

Coppermine

Bathurst Inlet

BRISTOL BAY

Iliamna Lake

MT. McKINLEY 20,300

ALASKA RANGE

MT. SANFORD 16,208

Dawson

Norman Wells

Great Bear Lake

Port Radium

Dupuwn Lake

Alaska Peninsula

COOK INLET

Anchorage

Kenai Pen.

Seward

Fort Selkirk

SELKIRK RANGE

AFOGNAKI.

Kodiak

KODIAK I.

GULF OF ALASKA

Cordova

LOGAN 19,850

ST. ELIAS RANGE

Whitehorse

Fort Simpson

Fort Providence

Hay River

Yellowknife

Great Slave Lake

Fort Smith

Mackenzie

Skagway

Juneau

ROCKY

CARIBOU MTS

Slave

Uranium City

ALEXANDER ARCHIPELAGO

Sitka

SHANE MTS.

Peace

Lake Athabasca

Fort Chipewyan

Athabasca

Reindeer Lake

DIXON ENTRANCE

Prince Rupert

Skeena

Peace River

Fort McMurray

QUEEN CHARLOTTE ISLANDS

Kitimat

Prince George

MOUNTAINS

Lesser Slave Lake

Grande Prairie

C A N A D A

Beauval

Flin Flon

HECATE STR.

Fraser

MT. ROBSON 12,972

Yellowhead Pass

Edmonton

Prince Albert

The Pas

QUEEN CHARLOTTE SOUND

Cape Scott

COAST RANGE

Kicking Horse Pass

N. Battleford

Saskatoon

North Saskatchewan

Lake Winnipegosis

VANCOUVER ISLAND

MT. WASHINGTON

Kamloops

Banff

Calgary

Hanna

South Saskatchewan

Yorkton

Assiniboine

Vancouver

Nelson

Fernie

Medicine Hat

Swift Current

Regina

Moose Jaw

JUAN DE FUCA STRAIT

Cape Flattery

Victoria

PUGET SOUND

Trail

Lethbridge

Weyburn

Brando

MT. OLYMPUS 7,955

Seattle

Tacoma

Cote

Olympia

Grand Coulee Dam

Spokane

Fort Peck Reservoir

Missouri

Minot

Garrison Reservoir

Portland

Columbia

Columbia

BITTERROOT

Helena

Great Falls

CASCADE RANGE

Salem

BLUE MTS.

Plateau

Butte

BEARTOOTH

Billings

Yellowstone

Cabo Blanco

Sage Plains

SALMON RIVER MTS.

Boise

Wind River MTS.

BIG HORN MTS.

Lead

Rapid City

Klamath Falls

U N I T E D

Snake

Twin Falls

BLACK HILLS

Eureka

Cape Mendocino

MT. SHASTA 14,162

S T A T E S

Great Salt Lake

D

North Platte

100 0 100 200 300 400 500 Miles

16

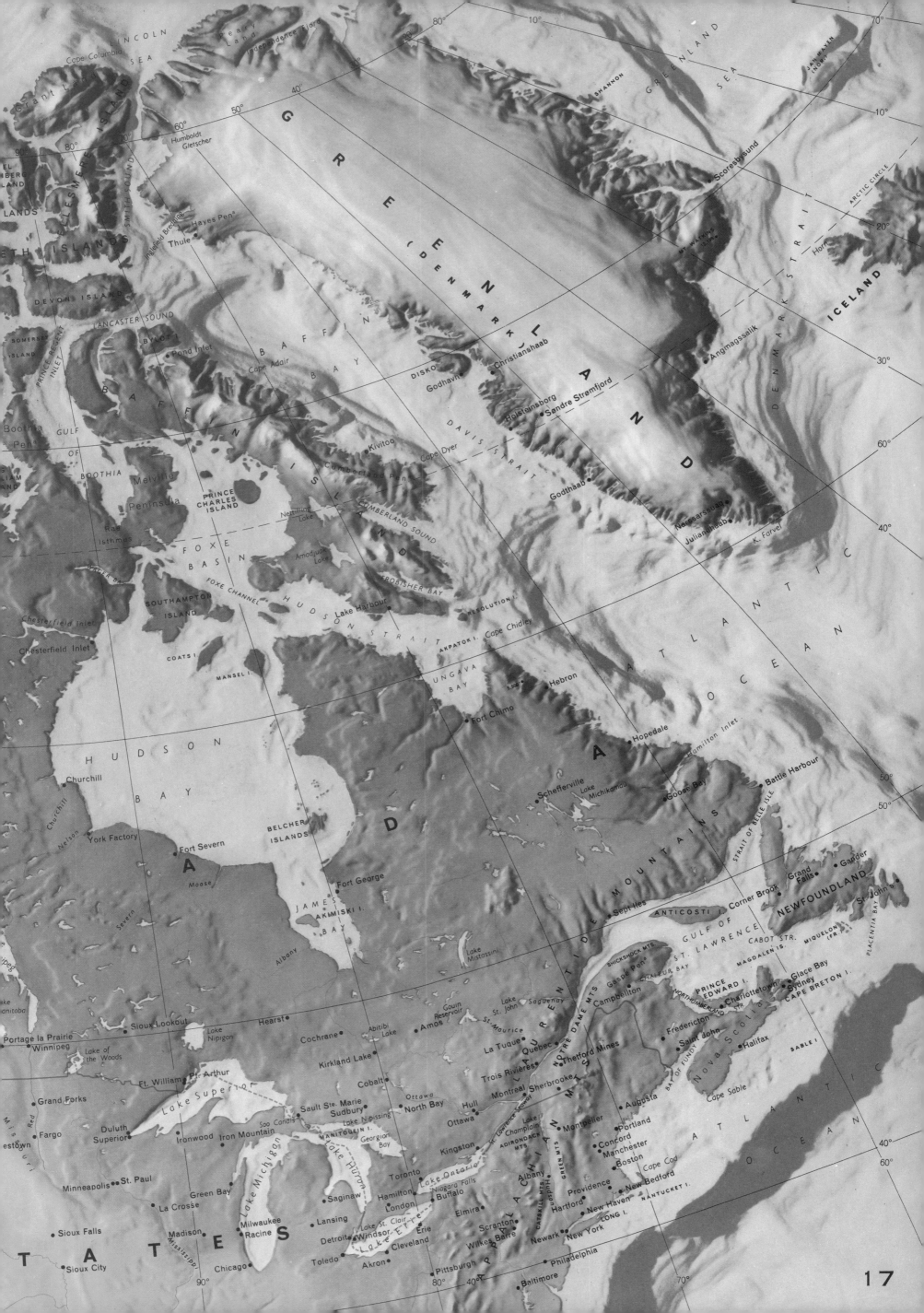

UNITED STATES
OF AMERICA
AND MEXICO

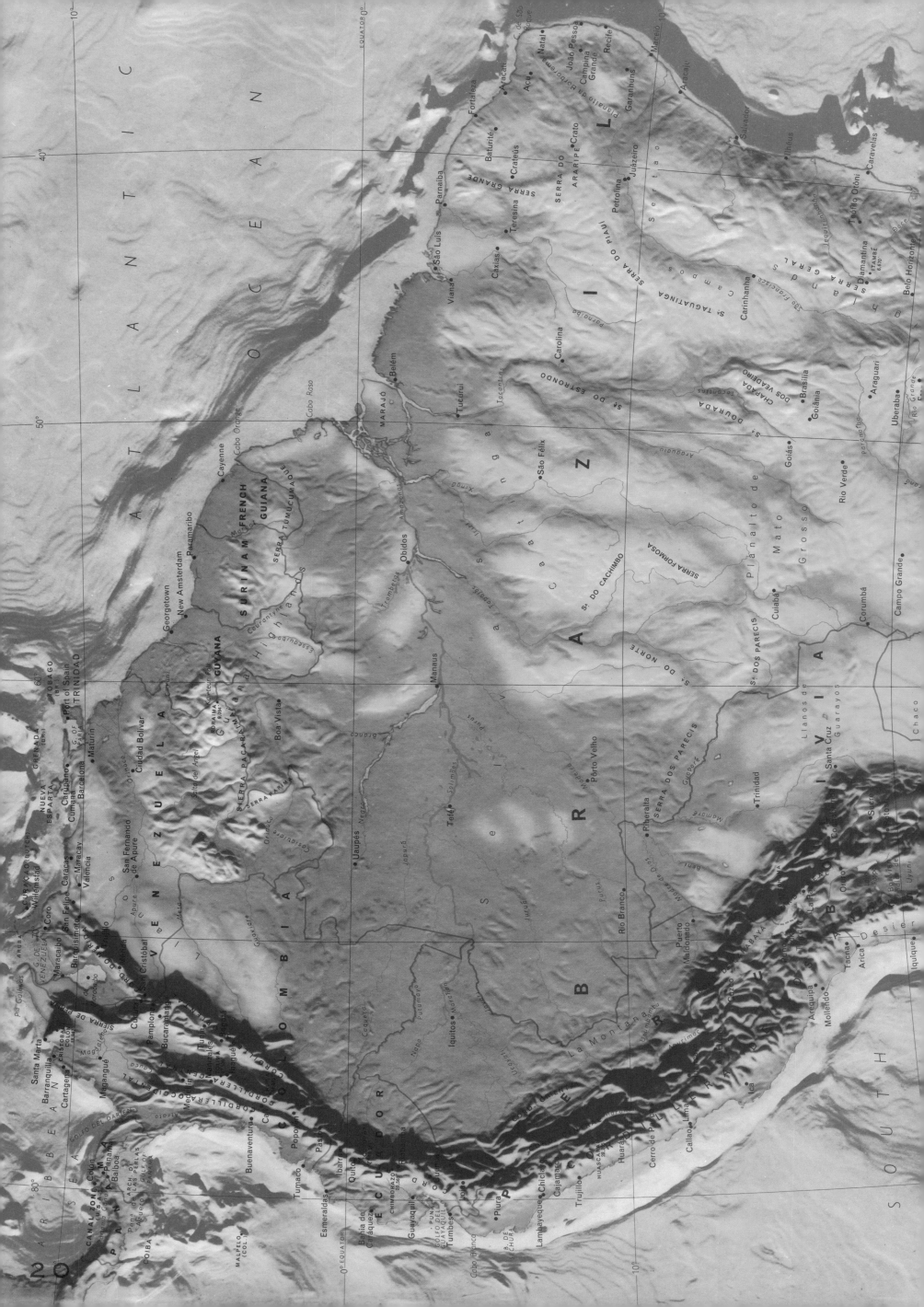

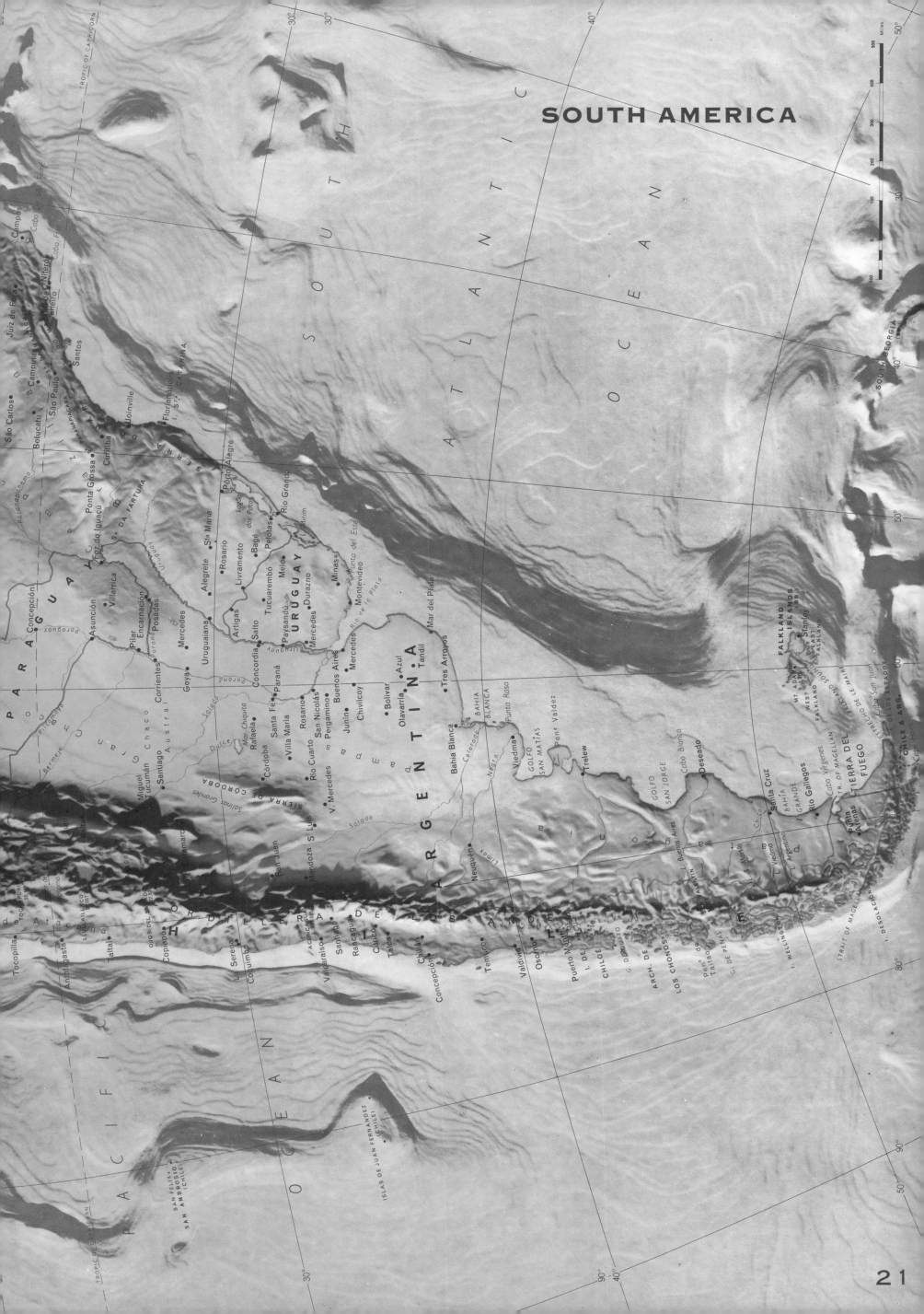

SOUTH AMERICA

SOUTH ATLANTIC OCEAN

PACIFIC OCEAN

ARGENTINA

URUGUAY

PARAGUAY

CHILE

BRAZIL

TIERRA DEL FUEGO

FALKLAND ISLANDS

SOUTH GEORGIA

Buenos Aires

Montevideo

Asunción

Santiago

Córdoba

Rosario

Bahía Blanca

CORDILLERA DE LOS ANDES

STRAIT OF MAGELLAN

Punta Arenas

21

AUSTRALASIA

THE FAR EAST

24

NORTHERN AFRICA

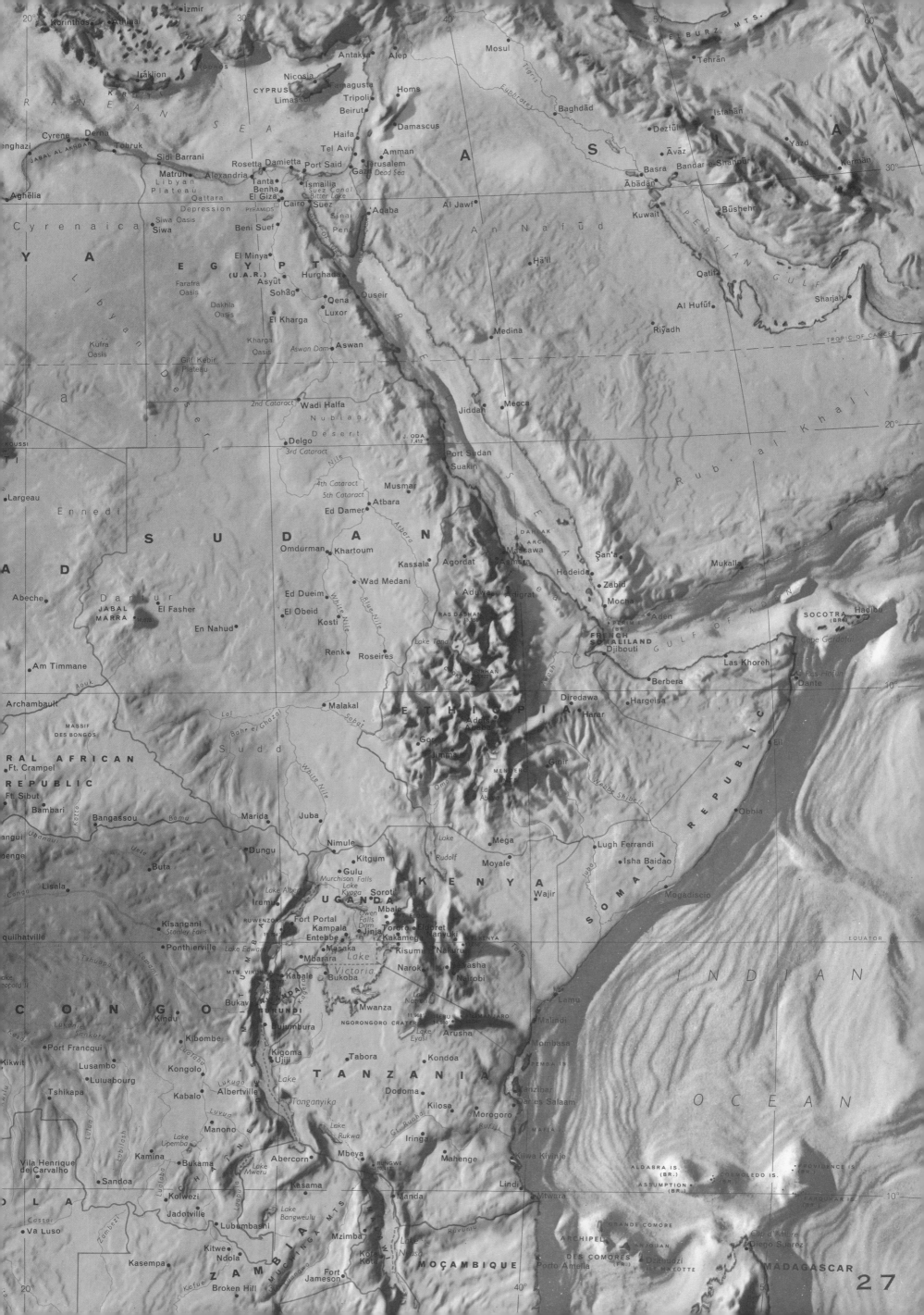

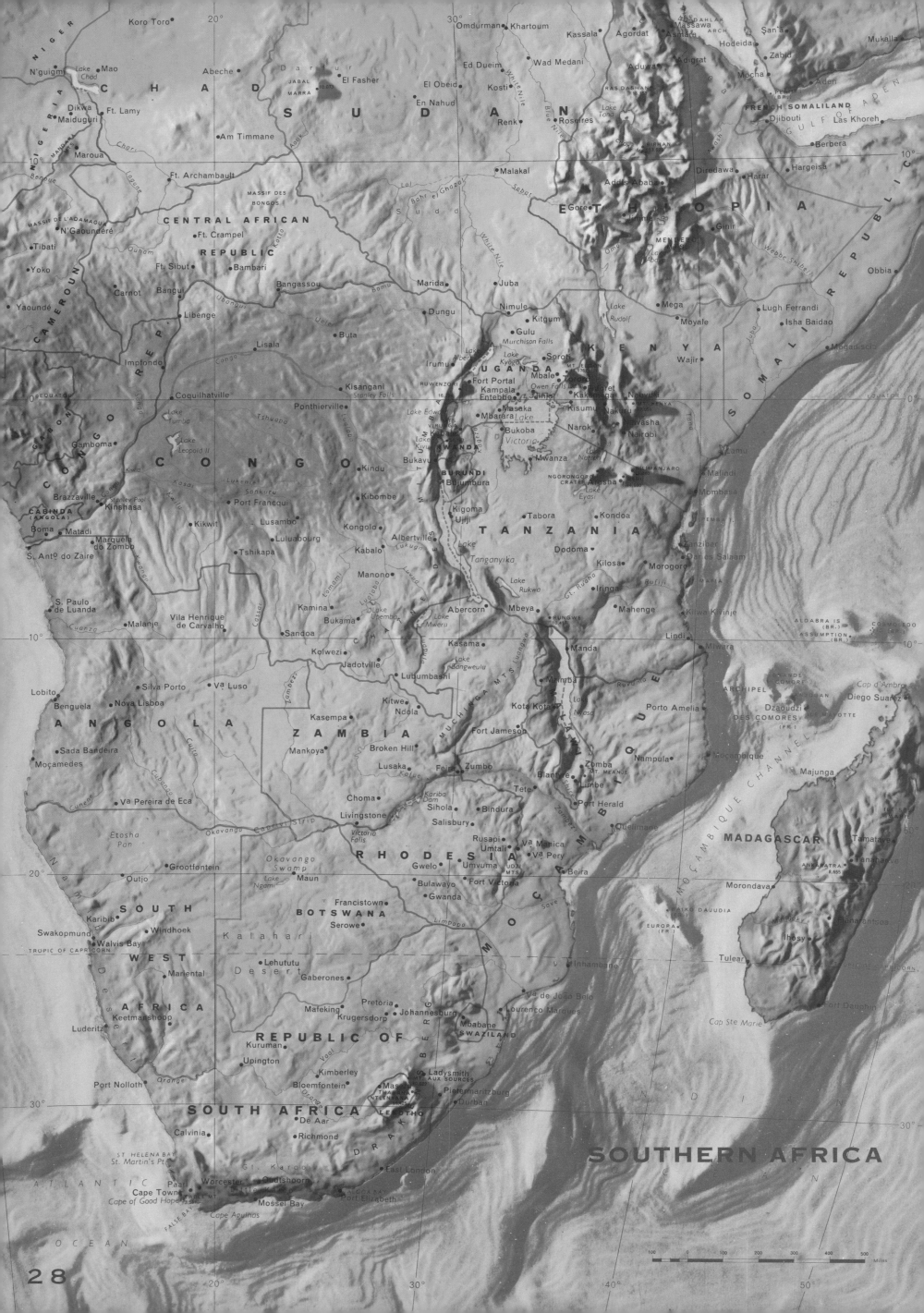

SOUTHERN AFRICA

28

THE COUNTRIES OF THE WORLD

CONTENTS

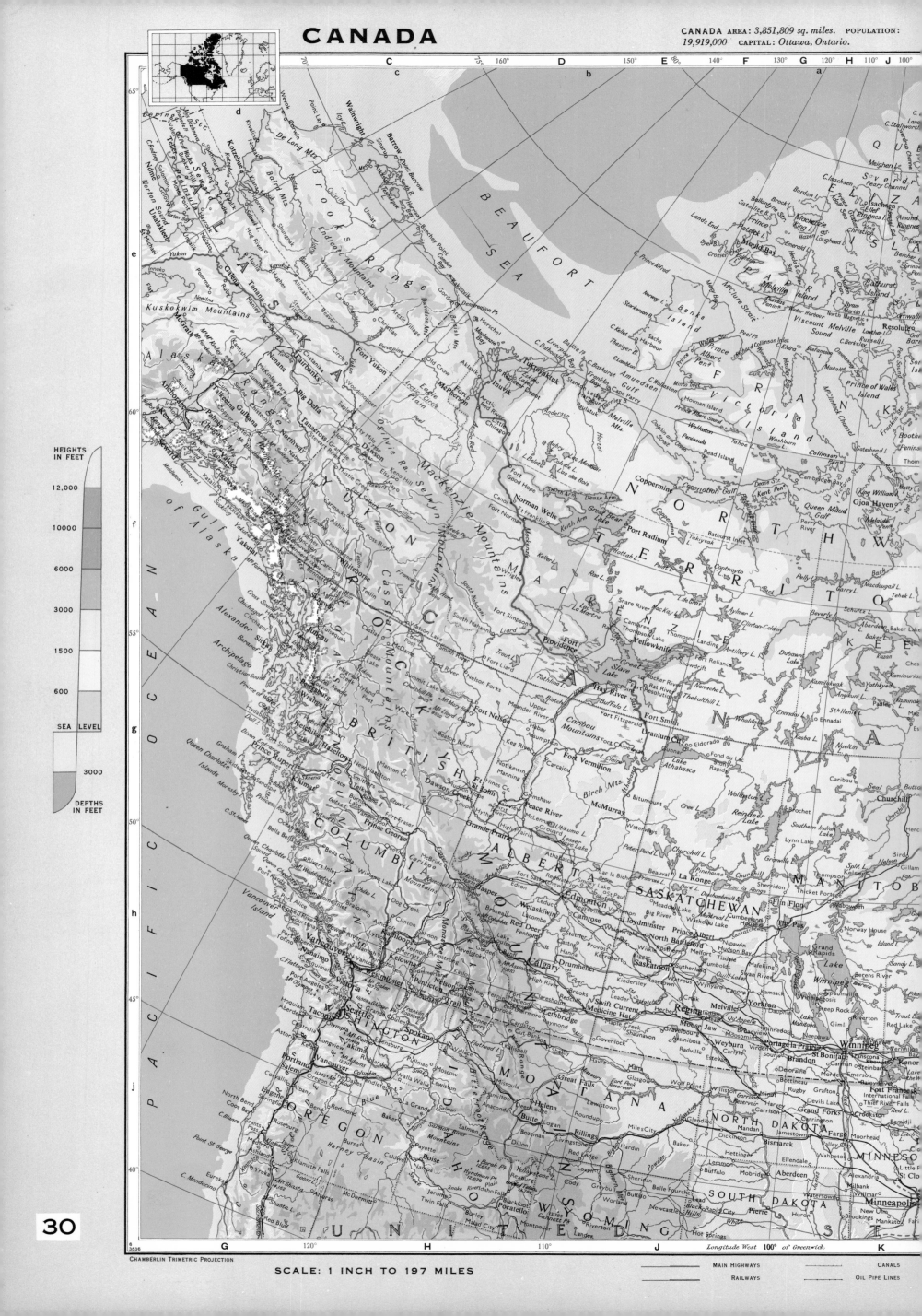

CANADA

CANADA AREA: 3,851,809 sq. miles. POPULATION: 19,919,000 CAPITAL: Ottawa, Ontario.

SCALE: 1 INCH TO 197 MILES

CHAMBERLIN TRIMETRIC PROJECTION

30

Canada, the world's second largest country after Russia, 5,780 miles at its widest and bordering the United States for 3,986 miles, comprises a massive central upland or great Shield, surrounded by inner flanking lowlands and outer marginal mountains. The Shield covers nearly half the country and is increasingly a source of mineral wealth.

SCALE IN MILES

SCALE: 1 INCH TO 197 MILES

© JOHN BARTHOLOMEW & SON LTD.

INTERNATIONAL BOUNDARIES
PROVINCE AND STATE BOUNDARIES
SWAMP AND FLOOD AREAS
GLACIERS AND ICECAPS
SPOT HEIGHTS IN FEET   9750

Rimming the Atlantic, is a succession of
mountain arcs with highlands and lowlands

HEIGHTS
IN FEET

3000

1500

600

300

SEA LEVEL

600

3000

DEPTHS
IN FEET

32

CONIC PROJECTION

SCALE: 1 INCH TO 47 MILES

ARTERIAL ROADS
OTHER MAIN ROADS
TRACKS
RAILWAYS
MAIN CIVIL AIRPORTS

LABRADOR

NEWFOUNDLAND

ATLANTIC OCEAN

GULF OF ST. LAWRENCE

CABOT STRAIT

CAPE BRETON ISLAND

NOVA SCOTIA

SAINT-PIERRE & MIQUELON
(To France)

PLACENTIA BAY

St. John's

Corner Brook

Gander

Sydney

SABLE ISLAND BANK

SCALE IN MILES

INTERNATIONAL BOUNDARIES
PROVINCIAL BOUNDARIES
SWAMP AND FLOOD AREAS
SPOT HEIGHTS IN FEET   △ 3700

SCALE: 1 INCH TO 47 MILES

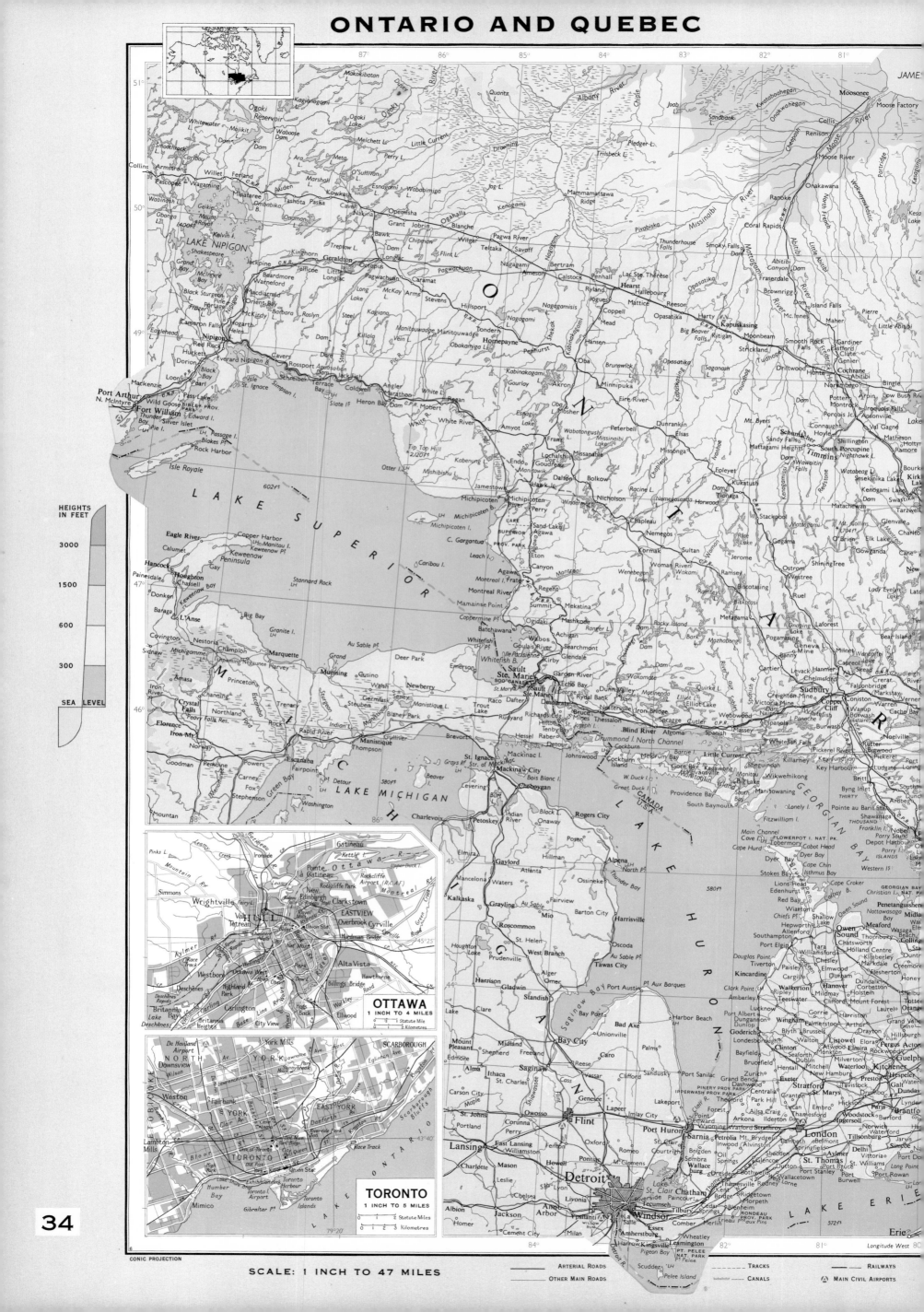

ONTARIO AND QUEBEC

HEIGHTS IN FEET

3000
1500
600
300
SEA LEVEL

LAKE SUPERIOR

LAKE NIPIGON

LAKE MICHIGAN

LAKE HURON

GEORGIAN BAY

LAKE ONTARIO

LAKE ERIE

JAMES

OTTAWA
1 INCH TO 4 MILES

Statute Mile
Kilometres

HULL

TORONTO
1 INCH TO 5 MILES

Statute Miles

Kilometres

Detroit

Windsor

34

CONIC PROJECTION

SCALE: 1 INCH TO 47 MILES

ARTERIAL ROADS ———— TRACKS ———— RAILWAYS ————
OTHER MAIN ROADS ———— CANALS ———— MAIN CIVIL AIRPORTS ▲

QUÉBEC

QUEBEC
1 INCH TO 2 MILES
Statute Miles
Kilometres

SCALE IN MILES

50
100
150
200
250
300
350
400
450
500

Q U E B E C

PARC DE LA VÉRENDRYE

PARC DES LAURENTIDES

PARC DE LA MONTAGNE TREMBLANTE

O N T A R I O

ALGONQUIN PROVINCIAL PARK

OTTAWA

Montreal

Québec

Sherbrooke

Toronto

LAKE ONTARIO 246 ft.

Niagara Falls
Buffalo
Rochester
Syracuse
Utica

N E W   Y O R K

CANADA
U.S.A.

MONTREAL
1 INCH TO 5 MILES

OUTREMONT
WESTMOUNT
CÔTE ST LUC
VERDUN
LACHINE

Caughnawaga Indian Reservation

35

© John Bartholomew & Son Ltd.

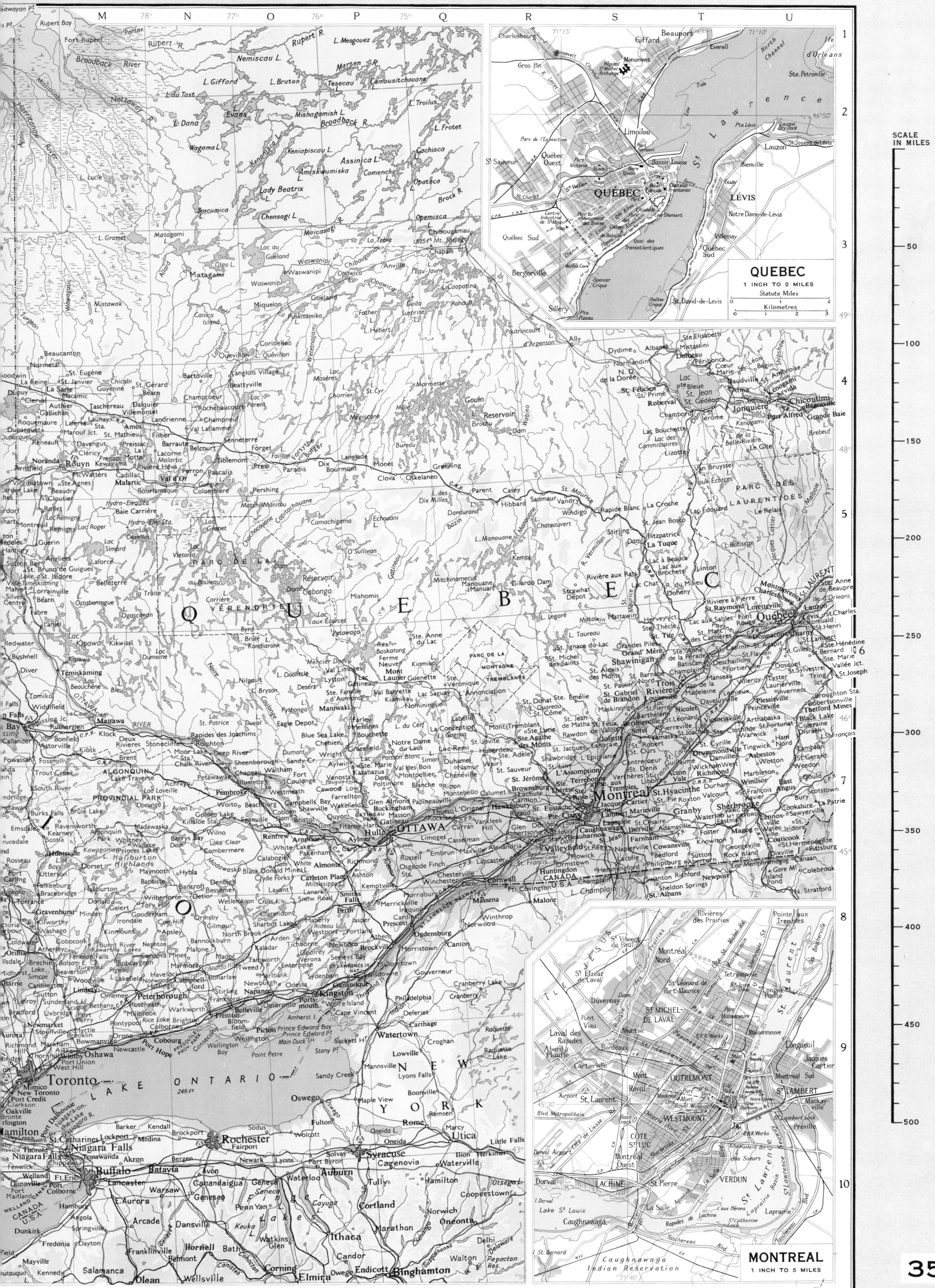

INTERNATIONAL BOUNDARIES
PROVINCIAL BOUNDARIES
SWAMP AND FLOOD AREAS
SPOT HEIGHTS IN FEET   2,120 ft.

SCALE: 1 INCH TO 47 MILES

Canada's prairies, taking in large areas of three provinces, were formed by deposits from the Pre-Cambrian Shield and from marginal mountains (the Rockies) laid down

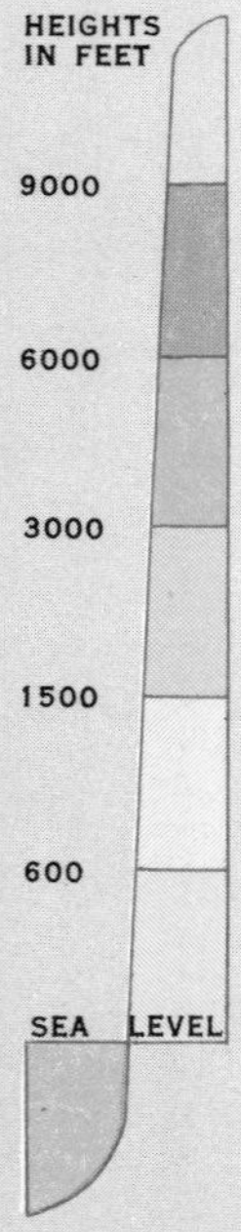

HEIGHTS IN FEET

9000
6000
3000
1500
600
SEA LEVEL

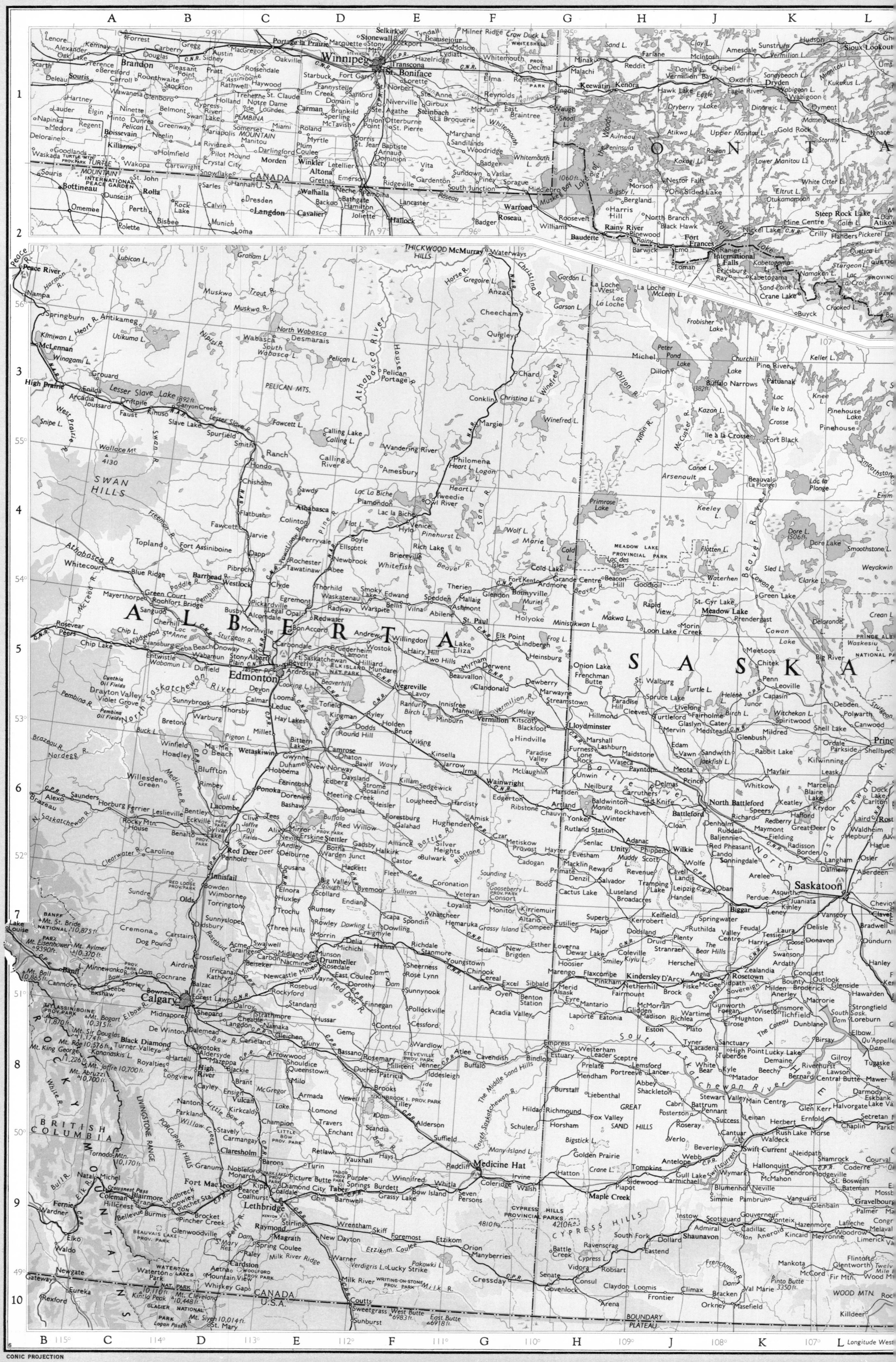

ALBERTA

SASKATCHEWAN

BRITISH COLUMBIA

MANITOBA

ONTARIO

CANADA
U.S.A.

SCALE: 1 INCH TO 47 MILES

CONIC PROJECTION

ARTERIAL ROADS TRACKS RAILWAYS
OTHER MAIN ROADS CANALS MAIN CIVIL AIRPORTS

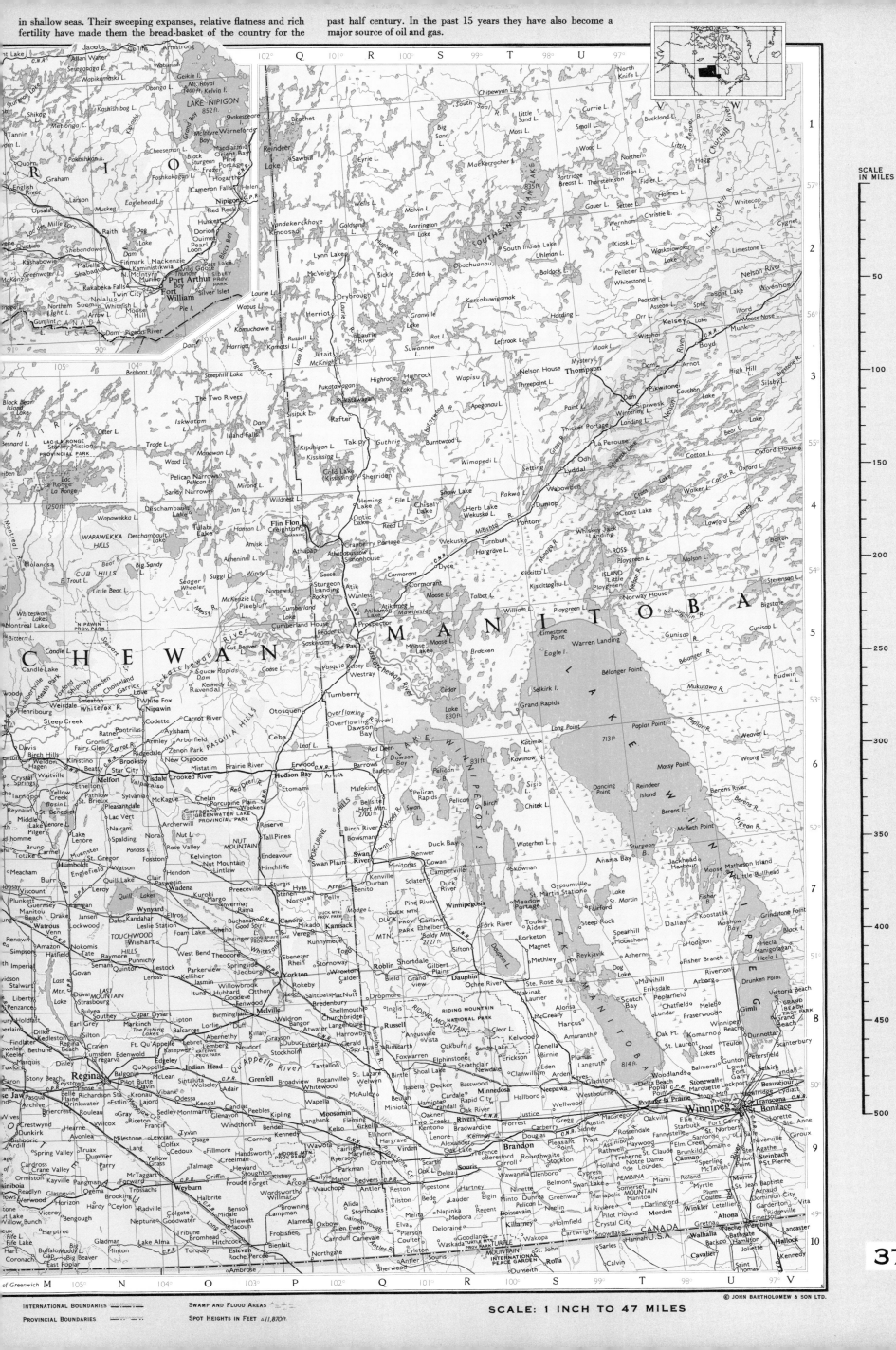

SCALE IN MILES

SCALE: 1 INCH TO 47 MILES

© JOHN BARTHOLOMEW & SON LTD.

INTERNATIONAL BOUNDARIES
PROVINCIAL BOUNDARIES
SWAMP AND FLOOD AREAS
SPOT HEIGHTS IN FEET

37

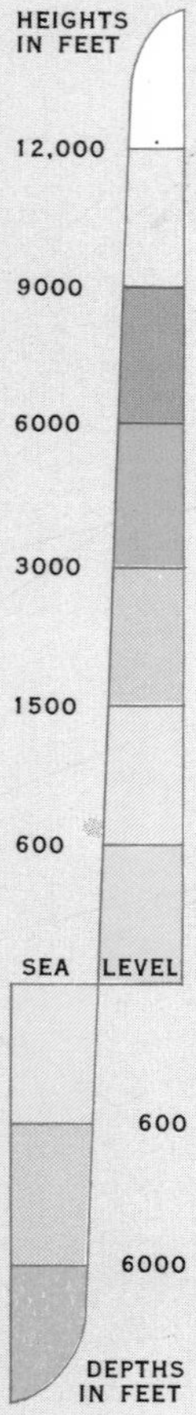

HEIGHTS
IN FEET

12,000

9000

6000

3000

1500

600

SEA LEVEL

600

6000

DEPTHS
IN FEET

DISTRICT OF KEEWATIN

NORTH WEST TERRITORIES

DISTRICT OF MACKENZIE

DISTRICT OF FRANKLIN

VICTORIA ISLAND

BEAUFORT SEA

Amundsen Gulf

Coronation Gulf

Queen Maud Gulf

GREAT BEAR LAKE

GREAT SLAVE LAKE

Yellowknife

Port Radium

Coppermine

MACKENZIE MOUNTAINS

Mackenzie River

Norman Wells

Fort Norman

Fort Good Hope

Fort McPherson

Tuktoyaktuk

Aklavik

YUKON TERRITORY

Dawson

Whitehorse

ALASKA

Brooks Range

Ogilvie Mountains

Mackenzie Mountains

Fort Simpson

Fort Liard

Fort Resolution

Hay River

Fort Smith

Uranium City

Lake Athabasca

Skagway

38

CONIC PROJECTION

SCALE: 1 INCH TO 94 MILES

ARTERIAL ROADS	RAILWAYS
OTHER MAIN ROADS	MAIN CIVIL AIRPORTS
TRACKS	
	CANALS
	OIL PIPE LINES

The western Cordilleras, second important source of Canadian mineral wealth, 500 miles wide and 1,400 miles long, are the greatest sweep of mountains in the country. They comprise the Rocky Mountains, the interior basins and plateaux, the Coast Range, the Inner Passage along the coast, and the outer system of islands.

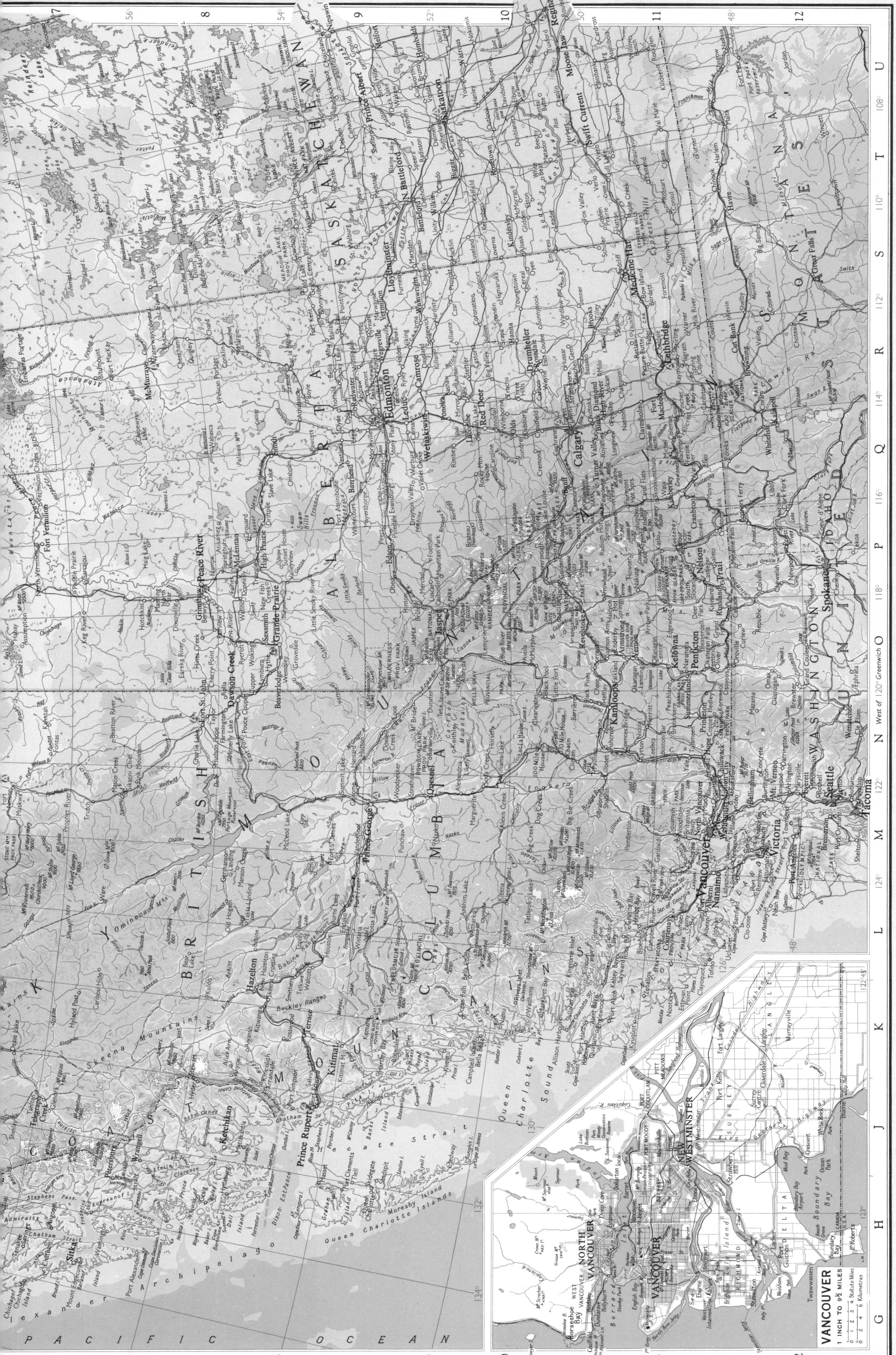

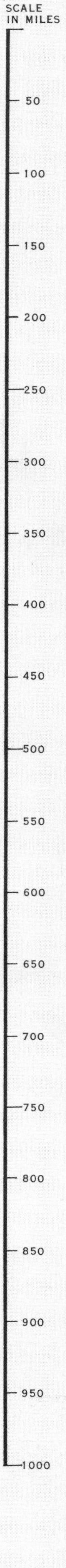

SCALE IN MILES

50
100
150
200
250
300
350
400
450
500
550
600
650
700
750
800
850
900
950
1000

VANCOUVER
1 INCH TO 9¾ MILES

INTERNATIONAL BOUNDARIES
PROVINCIAL BOUNDARIES

SWAMP AND FLOOD AREAS
GLACIERS AND ICECAPS
SPOT HEIGHTS IN FEET   ▲ 19,850

SCALE: 1 INCH TO 94 MILES

39

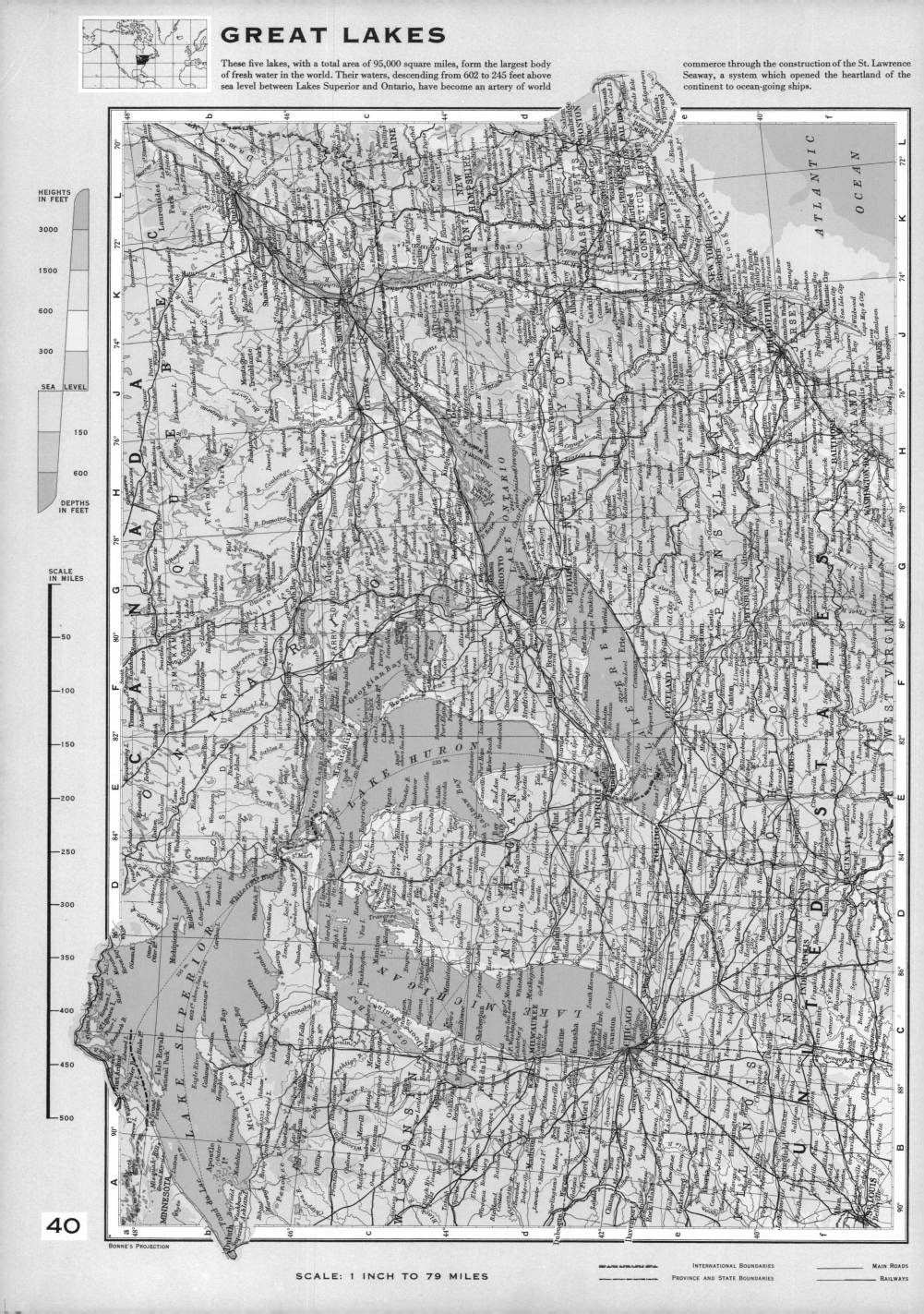

GREAT LAKES

These five lakes, with a total area of 95,000 square miles, form the largest body of fresh water in the world. Their waters, descending from 602 to 245 feet above sea level between Lakes Superior and Ontario, have become an artery of world commerce through the construction of the St. Lawrence Seaway, a system which opened the heartland of the continent to ocean-going ships.

HEIGHTS
IN FEET

3000
1500
600
300

SEA LEVEL

150
600

DEPTHS
IN FEET

SCALE
IN MILES

50
100
150
200
250
300
350
400
450
500

BONNE'S PROJECTION

SCALE: 1 INCH TO 79 MILES

INTERNATIONAL BOUNDARIES   MAIN ROADS

PROVINCE AND STATE BOUNDARIES   RAILWAYS

THE ARCTIC

The Asian and North American continents almost meet at the narrow and shallow Bering Strait, only 45 miles across. Between them lies the Arctic Ocean, nearly enclosed and always covered with drifting ice. Another outstanding feature of this map is the high plateau of Greenland, covered with ice up to 11,000 feet thick, yet reaching down to the same latitude as Oslo and Leningrad.

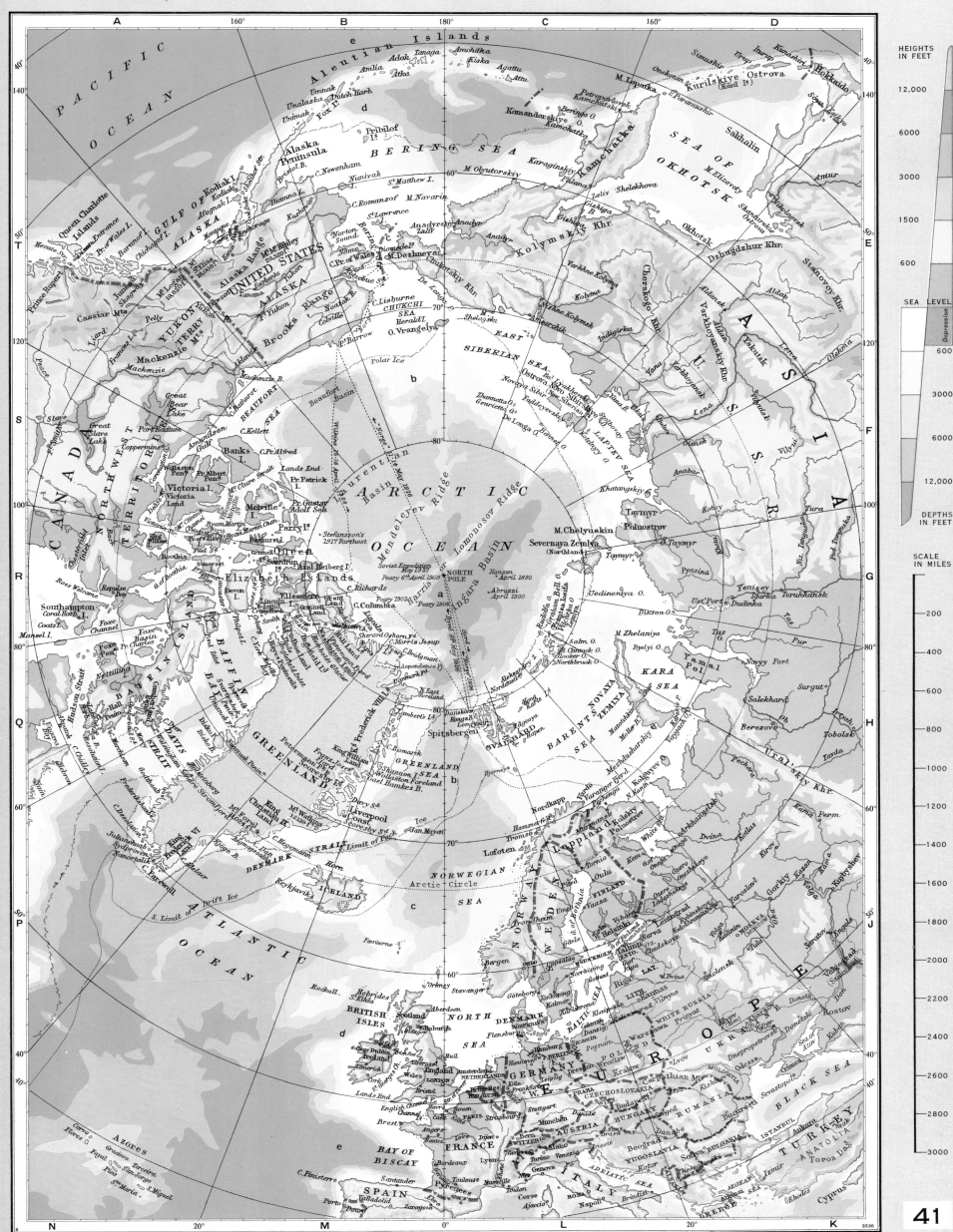

HEIGHTS
IN FEET

12,000

6000

3000

1500

600

SEA LEVEL

Depression

600

3000

6000

12,000

DEPTHS
IN FEET

SCALE
IN MILES

200

400

600

800

1000

1200

1400

1600

1800

2000

2200

2400

2600

2800

3000

41

INTERNATIONAL BOUNDARIES

LAMBERT'S AZIMUTHAL EQUAL-AREA PROJECTION

SCALE: 1 INCH TO 474 MILES

UNITED STATES OF AMERICA

AREA: 3,615,212 sq. miles.   POPULATION:
196,842,000.   CAPITAL: Washington, D.C.
CURRENCY: 100 cents=1 dollar.
The United States can be divided into six

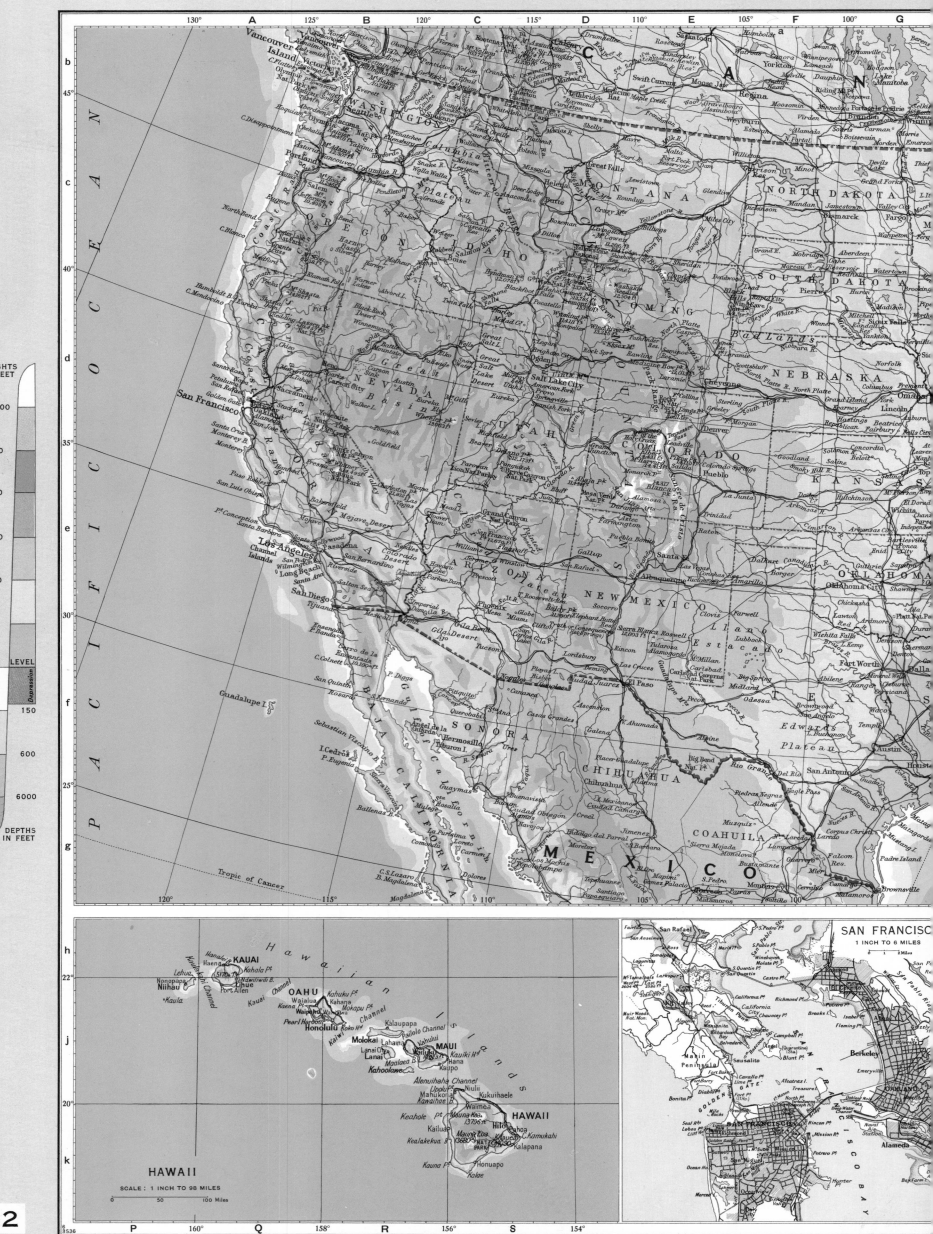

HEIGHTS
IN FEET

12,000

9000

6000

3000

1500

600

SEA LEVEL

150

600

6000

DEPTHS
IN FEET

HAWAII

SCALE: 1 INCH TO 98 MILES

0   50   100 Miles

SAN FRANCISCO

1 INCH TO 6 MILES

CONIC PROJECTION

SCALE: 1 INCH TO 197 MILES

MAIN ROADS

RAILWAYS

north–south sections. Reading the map from east to west, these are—a broad plain edging the Atlantic; the Appalachian Mountains; the Mississippi Basin; the Great Plains; the Rocky Mountains, and beyond, and along the Pacific coast, more mountains interspersed with fertile valleys. The state of Alaska, in the extreme north-west, is separated from the main body of the land by Western Canada. The northern part of the State lies within the Arctic Circle, and to the west it is separated from the U.S.S.R. by the Bering Strait. Hawaii consists of 20 islands (eight inhabited) in the North Pacific some 2,000 miles from San Francisco.

SCALE IN MILES

NEW YORK
1 INCH TO 6 MILES

ALASKA
SCALE: 1 INCH TO 394 MILES

© JOHN BARTHOLOMEW & SON LTD.

43

INTERNATIONAL BOUNDARIES
STATE BOUNDARIES

SCALE: 1 INCH TO 197 MILES

MIDDLE ATLANTIC STATES

The Atlantic seaboard in this north-east area of the United States is flanked by lowlands. The broken coastline is deeply penetrated by Chesa-peake, Delaware and Narragansett Bays. To the west and north of the lowlands lie the Appalachian, Catskill and Adirondack Mountains, while to the north-west is the Allegheny Plateau. To the south is Washington, in the District of Columbia, the seat of the U.S. Federal Government.

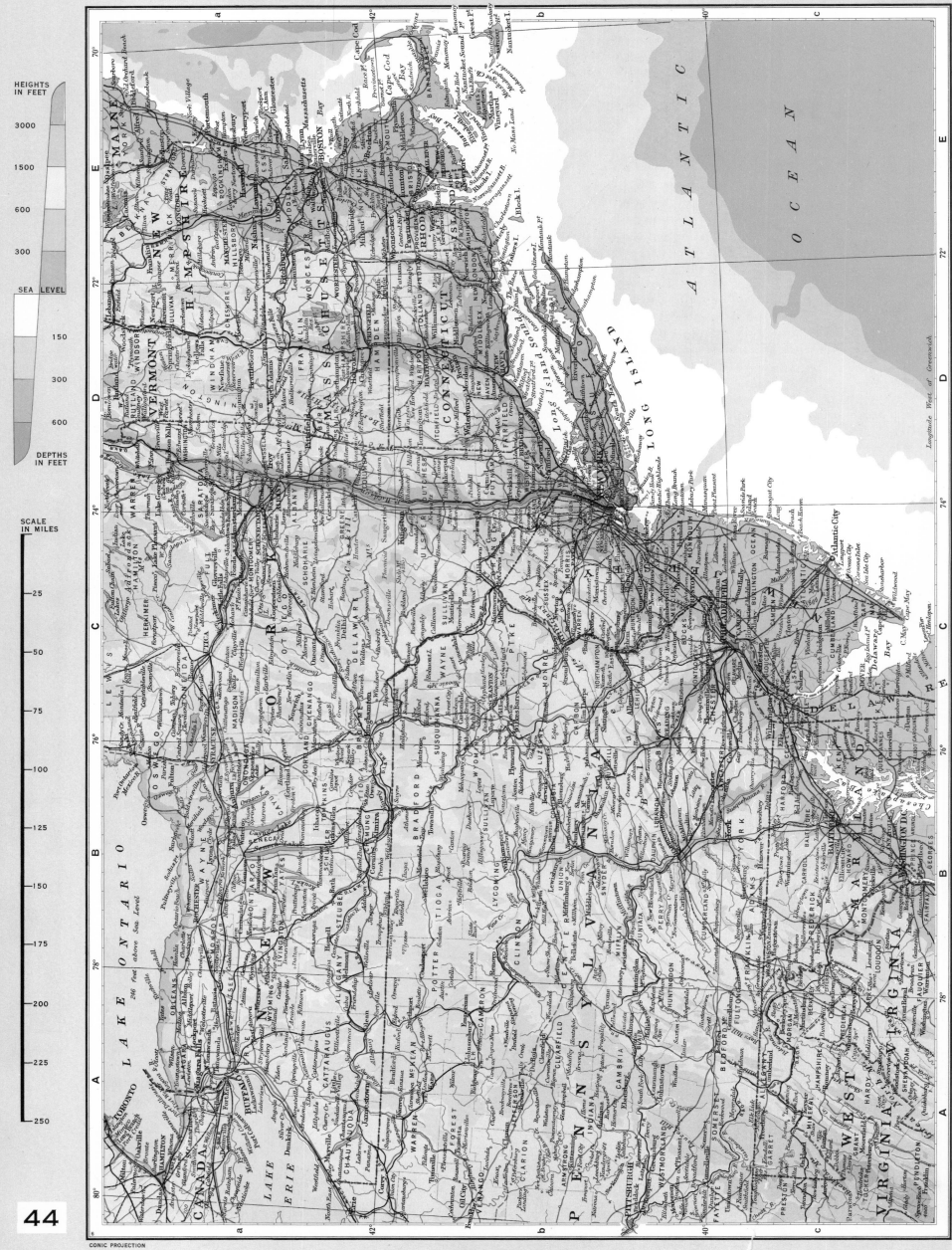

HEIGHTS IN FEET

3000
1500
600
300
SEA LEVEL
150
300
600

DEPTHS IN FEET

SCALE IN MILES

25
50
75
100
125
150
175
200
225
250

CONIC PROJECTION

SCALE: 1 INCH TO 39 MILES

Main Roads
Railways

PACIFIC COAST

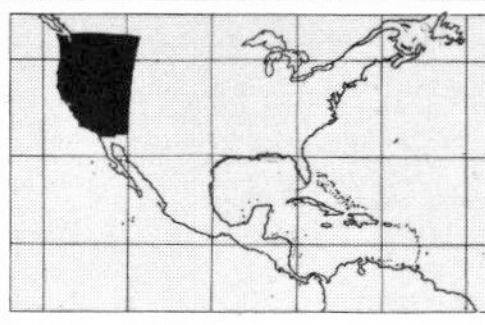

The map shows the States of Washington, Oregon, California and Nevada. The Coast Ranges on the west are separated by the Willamette Valley and the Central Valley of California from the Cascade Mountains and the Sierra Nevada. Beyond lies an extensive area of high basins, plateaux and ranges.

HEIGHTS IN FEET

12,000
9000
6000
3000
1500
600
300

SEA LEVEL

Depression

150
600
6000

DEPTHS IN FEET

SCALE IN MILES

50
100
150
200
250
300
350
400
450

INTERNATIONAL BOUNDARIES

STATE BOUNDARIES

SCALE: 1 INCH TO 79 MILES

Longitude West of Greenwich

Bonne's Projection

MEXICO GUATEMALA, HONDURAS, BRITISH HONDURAS, EL SALVADOR

MEXICO AREA: 761,600 sq. miles. POP: 44,145,000. CAP: Mexico City.
GUATEMALA AREA: 42,042 sq. miles. POP: 4,575,000. CAP: Guatemala City.
HONDURAS AREA: 43,277 sq. miles. POP: 2,363,000. CAP: Tegucigalpa.

BRITISH HONDURAS AREA: 8,867 sq. miles. POP: 109,000. CAP: Belize.
EL SALVADOR AREA: 8,260 sq. miles. POP: 3,037,000. CAP: San Salvador.

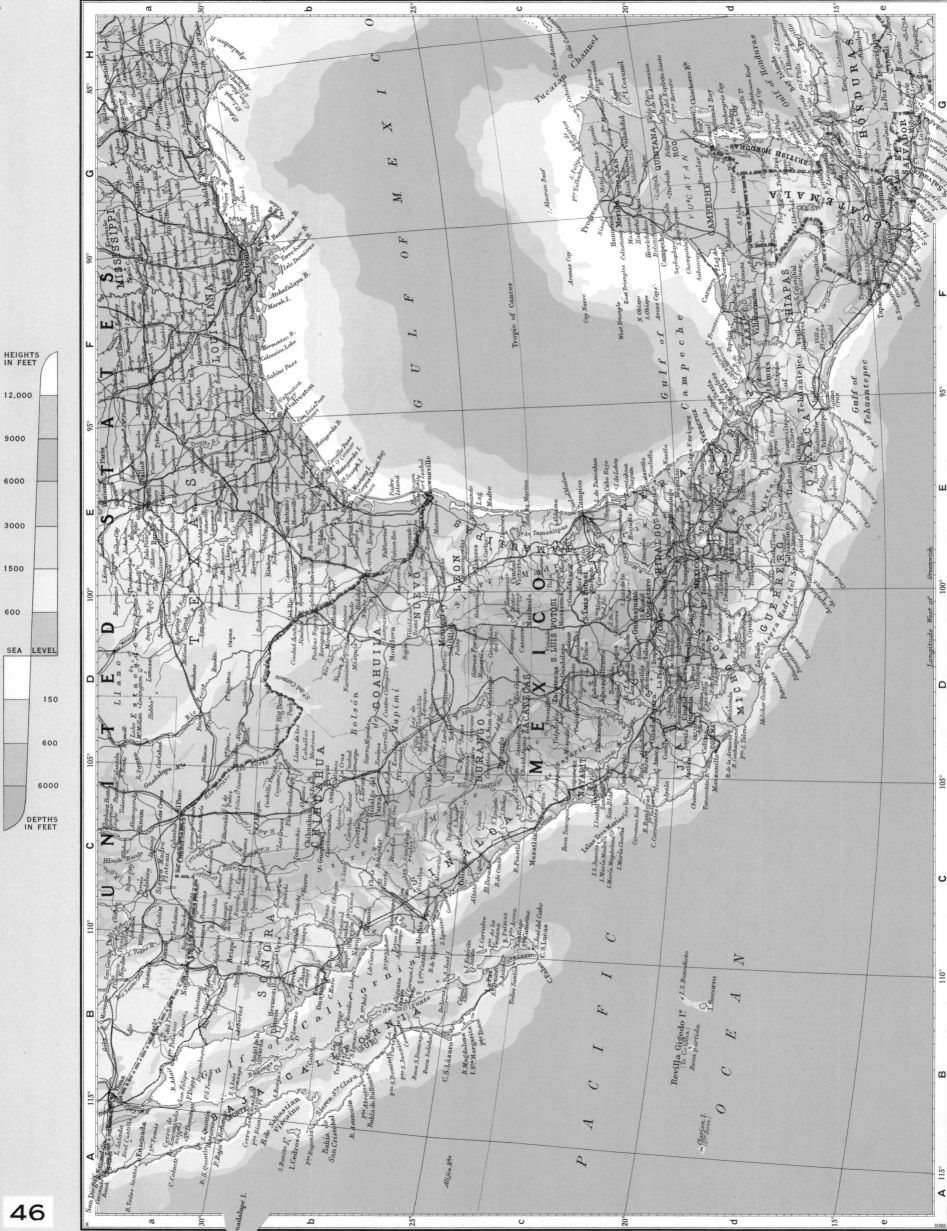

HEIGHTS
IN FEET

12,000
9000
6000
3000
1500
600

SEA LEVEL

150
600
6000

DEPTHS
IN FEET

GULF OF MEXICO

PACIFIC OCEAN

46

BONNE'S PROJECTION

SCALE: 1 INCH TO 158 MILES

INTERNATIONAL BOUNDARIES
STATE BOUNDARIES

NICARAGUA AREA: *57,143 sq. miles.* POPULATION: *1,655,000.* CAP: *Managua.*
COSTA RICA AREA: *19,695 sq. miles.* POPULATION: *1,486,000.* CAP: *San José.*
PANAMA AREA: *28,575 sq. miles.* POPULATION: *1,287,000.* CAP: *Panama City.*

CUBA AREA: *44,218 sq. miles.* POPULATION: *7,833,000.* CAP: *Havana.*
JAMAICA AREA: *4,232 sq. miles.* POPULATION: *1,839,000.* CAP: *Kingston.*

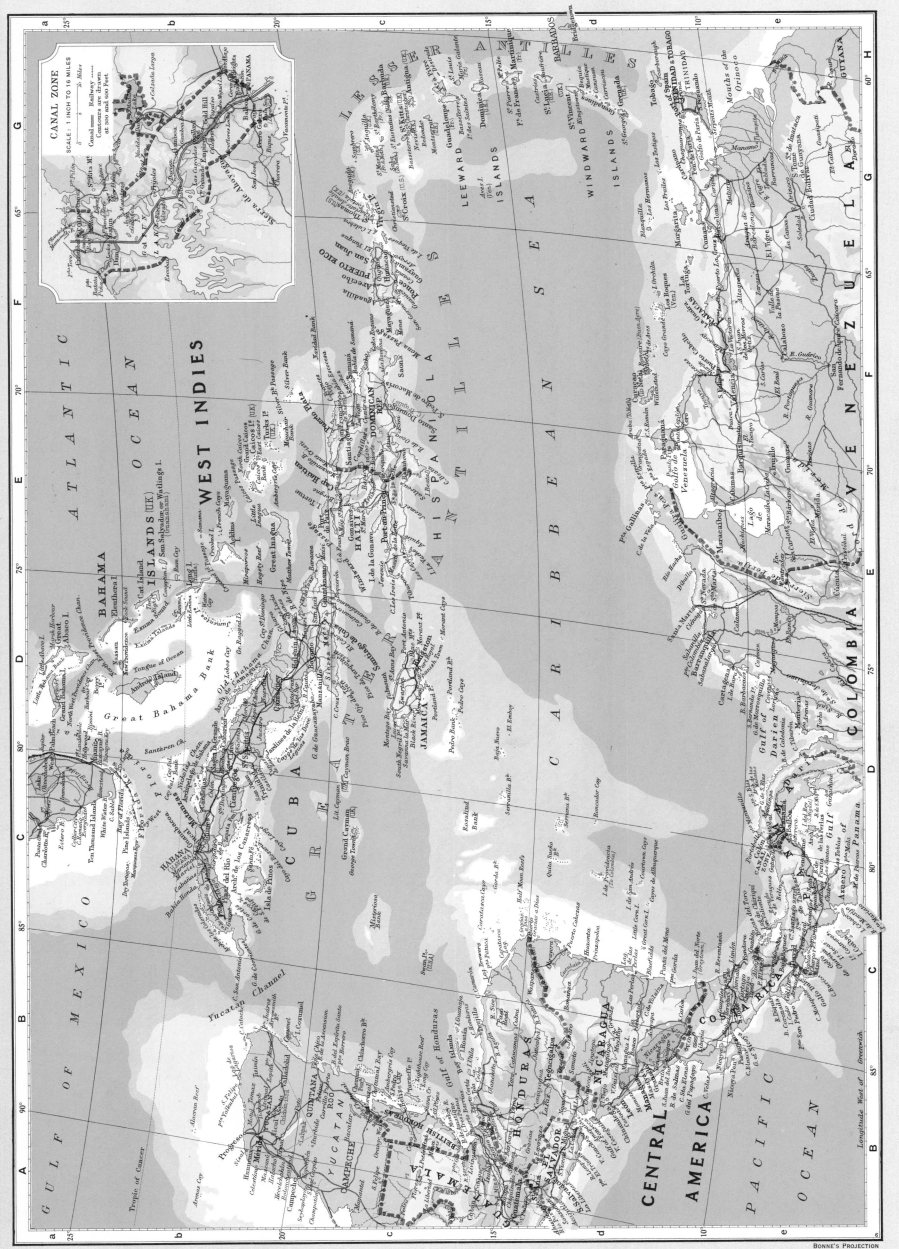

MAIN ROADS ⎯⎯⎯⎯⎯
RAILWAYS ⎯⎯⎯⎯⎯

SCALE: 1 INCH TO 158 MILES

SCALE IN MILES

BONNE'S PROJECTION

47

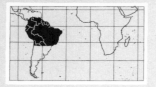

SOUTH AMERICA - NORTH

BRAZIL, PERU, ECUADOR, COLOMBIA, VENEZUELA

BRAZIL AREA: 3,286,170 sq. miles. POPULATION: 84,679,000*.
CAPITAL: *Brasilia.*
BOLIVIA AREA: 424,163 sq. miles. POPULATION: 3,748,000.
CAPITAL: *La Paz.*

HEIGHTS
IN FEET

16,000

12,000

10,000

6000

3000

1500

600

SEA LEVEL

150

600

6000

DEPTHS
IN FEET

48

LAMBERT'S AZIMUTHAL EQUAL-AREA PROJECTION

SCALE: 1 INCH TO 197 MILES

MAIN ROADS

RAILWAYS

PERU AREA: *496,222 sq. miles.* POP:
12,012,000*. CAPITAL: *Lima.*
ECUADOR AREA: *104,506 sq. miles.*
POPULATION: *5,326,000*.* CAP: *Quito*

COLOMBIA AREA: *455,355 sq. miles.*
POPULATION: *18,068,000.* CAPITAL: *Bogotá.*
VENEZUELA AREA: *352,143 sq. miles.*
POPULATION: *9,030,000*.* CAP: *Caracas.*

GUYANA AREA: *83,000 sq. miles.*
POPULATION: *665,000.* CAPITAL: *Georgetown.*
SURINAM AREA: *55,000 sq. miles.*
POPULATION: *345,000.* CAPITAL: *Paramaribo.*

FRENCH GUIANA AREA: *35,100 sq. miles.*
POPULATION: *37,000.* CAPITAL: *Cayenne.*

*Figure excludes Indian jungle population.

SCALE IN MILES

SCALE: 1 INCH TO 197 MILES

49

© JOHN BARTHOLOMEW & SON LTD.

INTERNATIONAL BOUNDARIES

STATE AND PROVINCIAL BOUNDARIES

SOUTH AMERICA-SOUTH ARGENTINA, CHILE, PARAGUAY, URUGUAY

ARGENTINA AREA: *1,072,646 sq. miles.*
POPULATION: 22,691,000.
CAPITAL: *Buenos Aires.*

CHILE AREA: *286,397 sq. miles.*
POPULATION: 8,591,000.
CAPITAL: *Santiago.*

PARAGUAY AREA: *157,047 sq. miles.*
POPULATION: 2,094,000.
CAPITAL: *Asunción.*

URUGUAY AREA: *72,172 sq. miles*
POPULATION: 2,749,000.
CAPITAL: *Montevideo.*

HEIGHTS
IN FEET

16,000
12,000
10,000
6000
3000
1500
600
SEA LEVEL
150
600
6000

DEPTHS
IN FEET

SCALE
IN MILES

100
200
300
400
500
600
700
800
900
1000

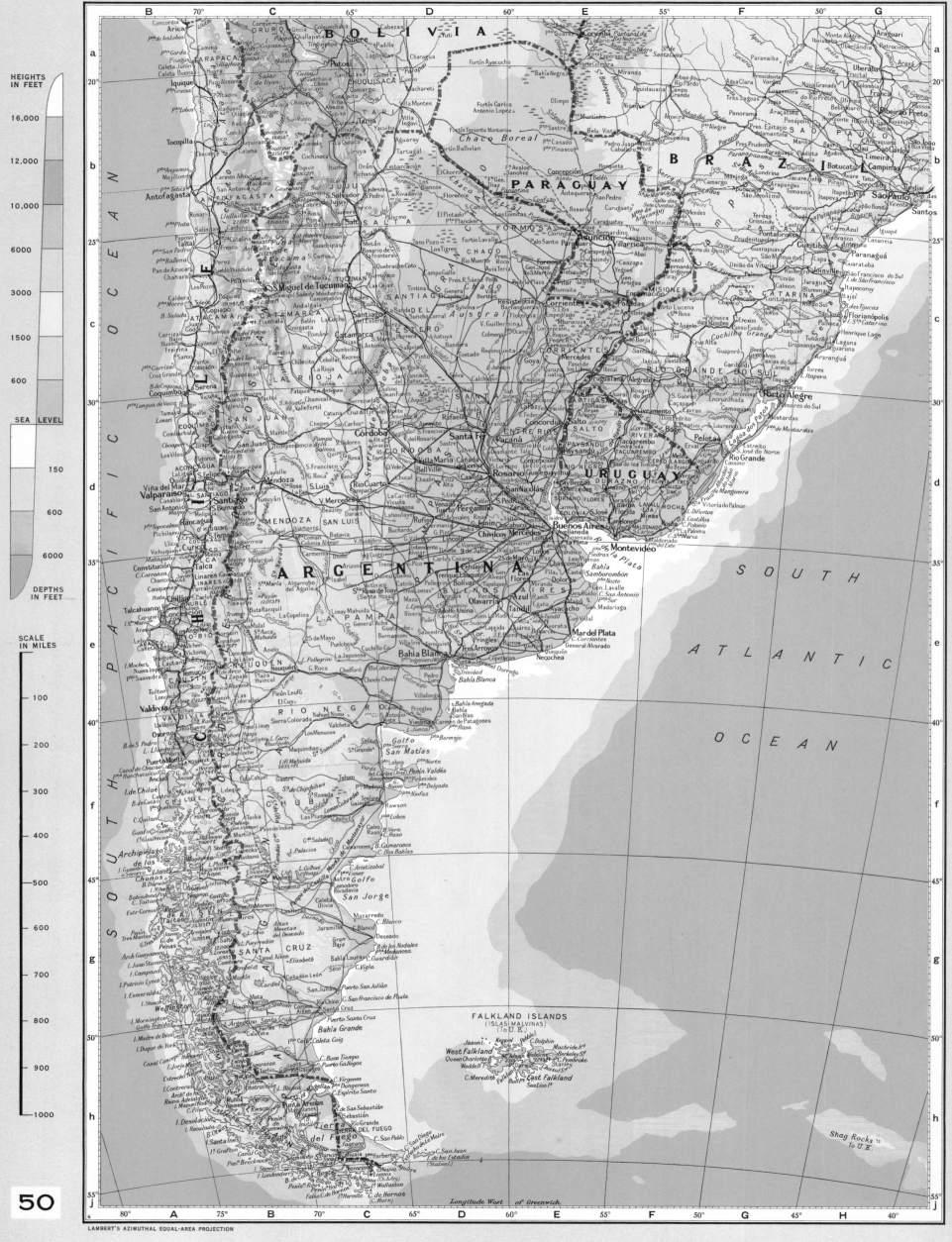

50

LAMBERT'S AZIMUTHAL EQUAL-AREA PROJECTION

SCALE: 1 INCH TO 197 MILES

INTERNATIONAL BOUNDARIES   MAIN ROADS
PROVINCIAL BOUNDARIES   RAILWAYS

NEW ZEALAND

AREA: *103,736 sq. miles.* POP: *2,676,000.* CAPITAL: *Wellington.* CURRENCY: *100 cents=1 dollar.* New Zealand includes North Island and South Island, the considerably smaller Stewart Island to the south, and a number of minor islands. The main islands are mountainous with rich coastal plains. North Island has volcanic peaks and hot springs. South Island includes the Southern Alps (Mount Cook 12,349 ft.) and the Tasman Glacier.

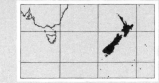

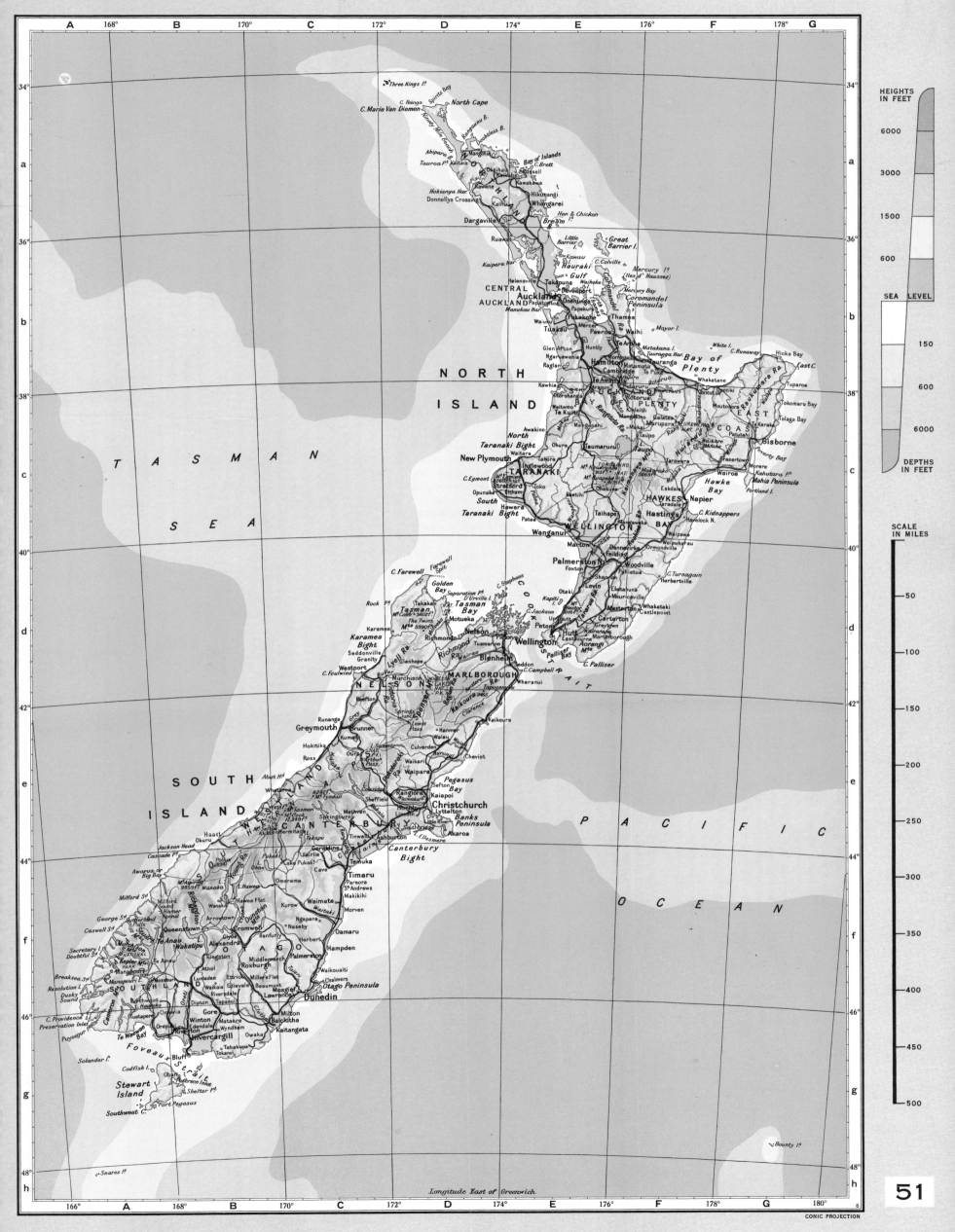

HEIGHTS IN FEET

6000
3000
1500
600

SEA LEVEL

150
600
6000

DEPTHS IN FEET

SCALE IN MILES

50
100
150
200
250
300
350
400
450
500

51

Longitude East of Greenwich

CONIC PROJECTION

SCALE: 1 INCH TO 79 MILES

AUSTRALIA

AREA: *2,971,081 sq. miles.* POPULATION: *11,541,000* (excluding full-blooded aborigines). CAP: *Canberra.* Australia, the largest island in the world, comprises six States and two Territories. Although two-fifths of Australia lie within the Tropic of Capricorn, the general climate is more temperate than that of corresponding regions in other parts of the world. Despite its great deserts, the country has vast

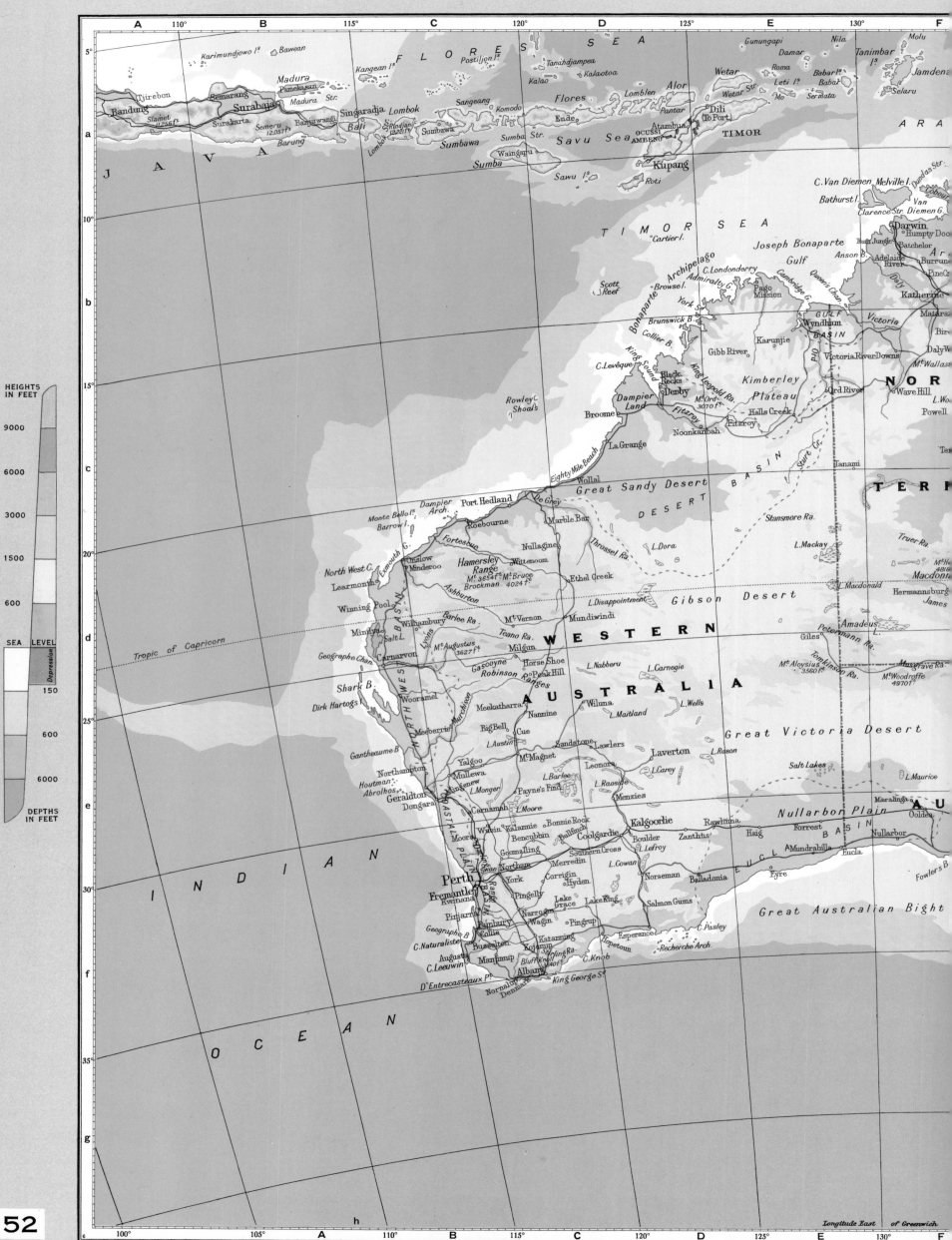

HEIGHTS
IN FEET

9000

6000

3000

1500

600

SEA LEVEL

Depression

150

600

6000

DEPTHS
IN FEET

BONNE'S PROJECTION

SCALE: 1 INCH TO 197 MILES

— MAIN ROADS

------- ARTESIAN BASINS

— RAILWAYS

acreages of fertile and well-watered land. Reading the map from east to west, one sees a narrow strip of fertile coastland, beyond which mountain ranges reach from Melbourne in the south right up to the Cape York Peninsula. These mountains, the Great Dividing Range, form a natural division between the coastal land and a fertile tableland, which is flanked on the west by an extensive inland plain. North of Spencer Gulf lies the Lake Eyre Basin, an inland drainage basin partly below sea level into which the rivers from the eastern plateau drain. Farther westwards, poorly watered plains give way to enormous deserts. Another strip of watered fertile land lies in the extreme south-west.

SCALE IN MILES

53

INTERNATIONAL BOUNDARIES

STATE BOUNDARIES

SCALE: 1 INCH TO 197 MILES

EURASIA

This vast land mass—the largest in the world—covers more than a quarter of the Earth's land surface and is inhabited by over three-quarters of its population. Across the whole area, from the Pyrénées to the backbone of W. Malaysia, runs an almost continuous belt of fold mountains, of which the highest, the Himalayas (Everest,

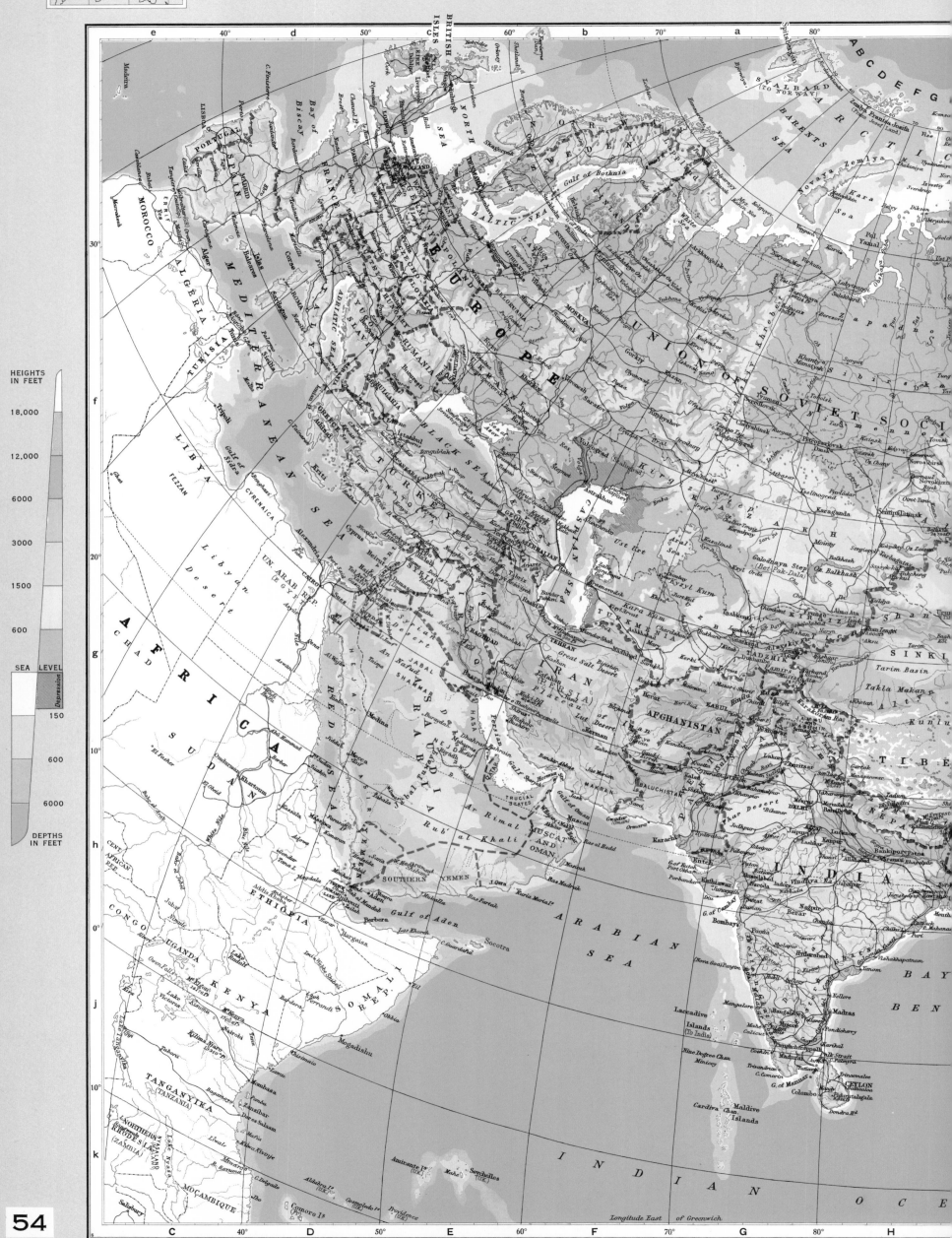

HEIGHTS IN FEET

18,000
12,000
6000
3000
1500
600
SEA LEVEL
Depression
150
600
6000
DEPTHS IN FEET

54

LAMBERT'S AZIMUTHAL EQUAL-AREA PROJECTION

SCALE: 1 INCH TO 474 MILES

INTERNATIONAL BOUNDARIES
STATE BOUNDARIES

29,028 feet), form a central branch. There is also an undersea range fringing the east as a chain of islands from the Aleutians south to the Philippines. Contrasting with the central highlands are the immense low-lying plains of northern Russia, while in between lies a great zone of desert stretching from Mongolia to Arabia. From the frozen tundra of the Arctic to the dense rain forests of W. Malaysia, there is every type of climate and soil, and for climatic reasons the population centres are mainly in the west, south and south-east. In India, for instance, the average population density is 392 per square mile; in Siberia it is less than five.

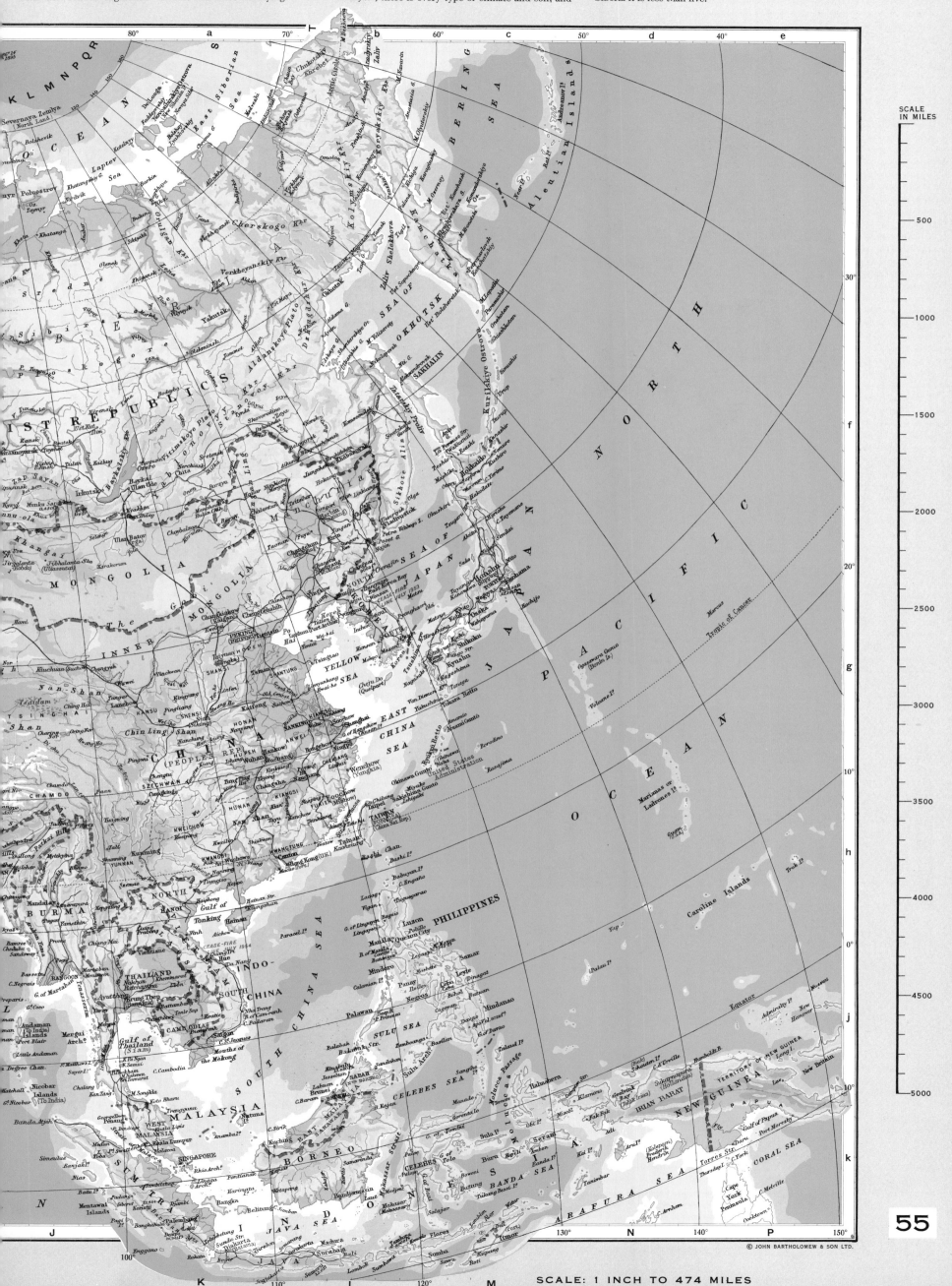

SCALE: 1 INCH TO 474 MILES

© JOHN BARTHOLOMEW & SON LTD.

EUROPE

Itself a peninsula of Asia, Europe is made up of smaller peninsulas such as Scandinavia, Iberia, Italy and Greece. Characteristic of these countries are north-south backbones of mountains, some of them offshoots of the great chain of fold mountains that winds across the entire continent from the Pyrénées to the Black Sea.

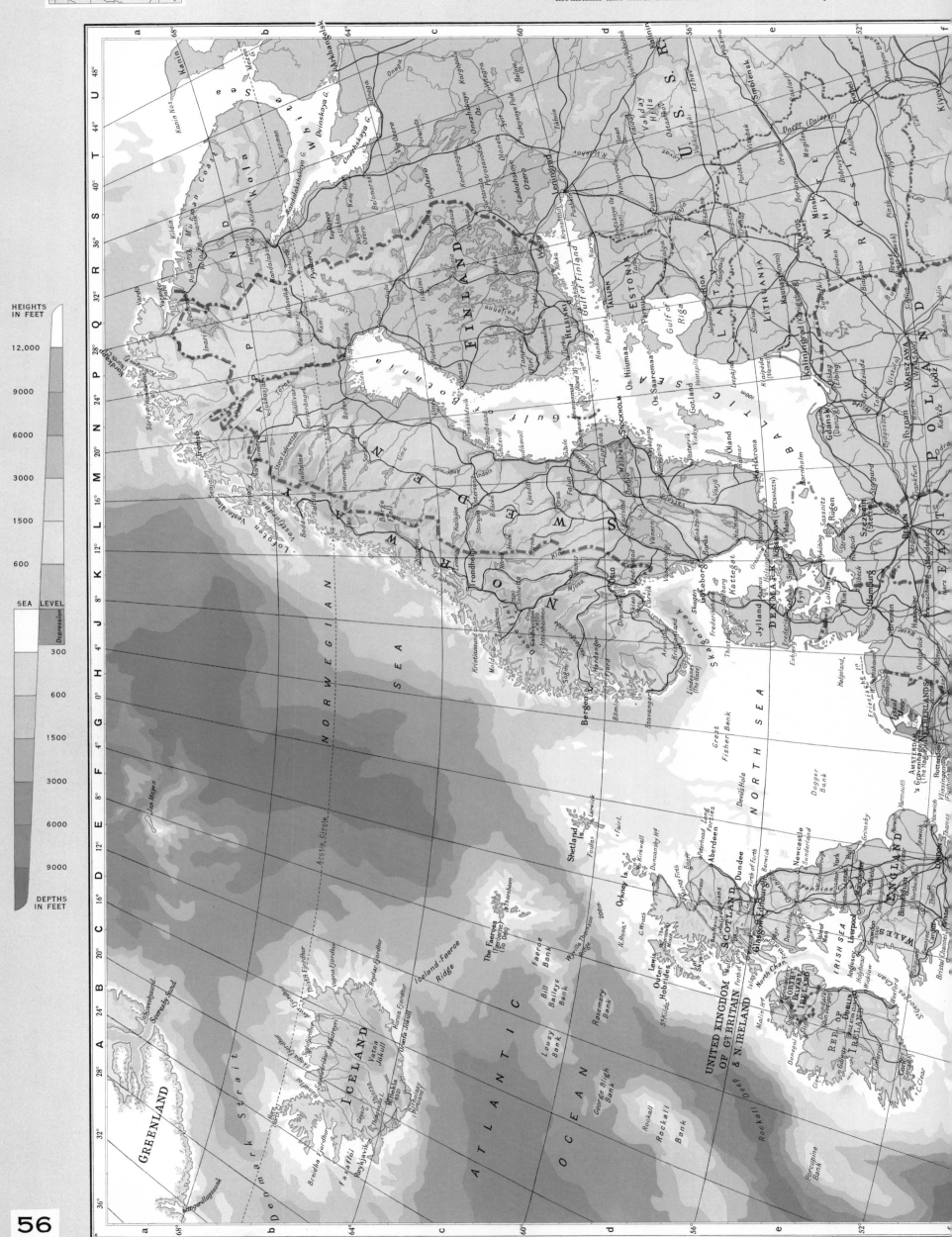

HEIGHTS
IN FEET

12,000
9000
6000
3000
1500
600
SEA LEVEL
Depression
300
600
1500
3000
6000
9000
DEPTHS
IN FEET

BONNE'S PROJECTION

SCALE: 1 INCH TO 158 MILES

MAIN ROADS
RAILWAYS

This east-west axis separates the other two major features of the map: the broad North European Plain stretching from Ireland to Russia, and the two basins of the Mediterranean, each as deep as the mountains are high.

This relatively small continent contains many striking geographical contrasts which are paralleled by the diversity of its peoples and cultures, among them the great Greek and Roman civilizations from which the whole world has

derived so much. The maritime outlook prevalent in the western areas of Europe led to the great explorations that took these people and their cultures to the farthest corners of the Earth.

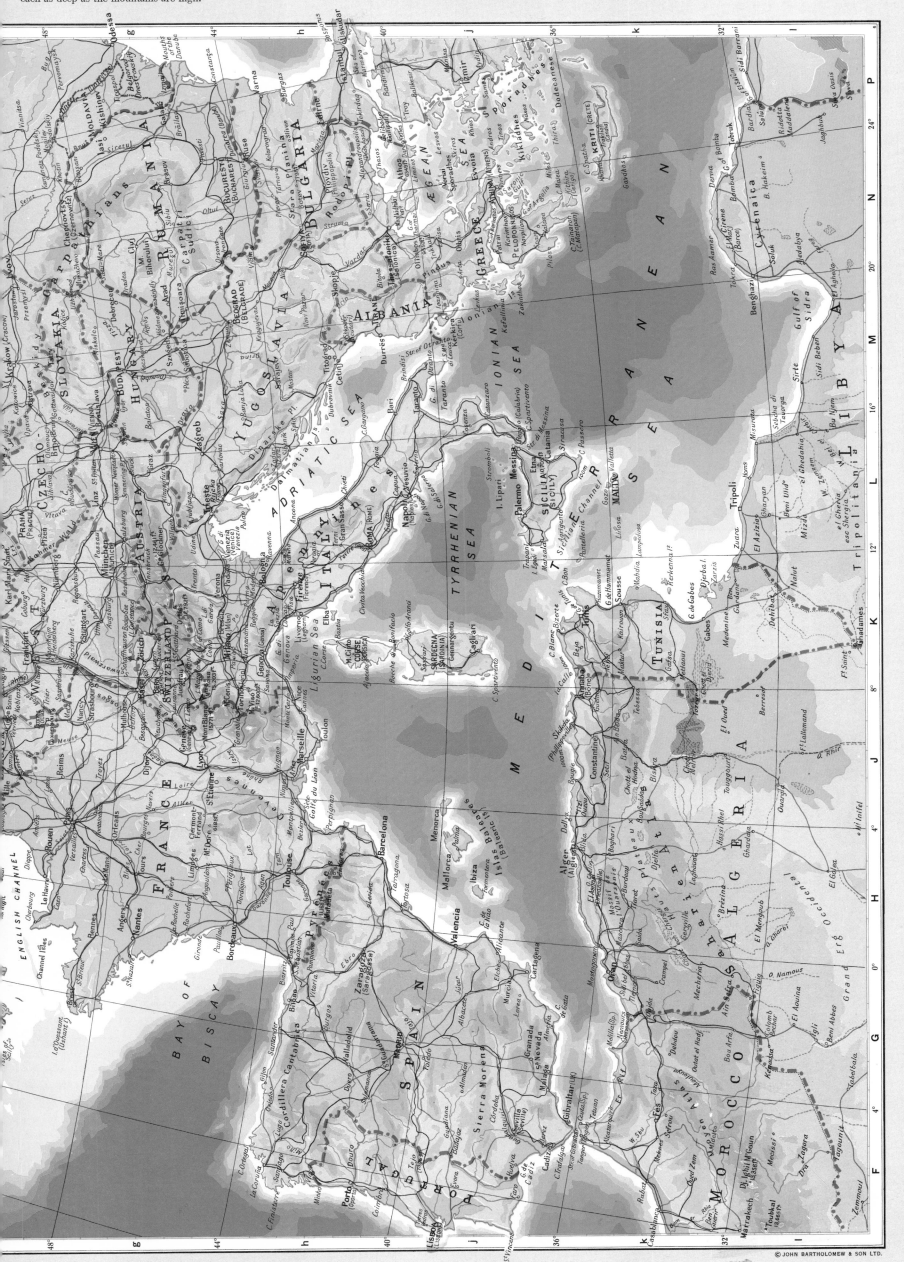

SCALE IN MILES

SCALE: 1 INCH TO 158 MILES

INTERNATIONAL BOUNDARIES

STATE BOUNDARIES

57

THE BRITISH ISLES

UNITED KINGDOM (ENGLAND: SCOTLAND: WALES: N. IRELAND)
AREA: 94,207 sq. miles. POPULATION: 54,965,000.
ENGLAND AREA: 50,327 sq. miles. POPULATION: 45,374,000.
WALES AREA: 8,016 sq. miles. POPULATION: 2,701,000.

HEIGHTS
IN FEET

3000
1500
600
300

SEA LEVEL
Depression

80
150
300
600
3000

DEPTHS
IN FEET

ZETLAND
(SHETLAND)

SCALE: 1 INCH TO 39 MILES

CONIC PROJECTION

MAIN ROADS
RAILWAYS

The British Isles, having regard to their relatively small area, show a structural variety matched by few European countries. A line drawn north-eastwards from the Exe to the Tees roughly separates Great Britain's ancient uplands (stretching from the Scottish Highlands to the moors of Devon and Cornwall) from the more recent rock formations found in the gentler slopes of the Cotswolds and Chilterns, East Anglia and the Weald. Signs of a one-time connection with the Continent are evident in the south, the fens of East Anglia having their counterpart in the low-lying flats of the Netherlands, and the chalk cliffs of Dover and the granitic cliffs of Cornwall in the coast of northern France.

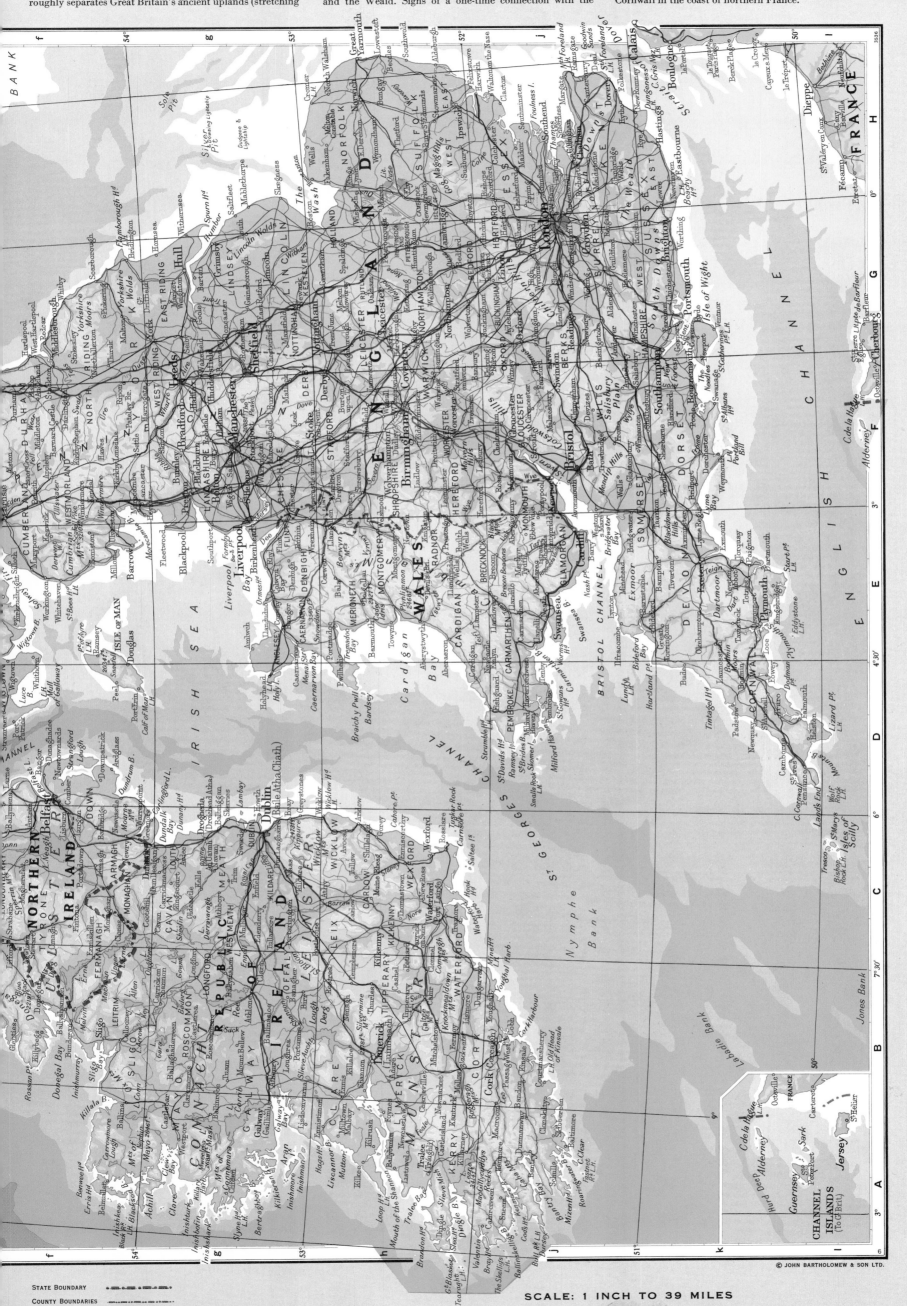

SCALE
IN MILES

25

50

75

100

125

150

175

200

225

250

275

300

325

350

375

400

59

STATE BOUNDARY

COUNTY BOUNDARIES

SCALE: 1 INCH TO 39 MILES

THE LOW COUNTRIES
BELGIUM, NETHERLANDS, LUXEMBOURG

BELGIUM AREA: *11,779 sq. miles.* POPULATION: *9,528,000.* CAPITAL: *Brussels.* CURRENCY: *100 centimes=1 franc.*

NETHERLANDS AREA: *12,978 sq. miles.* POPULATION: *12,455,000.* CAPITAL: *Amsterdam.* (GOVT: *The Hague.*) CURRENCY: *100 cents=1 guilder.*

LUXEMBOURG AREA: *998 sq. miles.* POPULATION: *335,000.* CAPITAL: *Luxembourg.* CURRENCY: *100 centimes=1 franc.*

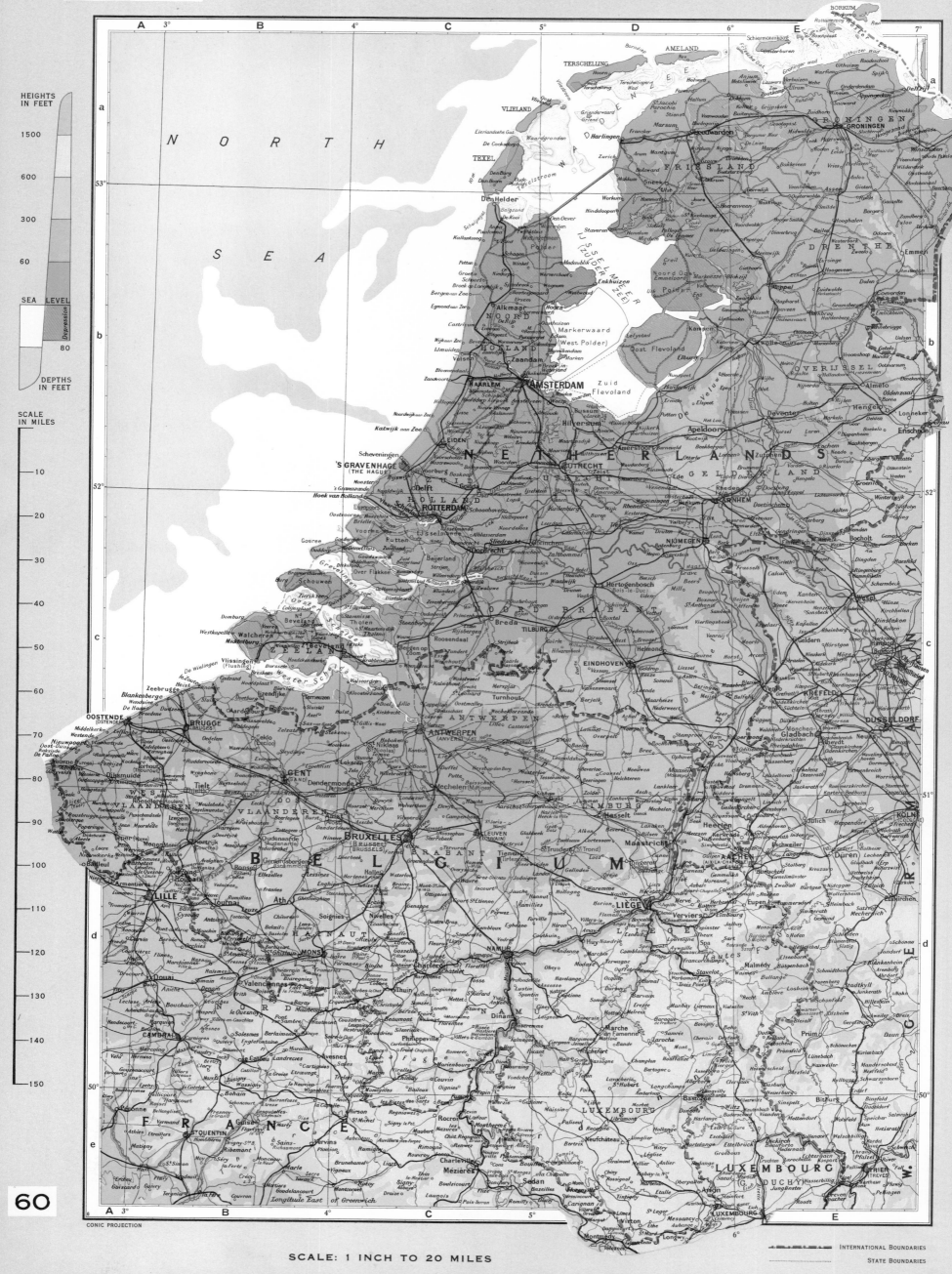

HEIGHTS IN FEET

1500
600
300
60
SEA LEVEL

DEPTHS IN FEET

SCALE IN MILES

60

CONIC PROJECTION

SCALE: 1 INCH TO 20 MILES

INTERNATIONAL BOUNDARIES
STATE BOUNDARIES

AREA: *15,941 sq. miles.* POPULATION: *5,945,000.*
CAPITAL: *Berne.* CURRENCY: *100 centimes=1
franc.* The Swiss Alps, rising to 15,203 feet

(Monte Rosa), cover more than half of Switzerland, making it the most mountainous country
in Europe. The country is divided into three

belts, running north-east to south-west, by the
broad valley of the Aare and the narrower one of
the Upper Rhein and Upper Rhône.

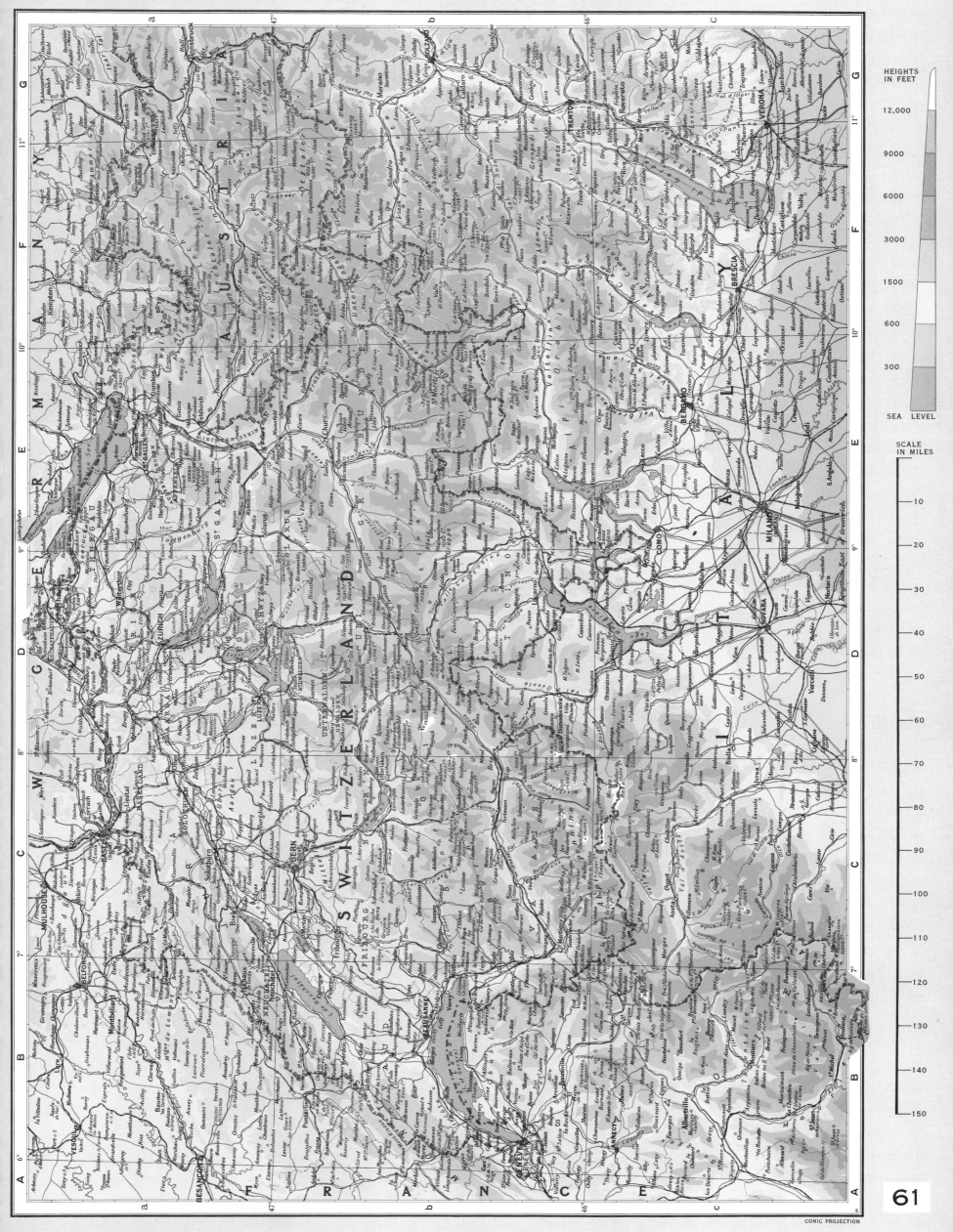

HEIGHTS
IN FEET

12,000
9000
6000
3000
1500
600
300
SEA LEVEL

SCALE
IN MILES

10
20
30
40
50
60
70
80
90
100
110
120
130
140
150

MAIN ROADS
RAILWAYS

CONIC PROJECTION

SCALE: 1 INCH TO 20 MILES

61

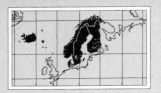

SCANDINAVIA AND BALTIC

NORWAY, SWEDEN, DENMARK, FINLAND, WITH ICELAND

NORWAY AREA: *125,198 sq. miles.* POPULATION: *3,753,000*
CAPITAL: *Oslo.* CURRENCY: *100 öre=1 krone.*
SWEDEN AREA *173,634 sq. miles.* POPULATION: *7,808,000.*
CAPITAL: *Stockholm.* CURRENCY: *100 öre=1 krona.*
From the backbone of mountains shared by Norway

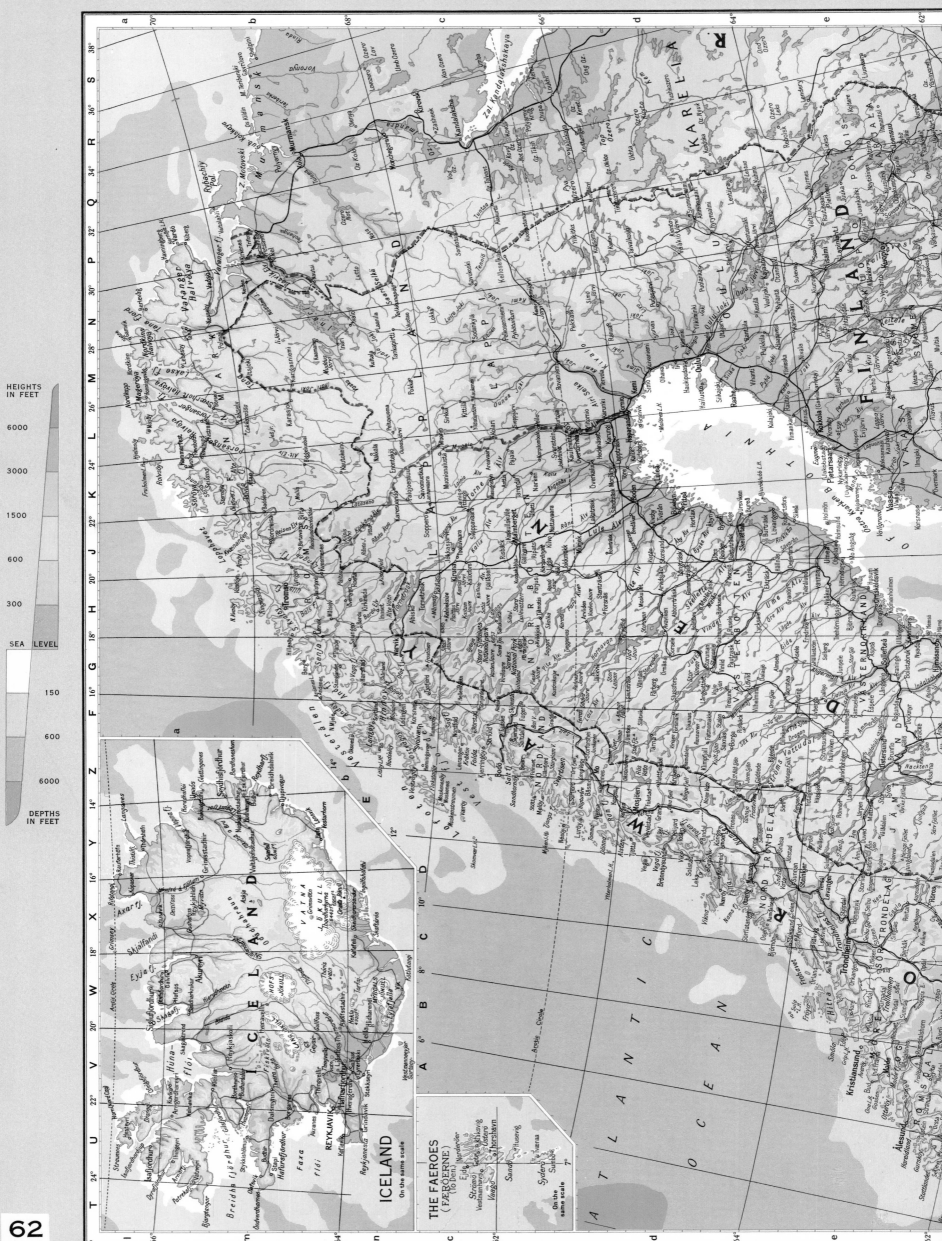

HEIGHTS IN FEET

6000
3000
1500
600
300
SEA LEVEL
150
600
6000

DEPTHS IN FEET

ICELAND
On the same scale

THE FAEROES
(FÆROERNE)
(To Denm.)
On the same scale

62

CONIC PROJECTION

SCALE: 1 INCH TO 71 MILES

MAIN ROADS
RAILWAYS

and Sweden come rivers that feed the many lakes on both sides. Norway continues as a high, rugged plateau, falling abruptly to a coastline broken by fjords and islands. Sweden, low-lying in the south, is better suited to cultivation and settlement.

DENMARK AREA: *16,619 sq. miles.* POPULATION: *4,797,000.* CAPITAL: *Copenhagen.* CURRENCY: *100 øre=1 krone.* Smallest and lowest-lying of the Scandinavian countries, Denmark rarely rises more than 500 feet above sea level. Besides the peninsula of Jutland, it comprises the four

main islands of Zealand, Fünen, Lolland and Falster.
FINLAND AREA: *130,119 sq. miles.* POPULATION: *4,639,000.* CAPITAL: *Helsinki.* CURRENCY: *100 pennis=1 markka.*
ICELAND AREA: *39,768 sq. miles.* POPULATION: *195,000.* CAPITAL: *Reykjavik.* CURRENCY: *100 aurar=1 króna.*

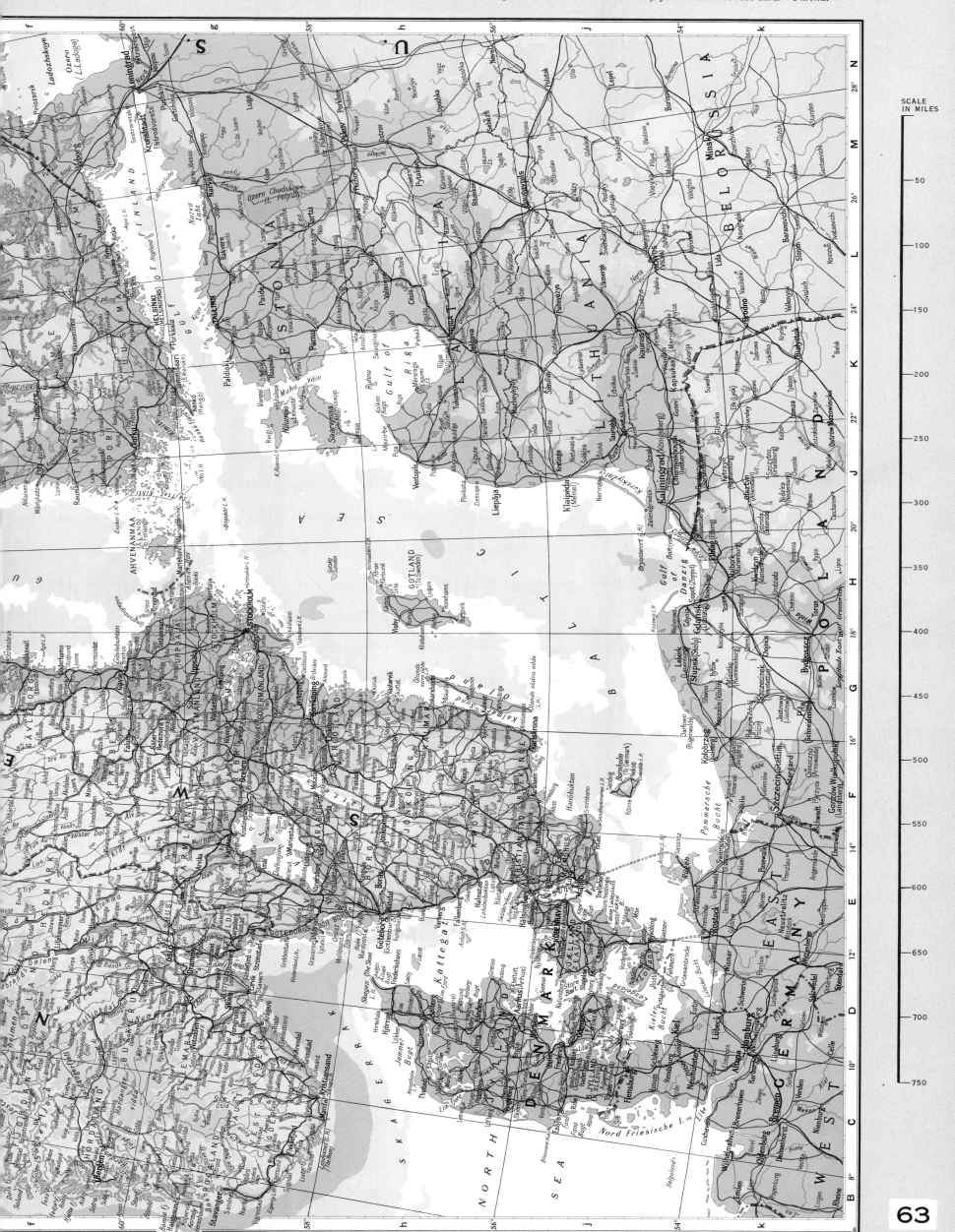

SCALE IN MILES

INTERNATIONAL BOUNDARIES
STATE BOUNDARIES

63

© JOHN BARTHOLOMEW & SON LTD.

SCALE: 1 INCH TO 71 MILES

CENTRAL EUROPE

GERMANY, POLAND, CZECHOSLOVAKIA, AUSTRIA

GERMANY (Fed. Republic) AREA: 95,913 sq. miles. POPULATION: 59,676,000. CAPITAL: Bonn. CURRENCY: 100 Pfennige=1 Deutsche Mark. EAST GERMANY AREA: 41,634 sq. miles. POPULATION: 17,067,000. CAPITAL: East Berlin. CURRENCY: 100 Pfennige=1 DM Ost. Germany is highest in the south, where the Bavarian Alps form a bound-

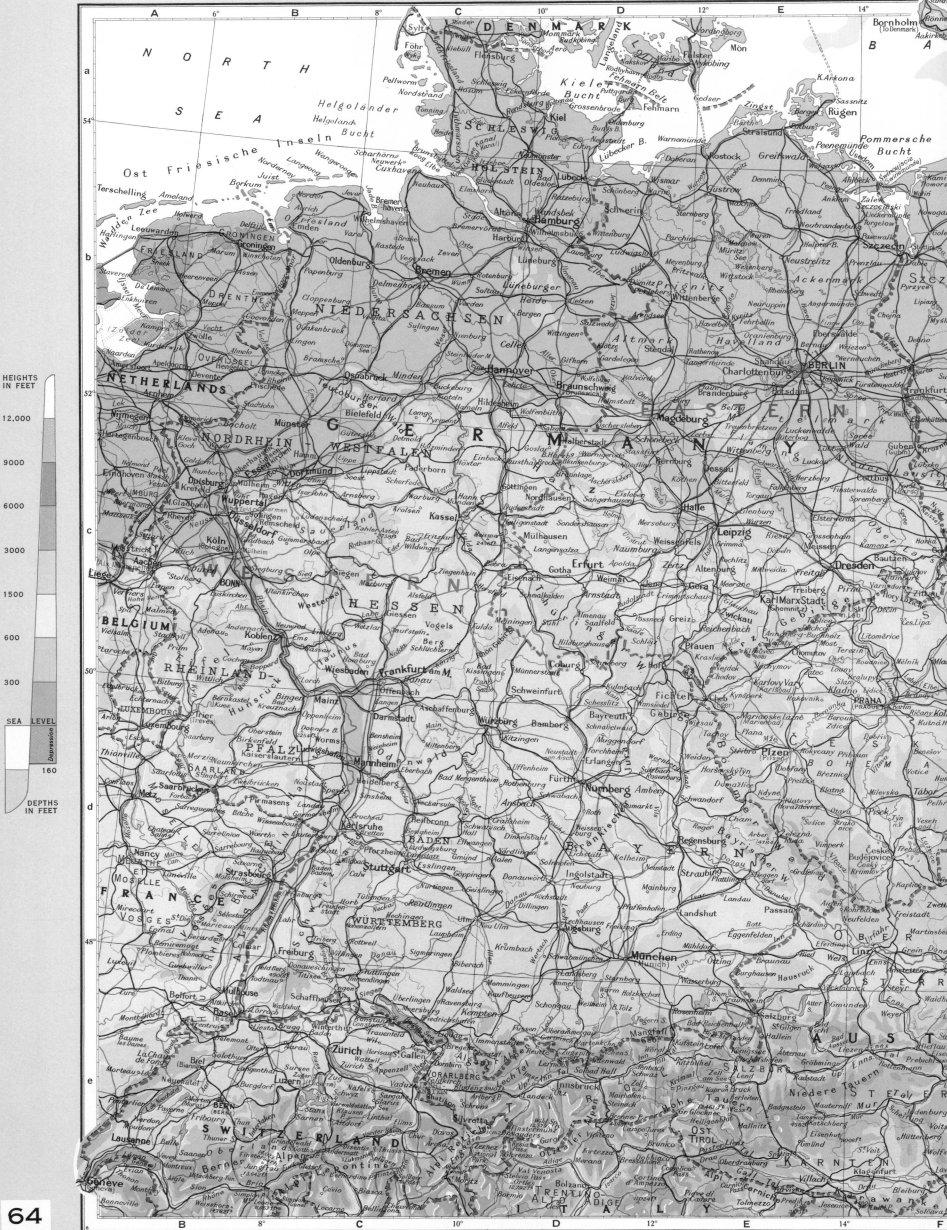

HEIGHTS IN FEET

12,000
9000
6000
3000
1500
600
300

SEA LEVEL

Depression

160

DEPTHS IN FEET

64

CONIC PROJECTION

SCALE: 1 INCH TO 47 MILES

MAIN ROADS
RAILWAYS

ary with Austria. Lower mountains in the centre give way to the North German Plain, now divided between East and West Germany. Except for the Danube, all important rivers—the Rhein, Ems, Weser, Elbe and Oder—follow this northwards slope, flowing into the Baltic or North Sea.

POLAND AREA: *120,664 sq. miles.* POPULATION: *31,698,000.* CAPITAL: *Warsaw.* CURRENCY: *100 groszy=1 zloty.* Except in the south, where it shares the Carpathians with Czechoslovakia, Poland is a vast plain connecting north Germany with the Russian steppes.

CZECHOSLOVAKIA AREA: *49,354 sq. miles.* POPULATION: *14,240,000.* CAPITAL: *Prague.* CURRENCY: *100 haler= 1 koruna.*
AUSTRIA AREA: *32,374 sq. miles.* POPULATION: *7,290,000.* CAPITAL: *Vienna.* CURRENCY: *100 Groschen=1 Schilling.*

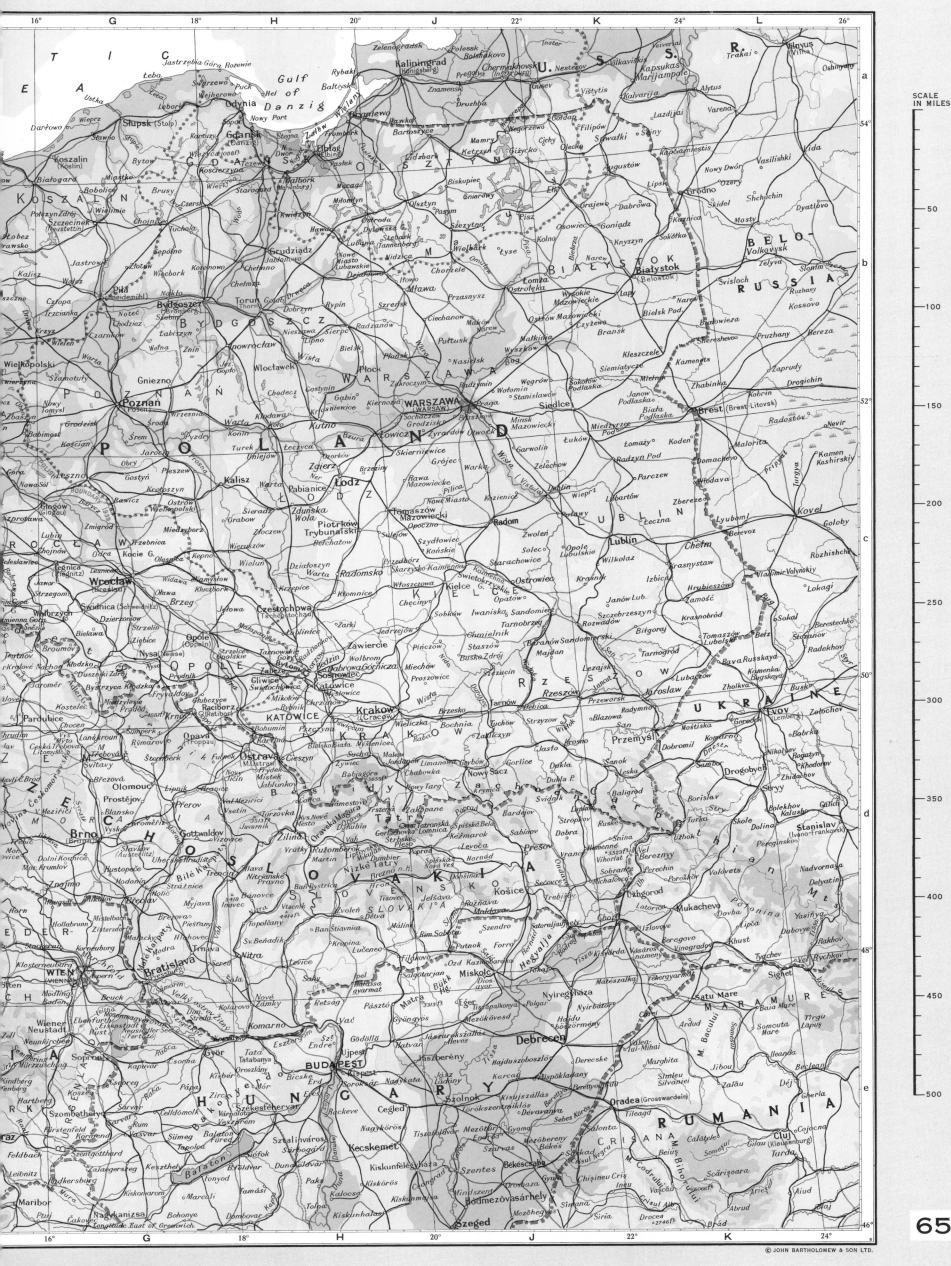

SCALE IN MILES

SCALE: 1 INCH TO 47 MILES

© JOHN BARTHOLOMEW & SON LTD.

INTERNATIONAL BOUNDARIES

STATE BOUNDARIES

IBERIAN PENINSULA

SPAIN, PORTUGAL

SPAIN AREA: 194,883 sq. miles. POPULATION: 31,871,000. CAPITAL: *Madrid.*
CURRENCY: 100 cèntimos=1 peseta.
PORTUGAL AREA: 35,453 sq. miles. POPULATION: 9,218,000. CAPITAL:
Lisbon. CURRENCY: 100 centavos=1 escudo. Roughly pentagonal in shape,

HEIGHTS
IN FEET

9000
6000
3000
1500
600
300

SEA LEVEL

150
600
6000

DEPTHS
IN FEET

66

CONIC PROJECTION

SCALE: 1 INCH TO 47 MILES

MAIN ROADS
RAILWAYS

the Iberian peninsula is divided between Spain, Portugal and the small state of Andorra. Seven-eighths of it is bordered by sea, the remainder by the high wall of the Pyrénées, which separates it from France and the land mass of Europe. Southwards, only eight and a half miles away at its nearest point, lies the continent of Africa. More than half the peninsula is covered by the Meseta, a high central plateau which is surrounded and traversed by mountain ranges. The rivers, notably the Tagus, flow mainly westwards. The four main islands of the Balearic group form a province of Spain; the Canary Islands are another province.

SCALE IN MILES

67

INTERNATIONAL BOUNDARIES
STATE BOUNDARIES

SCALE: 1 INCH TO 47 MILES

FRANCE
AND NORTHERN ALGERIA

AREA: *212,974 sq. miles.* POPULATION: *49,440,000.* CAPITAL: *Paris.*
CURRENCY: *100 centimes= 1 nouveau franc.* Around France are three seas,
into which flow the four great French rivers: the Seine into the English
Channel, the Loire and Garonne into the Atlantic, and the Rhône into

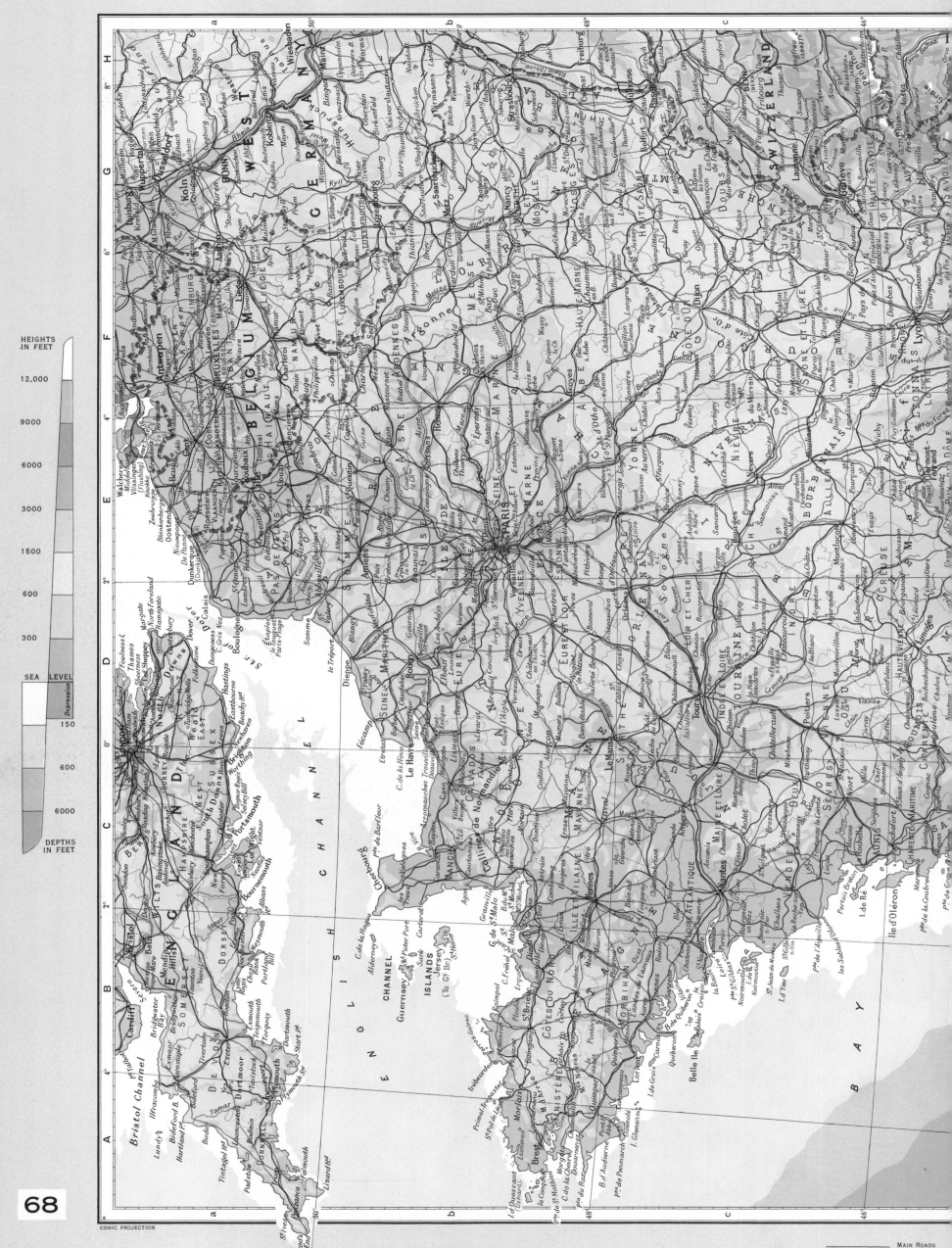

HEIGHTS
IN FEET

12,000
9000
6000
3000
1500
600
300

SEA LEVEL

Depression

150
600
6000

DEPTHS
IN FEET

CONIC PROJECTION

SCALE: 1 INCH TO 47 MILES

MAIN ROADS
RAILWAYS

the Mediterranean. This maritime outlook gives the country its mild and even climate. A line drawn from Sedan, in the north-east, to Bayonne, in the south-west, divides the country roughly into its upland and lowland halves. The north-western half is mainly low-lying and includes the broad plains of Normandy and Brittany. On France's eastern borders rise the high mountains of the Vosges, the Jura and the Alps (Mont Blanc, 15,771 feet, is one of the highest peaks in Europe). Running southwards from the centre is the Massif Central, while the Pyrénées in the south-west form a natural barrier between France and Spain.

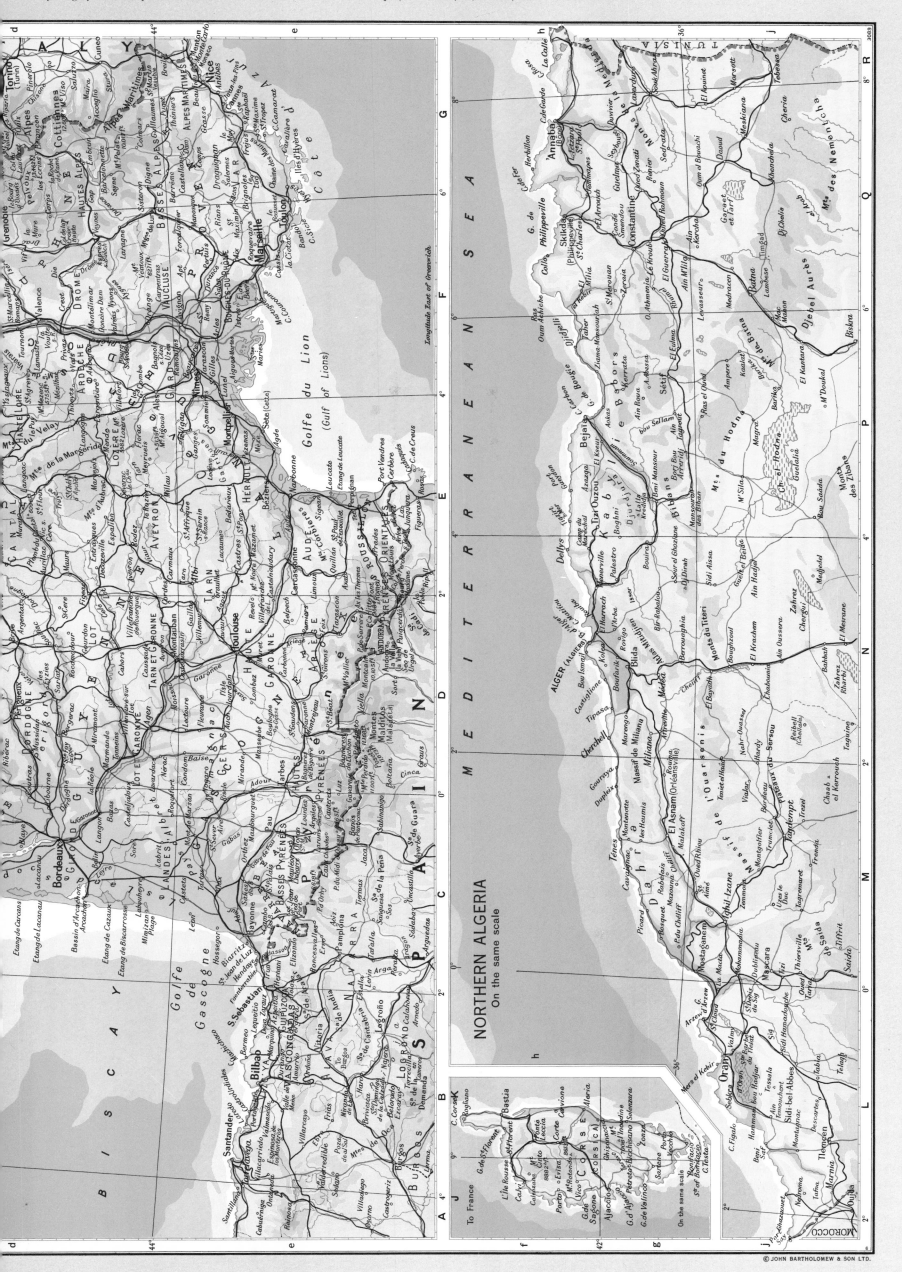

NORTHERN ALGERIA
On the same scale

SCALE IN MILES

50
100
150
200
250
300
350
400
450
500

INTERNATIONAL BOUNDARIES
DEPARTMENT BOUNDARIES

SCALE: 1 INCH TO 47 MILES

69

ITALY

AREA: *116,286 sq. miles.* POPULATION: *51,859,000.* CAPITAL: *Rome.* CURRENCY: *100 centesimi = 1 lira.*

Italy owes its boot-like shape to the Apennines which reach down the whole length of the country, culminating, across the Straits of Messina, in the island of Sicily. To the north the Alps encircle the peninsula like the head of a mushroom, shutting off Italy from the rest of Europe. The strange-shaped Dolomitic Alps (Dolomites) to the east form

HEIGHTS
IN FEET

12,000
9000
6000
3000
1500
600
300

SEA LEVEL

150
600
6000

DEPTHS
IN FEET

CONIC PROJECTION

SCALE: 1 INCH TO 47 MILES

MAIN ROADS
RAILWAYS

an important part of this mountain barrier which makes the country difficult to approach, and the names of the principal passes—the Simplon and St. Gotthard from Switzerland, and the Brenner from Austria—have become household words among travellers all over Europe.

Italy contains the only active volcanoes in Europe, notably Etna (the highest, 10,705 feet) in Sicily, and Vesuvius near Naples. Of the rivers, most of which are unnavigable, the longest is the Po (420 miles) which waters the fertile plain of Lombardy before entering the Adriatic through its delta between Venice and Ravenna. Other important rivers are the Tiber and the Arno.

SCALE IN MILES

SCALE: 1 INCH TO 47 MILES

INTERNATIONAL BOUNDARIES

REGIONAL BOUNDARIES

THE BALKANS

HUNGARY, RUMANIA, YUGOSLAVIA, BULGARIA, GREECE

HUNGARY AREA: 35,919 sq. miles. POPULATION: 10,179,000.
CAPITAL: *Budapest.* CURRENCY: 100 *fillér*=1 forint.
RUMANIA AREA: 91,699 sq. miles. POPULATION: 19,143,000.
CAPITAL: *Bucharest.* CURRENCY: 100 bani=1 leu.

HEIGHTS IN FEET

6000
3000
1500
600
300
SEA LEVEL
150
600
6000

CONIC PROJECTION

72

SCALE: 1 INCH TO 47 MILES

MAIN ROADS
RAILWAYS

YUGOSLAVIA AREA:98,766sq.miles.POPULATION:19,756,000.
CAPITAL: *Belgrade*. CURRENCY: *100 paras=1 dinar.*
BULGARIA AREA: 42,796 sq. miles. POPULATION: 8,258,000.
CAPITAL: *Sofia*. CURRENCY: *100 stotinki=1 (new) lev.*

GREECE AREA: 50,944 sq. miles. POPULATION : 8,612,000.
CAPITAL: *Athens*. CURRENCY: *100 lepta=1 drachma.*
The Balkan peninsula, with its broken coastline and many offshore islands, is separated from the rest

of Europe by the river Danube (1,770 miles long and western Europe's longest river) which flows eastwards from Hungary and through the Iron Gate, a gorge between the Carpathians and the barren Dinaric Alps in Yugoslavia.

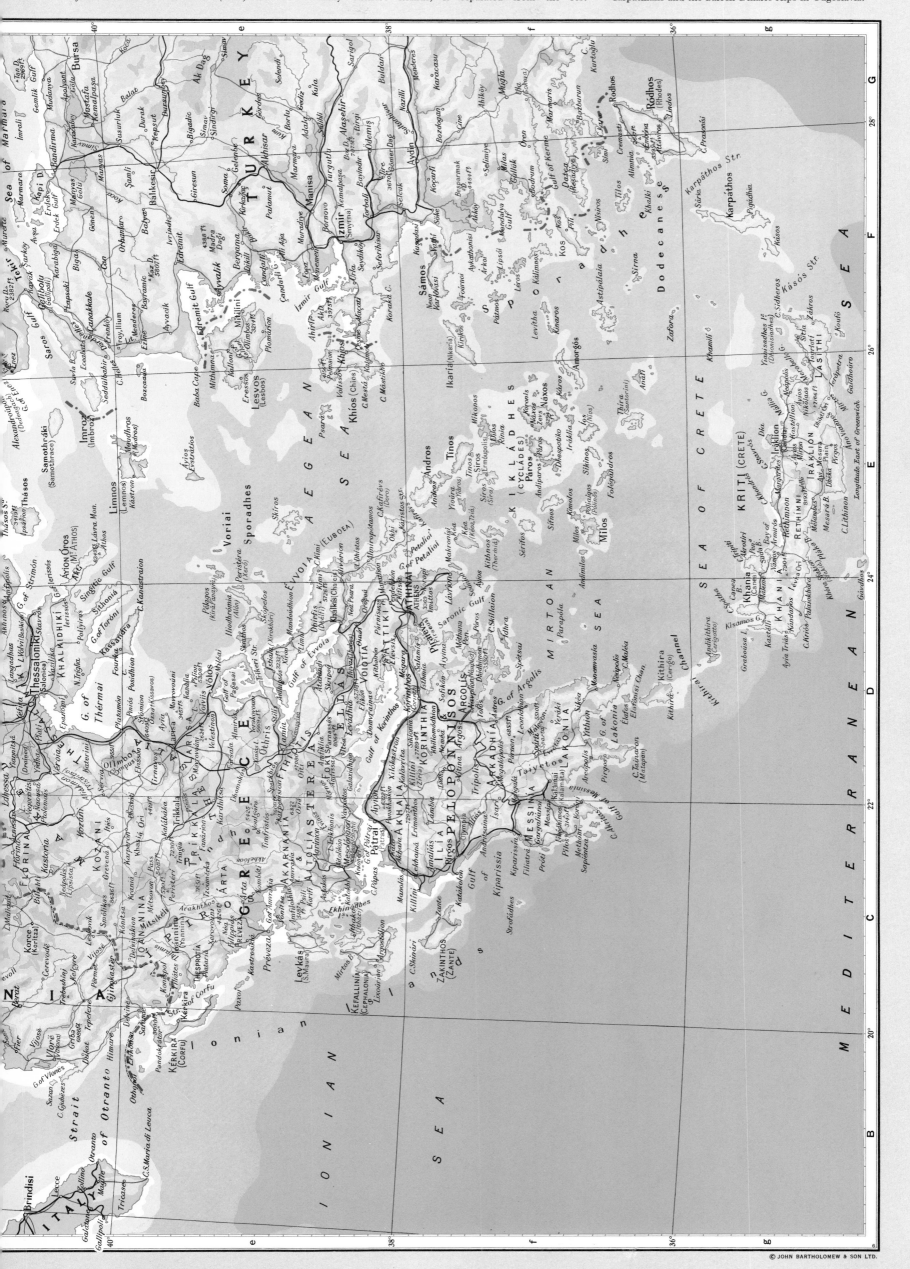

SCALE IN MILES

73

© JOHN BARTHOLOMEW & SON LTD.

INTERNATIONAL BOUNDARIES
PROVINCIAL BOUNDARIES

SCALE: 1 INCH TO 47 MILES

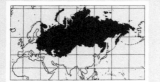

U.S.S.R.

AREA: *8,649,489 sq. miles.* POPULATION: *233,180,000.* CAPITAL: *Moscow.*
CURRENCY: *100 copecks=1 (new) rouble.*
The vast area of the U.S.S.R., straddling all Asia and half of Europe, shares
its immense boundaries with many countries in both continents. It is divided

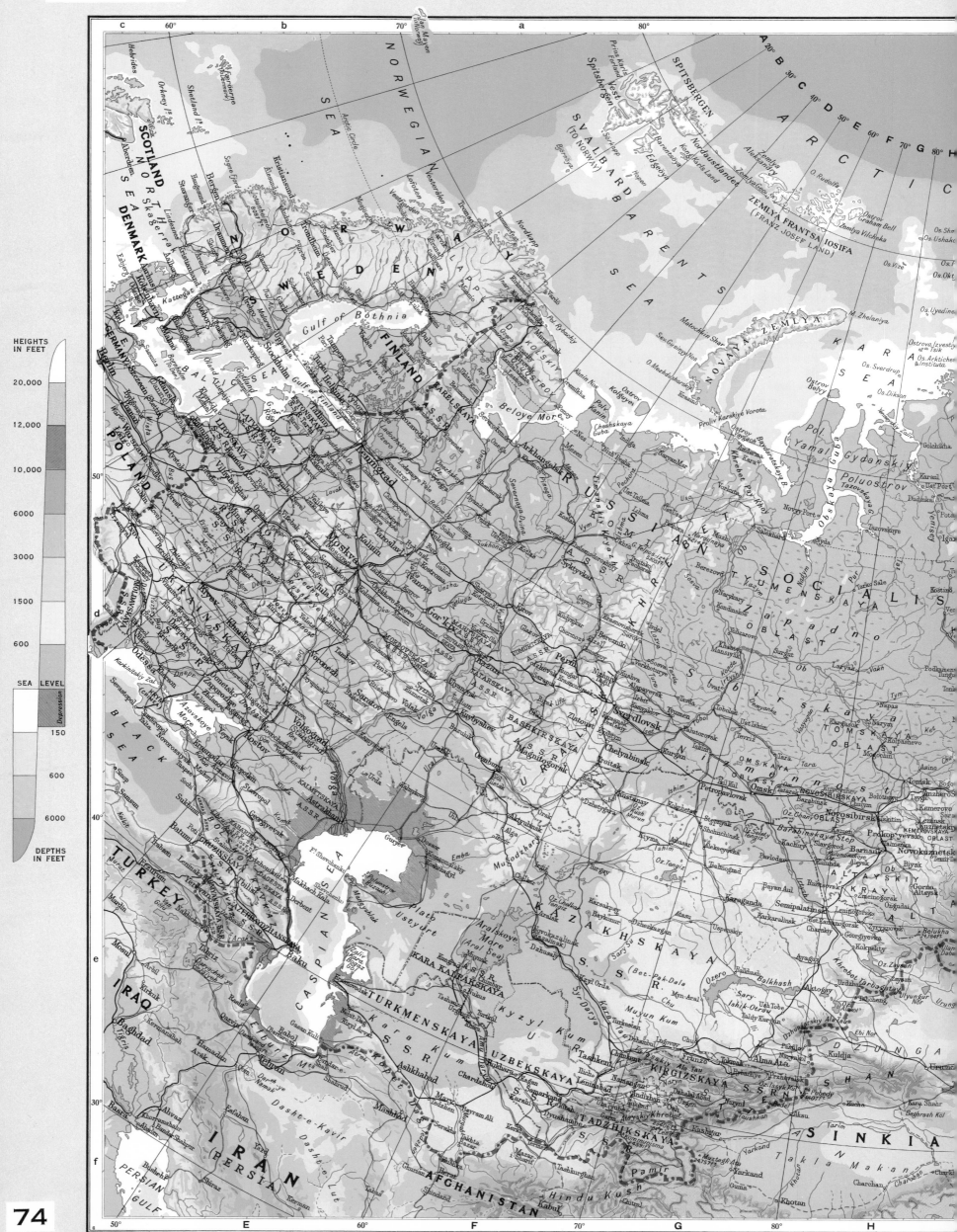

HEIGHTS
IN FEET

20,000

12,000

10,000

6000

3000

1500

600

SEA LEVEL

150

600

6000

DEPTHS
IN FEET

CONIC PROJECTION

SCALE: 1 INCH TO 276 MILES

MAIN ROADS

RAILWAYS

structurally into three regions from west to east: two plains, separated by the Uralski Khrebet (which also form a useful dividing line between Asia and Europe) and a vast region of hazardous country ending in the remote peninsula of Kamchatka. On the north—south axis there are likewise three zones. The frozen tundra of the Arctic merges into forests and fertile plains, which end at the borders of the great desert belt stretching from Mongolia to the Caspian. In fact, the U.S.S.R. is hemmed in on three fronts by hot or cold deserts or mountains, so that easy access is found only on the western side, through Europe.

SCALE IN MILES

100
200
300
400
500
600
700
800
900
1000
1100
1200
1300
1400
1500
1600
1700
1800
1900
2000
2100
2200
2300
2400
2500
2600
2700
2800
2900
3000

© JOHN BARTHOLOMEW & SON LTD.

INTERNATIONAL BOUNDARIES
STATE BOUNDARIES

SCALE: 1 INCH TO 276 MILES

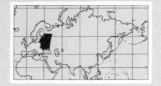

EUROPEAN RUSSIA

The area between the Baltic and the Black Sea is part of the enormous Russian Plain which stretches unbroken to the Central Russian uplands, before continuing eastwards. The comparatively low land in this district is shown up by the meandering rivers and the lakes and marshes of the Pripyat region. To the south, the mild undulations of the Ukrainian steppe interrupt the monotony of the northern plain.

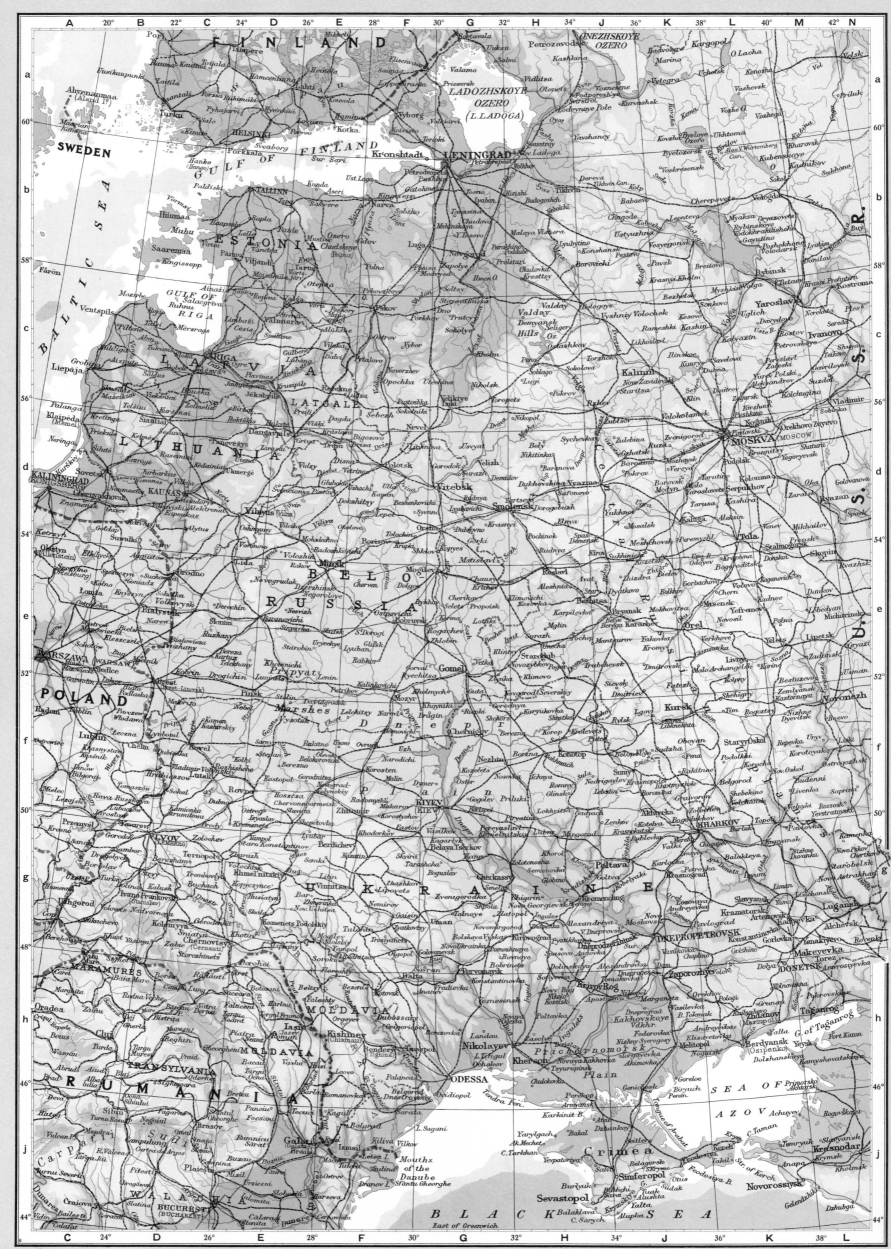

HEIGHTS
IN FEET

6000

3000

1500

600

300

SEA LEVEL

Depression

160

600

DEPTHS
IN FEET

CONIC PROJECTION

SCALE: 1 INCH TO 94 MILES

━━━━━━ INTERNATIONAL BOUNDARIES

------- STATE BOUNDARIES

THE VOLGA BASIN

This map shows the highest and the lowest parts of European Russia, from the Urals, up to 5,500 feet high, to the northern end of the Caspian, 50 feet below sea level. The two main rivers are the Don, and the 2,400-mile-long Volga which flows through several immense artificial lakes, recently created. The huge, low-lying plain that circles the northern end of the Caspian is the largest area of inland drainage in the world.

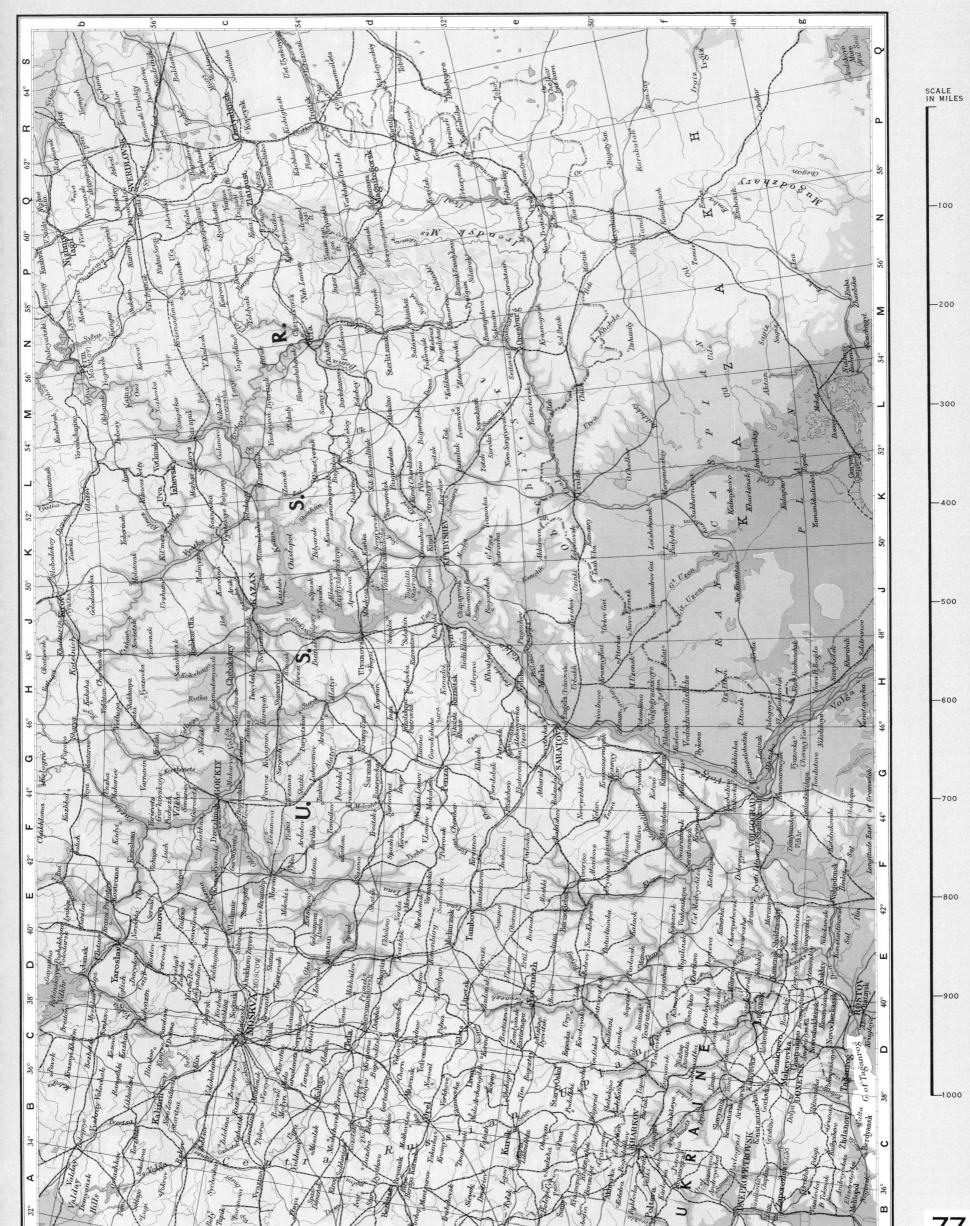

SCALE IN MILES

MAIN ROADS

RAILWAYS

CONIC PROJECTION

SCALE: 1 INCH TO 94 MILES

77

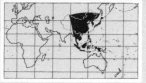

THE FAR EAST

NORTH KOREA, SOUTH KOREA, PHILIPPINES, INDONESIA

NORTH KOREA AREA: 46,540 sq. miles. POP: 12,100,000.
CAPITAL: *Pyongyang.* CURRENCY: 100 jun = 1 new won.
SOUTH KOREA AREA: 38,004 sq. miles. POPULATION:
29,086,000. CAP: *Seoul.* CURRENCY: 10 hwan = 1 won.

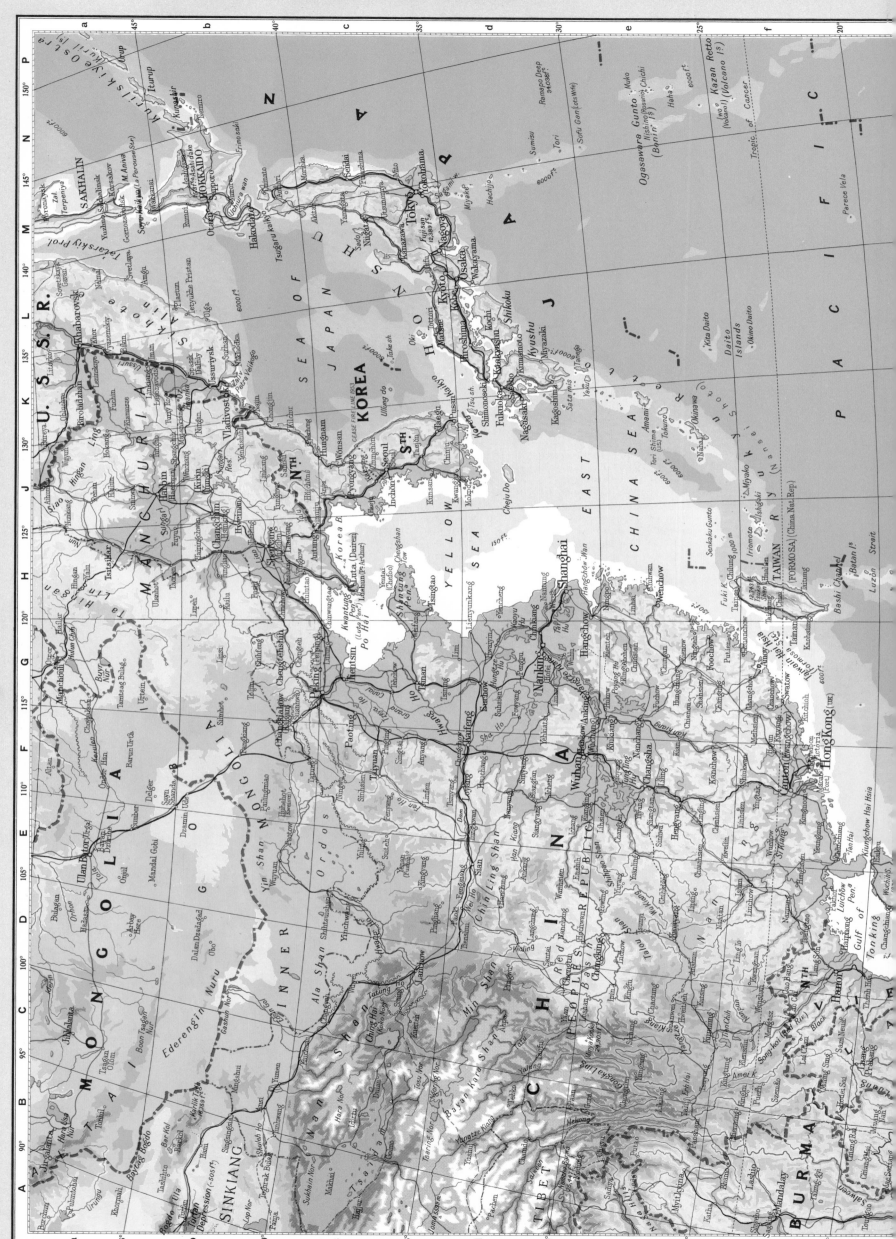

HEIGHTS
IN FEET

16,000

12,000

10,000

6000

3000

1500

600

SEA LEVEL

Depression

150

600

6000

78

BONNE'S PROJECTION

SCALE: 1 INCH TO 237 MILES

MAIN ROADS

RAILWAYS

PHILIPPINES AREA: *115,830 sq. miles.* POP: *33,477,000.*
CAPITAL: *Manila.* CURRENCY: *100 centaros=1 peso.*
INDONESIA AREA: *735,488 sq. miles.* POP: *104,500,000.*
CAPITAL: *Djakarta.* CURRENCY: *100 sen=1 rupiah.*

From the high Tibetan plateau to the deep ocean bed off the Philippines is a drop of nearly 50,000 feet. The shallow seas of the Indonesian Archipelago and the mainly volcanic formation of the mountainous islands curving round West

Malaysia to New Guinea are a marked contrast to the Himalayan fold mountains. The Philippines, some 7,000 islands, form the apex of a triangle based on Indonesia and pointing north to the equally mountainous islands of Japan.

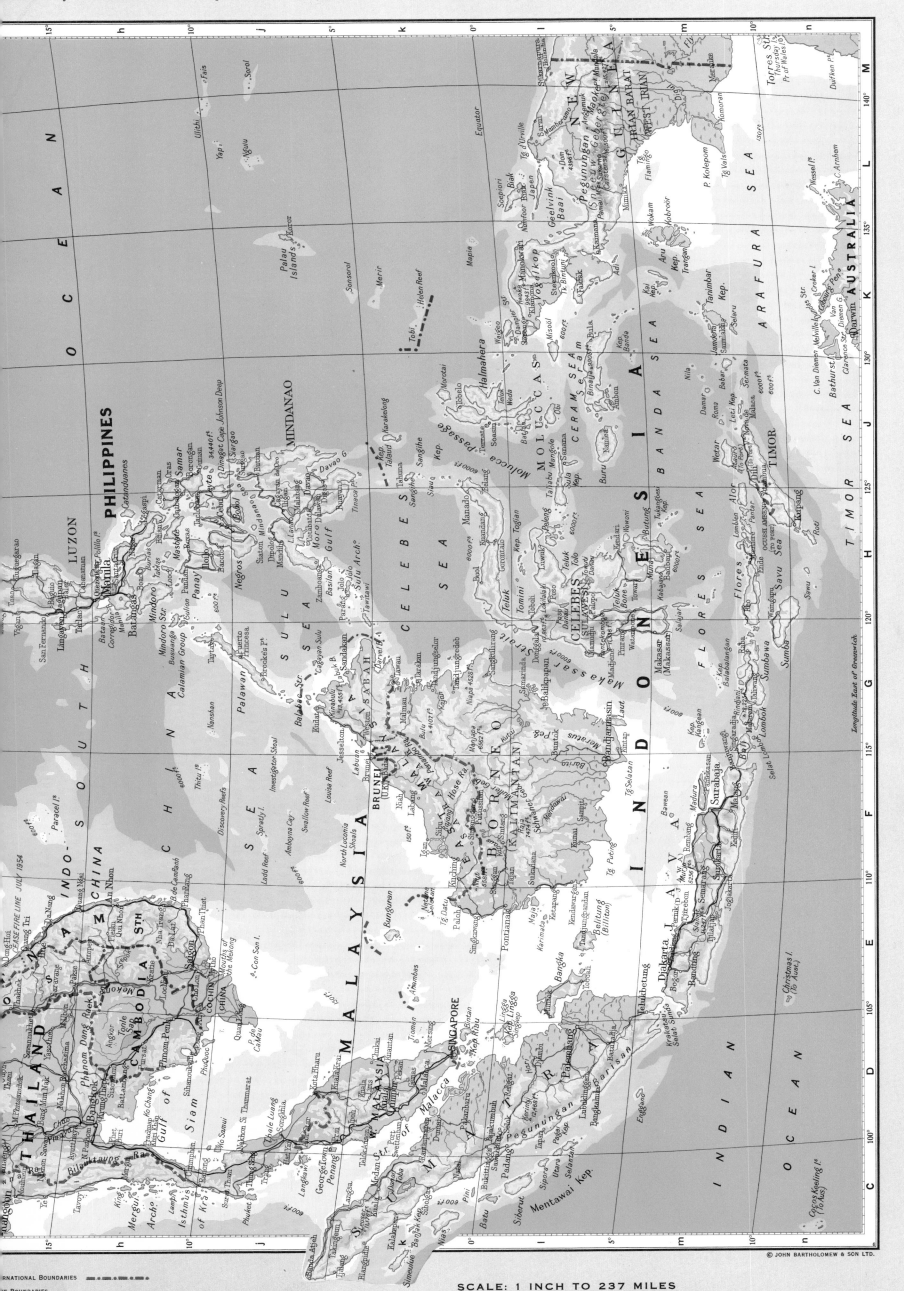

SCALE IN MILES

SCALE: 1 INCH TO 237 MILES

© JOHN BARTHOLOMEW & SON LTD.

x

INTERNATIONAL BOUNDARIES
STATE BOUNDARIES

EAST CHINA

CHINA AREA: *3,691,502 sq. miles.* POPULATION: *700,000,000.* CAPITAL: *Peking.* CURRENCY: *100 fen=1 yuan.*

Though half covered by mountains, China has the largest population of any country in the world, and also the largest area of fertile land. The eastern half of the map shows a semi-circle of low-lying land dotted with lakes, testifying

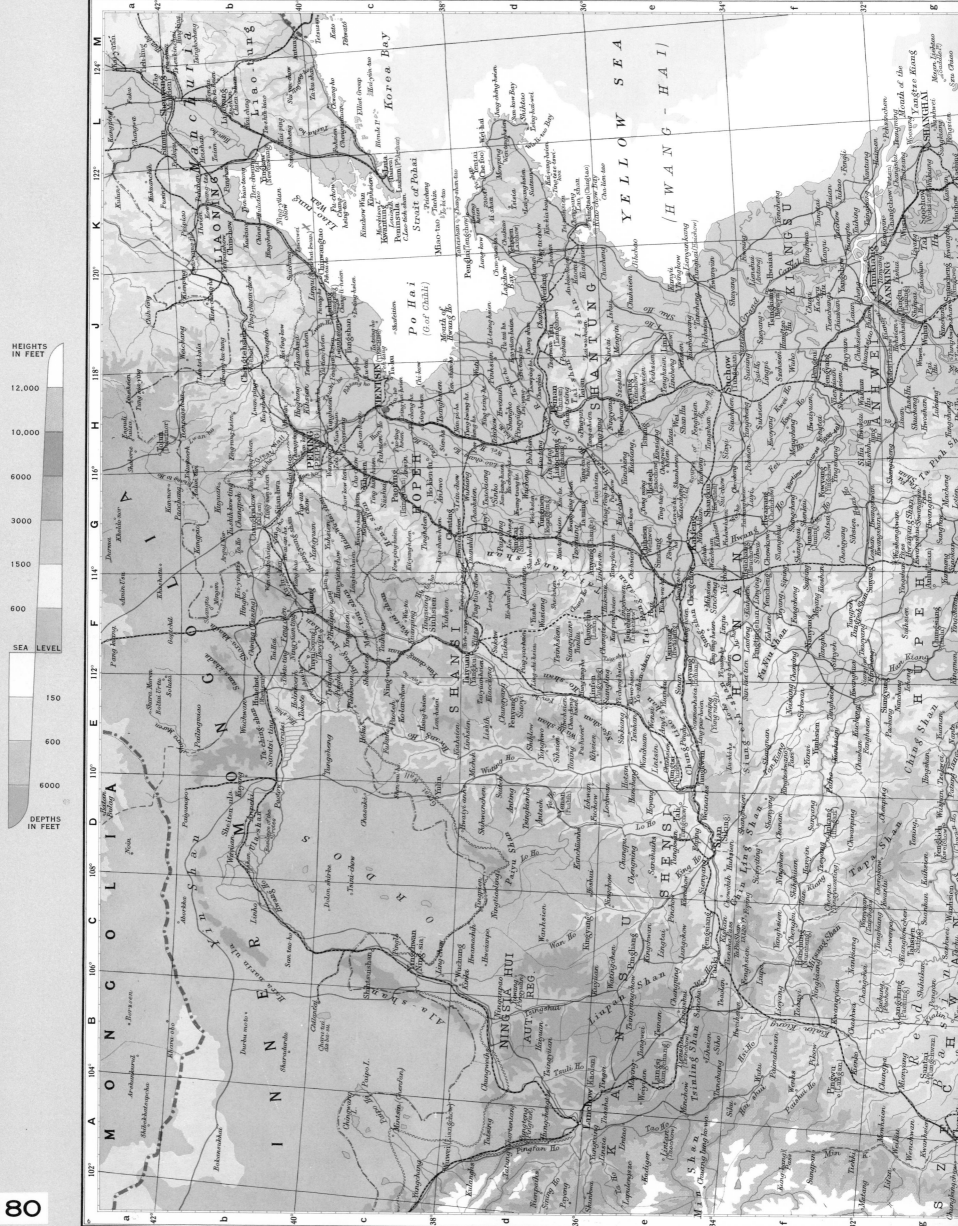

HEIGHTS IN FEET

12,000
10,000
6000
3000
1500
600
SEA LEVEL
150
600
6000

DEPTHS IN FEET

80

CONIC PROJECTION

SCALE: 1 INCH TO 94 MILES

—————— MAIN ROADS

- - - - - - RAILWAYS

to inadequate river drainage. This area is backed by vast mountain ranges running north-east to Siberia, and cut up by mountainous tracts on a south-east axis reaching down to the coast of Chekiang. Each of the three main rivers,

the Hwang Ho (Yellow River), the Yangtze Kiang and the Si Kiang, has a broad, well-watered valley, and together these valleys contain more than two-thirds of China's inhabitants. Sinkiang, the largest province, is mostly desert.

Another desert, the Gobi, which separates northern China from Outer Mongolia, covers nearly one-third of China's total area. China's jagged south-eastern coastline contrasts sharply with the smoother coastline north of Shanghai.

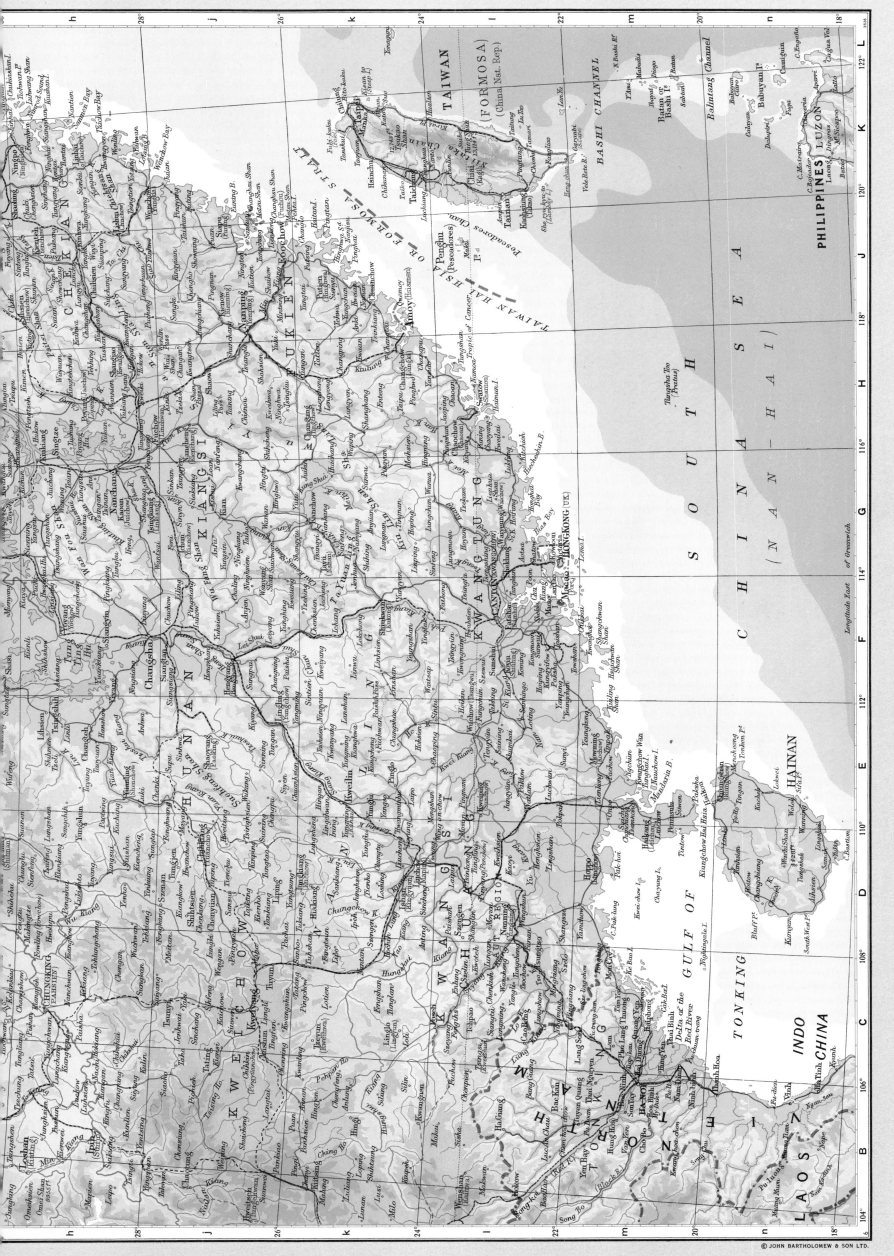

SCALE IN MILES

50
100
150
200
250
300
350
400
450
500
550
600
650
700
750
800
850
900
950
1000

INTERNATIONAL BOUNDARIES
PROVINCIAL BOUNDARIES

SCALE: 1 INCH TO 94 MILES

81

JAPAN

AREA: *142,719 sq. miles.* POPULATION: *98,865,000.*
CAPITAL: *Tokyo.* CURRENCY: *100 sen=1 yen.*
Japan consists of a group of four large islands and many smaller ones, stretching from north to south over a thousand miles and separated from China by the shallow Sea of Japan. The main island is Honshu, which is approximately the same size as Great Britain. Off Japan's east coast the Pacific Ocean is almost at its deepest.

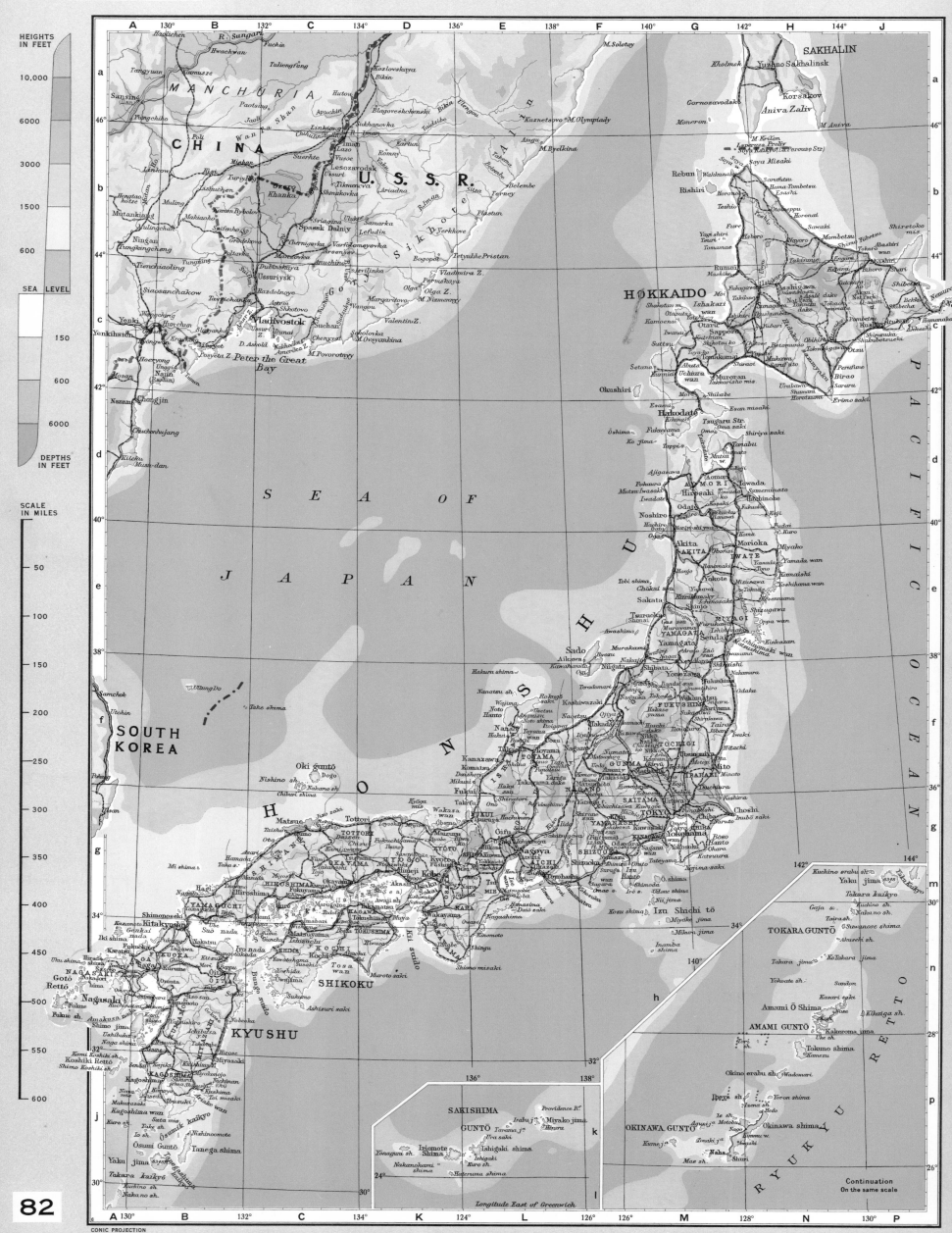

HEIGHTS IN FEET

10,000
6000
3000
1500
600
SEA LEVEL
150
600
6000

DEPTHS IN FEET

SCALE IN MILES

50
100
150
200
250
300
350
400
450
500
550
600

82

CONIC PROJECTION

SCALE: 1 INCH TO 94 MILES

INTERNATIONAL BOUNDARIES
PROVINCIAL BOUNDARIES

SOUTH-EAST ASIA

THAILAND AREA: 198,455 sq. miles. POPULA-
TION: 31,500,000. CAPITAL: *Bangkok.*
WEST MALAYSIA AREA: 50,690 sq. miles.
POPULATION: 8,298,000. CAPITAL: *Kuala Lumpur.*

NORTH VIETNAM AREA: 61,293 sq. miles.
POPULATION: 19,000,000. CAPITAL: *Hanoi.*
SOUTH VIETNAM AREA: 65,948 sq. miles.
POPULATION: 16,543,000. CAPITAL: *Saigon.*

LAOS AREA: 88,780 sq. miles. POP: 2,635,000
CAPITAL: *Luang Prabang.* (GOVT: *Vientiane.*)
CAMBODIA AREA: 69,900 sq. miles. POPULA
TION: 6,250,000. CAPITAL: *Phnom-Penh.*

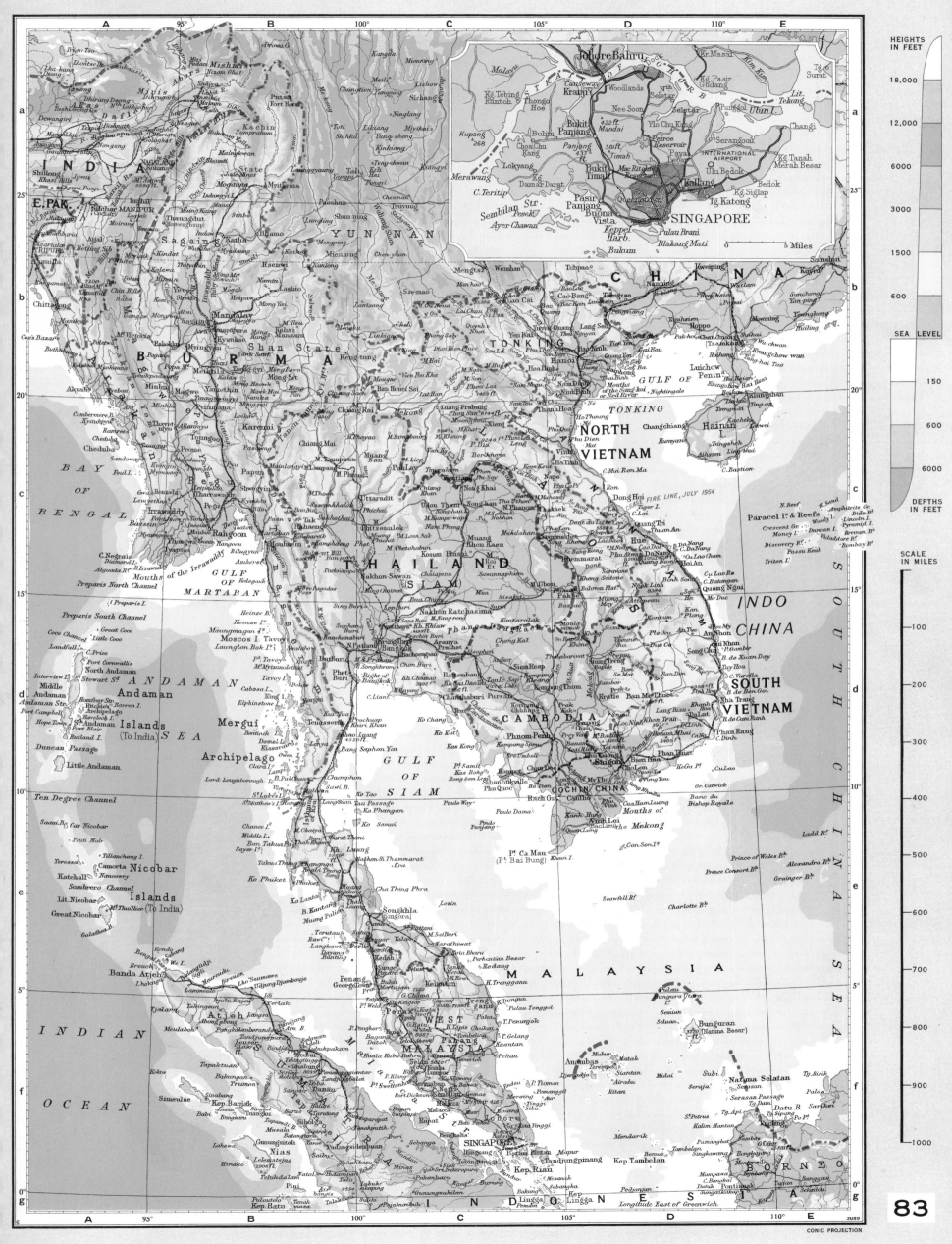

HEIGHTS
IN FEET

18,000
12,000
6000
3000
1500
600
SEA LEVEL
150
600
6000
DEPTHS
IN FEET

SCALE
IN MILES

100
200
300
400
500
600
700
800
900
1000

83

CONIC PROJECTION

MAIN ROADS
RAILWAYS

SCALE: 1 INCH TO 158 MILES

INDIA, PAKISTAN
CEYLON, BURMA

INDIA AREA: 1,229,215 sq. miles. POP: (excluding Kashmir-Jammu, Sikkim):
483,000,000. CAPITAL: Delhi. CURRENCY: 100 naye paise=1 rupee.
PAKISTAN AREA: 365,528 sq. miles. POP: (excl. Kashmir-Jammu, Gilgit, Baltistan):
105,044,000. CAP: Rawalpindi (Islamabad under construct.). CURRENCY: 100 paisas=1 ru

HEIGHTS
IN FEET

18,000

12,000

6000

3000

1500

600

SEA LEVEL

150

600

6000

DEPTHS
IN FEET

CONIC PROJECTION

SCALE: 1 INCH TO 158 MILES

———— MAIN ROADS

------------ RAILWAYS

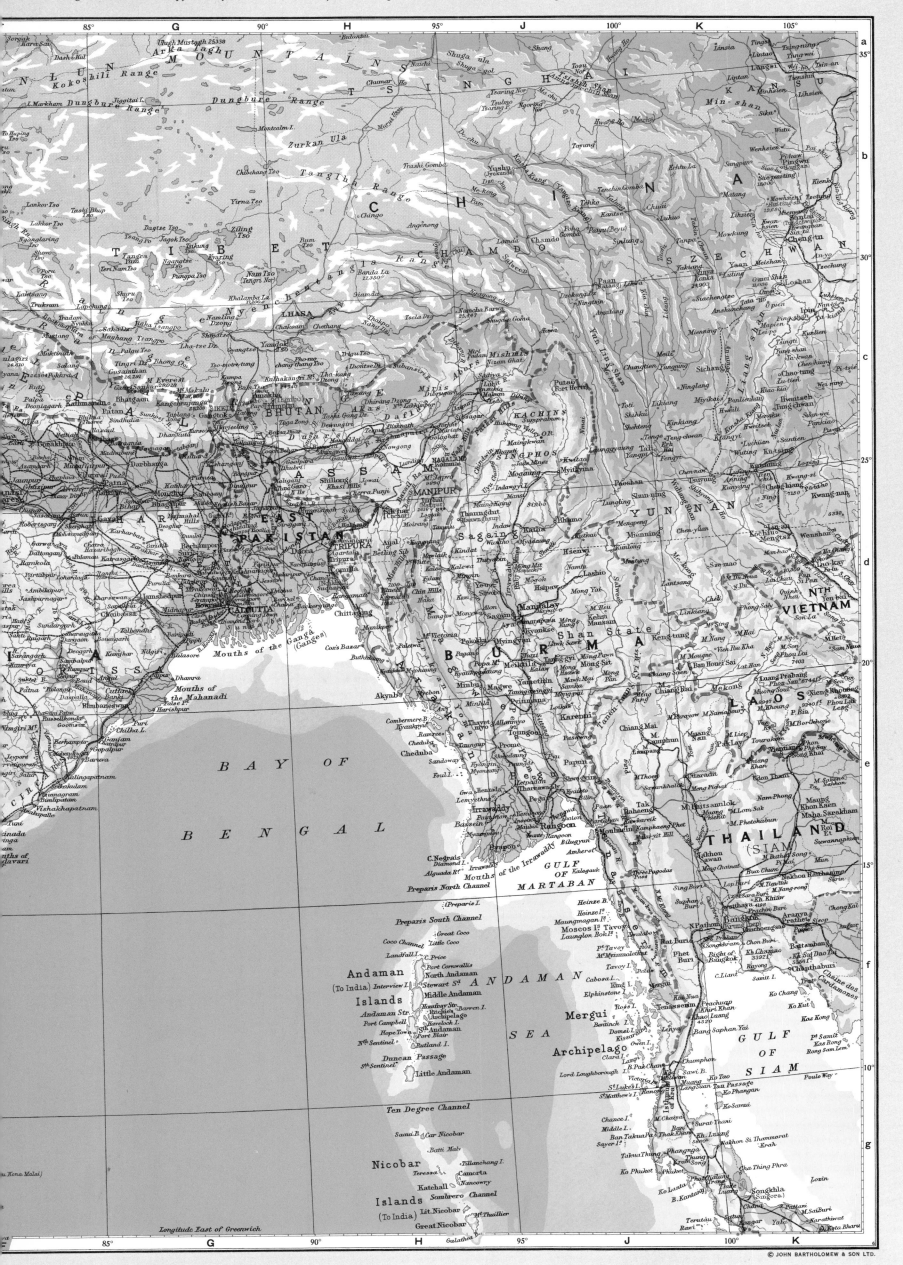

CEYLON AREA: 25,332 sq. miles. POPULATION: 11,500,000.
CAPITAL: *Colombo*. CURRENCY: *100 cents=rupee.*
BURMA AREA: 261,789 sq. miles. POPULATION: 25,246,000.
CAPITAL: *Rangoon*. CURRENCY: *100 pyas=1 kyat.*

The Indian peninsula falls into three main regions: the Himalayas, the great plains of the Indus and the Ganges, and the Deccan plateau. The mountains to the north virtually seal off the peninsula from the rest of Asia. Along the coast from the Gulf of Cambay down to Cape Comorin, runs the long mountain range of the Western Ghats. The high mountains of Burma are separated by the valley of the Irrawaddy and Sittang rivers.

SCALE IN MILES

85

SCALE: 1 INCH TO 158 MILES

© JOHN BARTHOLOMEW & SON LTD.

INTERNATIONAL BOUNDARIES
STATE BOUNDARIES

PUNJAB AND KASHMIR

To the north-west of the Indian peninsula a region of contrasts ranges from the arid deserts of the lower Indus plain to the perpetual snows of the high Himalayas in Kashmir, part of the district known as the Roof of the World. The area is intersected by the erratic courses of the Indus and its tributaries, which rise close to the eastward-flowing Brahmaputra River, shown on the opposite map.

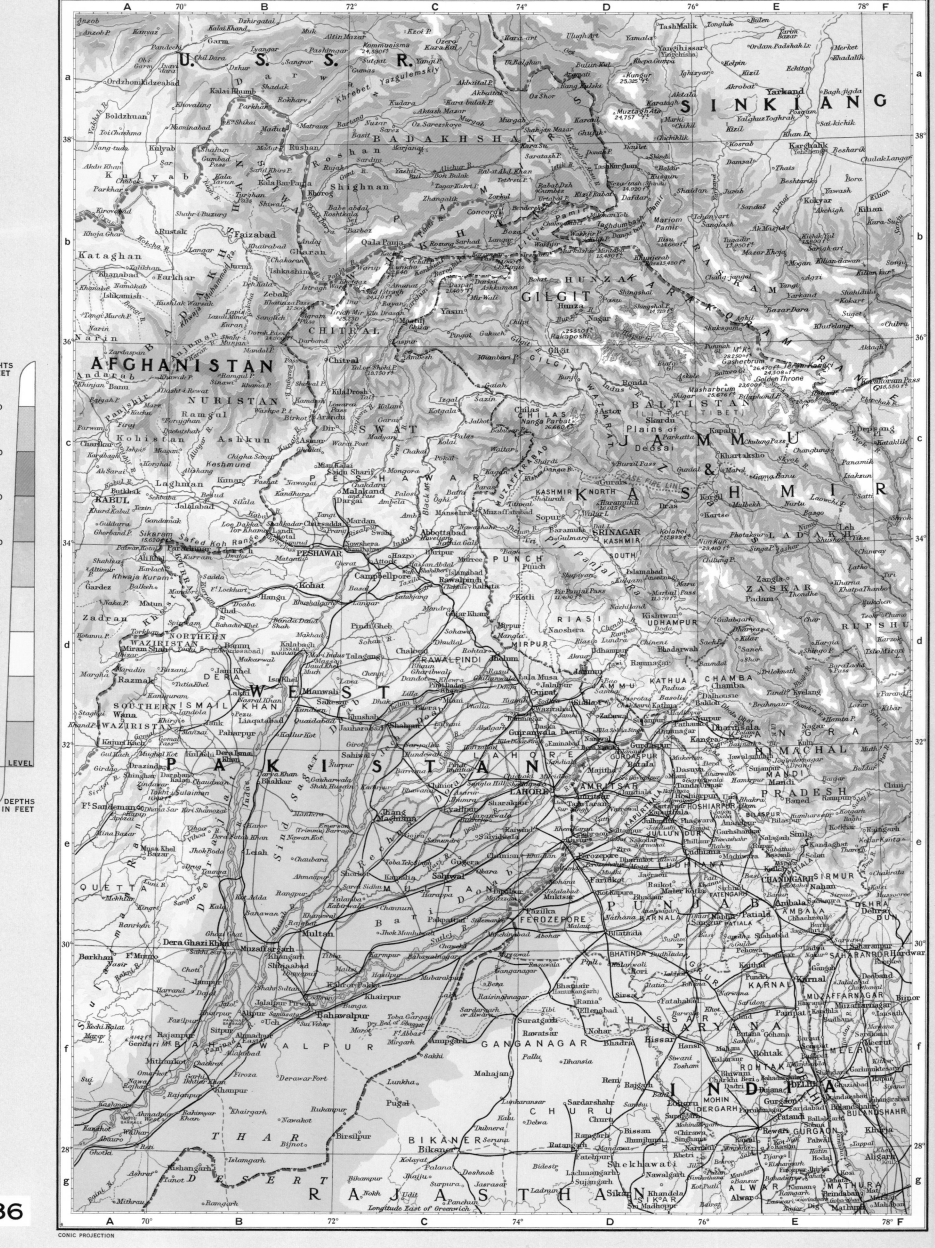

HEIGHTS
IN FEET

18000

16000

12000

10000

6000

3000

1500

600

SEA LEVEL

DEPTHS
IN FEET

CONIC PROJECTION

SCALE: 1 INCH TO 63 MILES

INTERNATIONAL BOUNDARIES

STATE BOUNDARIES

The Ganges valley is one of the most thickly populated regions in the world. The population is entirely dependent on the rivers that flow down from the north-west, across the plain, and through their many deltas into the Bay of Bengal. These rivers bring with them rich alluvial deposits and provide waters for irrigation. The largest river in the plain is revered throughout India as Mother Ganges.

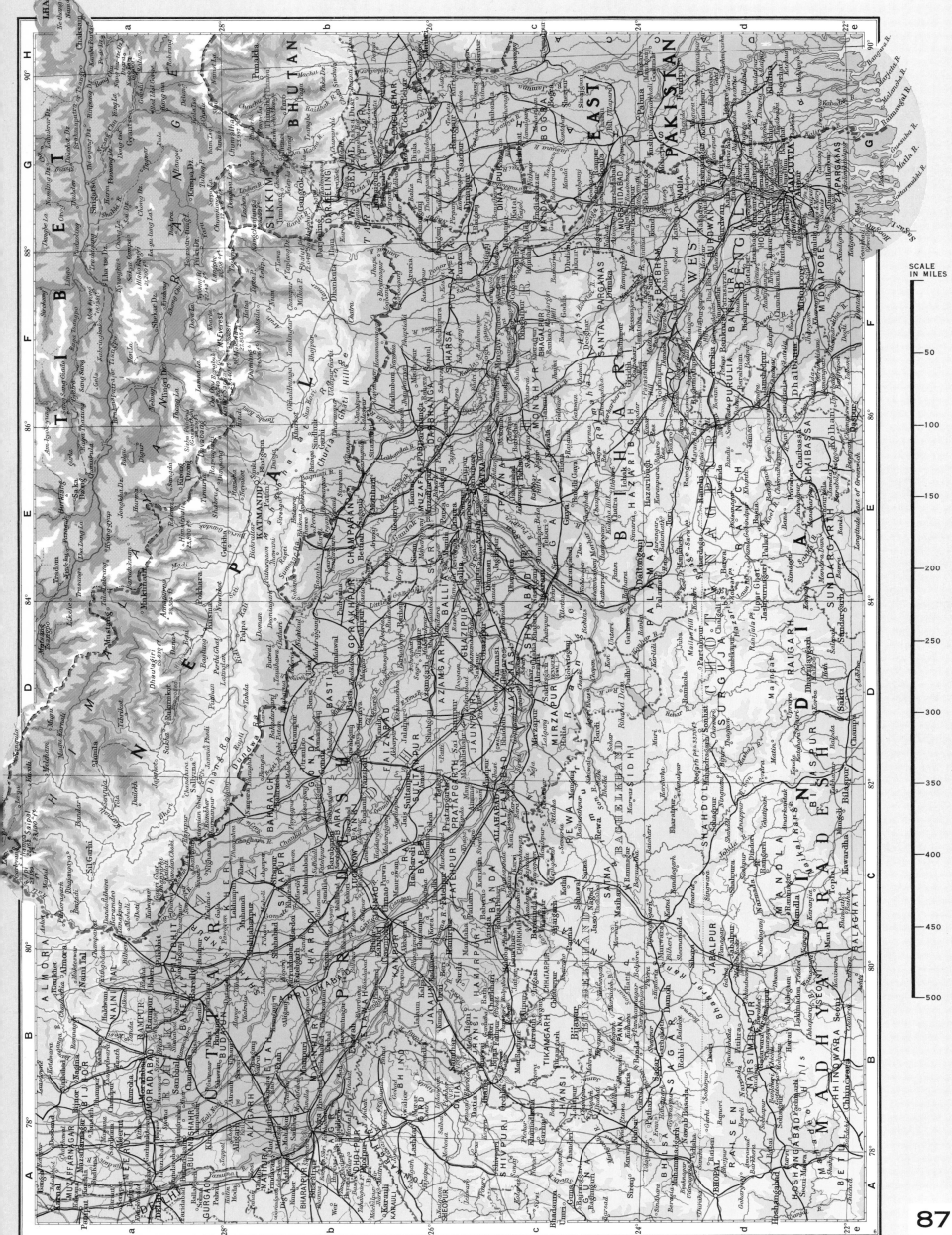

SCALE IN MILES

MAIN ROADS _____
RAILWAYS _____

CONIC PROJECTION

SCALE: 1 INCH TO 63 MILES

THE MIDDLE EAST
AND AFGHANISTAN

TURKEY AREA: 301,380 sq. miles. POPULATION: 32,901,000. CAPITAL:
Ankara. CURRENCY: 100 piastres (kurus) = 1 pound.
IRAQ AREA: 173,259 sq. miles. POPULATION: 8,338,000. CAPITAL:
Baghdad. CURRENCY: 1,000 fils = 1 dinar.

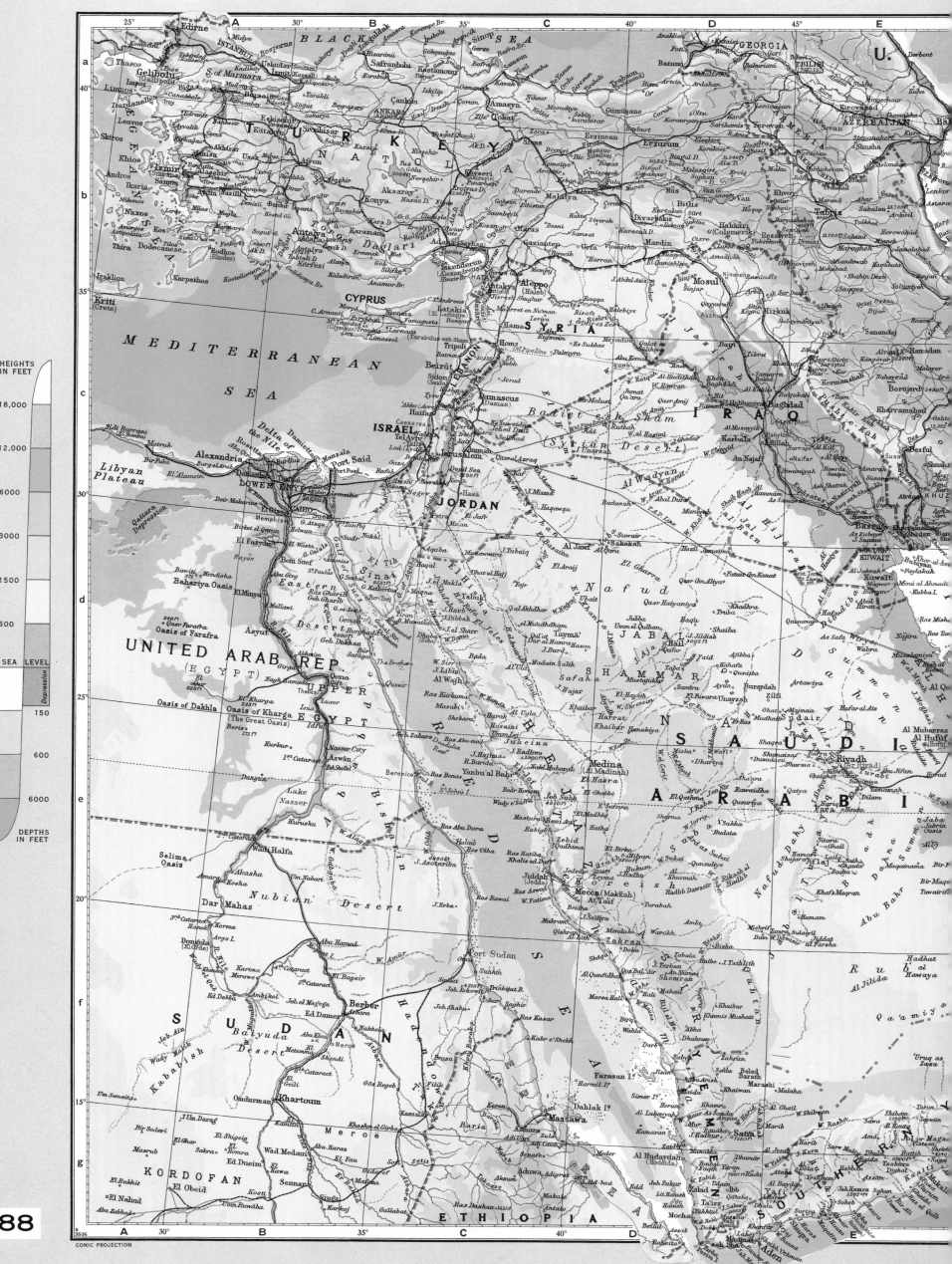

HEIGHTS
IN FEET

18,000

12,000

6000

3000

1500

600

SEA LEVEL

Depression

150

600

6000

DEPTHS
IN FEET

88

CONIC PROJECTION

SCALE: 1 INCH TO 158 MILES

MAIN ROADS

RAILWAYS

IRAN (PERSIA) AREA: 636,293 sq. miles. POPULATION: 25,780,000. CAPITAL: Tehran. CURRENCY: 100 dinars=1 rial. AFGHANISTAN AREA: 250,000 sq. miles. POP: 15,909,000, CAPITAL: Kabul. CURRENCY: 100 puls=1 afgháni.

SAUDI ARABIA AREA: 869,803 sq. miles. POPULATION: 6,750,000. CAPITALS: Mecca and Riyadh. CURRENCY: 20 qurush=1 rial.
The map shows the fold mountain belt widening from the

Georgian Caucasus into the broad plateau of Persia, and narrowing at the heights of the Hindu Kush. The deep rift of the Jordan and the Dead Sea broadens into the Red Sea, and continues south as the Great Rift Valley of Africa.

SCALE IN MILES

© JOHN BARTHOLOMEW & SON LTD.

INTERNATIONAL BOUNDARIES
STATE BOUNDARIES

SCALE: 1 INCH TO 158 MILES

THE LEVANT AND JORDAN

SYRIA AREA: 71,210 sq. miles.
POPULATION: 5,300,000.
CAPITAL: *Damascus*.
CURRENCY: *100 piastres = 1 pound.*

LEBANON AREA: 4,000 sq. miles.
POPULATION: 2,405,000.
CAPITAL: *Beirut*.
CURRENCY: *100 piastres = 1 pound.*

ISRAEL AREA: 7,992 sq. miles.
POPULATION: 2,629,000.
CAPITAL: *Jerusalem*.
CURRENCY: *100 agorot = 1 pound.*

JORDAN AREA: 37,737 sq. miles.
POPULATION: 1,976,000.
CAPITAL: *Amman*.
CURRENCY: *1,000 fils = 1 dinar.*

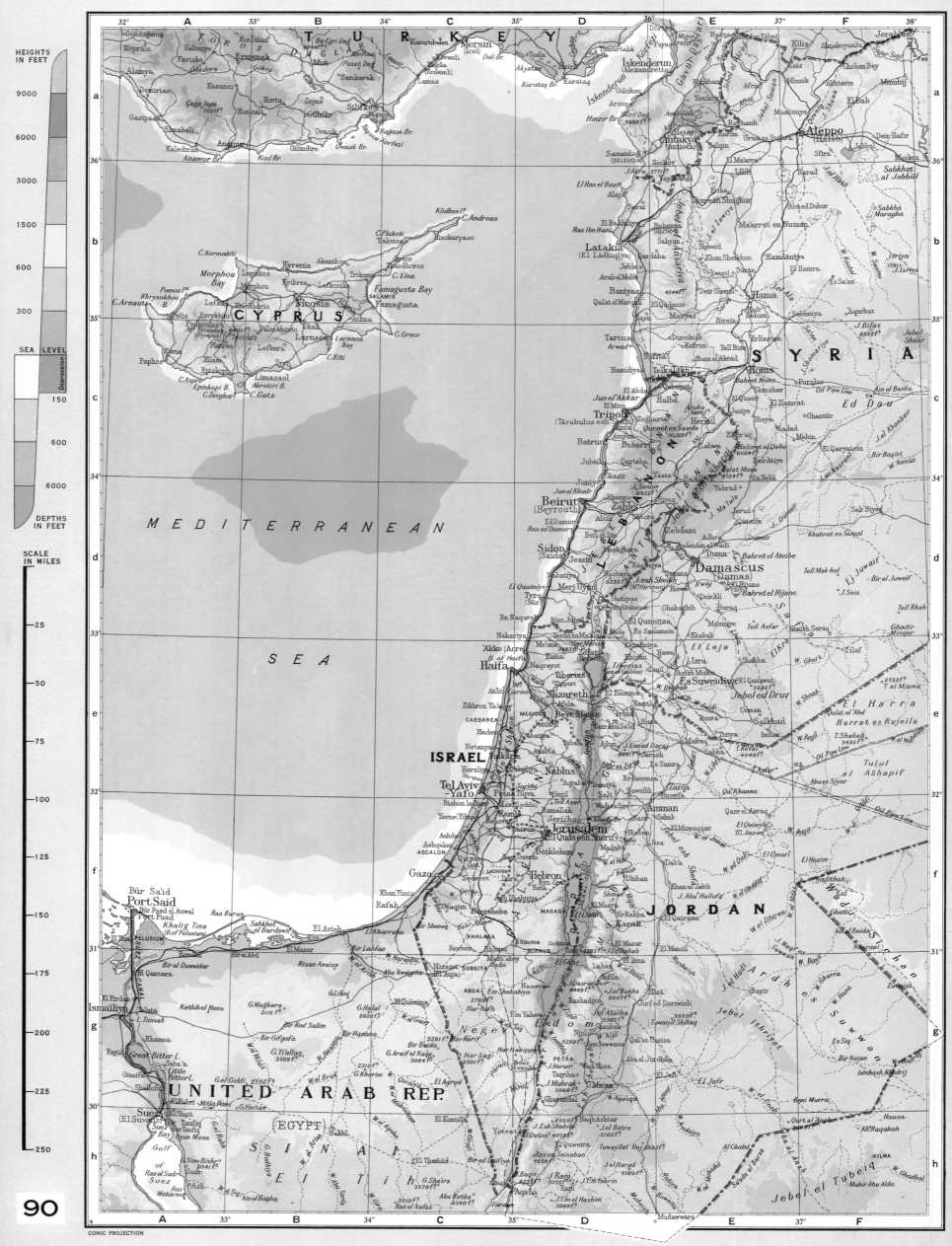

HEIGHTS IN FEET

9000
6000
3000
1500
600
300
SEA LEVEL

Depression

150
600
6000

DEPTHS IN FEET

SCALE IN MILES

25
50
75
100
125
150
175
200
225
250

90

CONIC PROJECTION

SCALE: 1 INCH TO 39 MILES

INTERNATIONAL BOUNDARIES
STATE BOUNDARIES
ARMISTICE LINE

SOUTHERN AFRICA

ZAMBIA	RHODESIA	S. WEST AFRICA	MALAWI	REP. OF S. AFRICA	BOTSWANA	MOÇAMBIQUE
AREA: 288,130 sq. m.	AREA: 150,333 sq. m.	AREA: 325,608 sq. m.	AREA: 49,066 sq. m.	AREA: 471,818 sq. m.	AREA: 220,000 sq. m.	AREA: 302,227 sq. m.
POP: 3,837,000.	POP: 4,400,000.	POP: 574,000.	POP: 4,042,000.	POP: 18,298,000.	POP: 580,000.	POP: 6,956,000.
CAP: Lusaka.	CAP: Salisbury.	CAP: Windhoek.	CAP: Zomba.	CAPS: Pretoria, Cape Town.	CAP: Gaberones.	CAP: Lourenço Marques.

HEIGHTS IN FEET

9000
6000
3000
1500
600
SEA LEVEL
150
600
6000
DEPTHS IN FEET

SCALE IN MILES

100
200
300
400
500
600
700
800
900
1000

THE CAPE
1 INCH TO 13 MILES

WITWATERSRAND
1 INCH TO 16 MILES

Limit of Gold-bearing Area

91

LAMBERT'S AZIMUTHAL EQUAL-AREA PROJECTION

MAIN ROADS ——
RAILWAYS ——

SCALE: 1 INCH TO 197 MILES

CENTRAL AND EAST AFRICA
CONGO, KENYA, UGANDA, TANZANIA, ETHIOPIA, MADAGASCAR

ANGOLA AREA: *481,351 sq. miles.* POP:
5,154,000. CAP: *Luanda.*
KENYA AREA: *224,960 sq. miles.* POP:
9,643,000. CAP: *Nairobi.*

HEIGHTS
IN FEET

12,000

9000

6000

3000

1500

600

SEA LEVEL

Depression

150

600

6000

DEPTHS
IN FEET

92

LAMBERT'S AZIMUTHAL EQUAL-AREA PROJECTION

SCALE: 1 INCH TO 197 MILES

———————— MAIN ROADS

———————— RAILWAYS

REP. OF THE CONGO AREA: 905,380 sq. miles. POP: (Africans only): 15,986,000. CAP: *Kinshasa*
CAMEROON REPUBLIC AREA: 183,568 sq. miles. POP: 5,229,000. CAP: *Yaoundé.*
UGANDA AREA: 93,981 sq. miles. POP: 7,740,000. CAPS: *Kampala, Entebbe.*
TANZANIA AREA: 362,720 sq. m. POP: 10,500,000. CAP: *Dar es Salaam.*
ETHIOPIA AREA: 471,776 sq. miles. POP: 23,000,000. CAP: *Addis Ababa.*
SOMALI REPUBLIC AREA: 246,200 sq. miles. POP: 2,500,000. CAP: *Mogadiscio.*
MALAGASY REP. AREA: 230,036 sq. miles. POP: 6,420,000. CAP: *Tananarive.*

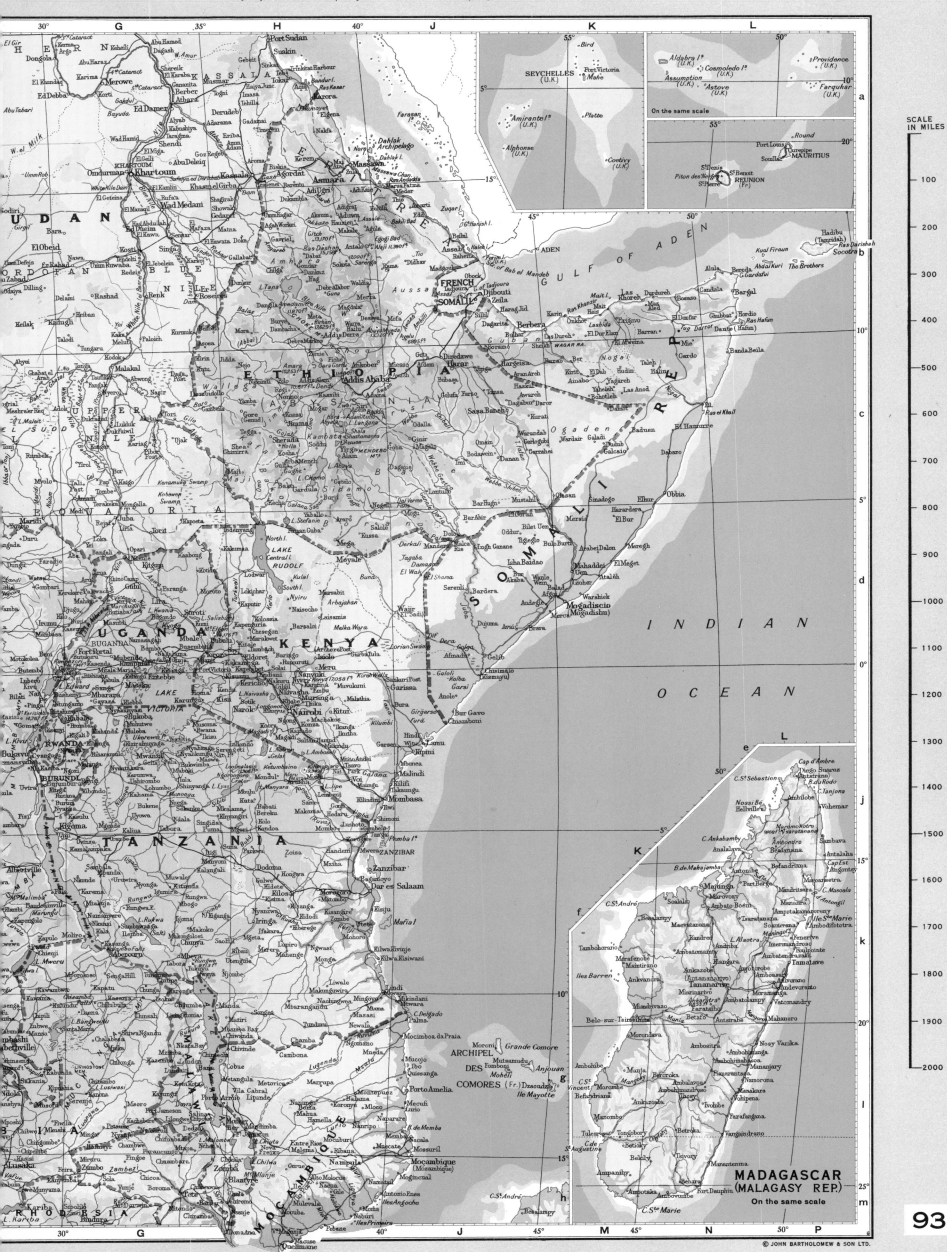

MADAGASCAR
(MALAGASY REP.)
On the same scale

SEYCHELLES (U.K.)

MAURITIUS

RÉUNION (Fr.)

SCALE IN MILES

93

© JOHN BARTHOLOMEW & SON LTD.

INTERNATIONAL BOUNDARIES
STATE BOUNDARIES

SCALE: 1 INCH TO 197 MILES

NORTH AND WEST AFRICA

MOROCCO, LIBYA, UNITED ARAB REP, SUDAN, GHANA, NIGERIA

MOROCCO AREA: *171,305 sq. miles.* POP:
13,451,000. CAP: *Rabat.*
TUNISIA AREA: *63,380 sq. miles.* POP:
4,458,000. CAP: *Tunis.*

HEIGHTS
IN FEET

12,000
9000
6000
3000
1500
600
SEA LEVEL
150
600
6000

DEPTHS
IN FEET

94

LAMBERT'S AZIMUTHAL EQUAL-AREA PROJECTION

MAIN ROADS
RAILWAYS

SCALE: 1 INCH TO 197 MILES

LIBYA AREA: 679,358 sq. miles. POP: 1,677,000. CAPS: Tripoli, Benghazi. UNITED ARAB REP. AREA: 386,198 sq. m. POP. 30,147,000. CAP: Cairo.

SUDAN AREA: 967,500 sq. miles. POP: 13,940,000. CAP: Khartoum. NIGERIA AREA: 356,668 sq. miles. POP 57,500,000. CAP: Lagos.

GHANA AREA: 92,100 sq. miles. POP: 7,945,000. CAP: Accra. LIBERIA AREA: 43,000 sq. miles. POP: 1,090,000. CAP: Monrovia.

SIERRA LEONE AREA: 27,699 sq. mile. POP: 2,403,000. CAP: Freetown. ALGERIA AREA: 919,591 sq. miles. POP: 12,102,000. CAP: Algiers.

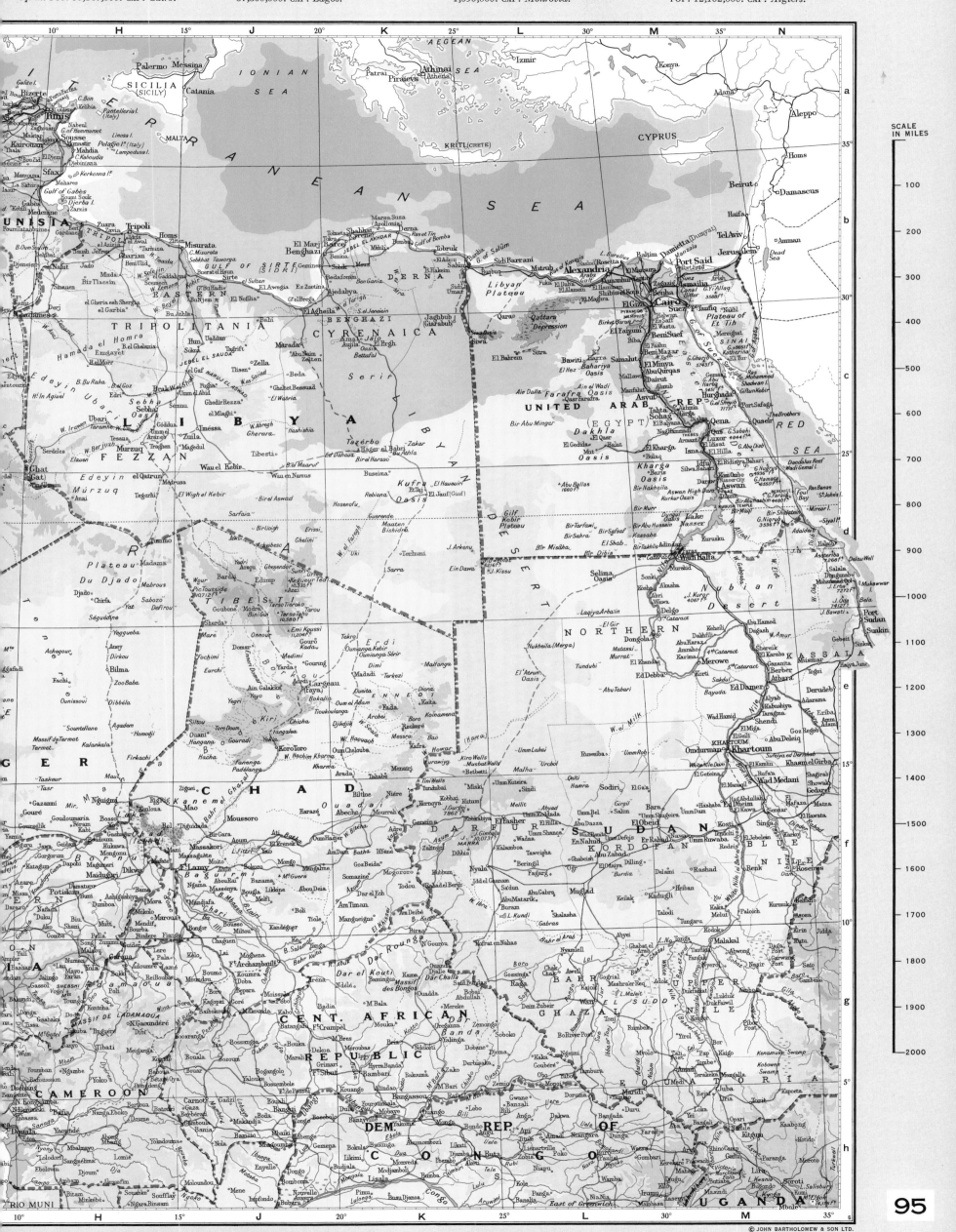

95

© JOHN BARTHOLOMEW & SON LTD.

INTERNATIONAL BOUNDARIES

STATE BOUNDARIES

SCALE: 1 INCH TO 197 MILES

SCALE IN MILES

INDIAN OCEAN

With an area of 28,350,000 square miles, the Indian Ocean is the third largest ocean in the world. It extends from the Indian Cape Comorin down to the Antarctic Continent, and in an east-west direction from Australia to Africa. A remarkable feature of this area is the central ridge of shallower water running down almost to the Antarctic Continent, somewhat similar to that in the Atlantic but with no counterpart in the Pacific.

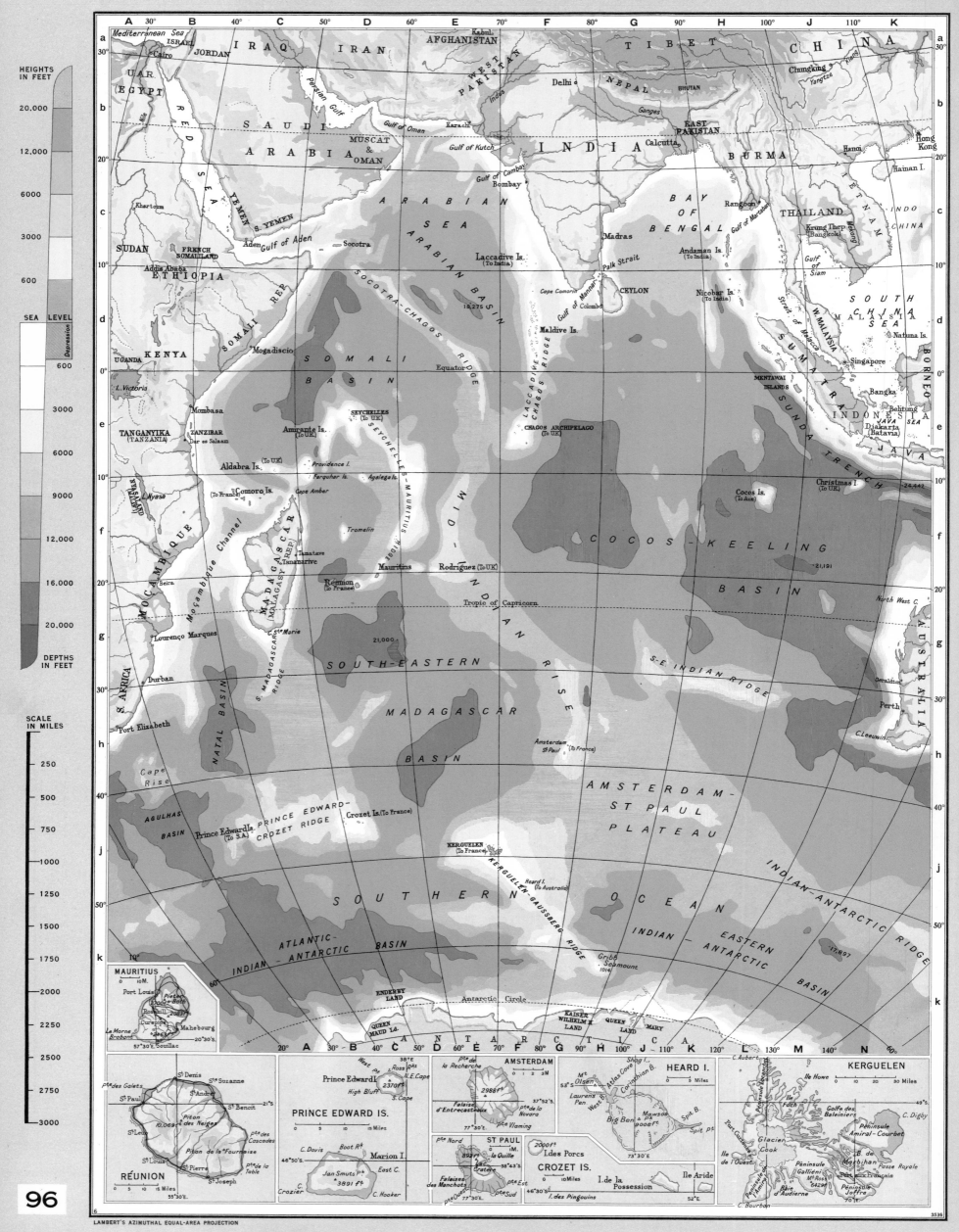

HEIGHTS IN FEET

20,000
12,000
6000
3000
600

SEA LEVEL

600
3000
6000
9000
12,000
16,000
20,000

DEPTHS IN FEET

SCALE IN MILES

250
500
750
1000
1250
1500
1750
2000
2250
2500
2750
3000

96

LAMBERT'S AZIMUTHAL EQUAL-AREA PROJECTION

SCALE: 1 INCH TO 632 MILES

ATLANTIC OCEAN

The Atlantic Ocean has an area of 31,839,306 square miles, and an average depth of 13,880 feet. It has the largest drainage area of all the oceans. Running southwards from Iceland to within a short distance of Antarctica is a well-defined central ridge, the curve of which follows the line of the African coast. Only the surface water on either side of this submarine barrier can cross it.

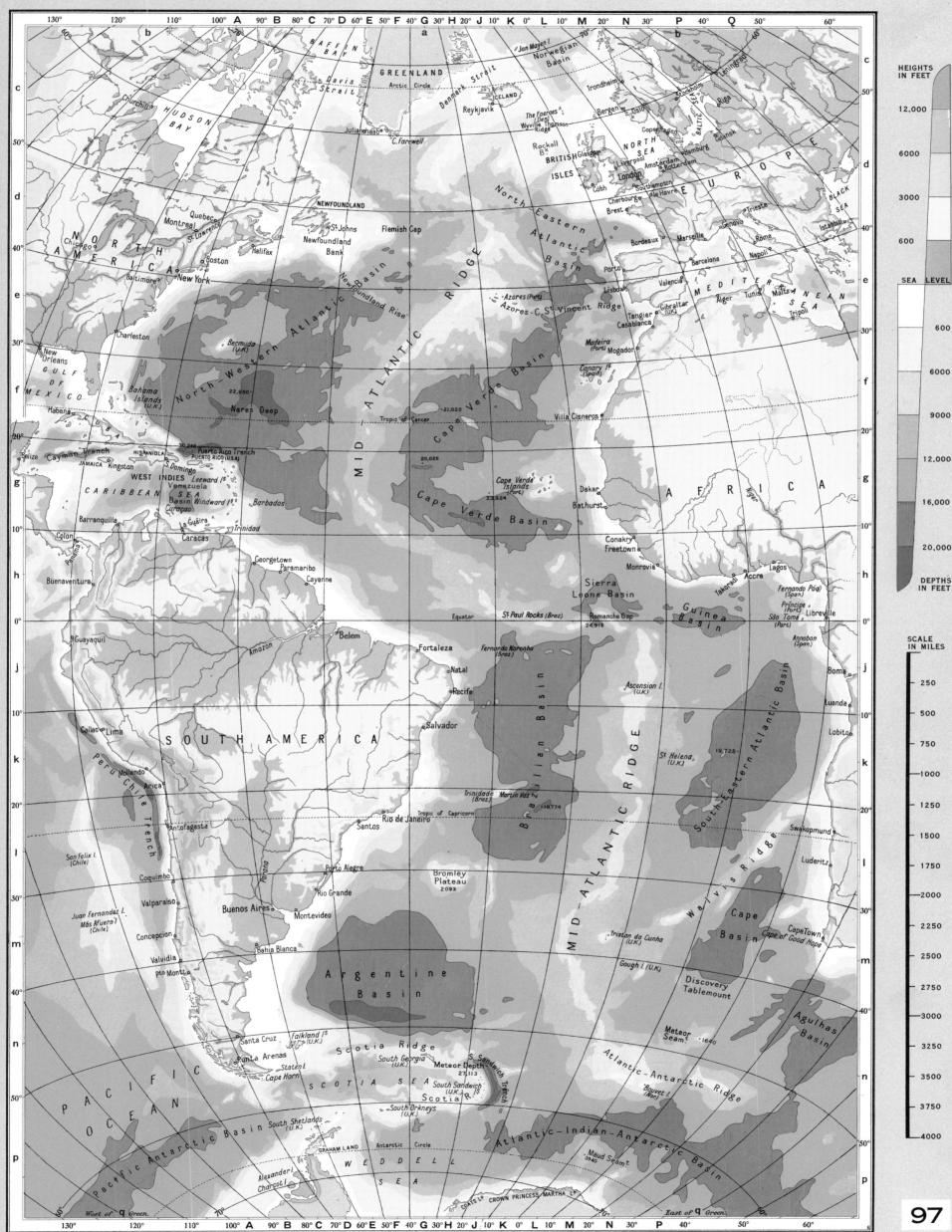

HEIGHTS IN FEET

12,000
6000
3000
600
SEA LEVEL
600
6000
9000
12,000
16,000
20,000

DEPTHS IN FEET

SCALE IN MILES

250
500
750
1000
1250
1500
1750
2000
2250
2500
2750
3000
3250
3500
3750
4000

97

LAMBERT'S AZIMUTHAL EQUAL-AREA PROJECTION

SCALE: 1 INCH TO 758 MILES

The Pacific, in area some 63,986,000 sq. miles, is the largest of the oceans. It is more than twice the size of the Atlantic, the next largest ocean, and occupies nearly half the Earth's surface. In the north it is almost landlocked, its only outlet to the Arctic Ocean being through the Bering Strait. It stretches 9,455 miles from this

HEIGHTS IN FEET

12,000
6000
3000
600

SEA LEVEL

Depression

600
3000
6000
9000
12,000
16,000
20,000

DEPTHS IN FEET

98

LAMBERT'S AZIMUTHAL EQUAL-AREA PROJECTION

SCALE: 1 INCH TO 711 MILES

strait to the Antarctic and at its broadest is 10,492 miles across. It has an average depth of about 14,000 feet, but in its deepest regions, which are off the Philippine Islands, a depth of 35,800 feet has been recorded. The islands of the Pacific fall into three main groups, Micronesia, Melanesia and Polynesia. Nearly all these islands are either volcanic or have a capping of coral over a submarine volcanic peak. The volcanic islands are very fertile and often mountainous, while the coral islands or atolls are mostly bare, desolate and low-lying. There are active volcanoes in the Solomon Islands, the New Hebrides and the Tonga group and Hawaii.

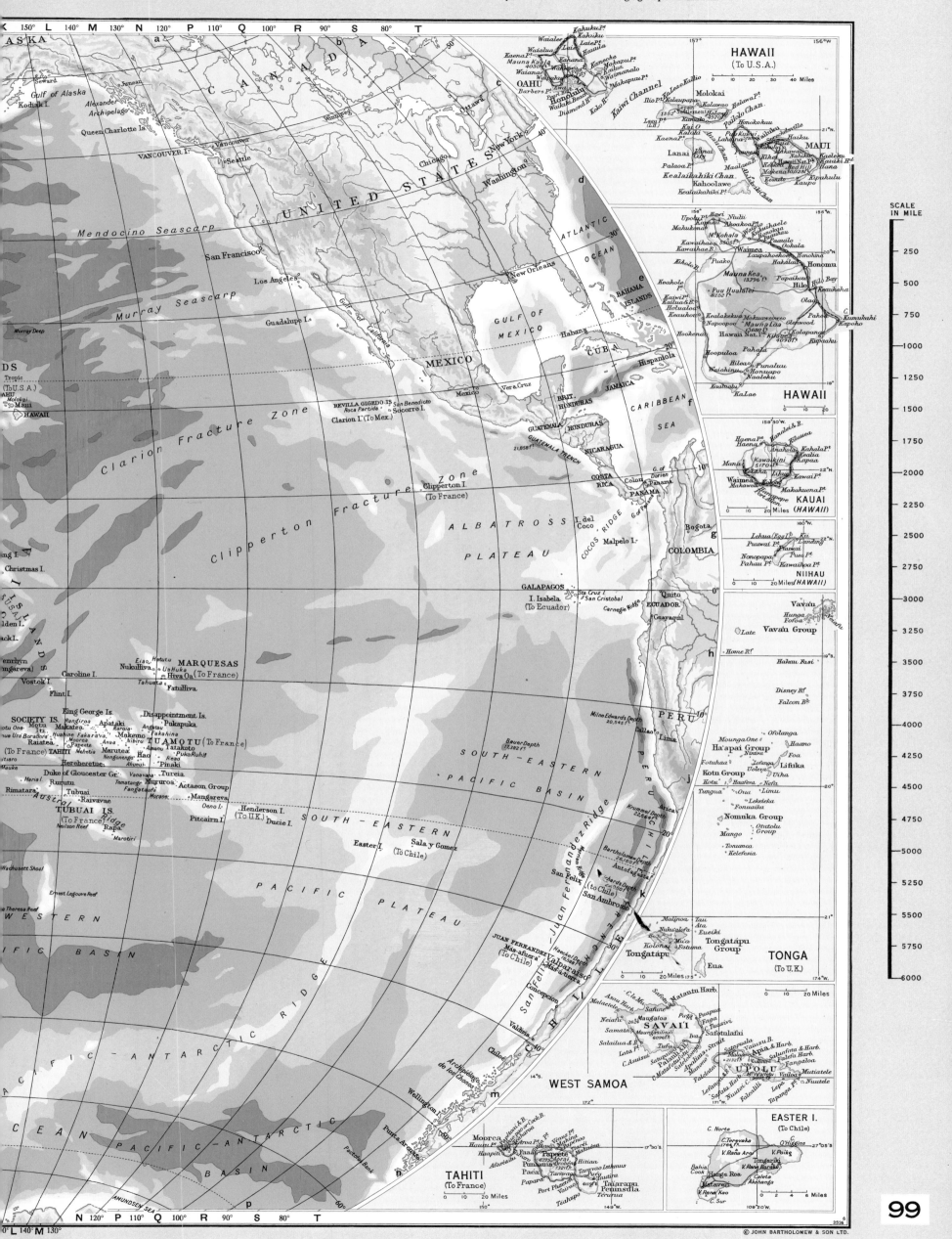

© JOHN BARTHOLOMEW & SON LTD.

SCALE: 1 INCH TO 711 MILES

THE ANTARCTIC

The Antarctic comprises those seas and lands round the South Pole which lie within the Antarctic Circle at 66° 33′ S. It has a total area of about four and a half million square miles. The continent is uniquely isolated, and is covered by an ice cap thousands of feet thick. Much of the rock surface beneath the ice is below sea level. If the ice cap were to melt, the sea level all over the Earth would rise by two or three hundred feet.

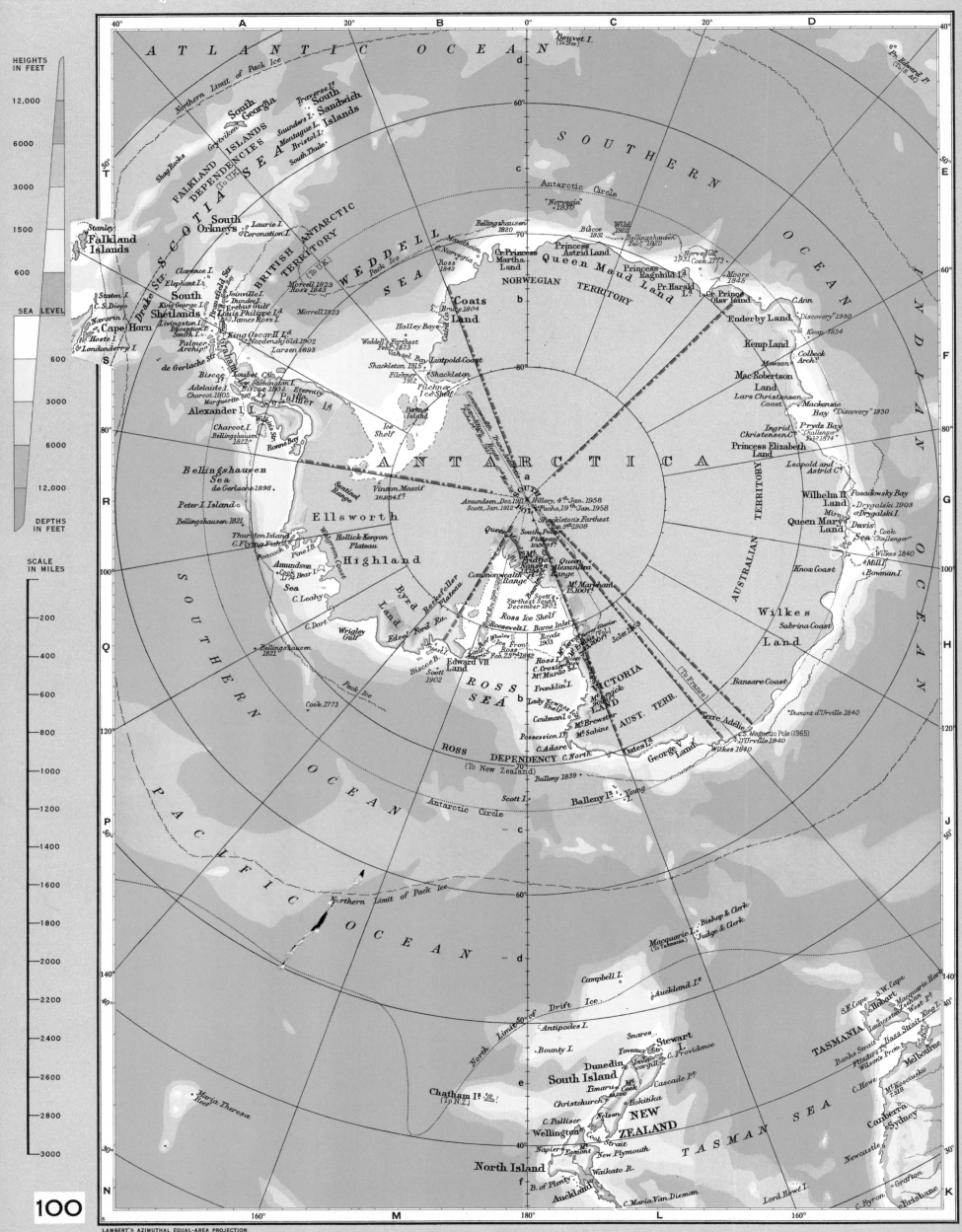

HEIGHTS IN FEET

12,000
6000
3000
1500
600
SEA LEVEL
600
3000
6000
12,000

DEPTHS IN FEET

SCALE IN MILES

200
400
600
800
1000
1200
1400
1600
1800
2000
2200
2400
2600
2800
3000

100

LAMBERT'S AZIMUTHAL EQUAL-AREA PROJECTION

SCALE: 1 INCH TO 474 MILES

INTERNATIONAL BOUNDARIES

THE WORLD AS WE KNOW IT

CONTENTS

OUR PLACE AMONG THE GALAXIES

*As the stars of the heaven, and as the sand
which is upon the sea shore*—GENESIS 22

FOR centuries man believed the Earth to be the centre of Creation. The true picture is far more awe-inspiring. We live on a small planet revolving round a star of only average size which is itself revolving, with thousands of millions of other stars, in one galaxy among millions in a Universe that may well be boundless.

Scientific observation has as yet revealed no limits to the Universe and has so far probed only a fraction of it. Yet to travel to the frontiers of that observed fraction, even at 186,300 miles per second (the speed of light) would take 6,000 million years, about 20,000 times the total period that human life is estimated to have existed on Earth.

The different bodies and structures in the Universe, all of which appear to be receding from us, range from single galaxies to mammoth clusters containing over 500 galaxies.

Although the cluster of galaxies to which our galaxy belongs is comparatively small (it has only 25 members), our galaxy itself, the Milky Way System, ranks among the larger of the known stellar systems. Counting its almost 100,000 million stars (of which the Sun with its family of planets is one) at the rate of one star a second would take about 2,500 years.

Seen edge-on from outside, the Milky Way System looks like a fairly flat disk with a thick cloud of stars near and round its centre. Seen at right angles, it looks like a giant Catherine wheel in which two main arms spiral out from the centre. The Sun lies in one of these arms. It is so far away from the centre that it needs about 225 million years to complete one orbit round the "hub" of the Catherine wheel. Calculated on the basis of the Sun's estimated age, it can have made only about 30 complete circuits.

The stars forming the Milky Way are not evenly distributed, but thin out from the central plane of the galaxy and from its bulbous centre. The myriads of stars forming the centre are hidden from the Earth by vast formations of cosmic dust and

BOUNDLESS SKY

Our Solar System is somewhere here

A barred spiral galaxy. The "bar" involves the nucleus and curves outwards to form trailing arms strongly indicative of rotation.

An elliptical galaxy. This shows no spiral structure and appears to be comparatively free from cosmic gas and dust.

A spiral galaxy, full view, with its central nucleus and trailing spiral arms. The whole vast complex of stars, dust and gas is rotating in a way that would tend to "wind up" the arms.

A spiral galaxy seen edge-on. The central bulge or nucleus is a great swarm of millions of stars. The dark markings in the central plane are caused by clouds of obscuring cosmic dust

are not directly visible. If we look in the direction of the plane, however, from our position slightly outside it, we see the stars distributed in greater depth and number, so that they appear to merge into a single luminous band. This bright streak in the sky has been known for centuries as the Milky Way, a name now given to the whole of the system.

Surrounding the galaxy and forming part of it are compact swarms of stars known as globular star clusters. Beyond them again lie thousands of millions of other galaxies with a considerable range in size and structure. The nearest comparable in size to our own is the Great Galaxy in Andromeda (centre of left-hand page), just over two million "light-years" away, a distance that light, in travelling at 186,300 miles per second, would take just over two million years to cover.

As man probes deeper into the Universe, the number of galaxies seems to grow as immense as the space through which they hurtle.

Our Solar System

The Milky Way, one of the millions of stellar galaxies in the Universe, is so vast that it would take a rocket, hurtling along its diameter at 100,000 miles per hour, 670 million years to make the journey from end to end. Travelling at the same speed across our solar system, from the Sun to its farthest dependent planet, Pluto, a rocket would take only four years and two months.

PISCIS AUSTRALIS
Fomalhaut

FORNAX

CETUS

AQUARIUS

PISCES

(Mira)

CAPRICORNUS

PEGASUS

ARIES

ERIDANUS

DELPHINUS

ANDROMEDA

TRIANGULUM

PLEIADES

TAURUS

SERPENS

AQUILA

Altair

CASSIOPEIA

Algol

HYADES

CYGNUS

Deneb

CEPHEUS

PERSEUS

Aldebaran

SAGITTARIUS

LYRA

Vega

Capella

AURIGA

Rigel

Bellatrix

Betelgeux

ORION

LEPUS

POLE STAR

DRACO

URSA MINOR

GEMINI

CANIS MAJOR

OPHIUCHUS

HERCULES

Mizar

Castor

Pollux

CANIS MINOR

Sirius

CORONA BOREALIS

URSA MAJOR

CANCER

SERPENS

BOOTES

45°

Procyon

SCORPIO

CANES VENATICI

Antares

LEO

Regulus

PUPPIS

Arcturus

Denebola

LIBRA

VIRGO

EQUATOR

CRATER

Spica

HYDRA

CORVUS

1st Magnitude   2nd Magnitude   3rd Magnitude

THE STARS AROUND US

THE LIGHT FROM MANY STARS STARTED ITS JOURNEY LONG BEFORE MAN APPEARED ON EARTH

For one star differeth from another in glory — 1 CORINTHIANS 15

WHEN we look at the stars we are looking back deep into the past; for we see them, not as they are now, but often as they were hundreds of years ago. The light we receive from most of them began its great journey long before we were born, and from the more distant stars long before man appeared on Earth.

Even light from the Sun – a mere 93 million miles away – takes eight minutes to reach the Earth. From the nearest star, Proxima Centauri in the Southern Hemisphere, it takes more than four years. Since light, travelling at 186,300 miles a second, covers some six million million miles in a year, this means that the distance between the Earth and Proxima Centauri is about 26 million million miles.

But the vast distances in space need a unit of measurement larger than the mile. Astronomers use the "light-year," which is the distance travelled by light in one year. In these terms,

Proxima Centauri is four and one-third light-years away from the Earth. The distance from Earth to the bright star Altair is about 16 light-years, to Vega 26 light-years, to Deneb 1,500 light-years, while some of the stars of the Milky Way are so far distant that their light takes thousands of years to reach us. The stars are therefore placed at great distances in space, not only from the Earth, but also from one another.

The stars vary greatly in size. Though our Sun seems large to us, and could easily contain the Earth a million times over, it is no more than an average star in the rest of the heavens. Some stars, called super-giants, make the Sun seem a tiny dwarf. Betelgeux, for instance, could contain not only the Sun and the Earth's orbit round it, but the entire orbit of the planet Mars – an orbit of some 284 million miles in diameter. At the other end of the scale are stars that are only a few thousandths of the Sun's size.

Stars also vary considerably in actual brightness, and so are graded into different "magnitudes." The brightest stars belong to the first magnitude, those slightly less bright to the second, and so on until we reach the sixth magnitude which consists of stars just visible to the naked eye on a very clear night. A star of the first magnitude is 100 times brighter than a star of the sixth magnitude. Compared with some first-magnitude stars, the Sun's light is like that of a glow-worm shining beside a searchlight.

Thus the brighter stars in the sky – like Rigel and Regulus – are not necessarily the nearest to us. Several very faint stars are in fact nearer to Earth than most of the bright ones, though the brilliant Alpha Centauri, in the Southern Hemisphere, and Altair, in the Northern Hemisphere, are fairly close neighbours – as stars go.

From earliest times, men have grouped the stars under names

TRIANGULUM
PEGASUS
ARIES
PISCES
CETUS
(Mira)
PLEIADES
AQUARIUS
DELPHINUS
PISCIS AUSTRALIS
CYGNUS
TAURUS
Fomalhaut
HYADES
FORNAX
PHOENIX
CAPRICORNUS
Altair
Aldebaran
ERIDANUS
GRUS
AQUILA
AURIGA
Achernar
SERPENS
Bellatrix
Rigel
HYDRUS
TUCANA
LYRA
ORION
LEPUS
COLUMBA
LESSER MAGELLANIC CLOUD
INDUS
Betelgeux
LARGER MAGELLANIC CLOUD
DORADO
SAGITTARIUS
Canopus
SOUTH POLE
TRIANG. AUST.
ARA
OPHIUCHUS
CANIS MAJOR
Sirius
CARINA
SCORPIO
PUPPIS
MUSCA
α Centauri
GEMINI
CRUX
β Centauri
Antares
CANIS MINOR
LUPUS
HERCULES
Procyon
CENTAURUS
45°
LIBRA
Castor
Pollux
SERPENS
HYDRA
CORONA BOREALIS
CANCER
CRATER
CORVUS
Spica
Regulus
VIRGO
EQUATOR
LEO
Arcturus
BOOTES
Denebola

4th Magnitude   The Milky Way

of animals and legendary heroes. A few of these constellation figures, as they are called, such as Orion and Corona Borealis (the Northern Crown), do look something like the figures they are supposed to represent, though most call for powerful feats of imagination. Among the brighter stars, however, some make definite patterns: five in Cygnus (the Swan) form a cross, and seven in Ursa Major (the Great Bear) suggest the Plough shape by which they are known.

The maps show the positions of the brightest stars in both Hemispheres. During one year, people living in the Northern Hemisphere can see all the stars on the left-hand map, but never those in the region of the Southern Cross, which are hidden by the Earth's bulk. Similarly, people living south of the Equator can see the stars on the right-hand map, but never the Plough or the North Pole Star. Only from the Equator would you eventually see almost every star in both Hemispheres.

Because the Earth rotates on its axis, the stars – like the Sun by day—appear to wheel from east to west across the sky. In the Northern Hemisphere, only Polaris, the Pole Star, seems to stand still because it is almost directly above the North Pole. Not only does it show the position of north, but its angular height above the northern horizon is roughly equal to the observer's latitude. Since the latitude of London is about 51½°N, the Pole Star, as seen from London, is about 51½° above the horizon.

The southern sky has no bright star like Polaris to mark

the position of the south celestial pole. To find this position we must draw a line from the tip of the Southern Cross to the bright star Achernar: the point above the South Pole lies midway along this line and slightly to the right of it.

With the naked eye, we can see from 2,000 to 2,500 stars on a clear night. Binoculars will show thousands more, and a large telescope can reach out to thousands of millions of stars. Most of these lie in the bright girdle of the Milky Way, once thought to be the road along which the souls of the dead travelled to heaven.

Many "stars" turn out to be not just single objects, but clusters of two, three or even more stars. Some of these "double stars," as they are called, are two stars held close together by the force of gravitation. Others only appear to be together because one happens to be almost behind the other in our line of sight, though they may in fact be an immense distance apart.

Of the larger star clusters, one of the finest is the Pleiades in the northern sky. When you first count the members of this group you will probably manage only six or seven, but on very clear nights this number can be pushed up to twelve or fourteen. A pair of binoculars will show many more, though it needs a really large telescope to reveal the 200 and more stars in this cluster. All these stars are travelling together through space. They form a moving family of suns all of which, presumably, had a common origin.

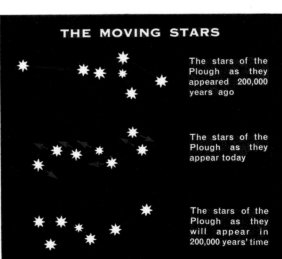

THE MOVING STARS

The stars of the Plough as they appeared 200,000 years ago

The stars of the Plough as they appear today

The stars of the Plough as they will appear in 200,000 years' time

The stars are never motionless in space, but move through it at tremendous speeds. The diagrams show the stars of the Plough as their positions are changing in relation to each other and as seen from the Earth. This motion is called the "proper motion" of the stars. It is not their motion in three-dimensional space, since we see only the two-dimensional aspect. As shown by the arrows, the five inner stars are travelling in approximately the same direction, forming a moving family of suns. The two outer stars, moving the opposite way, are not members of this group.

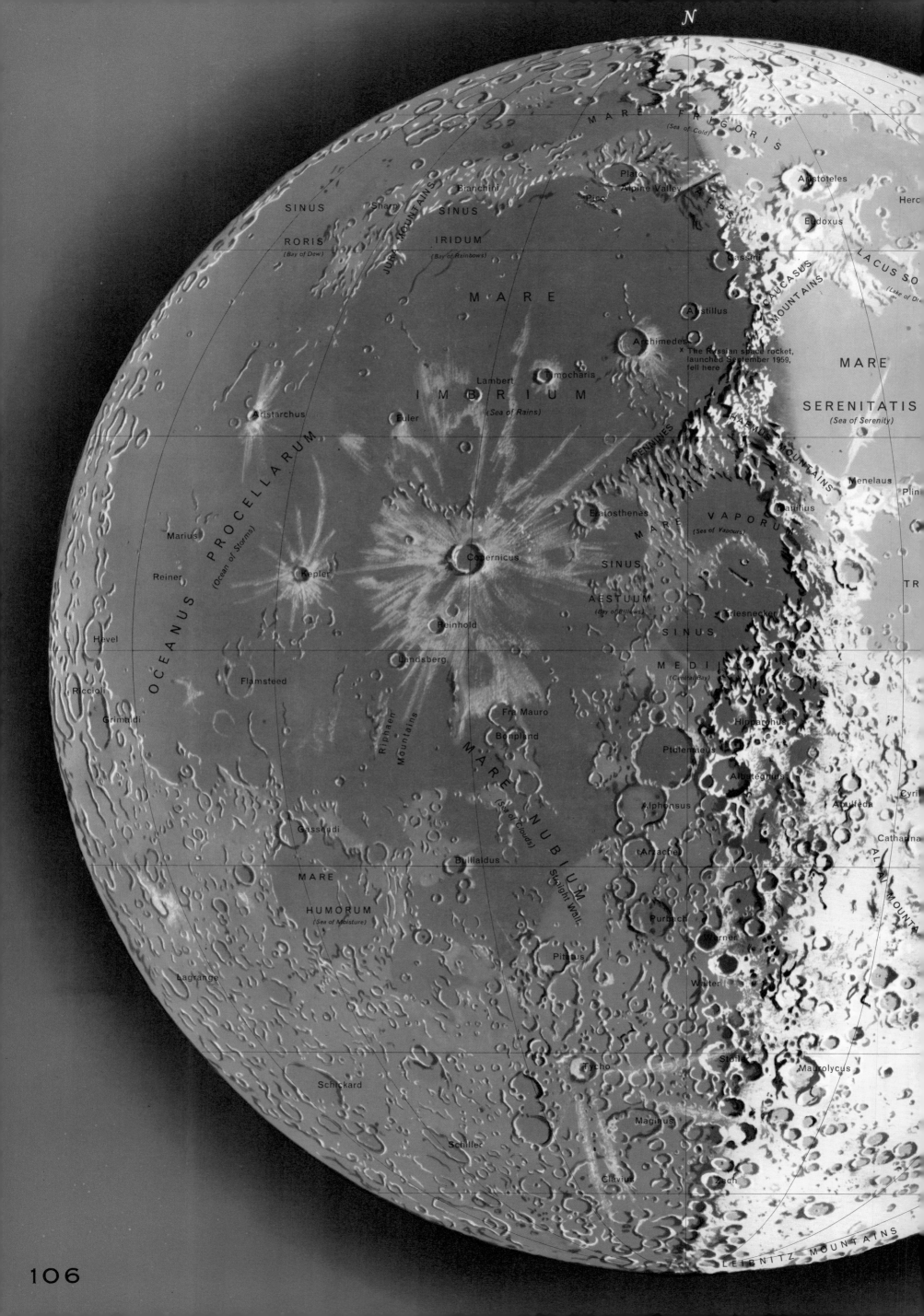

N

MARE FRIGORIS
(Sea of Cold)

Aristoteles
Herc

SINUS
RORIS
(Bay of Dew)

Bianchini

Plato

Sharp

Pico

Alpine Valley

Eudoxus

SINUS
IRIDUM
(Bay of Rainbows)

Cassini

CAUCASUS
MOUNTAINS

LACUS SO
(Lake of Dre

MARE

Aristillus

MARE
SERENITATIS
(Sea of Serenity)

Archimedes

× The Russian space rocket,
launched September 1959,
fell here

Timocharis

Lambert

IMBRIUM
(Sea of Rains)

Aristarchus

Euler

HAEMUS MOUNTAINS

Menelaus

Plin

Marius

Eratosthenes

Manilius

MARE   VAPORUM
(Sea of Vapours)

Reiner

Kepler

SINUS
AESTUUM
(Bay of Billows)

Triesnecker

TR

Reinhold

Hevel

SINUS

Landsberg

MEDII
(Central Bay)

Flamsteed

Hipparchus

Riccioli

Fra Mauro

Ptolemaeus

Abulfeda

Cyri

Grimaldi

Bonpland

Albategnius

MARE   NUBIUM
(Sea of Clouds)

Alphonsus

Cathanna

AL   AL   MOUNTA

Gassendi

Arzachel

Bullialdus

MARE

Purbach

HUMORUM
(Sea of Moisture)

Werner

Pitatus

Walter

Lagrange

Stofl

Maurolycus

Tycho

Schickard

Maginus

Schiller

Clavius

Zach

LEIBNITZ   MOUNTAINS

106

THE MOON

EARTH'S SATELLITE

He appointed the Moon for seasons—PSALM 104

THE Moon is unique in our Solar system. Many planets have satellites, but these are small in relation to their mother planets. The Moon is the only satellite of a size comparable to its planet, Earth.

MAIN FEATURES. The large map shows the near side of the Moon; the far side is hidden because the Moon rotates only once each time it travels round the Earth. (Since the Moon spins so slowly, its "day" lasts about two weeks, and is followed by two weeks of night.) The features marked on the map are all visible through good binoculars. They are best seen, not at full Moon when the Sun shines directly on them making no shadows, but when they are near the "terminator", or irregular edge of the Moon, and the Sun is lower in the lunar sky.

To the naked eye the Moon seems to be made up of bright and darker patches. The bright parts are mountains and craters which catch the light of the Sun; the large darker areas are the low-lying plains. Once thought to be seas, these plains are still called by such names as Mare Imbrium (Sea of Rains) and Oceanus Procellarum (Ocean of Storms) though in fact the Moon is entirely without water.

The mountains on the Moon are broad rather than high. The highest range is probably the Leibnitz Mountains near the Moon's south pole, with an estimated height of well over 20,000 feet. In relation to the Moon's size they appear higher still; a corresponding mountain range on Earth would tower 14 miles into the sky.

The most striking features are the many thousands of craters, named after philosophers and men of science. Either volcanic or meteoritic in origin, they range in size from pits of a mile or less across to magnificent walled plains such as Clavius, which is some 150 miles in diameter. Two of the finest are Copernicus and Tycho, both over 50 miles across and with walls rising to heights above two miles. From these two craters, and some others, bright streaks radiate for thousands of miles across mountains and valleys. The origin of these bright streaks is unknown; they seem, however, to be surface deposits of some kind.

SIZE AND GRAVITY. With a diameter about one-quarter of the Earth's, the Moon has a surface area less than half that of the Atlantic Ocean, and the part we can see is about the size of North America. Its gravitational pull is correspondingly smaller, only about one-sixth of the Earth's.

A six-foot man who could jump six feet on the Earth would be able to clear about 18 feet on the Moon, and his descent would be much slower. A space ship would need a velocity of only some 5,000 m.p.h. to take off from the Moon, compared with 25,000 m.p.h. required to escape from the Earth's gravity.

EFFECTS OF NO ATMOSPHERE. The Moon is without atmosphere, its gravity being too weak to hold down gas in any quantity. To an Earth-dweller, this produces some startling effects. The edges of shadows on the Moon are razor-sharp, unsoftened by mists or similar products of the atmosphere. There is no erosion due to weather, and the Moon's features have therefore undergone little major change since they were formed. There is no sound, which is a vibration transmitted through the air. Nor is there any twilight: day comes instantly because there is no atmosphere to be lit up before the Sun comes over the horizon. With no atmosphere to protect it from the Sun by day or to imprison the heat by night, the Moon has great extremes of temperature. At the equator, the day-time temperature at the Moon's surface rises to 100° C., as high as that of boiling water, and at night the temperature sinks to at least −168°C., as low as that of liquid air. Under these conditions no life as we know it can exist.

Average distance from Earth	238,856 miles	Mass in terms of Earth	1:81
Diameter	2,160 miles	Sidereal Period	27·3 days (approx.)
	(Earth's diameter 7,920 miles)	(time taken to make one complete circuit of Earth)	
Density	3·3 times that of water	Synodic Period	29·5 days (approx.)
	(Earth's density 5·5 times that of water)	(interval between one new Moon and the next)	

THE FAR SIDE OF THE MOON

Chart of the reverse side of the Moon, compiled from photographic positions obtained by the U.S. Orbiter vehicles and the Soviet Zond-3. When this chart was made in the autumn of 1967 only a very small portion of the far side of the moon had not been photographed.

Near the edge of the chart appear some features which can be identified on the map of the visible hemisphere: Mare Marginis and Mare Smythii. Mare Orientalis is of special interest as it can just be seen from Earth as a fore-shortened plain, but the far-side photographs have shown that it is of very complex structure, and it is of significance in studies of how the Moon's features were moulded. Two other interesting features are the dark-floored crater Tsiolkovskii and the dark patch of the Mare Moscoviae.

The names of features on the far side of the moon are under consideration by the International Astronomical Union.

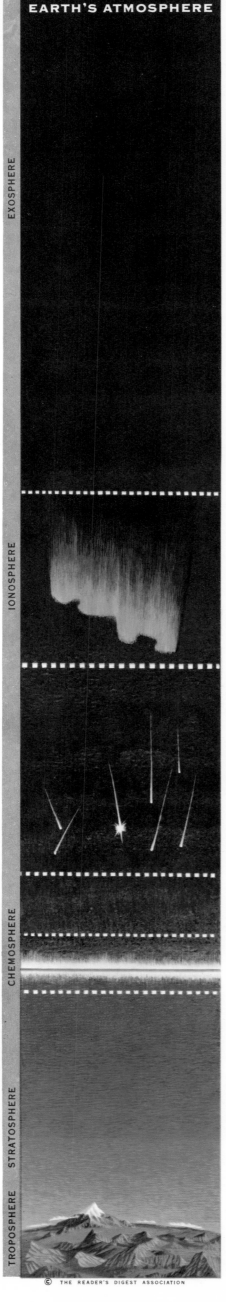

EARTH'S ATMOSPHERE

Earth's atmosphere, the blanket of gases surrounding the planet, is the element that, more than any other, enables life to exist. Without its protective insulation, temperatures would swing from unbearable cold at night to unbearable heat during the day. Air is composed of nitrogen (78 per cent), oxygen (21 per cent), argon (nearly one per cent) and small amounts of other gases. No one knows how far above the earth the atmosphere extends, but it is probably at least 1,000 miles. The air is not a uniform mass but can be divided into layers, each with its own characteristics.

EXOSPHERE

The air here is so rarefied that its density is only one million-millionth of that at ground level. Air particles move freely, some escaping into the near-vacuum of outer space.

(250 miles)

IONOSPHERE

In the ionosphere the air particles are electrically charged (ionized) by the Sun's ultra-violet radiation, and congregate in four main layers: D, E, F_1 and F_2. It is these layers which reflect radio waves back to the ground. The temperature increases rapidly from −73°C. at the D layer (at a height of about 45 miles) to perhaps as much as 1,600°C. at 200 miles.

F2 Layer (155 miles)

The glowing Auroras (Northern and Southern Lights) are thought to be caused when jets of atomic matter, shot out from the Sun, are deflected by the Earth's magnetic field towards the North and South Poles. They occur at varying heights between 40 and 600 miles.

F1 Layer (90-150 miles)

It is mainly in the lower ionosphere that meteors from outer space burn up as they meet the increased air resistance. F_2 and F_1 (bottom) layers (known as the Appleton layer—although at night the F_1 layer is absent) reflect short radio waves. E layer reflects long radio waves. Also called the Heaviside layer, it is the lowest stable layer. D layer is unstable and unpredictable, and is usually present only in daytime.

Meteors generally burn out above this level.

E Layer which extends about 30 miles above this line.
HYDROXYL ZONE where water vapour is broken up by sunlight into hydrogen atoms and molecules of one hydrogen and one oxygen atom (hydroxyl).

D Layer (45 miles)

CHEMOSPHERE

The chemosphere is defined mainly by an accumulation of ozone gas at about 20 to 30 miles high. Ozone absorbs some of the Sun's ultraviolet rays and is the Earth's main line of defence against the Sun's harmful effects. The ozone belt is marked by very high temperatures compared with those around it.

STRATOSPHERE

Throughout the ten-mile-thick layer of stratosphere, the temperature varies little, and is usually about −60°C. At the lower boundary, the tropopause, the direct effects of Earth's weather are not usually felt, and it is here that jet airliners fly to get above the weather.

TROPOSPHERE

From the ground to the tropopause the temperature drops steadily from about 15°C. at sea level (in temperate zones) to about −56°C. at seven miles (the average height of the troposphere) while the air thins out rapidly with increasing height. Air pressure at sea level is 14·7 lb. per square inch, but at six miles it is less than 4·9. The troposphere is the region of clouds and weather.

© THE READER'S DIGEST ASSOCIATION

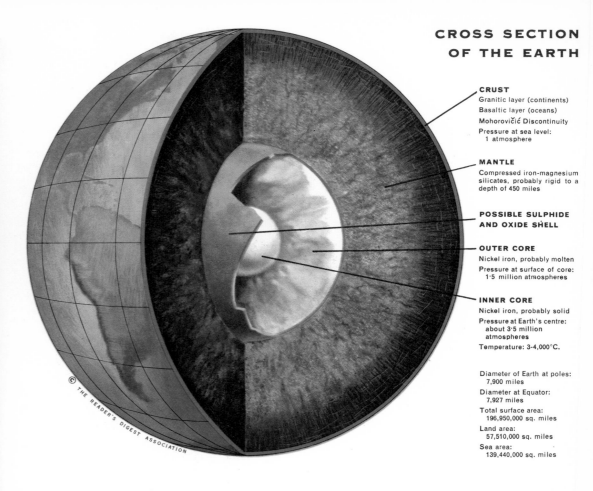

CROSS SECTION OF THE EARTH

CRUST
Granitic layer (continents)
Basaltic layer (oceans)
Mohorovičić Discontinuity
Pressure at sea level:
1 atmosphere

MANTLE
Compressed iron-magnesium silicates, probably rigid to a depth of 450 miles

POSSIBLE SULPHIDE AND OXIDE SHELL

OUTER CORE
Nickel iron, probably molten
Pressure at surface of core:
1·5 million atmospheres

INNER CORE
Nickel iron, probably solid
Pressure at Earth's centre:
about 3·5 million atmospheres
Temperature: 3-4,000°C.

Diameter of Earth at poles:
7,900 miles
Diameter at Equator:
7,927 miles
Total surface area:
196,950,000 sq. miles
Land area:
57,510,000 sq. miles
Sea area:
139,440,000 sq. miles

© THE READER'S DIGEST ASSOCIATION

THE EARTH'S STRUCTURE

Let the waters under the heaven be gathered together unto one place, and let the dry land appear — GENESIS 1

THE continental parts of the Earth's Crust are composed of many different kinds of rock which, as a whole, have the density and composition of granite. This granite layer is often called "sial" because of the predominance of *silica* and *alumina* in its composition. The granite layer, or "sial," floats on a denser layer, which has an average density and composition similar to that of the common black volcanic lava known as basalt. This so-called "basaltic" layer (termed "sima" because of its richness in *silica* and *magnesium*) directly underlies the ocean floor, and here forms the thinnest part of the Earth's Crust. In continental areas the granitic and basaltic layers together reach an average thickness of between 20 and 25 miles. In oceanic areas, the basaltic layer alone averages a thickness of about three miles.

Knowledge that the Earth could not consist entirely of these surface rocks came first from the planet's weight, measured by its pull of gravity; for these materials are far too light to account for a total mass of 6,600 million million tons. The density (weight per unit of volume) of rocks at the Earth's centre may in fact be as high as 16, compared with only 2·7 at the surface.

The best clues to what lies beneath the Earth's exterior are provided by records of earthquake shocks. Shock waves passing through the Earth are found to change their direction and speed at certain levels which are known as discontinuities. The first major discontinuity is at the base of the basaltic layer where the latter rests on the Mantle. This is named the Mohorovičić Discontinuity (Moho for short) after the Yugoslav scientist who discovered it. At this level a marked change in the velocity of earthquake waves takes place. This could indicate either an actual change in the chemical nature of the rocks or merely a change in their physical state; but precisely which we do not yet know.

The Mantle extends to a depth of 1,800 miles, where a second major discontinuity marks the beginning of the Outer Core. Although nothing is known directly about the rocks of the Earth's interior, it is widely accepted that the material near the inner edge of the Mantle is two to three times as heavy as the surface rocks.

The Outer Core, 1,310 miles thick, is probably formed of heavy metals (iron and nickel) in molten form; but because of the tremendous pressure, this fluid substance would be unlike any fluid we know on the Earth's surface. The next layer, the Inner Core, 850 miles thick, is believed to consist of the same materials as the Outer Core, but forced into a solid state by increased pressure—three million times greater at the centre of the Earth than at the surface. Temperature also increases sharply with descent into the Earth, until it may reach at least 4,000°C.

Some scientists believe that at the centre of the Earth there is a nucleus of high-density atoms, descended from the atoms that were the starting point of our solar system.

ROCKS AND THEIR ORIGINS

IGNEOUS | *Basalt* | *Granite*
SEDIMENTARY | *Shale* | *Sandstone* | *Limestone*
METAMORPHIC | *Schist* | *Gneiss*

IGNEOUS rocks are those that solidified directly from molten silicates, which geologists call magma. The Mantle obviously belongs to this category as do also the basaltic layer and much of the granitic layer. Igneous rocks include the fine-grained lavas, which have cooled quickly at the surface, and the coarse grained "plutonic" rocks which have cooled and crystallized slowly at depth.

Sedimentary rocks are formed when igneous rocks are eroded and laid down as sediment under the sea. Shale, which is mud layers compacted under great pressure, composes 80 per cent of these rocks. Others are sandstone —sand cemented into rock-form by other minerals—and limestone and chalk, which are in part the calcareous remains of countless marine creatures. Fossils are often found in the geologically younger sedimentary rocks.

Sedimentary and igneous rocks of all ages, which have been subjected to the intense pressures and heat in the roots of mountain chains, are now in a "metamorphosed" condition.

Because the older parts of the continents are criss-crossed with old eroded-down mountain chains these "metamorphic" rocks have a wide surface distribution. During metamorphism shales become schists, granite becomes gneiss, limestone becomes marble, and sandstone becomes quartzite. The changes involve re-crystallization, and the growth of new minerals from those composing the original rocks. The older metamorphic rocks are frequently rich in deposits of the base and precious metals.

108

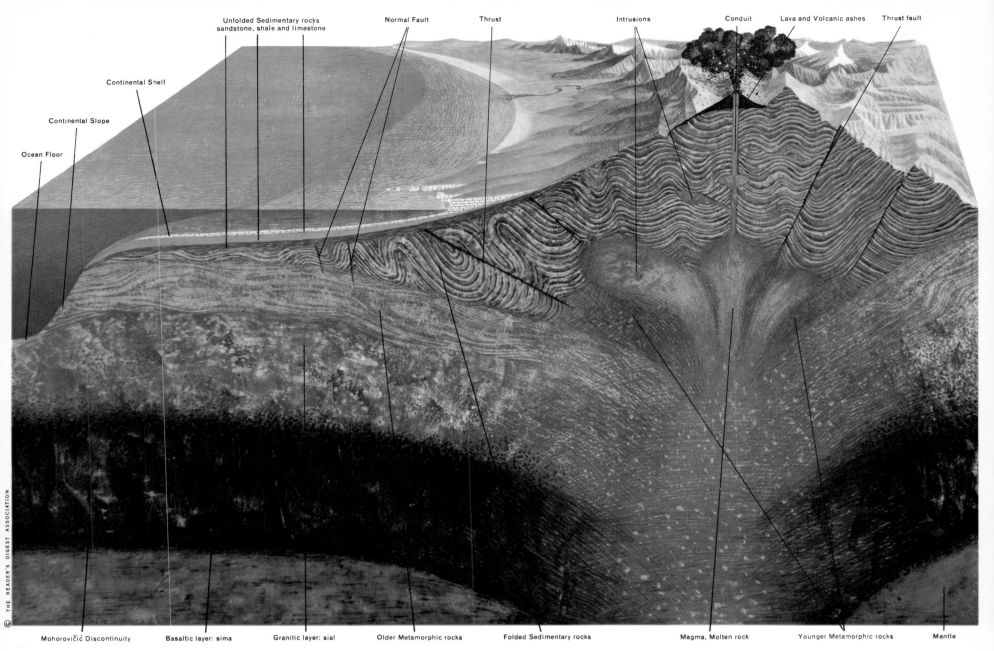

Ocean Floor · Continental Slope · Continental Shelf · Unfolded Sedimentary rocks sandstone, shale and limestone · Normal Fault · Thrust · Intrusions · Conduit · Lava and Volcanic ashes · Thrust fault

Mohorovičić Discontinuity · Basaltic layer: sima · Granitic layer: sial · Older Metamorphic rocks · Folded Sedimentary rocks · Magma, Molten rock · Younger Metamorphic rocks · Mantle

DIAGRAMMATIC SECTION THROUGH THE CRUST

In the great jig-saw of rocks that form the Earth's surface, the pieces are slowly and endlessly being rearranged. These changes originate deep in the Earth's interior.

The constant movements in the depths of the Earth mount in intensity from time to time, culminating in orogenies, profound disturbances in the Earth's Crust which give rise to great mountain ranges. The early stage of an orogeny is, paradoxically, downwarping of the Crust and formation of a sea-filled basin in which great thicknesses of sediments accumulate. Later the sides of the basin move towards each other, and the bottom moves up; the sedimentary rocks caught in this "vice" are folded and slide over each other, piling up into a great mountain chain. The fractures along which the sliding takes place are called "thrusts" or "thrust-faults". Heat and pressure in the depths of the downwarp—the "roots" of the mountain range—metamorphose the sedimentary rocks and cause molten granitic rock to form. This rises under great pressure with molten basalt from the Mantle, either crystallizing on the way up to form "intrusions", or drilling an outlet in the Earth's surface to pour out as volcanic lava and ashes. When the folded rocks appear above the sea surface, the destructive action of wind, rain, frost and waves begins. Eventually the mountains succumb; layers of sediment are deposited in places over the eroded rocks, and a surface of low relief with meandering rivers is all that is left.

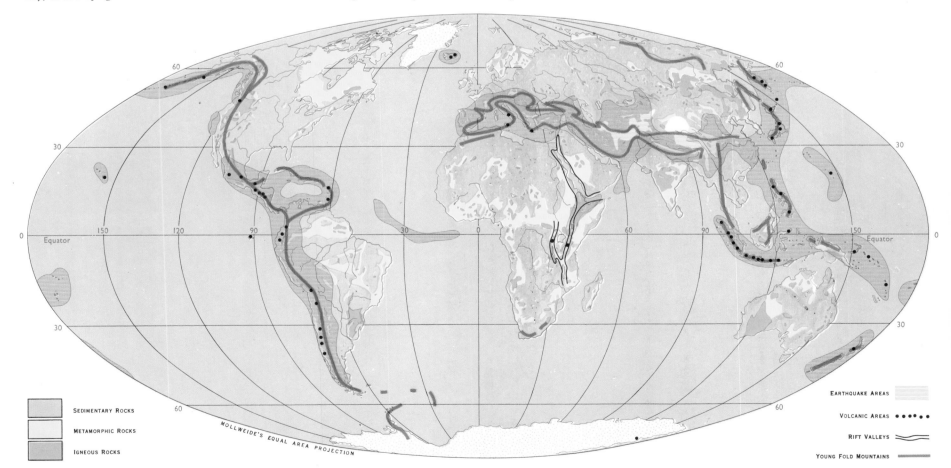

SEDIMENTARY ROCKS
METAMORPHIC ROCKS
IGNEOUS ROCKS

EARTHQUAKE AREAS
VOLCANIC AREAS
RIFT VALLEYS
YOUNG FOLD MOUNTAINS

MOLLWEIDE'S EQUAL AREA PROJECTION

THE ROCKS AND STRUCTURAL FEATURES OF THE EARTH'S CRUST

The map shows only the rocks to be seen on the surface of the Earth. The predominance of sedimentary rock is illusory, as these rocks form a thin skin over much thicker layers of metamorphic and igneous rock. Earthquake activity and active volcanoes indicate that the Earth's Crust is still unstable. Earthquakes are sudden adjustments of parts of the Crust in response to pressures generated during mountain-building and volcanic activity. Volcanoes are of two sorts: quiet outflows through tension cracks which reach down to chambers of molten rock; and explosively drilled pipes, generally in regions of active or recent mountain-building, through which bursts highly pressurized, gas-charged magma, giving violent eruptions. Present-day earthquakes and volcanic belts follow the more recent belts of mountain-building—The Alps, Himalayas, Rockies and Andes. The "Ring of Fire" round the Pacific is noteworthy; so is the Great Rift Valley extending north—south from the Jordan Valley to the Zambesi, along which the ground has sunk between parallel faults, with consequent volcanic activity.

109

Surely there is a mine for silver, and a place for gold which they refine. Iron is taken out of the earth, and brass is molten out of stone — JOB 28

FROM the prized flints of Stone-Age man to the uranium ores of the atomic scientist, minerals have contributed vitally to the growth of civilization. Man has long recognized their importance as the source of precious metals and precious stones, and of base metals such as copper, lead and zinc. Tomb paintings made in the Nile Valley nearly 5,000 years ago show craftsmen weighing malachite and

precious metals, smelting mineral ores and carving emeralds into gems.

Rocks are made up of minerals, and minerals themselves are composed of one or more of the 90-odd natural elements in the Earth's Crust. While a few elements, such as gold, are found in the pure state, the majority occur in chemical combination with other elements. Thus oxides are produced when

GALENA

Sulphide and chief ore of lead. Leaden pans for holding plants were used in the Hanging Gardens of Babylon. Lead is used in storage batteries, paint pigments, ammunition, solder, type and bearing metal, and as a safety shield with radio-active material.   *Missouri, U.S.A.*

FLUORITE (FLUORSPAR)

Calcium fluoride. Ornamental stone in Victorian times. Raw material for the production of hydrofluoric acid which is used in the aluminium, petroleum, steel and plastic industries; fluorite is used as a flux in steel-making and in the ceramic industry.   *Illinois, U.S.A.*

URANIUM MINERALS

Atomic energy developments are based on uranium. Uranium does not occur uncombined in nature but is present in over 150 minerals.

SPHALERITE

Sulphide and chief ore of zinc. Frequently occurs with galena. Zinc is used in die-castings, galvanizing steel, in brasses, dry battery cells; the oxide is used in rubber, paints, ceramics, cosmetics, etc. *Sullivan Mine, British Columbia*

ASBESTOS

A group of fire-resistant, fibrous silicate minerals. The long fibres can be spun into fabrics. The short fibres are mixed with cement to make asbestos board.   *Quebec, Canada*

PITCHBLENDE

Uranium oxides with other components. The massive variety of uraninite, the most important ore.   *Shinkolobwe, Katanga, Congo*

TORBERNITE

Hydrated copper-uranium phosphate. Green plates resemble a mica.   *Cornwall*

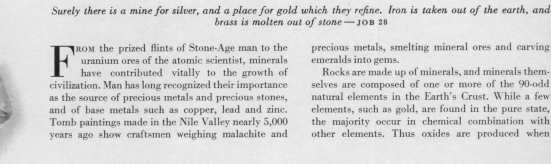

CASSITERITE

Oxide and chief ore of tin. Alloyed with copper, it was the basis of Bronze Age implements. Used in tin-plating, solders, bronze, bearing and type metal, pewter, and die-casting.   *W. Malaysia*

TOPAZ

Silicate of fluorine and aluminium. Used as gemstone and in refractories.   *Ouro Preto, Brazil*

OLIVINE

Magnesium-iron silicate. A common rock-forming mineral. Used as a moulding sand. Peridot and chrysolite are gem varieties.   *Zebirget, Egypt*

Sullivan Mine, British Columbia, *Sphalerite*
Minnesota, *Hematite* Quebec, *Asbestos*
U.S.A., *Garnet*   Sudbury, Ontario, *Pentlandite*
Illinois, *Fluorite*
Missouri, *Galena* W.Virginia, *Coal*
Texas, *Sulphur*

Mexico, *Silver*

Jamaica, *Bauxite*

Colombia, *Emerald*

Brazil, *Quartz*

Minas Gerais, *Aquamarine*
Ouro Preto, *Topaz*

Equator

 Oil

ALUMINA MINERALS

Although the most abundant metal in the Earth's Crust, aluminium does not occur in the free state, and commercial production did not start until the late 19th century. Alloys are used extensively in motor vehicles, aircraft, ships and domestic goods. Aluminium is used in electric transmission lines. Ruby and sapphire are gem varieties of corundum, a natural aluminium oxide.

CORUNDUM

Hardness only exceeded by diamond. Used as an abrasive in grinding optical glass. Mixed with magnetite and other minerals to form emery.   *Transvaal, South Africa*

SAPPHIRE

Corundum gemstones of whatever colour are sapphires with the exception of red (ruby); commonly blue.   *Ceylon*

RUBY

"Pigeon-blood" red variety. Large rubies are among the most precious of stones.   *Mogok, Burma*

BAUXITE

Rock composed of aluminium hydroxides. Chief ore of aluminium; also used in making abrasives, refractories, chemicals, high-alumina cement, insulating materials, as a catalyst by the oil industry, and as a flux in steel manufacture.   *Jamaica*

CINNABAR

Sulphide and chief ore of mercury (quick-silver). Mercury is used in the chemical, electrical and metal industries, and in scientific instruments, dental preparations, and detonators.   *Almaden, Spain*

COPPER MINERALS

Copper and gold were the first metals used by man. Both occur in the free state and are easily worked. Copper is used extensively in the electrical industry, also in bronze, brass and other alloys. About 12 of the 165 known copper minerals are commercially important.

IRON MINERALS

Iron is industry's indispensable metal. Although iron minerals occur abundantly, pure iron is too soft for use, so man learnt to harden it by adding carbon. Thus the Iron Age followed the Bronze Age in Europe and W.Asia. A moderate amount of carbon produces steel, an excess produces cast-iron.

AZURITE

Hydrated copper carbonate.   *Katanga, Congo*

CHALCOPYRITE

Copper-iron-sulphide. Crystals of chalcopyrite and quartz are shown. Most widespread and important ore of copper.   *Zambia*

MALACHITE

Hydrated copper carbonate. An ornamental stone as well as a valuable ore.   *Katanga, Congo*

MAGNETITE

Magnetic iron oxide. Crystals show octahedral form. Lodestone (leading-stone), a variety with magnetic polarity, was used in primitive compasses.   *Kiruna, Sweden*

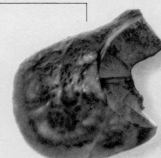

HEMATITE

Oxide of iron. The "kidney-ore" variety is shown. Used as an ornamental stone in signet rings, tie-pins and cuff links.   *Minnesota, U.S.A.*

110

TREASURES

EARTH'S CRUST

metals combine with oxygen, and sulphides when metals combine with sulphur. Minerals are formed in various ways, for example, by crystallization from molten lava, rather as ice crystals form when water freezes, and by crystallization from vapours, as in the formation of sulphur crystals by the cooling of sulphur-bearing vapours round active volcanoes.

Some 2,000 minerals have been recorded so far, and, although new minerals are still being discovered, it is unlikely that any large deposit of a new mineral will be found in the accessible parts of the Earth's

Crust. At depths below those of the present deepest mine, we may one day find new minerals that are stable at the high pressures and temperatures nearer the centre of the Earth. The advent of space travel opens up the possibility of the discovery of new minerals which would be stable on other planets where conditions are so different from our own.

This small selection of the Earth's minerals shows the variety of their natural forms and colours. Their more commercially important deposits and the locations of the world's oilfields are indicated on the map.

APATITE
Calcium phosphate. Chief constituent of phosphate-rock. Used in manufacture of fertilizers, cleansing products, smoke-bombs, pesticides, and phosphorus alloys.
Kola Peninsula, Russia

PENTLANDITE
Nickel-iron sulphide. Frequently occurs with chalcopyrite. Used extensively in stainless steels and other alloys; nickel is alloyed with copper to make Britain's "silver" coins and the U.S. five-cent "nickel".
Sudbury, Ontario

BERYLLIUM MINERALS
Beryllium is unusually light and strong and has valuable metallurgical properties. Used in alloys with copper, nickel, and aluminium, also in X-ray tubes, and nuclear reactors. Beryl is the commercial source of beryllium; aquamarine and emerald are gemstone varieties with similar composition.

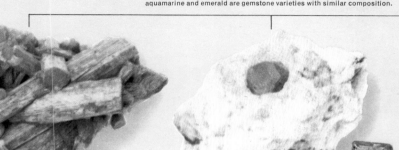

KAOLIN (CHINA CLAY)
Hydrated aluminium silicate. Used in paper, rubber, ceramics (notably porcelain and china), chemicals, cosmetics, insecticides and petroleum catalysts. *Cornwall*

ZIRCON
Zirconium silicate. Besides being a gemstone, zircon in mineral form is used as foundry sand and in abrasives and ceramics. Zirconium metal is used in nuclear reactors, steel alloys, and in the chemical and electrical industries.

BERYL
Silicate of beryllium and aluminium. Can occur in large crystals up to 25 tons in weight. Gemstone if clear and transparent.
Mocambique

EMERALD
Grass-green, unflawed stones exceeding six carats command high prices. Ranks with diamond and ruby as the most precious stone.
Colombia

AQUAMARINE
Sea-green variety.
Minas Gerais, Brazil

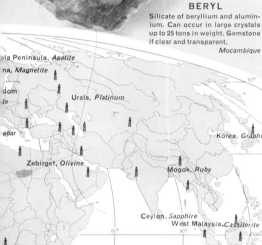

la Peninsula, *Apatite*
na, *Magnetite*
dom
Urals, *Platinum*
bar
Korea, *Graphite*
Zebirget, *Olivine*
Mogok, *Ruby*
Ceylon, *Sapphire*
West Malaysia, *Cassiterite*
Equator
Katanga,
hblende, *Azurite, Malachite*
Zambia, *Chalcopyrite*
Mocambique, *Beryl*
Transvaal, *Corundum*
Kimberley, *Diamond*
The Rand, *Gold*
New South Wales, *Opal*

CARBON MINERALS
Native crystalline carbon occurs as two important minerals: diamond and graphite. Coals consist largely of non-crystalline carbon of organic origin. Combination with hydrogen produces the natural hydrocarbons which constitute petroleums and bitumens.

DIAMOND
Hardest known mineral and the most valuable gemstone. Crystallized deep down at high temperature and pressure, and brought to surface in volcanic "kimberlite" pipes. Photograph shows a diamond in kimberlite. Most diamonds are minute and imperfect, and are used in industry for cutting or as abrasives.
Kimberley, South Africa

COAL
Bituminous coal showing banded structure. Besides being a fuel, coal is a source of coal gas, coke, tar, ammonia and many hydrocarbon chemicals. *United Kingdom*

GRAPHITE
One of the softest minerals. The "lead" in lead pencils. Used in foundry facings, steel-making, lubricants, refractory crucibles, electrical equipment, pigments and in atomic piles. *Korea*

SULPHUR (BRIMSTONE)
Native sulphur (illustrated), metallic sulphide ores, "sour" natural and refinery gas, and coal are all commercial sources of sulphur. Used in manufacture of sulphuric acid and many other chemicals, paper, rubber goods, steel, textiles. *Texas, U.S.A.*

PLATINUM
Native platinum usually contains variable amounts of the other platinum-group metals—palladium, iridium, osmium, rhodium and ruthenium—some of which are employed to harden pure platinum in commercial applications. Platinum is used in anti-corrosive chemical ware, electrical components and laboratory instruments. Platinum and palladium are both used as catalysts, and in jewellery, dentistry and medicine. *Urals*

SILVER
Specimen of native silver with milky-white quartz. Silver sulphides are important ores commonly associated with lead, copper and zinc ores. Used in coinage, plate, jewellery and dentistry, and in the photographic, electrical and chemical industries. *Mexico*

GOLD
Man used gold for decoration from early times. It is hardened by alloying with copper, silver, palladium or nickel for use in jewellery, dentistry and scientific equipment.
The Rand, South Africa

SILICA MINERALS
Silicon does not occur uncombined; but its oxide, quartz, and the large group of silicates are the most important rock-forming minerals. Silicon is the most abundant element in the Earth's Crust after oxygen; it is used in electronic components and alloys, and for manufacturing silicones. Chalcedony is a crystalline variety of quartz intimately mixed with opal and other constituents. Flint is a common dark grey-brown variety of chalcedony; precious varieties are shown below.

GARNET
Garnet is the name of a group of silicates. The photograph shows crystals in a metamorphic rock; garnet is also a semi-precious gemstone. The iron-aluminium garnet, almandine, is used as an abrasive. *U.S.A.*

OPAL
A hydrated non-crystalline form of silica (silicon dioxide) which shows a beautifully variegated play of colours or "fire". Gemstone. *New South Wales, Australia*

QUARTZ
One of the commonest minerals. High-grade quartz is used in crystal-controlled oscillator units (as in quartz-clocks) and other electronic instruments, also for optical purposes and in fused quartz ware. *Brazil*

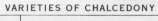

VARIETIES OF CHALCEDONY

HALITE (ROCK SALT)
Sodium chloride. Man requires about 12 lb. of salt a year. Apart from its use in food-seasoning and preserving, salt is chiefly used by the chemical industry. *Cheshire*

ONYX
An agate with regular bands in sharply contrasted colours.

CHRYSOPRASE
Apple-green variety coloured by nickel oxide.

CARNELIAN
Reddish variety coloured by ferric oxide.

AGATE
Greyish variety in which irregular bands conform to shape of original cavity. Easily stained and used for umbrella handles, brooches, etc., also in laboratory equipment.

111

THE AGES OF THE EARTH

And the Earth was waste and void — GENESIS 1

Of the 4,500 million and more years of the Earth's existence only the last 600 million years can be traced with accuracy. Almost nothing is known of conditions during the first 1,000 million years, before the Earth's Crust consolidated. The historian, relying on archaeological discoveries and the written records of ancient civilizations, can reach back a mere 6,000 years into the past, but the geologist can reconstruct the story in considerable detail for 600 million years before the historian's record begins. The geologist's evidence lies in the rocks and in the fossilized relics of plants and animals that many of the rocks contain.

Although little is known of the 3,000 million years which elapsed after consolidation of the Earth's Crust, the earliest and most primitive forms of life—seaweeds and invertebrate marine creatures—must have been evolving for many millions of years before their fossilized remains were first preserved in the rocks formed about 600 million years ago. The earliest vertebrates—primitive types of fish-like animals—did not appear for another 100 million years. Land plants first established themselves little more than 400 million years ago, and amphibious animals about 350 million years ago. Mammals, of which man, through his brain, is the most advanced, date back a little less than 250 million years; man himself has emerged only within the last million years.

The course of evolution has not been smooth and unbroken; some plants and animals evolved only to die out millions of years later, never to reappear; others have persisted almost unchanged. Major disturbances of the Earth's Crust caused important changes in geography and climate, which in turn influenced the evolution and distribution of animal and plant life. These major disturbances separate the four *eras* of geological history: the Proterozoic (first life), the Palaeozoic (ancient life), the Mesozoic (middle life), and the Cainozoic (modern life).

Within each of the four eras there were crustal disturbances which again broke up the geological record, but to a lesser degree. The rocks formed during the *periods* of time between these disturbances are grouped together as distinct *systems,* most of which have been named after the places where the rocks were first studied; e.g. the county of Devon, and the Jura Mountains of central Europe.

Thus, the evidence deduced from rocks and fossils reveals not only the general pattern of evolution in plant and animal life, but the development of the world's oceans, continents, mountain ranges and rivers, as well as changes in climatic conditions. From geological research we know that lion, rhinoceros, elephant and hippopotamus once roamed over the country we now call Britain, and that the summit of Mount Everest—where marine fossils have been found—is composed of limestone which was originally formed under the sea.

GEOLOGY OF CANADA

GEOLOGY OF NEWFOUNDLAND

CAINOZOIC FORMATIONS

- Mainly sedimentary and volcanic rocks

MESOZOIC FORMATIONS

- Mainly sedimentary and volcanic rocks
- Granites and other intrusive igneous rocks in western coast ranges

PALAEOZOIC FORMATIONS

- Mainly sedimentary and volcanic rocks (with some intrusive granites, gabbros, etc., in eastern provinces)

PROTEROZOIC AND OLDER FORMATIONS

- Mainly sedimentary rocks
- Mainly igneous (volcanic and intrusive) and metamorphic rocks (gneisses, schists, etc.)

ERA	GEOLOGICAL DIVISIONS	GEOGRAPHICAL CONDITIONS
CAINOZOIC (MODERN LIFE)	**Holocene** started 10 thousand years ago	The ice continues to retreat, causing the sea level to rise further. Britain, joined to Europe during the glacial period, is cut off from the Continent. Landscape much as we see it today. Climatic conditions gradually become more equable. In North Africa and the Middle East, increasing dryness produces deserts.
	Pleistocene started about 2 million years ago *lasted c 2 million years*	Ice-sheets and glaciers cover nearly all of Canada and much of Europe, America, Antarctica, and the Himalayas. The ice melts periodically, thus raising the sea level, and the land masses of North America and Europe, which have been pressed down by the enormous weight of the ice, begin to rise. (Scandinavia today continues to rise at a rate of a centimetre a year.) Melting ice forms the Great Lakes of North America, the lakes of Switzerland and Northern Italy. The tremendous weight of retreating glaciers cuts out the fjords of Norway. Landscape begins to take on present-day form and appearance. A period of abnormal and extreme climatic changes.
	Pliocene started about 7 million years ago *lasted c 5 million years*	Continents and oceans begin to take on their present form. Land subsidence leads to formation of the North Sea, the Black and Caspian Seas, the Sea of Aral. Formation of mountain ranges continues, though on a reduced scale. Climatic conditions are much like today's, but with a broader temperate zone.
	Miocene started about 26 million years ago *lasted 19 million years*	Period of great volcanism in North America. Powerful Earth movements lead to a further retreat of the sea. The Mediterranean becomes virtually a land-locked ocean. The European and Asian land masses are finally joined together. Increased rainfall leads to intense erosion in some parts. Further powerful movements in the Earth's Crust complete formation of the Alps and lead to formation of the Himalayas. Much volcanic activity. Climates tend to become more varied: dry and arid in some regions, cool and wet in others.
	Oligocene started about 38 million years ago *lasted 12 million years*	Throughout this period the land mass grows at the expense of the sea. Extensive movements of the Earth's Crust in the Americas and in Europe. Oligocene formations widespread in Florida and central America. The Alps begin to form. Warm, temperate conditions continue, but parts of the land mass experience a cycle of cooler winters.
	Eocene and Palaeocene (combined) started about 65 million years ago *lasted c 27 million years*	North America assumes approximately its present size and configuration at beginning of this period. The subsidence of much of Europe causes the seas to advance once again. Mountain ranges which began to form in the Cretaceous period continue to grow. Volcanic activity leads to the formation of the Atlantic and Indian Oceans, and causes vast amounts of lava to be deposited in areas as far apart as the Arctic, Scotland and Ireland, and southern India. Tropical conditions are more widespread than today, but glaciers exist on high mountain ranges in western North America.
MESOZOIC (MIDDLE LIFE)	**Cretaceous** chalk started about 136 million years ago *lasted 71 million years*	Final submergence of North American continent, but seas retreat before end of period leaving far-reaching swamps. The rivers flow slowly and form enormous deltas. Chalk formations accumulate in North America, Alaska and Mexico. Period of major mountain-building. The Rocky Mountains, the Andes, many European ranges and the Panama Ridge—giving rise to the Gulf Stream—begin to emerge. The climate continues to be mild, causing vegetation to grow abundantly as far north as Greenland, though parts of Australia appear to be covered by glaciers.
	Jurassic after Jura mountains in France and Switzerland started about 193 million years ago *lasted c 57 million years*	The seas advance again. Most land areas consist of forests or swampy plains with lakes and meandering rivers. The high mountains, already eroded by the arid climate of the previous period, are reduced to low hills by the wet conditions. Erosion prevails in eastern North American continent. Much of Asia and Europe is invaded by the sea. In Canada vast inland seas lay down rocks which now cover much of the great plains area. The climate is predominantly mild, becoming sub-tropical in some regions later in the period. There is sufficient rainfall to support luxuriant vegetation.
	Triassic after three-fold mountain system in Germany started about 225 million years ago *lasted c 32 million years*	In eastern Canada lava flows and erosion prevails, with infilling of local basins such as Bay of Fundy region. Deserts and shrub-covered mountains make up most of the Earth's land area. What is, today, Britain is covered by warm, salt lakes surrounded by deserts. Formation of marl and sandstone deposits in the warm seas. Hot, dry conditions prevail almost everywhere. Climate becomes wetter towards the end of the period.
PALAEOZOIC (ANCIENT LIFE)	**Permian** After Russian province of Perm started about 280 million years ago *lasted 55 million years*	Arms of the sea are cut off and turned into vast inland lakes by the warping of the Earth's Crust. The lakes start evaporating, a process that eventually leads to the formation of the world's chief potash deposits. A period of considerable Earth movements. Mountains form along North American eastern seaboard extending up into Maritimes and Newfoundland. Contrasting climatic conditions. Mainly arid in Northern Hemisphere, with widespread deserts and with occasional warm and humid zones, but ice-age conditions cover much of the Southern Hemisphere.
	Carboniferous the coal age (Upper Pennsylvanian and Lower Mississippian) started about 345 million years ago *lasted 65 million years*	Clear, shallow seas widespread in early period; about one-third of North America and most of Europe under water. Later, sea beds begin to rise, exposing great stretches of land. Other land areas sink, producing brackish swamps over much of North America and Europe, where mountain formations are much folded, faulted and uplifted. Chief coal-forming period, particularly in Northern Hemisphere, as in Canadian Maritimes and U.S. Appalachians. The land climate is extremely dry throughout most of the period, but in some regions it is warm and moist enough to encourage dense vegetation.
	Devonian after county of Devon where fossils of this period first found started about 395 million years ago *lasted 50 million years*	Land area increases at expense of sea. A period of extensive mountain-building, volcanic and igneous activity particularly in North America. Pebbles, sand and mud, washed off the newly-made mountains, form the "Old Red Sandstone" of north-west Europe. Warm and semi-arid climate over a large part of North America and in north-west Europe, with heavy seasonal rain. Equable conditions prevail elsewhere.
	Silurian after Celtic tribe, the Silures started about 435 million years ago *lasted c 40 million years*	The level of the seas tends to rise and fall periodically, causing regular changes in the land areas. Shallow seas spread over much of eastern United States and south-east Canada. Rocks formed in this period have been found in England, the Baltic and in the region of the Niagara Falls. New mountain ranges are beginning to form. Less volcanic activity than in Ordovician times. Generally warm and equable climate, but exceptionally dry in certain areas.
	Ordovician after Celtic tribe, the Ordovices started about 500 million years ago *lasted c 65 million years*	The seas continue to advance and retreat. Many areas of the sea floor become dry land as the shallow seas deposit ever-increasing amounts of sand and mud, as in North America. Rocks of Ordovician period have been found in parts of North America and north-west Europe. Mountain-building in these regions. Continent of North America subject to series of disturbances and volcanic activity. Volcanic eruptions on the floor of the sea creating huge volcanic beds. The climate appears warm and even, with no marked climatic zones.
	Cambrian after Cambria, Roman name for Wales started about 570 million years ago *lasted 70 million years*	Shallow seas cover much of the Earth. The seas tend to advance on and retreat from the land areas, some of which are probably little more than deserts. Cambrian rocks form in Wales, north-west Scotland and western England. Similar rock formations occur in the Canadian Rockies and in the U.S.A.—rocks from which the Grand Canyon is later carved form in this period. Considerable volcanic activity in Europe, but no evidence of important mountain-building in this period. Climatic conditions are moderately warm and equable.
PROTEROZOIC	**Pre-Cambrian**	Beginning as a whirling globe of inter-stellar gas, the Earth passes through a liquid state and forms a solidified crust. Thick, steamy atmosphere surrounds the planet. As the Earth's surface cools, water vapour condenses as rain to produce rivers and seas. The surface now forms a barren landscape of mountains, deserts, volcanoes and steaming lava fields. Many Pre-Cambrian rocks have been so crushed and altered by heat and by pressure of subsequent Earth movements that it is almost impossible to determine their original nature. Pre-Cambrian rocks exposed in British Columbia. The hot climate is broken up by a series of ice ages.

VEGETATION	LIFE IN THE SEA	LIFE ON LAND	EVOLUTION OF LIFE
With the retreat of the ice and the arrival of warmer summers, forests begin to spread all over Europe. Tundra vegetation (mossy, marshy plains) is replaced by birch and pine, followed by hazel and then by oak and elder.	Marine life much as it is today.	Man learns to domesticate animals and cultivate plants.	
Succeeding ice ages cause many plants in Europe to perish, leaving only hardier varieties—oak, willow, poplar, elm, hawthorn. In America and Asia, vegetation seeking warmer climates encounters no sea or mountain barriers, and more plants survive.	Marine life much as it is today.	Ape-like creatures develop enough intelligence to make stone implements for cutting up animals they have killed, thus marking the transition to primitive man. Probably originating in Africa, primitive man spreads to Asia and Europe. Alternating ice ages and warm periods change the migration habits of other mammals. In one glacial period, reindeer and Arctic fox roam southern England. In the warmer period, hippopotamuses live in the Thames, lions range as far north as Yorkshire. True elephants, horses, oxen first appear.	
Some plants of this period, such as the maidenhair tree, die out in Europe but survive in China and North America.	Giant sharks become extinct, as did creatures that grew to a great size in other periods. Marine life, both plant and animal, becomes much as it is today. There are only marginal developments from this period onwards.	The number of mammal species declines, with the notable exception of the man-like apes, which continue to develop and thrive. These apes come to include not only the forest-dwellers, but the species known as *Australopithecus* which walks upright in open country and may be ancestral to man. Elephants also thrive, and roam as far afield as Suffolk and Norfolk.	
Mild, damp climate in Europe and North America stimulates development of deciduous woods — maple, oak and poplar. Cedars and sequoias are established on higher ground. The great plains of North America become covered with prairie grasses.	Bony fish continue to increase in variety. Sharks, particularly abundant during this period, grow to enormous sizes, measuring over 60 feet in length, and having teeth six inches long.	*Proconsul,* a primitive anthropoid ape living in central Africa, migrates to Asia and Europe. A gibbon-like ape, known as *Pliopithecus,* is common in the forests of southern Europe. Elephants, steadily increasing in size, spread from Africa into Europe, Asia and North America. Long-legged waterbirds, ducks and pelicans live in rivers and lakes. Primitive penguins, some as tall as man, live in Antarctica.	
As a cooler climate affects some parts of the world, forests dwindle and grasslands spread, leading to an increase in grass-eating mammals.	A period in which new species of crabs, mussels and snails evolve.	The ancestors of modern cats, dogs and bears evolve. The number of plant-eating animals increases—small elephants with short trunks, and tusks in both upper and lower jaws, hoofed animals with odd numbers of toes, and giant rhinoceros. A tail-less, primitive ape, possibly related to the ancestors of man, appears.	
Flowering plants, including deciduous trees, become dominant. The warm climatic zone, which stretches right up to Greenland, allows palms to grow in the region of Bournemouth, and Malayan-type jungles in the region of London.	Marine reptiles have become extinct, but two groups of mammals—early whales and sea-cows—begin to adapt to life in the sea. Most species of fish in the ocean take on the shape and forms we know today.	Many varieties of modern mammals come into existence—ancestors of the elephant, the rhinoceros, the horse, the pig and cattle. Giant reptiles have disappeared, but crocodiles, turtles and land tortoises evolve, as do all groups of insects that we know today. Primitive monkeys and gibbons appear in Burma.	
A mild climate with alternating seasons—a feature of this period—encourages the growth of deciduous trees—fig, magnolia, poplar, plane. The parallel evolution of insects and nectar-bearing flowers encourages the spread of flowering plants.	Fish evolving in this period are closely related to the porbeagle sharks, rays and herrings of today. Marine life continues to be dominated by reptiles, giant turtles and mosasaurs—long, slender creatures resembling sea-serpents. Flying reptiles (pterosaurs) have a wing span of over 20 feet. (Their remains have been found in Yorkshire, Kent and Sussex.)	Giant reptiles, dinosaurs and pterosaurs, dominate life on land and in the air. Ichthyosaurs dominate life in the sea. Birds evolve into two types: one with well-developed wings, similar to modern birds, the other a sea-bird, almost wingless but with strongly developed legs for swimming. By the end of the period dinosaurs become extinct. Mammals remain inconspicuous throughout this period, but by its end placental mammals (whose young are nourished directly by the mother's blood until birth) have developed.	
Conifers, cycads, ferns and tree-ferns continue to flourish. Some cycads have flower-like cones—the first step in the evolution of flowers.	In the seas, the dominant animals are aquatic reptiles like ichthyosaurs. Rapid swimmers, they prey on fish and other marine creatures.	Reptiles increase in size and variety. Some take to the air; the first bird, *Archaeopteryx,* evolves feathers from scales, but retains many reptilian characteristics such as teeth, solid bones and a jointed tail. *Pterosaurus* develops wings made of skin stretched between body and fingers. Some reptiles, too large for survival on land (*Diplodocus,* length 84 feet, weight 35 tons), live in swamps and marshes. Mammals remain small and primitive, no bigger than rats, and live mostly in woodlands.	
Arid conditions in the Northern Hemisphere discourage the development of plant life at the beginning of the period. Later, wetter conditions stimulate the growth of conifers, cycads and ferns.	The first ichthyosaurs, carnivorous, fish-shaped reptiles, evolve in this period. So do flying fish and the first lobster-like creatures.	Reptiles continue to dominate life on land. The first mammals—warm-blooded creatures—evolve from the reptiles. Dinosaurs, no more than six inches long, are present for the first time. The first flies and termites appear.	
As seasonal differences of climate and temperature develop, evergreen plants begin to decrease in number, and deciduous plants, able to withstand periods of drought and frost, appear.	This period marks the end of the dominance by marine creatures, as animal and plant life on land increases.	Creatures capable of living on land increase in number and variety, ending the period of domination by marine creatures. As in the sea, however, animal life is predominantly reptilian. A great variety of insects begins to emerge.	
Giant evergreen trees, reaching heights of over 100 feet flourish in the tropical swamp of the period which knows no seasonal changes of temperature.	Amphibious creatures continue to develop. Living in swamp-land on the edge of lakes, they are small, salamander-like animals to begin with, but reach sizes of up to 15 feet by the end of the period. Marine life, both plant and animal, abounds in many varieties.	The reptile becomes the first creature to breed on land. Certain species of insects develop wings.	
Earth begins to look green, as plants with roots, stems and leaves evolve. They range from small, herb-like growths to trees of 40 feet or more in height. By the end of the period, various kinds of ferns, horsetails and seed-ferns have evolved.	Rapid evolution of vertebrate animals. Ancestors of all modern fish evolve. Primitive sharks, measuring up to 20 feet, appear. In consequence, this period has become known as the "Age of Fish." By the end of the period, the first amphibious animals have come into existence.	With land plants to feed on, the first invertebrate animals leave the sea and adapt themselves to life on land. They include millipedes, mites, spiders, and wingless insects.	
Plants first adapt themselves to life on land, but are still leafless. (Fossil remains have been found in Australia.)	New species of vertebrate animals develop in the sea. Appearance of sea-scorpions, heavily armoured animals reaching nine feet in length. (Fossil remains of Jamoytius, a primitive vertebrate of this period, have been found in Lanarkshire.) Plant life becomes more varied in structure, and coral reefs develop on a large scale.	First plants appear on land.	
Plant life confined to the sea.	All life still restricted to water, but first vertebrates appear. (Remains of ostracoderms—bony, armoured creatures—have been found in western U.S.A.) Plant life does not advance beyond seaweeds.	No life.	
Plant life confined to the sea.	Life exists only in the seas. All the major groups of invertebrates evolve. Seaweeds, still the only plants, provide food for these animals: worms, jellyfish, starfish, sponges — and trilobites, the dominant and most advanced animals, of which there are more than 1,000 species, ranging in size from a pin-head to 18 inches. (All now extinct.)	No life.	
Seaweeds are the only form of vegetation.	Life originates in the warm seas at some time during this period. (How it originated is a mystery.) It is very primitive, taking the form of seaweeds and mainly soft-bodied invertebrate animals.	No life.	

Evolution of Life diagram labels: Modern Man, Carnivores, Ancestral Man, Horses, Camels, Elephants, Whales, Apes, Bats, Grasses, Monkeys, Birds, Marsupials, Insectivores, Crocodiles, Early Mammals Evolving, Angiosperms, Turtles, Dinosaurs, Dinosaurs, Pterosaurs, Toothed Birds, Ichthyosaurs, Land Reptiles, Cycads, Plesiosaurs, Marine Reptiles, Theriodonts, Conifers, Ammonites, Cotylosaurs, Ferns, Seed Ferns, Crinoids, Labyrinthodonts, Insects, Scale Trees, Blastoids, Sharks, Clams, Cordaites, Brachiopods, Choanichthyes, Starfish, Corals, Cystoids, Nautiloids, Snails, Sponges, Trilobites, Algae.

Legend: MARINE LIFE, TERRESTRIAL PLANT LIFE, AERIAL LIFE, TERRESTRIAL ANIMAL LIFE, POINT OF EXTINCTION, EVOLUTION STILL CONTINUING.

THE GREAT OCEANS

And the gathering together of the waters called he Seas — GENESIS 1

Our world is awash with water. No other planet, as far as we know, has anything like a sea, but seven-tenths of the Earth is covered by great oceans, the Pacific alone having an area of more than 63 million square miles. The seas' average depth is 12,000 feet (two and a half miles) compared with an average land height of only 2,500 feet.

Beneath the surface there is no uniform mass of water, but a series of well-defined layers, each with its own characteristics, such as temperature, salt-content and marine life.

Coursing through these layers are fast currents, some of them hundreds of miles long and up to 100 miles wide. These currents not only affect the positions of fishing grounds, but may also influence the world's climate; for a change in the direction of a current can alter the weather far inland.

The sea bed is not merely land covered by water. It consists of a thin layer

The *continental shelves* are the threshold of the sea; submerged slabs of land, rather than the true ocean bed, with floors made of the same material as the adjacent land; the edge of this shelf is often nearly parallel to the coastline. They vary in width from a few miles to the 800 miles of the Russian Arctic and slope very gently to depths between 200 and 1,000 feet.

The *continental slopes* mark the edge of the continent. Sloping quickly to oceanic depths, they are the longest and highest escarpments known. Their average height is 12,000 feet, but some drop in unbroken slopes of 30,000 feet—a thousand feet higher than Mount Everest.

From the foot of the continental slopes the deep ocean basins reach out across half the surface of our planet. These basins, some two and a half miles down, are, in fact, ribbed with mountain ranges, pitted with deep valleys and floored by abyssal plains. The basins are carpeted with sediment, formed by the minute remains of creatures and rocks sifting down through the sea since time began. In places, the carpet is two miles thick—often built up at a rate of fractions of an inch in thousands of years. Scientists, lowering their instruments to the sea bed, take cores of the sediment, which they interpret like the rings in the trunk of a tree. One day they hope to sink a core right down to the hard rock beneath the sediment; they may then be able to trace the story of the oceans back to their very beginning.

Winding, steep-sided canyons cut across the edges of many continental slopes. Some may have been worn away by underwater currents; others, near the mouths of big rivers, were probably carved by slow erosion from the rivers when the sea was much shallower.

Challenger Deep is one of the deepest parts of the sea bed. Its floor lies 35,640 feet beneath the surface of the Pacific. There the water is perpetually near-freezing, yet forms of life are still to be found. The United States bathyscaphe *Trieste* touched bottom on 23rd January 1960 in Challenger Deep which is part of the Marianas Trench.

The volcanic island of Krakatoa completely disappeared in 1883 after the most explosive eruption ever recorded. When the volcano blew up, the sound was heard 3,000 miles away. Great tidal waves, which drowned tens of thousands of people, were felt even in the English Channel; and the volcanic dust tinged sunsets the world over for nearly a year. A thousand feet beneath the surface of Sunda Strait was a vast crater, all that remained of an island that had once stood 1,400 feet above the sea. In 1929, a new island suddenly emerged in the same place, it was named Anak Krakatoa—Child of Krakatoa.

Most mid-ocean islands are volcanic, thrust up through the sea bed by violent eruptions. The Hawaiian volcano Mauna Kea is the highest mountain on Earth. It rises sheer from the sea bed to 31,000 feet, of which only 13,823 feet show above the surface.

Coral is formed of the skeletons of tiny marine animals—yet the coral islands are the largest structures built by any living creature. The Great Barrier Reef of Australia, 1,260 miles long and 500 feet thick, is a vast coral honeycomb where fish, plant and rock forms make the most exotic jungle in the world. The coral atolls that dot the Pacific are monuments to sunken islands—and to the tiny creatures that build them, keeping pace with each island's descent into the sea bed. When the depth of Eniwetok atoll was measured, it was found that countless generations of coral animals had piled the atoll 4,000 feet thick on the submerged stump of island.

CONTINENTAL DRIFT

If the continents of the world are cut from a map, they can be made to fit together like the pieces of a jigsaw. Hence the theory that the Earth was originally one enormous continent, before it split up and the pieces drifted apart to their present positions. The theory, formulated earlier in this century, has recently won fresh scientific support. Magnetic measurements, showing which way rocks were facing when they were first formed, indicate that rocks all over the world were once differently orientated—in a pattern that seems to fit the theory of Continental Drift. Sandstones, some 200 million years old, found in Britain, suggest a Saharan climate; and the magnetic measurements indicate that Britain was then where the Sahara is now.

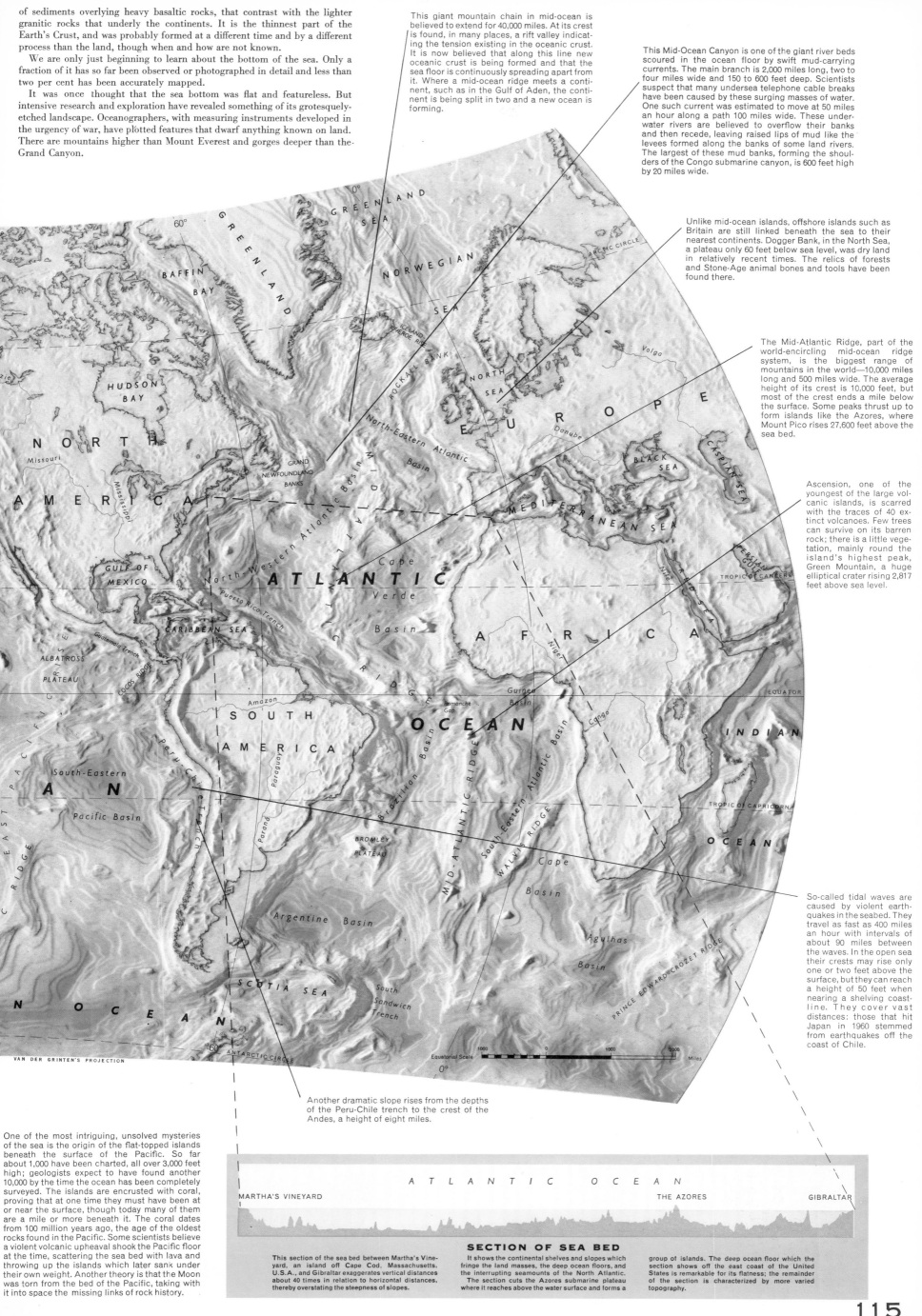

of sediments overlying heavy basaltic rocks, that contrast with the lighter granitic rocks that underly the continents. It is the thinnest part of the Earth's Crust, and was probably formed at a different time and by a different process than the land, though when and how are not known.

We are only just beginning to learn about the bottom of the sea. Only a fraction of it has so far been observed or photographed in detail and less than two per cent has been accurately mapped.

It was once thought that the sea bottom was flat and featureless. But intensive research and exploration have revealed something of its grotesquely-etched landscape. Oceanographers, with measuring instruments developed in the urgency of war, have plotted features that dwarf anything known on land. There are mountains higher than Mount Everest and gorges deeper than the Grand Canyon.

This giant mountain chain in mid-ocean is believed to extend for 40,000 miles. At its crest is found, in many places, a rift valley indicating the tension existing in the oceanic crust. It is now believed that along this line new oceanic crust is being formed and that the sea floor is continuously spreading apart from it. Where a mid-ocean ridge meets a continent, such as in the Gulf of Aden, the continent is being split in two and a new ocean is forming.

This Mid-Ocean Canyon is one of the giant river beds scoured in the ocean floor by swift mud-carrying currents. The main branch is 2,000 miles long, two to four miles wide and 150 to 600 feet deep. Scientists suspect that many undersea telephone cable breaks have been caused by these surging masses of water. One such current was estimated to move at 50 miles an hour along a path 100 miles wide. These underwater rivers are believed to overflow their banks and then recede, leaving raised lips of mud like the levees formed along the banks of some land rivers. The largest of these mud banks, forming the shoulders of the Congo submarine canyon, is 600 feet high by 20 miles wide.

Unlike mid-ocean islands, offshore islands such as Britain are still linked beneath the sea to their nearest continents. Dogger Bank, in the North Sea, a plateau only 60 feet below sea level, was dry land in relatively recent times. The relics of forests and Stone-Age animal bones and tools have been found there.

The Mid-Atlantic Ridge, part of the world-encircling mid-ocean ridge system, is the biggest range of mountains in the world—10,000 miles long and 500 miles wide. The average height of its crest is 10,000 feet, but most of the crest ends a mile below the surface. Some peaks thrust up to form islands like the Azores, where Mount Pico rises 27,600 feet above the sea bed.

Ascension, one of the youngest of the large volcanic islands, is scarred with the traces of 40 extinct volcanoes. Few trees can survive on its barren rock; there is a little vegetation, mainly round the island's highest peak, Green Mountain, a huge elliptical crater rising 2,817 feet above sea level.

So-called tidal waves are caused by violent earthquakes in the seabed. They travel as fast as 400 miles an hour with intervals of about 90 miles between the waves. In the open sea their crests may rise only one or two feet above the surface, but they can reach a height of 50 feet when nearing a shelving coastline. They cover vast distances: those that hit Japan in 1960 stemmed from earthquakes off the coast of Chile.

Another dramatic slope rises from the depths of the Peru-Chile trench to the crest of the Andes, a height of eight miles.

One of the most intriguing, unsolved mysteries of the sea is the origin of the flat-topped islands beneath the surface of the Pacific. So far about 1,000 have been charted, all over 3,000 feet high; geologists expect to have found another 10,000 by the time the ocean has been completely surveyed. The islands are encrusted with coral, proving that at one time they must have been at or near the surface, though today many of them are a mile or more beneath it. The coral dates from 100 million years ago, the age of the oldest rocks found in the Pacific. Some scientists believe a violent volcanic upheaval shook the Pacific floor at the time, scattering the sea bed with lava and throwing up the islands which later sank under their own weight. Another theory is that the Moon was torn from the bed of the Pacific, taking with it into space the missing links of rock history.

SECTION OF SEA BED

This section of the sea bed between Martha's Vineyard, an island off Cape Cod, Massachusetts, U.S.A., and Gibraltar exaggerates vertical distances about 40 times in relation to horizontal distances, thereby overstating the steepness of slopes.

It shows the continental shelves and slopes which fringe the land masses, the deep ocean floors, and the interrupting seamounts of the North Atlantic.

The section cuts the Azores submarine plateau where it reaches above the water surface and forms a group of islands. The deep ocean floor which the section shows off the east coast of the United States is remarkable for its flatness; the remainder of the section is characterized by more varied topography.

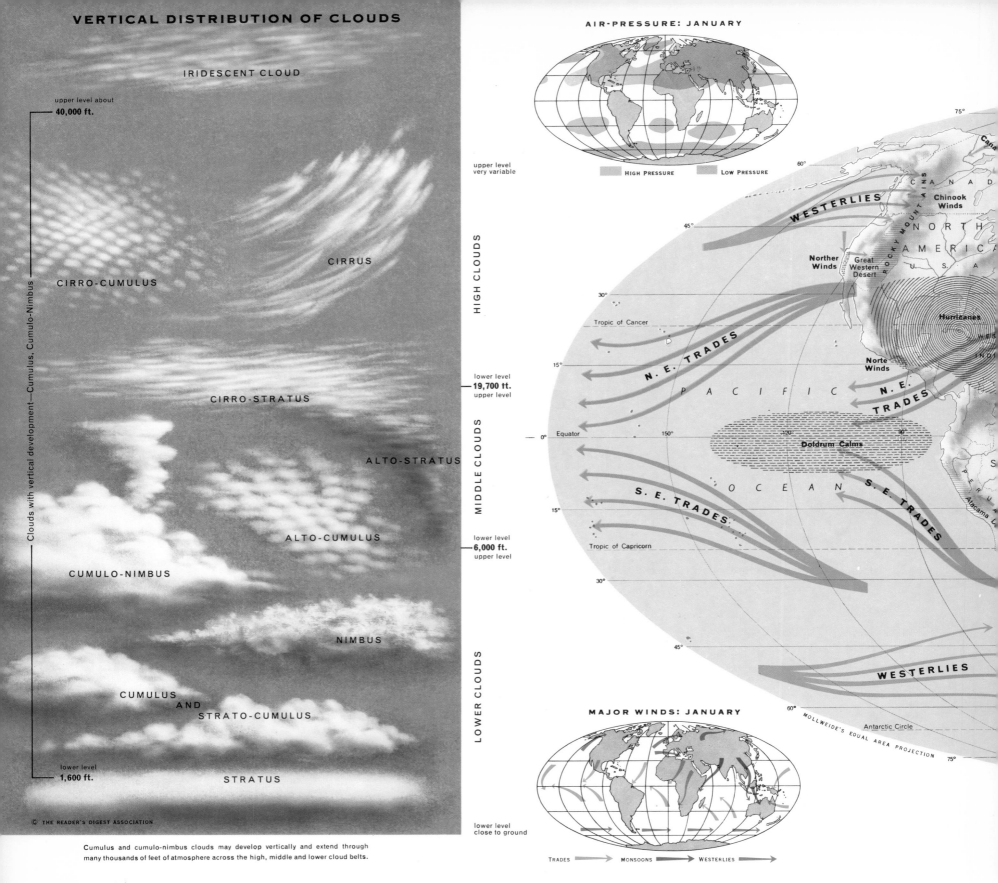

VERTICAL DISTRIBUTION OF CLOUDS

IRIDESCENT CLOUD

upper level about
40,000 ft.

CIRRUS

CIRRO-CUMULUS

HIGH CLOUDS

upper level very variable

CIRRO-STRATUS

lower level
19,700 ft.
upper level

ALTO-STRATUS

MIDDLE CLOUDS

ALTO-CUMULUS

lower level
6,000 ft.
upper level

CUMULO-NIMBUS

NIMBUS

LOWER CLOUDS

CUMULUS AND STRATO-CUMULUS

lower level
1,600 ft.

STRATUS

lower level close to ground

Clouds with vertical development—Cumulus, Cumulo-Nimbus

© THE READER'S DIGEST ASSOCIATION

Cumulus and cumulo-nimbus clouds may develop vertically and extend through many thousands of feet of atmosphere across the high, middle and lower cloud belts.

AIR-PRESSURE: JANUARY

HIGH PRESSURE   LOW PRESSURE

MAJOR WINDS: JANUARY

TRADES   MONSOONS   WESTERLIES

MOLLWEIDE'S EQUAL AREA PROJECTION

WESTERLIES · Chinook Winds · ROCKY MOUNTAINS · NORTH AMERICA · CANADA · Northers Winds · Great Western Desert · Hurricanes · N. E. TRADES · Norte Winds · PACIFIC OCEAN · Doldrum Calms · Equator · S. E. TRADES · Atacama · WESTERLIES · Antarctic Circle

HOW HOT IS IT?

ARCTIC OCEAN · Arctic Circle · NORTH AMERICA · Great Western Desert · Mississippi · EUROPE · ASIA · Yenisey · Gobi Desert · Sahara · Thar Desert · Arabian Desert · Yangtze · AFRICA · Amazon · SOUTH AMERICA · Atacama Desert · Congo · INDIAN OCEAN · ATLANTIC · PACIFIC OCEAN · Equator · Kalahari Desert · AUSTRALIA · Australian Desert · Patagonian Desert · WINKEL'S 'TRIPEL' PROJECTION

© THE READER'S DIGEST ASSOCIATION

ALWAYS COLD
WARM SUMMER / COLD WINTER
HOT SUMMER / COLD WINTER
COOL SUMMER / MILD WINTER
HOT SUMMER / WARM WINTER
ALWAYS HOT

Almost all our heat comes from the Sun, and the amount depends largely on how much of the Earth's atmosphere the Sun's rays must penetrate. The closer to vertical the Sun becomes, the lesser the amount of atmosphere to be penetrated and the more heat we receive, though clouds and the nature of the surface affect it. The Sun's rays give little heat to the air.

Air is mainly warmed by contact with the Earth's surface. The sea warms more slowly and parts with its heat more slowly, so that climates near oceans are more equable than those in the centre of continents.

The heat of the Tropics is, to some extent, distributed by ocean currents and winds. Thanks to the Gulf Stream and prevailing south-westerly winds the British Isles enjoy an average temperature of 50°F. Labrador, on the same latitude, does not enjoy these physical phenomena. It has an average temperature of 32°F.

Average temperatures fall as we rise above sea level at about one degree Fahrenheit for every 300 feet in Great Britain, so that high mountains are always cold.

PATTERNS

But there went up a mist from the earth, which watered the whole face of the ground—GENESIS 2

THE climates of the World are mainly dependent upon latitude. Within the Tropics the climate remains fairly stable, but outside the Tropics, climates, due to the twice-yearly swing of the Sun across the Equator, are seasonal. These swings of the Sun have the effect of shifting the belts of high pressure, as shown in the small pressure-maps.

Since the discovery of the barometer, we now know that the atmosphere has weight: where the atmosphere has piled up to give high pressure it tends to flow outwards on the surface of the Earth, just as water would do, and so becomes a wind. The rotation of the Earth causes winds to bend to the right in the Northern Hemisphere, and to the left in the Southern Hemisphere. In the North Atlantic, for example, the winds flowing towards the Equator are north-easterly and are known as the North East Trades, while the winds flowing towards the North Pole are south-westerly and are known as the Westerlies.

The flow of the major winds is shown diagrammatically on the large map; the shift in their flow from summer to winter is shown on the small wind-maps.

When the land becomes heated during the summer months, the air above tends to rise, and surface winds blow in to take its place, so that often at the coast there are land breezes at night, and sea breezes by day. This is better seen on a larger scale in the Monsoons, which blow inwards to the continent of Asia in the summer, and less strongly and outwards in the winter.

The major winds are not constant, since they are affected and complicated by cyclonic depressions.

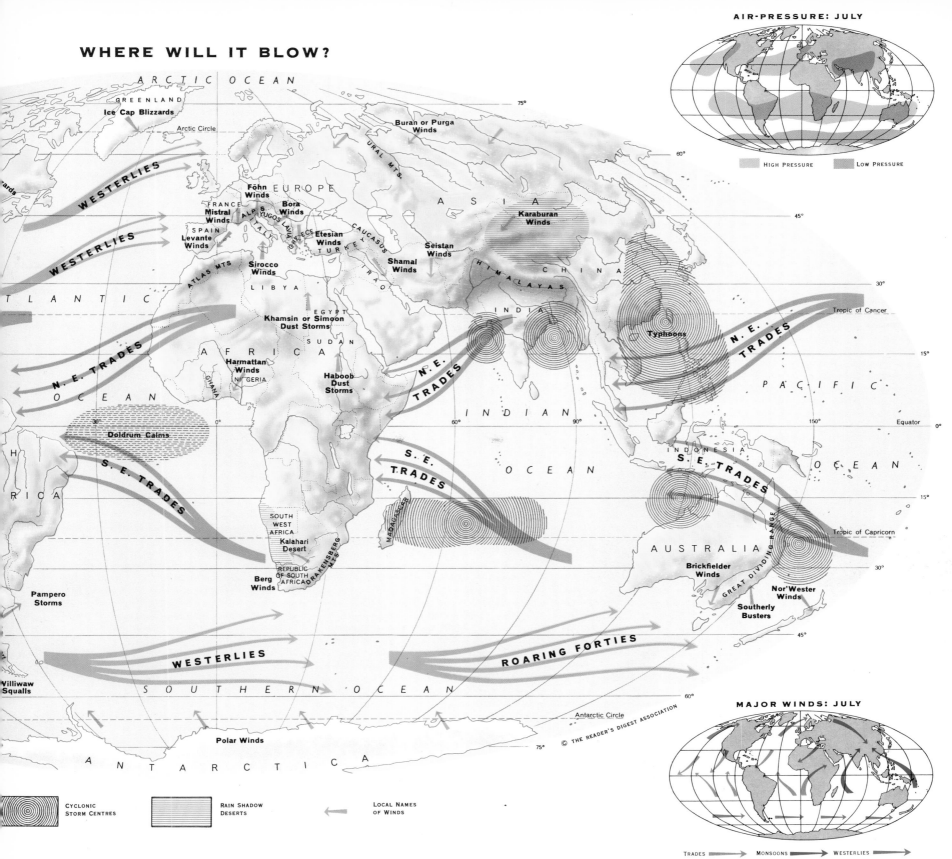

AIR-PRESSURE: JULY

HIGH PRESSURE   LOW PRESSURE

CYCLONIC
STORM CENTRES

RAIN SHADOW
DESERTS

LOCAL NAMES
OF WINDS

MAJOR WINDS: JULY

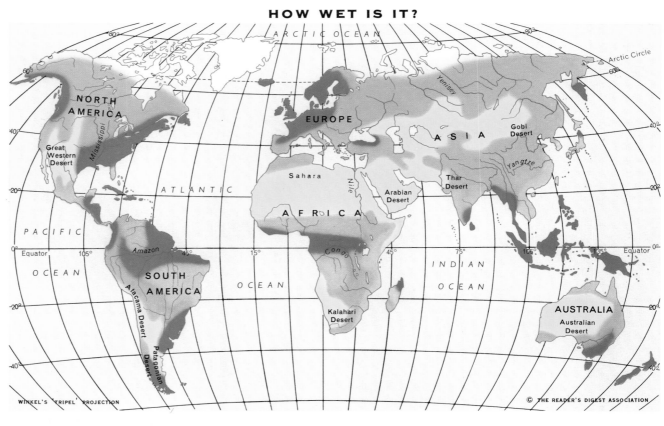

TRADES   MONSOONS   WESTERLIES

OF CLIMATE

The most constant winds are the South East Trades and the Westerlies in the higher latitudes of the Southern Hemisphere, where there is little land interference.

There are many local winds brought about by local conditions. Of those shown on the map, the Föhn of Switzerland and the Chinook of the Rockies in Canada are warm winds which blow down the mountains and melt the snows. A less pleasant warm wind is the Sirocco, which blows from North Africa across the Mediterranean to Northern Italy. The soft Etesian winds of the Aegean Sea are often mentioned in Greek literature. The cold Mistral, blowing down the Rhône Valley from the Alps, is an example of the unpleasant winds usually associated with high mountains adjacent to flat country. The vast Sahara Desert causes the Harmattan to bring dust to West Africa from November to March; but this wind, being dry, is a welcome change in West Africa's usually humid climate. The violent Pampero, blowing out to sea from Argentina, has long been known as a dangerous wind to sailing ships.

The Doldrums is a zone near the Equator where the rising of hot air creates calms and variable winds together with thunderstorms. In the days of sail, ships were often delayed in this area. A little farther away from the Equator there are occasional storms of great violence, known as typhoons in the East, as hurricanes in the Caribbean, and as tornadoes when they occur inland. These storms always follow a curved path, which can usually be forecast. All winds are slowed down by friction against the surface of the Earth, and produce eddies accompanied by rapid variations of air pressure. High up in the atmosphere winds are much more rapid, but much more steady.

HOW WET IS IT?

LIGHT SNOW

SELDOM RAINY

LIGHT SEASONAL RAIN

HEAVY SEASONAL RAIN

RAINFALL IN
EVERY MONTH

Moist air rises when winds force it against a mountain or blow it over heavier, colder air. As the moist air rises it cools and condenses into minute drops of water, forming clouds. When the droplets in the clouds become too heavy to be sustained, they fall as rain. Air is most likely to be moist over the sea and where temperatures are high. The wettest places of all are in the Tropics, where the sea air is blown against the windward slopes of high mountains. Rainfall belts move northwards and southwards following the ap-

parent movement of the Sun, so that some places, such as the Mediterranean, have most of their rain in the winter, while others, such as the Monsoon regions, have most in the summer.

The driest areas on Earth are where winds have blown for long distances over heated land. But a local dry area may be caused by a range of mountains extracting all the rain on its windward side, leaving what is called a rain-shadow on its leeward side. Such an area is the desert of Northern Chile.

117

FRONTIERS OF CULTIVATION

DEVELOPMENT OF THE NATURAL AND CULTIVATED AREAS OF THE WORLD

And the earth brought forth grass, herb yielding seed after its kind,
tree bearing fruit, wherein is the seed thereof, after its kind — GENESIS 1

ONLY about one-tenth of the world's land surface is at present under cultivation—little more than one acre per person.

The map shows the general distribution of vegetation—areas from which the natural vegetation has been cleared and the land cultivated for food and industrial crops such as fibres, cotton and rubber; areas where the natural vegetation is being utilized and developed; and areas which have remained in their natural state, with little or no vegetation.

In the areas of cultivation the maintenance of soil fertility is of the first importance. Bad husbandry, including the entire removal of trees, destroys the natural structure of the soil, with the result that it turns into dust, as in the great Dust Bowl of the United States, or into new man-made deserts, or is washed off unprotected slopes by rain, leaving behind bare unproductive subsoil, as in Yugoslavia and Greece.

The areas of *intensive* cultivation are those in which the optimum use is made of the soil. In Europe, the U.S.S.R., North America and parts of South America, South Africa and Australasia, cultivation of all kinds on a commercial scale is carried on, mainly with the aid of machinery. But in South and East Asia, where land is scarce and therefore precious, and the crops must support some of the densest rural populations in the world, much of the work is done with simple hand tools. Yet, even so, two crops of paddy rice a year are obtained as well as other kinds of cereal.

In the areas of *secondary* cultivation farming with crude tools and by means of rudimentary techniques predominates. The crops are largely grown for home consumption, though in some cases enough foods, such as cacao, oil-palm and peanuts, are grown for sale in local markets.

The areas of *shifting* cultivation are to be found near and among the tropical rain forests. Here land is generally cleared

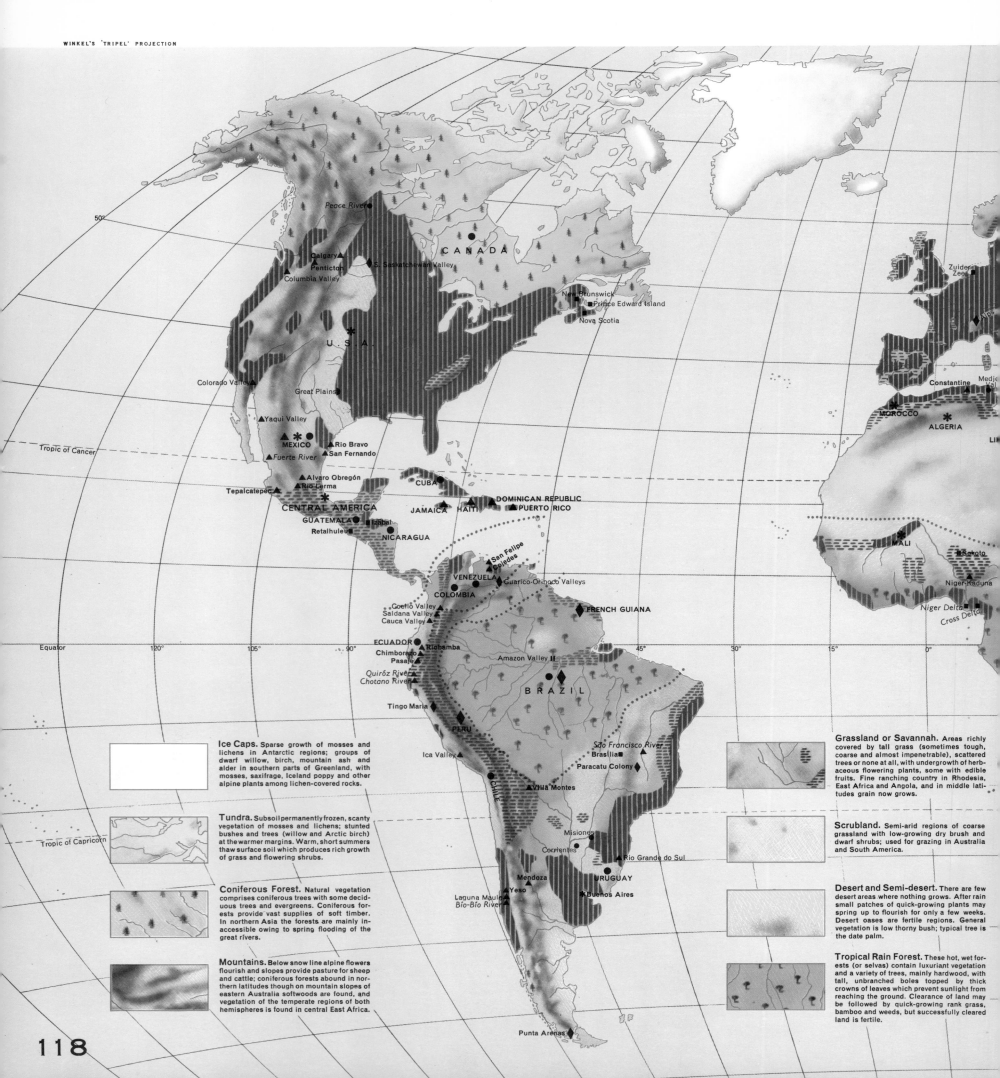

WINKEL'S 'TRIPEL' PROJECTION

Ice Caps. Sparse growth of mosses and lichens in Antarctic regions; groups of dwarf willow, birch, mountain ash and alder in southern parts of Greenland, with mosses, saxifrage, Iceland poppy and other alpine plants among lichen-covered rocks.

Tundra. Subsoil permanently frozen; scanty vegetation of mosses and lichens; stunted bushes and trees (willow and Arctic birch) at the warmer margins. Warm, short summers thaw the surface soil which produces rich growth of grass and flowering shrubs.

Coniferous Forest. Natural vegetation comprises coniferous trees with some deciduous trees and evergreens. Coniferous forests provide vast supplies of soft timber. In northern Asia the forests are mainly inaccessible owing to spring flooding of the great rivers.

Mountains. Below snow line alpine flowers flourish and slopes provide pasture for sheep and cattle; coniferous forests abound in northern latitudes though on mountain slopes of eastern Australia softwoods are found, and vegetation of the temperate regions of both hemispheres is found in central East Africa.

Grassland or Savannah. Areas richly covered by tall grass (sometimes tough, coarse and almost impenetrable), scattered trees or none at all, with undergrowth of herbaceous flowering plants, some with edible fruits. Fine ranching country in Rhodesia, East Africa and Angola, and in middle latitudes grain now grows.

Scrubland. Semi-arid regions of coarse grassland with low-growing dry brush and dwarf shrubs; used for grazing in Australia and South America.

Desert and Semi-desert. There are few desert areas where nothing grows. After rain small patches of quick-growing plants may spring up to flourish for only a few weeks. Desert oases are fertile regions. General vegetation is low thorny bush; typical tree is the date palm.

Tropical Rain Forest. These hot, wet forests (or selvas) contain luxuriant vegetation and a variety of trees, mainly hardwood, with tall, unbranched boles topped by thick crowns of leaves which prevent sunlight from reaching the ground. Clearance of land may be followed by quick-growing rank grass, bamboo and weeds, but successfully cleared land is fertile.

indiscriminately for individual needs, and after being wastefully denuded of its fertility by primitive farming methods, is abandoned.

Where land in the tropical rain forests is successfully cleared and maintained, it is fertile and suitable for the cultivation on a commercial scale of such plantation crops as rubber, tobacco, sugar, tea, oil-palm and cacao.

The areas of coniferous forest provide the major part of the world's soft timber—spruce, pine, fir—and by means of intensive afforestation some forests are being maintained and developed. The world's major logging and timber-working industries are found in North America and Europe.

The mountain slopes and much of the grassland and scrubland areas provide grazing for cattle and sheep and may thus be naturally maintained. Tropical grassland areas, when fully developed, may provide a variety of crops, such as maize, millet, cotton, sugar and groundnuts, with grain predominating in the more temperate regions.

Even in the deserts there are large areas of oases where the land is extremely fertile, and not only food crops are grown but grazing is also provided. The desert soil is often fine alluvial dust which, when irrigated, is exceptionally fertile, as in the Nile Valley, the Indus Plains and Lower Colorado. Some oases may cover hundreds of square miles.

But the patterns of cultivation vary from country to country according to their economic and social development. In the highly developed countries relatively few workers are able to provide sufficient of the right kind of food for the entire community. In the United States, for instance, 4,500,000 people (about 6 per cent of the working population) are employed on cultivation. On the other hand, in India 145,000,000 people (70 per cent of the working population) employed on cultivation produce barely enough food both in quantity and quality for the whole population of that country.

As the result of great advances in agricultural science since the Second World War, the yields in some areas such as North America, Europe, Australia and New Zealand have risen rapidly. In the less developed regions, post-war increases in agricultural production have been achieved mainly by bringing new land into cultivation. But as yet these areas have scarcely begun to benefit from applying scientific and improved technical methods of farming, so that only one-fifth of the world's agricultural output is produced with the aid of machines.

The symbols on the map show the areas where scientific and improved technical methods are being applied to improve the quality and yield of crops, and to bring back into cultivation land that is infertile or semi-arid. Of these techniques, irrigation and water conservation are of the first importance. Irrigation is one of man's earliest known ways of making the earth productive. In Egypt, in about 3000 B.C., the first Pharaoh built an embankment to control the flood waters of the Nile, and cultivation in Egypt today still depends on irrigated land. In China, ancient irrigation systems, some built 2,000 years ago, are still in use. In Latin America, the proper use of water supplies has now brought large areas of land under cultivation.

Other techniques which are being applied include the breeding of improved, disease-and-pest-resistant varieties of seed; the building up of soil fertility through the use of legumes and crop rotation; the introduction of new crops to provide a more varied and nutritious diet and to lessen a country's economic dependence on a single crop; forest conservation and afforestation; the better use of organic wastes as manures and the increased application of artificial fertilizers; better methods of cultivation, improved tools and the increased use of farm machinery; the reclamation and settlement of new lands; the control of pests, such as the locust and the tsetse fly.

By these methods, added to his own traditional skills, man is making the earth more fertile and so extending the frontiers of cultivation.

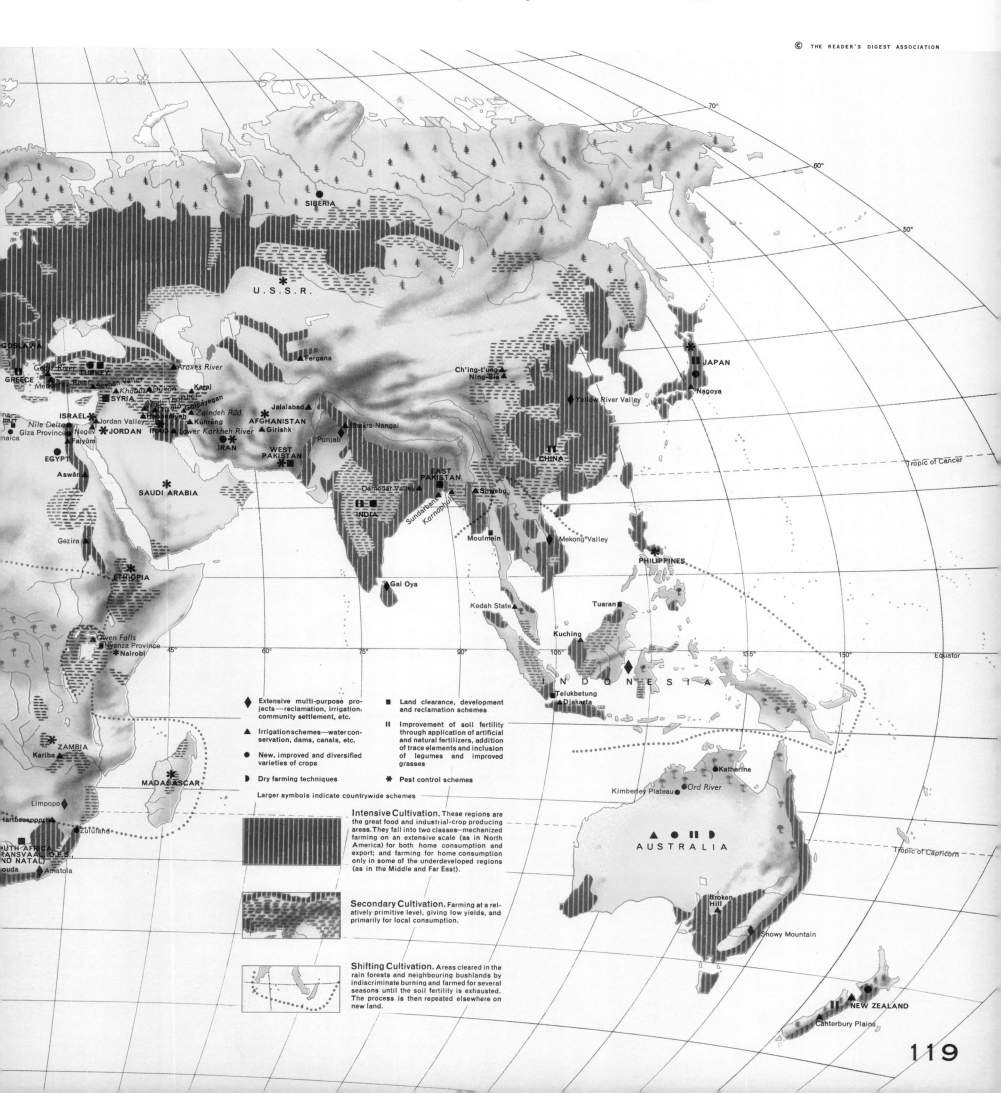

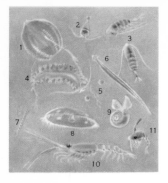

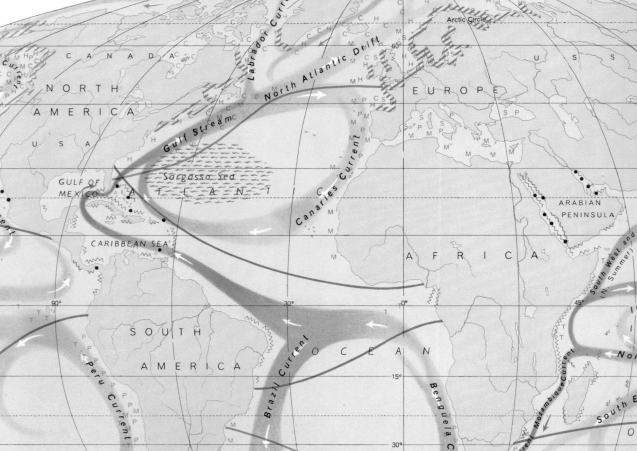

Various plankton, many times enlarged :—

1. *Pleurobrachia*, sea-gooseberry or comb-jelly
2. *Temora Longicornis*, a copepod crustacean
3. *Calanus Finmarchicus*, another copepod; principal food of herring
4. *Tomopteris*, a polychaet worm
5. Fish Eggs
6. *Sagitta*, an arrow worm
7. Diatoms, minute sea plants
8. *Obelia*, a medusa stage, produced by the fixed hydroids
9. Pteropod or sea butterfly
10. *Euphausia*, a shrimp - like crustacean, "Krill" the food of whales
11. Zoea, larva of crab

⌇⌇⌇ WARM CURRENTS	⁄⁄⁄⁄⁄⁄⁄ ATLANTIC SALMON	
～ COLD CURRENTS	⁄⁄⁄⁄⁄⁄⁄ PACIFIC SALMON	
～～～ FLOATING WEED	⌄⌄⌄⌄ CORAL REEFS	
	• • • • • • PEARLS	

LIFE IN THE SEA

And God said, Let the waters bring forth abundantly the moving creature that hath life—GENESIS 1

THE SEA, where life began, contains almost every main category of animal life—including mammals, the warm-blooded group to which man belongs. True fish are but a small section of the sea's community: whereas there are 15,000 known species of sea-fish, there are 60,000 known species of mollusc (the group which includes oysters, mussels, etc.).

In the sea, as on land, life depends largely on plants, and the plants of the ocean are almost as productive, acre for acre, as the plants on land. The pastures of the sea and the basis of its life cycle are countless myriads of free-floating, microscopic plants known as phytoplankton. These are the food of minute animals called zooplankton. Zooplankton are preyed upon by larger animal species, which themselves provide food for still bigger creatures. So continues a ruthless and never-ending cycle, for the plants in their turn are nourished by minerals derived in part from the decay of marine organisms.

Since most plants need sunlight for their survival, marine plants grow only within about 300 feet of the water's surface. A large part of sea life is, therefore, confined to this topmost layer, which is continually being refertilized by the action of the ocean currents.

The movement of currents, by which the oceans "plough" themselves, is caused by three main forces: the prevailing wind, the Earth's rotation and differences in the sea's density. Winds drive immense bodies of water before them, forming surface currents. At the same time, the Earth's rotation, which deflects moving things to the right in the Northern Hemisphere and to the left in the Southern Hemisphere, causes these ocean surface currents to move in a clockwise or anti-clockwise direction, as shown by the whirls on the map.

Where currents meet or diverge, where cold or salty water sinks beneath water that is less dense, or where coastal winds blow the surface water seawards, a circulation is set up which may penetrate to the ocean bottom. Surface water is then replaced by upwelling water rich in nutrient salts, which stimulate new growths of marine plants. Thus the herbivorous animal plankton thrives and the sea becomes fertile for fish. It is understandable that many of the world's great fisheries are found along the paths of ocean currents.

Beneath the sunlit 300-foot layer, life is sparser and creatures need special equipment for the fierce struggle for survival. Angler fish, with huge, expanding stomachs, can swallow creatures larger than themselves, and thus make one meal last a long time. Other fish, like *Gigantura*, have very sensitive tubular (telescopic) eyes that help them to see their prey in the near-darkness. Perhaps the most remarkable adaptation to life in the deep is that of certain deep-sea angler fish. Their reproduction depends on but one chance meeting in the barren depths, after which the female carries the male permanently with her. The male is much the smaller and is parasitic on his partner.

For the most part, however, the sea's species have not had to assume such specialized forms to cope with their environment. The oceans do not have the harsh seasonal and regional contrasts of land. Surface water temperature in any one region seldom varies more than a few degrees, and fish, whose bodies consist largely of fluid at the same temperature as their surroundings, do not, therefore, need any particular mechanism for keeping warm or cool. Again, the profusion of wings, limbs and other organs needed on land to overcome the burden of gravity is unnecessary for creatures whose element is the buoyant sea.

As few sea creatures have mechanisms, such as sweat glands, for adapting themselves to changing conditions, they are sensitive to the slightest variation in their surroundings. With some exceptions such as sharks and whales, which can range freely up and down the oceans, each species is confined to its own particular zone, where pressure, light, temperature and the quantity of salt in the water are more or less constant.

In this stable environment some creatures have remained unchanged throughout their entire history. The now-famous Coelacanth, one of a group of fish thought to have been extinct for 60 million years, has remained essentially like its relatives as they appear in fossils. It is considered the closest living relation of the long-extinct fish that is accepted as the ancestor of all land animals.

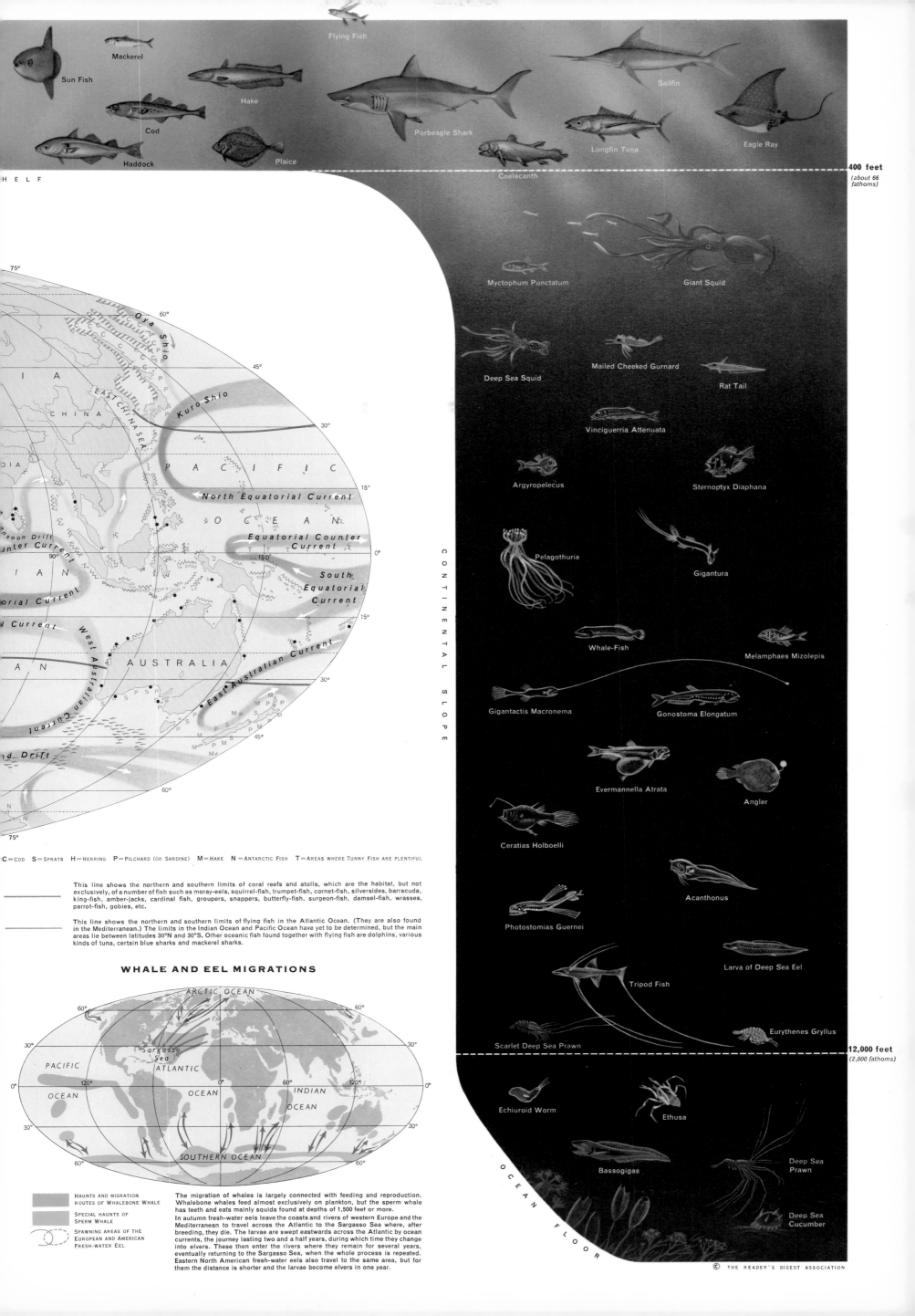

C=COD S=SPRATS H=HERRING P=PILCHARD (OR SARDINE) M=HAKE N=ANTARCTIC FISH T=AREAS WHERE TUNNY FISH ARE PLENTIFUL

This line shows the northern and southern limits of coral reefs and atolls, which are the habitat, but not exclusively, of a number of fish such as moray-eels, squirrel-fish, trumpet-fish, cornet-fish, silversides, barracuda, king-fish, amber-jacks, cardinal fish, groupers, snappers, butterfly-fish, surgeon-fish, damsel-fish, wrasses, parrot-fish, gobies, etc.

This line shows the northern and southern limits of flying fish in the Atlantic Ocean. (They are also found in the Mediterranean.) The limits in the Indian Ocean and Pacific Ocean have yet to be determined, but the main areas lie between latitudes 30°N and 30°S. Other oceanic fish found together with flying fish are dolphins, various kinds of tuna, certain blue sharks and mackerel sharks.

WHALE AND EEL MIGRATIONS

HAUNTS AND MIGRATION ROUTES OF WHALEBONE WHALE

SPECIAL HAUNTS OF SPERM WHALE

SPAWNING AREAS OF THE EUROPEAN AND AMERICAN FRESH-WATER EEL

The migration of whales is largely connected with feeding and reproduction. Whalebone whales feed almost exclusively on plankton, but the sperm whale has teeth and eats mainly squids found at depths of 1,500 feet or more.

In autumn fresh-water eels leave the coasts and rivers of western Europe and the Mediterranean to travel across the Atlantic to the Sargasso Sea where, after breeding, they die. The larvae are swept eastwards across the Atlantic by ocean currents, the journey lasting two and a half years, during which time they change into elvers. These then enter the rivers where they remain for several years, eventually returning to the Sargasso Sea, when the whole process is repeated. Eastern North American fresh-water eels also travel to the same area, but for them the distance is shorter and the larvae become elvers in one year.

400 feet (about 66 fathoms)

12,000 feet (2,000 fathoms)

BIRD MIGRATION

A MYSTERY OF ENDURANCE AND NAVIGATION

And let fowl fly above the earth in the open firmament of heaven — GENESIS 1

Golden Plover

Swallow

Bobolink

Ruff

White Stork

Arctic Tern

Greenland Wheatear

Sooty Shearwater

Arctic Warbler
Siberian Willow Warbler

Wandering Albatross

THERE are well over 8,000 known and named species of birds, and a great many of them are migratory. Despite all dangers of storms, droughts, and of man himself, millions of birds undertake twice-yearly journeys that span whole continents and oceans.

The great northern land masses of the Northern Hemisphere support a huge breeding population, which migrates south for the winter. The land areas south of the Equator are too small to support a comparable breeding population of land birds. Instead, there are great ocean masses which support vast sea bird populations, millions of which move north during the southern winter. The northern summer day is longer than the 12-hour day at the Equator, and therefore gives more time for hunting—a critical factor for birds whose young may eat many times their own weight in food during the time they are in the nest. When breeding is over and the young ones reared, glandular changes within the body, probably caused by the lengthening nights of approaching winter, stimulate the migratory instinct, but the *actual* moment of departure is influenced by the local weather conditions and the physical readiness of the birds themselves.

Before migrating, birds lay in stores of energy in the form of internal fat deposits. Some species may even double their body weight and in this way are enabled to stay on the wing for at least 90 hours and perhaps as long as 120. Ornithologists believe that some of the Greenland Wheatears, only a little larger than the House Sparrow, fly direct from Greenland to the north coast of Spain, an over-water flight of nearly 2,000 miles, and that the Blackpoll Warbler, smaller than the House Sparrow, may fly directly from New England to Venezuela. After such a journey a bird may have halved its starting weight and so must rest while it accumulates fresh stores of fat.

MORE than any other birds, the geese are symbolic of this incredible and complicated migratory instinct. Each fall, formation after formation come honking south, often following age-old fly-ways, to their restricted winter quarters. Canada Geese from the region of the Churchill and Severn Rivers head for east Texas. The small, dark Cackling Canadas of Alaska make for the interior valleys of California. For a few days the entire population of the Greater Snow Goose may be resting on the marshes of the St. Lawrence River.

Of all migrants, none travels farther than the Arctic Tern. After a short breeding season in the higher latitudes of the Northern Hemisphere (where long hours of summer daylight give ample time for feeding on the abundant supply of fish), some North American Arctic Terns cross the North Atlantic to join up with Arctic Terns from North-West Europe etc.; others pass down the western Atlantic, and Arctic Terns wearing rings fixed in Russia and Wales have been recovered in Australia. No other bird enjoys as much daylight during the year, but finding it involves an annual journey of about 22,000 miles.

Migratory birds often navigate with phenominal accuracy. The general direction of movements of some of them are indicated by the arrows on the map. The Pacific Golden Plover, which breeds in the extreme west of Alaska and in eastern Siberia, crosses the Pacific to make pinpoint arrivals on such small islands as Hawaii and Tonga. In one experi-

ment, a Manx Shearwater, captured and ringed in Wales, was flown to Boston, U.S.A., and released. Twelve and a half days later it arrived home, having crossed 3,000 miles of ocean.

Shearwaters are great travellers, and many from Britain winter off the coasts of Brazil and Argentina; one has even reached South Australia. One incredible young bird completed the 5,000-mile journey to Brazil in less than three weeks of leaving the nest. The Great Shearwater is among the fewer species that migrates northwards. It breeds on the lonely island of Tristan da Cunha in the South Atlantic, and spends the summer in the North Atlantic, penetrating as far as the Davis Strait off Greenland. Its cousin, the Sooty Shearwater (known to sailors as the Mutton Bird), also migrates northwards from its breeding areas in the Falkland Islands and small islands off Cape Horn, Tasmania and New Zealand. One bird, ringed in New Zealand, was recovered in the Sea of Okhotsk, to the north of Japan.

WHILE winter quarters are generally nearer the Equator than summer ones, they are not always directly south. East Siberian Willow Warblers (song-birds so small that three of them together weigh only one ounce) undertake the immense journey to East Africa. The Arctic Warbler spends the summer as far west as Northern Norway and winters in southeast Asia and Indonesia—thus crossing at right angles the path of the East Siberian Willow Warbler. One species of Shrike nests in central Asia and winters in equatorial Africa— 1,200 miles south, but 2,500 miles west.

The instinct to migrate brings together in huge flocks birds that are normally solitary. Even the most hospitable countryside cannot always provide sustenance for more than a few pairs of nesting birds per acre; and yet, with the onset of winter, birds collect in clouds that darken the northern skies. The Bobolink, or Rice Bird, is a solitary inhabitant of North American meadowlands. On the autumn migration flight, Bobolinks gather in immense flocks to invade the rice fields of the Carolinas and devastate the crops.

Size has little to do with the migration instinct. Tiny Humming Birds migrate 500 miles across the Gulf of Mexico. On the other hand, the Wandering Albatross, with a wing span of twelve feet, breeds on islands such as Tristan da Cunha, South Georgia, and Kerguelen, and spends the rest of the year soaring across the southern oceans, far from land. It is thought that these birds may circumnavigate the world several times between their breeding seasons.

The phenomenon of migration was known as long ago as Biblical times. The Book of Jeremiah notes the flight of White Storks, which leave the North European Plain in spectacular numbers and cross Israel and the Nile Valley. But, despite this long familiarity with migration, there is still much to be learned about it. How high do migrating birds fly? How do they navigate?

Radar has largely answered the altitude question: most migrations take place below 5,000 feet, but there are records of really small birds at 10,000, 15,000 and 20,000 feet.

Experiments with caged migrants suggest that they may use the sun and the stars as aids to navigation. Birds placed in a planetarium, beneath a replica of the night sky, turned at once in the direction of the southern winter quarters to which they were due to fly. Birds, it seems, are equipped with instincts that may surpass man's most elaborate instruments.

SPECIES	LENGTH IN INCHES	BREEDING AREA	WINTERING AREA	DISTANCE APART (approx.)
Arctic Skua (Parasitic Jaeger)	16½	Arctic America, Greenland, Arctic Europe, north Siberia	West Africa, Persian Gulf, Arabian Gulf, Australia, New Zealand, South America	4,000–8,000 miles
Arctic Tern	14–15	North Canada, Greenland, Iceland, north Europe	South and west African coasts, Antarctica	11,000 miles
Arctic Warbler	4½	North and north-east Europe, north Siberia	South-east Asia	4,000–7,000 miles
Blackpoll Warbler	5–5½	Alaska, east to Northern Labrador and New England	Colombia, Venezuela to French Guiana	2,500–5,000 miles
Black and white Cuckoo	13	India	East and south-east Africa	3,500–4,500 miles
Blue-cheeked Bee-eater	11	North India, west China	East Africa	4,000–5,500 miles

SPECIES	LENGTH IN INCHES	BREEDING AREA	WINTERING AREA	DISTANCE APART (approx.)
Bobolink	6½–8	South-east Canada, north-east and mid-west U.S.A.	Bolivia, Paraguay, Brazil	5,000 miles
Buff-breasted Sandpiper	7½	Arctic Canada	Argentina and Uruguay	6,000–8,000 miles
East Siberian Willow Warbler	4½	North-east Siberia	East Africa	8,000 miles
Great Shearwater	17–18	Tristan da Cunha	North Atlantic	6,000–8,000 miles
Long-tailed Cuckoo	16½	New Zealand	Samoa and Fiji	2,000 miles
Manx Shearwater	14	British Isles, Brittany, Atlantic Islands, Mediterranean	North and South Atlantic	500–5,000 miles
Needle-tailed Swift	7½	East Siberia, Japan	Australia, Tasmania	6,000–8,000 miles

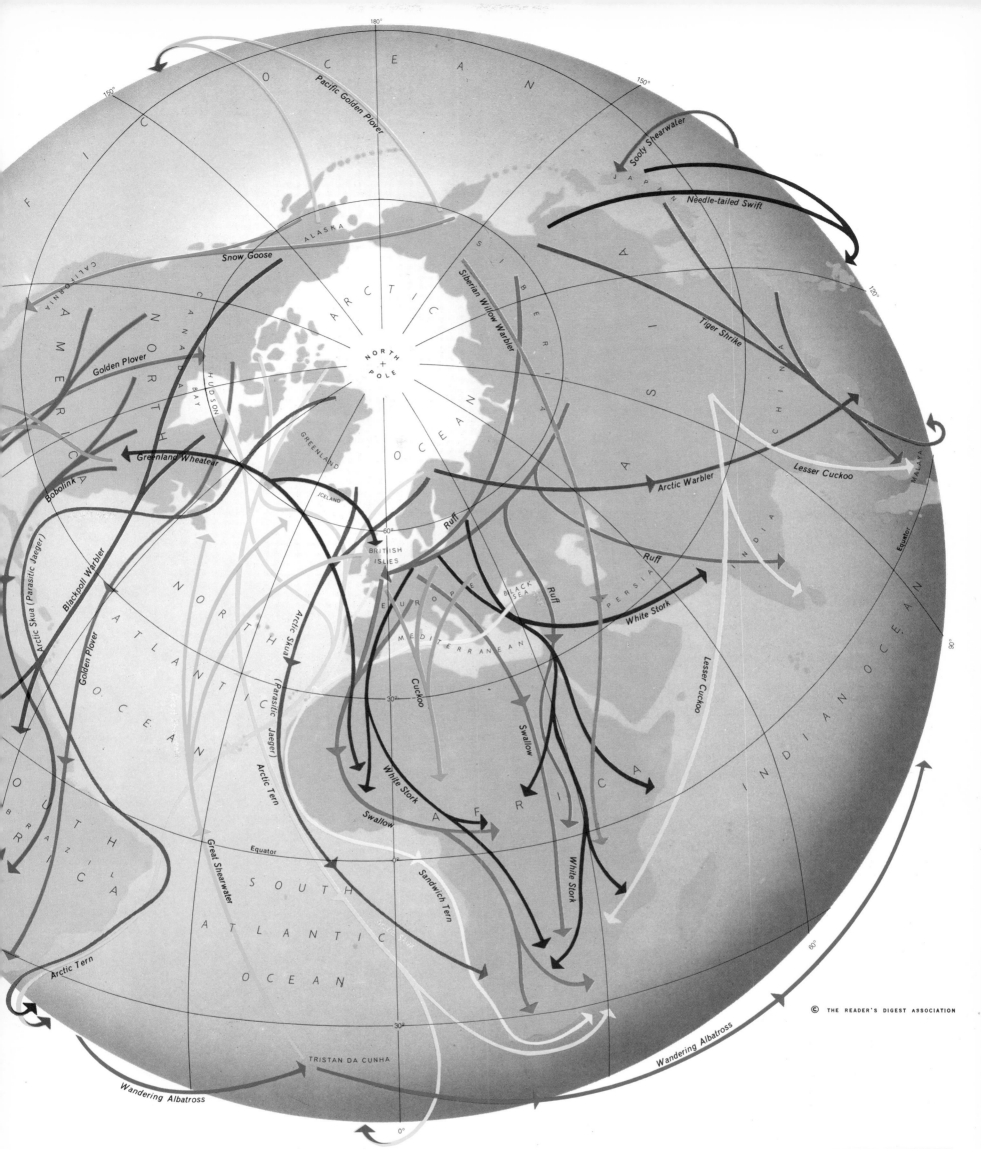

SPECIES	LENGTH IN INCHES	BREEDING AREA	WINTERING AREA	DISTANCE APART (APPROX.)
Pacific Golden Plover	10-11	West Alaska, north-east Siberia	Hawaii, Tonga, Indonesia, Australia	6,000-8,000 miles
Pintail (New World)	22	North-west Alaska east to Hudson Bay, south to Iowa, N. Colorado, S. California	Middle and southern United States to West Indies and Panama, west to Hawaii	1,000-4,000 miles
Ruff	8½-12	North and west Europe, Siberia	West Europe, South Africa, Iraq, Persia, India, Ceylon	3,000-6,000 miles
Sandwich Tern	16	Shores of North Sea and west Mediterranean, Black Sea	West and South Africa	1,000-5,000 miles
Scarlet Grosbeak	5¾	North-east Europe	India, south-east Asia	3,000-6,000 miles
Shining Cuckoo	7¼	New Zealand	Solomon Islands	1,800 miles

SPECIES	LENGTH IN INCHES	BREEDING AREA	WINTERING AREA	DISTANCE APART (APPROX.)
Snow Goose	25-30	East Siberia, Alaska, north-west Canada	West U.S.A. especially California	2,000-3,000 miles
Sooty Shearwater	16	New Zealand, Falkland Is., Cape Horn	North Atlantic, north Pacific	6,000-9,000 miles
Summer Tanager	7-7½	North America, north to as far as the Great Lakes	Mexico southwards to Peru	1,000-4,000 miles
Swallow (European)	7-7½	Europe, north to about 68°	Central and South Africa	5,000-7,000 miles
Tiger Shrike	7	China, east Siberia, Japan	Malaya, Sumatra, Celebes, Borneo	3,000-4,000 miles
Wandering Albatross	44-53	Tristan da Cunha, Gough Island	Southern oceans, chiefly south of 40°S.	unknown
White Stork	40	Mid-Europe	Tropical and South Africa	4,000-7,000 miles

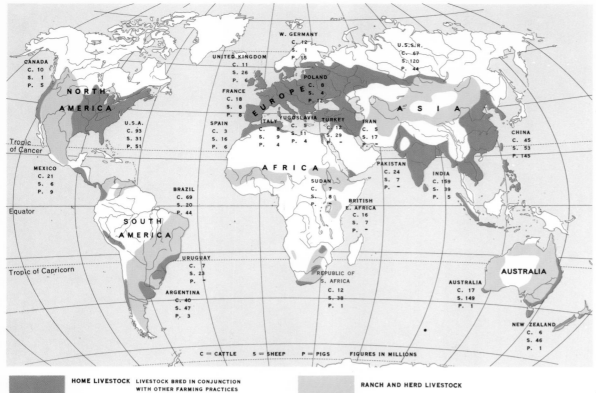

DISTRIBUTION OF LIVESTOCK

In all the areas of the world colonized by man, the domestication of certain mammals has invariably led to the extinction or near-extinction of the wilder species. The extent of man's advance has depended on the availability of pasture for animals which, through selective breeding, he adapted for his own purposes. Sheep, cattle, pigs, goats and horses (providing food, milk, clothing and transport) are of little interest zoologically but are vastly important economically. In areas with seasonal or scanty rainfall and sparse pasturage, domestic animals may be herded or ranched—a few to the square mile—over wide distances, and may be the primary factor in the regions' economy. In more favoured zones "mixed" farming is usual: animal husbandry and crop cultivation are practised in close conjunction with each other on the same farm unit. In either case wild animals are robbed of the territories best able to support them.

C = CATTLE S = SHEEP P = PIGS FIGURES IN MILLIONS

HOME LIVESTOCK LIVESTOCK BRED IN CONJUNCTION WITH OTHER FARMING PRACTICES RANCH AND HERD LIVESTOCK

THE SPREAD OF MAMMALS

Let the Earth bring forth the living creature after its kind — GENESIS 1

FROM the time terrestrial animal life began, some 350 million years ago, the face of the Earth has undergone immense changes, and even in the relatively recent period since mammals evolved from reptiles, more reshaping of land has occurred. It was once possible for species from Southern Asia to spread by age-long migration through Europe and, by means of a land-bridge where the Bering Strait is now, to the Americas. But barriers to migrations, and new avenues for them, have been appearing and disappearing since the time creatures first had need to travel in search of food and warmth.

For the most important animals of the present day—the warm-blooded mammals, of which man himself is one—the Earth has set strict limits. The geological changes that decided the patterns of movement also brought about changes in environment, and these changes, allied to other natural causes, speeded up the evolution of mammals, especially on the African, Euro-Asian and North American continents. One result is that mammals can now be grouped in five main regions, each of which is bounded by natural barriers—mountains, deserts and seas.

The formation of the Sahara Desert created one of the barriers to migration, so that the mammals to the south of the desert, living in tropical or semi-tropical conditions, have evolved in quite a different way from the mammals to the north of it. In Australia, the most primitive species of mammals in the world have

survived, for, with the disappearance of any land connection with Asia some 135 million years ago, they became isolated, and more active and dominating mammals were prevented from reaching the area. The Himalayas, formed about 25 million years ago, stopped any large-scale interchange of species between northern Asia and the Oriental Region; and the Bering Strait, during the recent Pleistocene Period, effectively cut off the Americas from Europe and Asia.

Some mammals learned to hunt in the air, like bats, others to live in trees, like monkeys, some to burrow under the ground, like moles, and still others, such as whales, went back to the sea from which life first came. And all of them developed characteristics according to their surroundings; the whales, for instance, developed layers of blubber under the skin to insulate them from the cold of the oceans, and some of the whales, because of the buoyancy of the water, were able to grow to a huge bulk and so become the largest of all mammals.

A natural spread took some mammals to the cold north, and these became more hairy, like the polar bear and the musk-ox. On the other hand, in the tropics, the elephant and the hippopotamus became almost hairless.

There are nearly 5,000 species of mammals, in bewildering varieties of shape and form. Among them are the primates, headed by man, whose unique specialization is that he can fashion his environment to suit his own needs.

The similarity between the marine animals on either side of the Central American isthmus suggests that here the sea, at one time, was unbroken. Wide rivers across the isthmus now form barriers to the migration of land animals, but the nine-banded armadillo, typical of the South American fauna, has continued to spread northwards, for while swimming it is able to gulp air to inflate its intestines, and thereby gain buoyancy for its heavy body.

The **Neotropical** Region (South America) is characterized by marsupials (opossum and small, shrew-like pouch-bearers) and edentates (mammals with few teeth or none at all, such as sloths, anteaters and armadillos). These were probably the region's only mammals until later Tertiary times when others, notably llamas, jaguars, pumas, some fox-like wolves and a few deer, arrived from the north across the land-bridge of Central America. Peccaries take the place of pigs of other regions, and the monkeys, although similar to those of Africa and Asia, form a distinct sub-order.

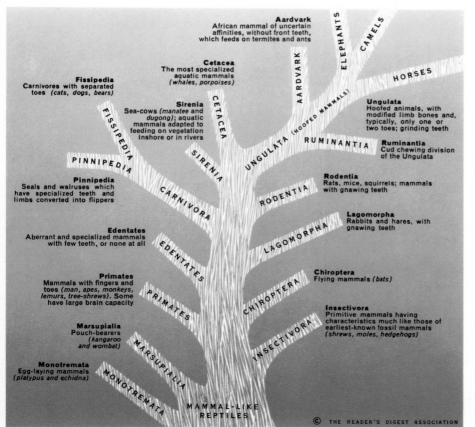

THE MAMMALIAN TREE

As mammals evolve and change their characteristics to suit their environments, their bony structures are the features which modify most slowly. In classifying mammals, therefore, emphasis is always placed on the character of the teeth, skull and skeleton. Where these features have become specialized, the animals are graded according to the degree of their specializations. On this basis man and the other primates appear low down on the genealogical tree, while the camel, elephant and whale are at the top. Man's preeminence in the world is due to his greater brain capacity, his grasping hand and his ability to use speech; but his limbs with their five digits and his face are still anatomically primitive.

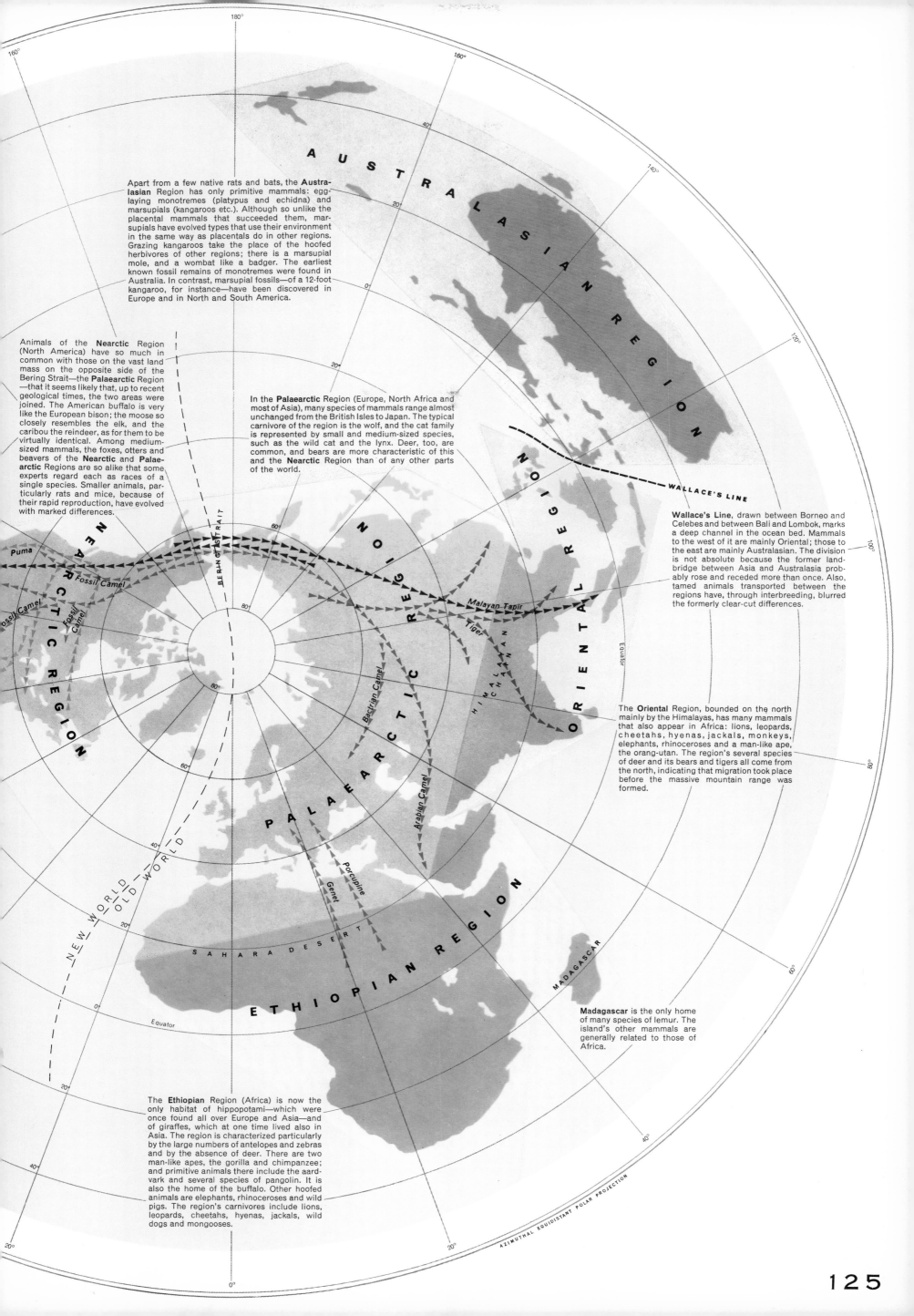

Apart from a few native rats and bats, the **Austra-lasian** Region has only primitive mammals: egg-laying monotremes (platypus and echidna) and marsupials (kangaroos etc.). Although so unlike the placental mammals that succeeded them, marsupials have evolved types that use their environment in the same way as placentals do in other regions. Grazing kangaroos take the place of the hoofed herbivores of other regions; there is a marsupial mole, and a wombat like a badger. The earliest known fossil remains of monotremes were found in Australia. In contrast, marsupial fossils—of a 12-foot kangaroo, for instance—have been discovered in Europe and in North and South America.

A U S T R A L A S I A N   R E G I O N

Animals of the **Nearctic** Region (North America) have so much in common with those on the vast land mass on the opposite side of the Bering Strait—the Palaearctic Region —that it seems likely that, up to recent geological times, the two areas were joined. The American buffalo is very like the European bison; the moose so closely resembles the elk, and the caribou the reindeer, as for them to be virtually identical. Among medium-sized mammals, the foxes, otters and beavers of the **Nearctic** and **Palae-arctic** Regions are so alike that some experts regard each as races of a single species. Smaller animals, particularly rats and mice, because of their rapid reproduction, have evolved with marked differences.

In the **Palaearctic** Region (Europe, North Africa and most of Asia), many species of mammals range almost unchanged from the British Isles to Japan. The typical carnivore of the region is the wolf, and the cat family is represented by small and medium-sized species, such as the wild cat and the lynx. Deer, too, are common, and bears are more characteristic of this and the **Nearctic** Region than of any other parts of the world.

Wallace's Line, drawn between Borneo and Celebes and between Bali and Lombok, marks a deep channel in the ocean bed. Mammals to the west of it are mainly Oriental; those to the east are mainly Australasian. The division is not absolute because the former land-bridge between Asia and Australasia probably rose and receded more than once. Also, tamed animals transported between the regions have, through interbreeding, blurred the formerly clear-cut differences.

WALLACE'S LINE

O R I E N T A L   R E G I O N

The **Oriental** Region, bounded on the north mainly by the Himalayas, has many mammals that also appear in Africa: lions, leopards, cheetahs, hyenas, jackals, monkeys, elephants, rhinoceroses and a man-like ape, the orang-utan. The region's several species of deer and its bears and tigers all come from the north, indicating that migration took place before the massive mountain range was formed.

N E A R C T I C   R E G I O N

Puma

Fossil Camel

Fossil Camel

Fossil Camel

BERING STRAIT

N O R T H   R E G I O N

Malayan Tapir

Tiger

HIMALAYAN CHAIN

Bactrian Camel

P A L A E A R C T I C   R E G I O N

Arabian Camel

Porcupine

Genet

NEW WORLD

OLD WORLD

S A H A R A   D E S E R T

E T H I O P I A N   R E G I O N

MADAGASCAR

Madagascar is the only home of many species of lemur. The island's other mammals are generally related to those of Africa.

Equator

The **Ethiopian** Region (Africa) is now the only habitat of hippopotami—which were once found all over Europe and Asia—and of giraffes, which at one time lived also in Asia. The region is characterized particularly by the large numbers of antelopes and zebras and by the absence of deer. There are two man-like apes, the gorilla and chimpanzee; and primitive animals there include the aard-vark and several species of pangolin. It is also the home of the buffalo. Other hoofed animals are elephants, rhinoceroses and wild pigs. The region's carnivores include lions, leopards, cheetahs, hyenas, jackals, wild dogs and mongooses.

AZIMUTHAL EQUIDISTANT POLAR PROJECTION

THE EVOLUTION OF MAN

When men began to multiply on the face of the earth—GENESIS 6

WE may learn something about early man in two different ways: by comparing the biology of man with that of other animals and so determining the degree of their relationship (taxonomy); and by looking at fossils and so determining their age and development (palaeontology).

By comparing man with other living creatures we know that he is a primate, having a large brain, a grasping hand with nails instead of claws, and eyesight which has been developed at the expense of his sense of smell. Primates include treeshrews, lemurs, monkeys and apes. Within this group man shows the greatest resemblance to apes, not only in his posture and means of locomotion, but in the development and co-

ordination of his brain and hands, and in the biochemistry of his blood. Man has, however, been distinguished from other primates, both living and fossil, by his ability to make and use tools.

The comparison of living forms enables us to estimate the affinities of fossils, even from their fragmentary remains; and by studying the tools and animal remains found with fossil men, we can discover something of their way of life and the environment in which they lived.

In the study of the modern races of man reference is made to inherited differences in anatomy, morphology and biochemistry. A race can be defined by using as many sorting criteria as can be seen or measured, such as colouring, hair and eye form, and

blood groups; but other criteria, such as stature and weight, which are closely related to nutrition, are of little help. Blood groups appear to be relatively stable criteria, and show marked differences in frequency in different populations. For example, though blood Group B is common among specialized Mongoloids, it is rare among South American Indians—an unspecialized Mongoloid group.

But any individual racial group is continually in a process of change through natural selection and intermarriage with neighbouring groups or migrants, so that a "pure" race does not exist.

The evolution of man and the present distribution of the races are shown on the accompanying maps and charts.

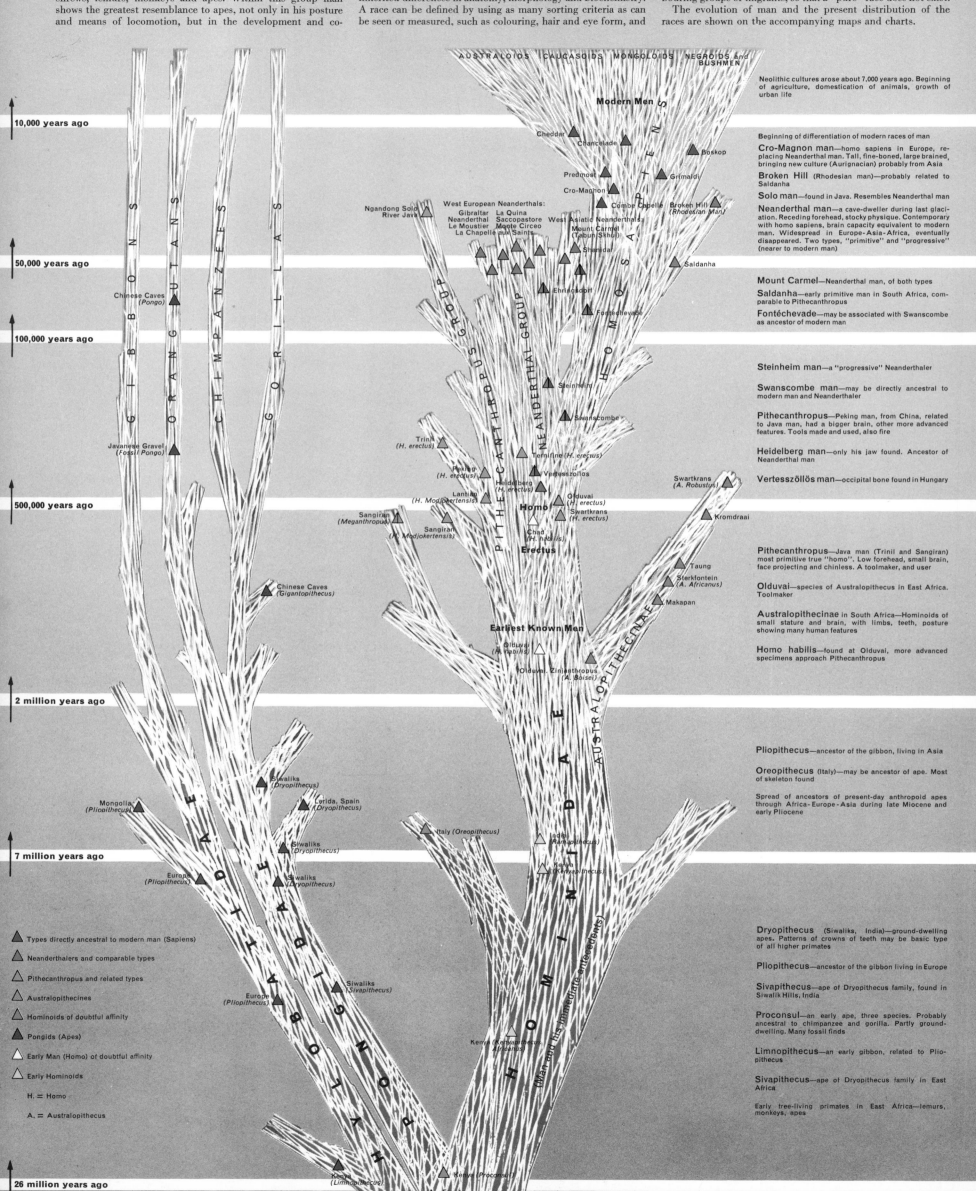

MAN'S ANCESTORS

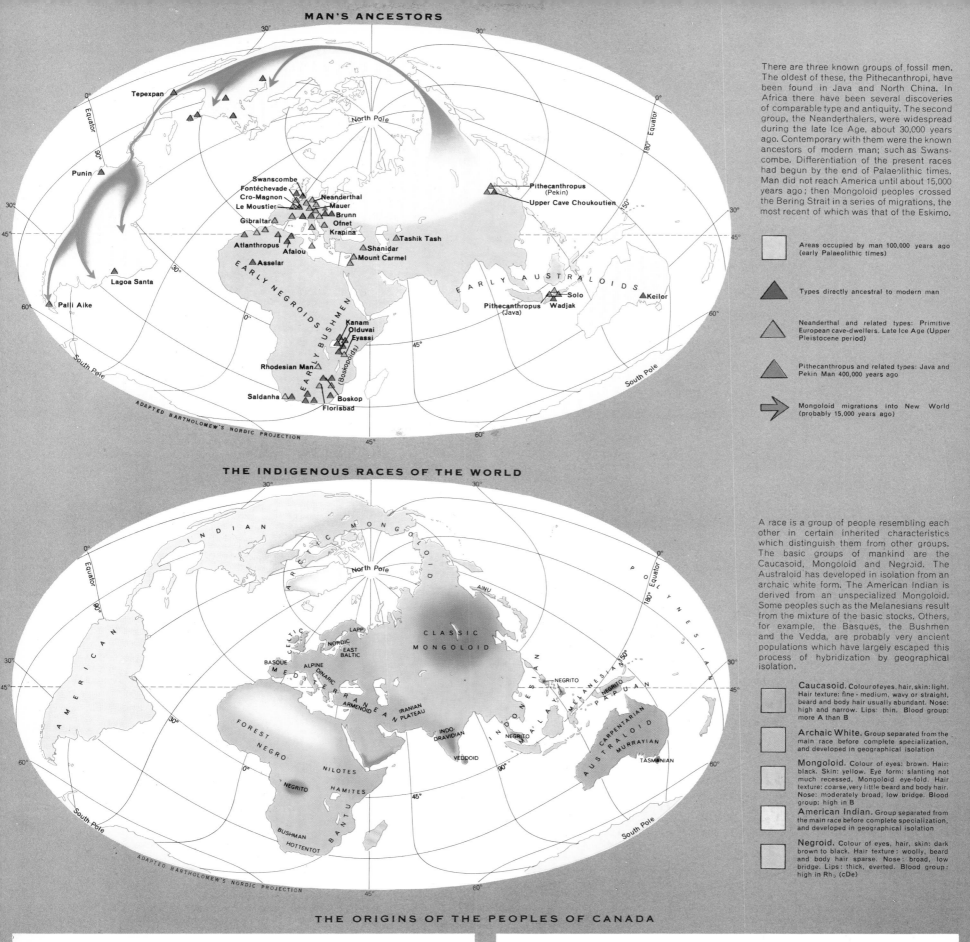

There are three known groups of fossil men. The oldest of these, the Pithecanthropi, have been found in Java and North China. In Africa there have been several discoveries of comparable type and antiquity. The second group, the Neanderthalers, were widespread during the late Ice Age, about 30,000 years ago. Contemporary with them were the known ancestors of modern man; such as Swanscombe. Differentiation of the present races had begun by the end of Palaeolithic times. Man did not reach America until about 15,000 years ago; then Mongoloid peoples crossed the Bering Strait in a series of migrations, the most recent of which was that of the Eskimo.

Areas occupied by man 100,000 years ago (early Palaeolithic times)

Types directly ancestral to modern man

Neanderthal and related types: Primitive European cave-dwellers. Late Ice Age (Upper Pleistocene period)

Pithecanthropus and related types: Java and Pekin Man 400,000 years ago

Mongoloid migrations into New World (probably 15,000 years ago)

Map labels: Tepexpan, Punin, Lagoa Santa, Palli Aike, Swanscombe, Fontéchevade, Cro-Magnon, Le Moustier, Gibraltar, Atlanthropus, Afalou, Asselar, Neanderthal, Mauer, Brunn, Ofnet, Krapina, Shanidar, Mount Carmel, Tashik Tash, EARLY NEGROIDS, EARLY BUSHMEN, Kanam, Olduvai, Eyassi, (Boskopoids), Rhodesian Man, Saldanha, Florisbad, Boskop, Pithecanthropus (Pekin), Upper Cave Choukoutien, EARLY AUSTRALOIDS, Pithecanthropus (Java), Solo, Wadjak, Keilor, North Pole, South Pole

ADAPTED BARTHOLOMEW'S NORDIC PROJECTION

THE INDIGENOUS RACES OF THE WORLD

A race is a group of people resembling each other in certain inherited characteristics which distinguish them from other groups. The basic groups of mankind are the Caucasoid, Mongoloid and Negroid. The Australoid has developed in isolation from an archaic white form. The American Indian is derived from an unspecialized Mongoloid. Some peoples such as the Melanesians result from the mixture of the basic stocks. Others, for example, the Basques, the Bushmen and the Vedda, are probably very ancient populations which have largely escaped this process of hybridization by geographical isolation.

Caucasoid. Colour of eyes, hair, skin: light. Hair texture: fine - medium, wavy or straight, beard and body hair usually abundant. Nose: high and narrow. Lips: thin. Blood group: more A than B.

Archaic White. Group separated from the main race before complete specialization, and developed in geographical isolation.

Mongoloid. Colour of eyes: brown. Hair: black. Skin: yellow. Eye form: slanting not much recessed, Mongoloid eye-fold. Hair texture: coarse, very little beard and body hair. Nose: moderately broad, low bridge. Blood group: high in B.

American Indian. Group separated from the main race before complete specialization, and developed in geographical isolation.

Negroid. Colour of eyes, hair, skin: dark brown to black. Hair texture: woolly, beard and body hair sparse. Nose: broad, low bridge. Lips: thick, everted. Blood group: high in Rh₃ (cDe)

Map labels: AMERICAN, ARCTIC MONGOLOID, CLASSIC MONGOLOID, AINU, CELTIC, LAPP, NORDIC, EAST BALTIC, BASQUE, ALPINE, DINARIC, MEDITERRANEAN, ARMENOID, IRANIAN PLATEAU, INDO-DRAVIDIAN, VEDDOID, NEGRITO, POLYNESIA, MELANESIA, PAPUAN, MALAY, INDONESIAN, CARPENTARIAN, AUSTRALOID, MURRAYIAN, TASMANIAN, FOREST NEGRO, NILOTES, HAMITES, BANTU, NEGRITO, BUSHMAN, HOTTENTOT, North Pole, South Pole

ADAPTED BARTHOLOMEW'S NORDIC PROJECTION

THE ORIGINS OF THE PEOPLES OF CANADA

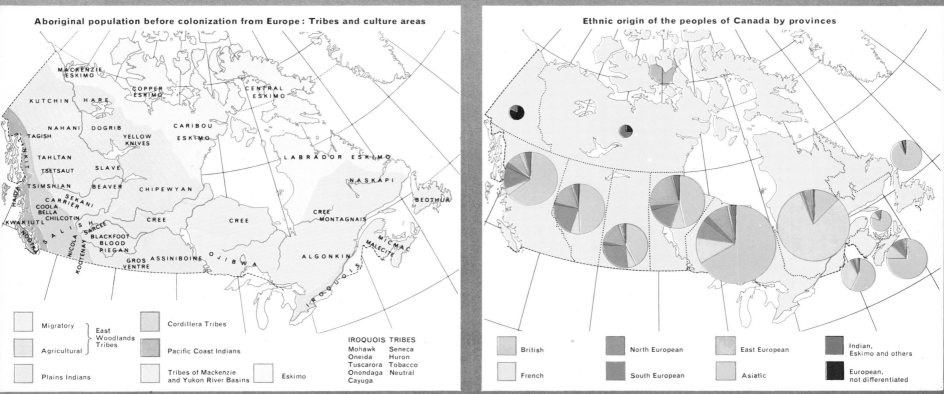

Aboriginal population before colonization from Europe: Tribes and culture areas

Map labels: MACKENZIE ESKIMO, COPPER ESKIMO, CENTRAL ESKIMO, KUTCHIN, HARE, NAHANI, DOGRIB, YELLOW KNIVES, CARIBOU ESKIMO, TAGISH, TAHLTAN, TSETSAUT, SLAVE, BEAVER, CHIPEWYAN, LABRADOR ESKIMO, NASKAPI, TSIMSHIAN, SEKANI, CARRIER, BELLA COOLA, CHILCOTIN, KWAKIUTL, SALISH, NICOLA, SARCEE, BLACKFOOT, BLOOD, PIEGAN, GROS VENTRE, ASSINIBOINE, CREE, CREE, OJIBWA, MONTAGNAIS, BEOTHUK, ALGONKIN, MICMAC, MALECITE, IROQUOIS, HAIDA, KOOTENAY, NOOTKA

Migratory
Agricultural — East Woodlands Tribes
Plains Indians
Cordillera Tribes
Pacific Coast Indians
Tribes of Mackenzie and Yukon River Basins
Eskimo

IROQUOIS TRIBES
Mohawk, Oneida, Tuscarora, Onondaga, Cayuga, Seneca, Huron, Tobacco, Neutral

Ethnic origin of the peoples of Canada by provinces

British
French
North European
South European
East European
Asiatic
Indian, Eskimo and others
European, not differentiated

The aboriginal population of Canada probably came from East Asia over the Bering Strait. The Eskimos show strong resemblances to Asiatic peoples.

At the time of the first European colonization, the native population of Canada was about 220,000. Today there are over 225,000 Indians and about 13,000 Eskimos, and these groups now show an annual increase in excess of the white population. Semi-permanent European settlements began in 1534 when Cartier claimed the St. Lawrence region for France. Colonization from Britain and other European countries did not gather momentum until after the American revolution. British Columbia was not settled until the late 19th century and population growth in this province is now among the most rapid in Canada. The Yukon and N.W. Territories remain comparatively undeveloped in spite of vast natural resources, but growing governmental interest holds promise for their future growth.

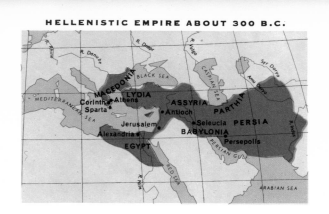

EGYPT AND BABYLONIA 2000-1500 B.C.

HELLENISTIC EMPIRE ABOUT 300 B.C.

ROMAN EMPIRE A.D. 180

THE GROWTH OF CIVILIZATIONS

A TIME CHART OF MAN'S PROGRESS THROUGH THE AGES

ALMOST all the great civilizations originated in river valleys, were nourished by trade, and came to maturity in cities. The conditions of life in the cities provided the intellectual stimulus in which philosophers and scientists could study the meaning of the Universe and the nature of matter; artists and writers could express the ideals and aspirations of their people through the medium of architecture, literature, painting and music.

The course of civilization can be traced in the five main geographical areas shown below. The progress of a civilization is marked by man's increasing control over Nature through applied mathematics and science, the evolution of writing, legal codes, and political and religious organizations. Political development usually began with the formation of city states, some of which expanded into empires or federations, but all have proved to be transient. Religions first exerted local, then national influence; and some spread beyond their countries of origin.

NEAR EAST

The union of the peoples of the Upper and Lower Nile some 5,000 years ago heralded the first major civilization in history. During its development, mathematics made possible the building of the Gizeh Pyramids; hieroglyphs were turned into alphabetic writing on stone and papyrus reed; and medicine was born. About 1500 B.C. the Egyptian Empire extended as far as Syria, but slowly declined after its failure to subdue the Hittites and Assyrians. A most vigorous civilization then developed in the fertile valleys of Mesopotamia. Here the Babylonians and Assyrians had adopted the cuneiform writing, the mathematical discoveries and the technical advances of the Sumerians—the first to found city states in the Tigris and Euphrates valleys. The Babylonian and Assyrian Empires spread east and west until they were checked by the rise of the Persians.

The Persian Empire extended from the Indus Valley to the Mediterranean, and embraced Zoroastrianism. Meanwhile in Egypt, settled in the "Promised Land" of Palestine. Their contribution was primarily religious, and paved the way for both Christianity and Islam.

After nearly a thousand years of Greek and Roman domination, another civilization was born in the Near East when, in the 7th century A.D., Arab rule and Islam spread as far as Persia and Spain. The Arabs preserved the knowledge of ancient science, philosophy and geography, translated Ptolemy, Euclid and Aristotle, and introduced into Europe the use of numerals and paper-making. Islam seemed seriously threatened when the Arabs were ousted from Spain and were defeated by the Turks in the Near East. The Turks, in taking over the Arab Empire, became Muslims, and the predominance of Islam continued. After being repelled in Central Europe, the Ottoman Empire began its slow decline. A revival of nationalism among the Arabs led to the foundation of the Arab League.

EUROPE

Western civilization originated in the Aegean, but received its real character from the cultures of Greece, Rome and Jerusalem. The Arabs and the Christian Church preserved different aspects of these cultures, and, in their development, carried them farther. The Greeks, entering the Aegean from the north, built city states which, though constantly at odds with one another, shared a common cultural development, used the alphabet brought to them by trading Phoenicians, and provided the starting points for most of our own ideas and ideals.

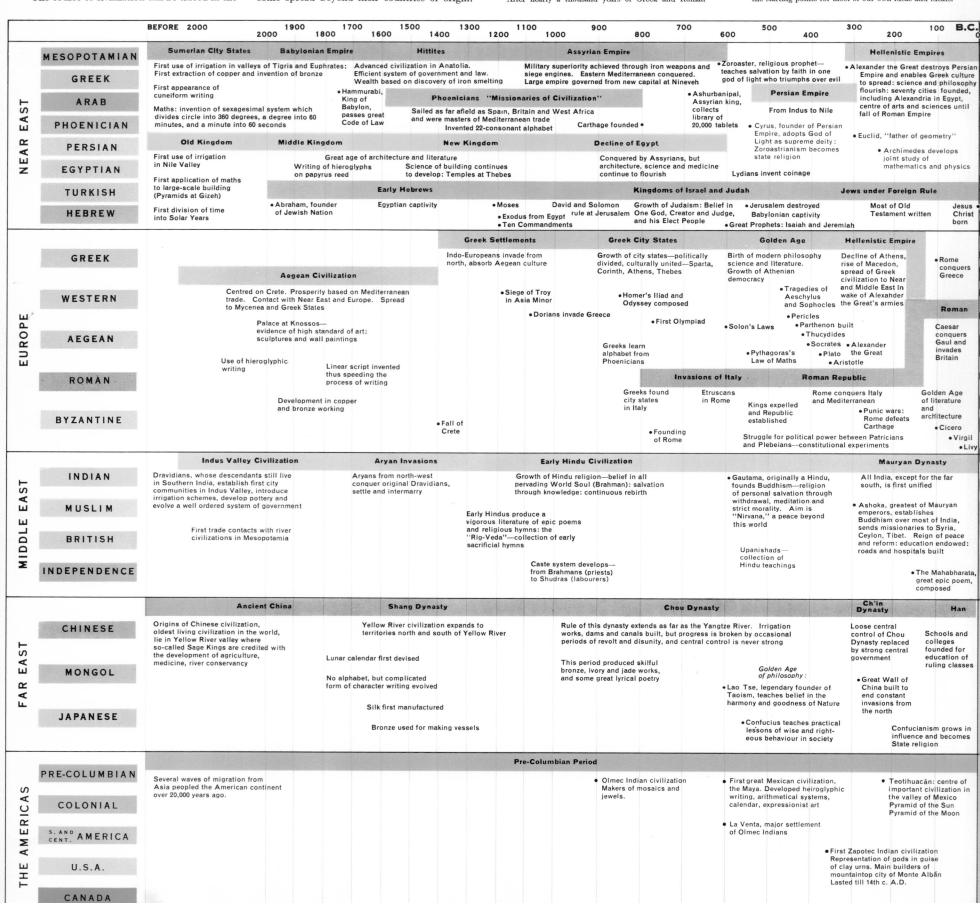

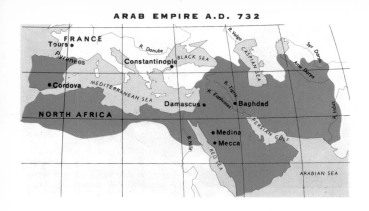

ARAB EMPIRE A.D. 732

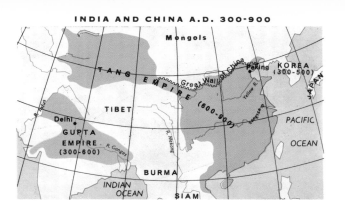

INDIA AND CHINA A.D. 300-900

Alexander the Great's victories over the Persian Empire carried Greek culture to the Near and Middle East. But it was spread still farther by the Romans, who conquered Greece and became masters of the Mediterranean and much of Europe. The Romans excelled as administrators. They created an enlightened and impartial system of law, an international language, imposing architecture, and a network of roads. The Roman Empire was divided into East and West in the 4th century A.D., but although the Western Empire disintegrated in the following century, the Eastern or Byzantine Empire, with Constantinople as its capital, resisted the onslaught of the Arabs and the Turks for nearly ten centuries, and spread its religion and culture to Bulgaria and Russia.

Meanwhile Christianity penetrated central Europe, the Church becoming responsible for the preservation of knowledge inherited from the past. The rebirth of classical learning during the Renaissance started a scientific and artistic revolution. Protestantism broke the religious supremacy of the Church of Rome. New lands were discovered, and European ideas spread to many parts of the world. The 19th century saw a great industrial revolution, brought about by the advance of science and technology and an unprecedented growth in population.

MIDDLE EAST—INDIA

Indian history is a record of constant invasions from the north-west, which brought contacts with foreign civilizations and an influx of alien races and religions. Until recently, political unity has never lasted long. The formative influences on Indian thought, art and society have been religious. India has produced many outstanding spiritual leaders from Buddha to Gandhi.

The ancient city civilization of the Indus Valley was destroyed by Aryan invaders, who intermingled with the original inhabitants and evolved the Hindu religion. In the 6th century B.C. Buddhism branched off from the main stream of Hinduism but made little impact until the 3rd century B.C., when Asoka, the greatest of the emperors of the Mauryan dynasty, patronized it, encouraged its adoption by the people and sent Buddhist missionaries to Burma and Ceylon. After Asoka's death came a revival of Hinduism in India. Buddhism rapidly lost its hold there, but spread to China, where it was widely accepted.

Hindu culture saw its golden age under the Gupta dynasty in the 3rd century A.D., when mathematics, astronomy, scholarship and architecture made great forward strides.

In the 10th century A.D., waves of Muhammadan invaders settled in India, and so initiated the long rivalry between Hindu and Muslim. In the 16th century new invaders, the Moguls, established Muhammadan rule over most of India. They produced great architecture, such as the Taj Mahal, and gave India many able and enlightened rulers. By the beginning of the 18th century the Mogul Empire had declined, and European powers were fighting one another for supremacy in the Indian sub-continent. Britain emerged from this struggle, to rule until 1947, when India and Pakistan became autonomous nations.

FAR EAST—CHINA

For centuries China was, geographically, almost inaccessible, and consequently its civilization developed in relative isolation. It absorbed its many invaders, and adapted their ideas to its own traditional culture.

The Chinese, the oldest living civilization, was more than once further advanced and more vigorous than other civilizations. It was practical and humanist, rather than religious. Originating in the Yellow River Valley, it spread north and south, reaching its first golden age in the 6th and 5th centuries B.C. under the Chou Dynasty. In this period the somewhat legendary Lao Tse founded Taoism. Later, under the same dynasty, Confucius taught a more active way of wise and righteous living through knowledge and adherence to a strict moral code. Confucianism was developed by Mencius, and became the official state religion under the Han Dynasty 2,000 years ago. The Han Emperors were the first rulers in the world to use a Civil Service (Mandarin class), entry into which was by competitive examination. Their reforms were made possible by the work of their predecessors, the Ch'in Dynasty, who imposed a large measure of central control for the first time, and built the Great Wall for protection against invasion from the north.

Buddhism spread from India to China during the 1st century A.D. It made an immediate appeal to the Chinese who, in turn, passed its teaching on to Korea and Japan.

After a period of disorder, and invasion by the Huns and Tartars, Chinese culture and scholarship flowered again, under the Tang and Sung Dynasties. Mongol invasions interrupted this golden age, but Kublai Khan, grandson of Ghengis Khan and the most enlightened and progressive of the Mongol Emperors, encouraged contact with the outside world. Under the Ming Dynasty, which drove out the Mongol Dynasty, the richness and variety of Chinese life became the envy of foreign traders, travellers and missionaries. But their successors, the Manchus, made a deliberate attempt to isolate China. This led to internal stagnation and, after the "Boxer Rebellion" in 1900, ended in the collapse of Imperial China. Sun-Yat-Sen proclaimed a republic in 1912, and after nearly forty years of almost continual civil strife and of war with Japan, the communists won control in 1949.

THE AMERICAS

No great early Indian civilization is known in North America. In Central and South America many Indian civilizations succeeded one another, as shown in the chart. All were notable for their architecture and art. The last of them, the Aztec and the Inca, were overthrown in the early 16th century by the Spaniards, who then divided the country between themselves and the Portuguese and imposed the Roman Catholic religion on the Indians. From the end of the 15th century North America and parts of South America were gradually colonized by other Europeans, who took with them their own civilization. From subsequent wars and revolutions, Canada, the United States, and the countries of Central and South America emerged as they are today.

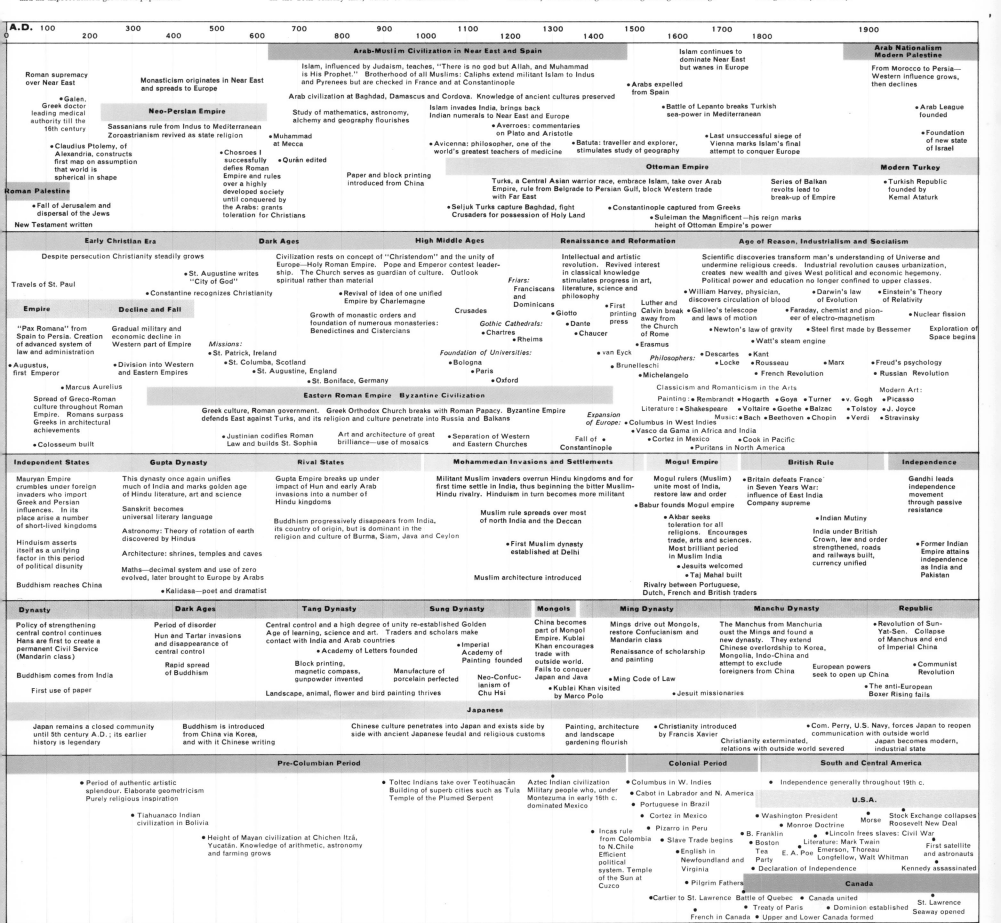

RELIGIONS—
THEIR ORIGINS AND ADHERENTS

In him we live, and move, and have our being—ACTS 17

RELIGION knows neither frontiers nor geographical barriers. With the exception of tribal religions which, though differing from one another in form and ritual, all seek to explain the mystery of life by insisting that Nature is animated by spirits, most religions have, for one reason or another, spread beyond the lands of their origins.

JUDAISM, which dates back to Moses in the 13th century B.C., when even the most advanced societies still worshipped a multiplicity of gods, is uncompromisingly monotheistic. After its

clash with Imperial Rome and the destruction of Jerusalem in A.D. 70 and 135, the Jews were expelled from the Holy Land, and a Jewish state was not again established in Palestine until 1948—almost 2,000 years later—although the majority of adherents of Judaism remain scattered throughout the world.

HINDUISM, the age-old religion of India, which honours many gods and goddesses—all of whom, however, are regarded as manifestations of the one divine spirit, Brahman—introduced into religious thinking the concept that spiritual peace and happiness can be attained only through physical and mental discipline (*yoga*—yoke). Its rigid caste divisions have been the target of innumerable reformers—among them men like Gandhi, Tagore and Bhave.

BUDDHISM, an offshoot of Hinduism, was founded by Gautama (563-483 B.C.) in North India and insists on rigid moral and

spiritual discipline in order to attain Nirvana, a condition where *karma* (deeds) have perished, the cycle of rebirth on earth has ceased, and supreme peace is attained. It spread widely throughout Asia, developing many local variations of philosophy, form and practice. In Japan, ZEN (meditation) Buddhism teaches enlightenment, while elsewhere many Buddhist teachers hold that salvation for all is possible only through the grace of Buddhas and *Bodhisattvas* (Beings of Enlightenment).

In China, from the 1st century A.D. onwards, Buddhism became mingled with the already established religions of CONFUCIANISM and TAOISM. Confucius' philosophy, which was of little influence in his own lifetime (551-479 B.C.), had been elaborated by subsequent generations of scholars both to provide a moral basis for the political structure of Imperial China and to embrace the hallowed forms of ancestor worship which

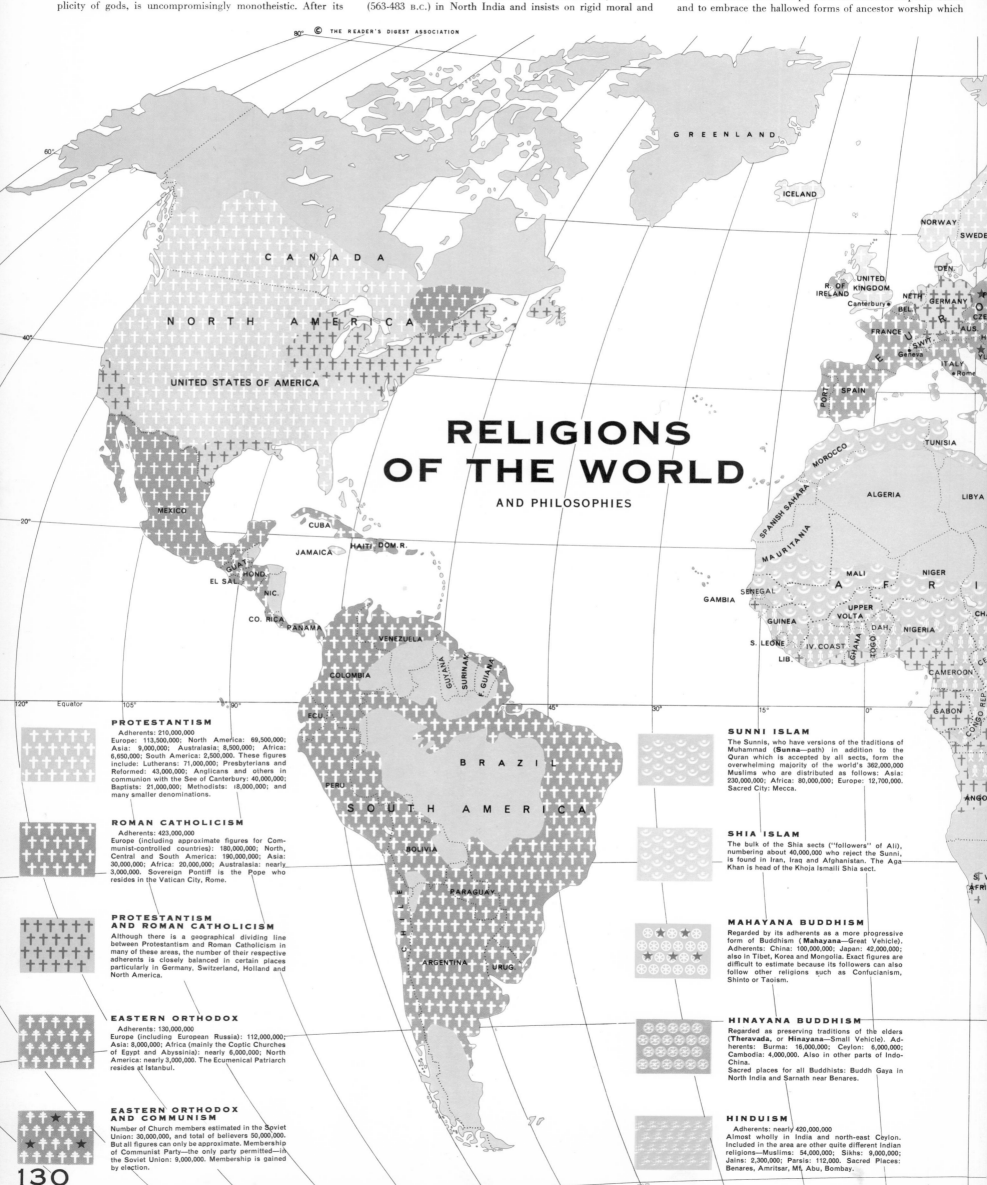

RELIGIONS OF THE WORLD
AND PHILOSOPHIES

PROTESTANTISM
Adherents: 210,000,000
Europe: 113,500,000; North America: 69,500,000; Asia: 9,000,000; Australasia: 8,500,000; Africa: 6,650,000; South America: 2,500,000. These figures include: Lutherans: 71,000,000; Presbyterians and Reformed: 43,000,000; Anglicans and others in communion with the See of Canterbury: 40,000,000; Baptists: 21,000,000; Methodists: 18,000,000; and many smaller denominations.

ROMAN CATHOLICISM
Adherents: 423,000,000
Europe (including approximate figures for Communist-controlled countries): 180,000,000; North, Central and South America: 190,000,000; Asia: 30,000,000; Africa: 20,000,000; Australasia: nearly 3,000,000. Sovereign Pontiff is the Pope who resides in the Vatican City, Rome.

PROTESTANTISM AND ROMAN CATHOLICISM
Although there is a geographical dividing line between Protestantism and Roman Catholicism in many of these areas, the number of their respective adherents is closely balanced in certain places particularly in Germany, Switzerland, Holland and North America.

EASTERN ORTHODOX
Adherents: 130,000,000
Europe (including European Russia): 112,000,000; Asia: 8,000,000; Africa (mainly the Coptic Churches of Egypt and Abyssinia): nearly 6,000,000; North America: nearly 3,000,000. The Ecumenical Patriarch resides at Istanbul.

EASTERN ORTHODOX AND COMMUNISM
Number of Church members estimated in the Soviet Union: 30,000,000, and total of believers 50,000,000. But all figures can only be approximate. Membership of Communist Party—the only party permitted—in the Soviet Union: 9,000,000. Membership is gained by election.

SUNNI ISLAM
The Sunnis, who have versions of the traditions of Muhammad (**Sunna**—path) in addition to the Quran which is accepted by all sects, form the overwhelming majority of the world's 362,000,000 Muslims who are distributed as follows: Asia: 230,000,000; Africa: 80,000,000; Europe: 12,700,000. Sacred City: Mecca.

SHIA ISLAM
The bulk of the Shia sects ("followers" of Ali), numbering about 40,000,000 who reject the Sunni, is found in Iran, Iraq and Afghanistan. The Aga Khan is head of the Khoja Ismaili Shia sect.

MAHAYANA BUDDHISM
Regarded by its adherents as a more progressive form of Buddhism (**Mahayana**—Great Vehicle). Adherents: China: 100,000,000; Japan: 42,000,000; also in Tibet, Korea and Mongolia. Exact figures are difficult to estimate because its followers can also follow other religions such as Confucianism, Shinto or Taoism.

HINAYANA BUDDHISM
Regarded as preserving traditions of the elders (**Theravada**, or **Hinayana**—Small Vehicle). Adherents: Burma: 16,000,000; Ceylon: 6,000,000; Cambodia: 4,000,000. Also in other parts of Indo-China.
Sacred places for all Buddhists: Buddh Gaya in North India and Sarnath near Benares.

HINDUISM
Adherents: nearly 420,000,000
Almost wholly in India and north-east Ceylon. Included in the area are other quite different Indian religions—Muslims: 54,000,000; Sikhs: 9,000,000; Jains: 2,300,000; Parsis: 112,000. Sacred Places: Benares, Amritsar, Mt. Abu, Bombay.

have always been practised in China; Taoism, based on the teachings of Lao Tse in the 6th century B.C., taught a quietist religion of living in the way (*tao*) of nature.

In Japan, from the 6th century A.D. onwards, Buddhism became mingled with the ancient religion of SHINTO, a nature worship of a multiplicity of deities honoured at shrines like that of Amaterasu, the Sun Goddess, at Ise, and many Japanese still attend the places of worship of both faiths.

One of the most active proselytizing faiths in the history of religion, ISLAM, was carried across Asia and Africa; it swept round the southern shores of the Mediterranean, crossed the Straits of Gibraltar into Spain and even penetrated into France after the death of its founder, Muhammad (A.D. 570-632). Almost a thousand years later, Islamic power penetrated far into Central Europe up to the walls of Vienna, and when the tide eventually

receded, it left behind, particularly in the Balkans, innumerable islands of Muslim communities.

The religion with the largest number of adherents and the most pronounced missionary zeal in the world today is CHRISTIANITY. It was founded in the 1st century A.D. by Jesus of Nazareth, who was accepted as the Christ, the Messiah or Anointed One, by his disciples who were then called Christians. His Crucifixion in Jerusalem and his Resurrection furnished the main articles of faith and the Symbol of the Cross.

Christianity spread quickly through the Roman Empire, where it became the official religion in the 4th century A.D., with the Pope in Rome—the successor of St. Peter, Christ's chief disciple—widely recognized as the supreme authority in a rapidly emerging Church hierarchy. The Eastern Church, which began in the Holy Land before there were any Christians in

Rome, rejected papal authority in the 11th century A.D.; and the Eastern Orthodox Church—comprising the historical patriarchal sees of Jerusalem, Antioch, Alexandria and Constantinople, to which was later added the patriarchate of Moscow (the largest today)—continued as a federation of mutually independent churches, standing in full communion with one another and united as equals. The ancient Armenian Jacobite, Syrian, Indian, and Coptic Abyssinian and Egyptian Churches are known, however, as the Separated Churches of the East.

A further rupture in Christian unity came in the 16th century with the Reformation movements of Protestantism, and Protestantism itself is now divided into many denominations. But the settlement of new continents has carried Christianity in one form or another to almost all parts of the world, and strong movements for Christian reunion are now in force.

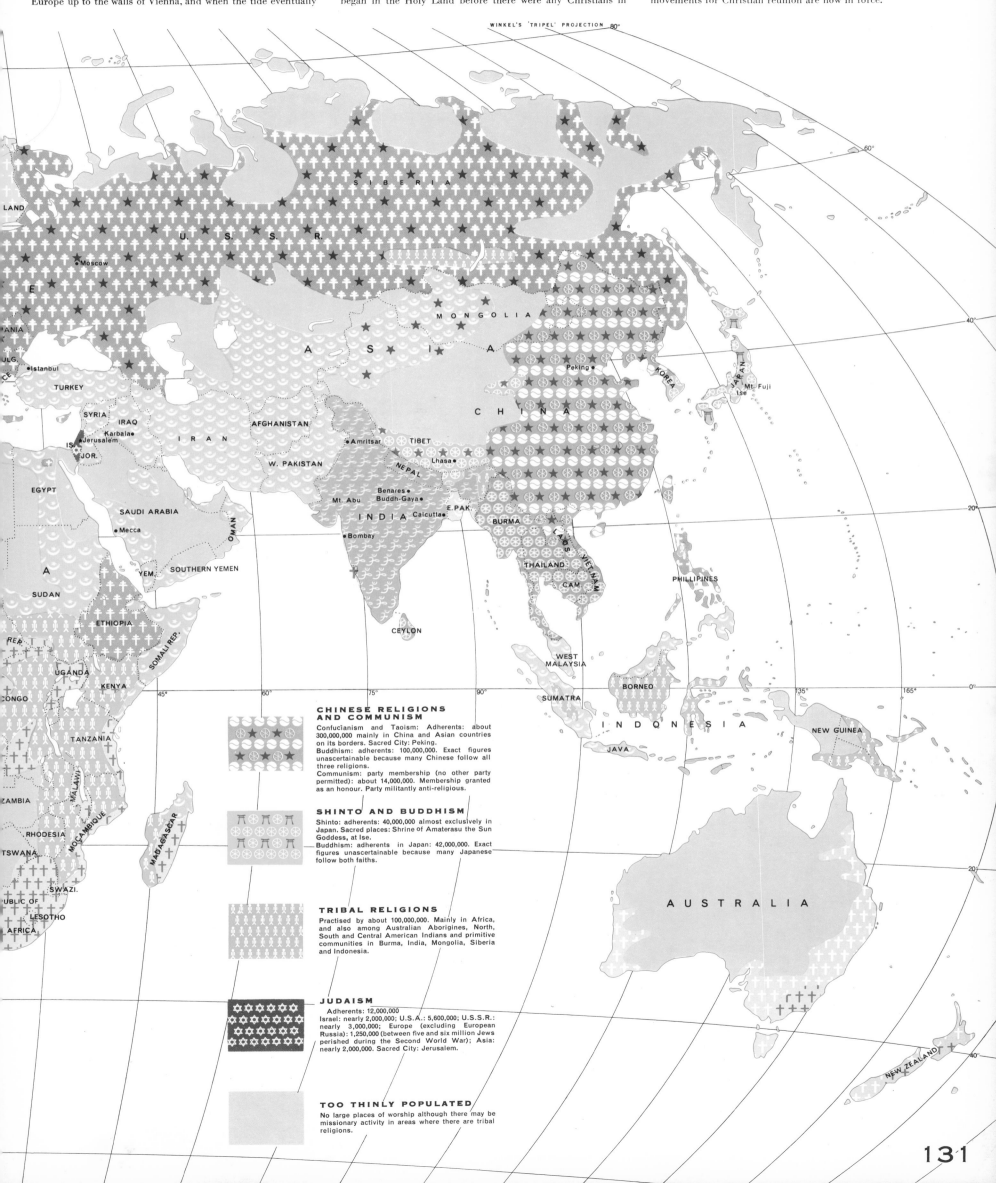

WINKEL'S 'TRIPEL' PROJECTION

**CHINESE RELIGIONS
AND COMMUNISM**
Confucianism and Taoism: Adherents: about 300,000,000 mainly in China and Asian countries on its borders. Sacred City: Peking.
Buddhism: adherents: 100,000,000. Exact figures unascertainable because many Chinese follow all three religions.
Communism: party membership (no other party permitted): about 14,000,000. Membership granted as an honour. Party militantly anti-religious.

SHINTO AND BUDDHISM
Shinto: adherents: 40,000,000 almost exclusively in Japan. Sacred places: Shrine of Amaterasu the Sun Goddess, at Ise.
Buddhism: adherents in Japan: 42,000,000. Exact figures unascertainable because many Japanese follow both faiths.

TRIBAL RELIGIONS
Practised by about 100,000,000. Mainly in Africa, and also among Australian Aborigines, North, South and Central American Indians and primitive communities in Burma, India, Mongolia, Siberia and Indonesia.

JUDAISM
Adherents: 12,000,000
Israel: nearly 2,000,000; U.S.A.: 5,600,000; U.S.S.R.: nearly 3,000,000; Europe (excluding European Russia): 1,250,000 (between five and six million Jews perished during the Second World War); Asia: nearly 2,000,000. Sacred City: Jerusalem.

TOO THINLY POPULATED
No large places of worship although there may be missionary activity in areas where there are tribal religions.

131

MOVEMENTS OF THE HEBREWS IN OLD TESTAMENT TIMES

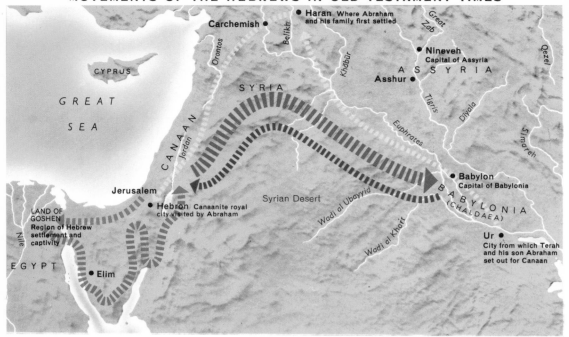

∙∙∙∙∙∙∙∙∙∙ c. 2000 B.C. Abraham, from Ur of the Chaldaeans, enters the land of Canaan in answer to God's call

▮▮▮▮▮▮▮▮ 18th cent. B.C. Increased Semitic migration into Egypt. Establishment of Hyksos rule

▶▶▶▶▶▶ c.1220 B.C. (?) Exodus from Egypt of Hebrew clans under Moses and the wanderings in the wilderness

▶▶▶▶▶▶ 597 B.C. Beginning of Jewish exile in Babylon

▶▶▶▶▶▶ After 539 B.C. Return of many Jews to the Holy Land after liberation by Cyrus

INVASIONS OF THE HOLY LAND

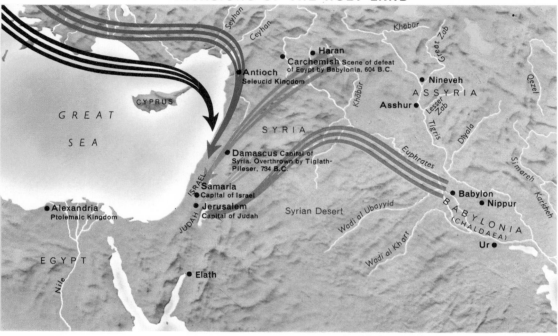

⟹ 842 B.C. Israel engaged in disastrous war with Syria

⟹ Assyrian invasions under Tiglath-Pileser III (745 B.C.), Sargon II (fall of Samaria, 721 B.C.), and Sennacherib (701 B.C. Siege of Jerusalem)

➤ 597 B.C. Siege of Jerusalem by Nebuchadrezzar and first deportation of Jews to Babylon. 586 B.C. Fall of Jerusalem and second deportation

➤ 198 B.C. Palestine falls to the Seleucidae. Rebellion of Jews under Judas Maccabaeus. 166 B.C., against Antiochus IV of Antioch

➤ 63 B.C. Pompey occupies Jerusalem. Thereafter Palestine becomes part of Roman province of Syria

THE JOURNEYS OF SAINT PAUL

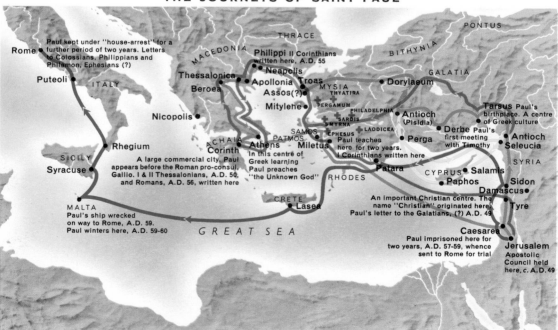

The first missionary journey to Cyprus and southern Asia Minor. Paul is accompanied by Barnabas and John Mark as far as Perga in Pamphylia. Paul's method was to address the local Jews first, whose reaction was invariably hostile. Thereupon he would turn to the Gentiles.

The second missionary journey took Paul through Asia Minor and Greece. This seems to have lasted some years, and included a two years stay at Corinth.

The third missionary journey took Paul through Asia Minor and Greece again. He remained two years at Ephesus, finally going up to Jerusalem in A.D. 56

Paul's journey to Rome, where he was kept in confinement in his own house for two more years. But the apostle seems finally to have been acquitted

✚ The seven churches of Asia Minor

BIBLE LANDS

And ye shall be my witnesses both in Jerusalem, and in all Judaea and Samaria, and unto the uttermost part of the earth— ACTS 1

THE OLD TESTAMENT

THE Old Testament relates the history of the Hebrew people during some 2,000 years. Their story begins with the migration from the city of Ur, in ancient Chaldaea, of a band of Semites led by Abraham in response to a divine call. Abraham, with his family, settled for a time at Haran in northern Syria, but later, about 2000 B.C., moved south into Canaan. Hebrew clans subsequently entered Egypt, and remained there for an unknown period.

The Exodus from Egypt under the leadership of Moses and the wanderings in the wilderness subsequently led them to the Promised Land—"a land flowing with milk and honey." Here eventually they united to form a nation under King Saul and his successors, David and Solomon; but with the division of the kingdom which followed Solomon's death they found themselves surrounded by powerful and hostile neighbours. In this precarious situation the prophets sought to teach the people that only religious purity, social righteousness and political neutrality would save them from extinction. Nevertheless a series of foreign invasions culminated in the destruction of Jerusalem in 586 B.C., when a large part of the nation was carried off in captivity to Babylon.

In 539 B.C. Babylon itself was captured by the Persian King Cyrus, who gave permission to the exiled Jews to return to their native land. A small number did so, and began to rebuild the Temple and with it the national life.

But the days of political independence were over. Persian rule gave way to Greek, and when Antiochus IV attempted to unite the heterogeneous elements of his realm on the basis of a common Hellenistic culture and religion, the Jews rebelled under the intrepid and not unsuccessful leadership of Judas Maccabaeus. The priest-kingdom of his descendents, however, succumbed in 63 B.C. to yet another foreign invader—Pompey and his Roman legions.

The troubled history and prolonged sufferings of the Jewish people convinced them, in the end, that their sole hope lay in God, who, in his own good time, they believed, would intervene in the course of world events by sending a Messianic king under whom they would at last find deliverance.

THE NEW TESTAMENT

The New Testament covers a period of some 60 years, beginning with the birth of Jesus in Bethlehem, the true date of which is probably about 4 B.C. Apart from the nativity stories and a single incident in Jesus' youth, the Gospels deal with a period of no more than three years, from the opening of His public ministry in Galilee to His death in Jerusalem at the hands of the Romans. The events leading up to the crucifixion and Christ's subsequent resurrection "on the third day" are recorded in detail, for these constituted the essence of the earliest Christian preaching and teaching.

From the moment of the descent of the Holy Spirit at the time of the Jewish feast of Pentecost, Jesus' followers set about the dangerous work of proclaiming the Christian message and baptizing converts—at first Jews, but later also Gentiles—into the "New Israel," the Church. In this work, Saul of Tarsus—St. Paul—himself a converted Pharisee, took the lead.

Paul's own mission was to the Gentile world, and his many journeys took him through Asia Minor to Greece and eventually to Rome itself. Of his death the New Testament makes no mention, but tradition awards him the martyr's crown.

In spite of persecution by the Romans and much public hostility, Christianity spread to Africa, Spain and Gaul in the first century A.D., and ultimately became the faith of the Roman Emperor.

PLAN OF JERUSALEM

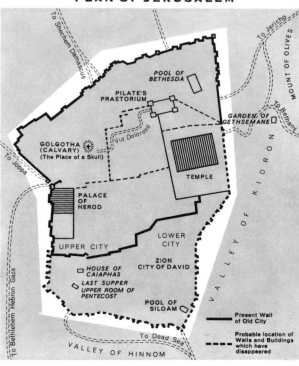

Present Wall of Old City

Probable location of Walls and Buildings which have disappeared

The sitings of the scene of the Last Supper and the Upper Room of Pentecost, the House of Caiaphas, the Way of the Cross (Via Dolorosa) and the Garden of Gethsemane are traditional only.

PALESTINE
IN THE TIME
OF JESUS

MT. HERMON

GREAT

SEA

(Mediterranean Sea)

• Tyre

P H O E N I C I A

I T U R A E A

• Caesarea Philippi Scene of Peter's
confession of faith: in recognition of
which Jesus promised him "the keys of
the Kingdom of Heaven".

• Ptolemais Formerly Acco.
Renamed by Ptolemy Philadelphus

Chorazin
A town cursed by Jesus
for its unbelief •

Beth-saida Home of
Andrew, Peter and Philip

S Y R O - G A L I L E E

Capernaum
'Here Jesus performed
many miracles and preached
in the synagogue

LAKE OF
GENNESARET
(Sea of Galilee)

• Cana
Scene of Jesus'
first recorded miracle

Tiberias
Founded by Herod
Antipas, A.D. 17-22

• Hippos

MT. CARMEL

• Nazareth
Home of Joseph and Mary

MT.
TABOR

• Abila

• Dora

Plain
of
Esdraelon

• Nain Here Jesus brought
to life the widow's son

• Gadara

Megiddo •

D E C A P O L I S

• Caesarea
Important centre of early
Christianity. Built by Herod

• Scythopolis

Plain of Sharon

Aenon
(Nr. Salim)
John the Baptist
baptized here

• Pella Thither Christians
said to have fled before
the siege of Jerusalem

• Sebaste (Samaria)
Rebuilt by Herod the Great

• Gerasa

S A M A R I A

MT. GERIZIM
Site of Samaritan temple
destroyed by John Hyrcanus,
128 B.C.

• Sychar
Jacob's Well

P
E
R
A
E
A

• Antipatris

• Alexandrium

• Joppa

Jordan

• Arimathea Home of Joseph,
a member of the Sanhedrin

• Philadelphia

• Lydda

• Ephraim

• Jamnia

• Emmaus
Scene of appearance
of the Risen Christ

Jericho Scene of healing by Jesus
of blind Bartimaeus. Mentioned also
in Parable of Good Samaritan

Jerusalem ■
Capital of Judaea.
Sacked by Romans,
A.D. 70

• Bethany
Home of Lazarus and his
sisters, Martha and Mary

Bethany
(or Bethabara)
Where John baptized

• Azotus

• Kh. Qumran
Essene centre
MS. scrolls
discovered near
here, A.D. 1947

• Bethlehem
Birthplace of Jesus

• Herodium

• Ashkelon

J U D A E A

S
A
L
T
S
E
A

(Dead Sea)

• Machaerus Fortress built by
Herod. Scene, according to
Josephus, of the Baptist's beheading

• Hebron

za

• Beer-sheba

I D U M A E A

THE GREAT EXPLORATIONS

As cold waters to a thirsty soul,
*so is good news from a far country—*PROVERBS 25

Only a small proportion of the world remains to be explored, for man has always been a wanderer and a searcher for new things.

As early as 700 B.C. Phoenician and Carthaginian traders were seeking fresh lands in the Mediterranean and beyond for their merchandise. About 470 B.C. Hanno, the Carthaginian, sailed with a large fleet as far as Sierra Leone, bringing back tales of gorillas and of a "land of fire". (This was probably on account of the grass fires lighted before the rains in many parts of Africa.)

In 330 B.C. the Greek, Pytheas, sailed round Britain and into the North Sea, but more important than his journey for those who were to come after him was his discovery of a means of calculating latitude.

The most important exploration of this period was made by Alexander the Great in the years 330–323 B.C., when, accompanied by land surveyors and scribes to record details of the countries through which he passed, he marched his armies through Persia to India, and, like a true explorer, returned by a different route.

In the Second and First Centuries B.C. the Romans, in the expansion of their Empire, penetrated up the Nile, as far north as the Baltic, and westwards across Europe.

Westward exploration was extended by the Norsemen, first by their discovery of Iceland about A.D. 867, then Greenland in A.D. 982, and finally by their reaching the mainland of North America about four years later.

At about the same time the Arabs were voyaging far afield in the Indian Ocean, ranging from Spain to China, and as far south as Madagascar. Their greatest traveller was Ibn Batuta, who visited every Moslem country in a remarkable series of journeys that lasted almost thirty years. Buddhist missionaries, passing to and fro from India to China across the deserts of Takla-Makan and Gobi, had come across what came to be known as the Jade Route, along which for centuries traders carried jade from the Himalayas to China in exchange for silk.

In the same period envoys were sent by the Pope to the Great Khan of the Mongol Empire, and thus opened up the way for the Polos, father and son—Venetian jewel merchants and the most famous land travellers of the age—who journeyed twice across Asia.

Meanwhile, ship-building and navigation in Europe had considerably advanced and more extended voyages were possible. By A.D. 1487 the Portuguese had coasted down Africa, and in that year the Cape of Good Hope was rounded by Bartholomew Diaz. Thus opened the Great Age of Discovery, and in thirty years all the unknown oceans were crossed—Columbus reaching America in 1492, Vasco da Gama reaching India in 1498, and Magellan sailing across the Pacific and round the whole world in 1521.

Following on the heels of Columbus, the Portuguese spread down through Brazil, and the Spaniards endeavoured to cross the continent that lay between them and the riches of the East. In 1513 Balboa crossed the Isthmus of Panama, and a few years later Cortez conquered Mexico, and by 1540 the Spaniards had reached the Gulf of California. The English and the French gained footings in North America, and, with the Dutch, began to seek a North-West Passage in the Arctic as a route to China. By A.D. 1650 the existence of all the continents except Antarctica had been proved.

Then followed the Age of Scientific Discovery, when expeditions by land and sea had exploration for knowledge as their aim. The greatest leader of such an expedition was Captain Cook who, in only three great voyages, explored Australia and New Zealand, circumnavigated Antarctica, and sailed through the Bering Strait. Exploration by land was slower, and it was not until the Nineteenth Century that English and American expeditions crossed North America, and South America was fully penetrated.

Africa was the last major continent to be crossed. Serious exploration was begun in 1795 by Mungo Park in West Africa, and thirty years later the Lander brothers found the mouth of the River Niger. In 1849, David Livingstone, who usually travelled alone and was perhaps the greatest land explorer ever known, began his journeys in Southern and Central Africa: his work was continued after his death by his friend, Stanley.

Major interest was then centred round the north and south Polar regions. In 1909 the American, Peary, was the first to reach the North Pole, and in 1958 the American submarine *Nautilus* travelled *beneath* it. In 1911 the Norwegian, Amundsen, was the first to reach the South Pole, followed a month later by the Englishman, Scott; and in 1955–58, Sir Vivian Fuchs led a British Commonwealth expedition which crossed the Antarctic continent from the Weddell Sea to the Ross Sea.

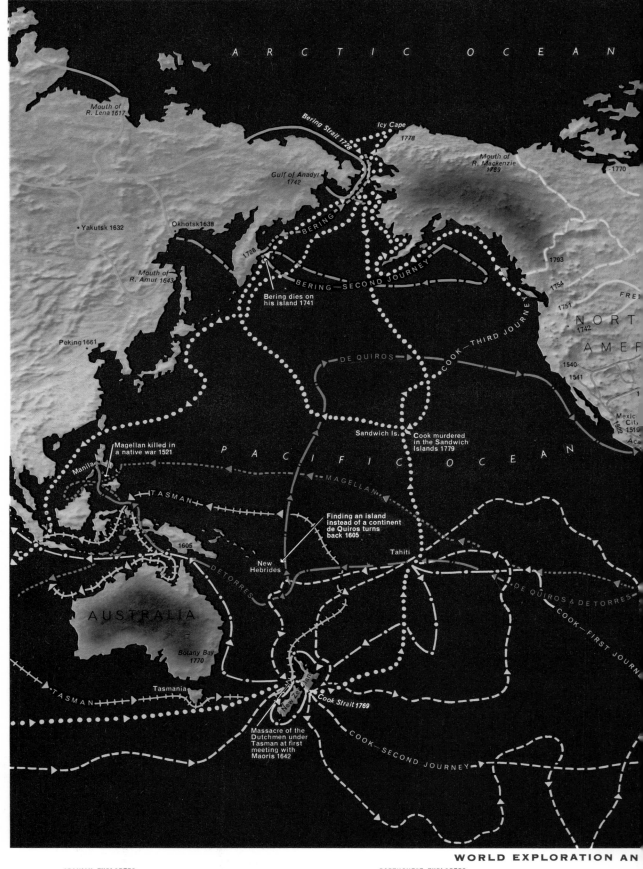

WORLD EXPLORATION AN

THE WORLD AS KNOWN IN 1490

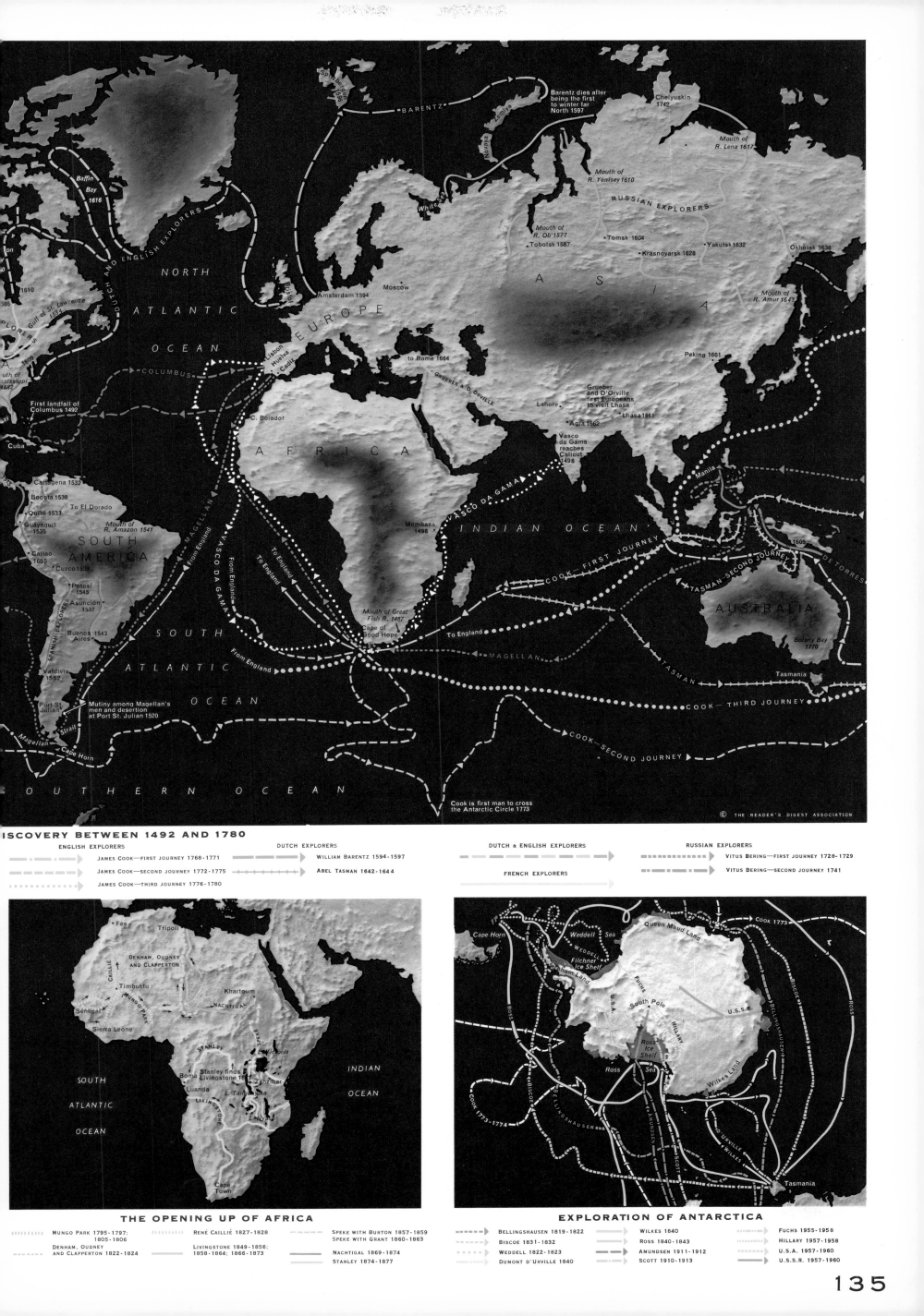

Baffin
Bay
1616

NORTH

ATLANTIC

OCEAN

Spitsbergen 1596

BARENTZ

Barentz dies after
being the first
to winter far
North 1597

Chelyuskin
1742

Mouth of
R. Lena 1617

Novaya Zemlya

White Sea

Mouth of
R. Yenisey 1610

RUSSIAN EXPLORERS

DUTCH AND ENGLISH EXPLORERS

Gulf of St. Lawrence
1534

Mouth of
Mississippi
1682

First landfall of
Columbus 1492

Amsterdam 1594

Moscow

ASIA

Mouth of
R. Ob 1577

Tobolsk 1587

Tomsk 1604

Krasnoyarsk 1628

Yakutsk 1632

Okhotsk 1638

Mouth of
R. Amur 1643

1610

COLUMBUS

EUROPE

Lisbon

Huelva

Cadiz

to Rome 1664

GRUEBER & D'ORVILLE

Peking 1661

Cuba

C. Bojador

AFRICA

Grueber
and D'Orville
first Europeans
to visit Lhasa

Lahore

Agra 1662

Lhasa 1661

Cartagena 1532

Bogotá 1538

To El Dorado

Quito 1533

Guayaquil
1535

Mouth of
R. Amazon 1541

SOUTH

AMERICA

Vasco
da Gama
reaches
Calicut
1498

Manila

Callao
1605

Cuzco 1533

Potosí
1545

Asunción
1537

Mombasa
1498

INDIAN OCEAN

VASCO DA GAMA

1605

DE TORRES

COOK—FIRST JOURNEY

MAGELLAN

From England

VASCO DA GAMA

From England

To England

To England

TASMAN—SECOND JOURNEY

AUSTRALIA

Buenos
Aires 1542

SPANISH EXPLORERS

SOUTH

Valdivia
1552

ATLANTIC

Mouth of Great
Fish R. 1487

Cape of
Good Hope

To England

Botany Bay
1770

Port St.
Julian

Mutiny among Magellan's
men and desertion
at Port St. Julian 1520

OCEAN

From England

MAGELLAN

TASMAN

Tasmania

Magellan

Strait

Cape Horn

SOUTHERN OCEAN

COOK—THIRD JOURNEY

COOK—SECOND JOURNEY

Cook is first man to cross
the Antarctic Circle 1773

© THE READER'S DIGEST ASSOCIATION

DISCOVERY BETWEEN 1492 AND 1780

ENGLISH EXPLORERS	DUTCH EXPLORERS	DUTCH & ENGLISH EXPLORERS	RUSSIAN EXPLORERS
JAMES COOK—FIRST JOURNEY 1768-1771	WILLIAM BARENTZ 1594-1597		VITUS BERING—FIRST JOURNEY 1728-1729
JAMES COOK—SECOND JOURNEY 1772-1775	ABEL TASMAN 1642-1644	FRENCH EXPLORERS	VITUS BERING—SECOND JOURNEY 1741
JAMES COOK—THIRD JOURNEY 1776-1780			

Fès

Tripoli

DENHAM, OUDNEY
AND CLAPPERTON

CAILLIÉ

Timbuktu

Khartoum

NACHTIGAL

MUNGO PARK

Sénégal

Sierra Leone

STANLEY

SPEKE

L. Victoria

SOUTH

ATLANTIC

OCEAN

Boma

Stanley finds
Livingstone 1871

Luanda

Zanzibar

L. Tanganyika

LIVINGSTONE

INDIAN

OCEAN

L. Nyasa

Cape
Town

Cape Horn

Weddell Sea

WEDDELL

Queen Maud Land

COOK 1773

Filchner
Ice Shelf

Graham Land

U.S.A.

FUCHS

ROSS

South Pole

U.S.S.R.

HILLARY

BELLINGHAUSEN

BISCOE

ROSS

COOK
1773-1774

BISCOE

BELLINGHAUSEN

Ross
Ice
Shelf

Ross
Sea

AMUNDSEN

SCOTT

Wilkes Land

D'URVILLE

WILKES

Tasmania

THE OPENING UP OF AFRICA

MUNGO PARK 1795-1797; 1805-1806	RENÉ CAILLIÉ 1827-1828	SPEKE WITH BURTON 1857-1859 SPEKE WITH GRANT 1860-1863
DENHAM, OUDNEY AND CLAPPERTON 1822-1824	LIVINGSTONE 1849-1856; 1858-1864; 1866-1873	NACHTIGAL 1869-1874
		STANLEY 1874-1877

EXPLORATION OF ANTARCTICA

BELLINGSHAUSEN 1819-1822	WILKES 1840	FUCHS 1955-1958
BISCOE 1831-1832	ROSS 1840-1843	HILLARY 1957-1958
WEDDELL 1822-1823	AMUNDSEN 1911-1912	U.S.A. 1957-1960
DUMONT D'URVILLE 1840	SCOTT 1910-1913	U.S.S.R. 1957-1960

Estimated World Population

Oceania	Africa	Central and S. America	N. America	U.S.S.R.	Europe
32 million	768 million	638 million	354 million	353 million	527 million

2000

2,000 Million   1,000 Million

1950

WORLD POPULATION

And God said unto them, Be fruitful, and multiply — GENESIS 1

In the middle of the 1800's the world's population was estimated to be 1,000 million; by the mid 1920's, less than a century later, the population had doubled; and in 1963 it had reached 3,000 million. After carefully considering the rates of birth, maternal and infant mortality, and the expectation of life in every country, the United Nations forecast that by A.D. 2000 the figure will have increased to over 6,000 million and that it may reach nearly 7,000 million. The phenomenal expansion is shown on the chart in the centre of these pages. The total population in 1966 of the four groups listed in the table below right is 3,296,335,000. It can be seen that while the populations of the Western Hemisphere and Australasia have steadily increased since 1900, the populations of Africa and Asia (with the exception of the U.S.S.R., China and Japan) show a much more rapid expansion. Improved food production and increasing medical knowledge are largely responsible for the expansion in these areas.

1900

MIGRATIONS SINCE A.D. 1650

1850

1800

© THE READER'S DIGEST ASSOCIATION

Movements of populations occur mainly for political, religious and economic reasons. The more important migrations of the past three hundred years are shown.

Europeans to U.S.A. During the 17th century about 500,000 people emigrated from Great Britain to settle in New England (*Mayflower* 1620), Virginia and Maryland (though some settled in the West Indies, mostly in Barbados), to be followed in the 18th century by three times that number (mainly Irish and Scots). In the 19th century the number further increased, and was added to by German, Austro-Hungarian and Italian immigrants. From 1900 to 1920 a total of 14,500,000 from many countries were admitted (1,042,000 in 1907—a peak for any one year). In the next 30 years only 5,500,000 were admitted, but during the years 1951-9 the rate of immigration increased to a total of 2,250,000. In the following six years the number of immigrants from Europe alone was 750,000.

Europeans to Canada During the 17th century Quebec Province was settled by the French, but later the majority of immigrants came from Great Britain. Until 1900 settlement was slow, but from 1900 to 1920 about 2,250,000 people entered the country, followed by 1,500,000 in the next 30 years. Thereafter immigration greatly increased, over 2,000,000 Europeans settling in Canada in 1951-67.

Europeans to South America South America has always mainly attracted the Spanish, Portuguese and Italians, Argentina and Brazil being their principal goals. Immigration was slow until the 1890's, but reached its peak before 1914. Between 1900 and 1920 about 3,000,000 people settled in Argentina, and about 1,500,000 in Brazil.

The Slave Trade Traffic in slaves from West Africa began in the 16th century, reaching its peak in the late 18th and early 19th centuries. About 20,000,000 slaves were taken mainly to the tobacco, sugar and coffee plantations of the Caribbean and Brazil. Many of them moved on to the cotton fields of the southern states of what is now the U.S.A.

Europeans to Australia and New Zealand The first white people settled in Australia in 1788, but immigration was slow until the period of the Gold Rush between 1850 and 1860. After 1860 it slowed down again until the turn of the century. Between 1901 and 1920 about 400,000 emigrated to Australia, mostly from the United Kingdom, but in the twenty years from 1945 over 2,500,000 settled in Australia, about half of whom were British. Emigration to New Zealand has followed much the same pattern, but on a smaller scale.

French to Algeria French traders became established in Algeria in the 16th century. In 1842 the country became a French colony, although Algiers had been captured in 1830. By 1848 government-sponsored settlers totalled 40,000, and in 1881 northern Algeria became a province of France. Settlement continued until the unrest preceding independence in 1963; then about four-fifths of the French population left for metropolitan France.

Europeans to Central and East Africa Few Europeans settled in Rhodesia before the discovery of the diamond deposits in 1880, development of which began in 1889 when Cecil Rhodes financed the trek to Salisbury. By 1960 nearly 300,000 had settled in Zambia and Rhodesia. East Africa was largely settled through official encouragement from 1906 onwards.

Dutch in South Africa The first Europeans to settle in the Cape were the Dutch in 1652. Emigrants from the British Isles did not arrive in any numbers until the late 18th century. In 1836 Dutch farmers (Boers) began their revolt against British rule in Cape Colony and made the Great Trek across the Orange River, to found the Orange Free State and the Transvaal. During the next ten years probably 14,000 Boers moved northwards. In the early 20th century there were mass movements of Africans (mostly from Moçambique, Basutoland, Bechuanaland and Nyasaland) to the Transvaal, especially to industrial Johannesburg.

Chinese to Other Parts of Asia From the middle of the 19th century the Chinese migrated in large numbers, mainly to Malaya, Indonesia, Burma and Ceylon. In 1948 there were 9,500,000 abroad, mostly in Asia, though over 200,000 were in the U.S.A. In the 1920's there were mass movements to Manchuria, Mongolia and Asiatic Russia.

Internal Migration in the U.S.S.R. Since 1918 great movements of European Russians to the east of the Urals have taken place. The Second World War accelerated industrial growth beyond the Urals, and a feature of the recent Five Year Plans has been the movement to and the settling of people in Kazakhstan and farther east.

Indians to Malaya and Africa In the mid 19th century Indians migrated to Ceylon, Burma and Malaya, Mauritius, Natal, East Africa and the West Indies. These migrations have continued on a small scale in the 20th century.

Migration between India and Pakistan After the 1947 partition of the former Indian Empire into India (Hindu majority) and Pakistan (Moslem majority) large religious minorities were left on either side of the border. Between 1947 and 1949 about 10,000,000 people were resettled.

Internal Migration in the U.S.A. From the end of the 18th century, when pioneers started the movement westwards, migration to the west has continued, as well as movement from the Atlantic seaboard to the south. In the fifteen years 1950-65 the population of California increased 75 per cent and that of Florida by over 100 per cent compared with a 23 per cent increase in the remainder of the U.S.A. Many negroes have moved north from the southern states; Puerto Ricans have settled in cities in the eastern states.

Jewish Migration Intermittent migrations of Jews from many countries into Palestine took place after the First World War, but since the formation of the State of Israel in 1948 many European Jews have been admitted. In 1949 over 239,000 settled in Israel, to be followed in the next fifteen years by nearly 900,000.

Internal Migration in Europe The Second World War left millions of displaced persons in Central Europe, who came mainly from Poland, Russia, the Baltic States, Hungary and the Balkans. Although the problem of resettlement was largely solved by 1951, it was not ended until the early 1960's.

Commonwealth to Great Britain In the 1950's increasing numbers of West Indians were attracted to Great Britain by better prospects of employment than at home. In the ten years 1951-60 the total number of immigrants was 175,000. In each of the three years following the Commonwealth Immigration Act, 1962, an average of 11,500 West Indians and 28,000 Indians and Pakistanis settled in Britain.

1750

1700

1650

. 2000: 6,130 million

China
1,045 million

Rest of Asia
2,413 million

1,000 Million   2,000 Million   3,000 Million

2000

1950

1900

1850

1800

1750

1700

1650

The Netherlands, with 960 people to the square mile, is the most densely populated country in the world. In Europe, England follows with 895 people to the square mile and Belgium with 809. Taiwan with 921 and South Korea with 765 head the list in Asia; Nigeria with 162 heads the list in Africa; and Puerto Rico with 776 people to the square mile is the most densely populated area in the Caribbean. Australia is over twenty-eight times as large, but less than a sixth as densely populated as New Zealand; the United States of America, with an area slightly less than that of Canada, has almost ten times Canada's population.

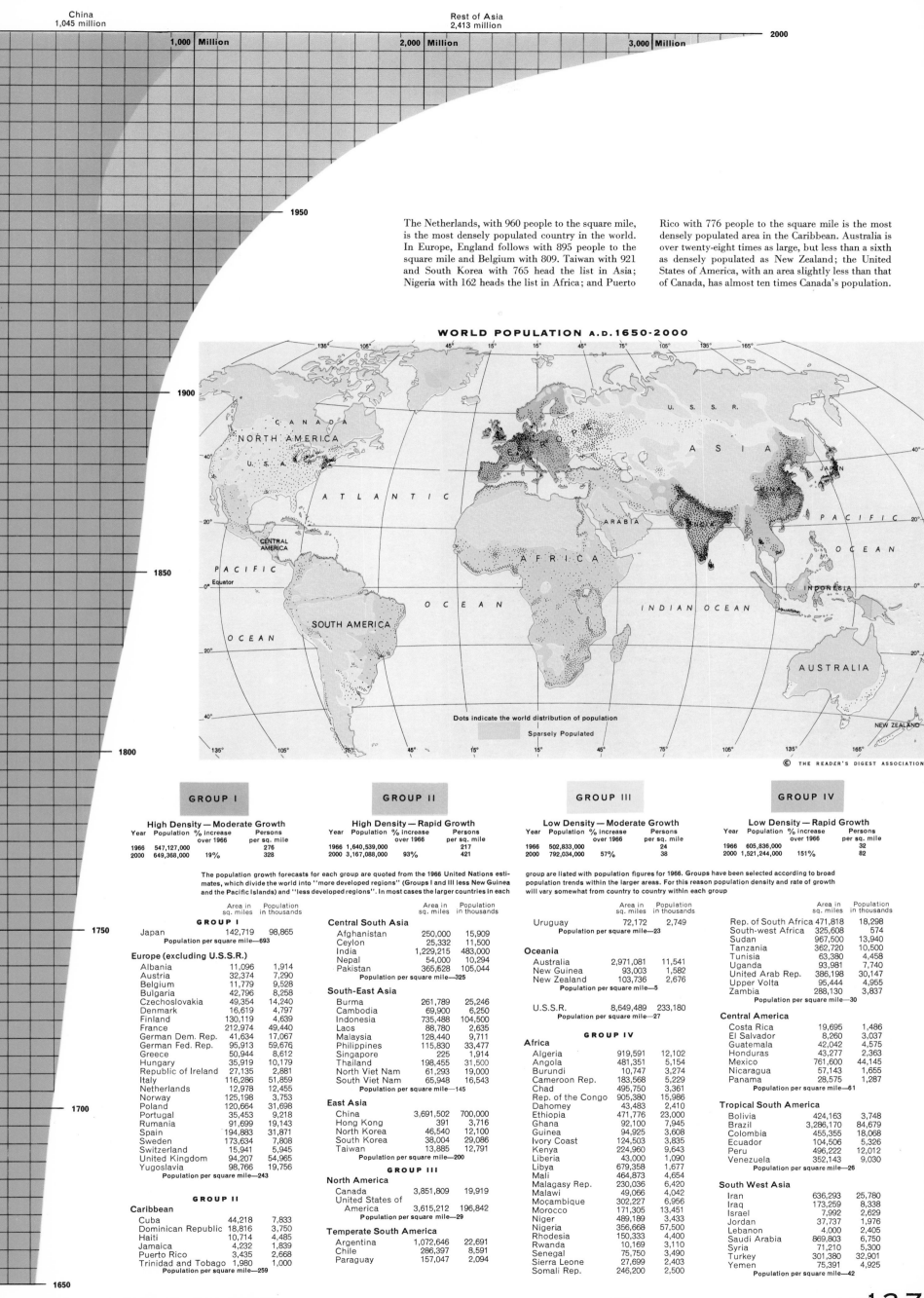

WORLD POPULATION A.D. 1650-2000

Dots indicate the world distribution of population

Sparsely Populated

© THE READER'S DIGEST ASSOCIATION

GROUP I

High Density — Moderate Growth

Year	Population	% increase over 1966	Persons per sq. mile
1966	547,127,000		276
2000	649,368,000	19%	328

GROUP II

High Density — Rapid Growth

Year	Population	% increase over 1966	Persons per sq. mile
1966	1,640,539,000		217
2000	3,167,088,000	93%	421

GROUP III

Low Density — Moderate Growth

Year	Population	% increase over 1966	Persons per sq. mile
1966	502,833,000		24
2000	792,034,000	57%	38

GROUP IV

Low Density — Rapid Growth

Year	Population	% increase over 1966	Persons per sq. mile
1966	605,836,000		32
2000	1,521,244,000	151%	82

The population growth forecasts for each group are quoted from the 1966 United Nations estimates, which divide the world into "more developed regions" (Groups I and III less New Guinea and the Pacific Islands) and "less developed regions". In most cases the larger countries in each group are listed with population figures for 1966. Groups have been selected according to broad population trends within the larger areas. For this reason population density and rate of growth will vary somewhat from country to country within each group.

	Area in sq. miles	Population in thousands
GROUP I		
Japan	142,719	98,865
Population per square mile—693		
Europe (excluding U.S.S.R.)		
Albania	11,096	1,914
Austria	32,374	7,290
Belgium	11,779	9,528
Bulgaria	42,796	8,258
Czechoslovakia	49,354	14,240
Denmark	16,619	4,797
Finland	130,119	4,639
France	212,974	49,440
German Dem. Rep.	41,634	17,067
German Fed. Rep.	95,913	59,676
Greece	50,944	8,612
Hungary	35,919	10,179
Republic of Ireland	27,135	2,881
Italy	116,286	51,859
Netherlands	12,978	12,455
Norway	125,198	3,753
Poland	120,664	31,698
Portugal	35,453	9,218
Rumania	91,699	19,143
Spain	194,883	31,871
Sweden	173,634	7,808
Switzerland	15,941	5,945
United Kingdom	94,207	54,965
Yugoslavia	98,766	19,756
Population per square mile—243		
GROUP II		
Caribbean		
Cuba	44,218	7,833
Dominican Republic	18,816	3,750
Haiti	10,714	4,485
Jamaica	4,232	1,839
Puerto Rico	3,435	2,668
Trinidad and Tobago	1,980	1,000
Population per square mile—259		

	Area in sq. miles	Population in thousands
Central South Asia		
Afghanistan	250,000	15,909
Ceylon	25,332	11,500
India	1,229,215	483,000
Nepal	54,000	10,294
Pakistan	365,528	105,044
Population per square mile—325		
South-East Asia		
Burma	261,789	25,246
Cambodia	69,900	6,250
Indonesia	735,848	104,500
Laos	88,780	2,635
Malaysia	128,440	9,711
Philippines	115,830	33,477
Singapore	225	1,914
Thailand	198,455	31,500
North Viet Nam	61,293	19,000
South Viet Nam	65,948	16,543
Population per square mile—145		
East Asia		
China	3,691,502	700,000
Hong Kong	391	3,716
North Korea	46,540	12,100
South Korea	38,004	29,086
Taiwan	13,885	12,791
Population per square mile—200		
GROUP III		
North America		
Canada	3,851,809	19,919
United States of America	3,615,212	196,842
Population per square mile—9		
Temperate South America		
Argentina	1,072,646	22,691
Chile	286,397	8,591
Paraguay	157,047	2,094

	Area in sq. miles	Population in thousands
Uruguay	72,172	2,749
Population per square mile—23		
Oceania		
Australia	2,971,081	11,541
New Guinea	93,003	1,582
New Zealand	103,736	2,676
Population per square mile—5		
U.S.S.R.	8,649,489	233,180
Population per square mile—27		
GROUP IV		
Africa		
Algeria	919,591	12,102
Angola	481,351	5,154
Burundi	10,747	3,274
Cameroon Rep.	183,568	5,229
Chad	495,750	3,361
Rep. of the Congo	905,380	15,986
Dahomey	43,483	2,410
Ethiopia	471,776	23,000
Ghana	92,100	7,945
Guinea	94,925	3,608
Ivory Coast	124,503	3,835
Kenya	224,960	9,643
Liberia	43,000	1,090
Libya	679,358	1,677
Mali	464,873	4,654
Malagasy Rep.	230,036	6,420
Malawi	49,066	4,042
Moçambique	302,227	6,956
Morocco	171,305	13,451
Niger	489,189	3,433
Nigeria	356,668	57,500
Rhodesia	150,333	4,400
Rwanda	10,169	3,110
Senegal	75,750	3,490
Sierra Leone	27,699	2,403
Somali Rep.	246,200	2,500

	Area in sq. miles	Population in thousands
Rep. of South Africa	471,818	18,298
South-west Africa	325,608	574
Sudan	967,500	13,940
Tanzania	362,720	10,500
Tunisia	63,380	4,458
Uganda	93,981	7,740
United Arab Rep.	386,198	30,147
Upper Volta	95,444	4,955
Zambia	288,130	3,837
Population per square mile—30		
Central America		
Costa Rica	19,695	1,486
El Salvador	8,260	3,037
Guatemala	42,042	4,575
Honduras	43,277	2,363
Mexico	761,600	44,145
Nicaragua	57,143	1,655
Panama	28,575	1,287
Population per square mile—61		
Tropical South America		
Bolivia	424,163	3,748
Brazil	3,286,170	84,679
Colombia	455,355	18,068
Ecuador	104,506	5,326
Peru	496,222	12,012
Venezuela	352,143	9,030
Population per square mile—26		
South West Asia		
Iran	636,293	25,780
Iraq	173,259	8,338
Israel	7,992	2,629
Jordan	37,737	1,976
Lebanon	4,000	2,405
Saudi Arabia	869,803	6,750
Syria	71,210	5,300
Turkey	301,380	32,901
Yemen	75,391	4,925
Population per square mile—42		

WHAT THE WORLD IS EATING

There is nothing better for a man than that he should eat and drink — ECCLESIASTES 2

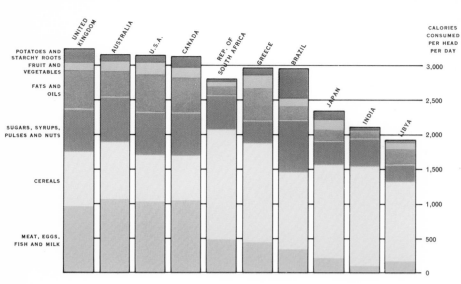

CALORIES CONSUMED PER HEAD PER DAY

EVERY day the world has to find food for more than 3,000 million human beings, and this number is steadily increasing.

We need sufficient food to give us energy (carbohydrates) and to provide the materials from which our bodies can be built and maintained (proteins), but to ensure good health our diet must include foods which provide vitamins and minerals as well.

Carbohydrates are obtained chiefly from cereals (wheat, maize, rye, oats, barley, rice, sorghums and millets), from roots and tubers (potatoes, sweet potatoes, yams and cassava), and from sugar. Proteins are obtained from meat and fish, from pulses (dry beans, peas, broad beans, lentils and chick-peas), and from nuts, oil-seeds and oil-containing fruit. Vitamins and minerals are obtained from fresh fruit and vegetables. But milk, closely followed by eggs, is a complete food in itself.

For the calculation of food values, our food consumption is measured in terms of calories. A well-balanced daily diet may contain as many as 2,000 to 3,000 calories.

Many of the well-developed countries of Western Europe, North and South America, Australia and New Zealand are able to produce or purchase enough food to ensure that a well-balanced diet is available to all their people. But in many under-developed countries primitive methods of cultivation still exist so that the amount of food produced is scarcely enough to meet the minimum requirements of the community. A daily diet of 2,000 calories or less, composed mainly of carbohydrates with only a small proportion of the vital and expensive proteins, is the typical diet of millions of people in these areas—a diet deficient in quantity and quality, resulting in the serious undernourishment of two-thirds of the world's population.

Shortages of food, in terms of quantity and quality, are not the only causes of malnutrition. Religious taboos, local customs and prejudices, ignorance of elementary hygiene and of the value of certain local foodstuffs often deny whole communities an adequate and health-giving diet. In some parts of the world, through ignorance of simple sterilization methods, mothers refuse to give their babies fresh milk because of its bad effect on them in the unsterilized state. In Uganda, tribal people value milk so little that they prefer to live on millet and root crops. In many parts of Africa cattle and goats are regarded as a measure of wealth, so that meat is rarely consumed.

Much is being done today by education, by the spread of scientific and technical knowledge, by advancing industrialization and by a proper distribution of surplus foodstuffs, to improve and increase food supplies for the rapidly growing population of the world.

TYPICAL CANADIAN DIET
Daily Consumption—oz.

Cereals	7·1
Roots and Tubers	6·5
Sugar and Syrups	4·8
Pulses and Nuts	0·5
Vegetables	6·9
Fruits	6·4
Meat and Fish	8·4
Eggs	1·6
Milk and Cheese	20·5
Oils and Fats	2·1
	64.8

TYPICAL U.S.A. DIET
Daily Consumption—oz.

Cereals	6·7
Roots and Tubers	4·7
Sugar and Syrups	4·6
Pulses and Nuts	·7
Vegetables	9·5
Fruits	7·9
Meat and Fish	8·3
Eggs	2·0
Milk and Cheese	18·8
Oils and Fats	2·1
	65·3

TYPICAL HONDURAS DIET
Daily Consumption—oz.

Cereals	11·1
Potatoes	·9
Sugar and Syrups	2·4
Pulses and Nuts	1·2
Vegetables	1·6
Fruits	26·1
Meat and Fish	1·2
Eggs	·4
Milk and Cheese	2·9
Oils and Fats	·4
	48·2

TYPICAL GAMBIAN DIE[T]
Daily Consumption—oz.
After H[arvest]

Cereals	15·4
Groundnuts	2·0
Fruits and Vegetables	2·0
Meat and Fish	1·4
Fats	·1
	20·9

TYPICAL CHILEAN DIET
Daily Consumption—oz.

Cereals	13·2
Roots and Tubers	6·9
Sugar	3·0
Pulses and Nuts	·7
Vegetables	6·5
Fruits	2·9
Meat and Fish	5·6
Eggs	·4
Milk	7·6
Oils and Fats	·7
	47·5

WINKEL'S 'TRIPEL' PROJECTION

COMPARISON OF POPULATION AND AGRICULTURAL PRODUCTION

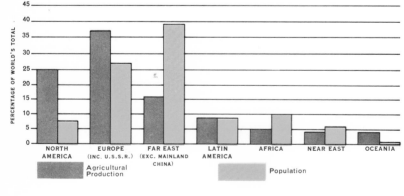

PERCENTAGE OF WORLD'S TOTAL

Agricultural Production
Population

WHEAT
WHEAT, of which there are about 650 varieties, is the most important and widely grown of all cereal crops, and is chiefly milled into flour. Wheat products are rich in carbohydrates; the whole grain contains also proteins, fats, minerals and vitamins. It is therefore a major energy food, and highly nutritious. The hard varieties are used mainly for bread, the soft for cakes, biscuits, pastry. One hard species, durum, is manufactured into spaghetti, macaroni, semolina, etc. Flat (unleavened) bread is eaten in much of Africa and Asia. In India wheat is combined with fat and made into pancake-like wafers called *chappattis*. A small part of the world's wheat production is processed into malt, dextrose and alcohol.

RYE, OATS, BARLEY
RYE is mainly produced in the poorer soils and wetter areas of the northern temperate regions, and is consumed largely in central and eastern European countries as "black" bread, which is very nutritious and more warmth-giving than other varieties of bread. OATS are hardy and also flourish in poorer soils. They have a high protein, fat and vitamin B content, and are principally used for breakfast foods, cakes, biscuits, etc. BARLEY thrives in most temperate climates and even under subarctic and subtropical conditions. It is chiefly grown in Europe for the manufacture of beer, though in parts of Scotland and Scandinavia it is made into barley bread. It is the staple food grain of North Africa and parts of Asia, where it is eaten as flatbread, porridge and pearl barley.

MAIZE
MAIZE (Indian corn), one of the most widely distributed food crops, although of great nutritive value, is not as nutritious as wheat. Sometimes the cob is roasted whole, but generally the grain is ground into meal and eaten as porridge, such as the "stirabout" of Ireland, or in cake form, such as the "johnny-cakes" of the U.S.A. It is eaten as a basic food in Mexico and in some parts of South America as *tortilla*, a flat pancake, often in conjunction with soups or fruit or vegetables such as sweet potatoes. In North America it is harvested early and eaten as "sweet corn". In northern Italy it is eaten as "polenta". Corn-flour is prepared from maize by a process of washing. Maize is used industrially as corn-starch, corn-oil and alcohol.

PRODUCTION OF MEAT AND FISH

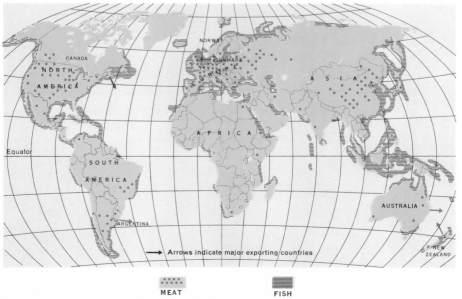

→ Arrows indicate major exporting countries

MEAT   FISH

PRODUCTION OF VEGETABLE OILS

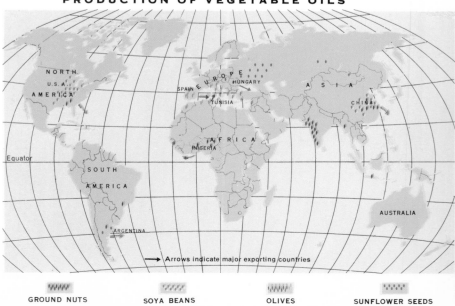

→ Arrows indicate major exporting countries

GROUND NUTS   SOYA BEANS   OLIVES   SUNFLOWER SEEDS

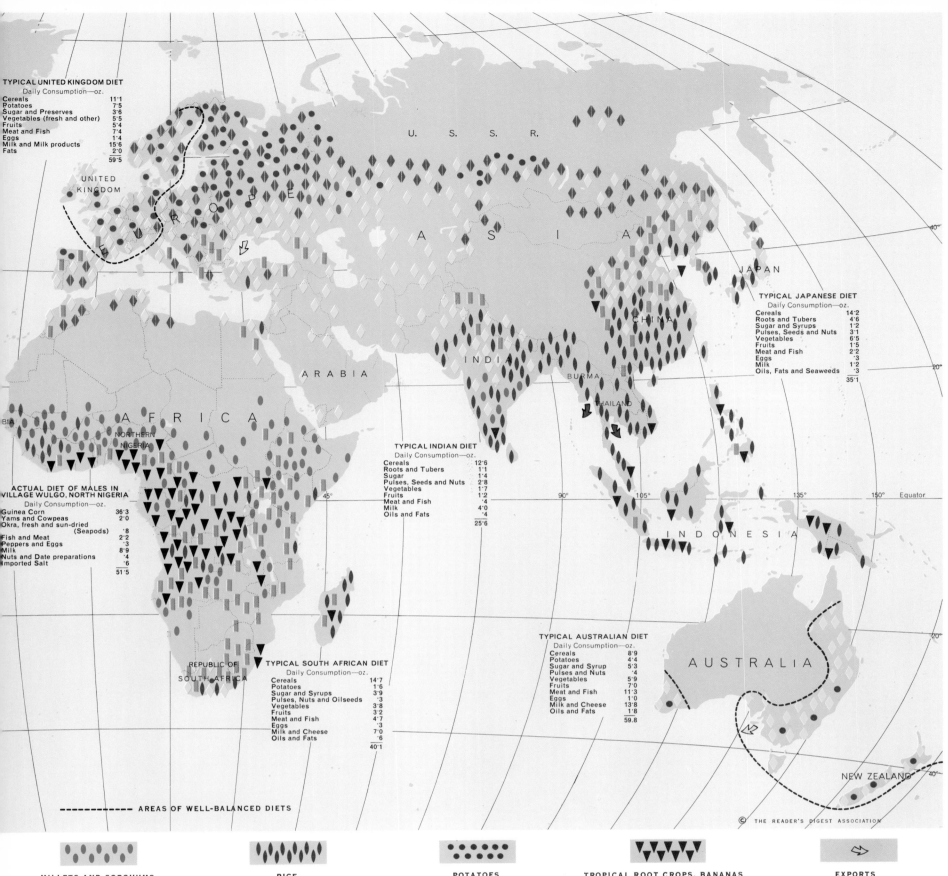

TYPICAL UNITED KINGDOM DIET
Daily Consumption — oz.

Cereals	11·1
Potatoes	7·5
Sugar and Preserves	3·6
Vegetables (fresh and other)	5·5
Fruits	5·4
Meat and Fish	7·4
Milk and Milk products	15·6
Fats	2·0
	59·5

TYPICAL JAPANESE DIET
Daily Consumption — oz.

Cereals	14·2
Roots and Tubers	4·6
Sugar and Syrups	1·2
Pulses, Seeds and Nuts	3·1
Vegetables	6·5
Fruits	1·5
Meat and Fish	2·2
Eggs	·3
Milk	1·2
Oils, Fats and Seaweeds	·3
	35·1

ACTUAL DIET OF MALES IN VILLAGE WULGO, NORTH NIGERIA
Daily Consumption — oz.

Guinea Corn	36·3
Yams and Cowpeas	2·0
Okra, fresh and sun-dried (Seapods)	·8
Fish and Meat	2·2
Peppers and Eggs	·3
Milk	8·9
Nuts and Date preparations	·3
Imported Salt	·6
	51·5

TYPICAL INDIAN DIET
Daily Consumption — oz.

Cereals	12·6
Roots and Tubers	1·1
Sugar	1·4
Pulses, Seeds and Nuts	2·8
Vegetables	1·7
Fruits	·4
Meat and Fish	·4
Milk	4·0
Oils and Fats	·6
	25·6

TYPICAL SOUTH AFRICAN DIET
Daily Consumption — oz.

Cereals	14·7
Potatoes	1·6
Sugar and Syrups	3·9
Pulses, Nuts and Oilseeds	·3
Vegetables	3·8
Fruits	1·6
Meat and Fish	4·7
Eggs	·3
Milk and Cheese	7·0
Oils and Fats	·6
	40·1

TYPICAL AUSTRALIAN DIET
Daily Consumption — oz.

Cereals	8·9
Potatoes	4·4
Sugar and Syrup	5·3
Pulses and Nuts	·4
Vegetables	5·9
Fruits	7·0
Meat and Fish	11·3
Eggs	1·0
Milk and Cheese	13·8
Oils and Fats	1·8
	59·8

- - - - - - AREAS OF WELL-BALANCED DIETS

© THE READER'S DIGEST ASSOCIATION

MILLETS AND SORGHUMS

MILLETS and SORGHUMS include a number of grain crops that respond to primitive methods of cultivation, and can withstand the drought and poor soil of some of the drier parts of the Tropics. The ear contains small round seeds which are pounded into flour, which is eaten as a gruel or porridge with a seasoned stew of vegetables, but rarely with meat. In West Africa it is made into balls of doughy paste (couscous). These balls, fried in palm or shea-nut oil are known as ''beignets'' or ''galettes'' and sold in the streets. In Northern China, millets and sorghums, as well as wheat, form the staple food. When grain is abundant, considerable quantities are brewed into beer; *pombe*, made from millet, is widely drunk in Africa. A variety of millet (prosbo)—eaten mainly as a thick porridge—is a staple food in the U.S.S.R.

RICE

There are more than 2,500 varieties of rice, more than 1,000 of them in India alone. Rice has a high energy value, though it is relatively poor nutritively. It yields more food per acre than any other grain and is widely grown and widely eaten in China, India, Japan, Burma, etc. It forms a major part of the food in these countries, where, on the whole, the diet is largely deficient in animal proteins. Among the higher income groups, the rice is always accompanied by meat and vegetables. It is commonly eaten with curry, which varies from the hot curries of India, Pakistan and Ceylon to the more subtle flavours of Malaysia and Indonesia. In China a favourite combination is with pork. The removal of its outer husk (polishing) deprives rice of much of its goodness. *Sake*, a popular and potent drink in Japan, *Arrak* in Java and *Chemshu* in China are all brewed from rice.

POTATOES

POTATOES, of which there are some 2,000 varieties, are grown in almost every country in the world, though they succeed best in the cooler regions. They contain carbohydrates, proteins, vitamins and mineral salts and are, therefore, a most valuable energy food. Among the white races they form an important part of every diet, and in some parts of Europe they are the staple food. They are generally eaten as a vegetable, but are also turned into flour and used for making bread, pastry and dumplings. Potatoes are also processed into starch and dextrose, and since the middle of the 19th century have replaced grain as a source of alcohol for commercial uses, particularly in Germany. Sweet potatoes are botanically quite different from ordinary potatoes and must be considered a tropical crop, although they have a similar food value.

TROPICAL ROOT CROPS, BANANAS

Three of the principal root crops are CASSAVA (manioc), YAMS and SWEET POTATOES. They are grown mainly in west and central Africa, the Malay Archipelago, and Latin America. The root of *sweet* cassava can be cooked and eaten directly, but the root of *bitter* cassava must be soaked in water for a few days before cooking, to extract the prussic acid. The cooked cassava is usually pounded into flour or meal and eaten as a porridge, often accompanied by yams or other vegetables. Sweet potatoes (called yams in America) grow better in drier areas, with less than 50 inches of rain. Although not root crops, BANANAS and PLANTAINS form a staple food in many tropical countries. Bananas are eaten raw and also cooked as a vegetable. Plantains are similar to bananas but contain less sugar and are usually eaten cooked. All these crops are low in protein.

EXPORTS

The arrows indicate those places from which the world's chief food cereals, wheat (yellow) and rice (brown) are exported. About 20 per cent of all the wheat produced is exported. Argentina exports one-third of her wheat production, mainly to Brazil, Peru and western Europe; Australia exports two-thirds and Canada one half, principally to Britain, China and Japan; the U.S.A. exports about half her production, mainly to India, Pakistan and Japan. The U.S.S.R. is an important exporter, but in bad harvest years she also becomes a large importer. In most years Britain is the world's largest single importer of wheat. Only about five per cent of the world's production of rice enters international trade, most of which is confined to south and south-east Asia—Burma and Thailand being the major exporters and Japan the largest importer.

PRODUCTION OF COFFEE, TEA AND SUGAR   PRODUCTION OF FRUIT

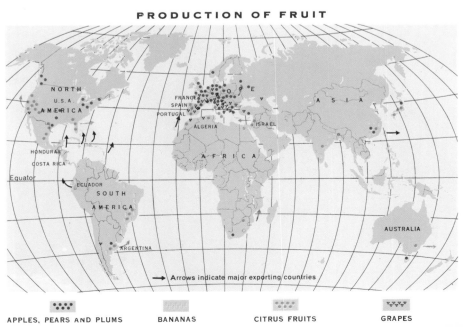

→ Arrows indicate major exporting countries

→ Arrows indicate major exporting/countries

BEET SUGAR	COFFEE	CANE SUGAR	TEA	APPLES, PEARS AND PLUMS	BANANAS	CITRUS FRUITS	GRAPES

WORLD HEALTH

I pray that in all things thou mayest prosper and be in health —3 JOHN

HEALTH may be defined as the balanced relationship of the mind, the body and the external environment. The maps on these pages are concerned with certain significant aspects of health which are related primarily to the effects of environment, diet and climate.

Types of diseases vary with latitude and with the standard of living of the community. In the more advanced communities the major health problems are cancer, diseases of the heart and circulation, and nervous and mental disorders, most of which are associated with middle and old age.

In tropical and near-tropical climates, where many of the under-developed countries are situated, infectious diseases account for the majority of deaths. The underlying causes can be found in poor hygiene and sanitation, in over-crowding and in dietary deficiencies. The very young are the most affected, and mortality in infancy and early childhood is high.

The sharp distinction which exists between the health of the peoples in advanced and under-developed countries can be seen in their expectation of life at birth, which is much lower in the under-developed countries.

It is in the under-developed regions that the population is generally increasing most rapidly, and where malnutrition and malaria are the world's most urgent health problems. The low standard of living results in inadequate supplies of food and, in particular, insufficient amounts of protein in the diet, which lead to deficiency diseases such as kwashiorkor, beriberi, pellagra, etc., and to the spread of infectious and parasitic diseases such as malaria, yellow fever, tuberculosis, cholera and bilharziasis.

Under the guidance of the United Nations Agencies (the World Health Organization, the Food and Agriculture Organization and the United Nations Children's Fund) these problems are being approached from many directions; in extending the production and consumption of cheap protein-rich foods; in the control of disease carriers such as the mosquito; in the development of preventive and curative medicine; and in improved sanitation and hygiene.

Government health organizations, often working in association with the United Nations Agencies, are actively concerned with these and many associated problems, such as the resistance to antibiotics and insecticides which some microbes, viruses, and insect and animal vectors have developed. Research into the use of new methods of prevention and control of the infectious diseases is being carried on. Mass campaigns for the eradication of yaws and smallpox and the control of leprosy and trachoma are in progress, and an international campaign against malaria is well advanced. The whole movement is towards the complete physical and mental well-being of man in every part of the world.

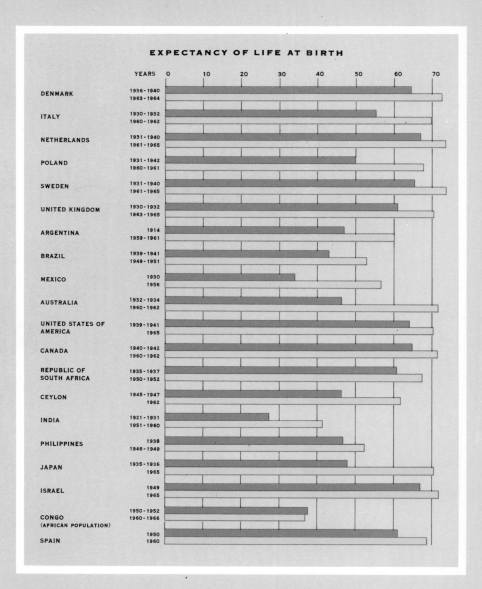

THE AREAS OF MALNUTRITION IN THE WORLD

Malnutrition uncommon

Malnutrition known to occur to an appreciable extent

No data, or sparsely inhabited

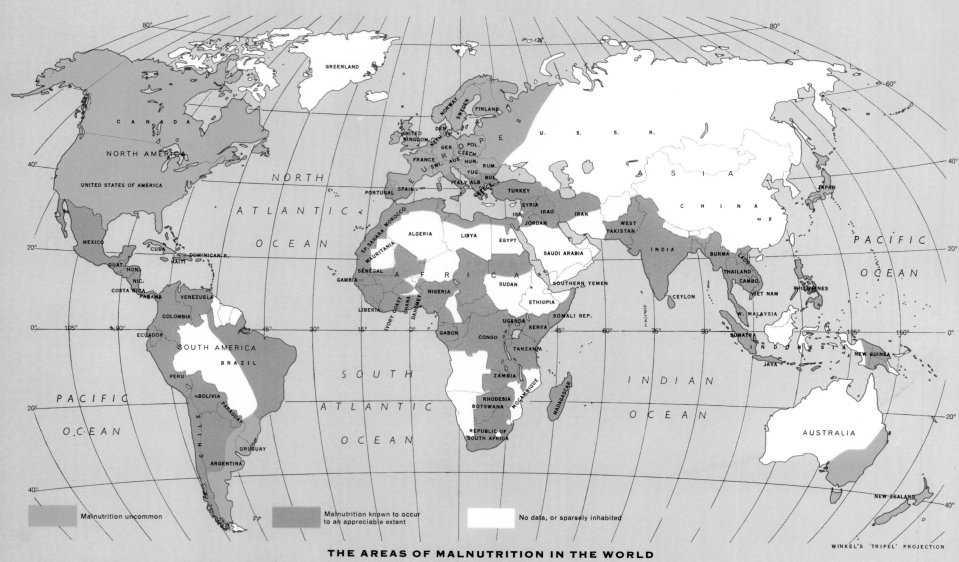

WINKEL'S 'TRIPEL' PROJECTION

The map shows roughly the areas where ill-health and disease due to diet deficiency are most common and serious. Undernutrition and malnutrition occur where the food requirements of a population are greater than its capacity for obtaining them from its own land by agriculture or from the lands of other nations by trade, that is, in countries where the birth rate is high and industrial development is low. A satisfactory diet must supply enough calories and also fulfil the body's requirements for proteins, fats, minerals and vitamins. Proteins are of special importance. The amount of animal protein in a diet often gives a rough idea of its nutritive value and an indication of the general standard of living of the population concerned. In areas of malnutrition protein supplies are much lower than in a well-fed country, such as Great Britain. In many of these areas the population is expanding rapidly and includes large numbers of young children. A sufficient quantity of protein is particularly necessary during the early years of life when the body is growing most quickly. Protein deficiency is, therefore, one of the most serious of nutritional problems.

The chart compares the birth weights and rate of increase in weight in well-nourished and malnourished infants and young children. During the early months of life a child can obtain the calories and nutrients it needs from its mother's milk, but in the period following weaning, from 6 months to 4 years, "critical" years when a good diet is particularly essential, a child in areas of malnutrition must usually subsist on his share of the meagre diet, mainly cereals and starchy roots, on which his family depends.

The high death rates in this age group, for example 1 in 11 live births in India and 1 in 17 in Mexico, as compared with 1 in 322 in Britain, are largely due to deficiencies in diet; kwashiorkor is prevalent in areas of protein deficiency, and other deficiency conditions are found in association with poor cereal diets. The common infectious diseases, such as measles and dysentery, are more likely to be fatal in children suffering from malnutrition.

While malnutrition is most prevalent in young children and expectant and nursing mothers, other groups also suffer. An insufficient and unbalanced diet impairs the health of people of all ages and thus affects their working capacity, with the result that the progress of entire communities may be retarded.

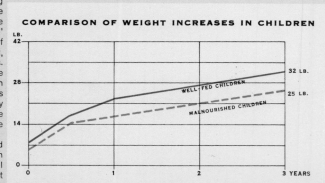

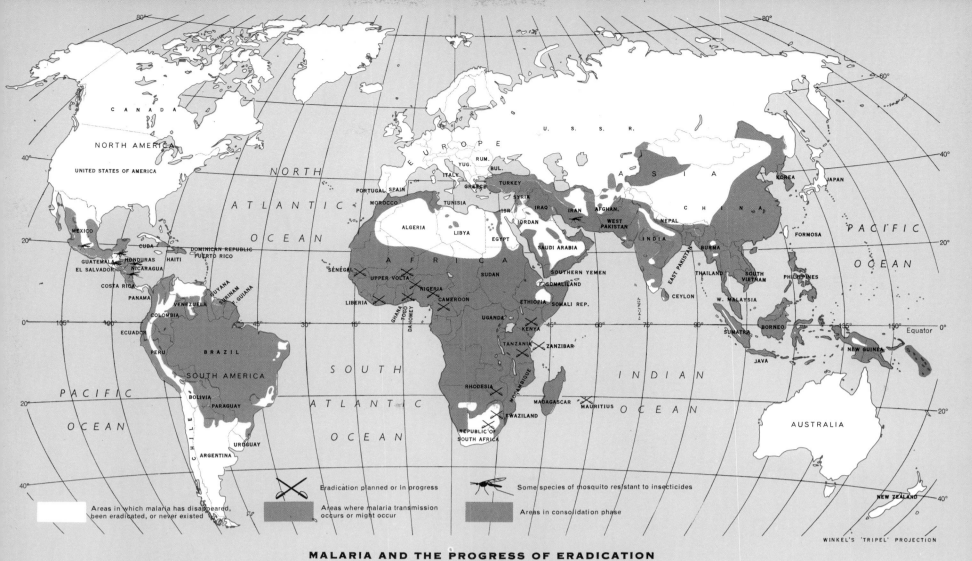

MALARIA AND THE PROGRESS OF ERADICATION

Malaria is a constant threat to half the world's population. It is man's greatest single health problem. It kills one person in five, striking first at a country's most precious possession, its children. In tropical Africa alone, one in ten of all under-fours dies from its direct effects and many thousands more from its indirect effects, for malaria weakens the organism and makes it more susceptible to other diseases. Bilharziasis, cholera, leprosy, yaws, yellow fever and tuberculosis take a heavy toll of life in tropical countries, but none is as widespread, or as costly in its effects, as malaria.

Malaria stunts man's physical and mental growth, bringing chronic ill-health to millions; it impedes the economic and social progress of a country. Hundreds of millions of working days are lost each year through the sickness it causes; vast tracts of fertile land in Africa, Asia, South and Central America, have been abandoned or left uncultivated because of its ravages.

For centuries the only effective remedy against malaria was quinine. But in 1939, armed with the knowledge accumulated since the discovery in 1880 of the cause of malaria and its communication from one person to another through *Anopheles* mosquito bites, scientists concentrated on eliminating the mosquito. D.D.T. and other insecticides sprayed on the inside walls of dwellings, where the mosquitos rest after biting, killed the insects and remained active for as long as six months after initial sprayings. By this simple method it was possible to protect the population for as little as two to three shillings per head per year. In 1948 the World Health Organization launched a series of spraying campaigns designed to

control malaria. Anti-malaria drugs, developed in the 1930's and found to be dramatically effective, particularly in the Second World War, were also used, but were more difficult to administer because of the widespread dispersal of the population in malarious areas. The number of people protected by World Health Organization campaigns increased from less than a million in 1949 to one hundred million in 1966.

In 1951 the mosquito counter-attacked. D.D.T. insecticides were becoming less effective, and in Greece the mosquito was developing a resistance to them. It became vital to interrupt the transmission of malaria and eradicate the disease before this sporadic resistance spread farther and made spraying campaigns ineffective. A world-wide campaign for the total eradication of malaria was launched.

Our map shows the progress of this campaign. By the end of 1966, of the 1,592 million people exposed to malaria, nearly 619 million were freed from its threat, 335 million were being protected by active eradication programmes, and a further 273 million will be protected within a few years. Greece, once the most malaria-ridden country in Europe, reduced its cases from one million in 1938 to very few in 1966. More than twenty countries have completely or virtually eliminated this disease, and a number of others have dramatically lowered their death rates at all ages.

Great progress has been made, but many millions of people still go unprotected. The attack on the mosquito becomes increasingly urgent as more and more species develop resistance to insecticides. Already 24 *Anopheles* species—half of them serious malaria carriers—are

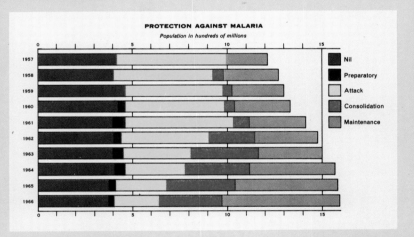

known to be immune to modern insecticides, including the most resistant species of all, *Anopheles gambiae*, which threatens over 90 per cent of the population of tropical Africa.

The total eradication of malaria is vital. Unless it is pursued energetically, the disease which has plagued man for thousands of years will spread anew throughout the world.

The above chart shows changes in the distribution of population in the originally malarious areas of the world (W.H.O. regions) by phase of malaria eradication between 1957 and 1966

HEALTH IN CANADA

Preventive, social and clinical medicine are now playing an increasingly vital part in the improvement of health.

At the beginning of the century infectious diseases—diphtheria, smallpox, typhoid and tuberculosis—accounted for about seventeen per cent of the deaths in Canada. Childbirth was often dangerous; many babies did not survive infancy; men, women and even children worked long hours; and malnutrition, insanitary living conditions and lack of public hygiene measures so encouraged the spread of sickness and disease that man's expectancy of life at birth was less than sixty years.

Higher standards in living conditions, advances in medical science and improved health care have drastically reduced the death rate from the infectious diseases. In 1966 these deaths accounted for one-half of one per cent of the total; diphtheria accounting for seven deaths compared with some 2,000 at the turn of the century, and tuberculosis deaths dropping from nearly 9,000 in 1901 to 669.

The conquest and control of these and other diseases, and the greatly improved health of the community, have come about not only by dramatic advances in medical science, but also by the development of preventive and social medicine. Better food, housing and sanitation; maternity clinics, child welfare and school health services, mass X-ray and industrial medicine; improvement in the hours and conditions of work; a new approach to the mentally ill and disabled; all have contributed to the health and well-being of the nation. The infant mortality rate of 1921 was 102 per 1,000 live births. By 1966 this had dropped dramatically to 23 per 1,000. The increase in life expectancy at one year of 4.8 years for men and 9.3 years for women from 1931-1961 indicates the better health of the people.

Accidents continue to account for an increasing number of deaths each year. In 1963 they were the leading cause of death among males aged 1 to 45 and one of the five major causes of death in older men. Health problems in recent years have tended to centre on the older age groups, and the proportion of deaths from causes which affect

them has increased. But deaths from causes that affect children and young people have declined. Cancer and cardiovascular diseases account for a large proportion of all deaths. Of the 147,367 deaths in 1963, cancer accounted for 25,077.

The increase in the figures for degenerative diseases is partly because medical science has learned to diagnose them more effectively, and partly because the population as a whole is living longer. But just as the infectious diseases are being conquered, so too it is hoped to overcome the degenerative disorders. Already early diagnosis of some forms of cancer has doubled and even trebled the rate of cure.

As medical science enables more and more people to live out the natural lifespan of threescore years and ten, and consequently to extend their working lives, the provision of special jobs for the older men and women to suit their slower reactions and declining manual dexterity, and of homes and hospital accommodation for the aged, are all part of the country's health programme.

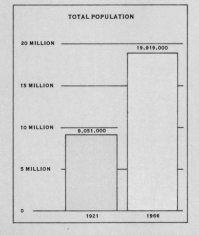

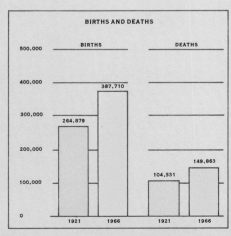

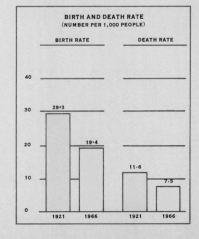

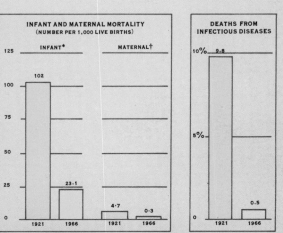

*Number of deaths of infants under 1 yr. per 1,000 live births

†Number of maternal deaths resulting from complications in pregnancy and childbirth per 1,000 live and still-births

THE MASS OF LAND

In full summer, from a point above central eastern Europe, the whole range of the Earth's surface structure can be seen. To the north a great plain stretches from the North Sea across Europe into Siberia, and finally merges into the close-packed ice-floes of the Arctic. To the south an immense desert barrier sweeps from the shores of the Atlantic in a giant scimitar curve across the north of Africa, Arabia, Turkestan, and to the Gobi. Except for the Chinese borderlands, this desert barrier has been dominated for a thousand years by the Muslim religion, so that both Europe and Christianity were shut off from the immemorial East until the Portuguese found a sea-way round Africa—an ocean ring-road round the Middle East. In Asia the mountains broaden out from the Caucasus to form the great wall of the mighty Himalayas with the Tibetan plateau behind them; and farther south lie the hot and densely populated lands of southern Asia.

In winter a view from the same point would reveal a dramatically unbroken sheet of snow stretching from the northern plain of Poland to the Pacific, demonstrating how the cold intensifies as the land recedes from the maritime western edges and reaches into the heart of the continent.

AROUND

And God saw every thing that he had made—GENESIS 1

These are views of the world as no man has ever seen it—a world exposed as a tangle of wild grandeur; as a blanket of water; as a globe roofed in ice; as illusions of light and shadow. Earth-bound man

WHERE MEN LIGHTEN THE DARKNESS

At night the populated areas of the world prick out patterns of light, clustered thickly where population is densest.

From a point directly above London we see a half-world in which live nine out of every ten of the people of the Earth. The lights of western Europe form a bright galaxy, for this region contains 85 towns with populations of 200,000 or over. Across the Atlantic, in the eastern United States, glow the lights of 40 towns of similar size. To the east are the bright clusters in Pakistan and India, in China, Japan and Indonesia—the homes of more than 1,200 million people.

Elsewhere are smaller concentrations of light—in California, on the banks of the Nile, round the coasts of the continents—almost everywhere except in the polar seas. Great black patches can be seen where unilluminated night broods over the circle of frozen northlands and over vast deserts and mountain ranges.

A CONTINENT OF ICE

Seen from a point directly over the South Pole, the Southern Hemisphere seems to be dominated by the shining ice cap that covers an island larger than the continent of Europe. In almost every direction the horizon is sea, although the tips of three continents extend into this half-world. Cape Horn, at the tip of South America, is 2,350 miles from the South Pole; Buenos Aires, the most southerly large town of South America, is 3,800 miles from it; the Cape of Good Hope, at the tip of Africa, with the port of Cape Town and the broadening mass of South Africa beyond, lies a similar distance away; Christchurch in New Zealand and Hobart in Tasmania, the largest towns near to the Pole, are 3,200 miles distant from it.

In this half-world there are only 25 towns with populations over 200,000. The stormy southern seas are deserted except for the icebergs which calve off the ice cap to drift far out into the ocean.

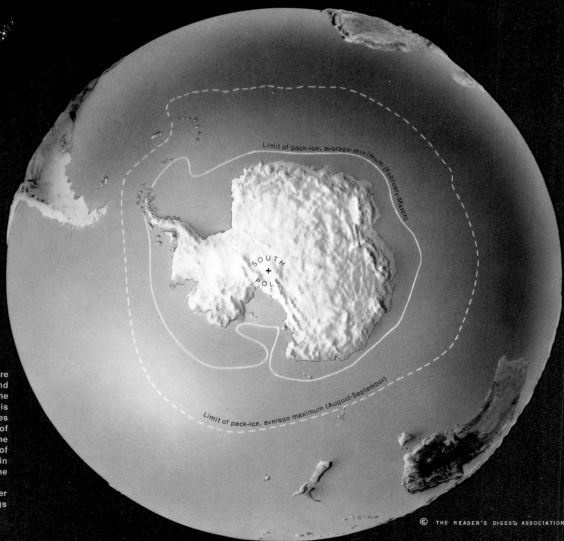

Limit of pack-ice, average minimum (February-March)

SOUTH POLE

Limit of pack-ice, average maximum (August-September)

142

THE WORLD

knows the broad truths of geography only from the jig-saw of the details he can see. Here the jig-saw has been completed; the world is seen in perspective.

Hold these pages 18 inches from your eyes. Each half-world will reveal the Earth just the size you would see it were you 25,000 miles out in space.

THE WATER PLANET

Tahiti is at the centre of this half-world—a half-world that is almost all water. The Pacific, largest of all oceans, shows its vast expanse. To the east and south of Tahiti are thousands of square miles of ocean without a single island or reef. In the western Pacific groups of tiny islands gleam white in the sunlight; far to the north Hawaii stands out as a solitary stepping stone on the 6,200 mile hop from North America to Asia. Solid land masses are far away, only just appearing on the horizon. To the south-west is Australia—with Sydney, a mere 3,801 miles from the island of Tahiti. The vast semicircle of the Americas serrates the opposite skyline; Vancouver is 4,888 miles away, Panama 5,180, Cape Horn 4,950. China and Japan lie out of sight. Tokyo is 5,893 miles from Tahiti.

Compare this hemisphere with the one to its left. There, millions of people live in the heart of Asia, and may be as far as three thousand miles from the open sea. Here, in the water hemisphere, live only a few hundred thousand people, thousands of miles from any sizeable land.

DAWN ADVANCES

Part of the world is in shadow: it is at a stage between "new Earth" and "full Earth."

Dawn, advancing at the rate of 15 degrees longitude every hour, is just reaching the Americas. The first rays of the rising sun break from the east on the hills of Nova Scotia and Brazil, while the glaciers of Greenland are already in full daylight. It is nine in London and breakfast is over, four in the morning in New York, an hour after midnight in San Francisco, and noon in Baghdad.

Only at the equinoxes in March and September does every place in the world have an equal number of hours of darkness and light. In June the tilt of the Earth's axis brings full daylight all round the clock to the North Pole. It is then midsummer in the Northern Hemisphere and midwinter in the Southern.

THE ROOF OF THE WORLD

The North Pole, with its monotonous waste of broken ice, is the hub of this crowded view. The floating ice of the North Pole merges into the surrounding land masses. Round the Arctic lies the expanse of frozen northlands of Russia and Canada. Below comes the belt of coniferous forest which rings the world from the Atlantic Ocean to the Pacific, and, jumping the 50-mile gap between Siberia and North America, sweeps on again round the globe from the Pacific Ocean to the Atlantic. Below the forest region, great towns describe another circle round the globe—Leningrad 2,070 miles from the North Pole, Glasgow 2,360, Quebec 3,000 and Edmonton 2,520. Along this ring of towns the transcontinental railways, the trunk roads, the busiest air-routes make a web of communications that is continued across the oceans by ships and planes navigating on "great circle" routes. Far on the horizon lies the belt of desert and mountain between temperate and tropical lands.

NORTH
+
POLE

FACTS ABOUT THE EARTH

Estimated age of the Earth . . at least 4,500 million years
Superficial area . . . . 196,950,000 sq. miles
Land surface . . . . 57,510,000 sq. miles
Water surface (71% of total area) . . 139,440,000 sq. miles
Equatorial circumference . . . . . . 24,902 miles
Meridional circumference . . . . . . 24,860 miles
Volume of the Earth . . . 260,000,000,000 cubic miles
Mass, or weight . . . 6,586,542,500,000,000,000,000 tons

It is estimated that the Earth attracts 14·9 tons of cosmic dust annually.

Highest point of the Earth's land surface—
Mount Everest . . . . 29,028 feet

Lowest point of the Earth's land surface—
Shores of the Dead Sea, Israel-Jordan 1,299 feet below sea level

Greatest ocean depth—Marianas Trench,
off the Philippines . . . . 36,198 feet below sea level

The Earth makes one complete revolution round the Sun every 365 days, 5 hours, 48 minutes and 46 seconds.

The Earth makes one complete rotation on its axis in 23 hours and 56 minutes.

The Earth revolves in its orbit round the Sun at a speed of 66,600 miles per hour.

The Earth rotates on its axis at an equatorial speed of more than 1,000 miles per hour.

CONTINENTS

	Area square miles	Mean Elevation feet	Highest Elevation feet	Lowest Elevation feet	Highest Recorded Temperature	Lowest Recorded Temperature
AFRICA	11,693,000	1,900	Mt. Kilimanjaro, *Tanzania* 19,340	Lake Assal, *Fr. Somaliland* 492 *below sea level*	Al Aziziyah, *Libya* 136·4°F	Semrir, *Morocco* —11·4°F
ANTARCTICA	5,150,000	6,000	Vinson Massif 16,864	Sea level	Hope Bay, *Graham Land* 59·4°F	Nr. Vostok —126·9°F
ASIA	16,943,000	3,000	Mt. Everest, *Nepal–Tibet* 29,028	Dead Sea, *Israel–Jordan* 1,299 *below sea level*	Jacobabad, *Pakistan* 127·1°F	Verkhoyansk, *Siberia* —89·9°F
AUSTRALIA	2,967,909	1,000	Mt. Kosciusko, *N. S. Wales* 7,316	Lake Eyre, *South Australia* 52 *below sea level*	Cloncurry, *Queensland* 127·5°F	Charlotte Pass, *N. S. Wales* —8·0°F
EUROPE*	4,053,300	980	Mt. El'brus, *U.S.S.R.* 18,482	Caspian Sea, *U.S.S.R.* 92 *below sea level*	Seville, *Spain* 124·0°F	Ust'-Shchugor, *U.S.S.R.* —67·0°F
NORTH AMERICA	9,365,000	2,000	Mt. McKinley, *Alaska* 20,320	Death Valley, *California* 282 *below sea level*	Death Valley, *California* 133·9°F	Snag, *Yukon* —81·0°F
SOUTH AMERICA	6,880,000	1,800	Mt. Aconcagua, *Argentina* 22,834	Salinas Grandes, *Argentina* 131 *below sea level*	Rivadavia, *Argentina* 120·0°F	Sarmiento, *Argentina* —27·4°F

* Including U.S.S.R. west of Ural'skiy Khrebet.

HIGHEST MOUNTAINS OF THE WORLD

	feet		feet		feet		feet
Everest, *Nepal-Tibet*	29,028	Nanda Devi, *India*	25,645	Muztagh Ata, *Sinkiang*	24,757	Mercedario, *Argentina*	22,211
K2 (Godwin Austen), *Kashmir-Sinkiang*	28,250	Rakaposhi, *Kashmir*	25,550	Kommunisma, (Pik), *U.S.S.R.*	24,590	Huascarán, *Peru*	22,205
Kangchenjunga, *Nepal-India*	28,209	Lamet, *India-Tibet*	25,447	Pobedy, (Pik), *U.S.S.R.-Sinkiang*	24,407	Llullaillaco, *Argentina-Chile*	22,057
Makalu, *Tibet-Nepal*	27,805	Namcha Barwa, *Tibet*	25,447	Chomolhari, *Bhutan-Tibet*	23,997	Kailas, *Tibet*	22,028
Dhaulagiri, *Nepal*	26,810	Gurla Mandhata, *Tibet*	25,355	Lenina, (Pik), *U.S.S.R.*	23,406	Yerupaja, *Peru*	21,759
Nanga Parbat, *Kashmir*	26,660	Ulugh Muztagh, *Tibet*	25,338	Aconcagua, *Argentina*	22,834	Ancohuma, *Bolivia*	21,490
Annapurna, *Nepal*	26,504	Kungur, *Sinkiang*	25,325	Illimani, *Bolivia*	22,579	Sajama, *Bolivia*	21,390
Gasherbrum, *Kashmir*	26,470	Tirich Mir, *Pakistan*	25,230	Ojos del Salado, *Chile-Argentina*	22,539	Illampu, *Bolivia*	21,276
Gosainthan, *Tibet*	26,291	Amne Machin, *China*	25,000	Bonete, *Argentina*	22,546	Coropuna, *Peru*	21,079
		Minya Konka, *China*	24,903	Tupungato, *Chile*	22,310	Chimborazo, *Ecuador*	20,577

The total number of active volcanoes is 485, and the most violent eruption on record is that of Krakatoa (Indonesia) in 1833

PRINCIPAL OCEANS AND SEAS OF THE WORLD

	Area sq. miles	Average Depth in feet	Greatest Depth in feet		Area sq. miles	Average Depth in feet	Greatest Depth in feet		Area sq. miles	Average Depth in feet	Greatest Depth in feet
Pacific Ocean	63,986,000	14,040	36,198	Bering Sea	878,000	1,665	13,422	Hudson Bay	472,000	440	1,500
Atlantic Ocean	31,530,000	12,880	30,143	Caribbean Sea	750,000	8,400	23,750	Japan, Sea of	405,000	4,835	10,200
Indian Ocean	28,350,000	13,000	22,968	Gulf of Mexico	700,000	4,700	12,426	North Sea	221,000	180	1,998
Arctic Ocean	5,541,600	4,200	17,850	Okhotsk, Sea of	582,000	3,000	12,621	Red Sea	178,000	1,490	7,254
Mediterranean Sea	1,145,000	4,500	14,435	East China Sea	480,000	610	10,500	Black Sea	168,500	4,300	7,362
South China Sea	895,000	5,400	16,456	Yellow Sea	480,000	160	348	Baltic Sea	158,000	221	1,300

LONGEST RIVERS OF THE WORLD

	miles		miles		miles		miles
Nile, *Africa*	4,090	Hwang Ho (Yellow), *China*	2,700	Volga, *U.S.S.R.*	2,290	Purus, *South America*	1,850
Amazon, *South America*	4,050	Lena, *U.S.S.R.*	2,645	Madeira, *South America*	2,100	Brahmaputra, *Asia*	1,800
Mississippi—Missouri, *U.S.A.*	3,760	Mackenzie, *Canada*	2,635	Paraná, *South America*	2,050	Orinoco, *South America*	1,800
Irtysh, *U.S.S.R.*	3,200	Mekong, *Asia*	2,600	Indus, *Asia*	1,980	São Francisco, *S. America*	1,800
Yangtze, *China*	3,100	Niger, *Africa*	2,600	Yukon, *Alaska*	1,979	Danube, *Europe*	1,770
Amur, *Asia*	2,900	Yenisey, *U.S.S.R.*	2,360	St. Lawrence, *Canada*	1,945	Salween, *Burma–China*	1,750
Congo, *Africa*	2,718	Murray—Darling, *Australia*	2,310	Rio Grande, *U.S.A.*	1,885	Euphrates, *Asia*	1,700

PRINCIPAL LAKES OF THE WORLD

	sq. miles		sq. miles		sq. miles		sq. miles
Caspian Sea, *U.S.S.R.–Iran (salt)*	170,000	Tanganyika, *East Central Africa*	12,700	Ontario, *U.S.A.–Canada*	7,540	Athabasca, *Canada*	3,058
Superior, *U.S.A.–Canada*	31,820	Great Bear, *Canada*	11,660	Balkhash, *U.S.S.R.*	7,050	Nicaragua, *Nicaragua*	3,000
Victoria, *East Central Africa*	26,200	Baykal, *U.S.S.R.*	11,580	Ladoga, *U.S.S.R.*	7,000	Reindeer, *Canada*	2,440
Aral, *U.S.S.R. (salt)*	24,400	Great Slave, *Canada*	11,170	Onega, *U.S.S.R.*	3,800	Torrens, *Australia (salt)*	2,400
Huron, *U.S.A.–Canada*	23,010	Erie, *U.S.A.–Canada*	9,940	Eyre, *Australia (salt)*	3,700	Koko Nor, *China (salt)*	2,300
Michigan, *U.S.A.*	22,400	Winnipeg, *Canada*	9,398	Rudolf, *Kenya (salt)*	3,500	Issyk-Kul', *U.S.S.R.*	2,276
Nyasa, *East Central Africa*	14,200	Chad, *North Central Africa*	8,000	Titicaca, *Peru-Bolivia*	3,200	Vänern, *Sweden*	2,150

SECTION FOUR

INDEX

PART ONE—CANADA

PAGES 30-40

LIST OF ABBREVIATIONS

Alta. Alberta
Arch. Archipelago, Archipel
Atl. Oc. Atlantic Ocean
B. Bay, Baie
B.C. British Columbia
Br. British
C. Cape, Cap.
Can. Canal
Chan. Channel
Co. County
Cr. Creek
Dist. District
E. East, Eastern
Fd. Fiord, Fjord
Fed. Dist. Federal District
Fr. French
G. Gulf
Gt. Great
Harb. Harbour
Hd. Head
Hist. Historical
I. Island, Islet, Île, Îlet
Internat. International
Is. Islands, Isles, Îles
Junc. Junction
L. Lake, Lac
Lit. Little
Lt. Ho. Light House
Man. Manitoba
Me. Maine
Mt. Mountain, Mount
N. North, Northern
Nat. National
N.B. New Brunswick
Nfd. Newfoundland
N.S. Nova Scotia
N.-W. Terr. North West Territories
Oc. Ocean
Ont. Ontario
Pac. Pacific
Pass. Passage
P.E.I. Prince Edward Island
Pen. Peninsula
Pk. Peak, Park
Plat. Plateau
Prom. Promontory
Prov. Province, Provincial
Pt., Pte. Point, Pointe
Que. Quebec
R. River, Rivière
Ra. Range
Reg. Region
Res. Reservoir
S. South, Southern
Sask. Saskatchewan
Sd. Sound
St., Ste. Saint, Sainte
Sta. Station
Str. Strait

Abbey, *Saskatchewan* 36 J 8
Abbotsford, *B.C.* 39 M 11
Abee, *Alberta* 36 E 4
Abercorn, *Quebec* 35 S 7
Aberdeen, *Saskatchewan* 36 L 6
Aberdeen L., *N.-W. Terr.* 38 Y 3
Abernethy, *Manitoba* 37 O 8
Abilene, *Alberta* 37 F 4
Abitau L., *N.-W. Terr.* 38 U 5
Abitibi, *Ontario* 34 K 3
Abitibi L., *Ontario* 34 K 4
Abitibi R., *Ontario* 34 J 2
Abitibi R., Little, *Ontario* 34 J 2
Abitibi Canyon Dam, *Ont.* 34 J 3
Abord à Plouffe, *Quebec* 35 Q 9
Abound, *Saskatchewan* 37 M 8
Abraham, Plains of, *Que.* 35 S 3
Abruzzi, Mt., *B.C.* 36 B 8
Acadia Valley, *Alberta* 36 G 7
Acheninni L., *Saskatchewan* 37 P 6
Achigan, *Ontario* 34 F 6
Achray, *Ontario* 35 N 7
Acme, *Alberta* 36 D 7
Acton, *Ontario* 34 K 9
Acton Vale, *Quebec* 35 S 7
Adair, *Manitoba* 37 O 8
Adamant Mt., *B.C.* 39 P 10
Adams L., *B.C.* 39 O 10
Adamsville, *Quebec* 35 S 7
Adanac, *Saskatchewan* 36 H 6
Adelaide Pen., *N.-W. Terr.* 38 Z 1
Adlavik Is., *Labrador* 31 O 7
Admiral, *Saskatchewan* 36 J 9
Admiralty Inlet, *N.-W. Terr.* 31 L 3
Admiralty I., *N.-W. Terr.* 38 X 1
Advocate Harbour, *Nova Scotia* 32 H 8
Aetna, *Alberta* 36 D 9
Again, R., *Quebec* 35 L 2
Agassiz, *British Columbia* 39 N 11
Agawa, *Ontario* 34 F 5
Agawa, R., *Ontario* 34 F 5
Agnes L., *Ontario* 37 L 2
Aguanish, *Quebec* 33 K 3
Aguanus R., *Quebec* 33 K 3
Aguasabon Dam, *Ontario* 34 C 4
Ahuntsic, *Quebec* 35 R 9
Aigle, L. à l', *Quebec* 32 G 2
Ailsa Craig, *Ontario* 34 J 9
Ainslie, L., *C. Breton I., Nova Scotia* 33 L 7
Airdrie, *Alberta* 36 C 7
Air Force I., *N.-W. Terr.* 31 M 4
Aishihik & L., *Yukon* 38 E 5
Aiyansh, *Br. Columbia* 39 J 8
Ajax, *Ontario* 35 L 9
Akimiski I., *James B., N.-W. Terr.* 31 L 7
Aklavik, *N.-W. Terr.* 38 F 1
Akpatok I., *N.-W. Terr.* 31 N 5
Akron, *Ontario* 34 F 4
Alameda, *Saskatchewan* 37 P 9
Alaska, *N. America* 30 C 4
Alaska Highway, *Alaska/Canada* 39 M 7
Albanel, *Quebec* 35 S 4
Albany, *Nova Scotia* 32 G 9
Albany R., *Ontario* 34 F 2
Alberni, *Vancouver I., B.C.* 39 L 11
Albert, *New Brunswick* 32 H 8
Alberta, prov., *Canada* 30 H 7
Alberta, Mt., *Alberta* 39 P 9
Alberton, *Prince Edward I.* 32 H 7
Albertville, *Saskatchewan* 37 M 5
Albreda, *Br. Columbia* 39 O 9
Alcantara L., *N.-W. Terr.* 38 T 5
Alcomdale, *Alberta* 36 D 5
Alderson, *Alberta* 36 F 8
Aldersyde, *Alberta* 36 D 8
Alert Bay, *Br. Columbia* 39 K 10
Alert, *N.-W. Terr.* 31 N 1
Alexander, *Manitoba* 37 R 9
Alexander C., *N.-W. Terr.* 38 U 1
Alexandria, *Br. Columbia* 39 M 9
Alexandria, *Ontario* 35 Q 7
Alexis B., *Labrador* 31 O 7
Alexis Creek, *B.C.* 39 M 9
Alexis R., *Labrador* 31 P 1
Alexo, *Alberta* 36 B 6
Algoma, *Ontario* 34 H 6
Algonquin Park, *Ontario* 35 M 7
Algonquin Prov. Park, *Ontario* 35 M 7
Alice Arm, *Br. Columbia* 39 J 8
Alida, *Saskatchewan* 37 Q 9
Alix, *Alberta* 36 D 6
Allan, *Saskatchewan* 36 L 7
Allan Water, *Ontario* 37 N 1
Allard, L., *Quebec* 32 J 3
Allard, R., *Quebec* 35 N 3
Allardville, *N.B.* 32 G 6
Allenford, *Ontario* 34 J 8
Alliance, *Alberta* 36 F 6
Allison Harbour, *B.C.* 39 K 10
Alliston, *Ontario* 34 L 8
Allumette I., *Quebec* 35 N 7
Ally, *Quebec* 35 R 3
Alma, *New Brunswick* 32 H 8
Alma, *Quebec* 35 T 4
Alma Pk., *Br. Columbia* 39 K 7
Almonte, *Ontario* 35 O 7
Alonsa, *Manitoba* 37 T 8
Alright I., *Madeleine Is., Quebec* 33 L 6
Alsask, *Saskatchewan* 36 H 7
Alsek, R., *Br. Columbia* 38 E 6
Altario, *Alberta* 36 G 7
Altona, *Manitoba* 37 U 9
Alvena, *Saskatchewan* 37 L 6
Alverstone, Mt., *Yukon* 38 D 5
Alvinston, *Ontario* 34 J 10
Amadjuak L., *N.-W. Terr.* 31 M 4
Amaranth, *Manitoba* 37 T 8
Amazon, *Saskatchewan* 37 M 7
Amberley, *Ontario* 34 J 8
Ambition, Mt., *B.C.* 39 H 7
Amesbury, *Alberta* 36 E 3
Amescale, *Ontario* 36 J 1
Ameson, *Ontario* 34 F 3
Amherst, *Nova Scotia* 32 H 8
Amherst I., *Ontario* 35 O 8
Amherst I, *Madeleine Is., Quebec* 33 L 6
Amherstburg, *Ontario* 34 G 10
Amisk, *Alberta* 36 F 6
Amisk L., *Saskatchewan* 37 P 4
Amiskwumiska L., *Que.* 35 O 2
Amos, *Quebec* 35 M 4
Amqui, *Quebec* 32 E 5
Amund Ringnes I., *N.-W. Terr.* 31 K 2
Amundsen G., *N.-W. Terr.* 38 L 1
Amyot, *Ontario* 34 F 4
Anahim Lake, *B.C.* 39 L 9
Anama Bay, *Manitoba* 37 T 7
Ancienne Lorette, airport, *Quebec* 35 T 6
Anderson B., *N.-W. Terr.* 38 V 1
Anderson, R., *N.-W. Terr.* 38 J 1
Andover, *New Brunswick* 32 E 7
Andrew, *Alberta* 36 E 5
Androscoggin R., *Maine* 32 B 9
Anerley, *Saskatchewan* 36 K 7
Aneroid, *Saskatchewan* 36 K 9
Angikuni L., *N.-W. Terr.* 31 K 5
Angler, *Ontario* 34 D 4
Anglia, *Saskatchewan* 36 J 7
Angliers, *Quebec* 35 L 5
Anguille, C. & Mts., *Newfoundland* 33 N 6
Angus, *Ontario* 34 L 8
Angusville, *Manitoba* 37 Q 8
Annacis I., *Br. Columbia* 39 J 12
Annapolis R., *Nova Scotia* 32 G 9
Annapolis Royal, *Nova S.* 32 G 9
Annieopsquotch Mts., *Newfoundland* 33 P 5
Anse-au-Griffon, *Quebec* 32 H 5
Anse au Loup, *Labrador* 33 Q 2
Ansonville, *Ontario* 34 K 4
Antelope, *Saskatchewan* 36 J 8
Anticosti I., *Quebec* 32 J 4
Antigonish, *Nova Scotia* 33 K 8
Antler, *Saskatchewan* 37 Q 9
Antler R., *Man./Sask.* 37 Q 9
Apenganau L., *Manitoba* 37 S 3
Anville, *Quebec* 35 P 3
Anyox, *Br. Columbia* 39 J 8
Anzac, *Alberta* 39 S 7
Apple River, *Nova Scotia* 32 H 8
Apsley, *Ontario* 35 M 8
Ara L., *Ontario* 34 C 2
Arabian L., *Quebec* 33 N 3
Arborfield, *Saskatchewan* 37 O 5
Arborg, *Manitoba* 37 U 8
Arcadia, *Alberta* 36 A 3
Archerwill, *Saskatchewan* 37 O 6
Archive, *Saskatchewan* 37 M 8
Arcola, *Saskatchewan* 37 P 9
Arctic Bay, *N.-W. Terr.* 31 L 3
Arctic Red, R., *N.-W. Terr.* 38 G 2
Arctic Red River, *N.-W. Terr.* 38 G 2
Ardath, *Saskatchewan* 36 K 7
Ardbeg, *Ontario* 34 K 7
Arden, *Manitoba* 36 S 8
Arden, *Ontario* 35 O 8
Ardill, *Saskatchewan* 37 M 9
Ardley, *Alberta* 36 D 6
Ardmore, *Alberta* 36 G 4
Ardrossan, *Alberta* 36 D 5
Arelee, *Saskatchewan* 36 K 6
Arena, *Saskatchewan* 36 H 9
Argenson, L. d', *Quebec* 35 R 3
Argent, R. à l', *Quebec* 32 C 3
Argenta, *B.C.* 39 P 10
Argentia, *Newfoundland* 33 S 6
Argyle, *Nova Scotia* 32 G 10
Arichat, *C. Breton I., N.S.* 33 M 8
Aristazabal I., *Br. Columbia* 39 J 9
Arkell, Mt., *Yukon* 38 F 5
Arkona, *Ontario* 34 J 9
Armada, *Alberta* 36 E 8
Armagh, *Quebec* 32 B 7
Armark L., *N.-W. Terr.* 38 X 2
Armit, *Saskatchewan* 37 Q 6
Armley, *Saskatchewan* 37 N 5
Arms, *Ontario* 34 D 3
Armstrong, *Br. Columbia* 39 O 10
Armstrong, *Ontario* 37 O 1
Arnaud, *Manitoba* 37 U 9
Arnand, R., *Quebec* 31 M 6
Arnot, *Manitoba* 37 V 3
Arnprior, *Ontario* 35 O 7
Arnstein, *Ontario* 34 L 7
Arntfield, *Quebec* 35 L 4
Aroostook Junc., *N.B.* 32 E 7
Arpin, *Ontario* 34 K 4
Arran, *Saskatchewan* 37 Q 7
Arrandale, *Br. Columbia* 39 J 8
Arrow L., *Ontario* 37 N 2
Arrow L., Lower, *B.C.* 39 O 11
Arrow L., Upper, *B.C.* 39 P 10
Arrow Park, *B.C.* 39 O 10
Arrowhead, *Br. Columbia* 39 P 10
Arrowwood, *Alberta* 36 D 8
Arsenault L., *Sask.* 36 J 3
Arseno L., *N.-W. Terr.* 38 Q 3
Arthabaska, *Quebec* 35 T 6
Arthur, *Ontario* 34 K 9
Artillery L., *N.-W. Terr.* 38 T 4
Artland, *Saskatchewan* 36 H 6
Arvida, *Quebec* 35 T 4
Asbestos, *Quebec* 35 T 7
Ashcroft, *Br. Columbia* 39 N 10
Ashern, *Manitoba* 37 T 7
Ashland, *Maine* 32 D 7
Ashmont, *Alberta* 36 F 4
Ashton, *Ontario* 35 O 7
Ashuanipi, L., *Quebec* 31 N 7
Ashuapmuchuan, R., *Que.* 35 R 3
Aspy B., *C. Breton I., N.S.* 33 M 7
Asquith, *Saskatchewan* 36 K 6
Assean L., *Manitoba* 37 V 2
Assigny, L., *Quebec* 32 G 2
Assiniboia, *Saskatchewan* 37 M 9
Assiniboine, Mt., *Br. Columbia/Alberta* 39 Q 10
Assiniboine R., *Manitoba/Saskatchewan* 37 T 9
Assinica L., *Quebec* 35 P 2
Assumption, *Alberta* 39 O 6
Astorville, *Ontario* 35 L 6
Athabasca, *Alberta* 36 D 4
Athabasca, L., *Sask./Alta.* 38 T 6
Athabasca, R., *Alberta* 39 S 7
Athapap, *Manitoba* 37 Q 4
Athapapuskow L., *Man.* 37 Q 4
Athens, *Ontario* 35 P 8
Atherley, *Ontario* 35 L 8
Aticonipi L., *Quebec* 33 N 2
Atik, *Manitoba* 37 Q 4
Atikameg, *Alberta* 36 B 3
Atikameg L., *Manitoba* 37 Q 4
Atikokan, *Ontario* 36 L 2
Atikonak L., *Labrador* 32 H 1
Atikwa L., *Ontario* 36 J 1
Atkinson Pt., *Br. Columbia* 39 G 11
Atkinson Pt., *N.-W. Terr.* 38 H 1
Atlee, *Alberta* 36 G 8
Atlin & L., *Br. Columbia* 38 G 6
Atnarko, *Br. Columbia* 39 L 9
Attawapiskat, *Ontario* 31 L 7
Attawapiskat, R. *Ontario* 31 L 7
Atwater, *Saskatchewan* 37 P 8
Atwood, *Ontario* 34 J 9
Aubry L., *N.-W. Terr.* 38 K 2
Auburn, *Maine* 32 B 9
Auden, *Ontario* 34 C 2
Augusta, *Maine* 32 C 9
Augusta Mt., *Yukon* 38 C 5
Aulneau Pen., *Ontario* 36 H 1
Aurora, *Ontario* 35 L 9
Auteuil L. d', *Quebec* 33 L 3
Authier, *Quebec* 35 M 4
Avalon Pen., *Newfoundland* 33 T 6
Avola, *Br. Columbia* 39 O 10
Avonlea, *Saskatchewan* 37 M 8
Awry L., *N.-W. Terr.* 38 Q 4
Axel Heiberg I., *N.-W. Terr.* 31 K 1
Aylen L., *Ontario* 35 N 7
Aylesbury, *Saskatchewan* 37 M 8
Aylesford, *Nova Scotia* 32 H 8
Aylesworth, Mt., *B.C.* 38 G 6
Aylmer, *Ontario* 34 K 10
Aylmer, *Quebec* 35 P 7
Aylmer L., *N.-W. Terr.* 38 T 3
Aylmer, Mt., *Alberta* 36 B 7
Aylsham, *Saskatchewan* 37 O 5
Aylwin, *Quebec* 35 O 7
Babbage, R., *Yukon* 38 D 1
Babine, *Br. Columbia* 39 K 8
Babine L., *Br. Columbia* 39 L 8
Babine Ra., *Br. Columbia* 39 K 8
Babine, R., *Br. Columbia* 39 K 8
Baccaro Pt., *Nova Scotia* 32 G 10
Bache Pen., *N.-W. Terr.* 31 M 2
Back L., *N.-W. Terr.* 38 T 4
Back R., *N.-W. Terr.* 38 Z 2
Backbone Ranges, *N.-W. Terr.* 38 J 4
Baddeck, *C. Breton I., N.S.* 33 M 7
Baden, *Manitoba* 37 Q 6
Badger, *Manitoba* 36 F 1
Badger, *Newfoundland* 33 Q 5
Baffin B., *Greenland/Canada* 31 M 3
Baffin I., *N.-W. Terr.* 31 L 3
Bagotville, *Quebec* 32 B 5
Baie Carrière, *Quebec* 35 N 5
Baie Comeau, *Quebec* 32 D 4
Baie-du-Milieu, *Quebec* 33 P 2
Baie du Vin, *New Brunswick* 32 G 6
Baie Johan Beetz, *Quebec* 32 K 3
Baie Ste. Catherine, *Que.* 32 C 5
Baie Ste. Clair, *Anticosti I., Quebec* 32 H 4
Baie St. Paul, *Quebec* 32 B 6
Baie-Trinité, *Quebec* 32 E 4
Baie Verte, *Newfoundland* 33 Q 4
Baillie Is., *N.-W. Terr.* 38 J 1
Baillie R., *N.-W. Terr.* 38 V 3
Baillie Hamilton I., *N.-W. Terr.* 31 K 2
Baker L., *N.-W. Terr.* 31 K 5
Baker Foreland, *N.-W. T.* 31 K 5
Baker Lake, *N.-W. Terr.* 31 K 5
Bala, *Ontario* 35 L 7
Balcarres, *Saskatchewan* 37 O 8
Baldock L., *Manitoba* 37 T 2
Baldwinton, *Saskatchewan* 36 H 6
Baldy Mt., *Manitoba* 37 R 7
Balfour, *Br. Columbia* 39 P 11
Balgonie, *Saskatchewan* 37 N 8
Baljennie, *Saskatchewan* 36 K 6
Ball, Mt., *Alberta* 36 B 7
Ballantyne Str., *N.-W. Terr.* 30 H 2
Balmoral, *Manitoba* 37 U 8
Balsam L., *Ontario* 35 M 8
Balzac, *Alberta* 36 D 7
Bamfield, *Br. Columbia* 39 L 11
Bancroft, *Ontario* 35 N 7
Banff, *Alberta* 39 Q 10
Banff Nat. Park, *Alberta* 39 P 10
Bangor, *Maine* 32 D 9
Bangor, *Saskatchewan* 37 P 8
Banks I., *Br. Columbia* 39 H 9
Banks I., *N.-W. Terr.* 30 G 3
Bannockburn, *Ontario* 35 N 8
Baptiste, *Ontario* 35 M 7
Barachois, *Quebec* 32 H 5
Barbara L., *Ontario* 34 C 3
Barbel, L., *Quebec* 32 D 2
Bardoux, L., *Quebec* 32 E 2
Barge Bay, *Labrador* 33 Q 2
Bar Harbor, *Maine* 32 D 9
Baring, C., *Victoria I., N.-W. Terr.* 38 P 1
Bark L., *Ontario* 34 H 6
Barkerville, *Br. Columbia* 39 N 9
Barlow, *Yukon* 38 E 4
Barlow L., *N.-W. Terr.* 38 W 4
Barn Mt., *Quebec* 32 H 5
Barnaby River, *N.B.* 32 G 7
Barnes Icecap, *N.-W. T.* 31 M 3
Barnet, *Br. Columbia* 39 H 11
Barnwell, *Alberta* 36 E 9
Barons, *Alberta* 36 D 9
Barraute, *Quebec* 35 N 4
Barrhead, *Alberta* 36 C 4
Barrie, *Ontario* 35 L 8
Barrie I., *Ontario* 34 H 6
Barrière, *Br. Columbia* 39 N 10
Barrington, *Nova Scotia* 32 G 10
Barrington L., *Manitoba* 37 R 1
Barrington Passage, *N.S.* 32 G 10
Barrow Str., *N.-W. Terr.* 31 K 3
Barrows, *Manitoba* 37 Q 6
Barrys Bay, *Ontario* 35 N 7
Bartibog, *N.B.* 32 G 6
Bartlett L., *N.-W. Terr.* 38 O 4
Bartlett's Harbour, *Newfoundland* 33 P 3
Bartouville, *Quebec* 35 N 4
Barwick, *Ontario* 36 H 2
Bashaw, *Alberta* 36 E 6
Basin L., *Saskatchewan* 37 M 6
Baskatong, Res., *Quebec* 35 P 6
Bassano, *Alberta* 36 E 8
Bass River, *Nova Scotia* 32 J 8
Basswood, *Manitoba* 37 R 8
Basswood L., *Minn./Ont.* 36 L 2
Bastille, L., *Quebec* 32 L 2
Batchawana, *Ontario* 34 F 6
Bateman, *Saskatchewan* 36 L 9
Bath, *Maine* 32 C 10
Bath, *New Brunswick* 32 E 7
Bathurst, *New Brunswick* 32 G 6
Bathurst, C., *N.-W. Terr.* 38 K 1
Bathurst Inlet, *N.-W. Terr.* 38 U 2
Bathurst I., *N.-W. Terr.* 30 J 2
Bathurst Inlet, *N.-W. Terr.* 38 T 2
Batiscan, *Quebec* 35 S 6
Batiscan, L., *Quebec* 35 T 5
Batoche, *Saskatchewan* 37 L 6
Battle R., *Alberta* 36 F 6
Battle Creek, *Sask.* 36 H 9
Battleford, *Saskatchewan* 36 J 6
Battle Harbour, *Labrador* 33 R 1
Battrum, *Saskatchewan* 36 J 8
Bauld, C., *Newfoundland* 33 R 2
Bawk, *Ontario* 34 D 3
Bawlf, *Alberta* 36 E 6
Bay Pt., *Br. Columbia* 39 K 10
Bay Bulls, *Newfoundland* 33 T 6
Bay de Verde, *Nfd.* 33 T 5
Bay du Nord, *Nfd.* 33 R 6
Bayfield, *Ontario* 34 J 9
Bayfield I., *Quebec* 33 O 2
Bayfield Mt., *Quebec* 32 F 5
Bay L'Argent, *Nfd.* 33 R 6
Bay Roberts, *Newfoundland* 33 T 6
Bays, L. of, *Ontario* 35 L 7
Baysville, *Ontario* 35 L 7
Bazin, R., *Quebec* 35 Q 5
Beachburg, *Ontario* 35 O 7
Beach Grove, *B.C.* 39 H 12
Beacon Hill, *Saskatchewan* 36 H 4
Beale, C., *Vancouver I., B.C.* 39 L 11
Beamsville, *Ontario* 35 L 9
Bear Creek, *Yukon* 38 D 4
Bear Creek, *Yukon* 38 E 5
Bear Hills, The, *Sask.* 36 J 7
Bear I., *James B., N.-W. T.* 31 L 7
Bear L., *Manitoba* 37 V 3
Bear Lake, *B.C.* 39 K 7
Beardmore, *Ontario* 34 C 3
Bear Head, *Anticosti I., Quebec* 33 K 4
Bear Island, *Ontario* 34 K 6
Béarn, *Quebec* 35 L 5
Béarn, *Quebec* 35 M 4
Bear River, *Nova Scotia* 32 G 9
Bearskin Lake, *Ontario* 31 K 7
Beatton R., *Br. Columbia* 39 N 7
Beatton River, *B.C.* 39 N 7
Beatty, *Saskatchewan* 37 N 6
Beattyville, *Quebec* 35 N 4
Beaucanton, *Quebec* 35 L 3
Beauceville, *Quebec* 32 B 7
Beauchêne, L., *Quebec* 35 M 6
Beaudry, *Quebec* 35 L 4
Beaufort Sea. *N.-W. T. etc.* 30 E 3
Beauharnois, *Quebec* 35 R 7
Beauharnois Power Can., *Quebec* 35 Q 7
Beaumont, *Newfoundland* 33 R 4
Beauport, *Quebec* 35 T 1
Beauséjour, *Manitoba* 37 V 8
Beauvais Lake Prov. Park, *Alberta* 36 C 9
Beauval, *Saskatchewan* 36 K 3
Beauvallon, *Alberta* 36 F 5
Beaver R., *Alberta* 36 F 4
Beaver R., *Saskatchewan* 36 K 4
Beaver, R., *Yukon* 38 L 5
Beaver Bank, *Nova Scotia* 32 J 9
Beaver Brook, *N.B.* 32 G 6
Beaver Creek, *Yukon* 38 C 4
Beaverdell, *B.C.* 39 O 11
Beaverhill L., *Alberta* 36 E 5
Beaverhill L., *N.-W. Terr.* 39 V 4
Beaver Island L., *Quebec* 33 O 2
Beaverlodge, *Alberta* 39 O 8
Beavermouth, *B.C.* 39 P 10
Beaverton, *Ontario* 35 L 8
Bede, *Manitoba* 37 R 9
Bedford, *Nova Scotia* 32 J 9
Bedford, *Quebec* 35 S 7
Beechey, L., *N.-W. Terr.* 38 U 3
Beechwood Hydro-Electric Sta., *New Brunswick* 32 E 6
Beechy, *Saskatchewan* 36 K 8
Begin, *Quebec* 35 T 4
Beiseker, *Alberta* 36 D 7
Bélanger Pt., *Manitoba* 37 U 5
Bélanger R., *Manitoba* 37 U 5
Belcher Chan., *N.-W. Terr.* 31 K 2
Belcher Is., *Hudson Bay, N.-W. Terr.* 31 M 6
Belcher Is., North, *Hudson Bay, N.-W. Terr.* 31 M 6
Belcourt, *Quebec* 35 N 4
Belfast, *Maine* 32 D 9
Belfast, *Prince Edward I.* 32 K 7
Bell I, *Harbour Main, Nfd.* 33 T 6
Bell I., *White B., Nfd.* 33 R 3
Bell Pen., *N.-W. Terr.* 31 L 5
Bell, R., *Quebec* 35 N 3
Bell, R., *Yukon* 38 E 2
Bella Bella, *Br. Columbia* 39 J 9
Bella Coola, *Br. Columbia* 39 K 9
Bellburns, *Newfoundland* 33 P 3
Belle B., *Newfoundland* 33 R 6
Belle I., *Newfoundland* 33 R 2
Belle Isle, Strait of, *Labrador/Newfoundland* 33 Q 2
Belle Isle Landing, *Belle Isle, Nfd.* 33 R 2
Belleoram, *Newfoundland* 33 R 6
Belle Plain, *Saskatchewan* 37 M 8
Belle-Rivière, L. de la, *Quebec* 35 T 4
Belleterre, *Quebec* 35 M 5
Belleville, *Ontario* 35 N 8
Bellevue, *Alberta* 36 C 9
Bellin, *Quebec* 31 N 5
Bellis, *Alberta* 36 E 4
Bellsite, *Manitoba* 37 Q 6
Belly R., *Alberta* 36 D 9
Belmont, *Manitoba* 37 S 9
Belmont, *Nova Scotia* 32 J 8
Belmont, *Ontario* 34 J 10
Belot, L., *N.-W. Terr.* 38 K 2
Benalto, *Alberta* 36 C 6
Bender, *Saskatchewan* 37 P 8
Bengough, *Saskatchewan* 37 M 9
Beniah L., *N.-W. Terr.* 38 R 4
Benito, *Manitoba* 37 Q 7
Bennet L., *Br. Columbia* 38 F 6
Bennett, *Br. Columbia* 38 F 6
Benny, *Ontario* 34 J 6
Benson, *Saskatchewan* 37 O 9
Bentley, *Alberta* 36 C 6
Benton, *New Brunswick* 32 E 7
Benton Station, *Alberta* 36 G 7
Berens, I., *Manitoba* 37 U 6
Berens R., *Manitoba* 37 V 6
Berens River, *Manitoba* 37 V 6
Beresford, *Manitoba* 37 R 9
Bergerville, dist., *Quebec* 35 R 3
Bergland, *Ontario* 36 H 1
Berkeley, C., *N.-W. Terr.* 30 J 3
Berland, R., *Alberta* 39 P 8
Berlinguet Inlet, *N.-W. T.* 31 L 3
Bernard, *Saskatchewan* 36 K 8
Bernard, L., *Quebec* 32 J 3
Bernard Harbour, *N.-W. Terr.* 38 Q 1
Bernier B., *N.-W. Terr.* 31 L 3
Berté, L., *Quebec* 32 D 3
Berthierville, *Quebec* 35 R 6
Bertram, *Ontario* 34 F 3
Berwick, *Nova Scotia* 32 H 8
Berwyn, *Alberta* 39 P 7
Besnard L., *Saskatchewan* 37 M 3
Bessemer, *Ontario* 35 N 7
Betchie, L., *Quebec* 32 C 4
Bethany, *Ontario* 35 M 8
Bethel, *Maine* 32 B 9
Bethoulat, L., *Quebec* 32 A 2
Bethune, *Saskatchewan* 37 M 8
Betsiamites, *Quebec* 32 C 5
Betsiamites R., *Quebec* 32 C 4
Beulah, *Manitoba* 37 Q 8
Beverley, *Saskatchewan* 36 J 8
Beverly, *Alberta* 36 D 5
Beverly L., *N.-W. Terr.* 38 X 3
Bexly, C., *N.-W. Terr.* 38 Q 1
Bic, *Quebec* 32 D 5
Bic, I. du, *Quebec* 32 D 5
Biche, L. la, *Alberta* 36 E 4
Bield, *Manitoba* 37 Q 7
Bienfait, *Saskatchewan* 37 P 9
Bienville, *Quebec* 35 T 2
Bienville, L., *Quebec* 31 M 6
Big I., *N.-W. Terr.* 31 M 5
Big I., *Gt. Slave L., N.-W. T.* 38 P 5
Big I., *Ontario* 36 G 1
Big L., *N.-W. Terr.* 38 R 3
Big Bar Creek, *B.C.* 39 M 10
Big Beaver, *Saskatchewan* 37 M 9
Big Beaver Falls, *Ontario* 34 H 3
Big Beaver House, *Ontario* 31 L 7
Big Caotibi L., *Quebec* 32 E 3
Big Creek, *B.C.* 39 M 10
Biggar, *Saskatchewan* 36 K 7
Bigger, Mt., *Br. Columbia* 38 E 6
Big Kalzas L., *Yukon* 38 F 4
Big Lake, *Ontario* 34 H 7
Big Muddy L., *Sask.* 37 M 9
Big Pond, *Cape Breton I.* 33 M 8
Big River, *Saskatchewan* 36 K 5

Big Salmon, R., *Yukon* 38 F 5
Big Sandy L., *Sask.* 37 N 4
Bigsby I., *Ontario* 36 H 1
Bigstick L., *Saskatchewan* 36 H 8
Bigstone L., *Manitoba* 37 W 5
Bigstone R., *Manitoba* 37 W 3
Big Trout L., *Ontario* 31 L 7
Big Valley, *Alberta* 36 E 6
Bigwood, *Ontario* 34 K 6
Billings Bridge, *Ontario* 34 D 9
Bindloss, *Alberta* 36 G 8
Bingham, *Maine* 32 C 8
Bingle, *Ontario* 34 K 4
Binscarth, *Manitoba* 37 Q 8
Birch I., *Manitoba* 37 S 6
Birch L., *Alberta* 36 F 5
Birch L., *N.-W. Terr.* 38 P 4
Birch L., *Saskatchewan* 36 J 5
Birch Mts., *Alberta* 39 R 7
Birch R., *Alberta* 39 R 6
Birch Hills, *Saskatchewan* 37 M 5
Birch River, *Manitoba* 37 Q 6
Bird, *Manitoba* 30 K 6
Bird Cove, *Newfoundland* 33 Q 2
Bird Rocks Lt. Ho., *Madeleine Is., Quebec* 33 L 6
Birmingham, *Saskatchewan* 37 P 8
Birnie, *Manitoba* 37 S 8
Birsay, *Saskatchewan* 36 L 7
Birtle, *Manitoba* 37 Q 8
Biscotasing, *Ontario* 34 H 5
Bishop L., *N.-W. Terr.* 38 P 3
Bishopric, *Saskatchewan* 37 M 8
Bishop's Falls, *Nfd.* 33 R 4
Biskotasi L., *Ontario* 34 H 5
Bison L., *Alberta* 39 P 7
Bistcho L., *Alberta* 38 O 6
Bittern L., *Saskatchewan* 37 M 5
Bittern Lake, *Alberta* 36 D 5
Bitumount, *Alberta* 39 S 7
Blache, L. De La, *Quebec* 32 C 3
Black B., *Ontario* 34 B 4
Black B., *Athabasca L., Saskatchewan* 38 T 6
Black I., *Manitoba* 37 V 7
Black L., *Saskatchewan* 38 V 6
Black Mts., *New Brunswick* 32 E 6
Black Bear Island L., *Sask.* 37 M 3
Black Birch L., *Sask.* 39 U 7
Blackburn, Mt., *Alaska* 30 E 6
Black Donald Mines, *Ont.* 35 O 7
Black Diamond, *Alberta* 36 C 8
Black Dome, pk., *B.C.* 39 K 9
Blackfoot, *Alberta* 36 G 5
Black Hawk, *Ontario* 36 H 2
Blackhead B., *Nfd.* 33 T 5
Blackie, *Alberta* 36 D 8
Black Lake, *Quebec* 35 T 6
Black Pines, *Br. Columbia* 39 N10
Black Pool, *Br. Columbia* 39 N10
Black Rocks, *Quebec* 33 N 3
Blacks Harbour, *N.B.* 32 F 8
Blackstone, R., *Yukon* 38 E 3
Black Sturgeon L., *Ont.* 34 B 3
Blackville, *New Brunswick* 32 G 7
Blackwater L., *N.-W. Terr.* 38 M 3
Bladworth, *Saskatchewan* 36 L 7
Blaine Lake, *Saskatchewan* 36 L 6
Blairmore, *Alberta* 36 C 9
Blanche, *Ontario* 34 E 2
Blanche, *Quebec* 35 P 7
Blanc Sablon, *Quebec* 33 P 2
Blenheim, *Ontario* 34 J 10
Bleu, L., *Quebec* 35 M 6
Blewett, *Sask.* 37 O 9
Blind River, *Ontario* 34 H 6
Bloedel, *Vancouver I., B.C.* 39 L 10
Bloomfield, *Ontario* 35 N 9
Blow, R., *Yukon* 38 E 1
Blucher, *Saskatchewan* 36 L 6
Blue R., *Br. Columbia* 38 J 6
Blueberry R., *Br. Columbia* 39 N 7
Blue Hills of Coteau, *Newfoundland* 33 O 6
Bluenose, L., *N.-W. Terr.* 38 O 1
Blue Ridge, *Alberta* 36 B 4
Blue River, *Br. Columbia* 39 O 9
Blue Sea Lake, *Quebec* 35 O 6
Bluffton, *Alberta* 36 C 6
Blumenhof, *Saskatchewan* 36 K 8
Blyth, *Ontario* 34 J 9
Boakview, *Ontario* 34 K 7
Bobcaygeon, *Ontario* 35 M 8
Bochart, *Quebec* 35 R 3
Bodo, *Alberta* 36 G 6
Bogart, Mt., *Alberta* 36 B 8
Boharm, *Saskatchewan* 37 M 8
Boiestown, *New Brunswick* 32 F 7
Bois, L. des, *N.-W. Terr.* 38 L 2
Boisdale, *Cape Breton I.* 33 M 7
Boissevain, *Manitoba* 37 R 9
Bolger, *Quebec* 35 O 4
Bolkow, *Ontario* 34 G 4
Bolton, *Ontario* 35 L 9
Bolton L., *Manitoba* 37 W 4
Bon Accord, *Alberta* 36 D 5
Bonarlaw, *Ontario* 35 N 8
Bonaventure, *Quebec* 32 G 5
Bonaventure I., *Quebec* 32 H 5
Bonavista & B., *Nfd.* 33 T 5
Boney River Sta., *New Brunswick* 32 F 8
Bonfield, *Ontario* 35 L 6
Bonheur, *Ontario* 37 L 1
Bonne Bay, *Newfoundland* 33 P 4
Bonne Espérance, *Quebec* 33 P 2
Bonnet Plume, R., *Yukon* 38 F 3
Bonny River, *N.B.* 32 F 8
Bonnyville, *Alberta* 36 G 4
Boothia, G. of, *N.-W. Terr.* 31 L 4
Boothia Pen. *N.-W. Terr.* 31 K 3
Bordeaux, *Quebec* 35 R 9
Borden, *Saskatchewan* 36 K 6
Borden I., *N.-W. Terr.* 30 H 2
Borden Pen., *N.-W. Terr.* 31 L 3
Boston Bar, *B.C.* 39 N11
Boswarlos, *Newfoundland* 33 O 5
Boswell, *B.C.* 39 P11
Botha, *Alberta* 36 E 6
Bothwell, *Ontario* 34 J 10
Botwood, *Newfoundland* 33 R 4
Boucher, L., *Quebec* 33 N 2
Boucherville, Is., *Quebec* 35 Q 7
Bouchette, *Quebec* 35 P 6
Boulain, L., *Quebec* 33 L 3
Bouleau, L. au, *Quebec* 35 N 5
Boundary B., *Br. Columbia* 39 H12
Boundary Mts., *Maine/Quebec* 32 B 8
Boundary Plat., *Mont./Sask.* 36 J 9
Boundary Bay, dist., *Vancouver* 39 H12
Boundary Bay Airport, *British Columbia* 39 H12
Bounty, *Saskatchewan* 36 K 7
Bourkes, *Ontario* 34 K 4
Bourlamaque, *Quebec* 35 N 4
Bourne, C., *N.-W. Terr.* 30 K 1
Bourmont, *Quebec* 35 P 4
Bow R., *Alberta* 36 D 8
Bowden, *Alberta* 36 C 7
Bowen I., *Br. Columbia* 39 M11
Bow Island, *Alberta* 36 F 9
Bowman B., *N.-W. Terr.* 31 M 4
Bowmanville, *Ontario* 35 M 9
Bowness, *Alberta* 36 C 7
Bowron Lake Prov. Park, *Br. Columbia* 39 N 9
Bowron R., *Br. Columbia* 39 N 9
Bowser L., *Br. Columbia* 39 J 7
Bowsman, *Manitoba* 37 Q 6
Bowyer I., *Br. Columbia* 39 G 10
Boyd, *Manitoba* 37 V 3
Boyd L., *N.-W. Terr.* 38 W 5
Boyd's Cove, *Nfd.* 33 S 4
Boyle, *Alberta* 36 E 4
Boylston, *Nova Scotia* 33 L 8
Brabant I., *Saskatchewan* 37 O 2
Bracebridge, *Ontario* 35 L 7
Bracken, *Saskatchewan* 36 J 9
Bracken L., *Manitoba* 37 S 5
Bradford, *Ontario* 35 L 8
Bradore Bay, *Que.* 35 P 2
Bradore Hills, *Que.* 35 P 2
Bradwardine, *Manitoba* 37 R 9
Bradwell, *Saskatchewan* 36 L 7
Bralorne, *Br. Columbia* 39 M10
Brampton, *Ontario* 35 L 9
Branch, *Newfoundland* 33 T 7
Brandon, *Manitoba* 37 S 9
Branston I., *Br. Columbia* 39 K11
Brant, *Alberta* 36 D 8
Brantford, *Ontario* 34 K 9
Bras d'Or, *C. Breton I., Nova Scotia* 33 M 7
Bras d'Or, L., *C. Breton I., Nova Scotia* 33 M 8
Bray I., *N.-W. Terr.* 31 M 4
Brazeau, *Alberta* 39 P 9
Brazeau, Mt., *Alberta* 39 P 9
Brazeau R., *Alberta* 39 P 9
Brazil Lake, *Nova Scotia* 32 G 10
Brébeuf, L., *Quebec* 32 B 5
Brechin, *Ontario* 35 L 8
Bredenbury, *Saskatchewan* 37 P 8
Bréhat, L., *Quebec* 32 B 1
Brent, *Ontario* 35 M 6
Breton, *Alberta* 36 C 5
Breton, C., *C. Breton I., Nova Scotia* 33 N 8
Brewer, *Maine* 32 D 9
Briconnet, L., *Quebec* 33 M 2
Bridge R., *Br. Columbia* 39 M10
Bridgeport, *Br. Columbia* 39 H11
Bridgetown, *Nova Scotia* 32 G 9
Bridgeville, *Nova Scotia* 32 K 8
Bridgewater, *Nova Scotia* 32 H 9
Bridgton, *Maine* 32 B 9
Brier I., *Nova Scotia* 32 F 9
Briercrest, *Saskatchewan* 37 M 8
Briereville, *Alberta* 36 F 4
Brigden, *Ontario* 34 H10
Brighouse, *Br. Columbia* 39 G 12
Brighton, *Ontario* 35 N 8
Brion I., *Madeleine Is., Quebec* 33 L 6
Bristol, *New Brunswick* 32 E 7
Bristol, *Quebec* 35 O 7
Britannia Bay, *Ontario* 34 C 9
Britannia Beach, *B.C.* 39 M11
British Columbia, prov., *Canada* 30 G 6
British Empire Ra., *N.-W. Territories* 31 L 1
Briton Cove, *Cape Breton I.* 33 M 7
Britt, *Ontario* 34 K 7
Broadacres, *Saskatchewan* 36 J 6
Broadback R., *Quebec* 31 M 7
Broadback R., *Quebec* 35 P 2
Broadview, *Saskatchewan* 37 P 8
Brochet, *Manitoba* 37 Q 1
Brochet, L., *Manitoba* 38 X 6
Brochet, L., *Quebec* 32 C 4
Brock, *Saskatchewan* 36 J 7
Brock I., *N.-W. Terr.* 30 H 2
Brock R., *Quebec* 35 Q 2
Brocket, *Alberta* 36 D 9
Brockville, *Ontario* 35 P 8
Broderick, *Saskatchewan* 36 L 7
Brodeur Pen., *N.-W. Terr.* 31 L 3
Bromhead, *Saskatchewan* 37 O 9
Bronte, *Ontario* 35 L 9
Brooch L., *Quebec* 32 D 3
Brookfield, *Nova Scotia* 32 J 8
Brooking, *Saskatchewan* 37 N 9
Brooklin, *Ontario* 35 L 9
Brooklyn, *Nova Scotia* 32 H 9
Brookmere, *Br. Columbia* 39 N11
Brooks, *Alberta* 36 F 8
Brooks Brook, *Yukon* 38 G 5
Brooksby, *Saskatchewan* 37 N 5
Broom B., *Anticosti I., Quebec* 33 K 4
Broughton Sta., *Quebec* 35 T 6
Browning, *Saskatchewan* 37 P 9
Brownlee, *Saskatchewan* 36 L 8
Brownrigg, *Ontario* 34 J 3
Brownsburg, *Quebec* 35 Q 7
Brownville Junc., *Maine* 32 C 8
Bruce, *Alberta* 36 F 5
Bruce Pen., *Ontario* 34 J 7
Brucefield, *Ontario* 34 J 9
Bruce Mines, *Ontario* 34 G 6
Bruederheim, *Alberta* 36 E 5
Brûlé, *Alberta* 39 O 9
Brûlé, L., *Quebec* 33 L 3
Brûle Lake, *Ontario* 35 M 7
Brunette, I., *Newfoundland* 33 R 6
Brunkild, *Manitoba* 37 U 9
Bruno, *Saskatchewan* 37 M 6
Brunswick, *Maine* 32 B 10
Brunswick L., *Ontario* 34 G 3
Brussels, *Ontario* 34 J 9
Bruton, L., *Quebec* 35 O 1
Bryson, L., *Quebec* 35 N 6
Buchan G., *N.-W. Terr.* 31 M 3
Buchanan, *Saskatchewan* 37 P 7
Buchans, *Newfoundland* 33 Q 5
Buchans Junction, *Newfoundland* 33 Q 5
Buck L., *Alberta* 36 C 5
Buckingham, *Quebec* 35 P 7
Buckland L., *Manitoba* 37 V 1
Buckley Ras., *B.C.* 39 K 8
Bucksport, *Maine* 32 D 9
Buctouche, *N.B.* 32 H 7
Buffalo, *Alberta* 36 G 8
Buffalo L., *Alberta* 36 E 6
Buffalo L., *N.-W. Terr.* 38 Q 5
Buffalo, R., *Alberta/N.-W. Terr.* 38 Q 6
Buffalo Gap, *Saskatchewan* 37 M 9
Buffalo Narrows, *Sask.* 36 J 3
Buffalo River, *N.-W. Terr.* 38 Q 5
Bulkley R., *Br. Columbia* 39 K 8
Bull R., *Br. Columbia* 36 B 9
Bullen, R., *N.-W. Terr.* 38 W 3
Bulwark, *Alberta* 36 F 6
Bulyea, *Saskatchewan* 37 N 8
Bumpus, Mt., *Victoria I.* 38 R 1
Buntzen, L., *Br. Columbia* 39 J 11
Burden, Mt., *Br. Columbia* 39 M 7
Burdett, *Alberta* 36 F 9
Burgeo, *Newfoundland* 33 P 6
Burin & Pen., *Nfd.* 33 R 6
Burke Chan., *Br. Columbia* 39 K 9
Burks Falls, *Ontario* 35 L 7
Burlington, *Newfoundland* 33 R 4
Burlington, *Ontario* 35 L 9
Burmis, *Alberta* 36 C 9
Burnaby, & L., *B.C.* 39 H11
Burnaby, Mt., *B.C.* 39 J 11
Burnside, R., *N.-W. Terr.* 38 T 2
Burns Lake, *Br. Columbia* 39 L 8
Burnsville, *New Brunswick* 32 G 6
Burnt L., *Labrador* 32 J 1
Burnt River, *Ontario* 35 M 8
Burntwood L. & R., *Manitoba* 37 R 3
Burr, *Saskatchewan* 37 M 6
Burrard Inlet, *B.C.* 39 G11
Burstall, *Saskatchewan* 36 H 8
Burtts Corner, *N.B.* 32 F 7
Burwash, *Ontario* 34 K 6
Burwash (Estaire) *Ont.* 34 K 6
Burwash Landing, *Yukon* 38 D 5
Bury, *Quebec* 35 T 7
Busby, *Alberta* 36 D 5
Bushell, *Saskatchewan* 38 T 6
Bushnell, *Ontario* 35 L 6
Bute Inlet, *Br. Columbia* 39 L 10
Butedale, *Br. Columbia* 39 J 9
Buttle L., *Br. Columbia* 39 L 11
Button B., *Manitoba* 31 K 6
Button Is., *N.-W. Terr.* 31 N 5
Button Is., *Quebec* 31 N 5
Buyck, *Minnesota* 36 K 2
Byam Martin Chan., *N.-W. Territories* 30 J 2
Byam Martin I., *N.-W. T.* 30 J 2
Byemoor, *Alberta* 36 E 6
Byers, Mt., *Ontario* 34 J 4
Bylot I., *N.-W. Terr.* 31 M 3
Byng Inlet, *Ontario* 34 K 7
Byron B., *Victoria I., N.-W. Territories* 38 T 1
Cabano, *Quebec* 32 D 6
Cabonga, Res., *Quebec* 35 O 5
Cabot Head, *Ontario* 34 J 7
Cabot Str., *Nfd./N.S.* 33 M 6
Cabri, *Saskatchewan* 36 J 8
Cacaoui L., *Quebec* 32 F 3
Cache Bay, *Ontario* 34 K 6
Cachisca L., *Quebec* 35 Q 2
Cacouna, *Quebec* 32 C 6
Cactus Lake, *Sask.* 36 H 6
Cadillac, *Quebec* 35 M 4
Cadillac, *Saskatchewan* 36 K 9
Cadogan, *Alberta* 36 G 6
Cadomin, *Alberta* 39 P 9
Cadotte, R., *Alberta* 39 P 7
Cains R., *New Brunswick* 32 G 7
Calabogie, *Ontario* 35 O 7
Calais, *Maine* 32 E 8
Calder, *Saskatchewan* 37 Q 7
Caledonia, *Nova Scotia* 32 G 9
Caledonia, *Nova Scotia* 33 K 8
Caledonia, *Ontario* 34 L 9
Calgary, *Alberta* 36 C 7
Callander, *Ontario* 35 L 6
Calling, L., *Alberta* 36 D 3
Calling Lake, *Alberta* 36 D 3
Calling River, *Alberta* 36 D 3
Callison Ranch, *B.C.* 39 H 6
Calm, L., *Ontario* 36 L 2
Calmar, *Alberta* 36 D 5
Calstock, *Ontario* 34 F 3
Calumet, *Quebec* 35 Q 7
Calvert I., *Br. Columbia* 39 J 10
Camachigama, L., *Quebec* 35 O 5
Cambell River, *B.C.* 30 G 7
Cambridge Bay, *Victoria I.* 38 V 1
Camden, *Maine* 32 C 9
Cameron Falls, *Ontario* 34 B 3
Cameron Hills, *Alberta* 38 O 6
Camlaren, *N.-W. Terr.* 38 R 4
Camousitchouane L., *Quebec* 35 P 1
Campania I., *Br. Columbia* 39 J 9
Campbell B., *N.-W. Terr.* 38 V 1
Campbell Cr., *B.C.* 39 K12
Campbell, L., *N.-W. Terr.* 38 U 4
Campbell, L., *N.-W. Terr.* 38 G 1
Campbell, Mt., *Yukon* 38 D 3
Campbellford, *Ontario* 35 N 8
Campbell Island, *B.C.* 39 J 9
Campbell River, *Vancouver I., B.C.* 39 L 11
Campbells Bay, *Quebec* 35 O 7
Campbellton, *N.B.* 32 F 6
Campbellton, *Nfd.* 33 S 4
Camperville, *Manitoba* 37 R 7
Campobello I., *N.B.* 32 F 9
Camrose, *Alberta* 36 E 5
Camsell, L., *N.-W. Terr.* 38 S 4
Camsell Ra., *N.-W. Terr.* 38 M 4
Camsel Portage, *Sask.* 38 T 6
Canaan R., *N.B.* 32 G 8
Canaan, *N.B.* 32 G 7
Canada Bay, *Newfoundland* 33 Q 3
Canal Flats, *Br. Columbia* 39 Q10
Candiac, *Manitoba* 37 P 8
Candle L., *Saskatchewan* 37 M 5
Candle Lake, *Sask.* 37 M 5
Cando, *Saskatchewan* 36 J 6
Cane, *Ontario* 34 K 5
Canica Island, *Quebec* 35 N 3
Canim L., *Br. Columbia* 39 N10
Canmore, *Alberta* 36 B 7
Canning, *Nova Scotia* 32 H 8
Cannington, *Ontario* 35 L 8
Canoe L., *Saskatchewan* 36 J 3
Canoe R., *Br. Columbia* 39 O 9
Canoe Passage, *B.C.* 39 G 12
Canol, *N.-W. Territories* 38 K 3
Canora, *Saskatchewan* 37 P 7
Canso, *Nova Scotia* 33 M 8
Canso, C., *Nova Scotia* 33 M 8
Canso, Strait of, *N.S.* 33 L 8
Cantaur, *Saskatchewan* 36 J 8
Canterbury Sta., *N.B.* 32 E 8
Canwood, *Saskatchewan* 36 L 5
Canyon, *Ontario* 34 F 5
Canyon, *Yukon* 38 E 5
Canyon Creek, *Alberta* 36 B 3
Canyon Ras, *N.-W. Terr.* 38 K 4
Caopacho L., *Quebec* 32 F 1
Caopacho R., *Quebec* 32 F 2
Caopatina, L., *Quebec* 35 Q 3
Capassin, *Saskatchewan* 36 K 5
Cap Chat, *Quebec* 32 F 4
Cap de la Madeleine, *Que.* 35 S 6
Cap-d'Espoir, *New Brunswick* 32 H 5
Cape Breton I., *N.S.* 33 N 7
Cape Breton Highlands Nat. Park, *C. Breton I., N.S.* 33 M 7
Cape Broyle, *Nfd.* 33 T 6
Cape Charles, *Labrador* 33 R 1
Cape Dorset, *N.-W. Terr.* 31 M 5
Cape Dyer, *N.-W. Terr.* 31 N 4
Cape Hopes Advance, *Que.* 31 N 5
Cape La Hune, *Nfd.* 33 Q 6
Cape Parry, *N.-W. Terr.* 38 L 1
Cape Race, *Nfd.* 33 T 7
Cape Ray, *Newfoundland* 33 N 6
Cape Sable I., *N.S.* 32 G 10
Cape St. Mary Lt. Ho., *Nova Scotia* 32 F 9
Cape Tormentine, *N.B.* 32 J 7
Capilano R., *Br. Columbia* 39 H11
Capitachouane, R., *Que.* 35 O 5
Caplan, *Quebec* 32 G 5
Capreol, *Ontario* 34 K 6
Capstick, *Cape Breton I.* 33 M 7
Caramat, *Ontario* 34 D 3
Caraquet & B., *N.B.* 32 H 6
Carberry, *Manitoba* 37 S 9
Carbon, *Alberta* 36 D 7
Carbondale, *Alberta* 36 D 5
Carbonear, *Newfoundland* 33 T 6
Carcajou, *Alberta* 39 P 7
Carcajou, R., *N.-W. Terr.* 38 J 3
Carcross, *Yukon* 38 F 5
Cardale, *Manitoba* 37 R 8
Cardigan, *P.E.I.* 32 K 7
Cardigan B., *P. Edward I.* 32 K 7
Cardinal, *Ontario* 35 P 8
Cardross, *Saskatchewan* 37 M 9
Cardston, *Alberta* 36 D 9
Carey L., *N.-W. Terr.* 38 W 4
Cargill, *Ontario* 34 J 8
Cariboo Mts., *B.C.* 39 N 9
Caribou, *Maine* 32 E 7
Caribou, *Manitoba* 31 K 6
Caribou I., *Nova Scotia* 32 K 8
Caribou I., *Ontario* 34 E 5
Caribou Is., *Gt. Slave L., N.-W. Territories* 38 R 5
Caribou L., *Ontario* 34 A 2
Caribou Mts., *Alberta* 39 Q 6
Caribou R., *N.-W. Terr.* 38 K 5
Caribou R., *Yukon* 38 F 2
Caribou Hide, *B.C.* 39 K 7
Carievale, *Saskatchewan* 37 Q 9
Carillon, *Quebec* 35 Q 7
Carleton, *Quebec* 32 F 5
Carleton, Mt., *N.B.* 32 F 6
Carleton Pt., *Anticosti I., Quebec* 32 K 4
Carleton Place, *Ontario* 35 O 7
Carlington, *Ontario* 34 C 9
Carlton, *Saskatchewan* 36 L 6
Carlyle, *Saskatchewan* 37 P 9
Carmacks, *Yukon* 38 E 4
Carman, *Manitoba* 37 U 9
Carmangay, *Alberta* 36 D 8
Carmanville, *Nfd.* 33 S 4
Carmel, *Sask.* 37 M 6
Carmichael, *Sask.* 36 J 8
Carnduff, *Saskatchewan* 37 Q 9
Carnwath, R., *N.-W. Terr.* 38 J 2
Caroline, *Alberta* 36 C 6
Caron, *Saskatchewan* 37 M 8
Carp, *Ontario* 35 O 7
Carp L., *Br. Columbia* 39 M 8
Carragana, *Sask.* 37 O 6
Carrière, L., *Quebec* 35 N 5
Carroll, *Manitoba* 37 R 9
Carrot R., *Manitoba* 37 V 4
Carrot R., *Saskatchewan* 37 N 5
Carrot River, *Sask.* 37 O 5
Carruthers, *Saskatchewan* 36 H 6
Carseland, *Alberta* 36 D 8
Carstairs, *Alberta* 36 C 7
Carswell L., *Sask.* 39 T 6
Cartier, *Ontario* 34 J 6
Cartierville, *Quebec* 35 R 9
Cartierville Airport, *Que.* 35 Q 9
Cartwright, *Labrador* 31 O 7
Cartwright, *Manitoba* 37 S 9
Casapedia, *Quebec* 32 G 5
Casapedia R., *Quebec* 32 F 5
Cascade, *Br. Columbia* 39 O11
Cascade Mts., *Canada/U.S.A.* 39 N11
Casey, *Quebec* 35 Q 5
Casselman, *Ontario* 35 P 7
Cassiar, *Br. Columbia* 38 H 6
Cassiar Mts., *B.C.* 38 H 6
Castine, *Maine* 32 D 9
Castlegar, *Br. Columbia* 39 P11
Castor, *Alberta* 36 F 6
Catalina, *Newfoundland* 33 T 5
Cater, *Saskatchewan* 36 J 5
Cat Lake, *Ontario* 31 K 7
Cauchon L., *Manitoba* 37 V 3
Caughnawaga, *Quebec* 35 Q 8
Caughnawaga Ind. Res., *Quebec* 35 R 10
Caulfield, *Vancouver* 39 F 11
Causapscal, *Quebec* 32 E 5
Cavell, *Ontario* 34 C 2
Cavell, *Saskatchewan* 36 J 6
Cavendish, *Alberta* 36 G 8
Cavers, *Ontario* 34 C 4
Cawood, *Quebec* 35 O 7
Cayley, *Alberta* 36 D 8
Cayuga, *Ontario* 34 L 10
Ceba, *Saskatchewan* 37 P 5
Cedar L., *Manitoba* 37 R 5
Cedar Springs, *Ontario* 34 H10
Cedoux, *Manitoba* 37 O 9
Central Butte, *Sask.* 36 L 8
Centralia, *Ontario* 34 J 9
Centreville, *N.B.* 32 E 7
Centreville, *N.S.* 32 F 9
Cereal, *Alberta* 36 G 7
Cerf, L. du, *Quebec* 35 P 6
Cessford, *Alberta* 36 F 7
Ceylon, *Sask.* 37 N 9
Chaleur, B. de., *Que./New Brunswick* 32 H 5
Chalk River, *Ontario* 35 N 6
Challenger Mts., *N.-W. T.* 31 L 1
Chamberlain, *Sask.* 37 M 8
Chamberlain L., *Maine* 32 C 7
Chambord, *Quebec* 35 S 4
Champagne, *Yukon* 38 E 5
Champcoeur, *Quebec* 35 N 4
Champion, *Alberta* 36 D 8
Champlain, *Quebec* 35 S 6
Champneuf, *Quebec* 35 N 4
Chandler, *Quebec* 32 H 5
Change Island, *Nfd.* 33 S 4
Channel, *Newfoundland* 33 N 6
Channel-Port-aux-Basques, *Newfoundland* 31 O 8
Channing, airfield, *Man.* 37 Q 4
Chantrey Inlet, *N.-W. T.* 38 Z 1
Chapais, *Quebec* 35 Q 3
Chapeau, *Quebec* 35 N 7
Chapelle, L. de la, *Quebec* 33 L 3
Chapleau, *Ontario* 34 G 5
Chapleau, R., *Ontario* 34 G 4
Chaplin, *Saskatchewan* 36 L 8
Chapman, airfield, *Sask.* 36 H 5
Chapman Is., *N.-W. Terr.* 38 T 1
Chapman Lake, *Yukon* 38 E 3
Chapman, Mt., *B.C.* 39 O10
Chaput Hughes, *Ontario* 34 K 4
Chard, *Alberta* 39 S 8
Charles I., *N.-W. Terr.* 31 M 5
Charles L., *Alberta* 38 S 6
Charlesbourg, *Quebec* 35 R 1
Charlie Lake, *B.C.* 39 N 7
Charlotte L., *B.C.* 39 L 9
Charlottetown, *Prince Edward I.* 32 J 7
Charlton, *Ontario* 34 K 5
Charlton I., *James Bay, N.-W. Territories* 31 M 7
Charny, *Quebec* 32 A 7
Charterville, *Quebec* 32 A 8
Chase, *Br. Columbia* 39 O10
Chasm, *Br. Columbia* 39 N10
Château Richer, *Quebec* 32 A 6
Chateauvert, L., *Quebec* 35 R 5
Chatfield, *Manitoba* 37 U 8
Chatham, *New Brunswick* 32 G 6
Chatham, *Ontario* 34 H10
Chatham Sd., *Br. Columbia* 39 H 8
Chatsworth, *Ontario* 34 K 8
Chaudière Falls, *Quebec* 34 C 8
Chauvin, *Alberta* 36 G 6
Cheadle, *Alberta* 36 D 7
Chedabucto B., *N.S.* 33 L 8
Cheecham, *Alberta* 39 S 7
Cheepash, R., *Ontario* 34 J 2
Cheeseman L., *Ontario* 37 O 1
Chelan, *Saskatchewan* 37 O 6
Chelmsford, *Ontario* 34 J 6
Chemainus, *Br. Columbia* 39 M11
Chemquasabamticook L., *Maine/Quebec* 32 B 7
Chénéville, *Quebec* 35 P 7
Chenier, *Quebec* 35 O 6
Chenil, L., *Quebec* 33 N 2
Chensagi L., *Quebec* 35 O 2
Cherhill, *Alberta* 36 C 5
Cherryfield, *Maine* 32 D 9
Cherry Point, *Alberta* 39 O 7
Chesley, *Ontario* 34 J 8
Chester, *Nova Scotia* 32 H 9
Chester Basin, *Nova Scotia* 32 H 9
Chesterfield Inlet, *N.-W. Territories* 31 K 5
Chesterville, *Ontario* 35 P 7
Chesuncook L., *Maine* 32 C 8
Cheticamp, *Cape Breton I., Nova Scotia* 33 L 7
Cheviot, *Saskatchewan* 36 L 6
Chibougamau, *Quebec* 35 Q 3
Chibougamau L., *Quebec* 35 Q 3
Chibougamau R., *Quebec* 35 P 3
Chicobi, L., *Quebec* 35 M 4
Chicotte, *Anticosti I., Que.* 32 J 4
Chicoutimi, *Quebec* 32 A 5
Chicoutimi, R., *Quebec* 35 T 5
Chidley, C., *Quebec* 31 N 5
Chiefs Pt., *Ontario* 34 J 8
Chignecto B., *N.S./N.B.* 32 H 8
Chilcotin, R., *B.C.* 39 M10
Chilko L., *Br. Columbia* 39 L 10
Chilko, R., *Br. Columbia* 39 M10
Chilliwack, *Br. Columbia* 39 N11
Chimney Cove, *Nfld.* 33 O 4
Chin, *Alberta* 36 E 9
Chin, C., *Ontario* 34 J 7
Chinchaga, R., *Alberta* 39 O 6
Chinook, *Alberta* 36 G 7
Chip L., *Alberta* 36 B 5
Chipewyan L., *Manitoba* 37 T 1
Chipie R., *Ontario* 34 G 1
Chip Lake, *Alberta* 36 B 5
Chipewyan Lake, *Alberta* 38 R 7
Chipman, *New Brunswick* 32 G 7
Chipman L., *Ontario* 34 D 3
Chippawa, *Ontario* 35 L 9
Chiputneticook Ls., *Maine/N.B.* 32 E 8
Chisholm, *Alberta* 36 C 4
Chitek, *Saskatchewan* 36 K 5
Chitek L., *Manitoba* 37 S 6
Chochocouane, R., *Que.* 35 O 5
Choiceland, *Saskatchewan* 37 N 5
Chown Mt., *Alberta* 39 O 9
Christian, C., *N.-W. Terr.* 31 N 3
Christian I., *Ontario* 34 K 8
Christianshåb, *Greenland* 31 O 4
Christie B., *N.-W. Terr.* 38 S 4
Christie L., *Manitoba* 37 V 2
Christina L., *Alberta* 36 F 3
Christina R., *Alberta* 36 G 2
Chudleigh, *Ontario* 34 K 6
Churchbridge, *Sask.* 37 Q 8
Churchill, *Manitoba* 31 K 6
Churchill, C., *Manitoba* 31 K 6
Churchill L., *Sask.* 36 J 2
Churchill Pk., *B.C.* 39 L 6
Churchill R., *Canada* 30 J 6
Churchill R., Lit., *Man.* 37 W 2
Church Point, *Nova Scotia* 32 F 9
Chute-aux-Outardes, *Quebec* 32 D 4
Chute-des-Passes, *Quebec* 32 A 4
City View, *Ontario* 34 C 9
Clair, *Saskatchewan* 37 N 6
Claire, L., *Alberta* 39 R 6
Clairs, *New Brunswick* 32 D 6
Clandonald, *Alberta* 36 G 5
Clanwilliam, *Manitoba* 37 S 8
Clarendon, *Ontario* 35 O 8
Clarenville, *Newfoundland* 33 S 5
Claresholm, *Alberta* 36 D 8
Clark, Mt., *N.-W. Terr.* 38 L 3
Clark Pt., *Ontario* 34 J 8
Clarke L., *Saskatchewan* 36 K 4
Clarke, R., *N.-W. Terr.* 38 W 4
Clarke City, *Quebec* 32 F 3
Clark's Harbour, *N.S.* 32 G10
Clarkson, *Ontario* 35 L 9
Clavet, *Saskatchewan* 36 L 6
Clay L., *Ontario* 36 J 1
Claydon, *Saskatchewan* 36 H 9
Clayoquot, *B.C.* 39 K11
Clear L., *Manitoba* 37 S 8
Clear, L., *Ontario* 35 N 7
Clear Hills, *Alberta* 39 O 7
Clearwater L., *Quebec* 31 M 6
Clearwater, R., *Alberta* 39 S 7
Clearwater R., *Alberta* 36 B 6
Clearwater Sta., *B.C.* 39 N10
Cleeves, *Saskatchewan* 36 H 5
Clements Markham Inlet, *N.-W. Terr.* 31 N 1
Clementsport, *N.S.* 32 G 9
Clementsvale, *N.S.* 32 G 9
Cléricy, *Quebec* 35 M 4
Clerval, *Quebec* 35 L 4
Clifford, *Ontario* 34 K 9
Clifton Pt., *N.-W. Terr.* 38 O 1
Climax, *Saskatchewan* 36 J 9
Cline Mt., *Alberta* 39 P 9
Clinton, *Br. Columbia* 39 N10
Clinton, *Ontario* 34 J 9
Clinton-Colden L., *N.-W. Territories* 38 U 4
Clive, *Alberta* 36 D 6
Clive L., *N.-W. Terr.* 38 O 4
Cloan, *Saskatchewan* 36 J 6
Clo-oorse, *Br. Columbia* 39 L 11
Cloudberry Pt., *Quebec* 33 M 3
Cloutier, *Quebec* 35 L 4
Clova, *Quebec* 35 P 4
Cloverdale, *Br. Columbia* 39 K12
Cluny, *Alberta* 36 E 8
Clut L., *N.-W. Terr.* 38 P 3
Clute, *Ontario* 34 K 3
Clyde, *Alberta* 36 D 4
Clyde, *N.-W. Territories* 31 N 3
Clyde Forks, *Ont.* 35 O 7
Clyde Inlet, *N.-W. Terr.* 31 N 3
Clyde R., *Nova Scotia* 32 G10
Coacoachou L., *Quebec* 33 M 3
Coal R., *Yukon* 38 K 5
Coal River, *B.C.* 38 K 5
Coaldale, *Alberta* 36 E 9
Coalhurst, *Alberta* 36 E 9
Coast Mts., *Br. Columbia* 39 G 7
Coast of Labrador, dist., *Newfoundland* 31 N 7
Coast Ra., *Oregon etc.* 30 G 9
Coaticook, *Quebec* 34 T 7
Coats I., *N.-W. Terr.* 31 L 5
Cobalt, *Ontario* 35 L 5
Cobden, *Ontario* 35 O 7
Cobequid B. & Mts., *Nova Scotia* 32 J 8
Coboconk, *Ontario* 35 M 8
Cobourg, *Ontario* 35 M 9
Coburg I., *N.-W. Terr.* 31 M 2
Cochrane, *Alberta* 36 C 7
Cochrane, *Ontario* 34 J 3
Cochrane, R., *Sask.* 38 W 6
Cockburn I., *Ontario* 34 G 7
Cockburn Island, *Ontario* 34 G 7
Cod I., *Labrador* 31 N 6
Coderre, *Saskatchewan* 36 L 8
Codette, *Saskatchewan* 37 N 5
Codroy, *Newfoundland* 33 N 6
Codroy Pond, *Nfd.* 33 O 5
Codys, *New Brunswick* 32 G 8
Coe Hill, *Ontario* 35 N 8
Coffee Creek, *Yukon* 38 D 4
Coffin I., *Madeleine Is., Quebec* 33 L 6
Colborne, *Ontario* 35 N 8
Cold L., *Alberta* 36 G 4
Cold Lake, *Alberta* 36 G 4
Cold Lake (Kississing), *Manitoba* 37 Q 3
Cold Spring Pond, *Nfd.* 33 Q 5
Coldwater, *Ontario* 35 L 8
Coldwell, *Ontario* 34 D 4
Coleman, *Alberta* 36 C 9
Coleraine, *Quebec* 35 T 7
Coleridge, *Alberta* 36 G 9
Coleville, *Saskatchewan* 36 H 7
Colfax, *Manitoba* 37 O 9
Colgate, *Saskatchewan* 37 N 9
Colinton, *Alberta* 36 D 4
Collingwood, *Ontario* 34 K 8
Collins, *Ontario* 37 O 1
Collins, Mt., *Ontario* 34 K 5
Collinson Pen., *Victoria I.* 38 X 1
Collis, *Ontario* 34 J 1
Colombière, *Quebec* 35 N 4
Colonsay, *Saskatchewan* 37 M 7
Colpoy B., *Ontario* 34 K 8
Columbia, C., *N.-W. Terr.* 31 M 1
Columbia, Mt., *B.C.* 39 P 9
Columbia R., *B.C.* 39 P 10
Columbia Lake, *B.C.* 39 Q10
Colville L., *N.-W. Terr.* 38 L 2
Colville Mts., *Victoria I., N.-W. Territories* 38 Q 1
Comber, *Ontario* 34 H10
Combermere, *Ontario* 35 N 7
Comencho L., *Quebec* 35 P 2
Commanda, *Ontario* 35 L 7
Commissaires, L. des, *Quebec* 35 S 4
Committee B., *N.-W. T.* 31 L 4
Compeer, *Alberta* 36 G 7
Conception B., *Nfd.* 33 T 6
Conception Harbour, *Newfoundland* 33 T 6
Conche, *Newfoundland* 33 R 3
Coney Arm, *Nfd.* 33 Q 4
Confusion B., *Nfd.* 33 R 3
Congress, *Saskatchewan* 36 L 9
Coniston, *Ontario* 34 K 6
Conklin, *Alberta* 39 S 8

Resolution I., *N.-W. Terr.* 31 N 5
Resolution L., *Quebec* 31 N 6
Restigouche, *Quebec* 32 F 5
Restigouche R., *N.B.* 98 E 6
Reston, *Manitoba* 37 Q 9
Restoule *Ontario* 35 L 6
Retlaw, *Alberta* 36 E 8
Revelstoke, *Br. Columbia* 39 O10
Revenue, *Saskatchewan* 36 J 6
Reward, *Saskatchewan* 36 H 6
Rexton, *New Brunswick* 32 H 7
Reykjavik, *Manitoba* 37 T 7
Reynaud, R.au, *Quebec* 32 H 5
Reynaud, *Saskatchewan* 37 M 6
Reynolds, *Manitoba* 36 F 1
Rhein, *Saskatchewan* 37 P 7
Rib Lake, *Ontario* 35 L 5
Ribstone, *Alberta* 36 G 6
Ribstone Cr., *Alberta* 36 F 6
Rice L., *Ontario* 35 M 8
Rice L., *Ontario* 34 H 5
Riceton, *Saskatchewan* 37 N 8
Richard, *Saskatchewan* 36 K 6
Richard Collinson Inlet, *N.-W. Territories* 30 H 3
Richards I., *N.-W. Terr.* 38 F 1
Richards Landing, *Ontario* 34 F 6
Richardson I., *Great Bear L., N.-W. Territories* 38 O 3
Richardson Is., *N.-W. T.* 38 S 1
Richardson Mts., *Yukon/N.-W. Terr.* 38 A 1
Richardson R., *Alberta* 39 S 6
Richardson, R., *N.-W. T.* 38 P 2
Richardson Sta., *Sask.* 37 N 8
Richdale, *Alberta* 36 F 7
Riche Pt., *Nfd.* 33 P 3
Richelieu, R., *Quebec* 35 R 7
Richibucto, *N.B.* 32 H 7
Rich Lake, *Alberta* 36 F 4
Richlea, *Saskatchewan* 36 J 7
Richmond, *Ontario* 35 P 7
Richmond, *Prince Ed. I.* 32 H 7
Richmond, *Quebec* 35 S 7
Richmond, co., *B.C.* 39 G 12
Richmond Hill, *Ontario* 35 M 9
Richmound, *Saskatchewan* 36 H 8
Rideau Can., *Ontario* 35 P 8
Rideau L., *Ontario* 35 O 8
Rideau, R., *Ontario* 35 P 7
Ridge, R., *Ontario* 34 F 2
Ridgedale, *Saskatchewan* 37 N 5
Ridgemont, *Ontario* 34 D 9
Ridgetown, *Ontario* 34 J 10
Ridgeville, *Manitoba* 37 V 9
Riding Mt., ra., *Manitoba* 37 R 8
Riding Mt. Nat. Park, *Man.* 37 R 8
Ridpath, *Saskatchewan* 36 J 7
Rigaud, *Quebec* 35 Q 7
Rigolet, *Labrador* 31 O 7
Rimbey, *Alberta* 36 C 6
Rimouski & R., *Quebec* 32 D 5
Riou L., *Saskatchewan* 38 U 6
Ripault, L., *Quebec* 32 K 2
Ripley, *Ontario* 34 J 8
Ripon, *Quebec* 35 P 7
Ritch I., *Great Bear L., N.-W. Territories* 38 O 2
River Denys, *Cape Breton I.* 33 L 8
Riverhead, *Newfoundland* 33 T 6
River Hébert, *N.S.* 32 H 8
Riverhurst, *Saskatchewan* 36 L 8
River John, *Nova Scotia* 32 J 8
River of Ponds, *Nfd.* 33 P 3
Riverport, *Nova Scotia* 32 H 9
Rivers, *Manitoba* 37 R 8
Rivers, L. of the, *Sask.* 37 M 9
Riverside, *Ontario* 34 H10
Rivers Inlet, *Br. Columbia* 39 K10
Riverton, *Manitoba* 37 U 8
River Valley, *Ontario* 34 K 6
Rivière-à-Claude, *Que.* 32 G 4
Rivière-à-la-Loutre, *Anticosti I., Quebec* 32 J 4
Rivière à Pierre, *Quebec* 35 S 6
Rivière-au-Renard, *Que.* 32 H 5
Rivière aux Graines, *Que.* 32 G 3
Rivière aux Rats, *Quebec* 35 S 5
Rivière Bleue, *Quebec* 32 C 6
Rivière-de-la-Chaloupe, *Anticosti I., Quebec* 32 K 4
Rivière du Loup, *Quebec* 32 C 6
Rivière du Milieu, *Quebec* 35 S 5
Rivière du Moulin, *Que.* 32 B 5
Rivière Héva, *Quebec* 35 M 4
Rivière la Madeleine, *Que.* 32 G 4
Rivière Ouelle, *Quebec* 32 B 6
Rivière Pentecôte, *Que.* 32 E 4
Rivière Pigou, *Quebec* 32 G 3
Rivières des Prairies, *Quebec* 35 S 8
Rivière St. Jean, *Quebec* 32 H 3
Rivière Verte, *N.B.* 32 D 6
Rivière Verte, *Quebec* 32 C 6
Robe Noire, L. de la, *Quebec* 32 K 3
Robertson Chan, *N.-W. Terr./Greenland* 31 N 1
Robertson L., *Quebec* 33 N 2
Robertsonville, *Quebec* 35 T 6
Robertville, *N.B.* 32 G 6
Roberval, *Quebec* 35 S 4
Robinson, *Yukon* 38 F 5
Robinson's, *Nfd.* 33 O 5
Robinsonville, *N.B.* 32 F 6
Robles del Rio. *See* Carmel Valley
Roblin, *Manitoba* 37 Q 7
Robsart, *Saskatchewan* 36 H 9
Robson, Mt., *Br. Columbia* 39 O 9
Rocanville, *Saskatchewan* 37 Q 8
Rochebaucourt, *Quebec* 35 N 4
Roche Percée, *Sask.* 37 P 9
Rocher, L. du, *Quebec* 33 O 2
Rocher River, *N.-W. T.* 38 R 5
Rochers, R. aux, *Quebec* 32 E 3
Rochester, *Alberta* 36 D 4
Rochfort Bridge, *Alberta* 36 B 5
Rock, R., *Yukon* 38 E 2
Rock, R., *Yukon* 38 K 5
Rock Bay, *Vancouver I., British Columbia* 39 L 10
Rockcliffe Airport, *Ottawa, Ontario* 34 D 8
Rockcliffe Park, *Ottawa, Ontario* 34 D 8
Rockglen, *Saskatchewan* 37 M 9
Rockhaven, *Sask.* 36 J 6
Rock Island, *Quebec* 35 S 7
Rockland, *Maine* 32 C 9
Rockland, *Ontario* 35 P 7
Rocknest L., *N.-W. Terr.* 38 Q 3
Rockwood, *Ontario* 34 K 9
Rocky L., *Manitoba* 37 Q 4
Rockyford, *Alberta* 36 D 7
Rocky Island L., *Ontario* 34 G 6
Rocky Mountain House, *Alberta* 36 C 6
Roddickton, *Nfd.* 33 Q 3
Rodney, *Ontario* 34 J 10
Roes Welcome Sd., *N.-W. Territories* 31 L 5
Roger, L., *Quebec* 35 M 5
Rogers, Mt., *Br. Columbia* 39 P 10
Rogersville, *N.B.* 32 G 7
Rohault, L., *Quebec* 35 Q 3
Rokeby, *Saskatchewan* 37 P 7
Roland, *Manitoba* 37 U 9
Rolla, *Br. Columbia* 39 N 8
Rollet, *Quebec* 35 L 5
Rolphton, *Ontario* 35 N 6
Romaine R., *Quebec* 32 J 3
Rondeau Prov. Park, *Ont.* 34 J 10
Ronge, Lac la, *Sask.* 30 J 6
Roosevelt, Mt., *B.C.* 39 L 6
Rooseveltown, *New York* 35 S 2
Root, R., *N.-W. Terr.* 38 L 4
Roquemaure, *Quebec* 35 L 4
Rorey L., *N.-W. Terr.* 38 J 2
Rorketon, *Manitoba* 37 S 7
Rosaire, *Quebec* 32 B 7
Rosalind, *Alberta* 36 E 6
Rose I., *Br. Columbia* 39 H12
Rose Pt., *Graham I., B.C.* 39 H 8
Rose Blanche, *Nfd.* 33 O 6
Rosebud, *Alberta* 36 E 7
Rosebud R., *Alberta* 36 D 7
Rosedale, *Alberta* 36 E 7
Roseheath, *Ontario* 35 M 8
Rose Lynn, *Alberta* 36 F 7
Rosemary, *Alberta* 36 E 8
Roseray, *Saskatchewan* 36 J 8
Rosetown, *Saskatchewan* 36 K 7
Rose Valley, *Sask.* 37 O 6
Rosevear, *Alberta* 36 A 5
Rosiers, C. des, *Quebec* 32 H 5
Roslyn L., *Ontario* 34 C 3
Ross I., *Manitoba* 37 U 4
Ross, R., *Yukon* 38 H 4
Rosseau, *Ontario* 35 L 7
Rossendale, *Manitoba* 37 T 9
Rossignol, L., *N.S.* 32 G 9
Rossland, *Br. Columbia* 39 P 11
Rossport, *Ontario* 34 C 4
Ross River, *Yukon* 38 G 4
Rossway, *Nova Scotia* 32 G 9
Rosswood, *Br. Columbia* 39 J 8
Rosthern, *Saskatchewan* 36 L 6
Rothesay, *N.B.* 32 G 8
Rouleau, *Saskatchewan* 37 N 8
Round Pond, *Nfd.*, 33 R 5
Round Harbour, *Nfd.* 33 R 4
Round Hill, *Alberta* 36 E 5
Roundrock L., *N.-W. T.* 39 R 3
Rounthwaite, *Manitoba* 37 S 9
Routhierville, *Quebec* 32 E 5
Rouvray, L., *Quebec* 32 B 4
Rouyn, *Quebec* 35 M 4
Rowan L., *Ontario* 36 J 1
Rowley, *Alberta* 36 E 7
Rowley I., *N.-W. Terr.* 31 M 4
Roxton, *Quebec* 35 S 7
Roy, L., *Quebec* 32 C 4
Royal, Mt., *Ontario* 34 B 3
Royal Geographical Society Is., *N.-W. Territories* 38 X 1
Royalties, *Alberta* 36 C 8
Ruddell, *Saskatchewan* 36 K 6
Ruel, *Ontario* 34 J 5
Rufus L., *N.-W. Terr.* 38 J 1
Rumsey, *Alberta* 36 E 7
Runnymede, *Saskatchewan* 37 Q 7
Rupert B., *Quebec* 35 L 1
Rupert, R., *Quebec* 31 M 7
Rupert R., *Quebec* 31 N 1
Rush Lake, *Saskatchewan* 36 K 8
Russell, *Manitoba* 37 Q 8
Russell, *Ontario* 31 P 7
Russell I., *N.-W. Terr.* 31 K 3
Russell L., *Manitoba* 37 Q 2
Russell L., *N.-W. Terr.* 38 Q 4
Russell L., *Saskatchewan* 39 V 7
Rutherglen, *Ontario* 35 L 6
Ruthilda, *Saskatchewan* 36 J 7
Rutland Station, *Sask.* 36 H 7
Rutledge L., *N.-W. Terr.* 38 S 5
Rutter, *Ontario* 34 K 6
Rycroft, *Alberta* 39 O 8
Rydal Bank, *Ontario* 34 F 6
Ryerson, *Saskatchewan* 37 Q 9
Ryland, *Ontario* 34 E 4
Ryley, *Alberta* 36 E 5
Saanich, *Br. Columbia* 39 M11
Sable C., *Nova Scotia* 32 G10
Sable I., *Nova Scotia* 33 N10
Sable Island Bank, *N.S.* 33 M10
Sable River, *Nova Scotia* 32 G10
Sables, R. aux, *Ontario* 34 H 6
Sachigo, R., *Ontario* 31 K 7
Sachs Harbour, *N.-W. T.* 30 G 3
Sackville, *N.B.* 32 H 8
Saco, *Maine* 32 B 10
Sacré-Coeur Saguenay, *Quebec* 32 C 5
Saganaga L., *Ontario* 37 Q 10
Saganash L., *Ontario* 34 H 3
Saglek B., *Labrador* 31 N 6
Saglouc, *Quebec* 31 M 5
Saguenay, R., *Quebec* 32 B 5
Ste. Adelaide, *Quebec* 32 F 4
Ste. Adèle, *Quebec* 35 Q 7
St. Agapit, *Manitoba* 35 T 6
Ste. Agathe, *Manitoba* 37 U 9
Ste. Agathe des Monts, *Quebec* 35 Q 6
Ste. Agnes, *Ontario* 35 U 3
St. Alban's, *Nfd.* 33 R 6
St. Albert, *Alberta* 36 D 5
St. Alexandre, *Quebec* 32 C 6
St.AlexisdesMonts, *Quebec* 35 R 6
St. Ambroise, *Quebec* 35 T 4
St. Anaclet, *Quebec* 32 D 5
St. Andrew's, *N.B.* 32 E 8
St. Andrew's, *Nfd.* 33 N 6
St. Andrew's Chan., *Cape Breton I.* 33 M 7
St. Ann B., *C. Breton I., Nova Scotia* 33 M 7
Ste. Ann, *Manitoba* 37 E 1
Ste. Anne, L., *Quebec* 32 E 3
Ste. Anne, R., *Quebec* 32 B 6
Ste. Anne de Beaupré, *Quebec* 32 B 6
Ste. Anne de Chicoutimi, *Quebec* 32 A 5
Ste. Anne de la Pérade, *Quebec* 35 S 6
Ste. Anne de la Pocatière, *Quebec* 32 B 6
Ste. Anne-des-Monts, *Que.* 32 F 4
Ste. Anne du Lac, *Que.* 35 P 6
St. Anns, *C. Breton I., N.S.* 33 M 7
St. Anthony, *Nfd.* 33 R 2
St. Antonin, *Quebec* 32 C 6
St. Arsène, *Quebec* 32 C 6
St. Athanase, *Quebec* 32 C 6
St. Aubert, *Quebec* 32 B 6
St. Augustin B., *Quebec* 33 O 2
St. Augustin-Saguenay, *Quebec* 33 O 2
St. Augustin R., *Quebec* 33 N 2
St. Barnabé Nord, *Quebec* 35 S 6
St. Barthélemi, *Quebec* 35 R 6
St. Benedict, *Sask.* 37 M 6
St. Benoit Labre, *Quebec* 32 B 7
St. Bernard, I., *Quebec* 35 Q10
Ste. Blandine, *Quebec* 32 D 5
St. Boniface, *Manitoba* 37 U 9
St. Boswells, *Sask.* 36 L 8
St. Brendan's, *Nfd.* 33 T 5
St. Bride, Mt., *Alberta* 36 B 7
St. Bride's, *Nfd.* 33 S 7
St. Brieux, *Sask.* 37 N 6
St. Bruno de Guigues, *Que.* 35 L 5
St. Camille, *Quebec* 32 B 7
St. Casimir, *Quebec* 35 S 6
St. Catharines, *Ontario* 35 L 9
St. Catherine Lock, *Que.* 35 S 10
St. Cécile, *Quebec* 32 B 8
St. Césaire, *Quebec* 35 R 7
St. Charles, *Quebec* 32 B 7
St. Charles R., *Quebec* 33 P 8
St. Clair, L., *Ont./Mich.* 34 H10
St. Clair R., *Ont./Mich.* 34 H10
St. Claude, *Manitoba* 37 T 9
St. Clement, *Quebec* 32 C 6
Ste. Clothilde, *Quebec* 35 S 7
St. Cœur de Marie, *Que.* 35 T 4
St. Côme. *See* Linière
St. Côme, *Quebec* 35 R 6
Ste. Croix, *N.B.* 32 E 8
Ste. Croix R., *Maine/N.B.* 32 E 8
St. Cyprien, *Quebec* 32 C 6
St. Cyrille, *Quebec* 35 S 7
St. Cyr Lake, *Sask.* 36 J 4
St. Damien, *Quebec* 32 B 7
St. David-de-Lévis, *Que.* 35 S 3
St. David's, *Newfoundland* 33 O 5
St. Denis, *Quebec* 32 C 6
St. Denis, *Quebec* 35 R 7
St. Donat, *Quebec* 35 Q 6
St. Elias, Mt., *Yukon* 38 C 5
St. Elias Mts., *Yukon/Alaska* 38 C 5
Ste. Elisabeth, *Quebec* 35 S 4
St. Eloi, *Quebec* 32 C 5
St. Elzéar de Laval, *Que.* 35 R 8
Ste. Émélie de l'Énergie, *Quebec* 35 R 6
St. Éphrem, *Quebec* 32 B 7
St. Eugène, *Quebec* 35 M 4
St. Eugène, *Quebec* 35 S 4
St. Eusèbe, *Quebec* 32 D 6
St. Eustache, *Quebec* 35 Q 7
St. Fabien, *Quebec* 32 D 5
Ste. Famille, *Quebec* 32 B 7
Ste. Famille d'Aumond, *Quebec* 35 P 6
St. Félicien, *Quebec* 35 S 4
Ste. Félicité, *Quebec* 32 E 5
St. Félix de Valois, *Que.* 35 R 6
St. Fintan's, *Nfd.* 33 O 5
St. Flavien, *Quebec* 35 T 6
Ste. Florence, *Quebec* 32 E 5
St. Fortunat, *Quebec* 35 T 7
St. Francis, *Maine* 32 D 6
St. Francis, C., *Nfd.* 33 T 6
St. Francis, L., *Quebec* 35 Q 7
St. François, L., *Quebec* 35 T 7
St. François, R., *Quebec* 35 S 7
St. François Xavier, *Que.* 35 S 7
St. Gabriel de Brandon, *Quebec* 35 R 6
St. Gédéon, *Quebec* 32 B 8
St. Gédéon, *Quebec* 35 T 4
Ste. Geneviève B., *Nfd.* 33 Q 2
St. George, *N.B.* 32 F 8
St. George, C., *Nfd.* 33 N 5
St. George's, *Nfd.* 33 O 5
St. Georges, *Quebec* 32 B 7
St. Georges, *Quebec* 35 S 6
St. George's B., *Nfd.* 33 N 5
St. Gérard, *Quebec* 35 S 7
St. Gérard, *Quebec* 35 T 7
Ste. Germaine, *Quebec* 32 B 7
St. Gervais, *Quebec* 32 B 7
St. Giles, *Quebec* 32 B 7
St. Godfroy, *Quebec* 32 G 5
St. Gregor, *Saskatchewan* 37 N 6
St. Gregory, Mt., *Newf.* 33 O 4
St. Guillaume, *Quebec* 35 S 7
Ste. Hélène, *Quebec* 32 C 6
Ste. Hélène, I., *Quebec* 35 S 9
St. Helier, *Quebec* 32 H 4
St. Hénédine, *Quebec* 32 B 7
St. Henri, *Quebec* 32 A 7
St. Herménégilde, *Que.* 35 T 7
St. Hyacinthe, *Quebec* 35 S 7
St. Honoré, *Quebec* 32 C 6
St. Honoré, *Quebec* 32 A 5
St. Ignace, *Ontario* 34 B 4
St. Ignace du Lac, *Quebec* 35 R 6
St. Irénée, *Quebec* 32 B 6
St. Isidore, *Quebec* 36 L 5
St. Isidore, *Quebec* 35 S 7
St. Jacques, *N.B.* 32 D 6
St. Jacques, *Quebec* 35 R 7
St. James, C., *Br. Columbia* 39 H 9
St. Janvier, *Quebec* 35 L 4
St. Jean, *Quebec* 35 R 7
St. Jean, L., *Quebec* 35 S 4
St. Jean, R., *Quebec* 32 H 3
St. Jean Baptiste, *Man.* 37 U 9
St. Jean Bosco, *Quebec* 35 S 5
St. Jean de Dieu, *Quebec* 32 C 5
St. Jean de Matha, *Que.* 35 R 6
St. Jean Port Joli, *Quebec* 32 B 6
St. Jérôme, *Quebec* 35 Q 7
St. Jérôme, *Quebec* 35 T 4
St. Joachim, *Quebec* 35 T 5
St. Joachim, *Quebec* 32 B 6
St. John, *New Brunswick* 32 F 8
St. John B. & I., *Nfd.* 33 P 3
St. John R., *Maine/N.B.* 32 E 7
St. John R., *Quebec* 32 G 5
St. John's, *Nfd.* 33 T 6
St. Joseph, *Quebec* 32 B 7
St. Joseph I., *Ontario* 34 G 6
St. Joseph, L., *Ontario* 31 K 7
St. Joseph d'Alma. *See* Alma
St. Joseph de Lévis, *Que.* 35 U 2
St. Joseph's, *Nfd.* 33 T 6
St. Jovite, *Quebec* 35 Q 6
St. Lambert, *Quebec* 35 T 6
St. Lambert, *Quebec* 35 R 7
St. Laurent, *Manitoba* 37 U 8
St. Laurent, *Quebec* 35 R 9
St. Laurent R., *Quebec* 33 Q 9
St. Lawrence, *Nfd.* 33 R 7
St. Lawrence, C., *C. Breton I., Nova Scotia* 33 M 6
St. Lawrence, G. of, *Canada* 32 K 6
St. Lawrence I., *Bering Sea* 30 B 5
St. Lawrence Islands Nat. Pk., *Ontario* 35 O 8
St. Lawrence R., *Canada/U.S.A.* 31 N 8
St. Lawrence Seaway, *Quebec/N.Y.* 35 P 8
St. Lazare, *Manitoba* 37 Q 8
St. Léon, *Quebec* 35 T 4
St. Léon, *Quebec* 32 E 5
St. Leonard, *N.B.* 32 E 6
St. Léonard, *Quebec* 35 S 6
St. Léonard de Port Maurice, *Quebec* 35 R 8
St. Léon-de-Standon, *Que.* 32 B 7
St. Lewis R., *Labrador* 33 P 1
St. Liboire, *Quebec* 35 S 7
St. Lin, *Quebec* 35 R 7
St. Louis, *Prince Ed. I.* 32 H 7
St. Louis, *Saskatchewan* 37 M 6
St. Louis, L., *Quebec* 35 R 7
St. Louis de Kent, *N.B.* 32 H 7
St. Louis du Ha Ha, *Que.* 32 D 6
Ste. Louise, *Quebec* 32 B 6
Ste. Lucie, *Quebec* 35 Q 6
St. Ludger, *Quebec* 32 B 8
St. Lunaire B., *Nfd.* 33 R 2
St. Malachie, *Quebec* 32 B 7
St. Marc des Carrières, *Quebec* 35 S 6
St. Marcel, *Quebec* 32 B 7
St. Margaret B., *N.S.* 32 J 9
St. Margaret B., *Nfd.* 33 P 2
Ste. Marguerite, R., *Que.* 32 B 5
Ste. Marguerite, R., *Que.* 32 F 3
Ste. Marie, *Quebec* 32 A 7
Ste. Marthe de Gaspé, *Quebec* 32 F 4
St. Martin, L., *Manitoba* 37 T 7
St. Martins, *N.B.* 32 G 8
St. Mary B., *Nova Scotia* 32 F 9
St. Mary, C., *Nova Scotia* 32 F 9
St. Mary Is, *Quebec* 33 N 3
St. Mary, Mt., *B.C.* 39 P 11
St. Mary Reefs, *Quebec* 33 N 3
St. Mary Res., *Alberta* 36 D 9
St. Mary's, *Nfd.* 33 T 7
St. Mary's, *Ontario* 34 J 9
St. Mary's B., *Nfd.* 33 S 7
St. Mary's C., *Nfd.* 33 S 7
St. Mary's R., *Nova Scotia* 33 K 8
St. Mathieu, *Quebec* 32 D 5
St. Mathieu, *Quebec* 35 M 4
St. Matthew I., *Bering Sea* 30 B 5
St. Maurice, R., *Quebec* 35 S 5
St. Maxine, *Quebec* 32 A 7
St. Michel de Laval, *Que.* 35 R 9
St. Michel des Saints, *Quebec* 35 R 6
St. Norbert, *Manitoba* 37 U 9
St. Omer, *Quebec* 32 F 5
St. Ours, *Quebec* 35 R 7
St. Pacôme, *Quebec* 33 C 6
St. Pamphile, *Quebec* 32 C 7
St. Pascal, *Quebec* 32 C 6
St. Patrice, L., *Quebec* 35 N 6
St. Paul, *Alberta* 36 F 4
St. Paul, *Quebec* 32 C 6
St. Paul I., *C. Breton I., Nova Scotia* 33 M 6
St. Paul R., *Quebec* 33 P 2
St. Paul-de-Montminy, *Quebec* 32 B 7
St. Paul du Nord, *Quebec* 32 C 5
St. Paulin, *Quebec* 35 R 6
St. Pauls Inlet, *Nfd.* 33 P 4
Ste. Perpétue, *Quebec* 32 C 6
St. Peter B., *Labrador* 33 R 1
St Peter Pt., *Quebec* 32 H 5
St. Peter's, *C. Breton I., Nova Scotia* 33 M 8
St. Peter's, *Prince Edward I.* 32 K 7
Ste. Petronille, *Quebec* 35 U 2
St. Philémon, *Quebec* 32 B 7
St. Pie, *Quebec* 35 S 7
St. Pierre, *Manitoba* 36 E 1
St. Pierre, *Quebec* 33 R10
St. Pierre & I., *Atlantic O.* 33 Q 7
St. Pierre, L., *Quebec* 35 S 6
St. Pierre & Miquelon, *Atlantic Oc.* 33 P 7
St. Prime, *Quebec* 35 S 4
St. Quentin, *N.B.* 32 E 6
St. Raphaël, *Quebec* 32 B 7
St. Raymond, *Quebec* 35 T 6
St. Rémi, *Quebec* 35 R 7
St. Robert, *Quebec* 35 R 7
St. Romaine, *Quebec* 32 A 8
Ste. Rose, *Quebec* 35 R 7
Ste. Rose du Dégelé, *Que.* 32 D 6
Ste. Rose du Lac, *Man.* 37 S 7
St. Samuel, *Quebec* 32 B 8
St. Sauveur, *Quebec* 35 R 7
St. Shott's, *Nfd.* 33 T 7
St. Siméon, *Quebec* 32 C 6
St. Simon, *Quebec* 32 C 5
St. Stephen, *N.B.* 32 E 8
St. Sylvestre, *Quebec* 32 A 7
Ste. Thècle, *Quebec* 35 S 6
St. Théophile, *Quebec* 32 B 8
Ste. Thérèse, *Quebec* 35 R 7
Ste. Thérèse, L., *N.-W. T.* 38 N 3
St. Thomas, *Ontario* 34 J 10
St. Tite, *Quebec* 35 S 6
St. Tite des Caps, *Quebec* 32 B 6
St. Urbain, *Quebec* 32 B 6
St. Vallier, *Quebec* 32 B 7
Ste. Véronique, *Quebec* 35 Q 6
St. Victor, *Quebec* 32 B 7
St. Vincent de Paul, *Que.* 35 R 8
St. Vincent's, *Nfd.* 33 T 7
St. Walburg, *Sask.* 36 H 5
St. Williams, *Ontario* 34 K10
St. Yvon, *Quebec* 32 H 4
Sakami L., *Quebec* 31 M 7
Salisbury, *New Brunswick* 32 G 7
Salisbury I., *N.-W. Terr.* 31 M 5
Salmo, *Br. Columbia* 39 P11
Salmon R., *Anticosti I., Quebec* 32 K 4
Salmon R., *New Brunswick* 32 G 7
Salmon, R., *Br. Columbia* 39 M 8
Salmon Arm, *Br. Columbia* 39 O10
Salmon Bay, *Quebec* 33 P 2
Saltcoats, *Saskatchewan* 37 P 7
Salt River, *N.-W. Terr.* 38 R 5
Salvador, *Saskatchewan* 36 H 6
Salvage, *Newfoundland* 33 T 5
Salvus, *Br. Columbia* 39 J 8
Sanctuary, *Saskatchewan* 36 J 7
Sand Hills, Great, *Sask.* 36 H 8
Sand Hills, Middle, *Alberta* 36 G 8
Sand L., *Ontario* 36 H 1
Sand L., Big, *Manitoba* 37 S 1
Sand L., Little, *Manitoba* 37 T 1
Sand R., *Alberta* 36 F 4
Sandbank L., *Ontario* 34 H 1
Sandfly L., *Sask.* 36 L 3
Sandilands, *Manitoba* 36 F 1
Sand Lake, *Ontario* 34 F 5
Sand Point L., *Minnesota* 36 K 2
Sandspit, *Moresby I., B.C.* 39 H 9
Sandtop, C., *Anticosti I., Quebec* 33 L 4
Sandwich B., *Labrador* 31 O 7
Sandwith, *Saskatchewan* 36 J 5
Sandy L., *Newfoundland* 33 Q 4
Sandy L., *Ontario* 31 K 7
Sandybeach L., *Ontario* 36 K 1
Sandy Creek, *Quebec* 35 O 7
Sandy Falls, *Ontario* 34 J 4
Sandy Lake, *Manitoba* 37 R 8
Sandy Lake, *Saskatchewan* 39 U 7
Sandy Narrows, *Sask.* 37 O 3
Sanford, *Maine* 32 B 10
Sanford, *Manitoba* 37 U 9
Sangudo, *Alberta* 36 C 5
Sanmaur, *Quebec* 35 R 5
Sante Agnes, *Quebec* 35 L 4
Sarnia, *Ontario* 34 H10
Sasamat, L., *Br. Columbia* 39 J 11
Sascumica L., *Quebec* 35 N 2
Saskatchewan, prov., *Canada* 30 J 7
Saskatchewan R., N., *Alberta/Saskatchewan* 36 K 6
Saskatchewan R., S., *Saskatchewan* 36 J 8
Saskatoon, *Sask.* 36 L 6
Saskeram L., *Manitoba* 37 Q 5
Satellite B., *N.-W. Terr.* 30 H 2
Saugeen, R., *Ontario* 34 J 8
Saugstad, Mt., *B.C.* 39 K 9
Saulnierville, *Nova Scotia* 32 F 9
Sault au Mouton, *Quebec* 32 C 5
Sault-aux-Cochons, R., *Quebec* 32 C 5
Sault Ste. Marie, *Ontario* 34 F 6
Saumur, L., *Quebec* 32 K 2
Saunders, *Alberta* 36 B 6
Sauterelles, L. aux, *Que.* 32 J 2
Savane R., *Quebec* 32 A 2
Savant Lake, *Ontario* 37 M 1
Savoff, *Ontario* 34 F 3
Savona, *Br. Columbia* 39 N10
Sawayan Pt., *Quebec* 35 L 1
Sawbill, *Manitoba* 37 Q 1
Sawdy, *Alberta* 36 D 4
Sawmill Bay, *N.-W. T.* 38 O 3
Sawyerville, *Quebec* 35 T 7
Sayabac, *Quebec* 32 E 5
Sayward, *Br. Columbia* 39 L 10
Scandia, *Alberta* 36 E 8
Scanterbury, *Manitoba* 37 V 8
Scapa, *Alberta* 36 F 7
Scarborough, *Ontario* 34 E 10
Scarborough Bluffs, *Ont.* 34 E 10
Scarth, *Manitoba* 37 R 9
Scatari I., *C. Breton I., Nova Scotia* 33 N 7
Sceptre, *Saskatchewan* 36 H 8
Schefferville, *Labrador* 31 N 7
Schreiber, *Ontario* 34 C 4
Schuler, *Alberta* 36 G 8
Schultz L., *N.-W. Terr.* 30 K 5
Schumacher, *Ontario* 34 J 4
Scie, R. à la, *Quebec* 33 R10
Sclater, *Manitoba* 37 R 7
Scollard, *Alberta* 36 E 7
Scotch Bay, *Manitoba* 37 T 8
Scotia, *Ontario* 35 L 7
Scotia Bay, *Br. Columbia* 38 G 6
Scotsburn, *Nova Scotia* 32 K 8
Scotsguard, *Saskatchewan* 36 J 9
Scotstown, *Quebec* 35 T 7
Scott, *Saskatchewan* 36 J 6
Scott, C., *Vancouver I., British Columbia* 39 J 10
Scott Inlet, *N.-W. Terr.* 31 M 3
Scott Is., *Br. Columbia* 39 J 10
Scott L., *Sask./N.-W. T.* 38 U 6
Scottsville, *Cape Breton I.* 33 L 7
Scout Lake, *Sask.* 37 M 9
Scudder, *Ontario* 34 H10
Scugog, L., *Ontario* 35 M 8
Sea I., *Br. Columbia* 39 G11
Seaforth, *Ontario* 34 J 9
Seager Wheeler L., *Sask.* 37 O 4
Seahorse Pt., *N.-W. Terr.* 31 L 5
Seal L., *N.-W. Terr.* 38 T 3
Seal, R., *Manitoba* 31 K 6
Seal Bight, *Labrador* 33 R 1
Seal Cove, *N.B.* 32 F 9
Seal Cove, *Newfoundland* 33 Q 4
Searchmont, *Ontario* 34 F 6
Searston, *Newfoundland* 33 N 6
Seattle, Mt., *Yukon/Alaska* 38 C 5
Seba Beach, *Alberta* 36 D 5
Sebago L., *Maine* 32 B10
Séchelles, L., *Quebec* 32 C 1
Sechelt, *Br. Columbia* 39 M11
Secretan, *Saskatchewan* 36 L 8
Sedalia, *Alberta* 36 G 7
Sedgewick, *Alberta* 36 F 6
Sedley, *Manitoba* 37 O 8
Seebe, *Alberta* 36 C 7
Seeleys Bay, *Ontario* 35 O 8
Seignelay, R., *Quebec* 32 C 1
Seldom, *Newfoundland* 33 S 4
Selkirk, *Manitoba* 37 V 8
Selkirk, *Ontario* 34 L 10
Selkirk I., *Manitoba* 37 S 5
Selkirk Mts., *B.C./Montana* 30 H 7
Selous, Mt., *Yukon* 38 G 4
Selwyn L., *N.-W. Terr.* 38 V 5
Selwyn Mts., *Yukon* 38 F 4
Semans, *Saskatchewan* 37 N 7
Senate, *Saskatchewan* 36 H 9
Senlac, *Saskatchewan* 36 H 6
Senneterre, *Quebec* 35 N 4
Sentinel Pk., *Br. Columbia* 39 N 8
Sept Îles, *Quebec* 32 F 3
Sept-Milles, L., *Quebec* 32 B 2
Serpent, R. au, *Quebec* 32 A 4
Serpentine R., *B.C.* 39 J 12
Seseganaga L., *Ontario* 37 N 1
Sesekinika Lake, *Ontario* 34 K 4
Settee L., *Manitoba* 37 U 1
Setting L., *Manitoba* 37 T 3
Seul, L., *Manitoba* 31 K 7
Seul, Lac, *Ontario* 31 K 7
Seven Islands. *See* Sept Îles
Seven Persons, *Alberta* 36 G 9
Seventy Mile House, *B.C.* 39 N10
Severn, *Ontario* 31 L 6
Severn, R., *Ontario* 31 L 6
Seward Glacier, *Yukon/Alaska* 38 C 5
Sexsmith, *Alberta* 39 O 8
Seymour, Mt., *B.C.* 39 H10
Seymour R., *B.C.* 39 H10
Shabaqua, *Ontario* 37 N 2
Shackleton, *Saskatchewan* 36 J 8
Shakespeare I., *Nipigon, L., Ontario* 34 B 3
Shalath, *Br. Columbia* 39 M10
Shallow B., *N.-W. Terr.* 38 F 1
Shallow Lake, *Ontario* 34 J 7
Shamrock, *Saskatchewan* 36 L 8
Sharbot Lake, *Ontario* 35 O 8
Shaunavon, *Saskatchewan* 36 J 9
Shawanaga, *Ontario* 34 K 7
Shawbridge, *Quebec* 35 Q 7
Shawinigan, *Quebec* 35 S 6
Shawville, *Quebec* 35 O 7
Shebandowan L., *Ontario* 37 M 2
Shedden, *Ontario* 34 J 10
Shediac, *New Brunswick* 32 H 7
Sheenborough, *Quebec* 35 N 7
Sheenjik R., *Alaska* 30 E 6
Sheep Cr., *Alberta* 39 O 9
Sheerness, *Alberta* 36 F 7
Sheet Harbour, *N.S.* 32 K 9
Sheguindah, *Ontario* 34 J 7
Sheho, *Saskatchewan* 37 O 7
Shehuen. *See* Chalia, R.
Shekak, R., *Ontario* 34 F 3
Shelburne, *Nova Scotia* 32 G10
Shelburne, *Ontario* 34 K 8
Sheldon Mt., *Yukon* 38 H 4
Sheldrake, *Quebec* 32 H 3
Shellbrook, *Sask.* 36 L 5
Shell Lake, *Sask.* 36 K 5
Shellmouth, *Manitoba* 37 Q 8
Shelter Bay, *Quebec* 32 F 3
Shepard, *Alberta* 36 D 7
Sheppard, Mt., *B.C.* 39 G 7
Sherard, C., *N.-W. Terr.* 31 L 3
Sherbrooke, *Nova Scotia* 32 L 8
Sherbrooke, *Quebec* 35 T 7
Sherbrooke L., *N.S.* 32 H 9
Sheridan, C., *N.-W. Terr.* 31 N 1
Sherman Basin, *N.-W. T.* 38 Z 2
Sherridon, *Manitoba* 37 Q 3
Sherwood L., *N.-W. T.* 38 W 5
Sheslay, *Br. Columbia* 39 H 6
Sheslay, R., *Br. Columbia* 39 H 6
Shickshock Mts., *Quebec* 32 F 5
Shigawake, *Quebec* 32 G 5
Shikag L., *Ontario* 37 M 1
Shillington, *Ontario* 34 K 4
Shining Tree, *Ontario* 34 J 5
Ship Cove, *Newfoundland* 33 S 6
Shipman, *Saskatchewan* 37 N 5
Shippegan & I., *N.B.* 32 H 6
Shipshaw Dam, *Quebec* 35 T 4
Shipshaw, R., *Quebec* 35 T 4
Shoal L., *Ontario* 36 G 1
Shoal Ls., *Manitoba* 37 U 8
Shoal Harbour, *Nfd.* 33 T 5
Shoal Lake, *Manitoba* 37 R 8
Shoe Cove, *Newfoundland* 33 R 4
Shortdale, *Manitoba* 37 R 7
Shouldice, *Alberta* 36 E 8
Shubenacadie, *Nova Scotia* 32 J 8
Shubenacadie L., *N.S.* 32 J 9
Shuswap L., *Br. Columbia* 39 O10
Sibbald, *Alberta* 36 G 7
Sibley Prov. Park, *Ont.* 34 B 4
Sickle L., *Manitoba* 37 R 2
Sid L., *N.-W. Terr.* 38 V 4
Sidewood, *Saskatchewan* 36 H 8
Sidney, *Manitoba* 37 S 9
Sidney, *Vancouver I., B.C.* 39 M11
Sifton, *Manitoba* 37 R 7
Sifton Pass, *Br. Columbia* 39 K 7
Sikanni Chief R., *B.C.* 39 M 7
Sillery, dist., *Quebec* 35 S 3
Silsby L., *Manitoba* 37 W 3
Silton, *Saskatchewan* 37 N 8
Silver Mt., pk., *Nfd.* 33 P 4
Silver R., *Nova Scotia* 32 G 9
Silver Centre, *Ontario* 35 L 5
Silver Heights, *Alberta* 36 F 6
Silver Islet, *Ontario* 34 B 4
Silver Star Prov. Park, *British Columbia* 39 O10
Silverthrone Mt., *B.C.* 39 K10
Simàrd, L., *Quebec* 35 M 5
Simcoe, *Ontario* 34 K10
Simcoe L., *Ontario* 35 L 8
Simmie, *Saskatchewan* 36 J 9
Simon L., *Quebec* 35 P 7
Simonette, R., *Alberta* 39 O 8
Simonhouse, *Manitoba* 37 Q 4
Simoom Sound, *B.C.* 39 K10
Simpson, *Saskatchewan* 37 M 7
Simpson B., *N.-W. Terr.* 38 Q 1
Simpson, Fort, *N.-W. Terr.* 30 G 5
Simpson I., *Ontario* 34 C 4
Simpson Is., *N.-W. Terr.* 38 R 5
Simpson L., *N.-W. Terr.* 38 K 1
Simpson Pen., *N.-W. Terr.* 31 L 4
Simpson Str., *N.-W. Terr.* 38 Y 1
Sintaluta, *Manitoba* 37 O 8
Sioux Lookout, *Ontario* 36 L 1
Sipiwesk, *Manitoba* 37 U 3
Sipiwesk L., *Manitoba* 37 U 3
Sir Alexander, Mt., *B.C.* 39 N 9
Sir Charles Hamilton Sd., *Newfoundland* 33 S 4
Sir Douglas, Mt., *Alberta/Br. Columbia* 36 B 8

Sir James McBrien, Mt., N.-W. Territories 38 J 4
Sir Sanford, Mt., B.C. 39 P 10
Sir Wilfred Laurier, Mt., British Columbia 39 O 9
Sisib L., Manitoba 37 S 6
Sisipuk L., Man./Sask. 37 Q 3
Sitidgi L., N.-W. Terr. 38 G 1
Skead, Ontario 34 K 4
Skead, Ontario 34 K 6
Skeena Mts., Br. Columbia 39 J 7
Skeena, R., Br. Columbia 39 J 8
Skeena Crossing, B.C. 39 K 8
Skidegate, Graham I., B.C. 39 G 9
Skiff, Alberta 36 F 9
Skookumchuk, B.C. 39 Q 11
Skowhegan, Maine 32 C 9
Skownan, Manitoba 37 S 7
Slate Is., Ontario 34 D 4
Slave L., Great, N.-W. T. 38 Q 5
Slave L., Lesser, Alberta 36 B 3
Slave Pt., Great Slave L., N.-W. Territories 38 Q 5
Slave R., N.-W. Terr. 38 R 5
Slave R., Lesser, Alberta 36 C 3
Slave Lake, Alberta 36 C 3
Sled L., Saskatchewan 36 K 4
Sleeper Is., N.-W. Terr. 31 M 6
Sleepers, The, Hudson Bay, Canada 31 L 6
Slocan, Br. Columbia 39 P 11
Slocan L., Br. Columbia 39 P 11
Sloko, R., Br. Columbia 38 G 6
Small L., Manitoba 37 U 1
Smart L., N.-W. Terr. 38 U 4
Smeaton, Saskatchewan 36 N 5
Smiley, Saskatchewan 36 H 7
Smith, Alberta 36 C 3
Smith Arm, bay, Great Bear L., N.-W. T. 38 M 2
Smith B., N.-W. Terr. 31 M 2
Smith I., Hudson B., N.-W. Territories 31 M 5
Smith, I., Quebec 31 M 5
Smith Pt., Nova Scotia 32 J 8
Smith Sd., N.-W. Terr. 31 M 2
Smithers, Br. Columbia 39 K 8
Smith River, Br. Columbia 38 K 6
Smiths Falls, Ontario 35 O 8
Smoking Mts., N.-W. T. 38 K 1
Smoky C., C. Breton I., Nova Scotia 33 M 7
Smoky, R., Alberta 39 P 8
Smoky R., Lit., Alberta 39 P 8
Smoky Falls, Ontario 34 H 2
Smoky Lake, Alberta 36 E 4
Smoothrock L., Ontario 34 A 2
Smooth Rock Falls, Ont. 34 J 4
Smoothstone L., Sask. 36 L 4
Smoothstone R., Sask. 36 L 3
Snag, Yukon 38 C 4
Snake, R., Yukon 38 G 3
Snare L., N.-W. Terr. 38 Q 3
Snare, L., Saskatchewan 39 U 6
Snare River, N.-W. Terr. 38 P 4
Snipe L., Alberta 36 A 3
Snowbird L., N.-W. Terr. 38 W 5
Snowden, Saskatchewan 37 N 5
Snowdrift, N.-W. Terr. 38 S 4
Snowdrift, R., N.-W. T. 38 S 4
Snowflake, Manitoba 37 T 9
Snow Lake, Manitoba 37 S 4
Snow Road, Ontario 35 O 8
Soda Creek, Br. Columbia 39 M 9
Sœurs, I. des, Quebec 35 S 10
Sombra, Ontario 34 H 10
Somerset, Manitoba 37 T 9
Somerset I., N.-W. Terr. 31 K 3
Sonningdale, Sask. 36 K 6
Sonora, Nova Scotia 33 L 8
Sooke, Br. Columbia 39 M 11
Sop's Arm, Newfoundland 33 Q 4
Sorel, Quebec 35 R 6
Sorrento, Br. Columbia 39 O 10
Soulanges Can., Quebec 35 Q 7
Sounding L., Alberta 36 G 6
Souris, Manitoba 37 R 9
Souris R., Man./N. Dak. 30 J 8
Souris, Prince Ed. I. 33 K 7
South B., Ontario 34 J 7
South Pt., Anticosti I., Que. 33 K 4
Southampton, N.S. 32 H 8
Southampton, Ontario 34 J 8
Southampton, C., N.-W. Territories 31 L 5
Southampton I., N.-W. T. 31 L 5
South Aulatsivik I., Labr. 31 N 6
South Baymouth, Ontario 34 H 7
South Brook, Nfd. 33 Q 4
South Brookfield, N.S. 32 H 9
Southend, Saskatchewan 39 W 7
Southern Harbour, Nfd. 33 S 6
Southey, Saskatchewan 37 N 8
South Fork, Sask. 36 J 9
South Harbour, Cape Breton I. 33 M 7
South Henik L., N.-W. T. 31 K 5
South Indian Lake, Man. 37 T 2
South Junction, Manitoba 36 F 1
South Lochaber, N.S. 33 K 8
South Nahanni, N.-W. T. 38 M 5
South Nelson, N.B. 32 G 7
South Paris, Maine 32 B 9
South Porcupine, Ontario 34 J 4
South River, Ontario 35 L 7
South Saskatchewan Dam, Saskatchewan 36 L 7
South Seal R., Manitoba 37 S 1
South Slocan, B.C. 39 P 11
Southwest C., Madeleine Is., Quebec 33 L 6
Southwest Pt., Anticosti I., Quebec 32 J 4
South Westminster, B.C. 39 J 12
Sovereign, Sask. 36 K 7
Sowden L., Ontario 37 M 1
Spalding, Saskatchewan 37 N 6
Spaniard's Bay, Nfd. 33 T 6
Spanish, Ontario 34 H 6
Spanish R., Ontario 34 J 6
Spearhill, Manitoba 37 T 7
Spedden, Alberta 36 F 4
Speers, Saskatchewan 36 K 6
Spence Bay, N.-W. Terr. 31 K 4
Spencer Crique, B., Que. 33 Q 9
Spences Bridge, B.C. 39 N 10
Sperling, Manitoba 37 U 9
Spirit River, Alberta 39 O 8
Spiritwood, Sask. 36 K 5
Split, C., Nova Scotia 32 H 8
Split L., Manitoba 37 V 2
Split Lake, Manitoba 37 V 2
Spondin, Alberta 36 F 7
Spragge, Ontario 34 H 6
Sprague, Manitoba 36 F 1
Springburn, Alberta 39 P 8
Spring Coulee, Alberta 36 D 9
Springdale, Newfoundland 33 Q 4
Springer, Mt., Quebec 35 Q 3
Springfield, N.B. 32 G 8
Springfield, Nova Scotia 32 H 9
Springfield, Ontario 34 K 10
Springhill, Nova Scotia 32 H 8
Springhill, Quebec 32 A 8
Springside, Saskatchewan 37 P 7
Spring Valley, Sask. 37 M 9
Springwater, Sask. 36 J 7
Spruce Brook, Nfd. 33 O 5
Sprucedale, Ontario 35 L 7
Spruce Lake, Sask. 36 H 5
Spurfield, Alberta 36 C 3
Spy Hill, Saskatchewan 37 Q 8
Squamish, Br. Columbia 39 M 11
Squattack, Quebec 32 D 6
Squaw L., Quebec 33 L 3
Stackpool, Ontario 34 J 5
Stagg L., N.-W. Terr. 38 Q 4
Stalin Mt., Br. Columbia 39 L 6
Stallworthy, C., N.-W. T. 31 K 1
Stalwart, Saskatchewan 37 M 7
Standard, Alberta 36 E 7
Stanley, New Brunswick 32 F 7
Stanley Mission, Sask. 37 N 3
Stanmore, Alberta 36 F 7
Stanton, N.-W. Terr. 38 J 1
Stapylton, N.-W. Terr. 38 P 1
Starbuck, Manitoba 37 U 9
Star City, Saskatchewan 37 N 6
Stave L., Br. Columbia 39 M 11
Stavely, Alberta 36 D 8
Stayner, Ontario 34 K 8
Steel L., Ontario 34 D 3
Steel R., Ontario 34 D 3
Steele, Mt., Yukon 38 C 5
Steen R., Alberta 38 P 6
Steep Creek, Sask. 37 M 5
Steephill L., Sask. 37 O 3
Steep Rock, Manitoba 37 T 7
Steep Rock Lake, Ont. 36 L 1
Stefansson I., N.-W. Terr. 30 J 3
Steinbach, Manitoba 37 V 9
Stellarton, Nova Scotia 32 K 8
Stenen, Saskatchewan 37 P 7
Stephenville, Nfd. 33 O 5
Stephenville Crossing, Newfoundland 33 O 5
Sterlet L., N.-W. Terr. 38 T 3
Stettler, Alberta 36 E 6
Stevens, Ontario 36 E 3
Stevenson, airfield, Man. 37 U 9
Stevenson L., Manitoba 37 W 5
Steveston, Lulu I., B.C. 39 G 12
Steveville Prov. Park, Alta. 36 F 8
Stewart, Br. Columbia 39 J 8
Stewart Cr., Sask. 37 N 5
Stewart, R., Yukon 38 D 4
Stewart, R., Yukon 38 D 4
Stewart River, Yukon 38 D 4
Stewart Valley, Sask. 36 K 8
Stewiacke, Nova Scotia 32 J 8
Stikine Ras., Br. Columbia 38 H 6
Stikine, R., Br. Columbia 39 H 7
Stirling, Alberta 36 E 9
Stirling, Ontario 35 N 8
Stirling, Quebec 35 S 5
Stockholm, Saskatchewan 37 P 8
Stockton, Manitoba 37 S 9
Stokes Bay, Ontario 34 J 7
Stonecliffe, Ontario 35 M 6
Stoneham, Quebec 32 A 7
Stone Mountain Prov. Park, British Columbia 39 L 6
Stonewall, Manitoba 37 U 8
Stoney Beach, Sask. 37 M 8
Stoney Creek, Ontario 35 L 9
Stony Mountain, Manitoba 37 U 8
Stony Plain, Alberta 36 D 5
Stony Rapids, Sask. 38 V 6
Stor I., N.-W. Terr. 31 L 2
Storkerson B., N.-W. T. 30 G 3
Stormy L., Ontario 36 K 1
Stornoway, Saskatchewan 37 P 7
Storthoaks, Saskatchewan 37 Q 9
Stouffville, Ontario 35 L 9
Stoughton, Manitoba 37 O 9
Strachan, Mt., B.C. 39 G 10
Stranraer, Saskatchewan 36 J 7
Strasbourg, Sask. 37 N 7
Stratford, Ontario 34 K 9
Stratford, Quebec 32 A 8
Strathclair, Manitoba 37 R 8
Strathcona Prov. Park, Vancouver I., B.C. 39 L 11
Strathlorne, C. Breton I., Nova Scotia 33 L 7
Strathmore, Alberta 36 D 7
Strathnaver, Br. Columbia 39 M 9
Strathroy, Ontario 34 J 10
Strawberry Hill, B.C. 39 J 12
Strawhat Depot, Quebec 35 R 5
Streamstown, Alberta 36 G 5
Strickland, Ontario 34 J 3
Strome, Alberta 36 E 6
Strongfield, Sask. 36 L 7
Stuart L. & R., B.C. 39 L 8
Stupendous Mt., B.C. 39 K 9
Sturgeon B., Manitoba 37 U 6
Sturgeon L., Alberta 39 P 8
Sturgeon L., Ontario 35 M 8
Sturgeon L., Ontario 37 L 2
Sturgeon L., Ontario 37 M 1
Sturgeon R., Alberta 36 C 5
Sturgeon R., Ontario 34 K 6
Sturgeon R., Sask. 36 L 6
Sturgeon Falls, Ontario 34 K 6
Sturgeon Landing, Sask. 37 Q 4
Sturgis, Saskatchewan 37 P 7
Success, Saskatchewan 36 J 8
Sudbury, Ontario 34 J 6
Suffield, Alberta 36 F 8
Suggi L., Saskatchewan 37 P 4
Sukunka, R., B.C. 39 N 8
Sullivan L., Alberta 36 F 6
Sullivan Bay, B.C. 39 K 10
Sultan, Ontario 34 H 5
Summerford, Nfd. 33 S 4
Summerland, Br. Columbia 39 O 11
Summerside, Prince Ed. I. 32 J 7
Summerville, Nfd. 33 T 5
Summit, Ontario 34 F 5
Summit Lake, B.C. 39 M 8
Sunderland, Ontario 35 L 8
Sundown, Manitoba 36 F 1
Sundre, Alberta 36 C 7
Sundridge, Ontario 35 L 7
Suni, Ontario 34 C 2
Sunnybrae, Nova Scotia 32 K 8
Sunnybrook, Alberta 36 C 5
Sunnynook, Alberta 36 F 7
Sunnyside, Newfoundland 33 T 6
Sunnyslope, Alberta 36 D 7
Sunset House, Alberta 39 P 8
Sunstrum, Ontario 36 K 1
Suomi, Ontario 37 M 2
Superb, Saskatchewan 36 H 7
Surf Inlet, Br. Columbia 39 J 9
Surprise, Br. Columbia 38 G 6
Surprise L., Br. Columbia 38 G 6
Surprise L., Quebec 35 Q 3
Surrey, co., Br. Columbia 39 J 12
Surrey Centre, B.C. 39 J 12
Sussex, New Brunswick 32 G 8
Sustut Pk., Br. Columbia 39 K 7
Sutton, Ontario 35 L 8
Sutton, Quebec 35 S 7
Sutton Bay, Ontario 35 L 5
Suwannee L., Manitoba 37 R 2
Sverdrup Chan., N.-W. T. 31 K 1
Sverdrup Is., N.-W. Terr. 30 J 2
Swalwell, Alberta 36 D 7
Swan Hills, Alberta 36 B 4
Swan L., Br. Columbia 39 J 8
Swan L., Manitoba 37 R 6
Swan R., Alberta 36 B 3
Swan R., Manitoba 37 Q 6
Swan Lake, Manitoba 37 T 9
Swan Plain, Saskatchewan 37 Q 6
Swan River, Manitoba 37 Q 6
Swansea, Ontario 34 C 10
Swanson, Saskatchewan 36 K 7
Swastika, Ontario 34 K 4
Swift, R., Br. Columbia 38 H 6
Swift Current, Nfd. 33 S 6
Swift Current, Sask. 36 K 8
Swiftcurrent Cr., Sask. 36 J 8
Swift River, Yukon 38 H 5
Sydenham, Ontario 35 O 8
Sydney, C. Breton I., N.S. 33 M 7
Sydney Mines, C. Breton I., Nova Scotia 33 M 7
Sylvania, Saskatchewan 37 N 6
Sylvan Lake, Alberta 36 C 6
Sylvester, Mt., Nfd. 33 R 5
Sylvia, Mt., Br. Columbia 39 L 6
Tabatière, La, Quebec 33 O 3
Taber, Alberta 36 E 9
Table Mt., Newfoundland 33 N 6
Tabor Prov. Park, Alta. 36 E 9
Tabusintac R., N.B. 32 G 6
Tadenet L., N.-W. Terr. 38 L 1
Tadoussac, Quebec 32 C 5
Tagish L., Br. Columbia 38 F 6
Tahi, R., Br. Columbia 38 G 6
Tahiryuak L., Victoria I., N.-W. Territories 38 R 1
Tahltan, Br. Columbia 39 H 6
Tahoe L., Victoria I., N.-W. Territories 38 T 1
Tahtsa, R., Br. Columbia 38 K 9
Takhini, R., N.-W. Terr. 38 F 5
Takipy, Manitoba 37 Q 3
Takiyuak L., N.-W. Terr. 38 R 2
Takla L., Br. Columbia 39 L 7
Takla Landing, B.C. 39 L 8
Taku, Br. Columbia 38 G 6
Taku, R., Br. Columbia 38 F 6
Taku Arm, L., Yukon 38 F 5
Talbot L., Manitoba 37 S 4
Talbot Inlet, N.-W. Terr. 31 M 2
Tall Pines, Saskatchewan 37 P 6
Talmage, Manitoba 37 O 9
Taltson River, N.-W. T. 38 R 5
Tamworth, Ontario 35 O 8
Tangier, Nova Scotia 32 K 9
Tangier Grand L., N.S. 32 K 9
Tannin, Ontario 37 M 1
Tantallon, Saskatchewan 37 Q 8
Tanzilla, R., Br. Columbia 38 H 6
Tara, Ontario 34 J 8
Tarnopol, Saskatchewan 37 M 6
Tarzwell, Ontario 34 K 4
Taschereau, Quebec 35 M 4
Taseko, Mt., Br. Columbia 39 M 10
Taseko, R., Br. Columbia 39 M 10
Tashota, Ontario 34 C 2
Tast, L. du, Quebec 35 N 1
Tatamagouche, N.S. 32 J 8
Tate, Saskatchewan 37 N 7
Tathlina L., N.-W. Terr. 38 P 5
Tatla L., Br. Columbia 39 L 10
Tatlayoko Lake, B.C. 39 L 10
Tatlow, Mt., Br. Columbia 39 M 10
Tatnam, C., Manitoba 31 K 6
Tatshenshini, R., B.C. 38 E 6
Taureau L., Quebec 35 R 6
Tavani, N.-W. Territories 31 K 5
Taverner B., N.-W. Terr. 31 M 4
Tavistock, Ontario 34 K 9
Tawatinaw & R., Alberta 36 D 4
Taylor, Br. Columbia 39 N 7
Taylor I., N.-W. Terr. 38 X 1
Taymouth, N.B. 32 F 7
Tazin L. & R., Sask. 38 T 6
Tebesjuak L., N.-W. T. 38 Y 4
Tecumseh, Ontario 34 H 10
Tees, Alberta 36 D 6
Teeswater, Ontario 34 J 9
Tehek L., N.-W. Terr. 31 K 4
Telegraph Creek, B.C. 39 H 7
Telkwa, Br. Columbia 39 K 8
Tellier, Quebec 32 F 3
Teltaka, Ontario 34 E 3
Temiscamie L., Quebec 32 A 2
Temiscamie R., Quebec 32 A 2
Temiscouata, L., Quebec 32 D 6
Témiskaming, Quebec 35 L 6
Tenby Bay, Ontario 34 G 6
Ten Mile L., Nfd. 33 Q 3
Tent L., N.-W. Terr. 38 T 4
Terence, Manitoba 37 R 9
Terrace, Br. Columbia 39 J 8
Terrace Bay, Ontario 34 C 4
Terra Nova & R., Nfd. 33 S 5
Terrebonne, Quebec 35 R 7
Terrence Bay, Nova Scotia 32 J 9
Terrenceville, Nfd. 33 S 6
Tescau L., Quebec 35 P 1
Teshekpuk L., Alaska 30 D 3
Teslin, Yukon 38 G 5
Teslin L., Yukon/B.C. 38 G 5
Teslin, R., Yukon/B.C. 38 F 5
Tessier, Saskatchewan 36 K 7
Tetachuck L., Br. Columbia 39 L 9
Tetagouche R., N.B. 32 F 6
Tête à la Baleine, Quebec 33 N 3
Tete Jaune Cache, B.C. 38 O 9
Tetreauville, Quebec 35 S 8
Teulon, Manitoba 37 U 8
Texada I., Br. Columbia 39 L 11
Thames, R., Ontario 34 H 10
Thamesville, Ontario 34 J 10
Thedford, Ontario 34 J 9
Thekulthili L., N.-W. T. 38 T 5
Thelon, R., N.-W. Terr. 38 W 3
Theodore, Saskatchewan 37 P 7
Therien, Alberta 36 F 4
Thesiger B., N.-W. Terr. 30 G 3
Thessalon, Ontario 34 G 6
Thetford Mines, Quebec 35 T 6
Thicket Portage, Man. 37 U 3
Thickwood Hills, Alberta 36 E 2
Thirty Thousand Is., Ont. 34 K 7
Thistle L., N.-W. Terr. 38 T 3
Thistle Creek, Yukon 38 D 4
Thoa R., N.-W. Terr. 38 T 5
Thom Bay, N.-W. Terr. 30 K 3
Thompson, Manitoba 37 U 3
Thompson, R., B.C. 39 N 10
Thompson Lake, N.-W. T. 38 R 4
Thompson Landing, N.-W. Territories 38 S 4
Thonokied L., N.-W. T. 38 T 3
Thorburn, N.S. 33 K 8
Thorhild, Alberta 36 D 4
Thornbury, Ontario 34 K 8
Thorndale, Ontario 34 J 9
Thornhill, Ontario 35 L 9
Thorold, Ontario 35 L 9
Thorsby, Alberta 36 C 5
Thorsteinson, L., Man. 37 U 1
Three Hills, Alberta 36 D 7
Threepoint L., Manitoba 37 T 3
Three Rivers, Quebec. See Trois Rivières
Three Rock Cove, Nfd. 33 N 5
Thubun Ls., N.-W. Terr. 38 S 5
Thule, Greenland 31 N 2
Thule Air Base. See Dundas
Thunder B., Ontario 37 O 2
Thunderhouse Falls, Ont. 34 G 2
Thurso, Quebec 35 P 7
Thutade L., Br. Columbia 39 K 7
Tiblemont, Quebec 34 N 4
Tichborne, Ontario 35 O 8
Tichfield, Saskatchewan 36 K 7
Tide L., Alberta 36 F 8
Tide Head, N.B. 32 F 6
Tidnish, Nova Scotia 32 J 8
Tignish, Prince Edward I. 32 H 7
Tika, Quebec 32 G 3
Tilbury, Ontario 34 H 10
Tilbury I., Br. Columbia 39 H 12
Tilley, Alberta 36 F 8
Tillsonburg, Ontario 34 K 10
Tilston, Manitoba 37 Q 9
Tilting, Newfoundland 33 S 4
Timagami, Ontario 35 L 5
Timagami L., Ontario 34 K 6
Timiskaming, L., Quebec/Ontario 35 L 5
Timmins, Ontario 34 J 4
Tingwick, Quebec 35 T 7
Tionaga, Ontario 34 H 4
Tip Top Hill, Ontario 34 D 4
Tisdale, Saskatchewan 37 N 6
Tiverton, Nova Scotia 32 F 9
Tiverton, Ontario 34 J 8
Tlell, Br. Columbia 39 H 9
Toad R., Br. Columbia 39 L 6
Toba Inlet, Br. Columbia 39 L 10
Tobermory, Ontario 34 J 7
Tobique R., N.B. 32 E 6
Todd Mt., N.B. 32 F 7
Tofield, Alberta 36 E 5
Tofino, Vancouver I., B.C. 39 L 11
Togo, Saskatchewan 37 Q 7
Tomiko, Ontario 35 L 6
Tompkins, Saskatchewan 36 J 8
Tondern, Ontario 34 E 3
Topland, Alberta 36 B 4
Topley Lodge, B.C. 39 K 8
Tor B., Nova Scotia 33 L 8
Torbay, Newfoundland 33 T 6
Tornado Mt., pk., Alberta/Br. Columbia 36 C 9
Torngat Mts., Labrador 31 N 6
Toronto, Ontario 35 L 9
Toronto Harb., Ontario 34 D 10
Toronto Island Airport, Ontario 34 D 10
Torquay, Saskatchewan 37 O 9
Torrance, Ontario 35 L 8
Torrington, Alberta 36 D 7
Tort, L. Le, Quebec 33 M 2
Tory Hill, Ontario 35 M 8
Tottenham, Ontario 35 L 8
Totzke, Saskatchewan 37 M 6
Touchwood Hills, reg., Saskatchewan 37 N 7
Toulnustouc R., Quebec 32 E 3
Tourgis L., N.-W. Terr. 38 U 3
Tourville, Quebec 32 B 6
Toutes Aides, Manitoba 37 S 7
Tracadie, N.B. 32 H 6
Tracadie, Nova Scotia 33 L 8
Tracy, New Brunswick 32 F 8
Trade L., Saskatchewan 37 O 3
Trail, Br. Columbia 39 P 11
Trainor L., N.-W. Terr. 38 N 5
Tramping Lake, Sask. 36 J 6
Trans-Canada Highway 35 N 8
Transcona, Manitoba 37 V 9
Travaillant L., N.-W. T. 38 G 2
Travers, Alberta 36 E 8
Tregarva, Saskatchewan 37 N 8
Treherne, Manitoba 37 T 9
Trembleur L., B.C. 39 L 8
Trenche, R., Quebec 35 S 5
Trent Can., Ontario 35 L 8
Trenton, Nova Scotia 32 K 8
Trenton, Ontario 35 N 8
Trepassey & B., Nfd. 33 T 7
Treptow L., Ontario 34 C 3
Triangle, Alberta 39 P 8
Tribune, Saskatchewan 37 O 9
Trilsbeck L., Ontario 34 F 2
Tring Junction, Quebec 32 B 7
Trinity, Newfoundland 33 T 5
Trinity, Newfoundland 33 T 5
Trinity B., Newfoundland 33 T 5
Triquet, L., Quebec 33 N 3
Trochu, Alberta 36 D 7
Troilus, L., Quebec 35 Q 2
Trois Pistoles, Quebec 32 C 5
Trois Rivières, Quebec 35 S 6
Trossachs, Saskatchewan 37 N 9
Trousers L., N.B. 32 F 6
Trout L., Br. Columbia 39 P 10
Trout L., N.-W. Terr. 38 N 5
Trout, R., Alberta 36 C 2
Trout, R., Br. Columbia 39 L 6
Trout, R., N.-W. Terr. 38 N 5
Trout Creek, Ontario 35 L 7
Trout Lake, Ontario 31 L 7
Trout River, Newfoundland 33 O 4
Truax, Saskatchewan 37 N 9
Truite, L. la, Quebec 35 M 5
Truro, Nova Scotia 32 J 8
Trutch, Br. Columbia 39 M 7
Trutch Cr., Br. Columbia 39 M 7
Tsitsutl Pk., Br. Columbia 39 L 9
Tuberose, Saskatchewan 36 J 8
Tuchodi, R., Br. Columbia 39 L 6
Tudhope, Ontario 34 J 4
Tugaske, Saskatchewan 36 L 8
Tuktoyaktuk, N.-W. Terr. 38 G 1
Tulabi Lake, Saskatchewan 37 O 4
Tulameen, Br. Columbia 39 N 11
Tulemalu L., N.-W. Terr. 38 Y 4
Tulsequah, Br. Columbia 39 G 6
Tunnel Dam, Ontario 34 G 6
Tunungayualuk I., Labr. 31 N 6
Tupper, Br. Columbia 39 N 8
Turgeon, R., Quebec 35 L 3
Turin, Alberta 36 E 9
Turnagain, R., B.C. 39 K 6
Turnberry, Manitoba 37 Q 5
Turnbull, Manitoba 37 S 4
Turner Valley, Alberta 36 C 8
Turnor L., Saskatchewan 39 T 7
Turtle L., Saskatchewan 36 J 5
Turtle Creek, N.B. 32 H 8
Turtleford, Saskatchewan 36 J 5
Turtle Mountain Prov. Park, Manitoba 37 R 9
Tusket, Nova Scotia 32 G 10
Tutshi L., Yukon 38 F 6
Tuxford, Saskatchewan 37 M 8
Tuya L., Br. Columbia 38 H 6
Twawwassen, B.C. 39 G 12
Tweed, Ontario 35 N 8
Tweedie, Alberta 36 F 4
Tweedsmuir Is., N.-W. T. 31 M 4
Tweedsmuir Provincial Park, British Columbia 39 K 9
Twelve Mile L., Sask. 36 L 9
Twillingate, Newfoundland 33 S 4
Twin Ls., N. & S., Nfd. 33 R 4
Two Brothers, Is., Hudson B., N.-W. Terr. 31 L 6
Twin City, Ontario 37 O 2
Twitya, R., N.-W. Terr. 38 J 3
Two Creeks, Manitoba 37 R 8
Two Hills, Alberta 36 F 5
Two Rivers, The, Sask. 39 W 8
Tyndall, Manitoba 37 V 8
Tyner, Saskatchewan 36 J 7
Tyne Valley, Prince Ed. I. 32 J 7
Tyrrell L., N.-W. Terr. 38 V 4
Tyvan, Manitoba 37 O 8
Ucluelet, Br. Columbia 39 L 11
Uhlman L., Manitoba 37 T 2
Umfreville, Ontario 36 L 1
Ungava B., Quebec 31 N 6
Union Point, Manitoba 37 U 9
United States Ra., N.-W. Territories 31 L 1
Unity, Saskatchewan 36 H 6
Unwin, Saskatchewan 36 H 6
Uplands, airport, Ontario 35 P 7
Upper Blackville, N.B. 32 G 7
Upper Duck I., Ontario 34 E 8
Upper Hay River, Alberta 39 P 6
Upper Humber R., Nfd. 33 P 5
Upper Kent, N.B. 32 E 7
Upper Laberge, Yukon 38 F 5
Upper Musquodoboit, Nova Scotia 32 K 8
Upper Stewiacke, N.S. 32 J 8
Upper Vaughan, N.S. 32 H 9
Upsala, Ontario 37 M 1
Upsalquitch & R., N.B. 32 F 6
Uranium City, Sask. 38 T 6
Urquhart L., N.-W. Terr. 38 G 1
Utik L., Manitoba 37 V 3
Utikuma L., Alberta 36 B 3
Utterson, Ontario 35 L 7
Uxbridge, Ontario 35 L 8
Val Barrette, Quebec 35 P 6
Val Brilliant, Quebec 32 E 5
Valcourt, Quebec 35 S 7
Val des Bois, Quebec 35 P 7
Val d'Or, Quebec 35 N 4
Val Gagné, Ontario 34 K 4
Val Laflamme, Quebec 35 N 4
Vallée Junction, Quebec 32 B 7
Valley, Nova Scotia 32 J 8
Valley Centre, Sask. 36 K 7
Valleyfield, Quebec 35 Q 7
Valleyview, Alberta 39 P 8
Val Limoges, Quebec 35 P 6
Val Marie, Saskatchewan 36 K 9
Valor, Saskatchewan 36 L 9
Valparaiso, Saskatchewan 37 N 6
Val Racine, Quebec 32 A 8
Val Tetreau, Quebec 34 C 8
Van Bruyssel, Quebec 35 S 5
Van Buren, Maine 32 E 6
Vancouver, Br. Columbia 39 M 11
Vancouver Airport, B.C. 39 G 11
Vancouver I., Br. Columbia 39 K 10
Vancouver, Mt., Yukon 30 F 5
Vancouver Heights, B.C. 39 H 11
Vandekerckhove L., Man. 37 Q 1
Vanderhoof, Br. Columbia 39 M 8
Vanguard, Saskatchewan 36 K 9
Vankleek Hill, Ontario 35 Q 7
Vanscoy, Saskatchewan 36 L 6
Vansittart I., N.-W. Terr 31 L 4
Vantage, Saskatchewan 37 L 9
Vassar, Manitoba 36 F 1
Vauxhall, Alberta 36 E 8
Vawn, Saskatchewan 36 J 5
Vegreville, Alberta 36 E 5
Vein L., Ontario 34 D 3
Venice, Alberta 36 E 4
Venn, Saskatchewan 37 M 7
Venosta, Quebec 35 O 7
Verchères, Quebec 35 R 7
Verdigris L., Alberta 36 F 9
Verdun, Quebec 35 S 10
Veregin, Saskatchewan 37 P 7
Verendrye, Parc de la, Quebec 35 N 5
Verlo, Saskatchewan 36 J 8
Vermilion L., Ontario 36 K 1
Vermilion & R., Alberta 36 G 5
Vermilion Bay, Ontario 36 J 1
Vermilion Chutes, Alberta 39 Q 6
Vermillion, R., Quebec 35 R 5
Verner, Ontario 34 K 6
Vernon, Br. Columbia 39 O 10
Vernon, Prince Edward I. 32 K 7
Verona, Ontario 35 O 8
Verte, B., N.S./N.B. 32 J 7
Verte, I., Quebec 32 C 5
Verton, L., Quebec 33 N 2
Verwood, Saskatchewan 37 M 9
Veteran, Alberta 36 F 6
Vibank, Manitoba 37 O 8
Viceroy, Saskatchewan 37 M 9
Victor L., Quebec 33 L 3
Victoria, Newfoundland 33 T 6
Victoria, Vancouver I., British Columbia 39 M 11
Victoria I., N.-W. Terr. 30 H 3
Victoria, L., Quebec 35 N 5
Victoria R., Nfd. 33 P 5
Victoria Str., N.-W. Terr. 38 X 1
Victoria Beach, Manitoba 37 V 8
Victoria Harbour, Ontario 35 L 8
Victoria Mine, Ontario 34 J 6
Victoriaville, Quebec 35 T 6
Vidora, Saskatchewan 36 H 9
Viger, Quebec 33 C 6
Viking, Alberta 36 F 5
Ville Marie, Quebec 35 L 5
Villemay, Quebec 35 T 3
Villemontel, Quebec 35 M 4
Villeroy, Quebec 35 T 6
Vilna, Alberta 36 F 4
Vingt-deuzième Mille, L. du, Quebec 32 J 3
Violet Grove, Alberta 36 B 5
Virden, Manitoba 37 R 9
Virginia Falls, N.-W. T. 38 K 5
Virginiatown, Ontario 35 L 4
Viscount, Saskatchewan 37 M 7
Viscount Melville Sd., N.-W. Territories 30 J 3
Vista, Manitoba 37 R 8
Vita, Manitoba 37 V 8
Vitré, L., Quebec 33 N 2
Vittoria, Ontario 34 K 10
Vonda, Saskatchewan 36 L 6
Vulcan, Alberta 36 D 8
Wababimiga L., Ontario 34 D 2
Wabamun & L., Alberta 36 C 5
Wabana, Newfoundland 33 T 6
Wabasca, Alberta 36 D 3
Wabasca L., North, Alta. 36 D 2
Wabasca L., South, Alta. 36 D 3
Wabasca, R., Alberta 39 Q 7
Wabatongushi L., Ontario 34 F 4
Wabigoon & L., Ontario 36 K 1
Wabinosh L., Ontario 37 N 1
Waboose Dam, Ontario 34 C 2
Wabos, Ontario 34 F 6
Wabowden, Manitoba 37 T 4
Wabush, Newfoundland 31 N 7
Waco, Quebec 32 G 2
Wacouno R., Quebec 32 G 2
Waddington, Mt., B.C. 39 L 10
Wadena, Saskatchewan 37 O 7
Wadham Is., Nfd. 33 T 4
Wadhams, Br. Columbia 39 K 10
Wadsley, Br. Columbia 39 G 11
Wagama L., Quebec 35 N 2
Wagaming, Ontario 34 B 2
Wager B., N.-W. Terr. 31 L 4
Wager Bay, N.-W. Terr. 31 K 4
Wahpeton, N. Dakota 30 K 8
Wainwright, Alberta 36 G 6
Waitville, Saskatchewan 37 M 6
Wakami L., Ontario 34 H 5
Wakaw, Saskatchewan 37 M 6
Wakefield, Quebec 35 P 7
Wakomata L., Ontario 34 G 6
Wakopa, Manitoba 37 S 9
Wakwayowkastic, R., Ontario 34 K 2
Walcott, Br. Columbia 39 K 8
Waldeck, Saskatchewan 36 K 8
Waldheim, Saskatchewan 36 L 6
Waldo, Br. Columbia 36 B 9
Waldoboro, Maine 32 C 9
Waldron, Saskatchewan 37 P 8
Wales I., N.-W. Terr. 31 L 4
Walker B., Victoria I., N.-W. Territories 38 O 1
Walker L., Manitoba 37 V 4
Walker L., Quebec 32 E 3
Walkerton, Ontario 34 J 8
Wallace, Nova Scotia 32 J 8
Wallace, Ontario 35 M 7
Wallace Mt., Alberta 36 B 3
Wallaceburg, Ontario 34 H 10
Wallacetown, Ontario 34 J 10
Walmsley L., N.-W. Terr. 38 T 4
Walsh, Alberta 36 G 9
Walsh, Mt., Yukon 38 D 5
Waltham Station, Quebec 35 O 7
Walton, Nova Scotia 32 J 8
Walton, Ontario 34 J 9
Wanapital L., Ontario 34 K 6
Wandering River, Alberta 36 E 3
Wanless, Manitoba 37 Q 4
Wanup, Ontario 34 K 6
Wapawekka Hills, Sask. 37 N 4
Wapawekka L., Sask. 37 N 4
Wapella, Saskatchewan 37 P 8
Wapikamaski, Ontario 37 N 1
Wapisu L., Manitoba 37 S 3
Wapiti, R., Alberta 39 O 8
Wapus L., Saskatchewan 37 P 2
Wapustagamau L., Quebec 33 O 2
Warburg, Alberta 36 C 5
Warden Junction, Alberta 36 E 6
Ward Hunt I., N.-W. T. 31 M 1
Wardlow, Alberta 36 F 8
Wardner, Br. Columbia 39 Q 11
Ware, Br. Columbia 39 L 7
Warkworth, Ontario 35 N 8
Warm Bay Hotsprings, British Columbia 38 G 6
Warneford, Ontario 34 B 3
Warner, Alberta 36 E 9
Warren, Ontario 34 K 6
Warren Pt., N.-W. Terr. 38 G 1
Warren Landing, Man. 37 U 5
Warspite, Alberta 36 E 4
Wartime, Saskatchewan 36 J 7
Warwick, Quebec 35 T 7
Wasa, British Columbia 39 Q 11
Wasaga Beach, Ontario 34 K 8

PART TWO—WORLD INDEX

PAGES 41-100

LIST OF ABBREVIATIONS

Afghan. Afghanistan
Afr. Africa
Ala. Alabama
Alta. Alberta
Alg. Algeria
Antarc. Antarctica
Arabia, Saudi-Arabia
Arch. Archipelago
Argent. Argentina
Ariz. Arizona
Ark. Arkansas
Aust. Australia
Aut. Autonomous
B. Bay, Bahia, Baie, Bucht
Baluch. Baluchistan
B.C. British Columbia
Belg., Belgium, Belgian
Bol. Bolivia
Br. British
Bulg. Bulgaria
C. Cape, Cabo, Cap
Cal. California
Can. Canal
Car. Carolina
Cel. Celebes
Cent. Central
Chan. Channel
Co. County
Col. Colony
Colo. Colorado
Colomb. Colombia
Conn. Connecticut
Cord. Cordillera
Cr. Creek
Czech. Czechoslovakia
Del. Delaware
Den. Denmark
Dep. Department
Des. Desert
Dist. District
Div. Division
Dom. Dominicana
E. East, Eastern
Ecua. Ecuador
E.I. East Indies
Eiln. Eilanden
Eire Republic of Ireland
Eng. England
Erit. Eritrea
Ethio. Ethiopia
Fd. Fjord
Fla. Florida
Fr. French, France
G. Gulf, Golfe, Golfo, Guba
Ga. Georgia
Geb. Gebirge (Mountains)
Ger. Germany
G.F. Goldfield
Grp. Group
Gt. Great
Guat. Guatemala
Harb. Harbour
Hd. Head
Hisp. Hispaniola
Hond. Honduras
Hung. Hungary
I., Is. Island, Islands, Île, Îles
Ia. Iowa
Ida. Idaho
Ill. Illinois
Ind. Indiana
Indon. Indonesia
It. Italian, Italy
Iv. Cst. Ivory Coast
Jeb. Jebel (Mountain)
Kan. Kansas
Kazakh. Kazakhskaya S.S.R.
Kep. Kepulauan (Islands)
Kirgiz. Kirgizskaya S.S.R.
Ky. Kentucky
L. Lake, Loch, Lough, Lago, Lac, Lagoon, Lagoa
La. Louisiana
Ld. Land
Leb. Lebanon
Lit. Little
Lith. Lithuania
Lr. Lower
Madag. Madagascar
Man. Manitoba
Mass. Massachusetts
Maur. Mauritania
Md. Maryland
Me. Maine
Mex. Mexico
Mich. Michigan
Minn. Minnesota
Miss. Mississippi
Mo. Missouri
Mong. Mongolia
Mont. Montana
Moçamb. Moçambique
Mt., Mte. Mount, Mont, Monte
N. North, Northern, New
Nat. National
N.B. New Brunswick
N.C. North Carolina
N. Dak. North Dakota
Neb. Nebraska
Nev. Nevada
Nfd. Newfoundland
N.H. New Hampshire
Nic. Nicaragua
N. Ire. Northern Ireland
N.J. New Jersey
N. Mex. New Mexico
N.S. Nova Scotia
N.S.W. New South Wales
N.-W. Terr. North-West Territories
N.Y. New York
N.Z. New Zealand
O. Ohio
O., Os., Ostrov (Island)
Ova., Ostrova (Islands)
Oc. Ocean
O.F.S. Orange Free State
Okla. Oklahoma
Ont. Ontario
Ore. Oregon
Oz. Ozero (Lake)
Pa. Pennsylvania
Pac. Pacific
Pak. Pakistan
Pan. Panama
Para. Paraguay
P.E.I. Prince Edward Island
Pen. Peninsula
Phil. Philippines
Pk. Peak, Park
Plat. Plateau
Pol. Poluostrov (Peninsula)
Port. Portuguese, Portugal
Princip. Principality
Prot. Protectorate
Prov. Province
Pt. Point, Pointe
Pta. Punta (Point)
Pto. Puerto
Qnsld. Queensland
Que. Quebec
R. River, Rio, Rivière
Ra. Range
Rep. Republic
Res. Reservoir
Rhod. Rhodesia
R.I. Rhode Island
Rum. Rumania
Russ. Russia
S. South, Southern
Sa. Serra, Sierra
Sard. Sardinia
Sask. Saskatchewan
S.C. South Carolina
Scot. Scotland
Sd. Sound
S. Dak. South Dakota
S. San, Santo
Set. Settlement
Sol. Solomon
Som. Somaliland
Sp. Spanish, Spain
S.S.R. Soviet Socialist Republic
St., Ste., Sta. Saint, Sainte, Santa
Str. Strait
Swed. Sweden
Switz. Switzerland
Tadzhik. Tadzhikskaya S.S.R.
Tan. Tanzania
Tenn. Tennessee
Terr. Territory
Tex. Texas
Trans. Transvaal
Turkmen. Turkmenskaya S.S.R.
Ukr. Ukraine
Up. Upper
U.S.A. United States of America
U.S.S.R. Union of Soviet Socialist Republics
Ut. Utah
Uzbek. Uzbekskaya S.S.R.
Va. Virginia
Val. Valley
Vdkhr. Vodokhranilishche (Reservoir)
Venez. Venezuela
Vict. Victoria
Vol. Volcano
Vt. Vermont
W. West, Western
Wash. Washington
W.I. West Indies
Wis. Wisconsin
Wyo. Wyoming
Yugosl. Yugoslavia

Aach **Alor**

Aachen, *Germany* **64 Ac**
Aalborg, *Denmark* **63 Dh**
Aalen, *Germany* **64 Dd**
Aalestrup, *Denmark* **63 Ch**
Aalsmeer, *Netherlands* **60 Cb**
Aalst. See Alost
Aalten, *Netherlands* **60 Ec**
Aarau, *Switzerland* **61 Da**
Aarberg, *Switzerland* **61 Ca**
Aarburg, *Switzerland* **61 Ca**
Aardenburg, *Netherlands* **60 Bc**
Aare, R., *Switzerland* **61 Ca**
Aargau, canton, *Switzerland* **61 Da**
Aarhus, *Denmark* **63 Dh**
Aars, *Denmark* **63 Ch**
Aarschot, *Belgium* **60 Cd**
Aba, *Congo* **93 Gd**
Abacaxis R., *Brazil* **48 Fe**
Abaco I., Gt., *Bahama Is.* **47 Da**
Abaco I., Lit., *Bahama Is.* **47 Da**
Abadan, *Persia* **88 Ec**
Abadeh, *Persia* **89 Fc**
Abaete, *Brazil* **49 Hd**
Abajo Pk., *Utah* **42 Ed**
Abakan, *Russia* **75 Jc**
Abal Dufaf, *Arabia* **88 Dc**
Abancay, *Peru* **48 Cf**
Abarqu, *Persia* **89 Fc**
Abashiri & B., *Japan* **82 Jb**
Abau, *Papua* **53 Jb**
Abaya L., *Ethiopia* **93 Hc**
Abbeville, *France* **68 Da**
Abbottabad, *W. Pakistan* **86 Cc**
Abdul Aziz, Jebel, *Syria* **88 Db**
Abdulino, *Russia* **77 Ld**
Abeche, *Chad* **95 Kf**
Abeele, *Belgium* **60 Ad**
Abelessa, *Algeria* **94 Fd**
Abengourou, *Ivory Coast* **94 Eg**
Abeokuta, *Nigeria* **94 Fg**
Aberaeron, *Wales* **59 Eh**
Aberdare, *Wales* **59 Ej**
Aberdeen, *S. Dakota* **43 Gb**
Aberdeen, *Washington* **45 Ab**
Aberdeen & co., *Scotland* **58 Fc**
Aberfeldy, *Scotland* **58 Ed**
Aberfoyle, *Scotland* **58 Ed**
Abergavenny, *Britain* **59 Ej**
Aberystwyth, *Wales* **59 Eh**
Abha, *Arabia* **88 Df**
Abidjan, *Ivory Coast* **94 Eg**
Ab-i-Istada L., *Afghanistan* **89 Jc**
Abilene, *Texas* **42 Ge**
Abingdon, *Virginia* **43 Kd**
Abington, *Massachusetts* **44 Ea**
Abisko, *Sweden* **62 Hb**
Abomey, *Dahomey* **94 Fg**
Abrantes, *Portugal* **66 Ac**
Abrets, les, *France* **68 Fd**
Abrud, *Rumania* **72 Da**
Abruzzi, dep., *It.* **70 Dd**
Abtenau, *Austria* **64 Ee**
Abu, *India* **84 Dd**
Abu al Abyad, *Trucial States* **89 Fe**
Abu Arish, *Arabia* **88 Df**
Abu Bahr, *Arabia* **88 Ee**
Abu Deleiq, *Sudan* **95 Me**
Abu Dhabi, *Trucial States* **89 Fe**
Abu ed Duhur, *Syria* **90 Fb**
Abu el Jurdhan, *Jordan* **90 Dg**
Abu Jifan, *Arabia* **88 Ee**
Abu Kemal, *Syria* **88 Dc**
Abumombozi, *Congo* **92 Ed**
Abunã, *Brazil* **48 De**
Abu Qurqas, *Egypt* **95 Mc**
Abuta, *Japan* **82 Gc**
Abuya Myeda, Mt., *Ethiopia* **93 Hb**
Abu Zabad, *Sudan* **95 Lf**
Abyei, *Sudan* **95 Lg**
Abyy, *Russia* **75 Pb**
Åbyn, *Sweden* **62 Jd**
Acajutla, *Salvador* **47 Bd**
Acambaro, *Mexico* **46 Dc**
Acaponeta, *Mexico* **46 Cc**
Acapulco, *Mexico* **46 Dd**
Acara & R., *Brazil* **49 Hd**
Acarigua, *Venezuela* **48 Db**
Acatlan, *Mexico* **46 Ed**
Accra, *Ghana* **94 Eg**
Achaguas, *Venezuela* **48 Db**
Achao, *Chile* **50 Bf**
Achill I., *Eire* **59 Ag**
Achinsk, *Russia* **75 Jc**
Achray, *Ontario* **40 Hc**
Acklins, I., *Bahamas Is.* **47 Eb**
Aconcagua, Mt., *Argentina* **50 Cd**
Açores, Is., *Atlantic Ocean* **94 Ba**
Acorizal, *Brazil* **49 Fg**
Acoyapa, *Nicaragua* **47 Bd**
Acre, *Israel* **90 De**
Actaeon Grp., *Tuamotu Arch.* **99 Mk**
Actonvale, *Quebec* **40 Kc**
Açu & R., *Brazil* **49 Ke**
Ada, *Oklahoma* **42 Ge**
Adak, I., *Aleutian Is.* **43 Vm**
Adalia. See Antalya
Adam, *Muscat & Oman* **89 Ge**
Adama, *Ethiopia* **93 Hc**
Adamello, Mt., *Italy* **70 Cb**
Adams, *New York* **40 Hd**
Adam's Bridge, *India-Ceylon* **84 Eg**
Adams, Mt., *Washington* **45 Cb**
Adam's Pk., *Ceylon* **84 Fg**
Adana, *Turkey* **88 Cb**
Adapazari, *Turkey* **88 Ba**
Adare, *Eire* **59 Bh**
Adare, C., *Antarctica* **100 Lb**
Adavale, *Queensland* **53 He**
Addis Ababa, *Ethiopia* **93 Hc**
Addis Derra, *Ethiopia* **93 Hb**
Addison, *New York* **44 Ba**
Adelaer, C., *Greenland* **41 Pc**
Adelaide, *Cape Province* **91 Df**
Adelaide, *S. Australia* **53 Gf**
Adelaide, I., *Antarctica* **100 Sc**
Adelaide River, *N. Terr., Aust.* **52 Fb**
Adelboden, *Switzerland* **61 Cb**
Ademuz, *Spain* **67 Eb**
Aden, *S. Yemen* **88 Eg**
Aden. See Southern Yemen, Republic of
Aden, G. of, *Africa-Arabia* **54 Dg**
Adh Dhahiriya, *Jordan* **90 Cf**
Adhoi, *India* **84 Dd**
Adhra, *Syria* **90 Ed**
Adi, I., *W. Irian* **79 Kl**
Adi Kaie, *Eritrea* **93 Hb**
Adilabad, *India* **84 Ee**
Adirondack Mts., *New York* **40 Jc**
Adi Ugri, *Eritrea* **93 Hb**
Admiralty G., *W. Australia* **52 Eb**
Admiralty Is., *Pacific Ocean* **98 Dh**
Adolfo Alsina, *Argentina* **50 De**
Adoni, *India* **84 Ee**
Adoumre, *Cameroon* **95 Hg**
Adour R., *France* **69 Ce**
Adra, *Spain* **66 Dd**
Adraj, *Arabia* **89 Fe**
Adrano, *Sicily* **71 Eg**
Adrar, *Algeria* **94 Ec**
Adria, *Italy* **70 Dc**
Adrian, *Michigan* **40 De**
Adriatic Sea, *Italy* **70 Ed**
Aduwa, *Ethiopia* **93 Hb**
Aegean Sea, *Greece* **73 Ee**
Aeltre, *Belgium* **60 Bc**
Æröskobing, *Denmark* **63 Dj**
Aesch, *Switzerland* **61 Ca**
Afferden, *Netherlands* **60 Ec**
Affua, *Brazil* **49 Gd**
Afghanistan, *Asia* **89 Hc**
Afif, *Arabia* **88 Ee**
Afogados de Ingazeira, *Brazil* **49 Ke**
Afognak I., *Alaska* **43 Xm**
Afrin, *Syria* **90 Ea**
Afula, *Israel* **90 De**
Afyon, *Turkey* **88 Bb**
Agab Workei, *Ethiopia* **93 Hb**
Agadès, *Niger* **94 Ge**
Agadir, *Morocco* **94 Db**
Agartala, *India* **85 Hd**
Agattu, I., *Aleutian Is.* **43 Um**
Agawa, *Ontario* **40 Db**
Agde, *France* **69 Ee**
Agen, *France* **69 Dd**
Agiabampo, *Mexico* **46 Cb**
Agira, *Sicily* **71 Eg**
Agnebilekrou, *Ivory Coast* **94 Eg**
Agno, *Switzerland* **61 Dc**
Agordat, *Eritrea* **93 Ha**
Agra, *India* **87 Bb**
Agram. See Zagreb
Agrigento, *Sicily* **71 Dg**
Agrihan, I., *Mariana Is.* **98 Df**
Agrinion, *Greece* **73 Ce**
Agropoli, *Italy* **71 Ee**
Agua Clara, *Brazil* **49 Gh**
Aguadas, *Colombia* **48 Bb**
Aguadilla, *Puerto Rico* **47 Fc**
Aguadulce, *Panama* **47 Ce**
Agua Prieta, *Mexico* **46 Ca**
Aguaray, *Argentina* **50 Db**
Aguascalientes, *Mexico* **46 Dc**
Agudo, *Spain* **66 Cc**
Agudos, *Brazil* **49 Hh**
Aguilar, *Spain* **66 Cd**
Aguilar de Campos, *Spain* **66 Ca**
Aguilas, *Spain* **67 Ed**
Aguirre, B., *Argentina* **50 Cj**
Agulhas C., *Cape Province* **91 Cf**
Agusta, *W. Australia* **52 Cf**
Ahar, *Persia* **88 Eb**
Ahmadnegar, *India* **84 De**
Ahmadpur, *W. Pakistan* **86 Bf**
Ahmedabad, *India* **84 Dd**
Ahraura, *India* **87 Dc**
Ahtopol, *Bulgaria* **72 Fc**
Ahuachapan, *Salvador* **47 Ad**
Ahualulco, *Mexico* **46 Dc**
Ahus, *Sweden* **63 Fj**
Ahvaz, *Persia* **88 Ec**
Ahvenanmaa, *Finland* **63 Hf**
Ahwar, *S. Yemen* **88 Eg**
Aigle, *Switzerland* **61 Bb**
Aihunkiu, *China* **78 Ja**
Aijal, *India* **85 Hd**
Aikawa, *Japan* **82 Fe**
Aileron, *N. Terr., Aust.* **53 Fd**
Aim, *Russia* **75 Nc**
Aimores, *Brazil* **49 Jg**
Ain, dep., *France* **68 Fc**
Ain Galakka, *Chad* **94 Je**
Ain Safra, *Mauritania* **94 Ce**
Ain Sefra, *Algeria* **94 Eb**
Aire, *France* **69 Ce**
Aire, R., *England* **59 Gg**
Airolo, *Switzerland* **61 Db**
Aisne, dep., *France* **68 Eb**
Aiun, El, *Sp. W. Africa* **94 Cc**
Aix, *France* **69 Fe**
Aix, Mt., *Washington* **45 Cb**
Aix-la-Chapelle. See Aachen
Aiyina I., *Greece* **73 Df**
Aiyion, *Greece* **73 Ce**
Aizpute, *Latvia* **63 Jh**
Ajaccio & G. d', *Corsica* **71 Be**
Ajaigarh, *India* **87 Cc**
Ajanta, *India* **84 Ed**
Ajanta Ra. See Sahiadriparvat
Ajib, *Muscat & Oman* **89 Ge**
Ajibba, *Arabia* **88 Dd**
Ajigasawa, *Japan* **82 Gd**
Ajlun, *Jordan* **90 De**
Ajmer, *India* **84 Dc**
Ajoewa, *Surinam* **49 Fc**
Akalkot, *India* **84 Ee**
Akan Nat. Park, *Japan* **82 Hc**
Akanthou, *Cyprus* **90 Bb**
Akaoka, *Japan* **82 Ch**
Akarnania & Aitolia, *Greece* **73 Ce**
Akaroa, *New Zealand* **51 De**
Akashi, *Japan* **82 Dg**
Akbarpur, *India* **87 Cb**
Akcha, *Afghanistan* **89 Jb**
Akhdhar, Jeb., *Muscat & Oman* **89 Ge**
Akhisar, *Turkey* **88 Ab**
Akhterin, *Syria* **90 Fa**
Akhtyrka, *Ukraine* **76 Jf**
Akita, *Japan* **82 Ge**
Akkrum, *Netherlands* **60 Da**
Akmolinsk, *Kazakh.* **74 Gc**
Ako, *Nigeria* **92 Cb**
Akola, *India* **84 Ed**
Akra, Jebel el, *Turkey* **90 Db**
Akron, *Ohio* **40 Fe**
Akrotiri Pen., *Crete* **73 Eg**
Aksaray, *Turkey* **88 Bb**
Aksehir, *Turkey* **88 Bb**
Aksha, *Russia* **75 Lc**
Äksi, *Estonia* **63 Mg**
Akti, *Greece* **73 Ed**
Aktyubinsk, *Kazakh.* **74 Ec**
Akure, *Nigeria* **94 Gg**
Akureyri, *Iceland* **62 Wm**
Akyab, *Burma* **85 Hd**
Akzhal, *Kazakh.* **74 Hd**
Alabama, state, *U.S.A.* **43 Je**
Alabama R., *Alabama* **43 Je**
Alaejos, *Spain* **66 Cb**
Alagoas, *Brazil* **49 Ke**
Alagoinhas, *Brazil* **49 Kf**
Alagon, *Spain* **67 Eb**
Alaja, *Syria* **90 Db**
Alajuela, *Costa Rica* **47 Cd**
Alam, *Ethiopia* **93 Hc**
Alameda, *California* **45 Bg**
Alamogordo, *New Mexico* **42 Ee**
Alamos, *Mexico* **46 Cb**
Alamosa, *Colorado* **42 Ed**
Åland. See Ahvenanmaa
Ålands Hav, *Swed.-Fin.* **63 Hg**
Alapayevsk, *Russia* **77 Qb**
Alapur, *India* **87 Bb**
Alasehir, *Turkey* **88 Ab**
Ala Shan, *China* **78 Dc**
Al Ashkharah, *Muscat & Oman* **89 Ge**
Alaska, state, *U.S.A.* **43 Xl**
Alaska, G. of, *Alaska* **43 Ym**
Alaska Pen., *Alaska* **43 Xm**
Alaska Ra., *Alaska* **43 Xl**
Alatyr, *Russia* **77 Hc**
Alavus, *Finland* **62 Ke**
Al 'Ayn, *Muscat & Oman* **89 Gf**
Alaysky Khrebet, *Kirgiz.* **74 Ge**
Alazeyskoye Plat., *Russia* **75 Pb**
Albacete, *Spain* **67 Ec**
Alba de Tormes, *Spain* **66 Cb**
Albaida, *Spain* **67 Ec**
Alba Iulia, *Rumania* **72 Da**
Albania, *S. Europe* **72 Cd**
Albany, *Georgia* **43 Ke**
Albany, *New York* **40 Kd**
Albany, *Oregon* **45 Bc**
Albany, *W. Australia* **52 Cf**
Albarracin, *Spain* **67 Eb**
Albergaria a-Velha, *Portug.* **66 Ab**
Alberique, *Spain* **67 Ec**
Albert L., *Congo* **93 Gd**
Albert Nat. Park, *Congo* **93 Fe**
Albert Edward Mt., *Papua* **53 Ja**
Albert Lea, *Minnesota* **43 Hc**
Albertville, *Congo* **93 Ff**
Albertville, *France* **68 Gd**
Albi, *France* **69 Ee**
Albina, *Surinam* **49 Gb**
Albion, *Michigan* **40 Dd**
Albion, *New York* **44 Aa**
Albocácer, *Spain* **67 Eb**
Albufeira, *Portugal* **66 Ad**
Albuñol, *Spain* **66 Dd**
Albuquerque, *New Mexico* **42 Ed**
Albuquerque, *Spain* **66 Bc**
Albury, *New South Wales* **53 Jg**
Alcacer do Sal, *Portugal* **66 Ac**
Alcala de Chisvert, *Spain* **67 Fb**
Alcala de Henares, *Spain* **66 Db**
Alcamo, *Sicily* **71 Dg**
Alcañices, *Spain* **66 Bb**
Alcañiz, *Spain* **67 Eb**
Alcantara, *Brazil* **49 Jd**
Alcantára, *Spain* **66 Bc**
Alcantarilla, *Spain* **67 Ed**
Alcaraz, *Spain* **67 Dc**
Alcatraz, I., *San Francisco* **42 Bd**
Alcázar de San Juan, *Spain* **66 Dc**
Alchevsk, *Ukraine* **76 Lg**
Alcira, *Spain* **67 Ec**
Alcobaça, *Portugal* **66 Ac**
Alcolea del Pinar, *Spain* **67 Db**
Alcoutim, *Portugal* **66 Bd**
Alcoy, *Spain* **67 Ec**
Alcuhemas, *Morocco* **94 Ea**
Aldabra Is., *Indian Ocean* **93 Ka**
Aldama, *Chihuahua, Mexico* **46 Cb**
Aldama, *Tamaulipas, Mexico* **46 Ec**
Aldan & R., *Russia* **75 Mc**
Aldeburgh, *England* **59 Jh**
Alderney, I., *Channel Is.* **59 Ak**
Aldershot, *England* **59 Gj**
Al Dola, *S. Yemen* **88 Eg**
Alegrete, *Brazil* **50 Ec**
Aleih, *Lebanon* **90 Dd**
Aleksandrov, *Russia* **76 Lc**
Aleksandrovsk Sakhalinskiy, *Russia* **75 Pc**
Aleksandry, Zemlya, *Arctic Ocean* **74 Da**
Alekseyevka, *Russia* **77 Hd**
Alekseyevka, *Kazakh.* **74 Gc**
Alençon, *France* **68 Db**
Alenquer, *Portugal* **66 Ac**
Alenquer, *Brazil* **49 Gd**
Aleppo, *Syria* **90 Fa**
Ales, *France* **69 Fd**
Aleshki, *Russia* **77 Ee**
Alessandria, *Italy* **70 Bc**
Ålesund, *Norway* **62 Be**
Aletschhorn, Mt., *Switz.* **61 Cb**
Aleutian Is., *Bering Sea* **43 Um**
Alexander Arch., *Alaska* **43 Zm**
Alexander I, I., *Antarctica* **100 Sc**
Alexandra, *New Zealand* **51 Bf**
Alexandretta. See Iskenderun
Alexandria, *Egypt* **95 Lb**
Alexandria, *Louisiana* **43 He**
Alexandria, *Ontario* **40 Jc**
Alexandria, *Virginia* **44 Bc**
Alexandrina, L., *S. Aust.* **53 Gg**
Alexandroupolis, *Greece* **73 Ed**
Alexikovo, *Russia* **77 Fe**
Aleysk, *Russia* **74 Hc**
Alfaro, *Spain* **67 Ea**
Al Fāw, *Iraq* **88 Ed**
Alfred, *Maine* **44 Ea**
Alga, *Kazakh.* **74 Ed**
Ålgård, *Norway* **63 Ag**
Al Garrobo del Aquila, *Argentina* **50 Ce**
Algauer Alpen, *Austria etc.* **64 De**
Algeciras, *Spain* **66 Cd**
Alger (Algiers), *Algeria* **69 Nf**
Algeria, *N.-W. Africa* **94 Eb**
Al Ghail, *Yemen* **88 Ef**
Alghero, *Sardinia* **71 Be**
Algoa B., *Cape Province* **91 Df**
Algoma, *Ontario* **40 Eb**
Algoma, *Wisconsin* **40 Cc**
Algonquin Park, *Ontario* **40 Gc**
Alguada Reef, *Burma* **85 He**
Alhama de Granada, *Spain* **66 Dd**
Al Hasa, *Arabia* **88 Ed**
Al Hauta, *S. Yemen* **88 Ef**
Al Hayy, *Iraq* **88 Ec**
Alhucemas I., *Spain* **66 De**
Alia, *Sicily* **71 Dg**
Aliaga, *Spain* **67 Eb**
Alibag, *India* **84 De**
Alicante, *Spain* **67 Ec**
Alice Springs, *N. Terr., Aust.* **53 Fd**
Alicudi, I., *Italy* **71 Ef**
Aliganj, *India* **87 Bb**
Aligarh, *India* **86 Fg**
Ali Khel, *Afghanistan* **89 Jc**
Alimnia, I., *Greece* **73 Ff**
Aling Kangri, *Tibet* **84 Fb**
Alingsås, *Sweden* **63 Eh**
Alipur, *India* **87 Gd**
Alipur, *India* **87 Gb**
Alipur, *W. Pakistan* **87 Bc**
Alipura, *India* **87 Bf**
Alirajpur, *India* **84 Dd**
Alivérion, *Greece* **73 Ee**
Al Jawf, *Arabia* **88 Cd**
Al Jesab, *Arabia* **88 Ef**
Aljustrel, *Portugal* **66 Ad**
Alken, *Belgium* **60 Dd**
Alkmar, *Netherlands* **60 Cb**
Al Kut, *Iraq* **88 Ec**
Allahabad, *India* **87 Cc**
Allanmyo, *Burma* **85 Je**
Allariz, *Spain* **66 Ba**
Allaykha, *Russia* **75 Pa**
Alle, *Belgium* **60 Ce**
Allegan, *Michigan* **40 Dd**
Allegheny Mts., *U.S.A.* **43 Kd**
Allegheny R., *Penn., etc.* **44 Aa**
Allen L., *Eire* **59 Bf**
Allenby Bridge, *Jordan* **90 Df**
Allentown, *Pennsylvania* **44 Cb**
Alleppey, *India* **84 Eg**
Alliance, *Ohio* **40 Fe**
Allier, dep., *France* **68 Ec**
Allier, R., *France* **68 Ed**
Alliston, *Ontario* **40 Gc**
Alloa, *Scotland* **58 Ed**
All Pines, *Brit. Honduras* **47 Bc**
Al Luhaygah, *Yemen* **88 Df**
Allumette I., *Quebec* **40 Hc**
Alma, *Michigan* **40 Dd**
Alma Ata, *Kazakh.* **74 Gd**
Almaden, *Spain* **66 Cc**
Almagro, *Spain* **66 Dc**
Almansa, *Spain* **67 Ec**
Almazán, *Spain* **67 Db**
Almeirim, *Brazil* **49 Gd**
Almeirim, *Portugal* **66 Ac**
Almelo, *Netherlands* **60 Eb**
Almeria & Gulf, *Spain* **67 Dd**
Almirante, *Panama* **47 Ce**
Almiropótamos, *Greece* **73 Ee**
Almirós, *Greece* **73 De**
Almodôvar, *Portugal* **66 Bd**
Almodóvar, *Spain* **66 Cc**
Almonte, *Ontario* **40 Hc**
Almora, *India* **87 Ba**
Almorox, *Spain* **66 Cb**
Almudebar, *Spain* **67 Ea**
Almunia de Doña Godina, la, *Spain* **67 Eb**
Al Musayyib, *Iraq* **88 Dc**
Al Muwaila, *Arabia* **88 Cd**
Alness, *Scotland* **58 Ec**
Alnwick, *England* **58 Fe**
Alocén, *Spain* **67 Db**
Aloja, *Latvia* **63 Lh**
Alon, *Burma* **85 Jd**
Alón. See Iliodhrómia, I.
Alor, I., *Indonesia* **79 Hm**
Alora, *Spain* **66 Cd**

Alor Star, W. Malaya 83 Ce
Alost, Belgium 60 Cd
Aloysius, Mt., W. Australia 52 Ee
Alpena, Michigan 40 Ec
Alpes-Maritimes, dep., Fr. 69 Ge
Alphen, Netherlands 60 Cb
Alpine, Texas 42 Fe
Alps, Mts., Cent. Europe 57 Jg
Al Qara, Arabia 88 Dd
Al Qayyara, Iraq 88 Db
Al Qunfidhah, Arabia 88 Df
Al Qurnah, Iraq 88 Ec
Als, I., Denmark 63 Cj
Alsten, Norway 62 Ed
Alston, England 59 Ff
Alšvanga, Latvia 63 Jh
Alta Gracia, Argentina 50 Dd
Altagracia, Venezuela 48 Ca
Altagracia de Orituco, Venez. 48 Db
Altai, Mts., Central Asia 74 Hc
Altamachi, Bolivia 48 Dg
Altamakha R., Georgia 43 Ke
Altamira, Brazil 49 Gd
Altamura, Italy 71 Fe
Altan Bulag, Mongolia 75 Kc
Altar, Mexico 46 Ba
Altata, Mexico 46 Cc
Altdorf, Switzerland 61 Db
Altea, Spain 67 Fc
Altenburg, Germany 64 Ec
Altin Koprü, Iraq 88 Db
Altmark, Germany 64 Db
Alto Araguaia, Brazil 49 Gg
Alto Longa, Brazil 49 Je
Alto Madeira, Brazil 48 Ee
Alto Molocue, Moçambique 93 Hh
Alton, Illinois 40 Af
Altona, Germany 64 Cb
Altona, New York 40 Kc
Altoona, Pennsylvania 44 Ab
Altstätten, Switzerland 61 Ea
Alturas, California 45 Ce
Altyn Tagh, China 54 He
Al Ugla, Arabia 88 Cd
Al 'Uj, Arabia 88 Ee
Alūksne, Latvia 63 Mh
Alula, Somalia 93 Lb
Alumine, Argentina 50 Be
Alupka, Russia 76 Jj
Alushta, Russia 76 Jj
Alvarado, Mexico 46 Ed
Alvear, Argentina 50 De
Alvesta, Sweden 63 Fh
Älvho, Sweden 63 Ff
Alvito, Portugal 66 Ac
Alvord, L., Oregon 45 Dd
Al Wajh, Arabia 88 Cd
Alwar, India 86 Eg
Alyab, Sudan 95 Me
Alytus, Lithuania 63 Lj
Amadeus L., N. Terr., Aust. 52 Ed
Amadi, Sudan 95 Mg
Amadiyah, Iraq 88 Db
Amakusa Nada, Japan 82 Ah
Amål, Sweden 63 Eg
Amalfi, Italy 71 Ee
Amaliás, Greece 73 Cf
Amami Gunto, Japan 82 Nn
Amanalco, Mexico 46 Dd
Amantea, Italy 71 Ef
Amapa, Brazil 49 Gc
Amapala, Honduras 47 Bd
Amarah, Iraq 88 Ec
Amarante, Brazil 49 Je
Amarapura, Burma 85 Jd
Amaravti, India 84 Ed
Amargosa, Brazil 49 Kf
Amarillo, Texas 42 Fd
Amasra, Turkey 88 Ba
Amasya, Turkey 88 Ca
Amatique, G. de, Guatemala 46 Gd
Amatitlan, Guatemala 46 Fe
Amazon, Mths. of the, Brazil 49 Hc
Amazonas, R., Brazil 49 Gd
Amb, W. Pakistan 86 Cc
Ambala, India 86 Ee
Ambalavca, Madagascar 93 Hl
Ambam, Cameroon 92 Cd
Ambar, Persia 89 Gc
Ambarchik, Russia 75 Rb
Ambato, Ecuador 48 Bd
Ambato-Boéni, Madagascar 93 Nk
Amberg, Germany 64 Dd
Ambergris Cay, Bahama Is. 47 Eb
Ambergris Cay, Brit. Hond. 47 Bc
Ambérieu, France 68 Fc
Ambert, France 68 Ed
Ambikapur, India 87 Dd
Ambilobe, Madagascar 93 Nj
Amblève, Belgium 60 Ed
Ambohimahasoa, Madag. 93 Nl
Ambon, I., Indonesia 79 Jl
Ambositra, Madagascar 93 Nl
Ambrim, I., New Hebrides 98 Fj
Ambriz, Angola 92 Cf
Ambrizete, Angola 92 Cf
Amchitka, I., Aleutian Is. 43 Um
Amd, Aden 88 Ef
Amderma, Russia 74 Fb
Ameca, Mexico 46 Dc
Ameland I., Netherlands 60 Da
American Fork, Utah 42 Dc
Americus, Georgia 43 Ke
Amerongen, Netherlands 60 Db
Amersfoort, Netherlands 60 Db
Amesbury, Massachusetts 44 Ea
Amethi, India 87 Cb
Amfiklia, Greece 73 De
Amfilokhia, Greece 73 Ce
Amga & R., Russia 75 Nb
Amgu, Russia 75 Nd
Amherst, Burma 85 Je
Amherst, Massachusetts 44 Da
Amherst I., Ontario 40 Hc
Amherstburg, Ontario 40 Ed
Amiens, France 68 Eb
Amik Lake, Ontario 40 Gc
Amindivi, I., India 84 Df
Amingaon, India 85 Hc
Aminuis, S.-W. Africa 91 Bd
Amirante Is., Indian Ocean 96 De
Amla, Arabia 88 De
Amlwch, Wales 59 Eg
Amm Adam, Sudan 95 Ne
Amman, Jordan 90 Df
Amol, Persia 89 Fb
Amorgós, I., Greece 73 Ef
Amoy, China 81 Jk
Amparo, Brazil 49 Hh
Amraho, Sudan 95 Me
Amran, Yemen 88 Df
Amreli, India 84 Dd
Amriswil, Switzerland 61 Ea
Amritsar, India 86 De
Amroha, India 87 Ba
Amstelveen, Netherlands 60 Cb
Amsterdam, Netherlands 60 Cb
Amsterdam, New York 44 Ca
Amsterdam, I., Indian Ocean 96 Fh
Am Timan, Chad 95 Kf
Amu Darya, Turkmen 74 Fd
Amundsen Sea, Antarctica 100 Qb
Amur, R., Russia-China 75 Mc
Amyun, Lebanon 90 Dc
An, Burma 85 He
Anabta, Jordan 90 De
Anaconda, Montana 45 Gb
Anadyr & R., Russia 75 Sb
Anadyrskiy Zaliv, Russia 75 Tb
Anáfi, I., Greece 73 Ef
Anah, Iraq 88 Dc
Anai, Libya 95 Hd
Anaimalai Hills, India 84 Ef
Anaiza. See Unayzah
Anakapalle, India 85 Fe
Analalava, Madagascar 93 Nj
Anama, Brazil 48 Ed
Anambas Kep., Indonesia 79 Ek
Anamizu, Japan 82 Ef
Anandpur, India 86 Ee
Anantapur, India 84 Ef
Anápolis, Brazil 49 Hg
Anar, Persia 89 Gc
Anarak, Persia 89 Fc
Anardarra, Afghanistan 89 Hc
Anatolia, Turkey 88 Bb
Añatuya, Argentina 50 Dc
Anchorage, Alaska 43 Yl
Anchuras, Spain 66 Cc
Ancohuma, Mt., Bolivia 48 Dg
Ancon, Peru 48 Bf
Ancona, Italy 70 Dd
Ancud, Chile 50 Bf
And Fd., Norway 62 Gb
Andacollo, Argentina 50 Be
Andalgala, Argentina 50 Cc
Åndalsnes, Norway 62 Be
Andaman Is. & Str., Bay of Bengal 85 Hf
Andaman Sea, Bay of Bengal 85 Hf
Andeer, Switzerland 61 Eb
Andelfingen, Switzerland 61 Da
Andenne, Belgium 60 Dd
Andermatt, Switzerland 61 Db
Anderson, Indiana 40 De
Anderson, S. Carolina 43 Ke
Andes, Cord. de los, South America 50 Cc
Andevoranto, Madagascar 93 Nk
Andhra Pradesh, India 84 Ee
Andikíthira I., Greece 73 Dg
Andímilos, I., Greece 73 Ef
Andíparos, I., Greece 73 Ef
Andizhan, Uzbek. 74 Gd
Andkhui, Afghanistan 89 Jb
Andoas, Ecuador 48 Bd
Andorra & rep., Pyrenees 67 Fa
Andover, Massachusetts 44 Ea
Andöy, Norway 62 Fb
Andrade, Moçambique 91 Fc
Andreanof Is., Aleutian Is. 43 Vm
Andreas, C., Cyprus 90 Cb
Andrelândia, Brazil 49 Jh
Andreyevka, Ukraine 76 Jg
Andria, Italy 71 Fe
Andriba, Madagascar 93 Nk
Andritsaina, Greece 73 Cf
Andros I., Bahama Is. 47 Db
Andros, I., Greece 73 Ef
Anegada, B., Argentina 50 Df
Anegada, I., Virgin Is. 47 Gc
Anelo, Argentina 50 Ce
Aney, Niger 95 He
Anfa, Lebanon 90 Dc
Angangueo, Mexico 46 Dd
Angel Fall, Venezuela 48 Eb
Angel de la Guarda, I., Mex. 46 Bb
Angelholm, Sweden 63 Eh
Angers, France 68 Cc
Angkor, Cambodia 83 Cd
Anglesey, Wales 59 Eg
Angliers, Quebec 40 Gb
Angmagssalik, Greenland 41 Nc
Angol, Chile 50 Be
Angola, New York 44 Aa
Angola, W. Africa 92 Dg
Agontsy, Madagascar 93 Pk
Angora. See Ankara
Angoulême, France 68 Dd
Angoumois, prov., France 68 Dd
Angra, Brazil 49 Jh
Anguilla, I., Leeward Is. 47 Gc
Angul, India 85 Gd
Angus, co., Scotland 58 Ed
Anholt, I., Denmark 63 Dh
An-hui. See Anhwei
Anhwei, prov., China 80 Hf
Anina, Rumania 72 Cb
Anjengo, India 84 Eg
Anjou, prov., France 68 Cc
Anjouan I., Comores, Arch. des 93 Jg
Anjozorobe, Madagascar 93 Nk
Ankacho, Russia 75 Kb
Ankang, China 80 Df
Ankara, Turkey 88 Ba
Anking. See Hwaining
Ankober, Ethiopia 93 Hc
Ankwo, China 80 Gc
Anlier, Belgium 60 De
Anlu, China 80 Fg
Anlu. See Chungsiang
Ann C., Antarctica 100 Ec
Ann C., Massachusetts 44 Ea
Anna, Russia 77 Ee
Annaba (Bône), Algeria 95 Ga
Annai, Guyana 48 Fc
An Najaf, Iraq 88 Dc
Annam, Vietnam 83 Dc
Annan, Scotland 58 Ee
Annapolis, Maryland 44 Bc
Ann Arbor, Michigan 40 Ed
An Nasiriyah, Iraq 88 Ec
Annecy & L. d', France 68 Gd
Anniston, Alabama 43 Je
Annobon I., Gulf of Guinea 92 Be
Annonay, France 69 Fd
An Numas, Arabia 88 Df
Anole, Somalia 93 Je
Ano Viánnos, Crete 73 Eg
Anpehi, China 80 Db
Ansariya, Jebel el, Syria 90 Eb
Ansbach, Germany 64 Dd
Anshan, China 78 Hb
Anshun, China 81 Bj
Ansi, China 78 Cb
Ansin, China 80 Gc
Anson, B., N. Terr., Aust. 52 Eb
Ansongo, Mali 94 Fe
Ansonia, Connecticut 44 Db
Anta, Peru 48 Cf
Antakya (Antioch), Turkey 90 Ea
Antalo, Ethiopia 93 Hb
Antalya, Turkey 88 Bb
Antalya, G. of, Turkey 88 Bb
Antarctica 100
Antequera, Paraguay 50 Eb
Antequera, Spain 66 Cd
Anthony Lagoon, N.T., Aust. 53 Gc
Antibes, France 69 Ge
Antigo, Wisconsin 40 Bc
Antigua, I., Leeward Is. 47 Gc
Antilhue, Chile 50 Be
Antilla, Cuba 47 Db
Antilles, Greater, W.I. 47
Antilles, Lesser, West Indies 47
Antioquia, Colombia 48 Bb
Antipodes Is., Pacific Islands 98 Gm
Antivari. See Bar
Antofagasta, Chile 50 Bb
Antofagasta de la S., Arg. 50 Cc
Antofalla, Mt., Argentina 50 Cc
Antoing, Belgium 60 Bd
Antongil, B. d', Madagascar 93 Nk
Antrain, France 68 Cb
Antrim & co., N. Ireland 59 Cf
Antrim Hills, N. Ireland 58 Ce
Antsirabe, Madagascar 93 Nk
Antsirane, Madagascar 93 Nj
Antsla, Estonia 63 Mh
Antung, China 80 Mb
Antwerp. See Antwerpen
Antwerpen & prov., Belg. 60 Cc
Anupgarh, India 86 Cf
Anupshahr, India 87 Ba
Anuradhapura, Ceylon 84 Fg
Anvers. See Antwerpen
Anyang, China 80 Gd
Anyi, China 80 Ee
Anykščiai, Lithuania 63 Lj
Anzhero Sudzhensk, Russia 74 Hc
Aomori, Japan 82 Gd
Aonla, India 87 Ba
Aorangi Mts., New Zealand 51 Ed
Aosta, Italy 70 Ac
Aoudéras, Niger 94 Ge
Apakova, Russia 77 Jc
Apalachee B., Florida 43 Kf
Apalachicola, R., Florida 43 Kf
Aparri, Philippines 79 Hg
Apataki, I., Tuamotu Arch. 99 Lj
Apatin, Yugoslavia 72 Bb
Ape, Latvia 63 Mh
Apeldoorn, Netherlands 60 Db
Apennines, Mts., Italy 57 Kh
Api, Mt., Nepal 87 Ca
Apiai, Brazil 50 Gb
Apodi, Brazil 49 Ke
Apolo, Bolivia 48 Df
Apostle Is., Wisconsin 40 Ab
Apostoles, Argentina 50 Ec
Apoteri, Guyana 48 Fc
Apozai, W. Pakistan 84 Cb
Appalachian Mts., U.S.A. 43 Kd
Appenzell & canton, Switz. 61 Ea
Applecross, Scotland 58 Dc
Appleton, Wisconsin 40 Bc
Apt, France 69 Fe
Aqaba, Jordan 90 Dh
Aqarbat, Syria 90 Fb
'Aqda, Persia 89 Fc
Aqiq, Sudan 93 Ha
Aqraba, Jordan 90 De
Aquidauana, Brazil 49 Fh
Aquila, L', Italy 70 Dd
Aquin, Haiti 47 Ec
Arabia (Saudi Kingdom), W. Asia 88
Arabian Sea, S. Asia 54 Fg
Aracju, Brazil 49 Kf
Aracati, Brazil 49 Kd
Aracruz, Brazil 49 Kh
Araçuai, Brazil 49 Jg
Arad, Rumania 72 Ca
Arada, Chad 95 Ke
Arafura Sea, Indonesia 79 Km
Aragua de Barcelona, Venez. 48 Eb
Araguacema, Brazil 49 He
Araguaia, R., Brazil 49 He
Araguari, Brazil 49 Hg
Arak, Persia 88 Ec
Arakaka, Guyana 48 Fb
Arakan. See Myohaung
Arakan Yoma, Burma 85 Hd
Araks, R., Persia, etc. 74 De
Aral'sk, Kazakh. 74 Fd
Aral'skoye More (Aral Sea), Kazakh.-Uzb. 74 Ed
Aramac, Queensland 53 Jd
Arambagh, India 87 Fd
Aran Is., Eire 59 Ag
Aranda de Duero, Spain 66 Db
Arandu, W. Pakistan 86 Bc
Arani, Bolivia 48 Dg
Aranjuez, Spain 66 Db
Aranya, Siam 83 Cd
Arapey, Uruguay 50 Ed
Arapkir, Turkey 88 Cb
Arapuni, New Zealand 51 Ec
Ararangua, Brazil 50 Gc
Ararat, Victoria 53 Hg
Ararat, Mt., Turkey 88 Db
Araria, India 87 Fb
Araty, Brazil 48 Ce
Arauca, Colombia 48 Cb
Arauco, Chile 50 Be
Aravalli Ra., India 84 Dc
Araxa, Brazil 49 Hg
Arbai Khere, Mongolia 78 Da
Arbatax, Sardinia 71 Bf
Arbil, Iraq 88 Db
Arboga, Sweden 63 Fg
Arbois, France 68 Fc
Arbon, Switzerland 61 Ea
Arbroath, Scotland 58 Fd
Arcade, New York 40 Gd
Arcadia, Michigan 40 Cc
Arcen, Netherlands 60 Ec
Archbald, Pennsylvania 44 Cb
Archidona, Spain 66 Cd
Arcot, India 84 Ef
Arctic Ocean 41
Ardabil, Persia 88 Eb
Ardahan, Turkey 88 Da
Ardakan, Persia 89 Fc
Årdal, Norway 63 Bf
Ardal, Persia 89 Fc
Ardatov, Russia 77 Fc
Ardèche, dep., France 69 Fd
Ardennes, dep., France 68 Fb
Ardennes Mts., Belgium, etc. 68 Fa
Ardestan, Persia 89 Fc
Ardez, Switzerland 61 Fb
Ardglass, N. Ireland 59 Df
Ardino, Bulgaria 72 Ed
Ardmore, Oklahoma 42 Ge
Ardrishaig, Scotland 58 De
Ardrossan, Scotland 58 De
Ardud, Rumania 65 Ke
Arecibo, Puerto Rico 47 Fc
Areia Branco, Brazil 49 Kd
Arenales, Argentina 50 Dd
Arenales, Mt., Chile 50 Bg
Arenas de San Pedro, Spain 66 Cb
Arendal, Norway 63 Cg
Arenys de Mar, Spain 67 Gb
Arequipa, Peru 48 Cg
Areré, Brazil 49 Gd
Arévalo, Spain 66 Cb
Arezzo, Italy 70 Cd
Argentan, France 68 Cb
Argentat, France 69 Dd
Argentina, rep., S. America 50
Argentino, L., Argentina 50 Bh
Argent-sur-Sauldre, France 68 Ec
Argo, Sudan 95 Me
Argolis, G. of, Greece 73 Df
Argonne, France 68 Fb
Argos, Greece 73 Df
Arguedas, Spain 67 Ea
Argun, R., Russia-Manchuria 75 Lc
Argungu, Nigeria 94 Ff
Argyll, co., Scotland 58 Dd
Ariake Wan, Japan 82 Bj
Ariano Irpino, Italy 71 Ee
Arica, Chile 50 Ba
Arica, Colombia 48 Cd
Ariège, dep., France 69 De
Arilje, Yugoslavia 72 Cc
Arima, Brazil 48 Ee
Arinda, Guyana 48 Fc
Aripuana, Brazil 48 Ee
Ariquemes, Brazil 48 Ee
Arisaig, Scotland 58 Dd
Arivechi, Mexico 46 Cb
Ariza, Spain 67 Db
Arizona, Argentina 50 Ce
Arizona, state, U.S.A. 42 De
Arizpe, Mexico 46 Ba
Arka, Russia 75 Pb
Arka, S. Yemen 88 Eg
Arkadhía, Greece 73 Df
Arkansas, state, U.S.A. 43 He
Arkansas R., Ark.-Oklahoma 43 Hd
Arkansas City, Arkansas 43 He
Arkansas City, Kansas 42 Gd
Arkhangel'sk, Russia 74 Db
Arklow, Eire 59 Ch
Arkoi, I., Greece 73 Ff
Arles, France 69 Fe
Arlon, Belgium 60 De
Arltunga, N. Terr., Aust. 53 Fd
Armagh & co., N. Ireland 59 Cf
Armenia, Colombia 48 Bc
Armenia. See Armyanskaya S.S.R.
Armentières, France 68 Ea
Armidale, New S. Wales 53 Kf
Armirós, B. of, Crete 73 Eg
Armori, India 84 Fd
Armyanskaya S.S.R., U.S.S.R. 74 Dd
Arnauti, C., Cyprus 90 Ab
Arnhem, Netherlands 60 Dc
Arnhem, C., N. Terr., Aust. 53 Gb
Arnhem Ld., N. Terr., Aust. 52 Fb
Arni, India 84 Ef
Arnissa, Greece 73 Cd
Arnöy, Norway 62 Ja
Arnprior, Ontario 40 Hc
Arnsberg, Germany 64 Cc
Arnstadt, Germany 64 Dc
Aroe Eiln. See Aru Kep.
Arolla, Switzerland 61 Cb
Arorae, I., Gilbert Is. 98 Gh
Arosa, Switzerland 61 Eb
Arrah, India 87 Ec
Arraias, Brazil 49 Hf
Arran I., Scotland 58 De
Arras, France 68 Ea
Arroba, Spain 66 Cc
Arromanches, France 68 Cb
Arronches, Portugal 66 Bc
Arrow, L., Eire 59 Bf
Arrowtown, New Zealand 51 Bf
Arroyito, Argentina 50 Dd
Arroyo, Puerto Rico 47 Fc
Arsk, Russia 77 Jb
Arta, Greece 73 Ce
Artawiya, Arabia 88 Ed
Artemovsk, Russia 75 Jc
Artemovsk, Ukraine 76 Kg
Artemovskiy, Russia 75 Lc
Artemovskiy, Russia 77 Qb
Artenay, France 68 Db
Artibonite, R., Haiti 47 Ec
Artigas, Uruguay 50 Ed
Artois, prov., France 68 Ea
Artvin, Turkey 88 Da
Aru, Congo 93 Gd
Aruba, I., Caribbean 47 Fd
Aruanã, Brazil 49 Gf
Aru Kep., Indonesia 79 Km
Arumá, Brazil 48 Ed
Arundel, Quebec 40 Jc
Aruppukkottai, India 84 Eg
Arusha, Tanzania 93 He
Aru Tso, Tibet 85 Fb
Arvika, Sweden 63 Eg
Arzamas, Russia 77 Fc
Arzew, Algeria 94 Ea
Arzua, Spain 66 Aa
Aš, Czechoslovakia 64 Ec
Asahigawa, Japan 82 Hc
Asansol, India 87 Fd
Åsarna, Sweden 62 Fe
Asbestos, Quebec 40 Lc
Asbury Park, New Jersey 44 Db
Ascension, Bolivia 48 Eg
Ascension, B. de la, Mexico 46 Gd
Ascension I., Atlantic Ocean 97 Jj
Asch, Belgium 60 Dc
Aschaffenburg, Germany 64 Cd
Ascoli, Italy 70 Dd
Ascona, Switzerland 61 Db
Ascotan, Chile 50 Cb
Aseda, Sweden 63 Fh
Åsele, Sweden 62 Gd
Åsen, Sweden 63 Ef
Asenovgrad, Bulgaria 72 Ed
Ash, Muscat & Oman 89 Ge
Ashburton, New Zealand 51 Ce
Ashburton, R., W. Aust. 52 Cd
Ashdod, Israel 90 Cf
Asheville, N. Carolina 43 Kd
Ashkhabad, Turkmen 74 Ee
Ashland, Kentucky 43 Kd
Ashland, Ohio 40 Ee
Ashland, Oregon 45 Bd
Ashland, Pennsylvania 44 Bb
Ashland, Wisconsin 40 Ab
Ashqelon, Israel 90 Cf
Ash Shihr, S. Yemen 88 Eg
Ashtabula, Ohio 40 Fe
Ashūrādehye Bozorg, Persia 89 Fb
Asinara, I. & G. di, Sardinia 71 Be
Asino, Russia 74 Hc
Asir, Arabia 88 Df
Askersund, Sweden 63 Fg
Askvoll, Norway 63 Af
Aslandus, Persia 88 Eb
Asmara, Eritrea 93 Ha
Aspern, Austria 65 Gd
Aspinaje, Brazil 49 Hf
Aspiring, Mt., New Zealand 51 Bf
Aspres-sur-Buech, France 69 Fd
Aspro, C., Cyprus 90 Ac
Assab, Eritrea 93 Jb
As Safa, Arabia 88 Ed
Assam, India 85 Hc
As Sauda, Yemen 88 Df
Assaye, India 84 Ed
Assche, Belgium 60 Cd
Assen, Netherlands 60 Ea
Asshur, Iraq 88 Db
Assumar, Portugal 66 Bc
Asten, Netherlands 60 Dc
Asti, Italy 70 Bc
Asripálaia, I., Greece 73 Ff
Astor, Kashmir 86 Dc
Astorga, Spain 66 Ba
Astoria, Oregon 45 Bb
Astrakhan, Russia 74 Dd
Asträsk, Sweden 62 Hd
Astros, Greece 73 Df
Astudillo, Spain 66 Ca
Asuncion, Paraguay 50 Ec
Aswân, Egypt 95 Md
Aswân High Dam, Egypt 95 Md
Asyût, Egypt 95 Mc
Atacama Des., Chile 50 Cb
Atakpame, Togo 94 Fg
Atalaia, Brazil 49 Ke
Atalándi, Greece 73 De
Atalèh, Somali Rep. 93 Kd
Atambua, Timor I., Indon. 79 Hm
Atar, Mauritania 94 Cd
Atara, Yemen 88 Eg
Ataran, R., Burma 85 Je
Atauba, Brazil 48 Ed
Atbara, Sudan 95 Me
Atbasar, Kazakh. 74 Fc
Atchafalaya B., Louisiana 43 Hf
Atchison, Kansas 42 Gd
Ateca, Spain 67 Eb
Ath, Belgium 60 Bd
Athboy, Eire 59 Cg
Athenry, Eire 59 Bg
Athens, Georgia 43 Ke
Athens, Greece 73 Df
Atherton, Qnsld. 53 Hc
Atherton Plat., Queensland 53 Hc
Athinai, Greece 73 Df
Athlone, Eire 59 Bg
Athna, Cyprus 90 Bb
Athol, Massachusetts 44 Da
Athol, New Zealand 51 Bf
Athy, Eire 59 Ch
Atico, Peru 48 Cg
Atienza, Spain 66 Db
Atka, Russia 75 Qb
Atka, I., Aleutian Is. 43 Vm
Atkarsk, Russia 77 Ge
Atlanta, Georgia 43 Ke
Atlanta, Michigan 40 Dc
Atlantic City, New Jersey 44 Cc
Atlit, Israel 90 Ce
Atrauli, India 87 Bb
Atsuta, Japan 82 Eg
Attica, New York 44 Aa
Attiki, Greece 73 De
Attleboro, Massachusetts 44 Eb
Attock, W. Pakistan 86 Cd
Attu, I., Aleutian Is. 43 Um
Atukesi, Japan 82 Jc
Atupi, Brazil 49 Gc
Aube, dep., France 68 Fb
Aubel, Belgium 60 Dd
Aubenas, France 69 Fd
Aubonne, Switzerland 61 Bb
Auburn, Indiana 40 De
Auburn, Nebraska 42 Gc
Auburn, New York 44 Ba
Aubusson, France 68 Ed
Auce, Latvia 63 Kh
Auch, France 69 De
Auckland, New Zealand 51 Eb
Auckland Is., Pacific Ocean 98 Fn
Aude, dep., France 69 Ee
Audegle, Somalia 93 Jd
Audenarde, Belgium 60 Bd
Audierne, B. d', France 68 Ac
Aufa, Lebanon 90 Df
Augathella, Qnsld. 53 Je
Augsburg, Germany 64 Dd
Augusta, Georgia 43 Ke
Augusta, Sicily 71 Eg
Augusta, Wisconsin 40 Ac
Augustów, Poland 65 Kb
Augustus, Mt., W. Australia 52 Cd
Auletta, Italy 71 Ee
Aunis, prov., France 68 Cc
Aura, Finland 63 Kf
Auraiya, India 87 Bb
Aurangabad, India 87 Ec
Aurangabad, India 84 De
Auray, France 68 Bc
Aurillac, France 69 Ed
Aurora, Illinois 40 Be
Aurora, New York 44 Ba
Aurora, Ontario 40 Gd
Aus, S.-W. Africa 91 Be
Au Sable, Michigan 40 Ec
Au Sable Forks, New York 40 Kc
Austin, Minnesota 43 Hc
Austin, Nevada 45 Ef
Austin, Texas 42 Ge
Austin, L., W. Australia 52 Ce
Austral Is., Pacific Ocean 99 Kk
Australia 52
Australian Alps, Vict.-N.S.W. 53 Jg
Austria, Central Europe 57 Lg
Autlan, Mexico 46 Dd
Autse. See Auce
Autun, France 68 Fc
Auvergne, prov., France 69 Ed
Auxerre, France 68 Ec
Aux Sources, Mt., Lesotho 91 De
Ava, Burma 85 Jd
Avallon, France 68 Ec
Avanoas, S.-W. Africa 91 Ac
Avare, Brazil 49 Hh
Avaviken, Sweden 62 Hd
Aveiro, Brazil 49 Gd
Aveiro, Portugal 66 Ab
Avelghem, Belgium 60 Bd
Avellanada, Argentina 50 Ed
Avellino, Italy 71 Ee
Avenir, French Guiana 49 Gc
Averöy, Norway 62 Be
Aversa, Italy 71 Ee
Avesnes, France 68 Ea
Avesta, Sweden 63 Gf
Aveyron, dep., France 69 Ed
Avezzano, Italy 71 De
Aviá Teria, Argentina 50 Dc
Aviemore, Scotland 58 Ec
Avigliano, Italy 71 Ee
Avignon, France 69 Fe
Avila, Spain 66 Cb
Aviz, Portugal 66 Bc
Avola, Sicily 71 Eg
Avranches, France 68 Cb
Awaji Shima, Japan 82 Dg
Awakino, New Zealand 51 Ec
Awe, L., Scotland 58 Dd
Awusa, L., Ethiopia 93 Hc
Axat, France 69 Ee
Axel, Netherlands 60 Bc
Axinim, Brazil 48 Fd
Axios, R. See Vardar, R.
Axminster, England 59 Ek
Ayabaca, Peru 48 Bd
Ayacucho, Argentina 50 Ee
Ayacucho, Peru 48 Cf
Ayaguz, Kazakh. 74 Hd
Ayamonte, Spain 66 Bd
Ayan, Russia 75 Nc
Ayancik, Turkey 88 Ba
Ayaviri, Peru 48 C
Aydin, Turkey 88 Ab
Ayerbe, Spain 67 Ea
Ayia, Greece 73 De
Ayion Oros, Greece 73 Ed
Ayios Evstrátios, Greece 73 Ee
Aykathonisi, Greece 73 Ff
Aylesbury, England 59 Gj
Aylmer, Ontario 40 Fd
Aylwin, Quebec 40 Hb
Ayodhya, India 87 Db
Ayon, Ostrov, Russia 75 Ra
Ayora, Spain 67 Ec
Ayr, Queensland 53 Jc
Ayr & R., Scotland 58 De
Ayr, co., Scotland 58 De
Ayun, Arabia 88 Dd
Ayutla, Guatemala 46 Fe
Ayutla, Mexico 46 Ed
Ayvalik, Turkey 88 Ab
Aywaille, Belgium 60 Dd
Azaila, Spain 67 Eb
Azamgarh, India 87 Db
Azare, Nigeria 95 Hf
Azaz, Syria 90 Fa
Azerbaidshan. See Azerbaydzhanskaya S.S.R.
Azerbaydzhanskaya S.S.R., U.S.S.R. 74 Dd
Azogues, Ecuador 48 Bd
Azores Is., Atlantic Ocean 94 Aa
Azov, Sea of, Russia 76 Kj
Azpeitia, Spain 69 Be
Aztec, New Mexico 42 Ed
Azua, Rep. Dominicana 47 Ec
Azuaga, Spain 66 Cc
Azufre, Mt., Chile 50 Cc
Azul, Argentina 50 Ee
Azzan, S. Yemen 88 Eg
Az Zubayr, Iraq 88 Ec
Baalbek, Lebanon 90 Ec
Baarle Nassau, Netherlands 60 Cc
Baarn, Netherlands 60 Db
Babahoya, Ecuador 48 Bd
Babar, I., Indonesia 79 Jm
Babati, Tanzania 93 He
Bab el Mandeb, Red Sea 93 Jb
Babenna, Syria 90 Eb
Babōl, Persia 89 Fb
Babura, Nigeria 92 Bb
Babuyan Is., Philippines 78 Hg
Babylon, Iraq 88 Dc
Bacabal, Brazil 49 Fe
Bacadehuachi, Mexico 46 Cb
Bacalar, Mexico 46 Gd
Bacău, Rumania 72 Fa
Bacerac, Mexico 46 Ca
Backa Topola, Yugoslavia 72 Bb
Backbone Mts., W. Va.-Maryland 44 Ac
Bäckefors, Sweden 63 Eg
Backergunge, East Pakistan 85 Hd
Bac Lieu, S. Vietnam 83 De
Bac-Ninh, N. Vietnam 83 Db
Bacoachic, Mexico 46 Ca
Bacolod, Philippines 79 Hh
Bada, Arabia 88 Cd
Badajos, Brazil 49 Hd
Badajoz, Spain 66 Bc
Badalona, Spain 67 Gb
Badarma, Russia 75 Kc
Badas, Brunei 79 Fk
Bad Axe, Michigan 40 Ed
Baden, Germany 64 Cd
Baden, Switzerland 61 Da
Baden-Baden, Germany 64 Cd
Badia, Arabia 88 Ee
Badin, W. Pakistan 84 Cd
Badiya, Muscat & Oman 89 Ge
Bad Kissingen, Germany 64 Dc
Bad Lands, Nebraska, etc. 42 Fc
Badon, Senegal 94 Cf
Badrinath, India 84 Eb
Baduen, Somalia 93 Kc
Badulla, Ceylon 84 Fg
Baelen, Belgium 60 Dc
Baena, Spain 66 Cd
Baerle-Duc, Belgium 60 Cc

Caibarien, Cuba 47 Db
Caicara, Bolivar, Venezuela 48 Db
Caicara, Monagas, Venezuela 48 Eb
Caicos Is., Bahama Is. 47 Eb
Cailloma, Peru 48 Cg
Caimanera, Cuba 47 Dc
Caird Coast, Antarctica 100 Ab
Cairngorms, Scotland 58 Ec
Cairns, Queensland 53 Jc
Cairo, Egypt 95 Mb
Cairo, Illinois 43 Jd
Caithness, co., Scotland 58 Eb
Cajamarca, Peru 48 Be
Cajazeiras, Brazil 49 Ke
Cakovec, Yugoslavia 71 Fb
Cala, Spain 66 Bd
Calabar, Nigeria 94 Gg
Calabozo, Venezuela 48 Db
Calabria, dep., Italy 71 Ff
Calacoto, Bolivia 48 Dg
Calafat, Rumania 72 Dc
Calafate, Argentina 50 Bh
Calais, France 68 Da
Calama, Brazil 48 Ee
Calama, Chile 50 Cb
Calamar, Colombia 48 Ca
Calamar, Colombia 48 Cc
Calamian Group, Phil. 79 Gh
Calamocha, Spain 67 Eb
Calanaque, Brazil 48 Ed
Calaoria. See Reggio Calabria
Calatayud, Spain 67 Eb
Calava C., Sicily 71 Ef
Calbuco, Chile 50 Bf
Calceta, Ecuador 48 Bd
Calchaqui, Argentina 50 Dc
Calçoene, Brazil 49 Gc
Calcutta, India 85 Gd
Caldas da Rainha, Portugal 66 Ac
Caldera, Chile 50 Bc
Caldwell, Idaho 45 Ed
Calella, Spain 67 Gb
Calenzana, Corsica 69 Jf
Caleta Buena, Chile 50 Ba
Caleta Junin, Chile 50 Ba
Caleta Olivia, Argentina 50 Cg
Cali, Colombia 48 Bc
Calicut. See Kozhikode
California, G. of, Mexico 46 Bb
California, state, U.S.A. 42 Bd
Calimali, Mexico 46 Bb
Calingasta, Argentina 50 Cd
Callabonna L., S. Aust. 53 He
Callander, Ontario 40 Gb
Callander, Scotland 58 Ed
Callao, Peru 48 Bf
Callasa de Ensarria, Spain 67 Ec
Calmon, Brazil 50 Fc
Calmpthout, Belgium 60 Cc
Caltagirone, Sicily 71 Eg
Caltanissetta, Sicily 71 Eg
Calulo, Angola 92 Dg
Calumet. See Hancock
Calumet I., Quebec 40 Hc
Calunda, Angola 92 Eg
Calvados, dep., France 68 Cb
Calvillo, Mexico 46 Dc
Calvinia, Cape Province 91 Cf
Camabatela, Angola 92 Df
Camaguey, Cuba 47 Db
Camaguey, Is. de, Cuba 47 Db
Camana, Peru 48 Cg
Camara, Brazil 48 Ed
Camarat C. France 68 Ge
Camargo, Bolivia 48 Dh
Camargo, Mexico 46 Eb
Camarones & B., Argentina 50 Cf
Ca-Mau, S. Vietnam 83 De
Ca-Mau, Pt. S. Vietnam 83 Ce
Cambados, Spain 66 Aa
Cambay, India 84 Dd
Cambay, G. of, India 84 Dd
Cambodia, Indo-China 83 Cd
Cambodia, C. See Ca-Mau Pt.
Cambona, Moçambique 93 Hg
Cambrai, France 68 Ea
Cambrian Mts., Wales 59 Eh
Cambridge, Massachusetts 44 Ea
Cambridge, New Zealand 51 Eb
Cambridge & Isle of Ely, co., England 59 Hh
Cambridge G., W. Australia 52 Eb
Camden, Arkansas 43 He
Camden, Delaware 44 Cc
Camden, New Jersey 44 Cc
Camden, New York 40 Jd
Camedo, Switzerland 61 Db
Cameron Mts., New Zealand 51 Ag
Cameroon, Cent. Africa 95 Hg
Cameroons Mt., Cameroon 94 Gg
Camerota, Italy 71 Ef
Cameta, Brazil 49 Hd
Camina, Chile 50 Ca
Caminha, Portugal 66 Ab
Caminreal, Spain 67 Eb
Camoa, Mexico 46 Cb
Camocim, Brazil 49 Jd
Camooweal, Queensland 53 Gd
Camopi, Fr. Guiana 49 Gc
Camorta I., Nicobar Is. 85 Hg
Campana, Argentina 50 Ed
Campana, I., Chile 50 Ag
Campania, dep., Italy 71 Ee
Campas, Mexico 46 Ca
Campbell I., Pacific Ocean 98 Fn
Campbellford, Ontario 40 Hc
Campbellpore, W. Pakistan 86 Cd
Campbeltown, Scotland 58 De
Campeche & state, Mexico 46 Fd
Campeche, G. of, Mexico 46 Fd
Campiglia Marittima, Italy 70 Cd
Campillos, Spain 66 Cd
Campina Grande, Brazil 49 Ke
Campinas, Brazil 49 Hh
Campoalegre, Colombia 48 Bc
Campobasso, Italy 71 Ee
Campo Belo, Brazil 49 Hh
Campo Formosa, Brazil 49 Jf
Campo Gallo, Argentina 50 Dc
Campo Grande, Brazil 49 Gh
Campo Maior, Brazil 49 Jd
Campo Maior, Portugal 66 Bc
Campos, Brazil 49 Jh
Campos Sales, Brazil 49 Je
Campos Novos, Brazil 50 Fc
Campulung, Rumania 72 Eb
Canaan, New Hampshire 40 Ld
Cañada de Gomez, Argent. 50 Dd
Canadian R., Oklahoma, etc. 42 Fd
Cañadon León, Argent. 50 Ch
Canakkale, Turkey 88 Aa
Canama, Brazil 48 Ce
Canandaigua, New York 44 Ba
Canandaigua L., New York 44 Ba
Cananea, Mexico 46 Ba
Cananeia, Brazil 50 Gc
Canarias, Islas, Atlantic Oc. 94 Bc
Canarreos, Arch de los, Cuba 47 Cb
Canary Is. See Canarias
Canas, Portugal 66 Bb
Canaseraga, New York 44 Ba
Canatlan, Mexico 46 Dc
Cañaveral, Spain 66 Bc
Canaveral, C. See Kennedy, C.
Cañaveras, Spain 67 Db
Canavieiras, Brazil 49 Kg
Canberra, Cap. Terr., Aust. 53 Jg
Candasnos, Spain 67 Eb
Candia. See Iráklion
Canea. See Khania
Canella, Brazil 50 Fc
Canelones, Uruguay 50 Ed
Canete, Chile 50 Be
Canete, Peru 48 Bf
Cañete, Spain 67 Eb
Cangamba, Angola 92 Dg
Cangandala, Angola 92 Df
Cangas, Spain 66 Ba
Canguaretama, Brazil 49 Le
Canha, Portugal 66 Ac
Canicatti, Sicily 71 Dg
Çankiri, Turkey 88 Ba
Canna, I., Scotland 58 Cc
Cannanore, India 84 Ef
Cannes, France 69 Ge
Canosa, Italy 71 Fe
Cantabrica, Cord., Spain 66 Ca
Cantal, dep., France 69 Ed
Cantanhede, Portugal 66 Ab
Canterbury, England 59 Hj
Canterbury Bight, N.Z. 51 Df
Canterbury Plains, N.Z. 51 Cf
Can Tho, S. Vietnam 83 De
Canton, China 81 Fl
Canton, New York 40 Jc
Canton, Ohio 40 Fe
Canton I., Phoenix Is. 98 Hh
Canuelas, Argentina 50 Ee
Canutama, Brazil 48 Ee
Cao Bang, N. Vietnam 83 Db
Capabarida, Venezuela 48 Ca
Capakçur. See Bingol
Capana, Brazil 48 Ee
Capao Bonito, Brazil 50 Gb
Cape Barren I., Tasmania 53 Jh
Cape Canaveral, Florida 43 Kf
Cape Clear, Eire 59 Aj
Cape Coast, Ghana 94 Eg
Cape Cod B., Massachusetts 44 Eb
Cape Fear R., N. Carolina 43 Le
Cape Girardeau, Missouri 43 Hd
Capelinha, Brazil 49 Jg
Capelle, la, France 68 Eb
Cape May, New Jersey 44 Cc
Cape May Court House, New Jersey 44 Cc
Cape Province (Cape of Good Hope), South Africa 91 Cf
Cape Town, Cape Province 91 Bf
Cape Verde Is., Atlantic Oc. 94 Bh
Cape York Pen., Queensland 53 Hb
Cap Haitien, Haiti 47 Ec
Capilla, Argentina 50 Ed
Capilla del Monte, Argentina 50 Dd
Capim, Brazil 49 Hd
Capo Bonito, Brazil 70 Bd
Capraia, I., Italy 70 Bd
Capreol, Ontario 40 Fb
Caprera, I., Sardinia 71 Be
Capri, I., Italy 71 Ee
Capricorn Chan., Qnsld. 53 Kd
Caprivi Strip, S.-W. Africa 91 Cc
Carabaya, Cord. de, Peru 48 Cf
Caracaraí, Brazil 48 Ec
Caracas, Venezuela 48 Da
Caracol, Brazil 49 Je
Caraguatay, Paraguay 50 Ec
Caransebes, Rumania 72 Db
Carapegua, Paraguay 50 Ec
Caras, Peru 48 Be
Caratasca Lag., Honduras 47 Cc
Caratinga, Brazil 49 Jg
Carauari, Brazil 48 Dd
Caravaca, Spain 67 Dc
Caravelas, Brazil 49 Kg
Caraveli, Peru 48 Cg
Carballino, Spain 66 Aa
Carballo, Spain 66 Aa
Carbonara C., Sardinia 71 Bf
Carbondale, Pennsylvania 44 Cb
Carcassonne, France 69 Ee
Cardamom Hills, India 84 Eg
Cardenas, Cuba 47 Cb
Cardenas, Mexico 46 Ec
Cardiel, L., Argentina 50 Bg
Cardiff, Wales 59 Ej
Cardigan & B., Wales 59 Dh
Cardigan, co., Wales 59 Eh
Cardona, Spain 67 Fb
Cardwell, Queensland 53 Jc
Carey, L., W. Australia 52 De
Carhaix, France 68 Bb
Carhue. See Adolfo Alsina
Caribbean Sea, West Indies 47 Dd
Caribrod. See Dimitrovgrad
Carichic, Mexico 46 Cb
Cariñena, Spain 67 Eb
Carinhanha, Brazil 49 Jf
Caripito, Venezuela 48 Ea
Carius, Brazil 49 Ke
Carlet, Spain 67 Ec
Carleton Place, Ontario 40 Hc
Carlingford L., Eire 59 Dg
Carlisle, England 59 Ff
Carlisle, Pennsylvania 44 Bb
Carlos Casares, Argentina 50 De
Carlow & co., Eire 59 Ch
Carlsbad Caverns Nat. Park, New Mexico 42 Fe
Carmarthen & co., Wales 59 Ej
Carmarthen B., Wales 59 Dj
Carmaux, France 69 Ed
Carmel, New York 44 Db
Carmel, Mt., Israel 90 De
Carmelo, Uruguay 50 Ed
Carmen, Bolivia 48 Df
Carmen, Colombia 48 Bb
Carmen, Mexico 46 Fd
Carmen I., Mexico 46 Bb
Carmen Alto, Chile 50 Cb
Carmen de Patagones, Argentina 50 Df
Carmensa, Argentina 50 Ce
Carmona, Spain 66 Cd
Carnamah, W. Aust. 52 Ce
Carnarvon, Cape Province 91 Cf
Carnarvon, W. Australia 52 Bd
Carndonagh, Eire 58 Ce
Carnegie, L., W. Australia 52 De
Carnot, Cent. Afr. Rep. 95 Jh
Carnsore Pt., Eire 59 Ch
Caro, Michigan 40 Ed
Carolina, Brazil 49 He
Carolina, Transvaal 91 Ee
Caroline I., Pacific Ocean 99 Kh
Caroline Is., Pacific Ocean 98 Dg
Carora, Venezuela 48 Ca
Carpathian Mts., Cent. Eur. 57 Nf
Carpatii Sudici, Rumania 72 Db
Carpentaria, G. of, Aust. 53 Gb
Carrara, Italy 70 Cc
Carreño, Spain 66 Ca
Carrickmacross, Eire 59 Cg
Carrick-on-Shannon, Eire 59 Bg
Carrick-on-Suir, Eire 59 Ch
Carrión-de-los-Condes, Sp. 66 Ca
Carrowmore L., Eire 59 Af
Carroz, le, Switzerland 61 Bb
Carsamba, Turkey 88 Ca
Carson City, Nevada 45 Df
Carson Sink, Nevada 45 Df
Carstairs, Scotland 58 Ee
Carstensz, Mt., New Guinea 79 Ll
Cartagena, Colombia 48 Ba
Cartagena, Spain 67 Ed
Cartago, Colombia 48 Bc
Cartago, Costa Rica 47 Ce
Cartaxo, Portugal 66 Ac
Cartaya, Spain 66 Bd
Carteret, France 68 Cb
Carterton, New Zealand 51 Ed
Carthage, Missouri 43 Hd
Carthage, New York 40 Jd
Cartier, Ontario 40 Fb
Carupano, Venezuela 48 Ea
Carutaperá, Brazil 49 Hd
Carvoeiro, Brazil 48 Ed
Casablanca, Chile 50 Bd
Casablanca, Morocco 94 Db
Casaccia, Switzerland 61 Eb
Casas Grandes, Mexico 46 Ca
Casas Ibañez, Spain 67 Ec
Cascade Ra., Oregon, etc. 42 Bc
Cascais, Portugal 66 Ac
Caserta, Italy 71 Ee
Caseville, Michigan 40 Ed
Cashel, Eire 59 Bh
Casilda, Argentina 50 Dd
Casilda, Cuba 47 Db
Casino, New South Wales 53 Ke
Casma, Peru 48 Be
Casmalia, California 45 Ch
Caspe, Spain 67 Eb
Casper, Wyoming 42 Ec
Caspian Sea, Europe-Asia 54 Dd
Cassai, Angola 92 Eg
Cassamba, Angola 92 Eg
Cassel, France 68 Ea
Cassinga, Angola 91 Bc
Cassino, Brazil 50 Fd
Cassino, Italy 71 De
Cassis, France 69 Fe
Cassopolis, Michigan 40 Ce
Cassou, Upper Volta 94 Ef
Castanhal, Brazil 48 Ee
Castanheiro, Brazil 48 Dd
Castaño, Argentina 50 Cd
Castasegna, Switzerland 61 Eb
Casteljaloux, France 69 Cd
Castellammare & G. di, Sicily 71 Df
Castellammare di Stabia, It. 71 Ee
Castellane, France 69 Ge
Castellar de Santiago, Spain 66 Dc
Castelli, Argentina 50 Ee
Castellón de la Plana, Spain 67 Ec
Castellote, Spain 67 Eb
Castelnaudary, France 69 Ee
Castelo Branco, Portugal 66 Bc
Castelo de Vide, Portugal 66 Bc
Castelsarrasin, France 69 De
Castelvetrano, Sicily 71 Dg
Casterle, Belgium 60 Cc
Castets, France 69 Ce
Castilletes, Colombia 48 Ca
Castillo, Mt., Chile 50 Bg
Castlebar, Eire 59 Ag
Castle Douglas, Scotland 59 Ef
Castlerea, Eire 59 Bg
Castlereagh, R., N.S.W. 53 Jf
Castle Rock, Mt., Oregon 45 Dc
Castres, France 69 Ee
Castro, Brazil 50 Fb
Castro, Chile 50 Bf
Castro Marin, Portugal 66 Bd
Castropol, Spain 66 Ba
Castrovillari, Italy 71 Ff
Castuera, Spain 66 Cc
Cat I., Bahama Is. 47 Db
Catabola, Angola 92 Dg
Catamaran, Tasmania 53 Jh
Catamarca, Argentina 50 Cc
Catanduanes, I., Philippines 79 Hh
Catania & G. di, Sicily 71 Eg
Catanzaro, Italy 71 Ff
Catarman, Philippines 79 Hh
Catastrophe, C., S. Australia 53 Gg
Cateau, le, France 68 Ea
Catonsville, Maryland 44 Bc
Catorce, Mexico 46 Dc
Catrilo, Argentina 50 De
Catskill & Mts., New York 44 Ca
Cattaraugus, New York 44 Aa
Catuna, Argentina 50 Cd
Caungula, Angola 92 Df
Cauquenes, Chile 50 Be
Cauto, R., Cuba 47 Db
Cauvery R., India 84 Ef
Cavalcante, Brazil 49 Hf
Cavan & co., Eire 59 Cg
Cave, New Zealand 51 Cf
Cavergno, Switzerland 61 Db
Caviana, I., Brazil 49 Gc
Cawnpore. See Kanpur
Caxias, Brazil 48 Cd
Caxias, Brazil 49 Jd
Caxias do Sul, Brazil 50 Fc
Cayambe, Ecuador 48 Bc
Cayenne, French Guiana 49 Gc
Cayes, Les, Haiti 47 Ec
Cayman Is., W. Indies 47 Cc
Cayo, British Honduras 47 Bc
Cayuga, Ontario 40 Gd
Cayuga L., New York 44 Ba
Cazage, Angola 92 Eg
Cazalla de la Sierra, Spain 66 Cd
Cazenovia, New York 44 Ca
Cazin, Yugoslavia 70 Ec
Cazorla, Spain 66 Dd
Ceanannus Mór. See Kells
Ceará. See Fortaleza
Ceara Mirim, Brazil 49 Ke
Cebaco, I., Panama 47 Ce
Cebollar, Argentina 50 Cc
Cebollera, sa., Spain 67 Db
Cebu, Philippines 79 Hh
Ceclavin, Spain 66 Bc
Cedar Mts., Oregon 45 Ed
Cedar Ra., Utah 45 Ge
Cedarburg, Wisconsin 40 Cd
Cedar City, Utah 45 Gg
Cedar Key, Florida 43 Kf
Cedar Rapids, Iowa 43 Hc
Cedar Springs, Michigan 40 Dd
Cedral, Mexico 46 Dc
Cedros, I., Mexico 46 Ab
Ceduna, S. Australia 53 Ff
Cefalu, Sicily 71 Ef
Cegled, Hungary 65 He
Cehegin, Spain 67 Ec
Ceiba, La, Honduras 46 Gd
Cejal, Colombia 48 Dc
Celanova, Spain 66 Ba
Celaya, Mexico 46 Dc
Celebes, I., Indonesia 79 Gl
Celebes Sea, Indonesia 79 Hk
Celje, Yugoslavia 70 Eb
Cella, Spain 67 Eb
Celle, Germany 64 Cb
Celles, Belgium 60 Bd
Çemişgezek, Turkey 88 Cb
Cenis, Mte., France 70 Ac
Centerville, Iowa 43 Hc
Central, Cord., Peru 48 Be
Central, Cord., Rep. Dom. 47 Ec
Central African Republic, Cent. Africa 95 Jg
Central America 47 Bd
Centralia, Illinois 40 Bf
Centralia, Washington 45 Bb
Central Lake, Michigan 40 Dc
Cephalonia. See Kefallinia
Ceram Sea, Indonesia 79 Jl
Cerignola, Italy 71 Ee
Cerigo. See Kithira I.
Cerigotto. See Andikithira
Cerknica, Yugoslavia 70 Ec
Çermik, Turkey 88 Cb
Cernauti. See Chernovtsy
Cerralvo, Mexico 46 Eb
Cerralvo, I., Mexico 46 Cc
Cerreto Sannita, Italy 71 Ee
Cerro de Pasco, Peru 48 Bf
Cervera de Pisuerga, Spain 66 Ca
Cesena, Italy 70 Dc
Cesis, Latvia 63 Lh
Ceská Lipa, Czechoslovakia 64 Fc
České Budějovice, Czech. 64 Fd
Cessnock, New S. Wales 53 Kf
Cetinje, Yugoslavia 72 Bc
Cetraro, Italy 71 Ef
Cette. See Sete
Ceuta, N. Africa 94 Da
Ceuta, B. de, Mexico 46 Cc
Cevennes, France 69 Ee
Cevio, Switzerland 61 Db
Ceylon, I., Indian Ocean 84 Eg
Chablis, France 68 Ec
Chacabuco, Argentina 50 Dd
Chacance, Chile 50 Cb
Chachapoyas, Peru 48 Be
Chachwengsao, Siam 83 Cd
Chad (Tchad), Cent. Africa 95 Jf
Chad (Tchad) L., Chad 95 Hf
Chagai, W. Pakistan 84 Bc
Chagda, Russia 75 Nc
Chagny, France 68 Fc
Chagode, Russia 76 Jb
Chagos Arch., Indian Ocean 96 Fe
Chaguaramas, Trinidad 48 Ea
Chāh Bahār, Persia 89 Hd
Chaibassa, India 87 Ed
Chaise Dieu, France 69 Ed
Chakansur, Afghanistan 89 Hc
Chakia, India 87 Dc
Chaksam, Tibet 85 Hc
Chakwal, W. Pakistan 86 Cd
Chala, Peru 48 Cg
Chalchihuites, Mexico 46 Dc
Chalcis. See Khalkis
Chalham, I., Chile 50 Ch
Chalhuanca, Peru 48 Cf
Chaling, China 81 Fj
Chalisgaon, India 84 Dd
Chalk River, Ontario 40 Hc
Challapata, Bolivia 48 Dg
Châlons-sur-Marne, France 68 Fb
Châlons-sur-Saône, France 68 Fc
Chalus, France 68 Dd
Cham, Germany 64 Ed
Chaman, W. Pakistan 84 Cb
Chamba, India 86 Ed
Chamba, Tanzania 93 Hg
Chambal R., India 84 Ec
Chambersburg, Pennsylvania 44 Bc
Chambéry, France 68 Fd
Chambica, Brazil 49 Hd
Chamdo, China 78 Cd
Chamical, Argentina 50 Cd
Chamo, L., Ethiopia 93 Hc
Chamonix, France 68 Gd
Champa, India 87 De
Champagne, prov., France 68 Eb
Champaign, Illinois 40 Be
Champerico, Guatemala 46 Fe
Champlain L., N.Y.-Vermont 40 Kc
Champlitte, France 68 Fc
Champion, Belgium 60 Dd
Chamusca, Portugal 66 Ac
Chan-ching. See Tsamkong
Chanco, Chile 50 Be
Chancy, Switzerland 61 Ab
Chanda, India 84 Ed
Chandausi, India 87 Ba
Chanderi, India 87 Bc
Chandernagore, India 87 Gd
Chandigarh, India 86 Ee
Chandod, India 84 Dd
Chandpur, East Pakistan 85 Hd
Chandpur, India 87 Ba
Chandrakona, India 87 Fd
Chanduria, East Pakistan 87 Gd
Chanf, Persia 89 Hd
Chang-chia-k'on. See Changkiakow
Changchih, China 80 Fd
Changchow, China 81 Hk
Changchow, China 80 Kg
Changchun, China 78 Jb
Changhua, Taiwan 81 Kk
Changkiakow, China 80 Gb
Changlo, China 80 Jd
Changpeh, China 80 Gb
Changping, China 80 Hb
Changpu, China 81 Hk
Changsha, China 81 Fh
Changshan, China 81 Jh
Changte. See Anyang
Changteh, China 81 Eh
Changting, China 81 Hk
Changyeh, China 78 Dc
Channel Is., California 42 Be
Channel Is., English Channel 59 Al
Chantada, Spain 66 Ba
Chanthaburi, Siam 83 Cd
Chantilly, France 68 Eb
Chanute, Kansas 42 Gd
Chany, Oz., Russia 74 Gc
Chao, R., Siam 79 Dg
Chaoan, China 81 Hl
Chaochow, China 81 Hl
Chao Hu, China 80 Hg
Chaotung, China 81 Aj
Chapala, L., Mexico 46 Dc
Chapayevsk, Russia 77 Jd
Chapleau, Ontario 40 Eb
Chapra, India 87 Ec
Char, Mauritania 94 Cd
Chara, Russia 75 Lc
Charagua, Bolivia 48 Eg
Charana, Bolivia 48 Dg
Charco Azul B., Panama 47 Ce
Charcot, I., Antarctica 100 Sc
Chardzhou, Turkmen 74 Fe
Charente, dep., France 68 Dd
Charente, R., France 68 Cd
Charente-Maritime, dep., France 68 Cd
Chari R., Chad 95 Jf
Charikar, Afghanistan 89 Jc
Charité, la, France 68 Ec
Charkhari, India 87 Bc
Charleroi, Belgium 60 Cd
Charles C., Virginia 43 Ld
Charles City, Iowa 43 Hc
Charles L., Louisiana 43 He
Charles R., Massachusetts 44 Ea
Charleston, S. Carolina 43 Le
Charleston, W. Virginia 43 Kd
Charleston Pk., Nevada 45 Fg
Charles Town, W. Virginia 44 Bc
Charleville, Eire 59 Bh
Charleville, France 68 Fb
Charleville, Queensland 53 Je
Charlevoix, Michigan 40 Dc
Charlotte, Michigan 40 Dd
Charlotte, New York 40 Hd
Charlotte, N. Carolina 43 Kd
Charlotte Amalie, Virgin Is. 47 Gc
Charlotte Harbor, Florida 43 Kf
Charlottenburg, Germany 64 Eb
Charlottesville, Virginia 43 Ld
Charlton, Victoria 53 Hg
Charmey, Switzerland 61 Cb
Charolles, France 68 Fc
Charsadda, W. Pakistan 86 Cc
Charters Towers, Queensland 53 Jd
Chartres, France 68 Db
Chartreuse, France 68 Fd
Charvonnex, France 61 Bc
Chascomus, Argentina 50 Ee
Chasseneuil, France 68 Dd
Châteaubriant, France 68 Cc
Château Chinon, France 68 Ec
Château-du-Loir, France 68 Dc
Châteaudun, France 68 Db
Château Gontier, France 68 Cc
Château-la-Valliere, France 68 Dc
Châteaulin, France 68 Ab
Châteauneuf-en-Thymerais, France 68 Db
Châteaurenault, France 68 Dc
Châteauroux, France 68 Dc
Chateau Salins, France 68 Gb
Château Thierry, France 68 Eb
Châteauvillain, France 68 Fb
Châtelet, Belgium 60 Cd
Châtellerault, France 68 Dc
Châtel-St Denis, Switz. 61 Bb
Chatham, England 59 Hj
Chatham, New York 40 Kd
Chatham, Ontario 40 Ed
Chatham Is., Pacific Ocean 99 Hm
Cha Thing Phra, Siam 83 Ce
Châtillon-sur-Seine, France 68 Fc
Chatra, India 87 Ec
Chatrapur, India 85 Ge
Châtre, la, France 68 Ec
Chattahoochee R., Georgia 43 Ke
Chattanooga, Tennessee 43 Jd
Chaudiere R., Quebec 40 Lb
Chau-doc, S. Vietnam 83 Cd
Chauka R., India 87 Cb
Chaumont-en-Bassigny, Fr. 68 Fb
Chaunskaya Guba, Russia 75 Rb
Chausa, India 87 Dc
Chautauqua L., New York 44 Aa
Chaux de Fonds, la, Switz. 61 Ba
Chaves, Brazil 49 Hd
Chaves, Portugal 66 Bb
Chayu, Tibet 78 Ce
Chazon, Argentina 50 Dd
Cheb, Czechoslovakia 64 Ec
Cheboksary, Russia 77 Hb
Cheboygan, Michigan 40 Dc
Cheduba & I., Burma 85 He
Che foo. See Yentai
Chehalis, Washington 45 Bb
Cheju Do, Korea 78 Jd
Chekiang, prov., China 81 Jh
Chekunda, Russia 75 Nc
Chelforó, Argentina 50 Ce
Chelkar, Kazakh. 74 Ed
Chelm, Poland 65 Kc
Chelmsford, England 59 Hj
Chelsea, Vermont 40 Kc
Chelsea, Wisconsin 40 Ac
Cheltenham, England 59 Fj
Chelva, Spain 67 Ec
Chelyabinsk, Russia 77 Qc
Chemba, Moçambique 91 Ec
Chembar, Russia 77 Fd
Chemnitz. See Karl Marx Stadt
Chenab R., W. Pakistan 86 Be
Chenchow. See Hwaiyang
Chenesht, Persia 89 Gc
Chengchow, China 80 Fe
Chengho, China 81 Jj
Chengshan Tow, China 78 Hc
Chêngtehshih, China 80 Hb
Chengtu, China 80 Bg
Chenhsien, China 81 Fk
Chennan. See Tchpao
Chenoa, Illinois 40 Be
Chenting, China 80 Gc
Chenyüan, China 81 Dj
Cheongkong, Hainan I. 78 Eg
Chepen, Peru 48 Be
Chepes, Argentina 50 Cd
Cher, R. & dep., France 68 Ec
Cherbourg, France 68 Cb
Cherchell, Algeria 94 Fa
Cheremkhovo, Russia 75 Kc
Cherepovets, Russia 76 Lb
Cherkassy, Ukraine 76 Gg
Chermoz, Russia 74 Ec
Chernigov, Ukraine 76 Gf
Chernikovsk, Russia 77 Nc
Chernovsk, Russia 77 Ja
Chernovtsy, Ukraine 76 Dg
Chernyakhovsk, Russia 63 Jj
Cherokee, Iowa 42 Gc
Cherrapungi, India 85 Hc
Cherskogo, Khrebet, Russia 75 Pb
Chertkovo, Ukraine 76 Lg
Chervenbryeg, Bulgaria 72 Ec
Chesapeake B., Maryland 43 Ld
Cheshire, co., England 59 Fg
Cheshskaya Guba, Russia 74 Db
Chesley, Ontario 40 Fc
Chester, England 59 Fg
Chester, Pennsylvania 44 Cc
Chesterfield, England 59 Gg
Chesterfield Is., Pacific Oc. 98 Ej
Chestertown, Maryland 44 Bc
Chethang, Tibet 85 Hc
Chetumal, Mexico 46 Gd
Chetumal B., Mexico 47 Bc
Cheviot, New Zealand 51 De
Cheviot, The, England 58 Fe
Cheviot Hills, Eng.-Scot. 58 Fe
Cheyenne, Wyoming 42 Fc
Cheyenne R., S. Dakota 42 Fc
Chhachrauli, India 86 Ee
Chhata, India 86 Eg
Chhatarpur, India 87 Bc
Chhibramau, India 87 Bb
Chhindwara, India 87 Bd
Chiai, Taiwan 81 Kl
Chia-mu-ssu. See Kiamusze
Chiang-hsi. See Kiangsi
Chiang-kan, Siam 83 Cc
Chiang Mai, Siam 83 Bc
Chiang Rai, Siam 83 Bc
Chiang-su. See Kiangsu
Chiapa, Mexico 46 Fd
Chiapas R. & state, Mexico 46 Fd
Chiasso, Switzerland 61 Ec
Chiavari, Italy 70 Bc
Chiba, Japan 82 Gg
Chibia, Angola 91 Ac
Chicago, Illinois 40 Ce
Chichagof I., Alaska 43 Zm
Chichester, England 59 Gk
Ch'i-ch'i-ha-erh. See Tsitsihar
Chickasha, Oklahoma 42 Ge
Chiclayo, Peru 48 Be
Chico, California 45 Cf
Chicoana, Argentina 50 Cc
Chicopee, Massachusetts 44 Da
Chicuma, Angola 92 Dd
Chicundo, Transvaal 91 Ed
Chidambaram, India 84 Ef
Chiengue, Angola 92 Dg
Chien-ou. See Kienow
Chieti, Italy 70 Ed
Chièvres, Belgium 60 Bd
Chihchow. See Kweichih
Chih-fêng, China 80 Ja
Chihkiang, China 81 Dj
Chihsien, China 80 Ge
Chihuahua & state, Mexico 46 Cb
Chikala, Malawi 93 Hg
Chik-Ballapur, India 84 Ef
Chikien, China 75 Mc
Chikmagalur, India 84 Ef
Chikwawa, Malawi 93 Gh
Chilant'ai, China 80 Bc
Chilas, Kashmir 86 Dc
Chilca, Pta. de, Peru 48 Bf
Chile, rep., S. America 50 Bf
Chilecito, Argentina 50 Cc
Chilete, Peru 48 Be
Chilia Veche, Rumania 72 Gb
Chi-lin. See Kirin
Chilka L., India 85 Ge
Chillan, Chile 50 Be
Chillicothe, Ohio 40 Ef
Chiloe, I. de, Chile 50 Bf
Chilonga, Zambia 93 Gg
Chilpancingo, Mexico 46 Ed
Chiltern Hills, England 59 Gj
Chilton, Wisconsin 40 Bc
Chiluane, Moçambique 91 Fd
Chilubula, Zambia 93 Gg
Chilumba, Malawi 91 Eb
Chilung, Taiwan 81 Kk
Chilwa L., Malawi 93 Hh
Chimay, Belgium 60 Cd
Chimbay, Uzbek. 74 Fd
Chimbote, Peru 48 Be
Chimkent, Kazakh. 74 Fd
China, Asia 55 Ke
Chi-nan. See Tsinan
Chinandega, Nicaragua 47 Bd
Chincha, Peru 48 Bf
Chin-chiang. See Tsingkiang
Chinchon, Spain 66 Db
Chinchow, China 78 Hb
Chindwin R., Burma 85 Jc
Ching Hai, China 78 Dc
Chingleput, India 84 Ff
Ching Shan, China 80 Eg
Ch'ing-tao. See Tsingtao
Chinguetta, Mauritania 94 Cd
Ch'ing-yuan. See Paoting
Chinhai, China 81 Kh
Chin Hills, Burma 85 Hd
Chin-hua. See Kinhwa
Chini, India 86 Fe
Chin-ning. See Tsining
Chiniot, W. Pakistan 86 Ce
Chinju, Korea 78 Jc
Chinkiang, China 80 Jf
Chin Ling Shan, China 78 Ed
Chinsura, India 87 Gd
Chinwangtao, China 80 Jc
Chioggia, Italy 70 Dc
Chios I. See Khíos, I.

Davis Str., Greenland 41 Pc
Davos Dorf, Switzerland 61 Eb
Davos Platz, Switzerland 61 Eb
Davy Sd., Greenland 41 Nb
Dawna Ra., Burma, etc. 85 Je
Dawson, R., Queensland 53 Je
Dax, France 69 Ce
Dayton, Ohio 40 Df
Daytona Beach, Florida 43 Kf
De Aar, Cape Province 91 Cf
Dead Sea, Jordan-Israel 90 Df
Deadwood, S. Dakota 42 Fc
Deal, England 59 Hj
Dean Funes, Argentina 50 Dd
Death Valley, California 45 Eg
Deauville, France 68 Cb
Debar, Yugoslavia 72 Cd
Debesy, Russia 77 Lb
Debica, Poland 65 Jc
Deblin, Poland 65 Jc
Debno, Poland 64 Fb
Debra Markos, Ethiopia 93 Hb
Debrecen, Hungary 65 Je
Decatur, Alabama 43 Je
Decatur, Illinois 40 Bf
Deccan, India 84 Ef
Deception, I., S. Shetlands 100 Sc
Děčín, Czechoslovakia 64 Fc
Decize, France 68 Ec
Dedeagach. See Alexandroúpolis
Dedham, Massachusetts 44 Ea
Dédougou, Upper Volta 94 Ef
Dedza, Malawi 93 Gg
Dee R., Scotland 58 Fc
Dee R., Wales 59 Eg
Deep Creek L., Maryland 44 Ac
Deer Lodge, Montana 45 Gb
Deerlyck, Belgium 60 Bd
Deesa, India 84 Da
Defferrari, Argentina 50 Ee
Degana, India 84 Dc
Degerfors, Sweden 62 Hd
De Gerlache Straits, Antarctica 100 Sc
De Grey, R., W. Australia 52 Cd
Deh Bid, Persia 89 Fc
Deh Dehdez, Persia 89 Fc
Dehra Dun, India 86 Fe
Dehrud, Persia 89 Fd
Deim Zubeir, Sudan 95 Lg
Deir Abu Said, Jordan 90 De
Deir 'Ali, Syria 90 Ed
Deir Atiye, Syria 90 Ec
Deir ez Zor, Syria 88 Cb
Deir Hafir, Syria 90 Fa
Deir Shemil, Syria 90 Eb
Déj, Rumania 65 Ke
De Jong's Pt., New Guinea 79 Lm
Dekalb, Illinois 40 Be
De Kastri, Russia 75 Pc
Delano Pk., Utah 42 Dd
Delavan, Wisconsin 40 Bd
Delaware, Ohio 40 Ee
Delaware, state, U.S.A. 43 Ld
Delaware B., Del.-N.J. 44 Cc
Delaware R., New Jersey, etc. 44 Cb
Delaware City, Delaware 44 Cc
Delden, Netherlands 60 Eb
Deleitosa, Spain 66 Cc
De Lemmer, Netherlands 60 Db
Delémont, Switzerland 61 Ca
Delfshaven, Netherlands 60 Cc
Delft, Netherlands 60 Cb
Delfzijl, Netherlands 60 Ea
Delger, Mongolia 78 Fa
Delgo, Sudan 95 Md
Delhi, India 84 Ec
Delhi, New York 44 Ca
Dellenbaugh, Mt., Arizona 45 Gg
Dellys, Algeria 94 Fa
Delmenhorst, Germany 64 Cb
Delta, Pennsylvania 44 Bc
Demanda, Sa. de la, Spain 66 Da
Demchok, Tibet 84 Eb
Deming, New Mexico 42 Ee
Demmin, Germany 64 Eb
Denbigh & co., Wales 59 Eg
Denderleeuw, Belgium 60 Cd
Dendermonde, Belgium 60 Cc
Dendi, Mt., Ethiopia 93 Hc
Denekamp, Netherlands 60 Eb
Den Helder, Netherlands 60 Cb
Denia, Spain 67 Ec
Deniliquin, New S. Wales 53 Jg
Denison, Texas 42 Ge
Denizli, Turkey 88 Ab
Denmark, kingdom, W.-Eur. 63 Cj
Denmark Str., Greenland, etc. 41 Nc
Den Oever, Netherlands 66 Db
Dent Blanche, Mt., Switz. 61 Cb
Denton, Maryland 40 Jf
Denton, Texas 42 Ge
D'Entrecasteaux Is., Papua 53 Ka
D'Entrecasteaux Pt., W. Aust. 52 Cf
Denver, Colorado 42 Fd
Deoband, India 86 Ef
Deobhog, India 85 Fd
Deogarh, India 85 Fd
Deoghar, India 87 Fc
Deoli, India 84 Ec
Deolia, India 84 Dd
Deori, India 87 Bd
De Panne, Belgium 60 Ac
De Pere, Wisconsin 40 Bc
Deposit, New York 40 Jd
Depot Harbour, Ontario 40 Fc
Dera, Syria 90 Ee
Dera Bugti, W. Pakistan 84 Cc
Dera Ghazi Khan, W. Pakistan 86 Be
Dera Ismail Khan, W. Pakistan 86 Be
Dera Nanak, India 86 Dd
Derbent, Russia 74 Dd
Derby, W. Australia 52 Dc
Derby & co., England 59 Fh
Derecske, Hungary 65 Je
Derg L., Eire 59 Bf
Derg L., Eire 59 Bh
De Rijp, Netherlands 60 Cb
De Ruyter, New York 44 Ca
Derna, Libya 95 Kb
Dernberg C., S.-W. Africa 91 Be
Derravaragh L., Eire 59 Cg
Derudeb, Sudan 95 Ne
Derventa, Yugoslavia 70 Gc
Derwent Water, England 59 Ef
Descalvados, Brazil 49 Fg
Deschaillons, Quebec 40 Kb
Deseado, R., Argentina 50 Cg
Des Moines & R., Iowa 43 Hc
Desna, R., Ukraine 76 Gf
Desolacion, I., Chile 50 Bh
Desolation C., Greenland 41 Pc
Dessau, Germany 64 Ec
Deta, Rumania 72 Cb
Detroit, Michigan 40 Ed
Dett, Rhodesia 91 Dc
Deurne, Netherlands 60 Dc
Deux Rivières, Ontario 40 Gb
Deux-Sèvres, dep., France 68 Cc
Déva, Rumania 72 Db
Dévávanya, Hungary 72 Ca
Deventer, Netherlands 60 Eb
Deveron R., Scotland 58 Fc
Devils Lake, N. Dakota 42 Gb
Devin, Bulgaria 72 Ed
Devizes, England 59 Fj
Devon, co., England 59 Ek
Devonport, England 59 Ek
Devonport, New Zealand 51 Eb
Devonport, Tasmania 53 Jh
Dewangiri, Bhutan 85 Hc
Deyhuk, Persia 89 Gc
Deynze, Belgium 60 Bd
Dezful, Persia 88 Ec
Dhaba, Arabia 88 Cd
Dhahran, Arabia 88 Fd
Dhak, W. Pakistan 86 Cd
Dhala, S. Yemen 88 Dg
Dhamār, Yemen 88 Dg
Dhampur, India 87 Ba
Dhamra, India 85 Gd
Dhamtari, India 84 Fd
Dhang Ra., Nepal 87 Ca
Dhangain, India 87 Ec
Dhankuta, Nepal 87 Fb
Dhariya, Arabia 88 De
Dharmjaygarh, India 87 Dd
Dharmkot, India 86 De
Dharmsala, India 86 Ed
Dharwar, India 84 Ee
Dhaulagiri, Mt., Nepal 87 Da
Dhayd, Trucial States 89 Gd
Dhiban, Jordan 90 Df
Dhidhimótikhon, Greece 72 Fd
Dhionisiadhes. See Yianisadhes Is.
Dhirang Jong, India 85 Hc
Dholera, India 84 Dd
Dholpur, India 87 Ab
Dhond, India 84 De
Dhubri, India 87 Hb
Dhula, S. Yemen 88 Ef
Dhulia, India 84 Dd
Dhurma, Arabia 88 Ee
Dhurwai, India 87 Bc
Dia I., Crete 73 Eg
Diamante, Argentina 50 Dd
Diamantina, Brazil 49 Jg
Diamantina, R., Queensland 53 Hd
Diamantino, Brazil 49 Ff
Diamond, I., Burma 85 He
Diamond Harbour, India 87 Gd
Dianópolis, Brazil 49 Hf
Dibbah, Jebel, Arabia 88 Cd
Dibbéla, Niger 95 He
Dibrugarh, India 85 Hc
Dickinson, N. Dakota 42 Fb
Die, France 69 Fd
Dien Bien Phu, N. Vietnam 83 Cb
Dieppe, France 68 Db
Diest, Belgium 60 Dd
Dieverbrug, Netherlands 60 Eb
Dig, India 86 Eg
Dighal, S. Yemen 88 Eg
Digne, France 69 Gd
Digoel, R., New Guinea 79 Lm
Digoin, France 68 Ec
Dijon, France 68 Fc
Diksmuide, Belgium 60 Ac
Dikwa, Nigeria 95 Hf
Dilam, Arabia 88 Ee
Dili, Timor I., Indonesia 79 Jm
Dillon, Montana 45 Gc
Dilolo, Angola 92 Eg
Dilolo, Congo 92 Eg
Dimbokro, Ivory Coast 94 Eg
Dimgarpur, India 84 Dd
Dimitrovgrad, Yugoslavia 72 Dc
Dimla, E. Pakistan 87 Gb
Dimona, Israel 90 Df
Dimotika. See Dhidhimótikhon
Dinagat, I., Philippines 79 Jh
Dinajpur, E. Pakistan 87 Gc
Dinan, France 68 Bb
Dinanagar, India 86 Dd
Dinant, Belgium 60 Cd
Dinapore, India 87 Ec
Dinar, Turkey 88 Bb
Dinard, France 68 Bb
Dinarske Planina, Yugoslavia 70 Fc
Dindigul, India 84 Ef
Dingle & B., Eire 59 Ah
Dingwall, Scotland 58 Dc
Dinteloord, Netherlands 60 Cc
Diourbel, Senegal 94 Bf
Dipalpur, W. Pakistan 86 Ce
Dipton, New Zealand 51 Bf
Dir, W. Pakistan 86 Bc
Direction, C., Queensland 53 Hb
Diredawa, Ethiopia 93 Jc
Diriamba, Nicaragua 47 Bd
Dirjaj, S. Yemen 88 Eg
Dirk Hartogs I., W. Aust. 52 Be
Dirksland, Netherlands 60 Cc
Dirranbandi, Queensland 52 Je
Disappointment, C., Wash. 45 Ab
Disappointment Is., Tuamotu Arch. 99 Lj
Disappointment, L., W. Aust. 52 Dd
Disentis, Switzerland 61 Db
Disko, B., Greenland 41 Pc
Disko, I., Greenland 41 Pc
Disna, Belorussia 76 Fd
Dison, Belgium 60 Dd
Diu, India 84 Dd
Diver, Ontario 40 Gb
Diviso, Colombia 48 Bc
Divrigi, Turkey 88 Cb
Diwaniyah, Iraq 88 Dc
Dix, Quebec 40 Ha
Dixmude, Belgium 60 Ac
Dixon, Illinois 40 Be
Diyarbakir, Turkey 88 Db
Dizah, Persia 89 Hd
Djakarta, Java 79 Em
Djambi, Sumatra 79 Dl
Djelfa, Algeria 94 Fb
Djeneien, Tunisia 95 Gb
Djerba, I., Tunisia 95 Hb
Djibouti, Fr. Somaliland 93 Jb
Djidjelh, Algeria 94 Ga
Djolu, Congo 92 Ed
Djougou, Dahomey 94 Fg
Djursholm, Sweden 63 Gg
Dmitriya Lapteva, Proliv, Russia 75 Pa
Dnepr R., Ukraine 76 Gf
Dneprodzerzhinsk, Ukraine 76 Jg
Dnepropetrovsk, Ukraine 76 Jg
Dnestr, R., Ukraine 76 Fh
Dnieper R. See Dnepr, R.
Dniester R. See Dnestr, R.
Dobbyn, Queensland 53 Hc
Dobele, Latvia 63 Kh
Doberan, Germany 64 Da
Dobra, Czechoslovakia 65 Jd
Dobřany, Czechoslovakia 64 Ed
Dobrich (Tolbukhin), Bulg. 72 Fc
Dobruja, Rumania 72 Gb
Dobryanski, Russia 77 Na
Dobrzyn, Poland 65 Hb
Doce Leguas, Cayos de las, Cuba 47 Db
Doctor Arroyo, Mexico 46 Dc
Dodecanese, Greece 73 Ff
Dodge City, Kansas 42 Fd
Dodgeville, Wisconsin 40 Ad
Dodman Pt., England 59 Dk
Dodoma, Tanzania 93 Hf
Doel, Belgium 60 Cc
Doesburg, Netherlands 60 Eb
Doetinchem, Netherlands 60 Ec
Dogger Bank, North Sea 56 He
Doha, Qatar 89 Fd
Dohad, India 84 Dd
Doka, Arabia 88 Df
Dokka, Yemen 88 Dg
Dokkum, Netherlands 60 Ea
Dol, France 68 Cb
Dolcigno. See Ulcinj
Dôle, France 68 Fc
Dolent, Mt., Switzerland 61 Cc
Dolgellau, Wales 59 Eh
Dolo, Ethiopia 93 Jd
Dolomitiche, Alpi, Italy 70 Cb
Dolores, Argentina 50 Ee
Dolores, Mexico 46 Bb
Dolores, Spain 67 Ec
Dolphin, C., Falkland Is. 50 Eh
Dolunnor. See Tolun
Dom, Mt., W. Irian 79 Ll
Domariaganj, India 87 Db
Domburg, Netherlands 60 Bc
Dome Rock Mts., Arizona 45 Fj
Domel, I., Burma 85 Jf
Domfront, France 68 Cb
Dominica, I., West Indies 47 Gc
Dominican Rep., W.I. 47 Ec
Domira Bay, Malawi 93 Gg
Dömitz, Germany 64 Db
Dom Pedrito, Brazil 50 Fd
Domuyo, Mt., Argentina 50 Be
Domvraina, Greece 73 De
Don, R., Russia 74 Cc
Don R., Scotland 58 Ec
Donaghadee, N. Ireland 59 Df
Donau, R. (Danube), Central Europe 64 Ed
Donaueschingen, Germany 64 Ce
Don Benito, Spain 66 Cc
Doncaster, England 59 Gg
Dondo, Angola 92 Cf
Donegal & co., Eire 59 Bf
Donegal B., Eire 59 Bf
Donets, R., Russia 77 Eg
Donetsk, Russia 76 Kh
Donga, Nigeria 95 Hg
Dongara, W. Australia 52 Be
Dongargarh, India 84 Fd
Donggala, Celebes 79 Gl
Dong-hoi, N. Vietnam 83 Dc
Dongo, Angola 92 Dg
Dongola, Sudan 95 Me
Donji Miholjac, Yugoslavia 70 Gc
Dönna, Norway 62 Ec
Donnellys Crossing, New Zealand 51 Da
Doon L., Scotland 58 Ee
Doorman, Mt., W. Irian 79 Ll
Doorn, Netherlands 60 Db
Dora, L., W. Australia 52 Dd
Doranda, India 87 Ed
Dorat le, France 68 Dc
Dorchester, England 59 Fk
Dordogne, dep., France 69 Dd
Dordogne R., France 69 Cd
Dordrecht, Netherlands 60 Cc
Dore, Mt., France 68 Ed
Dori, Upper Volta 94 Ef
Dornoch & Firth, Scotland 58 Ec
Dorokhsh, Persia 89 Gc
Dorotea, Sweden 62 Gd
Dorrego, Argentina 50 De
Dorset, co., England 59 Fk
Dortmund, Germany 62 Bc
Dos Bahias, C., Argentina 50 Cf
Doshi, Afghanistan 89 Jb
Dospat, Bulgaria 72 Dd
Dosso, Niger 94 Ff
Dossor, Kazakh. 74 Ed
Dothan, Alabama 43 Je
Douai, France 68 Ea
Douala, Cameroon 95 Gh
Douarnenez, France 68 Ab
Doubs, dep., France 68 Gc
Doubtless B., New Zealand 51 Da
Douglas, Arizona 42 Ee
Douglas, Cape Province 91 Ce
Douglas, I. of Man 59 Ef
Doullens, France 68 Ea
Doume, Cameroon 92 Cd
Douro & R., Spain-Portugal 66 Ab
Dover, Delaware 44 Cc
Dover, England 59 Hj
Dover, New Hampshire 44 Ea
Dover, New Jersey 44 Cb
Dover, Ohio 40 Fe
Dover, Str. of, Eng.-France 68 Da
Dovre Fjell, Norway 62 Ce
Dow L., Botswana 91 Cd
Dowa, Malawi 93 Gg
Down, co., N. Ireland 59 Cf
Downpatrick, N. Ireland 59 Df
Dow Polān, Persia 89 Fc
Doylestown, Pennsylvania 44 Cb
Drăgăsani, Rumania 72 Eb
Draguignan, France 69 Ge
Drake Str., Antarctica 100 Sd
Drakensberg, Mts., S. Africa 91 Df
Dráma, Greece 72 Ed
Drammen, Norway 63 Dg
Dranov I., Rumania 72 Gb
Dras, Kashmir 86 Dc
Drawsko, Poland 65 Fb
Drazinda, W. Pakistan 86 Ae
Drenthe, prov., Netherlands 60 Eb
Dresden, Germany 64 Ec
Dresden, Ontario 40 Ed
Dreux, France 68 Db
Drin G., Albania 72 Bd
Drina, R., Yugoslavia 72 Bc
Dröbak, Norway 63 Dg
Drogheda, Eire 59 Cg
Droichead Atha. See Drogheda
Droitwich, England 59 Fh
Drôme, dep. & R., France 69 Fd
Drummond I., Michigan 40 Ec
Drummondville, Quebec 40 Kc
Drunen, Netherlands 60 Dc
Druten, Netherlands 60 Dc
Druz, Jeb. ed, Syria 90 Ee
Drygalski I., Antarctica 100 Gc
Dschang, Cameroon 92 Cc
Dubayy, Trucial States 89 Gd
Dubbo, New S. Wales 53 Jf
Dublin, Georgia 43 Ke
Dublin & co., Eire 59 Cg
Dubno, Ukraine 76 Df
Du Bois, Pennsylvania 44 Ab
Dubrovnik, Yugoslavia 72 Bc
Dubuque, Iowa 43 Hc
Duchcov, Czechoslovakia 64 Ec
Ducie I., Pacific Ocean 99 Nk
Duck Is., Ontario 40 Ec
Dudinka, Russia 74 Hb
Dudley, England 59 Fh
Duero R., Spain 66 Cb
Duffel, Belgium 60 Cc
Dugi Otok, I., Yugoslavia 70 Ec
Duifken Pt., Queensland 53 Hb
Duisburg, Germany 64 Bc
Dujana, India 86 Ef
Duke of Gloucester Grp., Tuamotu Archipelago 99 Lk
Duk Faiwil, Sudan 95 Mg
Dulan, China 78 Cc
Dulce, G., Costa Rica 47 Ce
Duluth, Minnesota 43 Hb
Duma, Syria 90 Ed
Dumbarton, Scotland 58 Ee
Dum-Dum, India 87 Gd
Dumeir, Syria 90 Ed
Dumfries & co., Scotland 58 Ee
Dumka, India 87 Fc
Dumraon, India 87 Ec
Dunarea (Danube), R., Central Europe 57 Pg
Dunbarton, co., Scotland 58 Dd
Duncan Pass., Andaman Is. 85 Hf
Duncansby Head, Scotland 58 Fb
Dundalk, Eire 59 Cf
Dundalk B., Eire 59 Cg
Dundas, Ontario 40 Fd
Dundas Str., N. Terr., Aust. 52 Fb
Dún Dealgan. See Dundalk
Dundee, Natal 91 Ee
Dundee, Scotland 58 Fd
Dundee I., Antarctica 100 Tb
Dundrum B., N. Ireland 59 Df
Dungwa Ra., Nepal 87 Db
Dunedin, New Zealand 51 Cf
Dunfermline, Scotland 58 Ed
Dungarven, Eire 59 Bh
Dungbure Ra., Tibet 85 Fa
Dungeness, England 59 Hk
Dungu, Congo 93 Fd
Dunkeld, Scotland 58 Ed
Dunkerque (Dunkirk), Fr. 68 Ea
Dunkirk, New York 44 Aa
Dunkur, Ethiopia 93 Hb
Dunkwa, Ghana 94 Eg
Dúnlaoghaire, Eire 59 Cg
Dunmanway, Eire 59 Aj
Dunmara, N.T., Aust. 53 Fc
Dunnet Hd., Scotland 58 Eb
Duns, Scotland 58 Fe
Duque de York, I., Chile 50 Ah
Dura, Jordan 90 Df
Durango, Colorado 42 Ed
Durango & state, Mexico 46 Dc
Durant, Oklahoma 42 Ge
Durazno, Uruguay 50 Ed
Durazzo. See Durrës
Durban, Natal 91 Ee
Durbe, Latvia 63 Jh
Durbuy, Belgium 60 Dd
Durdevac, Yugoslavia 70 Fb
Durdureh, Somalia 93 Kb
Dureikish, Syria 90 Ec
Düren, Germany 64 Bc
Durga Str., W. Irian 53 Ga
Durham, N. Carolina 43 Ld
Durham, Ontario 40 Fc
Durham & co., England 59 Ff
Durness, Scotland 58 Db
Durrës, Albania 72 Bd
Dursey, I., Eire 59 Aj
Duruh, Persia 89 Hc
D'Urville I., New Zealand 51 Dd
Duryea, Pennsylvania 44 Cb
Dushanbe, Tadzhik 74 Fe
Dushore, Pennsylvania 44 Bb
Dusky Sound, New Zealand 51 Af
Düsseldorf, Germany 64 Bc
Dussen, Netherlands 60 Cc
Duszniki Zdrój, Poland 65 Gc
Dutch Harb., Aleutian Is. 43 Wm
Dutch Guiana. See Surinam
Duvan, Russia 77 Nc
Duwadami, Arabia 88 De
Dvina, R., Latvia 63 Lh
Dyatkovo, Russia 76 Je
Dyersburg, Tennessee 43 Jd
Dyle R., Belgium 60 Cd
Dyurtyuli, Russia 77 Mc
Dzamyn Ude, Mongolia 78 Eb
Dzep, Yugoslavia 72 Dc
Dzerzhinsk, Russia 77 Fb
Dzerzhinsk, Belorussia 76 Ee
Dzhagdy, Khrebet, Russia 75 Mc
Dzhalal Abad, Kirgiz. 74 Gd
Dzhalinda, Russia 75 Mc
Dzhambul, Kazakh. 74 Gd
Dzhetygara, Kazakh. 74 Fc
Dzhezkazgan, Kazakh. 74 Fd
Dzhugdzhur, Khrebet, Rus. 75 Nc
Dzhungarskiy Ala-Tau., Kazakh. 74 Gd
Dzhusaly, Kazakh. 74 Fd
Dzierzoniow, Poland 65 Gc
Eagle, Alaska 43 Yl
Eagle Pass, Texas 42 Ff
Eagle River, Wisconsin 40 Bc
Earlville, New York 44 Ca
Earn L., Scotland 58 Ed
East Aurora, New York 44 Aa
Eastbourne, England 59 Hk
Eastbourne, New Zealand 51 Ed
East Dereham, England 59 Hh
Easter I., Pacific Ocean 99 Qk
Eastern B., Maryland 44 Bc
Eastern States, India 84 Fd
East Liverpool, Ohio 40 Fe
East London, Cape Province 91 Df
East Lothian, co., Scotland 58 Fe
Easton, Maryland 44 Bc
Easton, Pennsylvania 44 Cb
East Pakistan, S. Asia 85 Gd
East Retford, England 59 Gg
East Riding, Yorks., Eng. 59 Gg
East St Louis, Illinois 43 Jd
Eaton Rapids, Michigan 40 Dd
Eau Claire, Wisconsin 43 Hc
Ebbw Vale, Britain 59 Ej
Ebensburg, Pennsylvania 44 Ab
Eberswalde, Germany 64 Eb
Eboli, Italy 71 Ee
Ebolowa, Cameroon 92 Cd
Ebro, R., Spain 67 Ea
Ecaussines, Belgium 60 Cd
Echallens, Switzerland 61 Bb
Echt, Netherlands 60 Dc
Echten, Netherlands 60 Eb
Echternach, Luxembourg 64 Bd
Echuca, Victoria 53 Hg
Eckeren, Belgium 60 Cc
Ecuador, rep., S. America 48 Bd
Edam, Netherlands 60 Db
Eday, I., Orkney Is. 58 Fa
Ed Damer, Sudan 95 Me
Ed Damur, Lebanon 90 Dd
Ed Debba, Sudan 95 Me
Eddrachillis B., Scotland 58 Db
Ed Dueim, Sudan 95 Mf
Ede, Netherlands 60 Db
Edebäck, Sweden 63 Ef
Eden, New York 44 Aa
Eden R., England 59 Ff
Edenburg, Orange Free State 91 De
Edendale, New Zealand 51 Bg
Edenderry, Eire 59 Cg
Ederengin Nuru, Mongolia 78 Cb
Edgeöya, I., Arctic Ocean 74 Ba
Edgerton, Wisconsin 40 Bd
Édhessa, Greece 73 Dd
Edievale, New Zealand 51 Bf
Edinburgh, Scotland 58 Ee
Edirne, Turkey 88 Aa
Edremit, Turkey 88 Ab
Edsele, Sweden 62 Ge
Edsel Ford Ra., Antarctica 100 Pb
Edsin Gol, China 78 Db
Edward L., Congo 93 Fe
Edwardesabad. See Bannu
Edwards, New York 40 Jc
Edwards Plat., Texas 42 Fe
Eecke, Belgium 60 Bd
Eeklo (Eecloo), Belgium 60 Bc
Efate, I., New Hebrides 98 Fj
Eferding, Austria 64 Ed
Effingham, Illinois 40 Bf
Egadi Is., Sicily 71 Dg
Egaña, Argentina 50 Ee
Eganville, Ontario 40 Hc
Eger. See Cheb
Eger, Hungary 65 Je
Egersund, Norway 63 Bg
Eggenfelden, Germany 64 Ed
Eghezee, Belgium 60 Cd
Egmont, Mt., New Zealand 51 Ec
Egridir, Turkey 88 Bb
Egypt (U.A.R.), N. Africa 95 Lc
Eibergen, Netherlands 60 Eb
Eichstätt, Germany 64 Dd
Eide, Norway 63 Bf
Eidsvoll, Norway 63 Df
Eifel, Mts., Germany 64 Bc
Eigg, I., Scotland 58 Cd
Eighty Mile Beach, W. Aust. 52 Dc
Eil, Somalia 93 Kc
Eilat, Israel 90 Ch
Eindhoven, Netherlands 60 Dc
Ein Yahav, Israel 90 Dg
Eire. See Ireland, Republic of
Eirunepe, Brazil 48 Ce
Eisden, Netherlands 60 Dd
Eisenach, Germany 64 Dc
Eisenerz, Austria 64 Fe
Eisleben, Germany 64 Dc
Ejutla, Mexico 46 Ed
Ekaterinoslav. See Dnepropetrovsk
Eketahana, New Zealand 51 Ed
Ekhinádhes Is., Greece 73 Ce
Eksjö, Sweden 63 Fh
Ekträsk, Sweden 62 Hd
El Abde, Lebanon 90 Dc
Elafónisi Chan, Greece 73 Df
Élafos I., Greece 73 Df
El Agheila, Libya 95 Jb
El Aina, Jordan 90 Dg
El Alamein, Egypt 95 Lb
El-Asnam (Orléansville), Algeria 94 Fa
Elasson, Greece 73 De
El Auja. See Nizana
Elâzig, Turkey 88 Cb
Elba, I., Italy 70 Cd
El Bab, Syria 90 Fa
El Bahluiye, Syria 90 Db
El Banco, Colombia 48 Cb
El Barco de Valdeorras, Sp. 66 Ba
Elbasan, Albania 72 Cd
El Baul, Venezuela 48 Db
El-Bayadh, Algeria 94 Fb
Elbe R., Germany 64 Db
Elbert, Mt., Colorado 42 Ed
Elbeuf, France 68 Db
Elbing. See Elblag
El-Birka, Arabia 88 Dc
Elbistan, Turkey 88 Cb
Elblag, Poland 65 Ha
El Br'aij, Syria 90 Ec
El'brus, Mt., Russia 74 Dd
Elburg, Netherlands 60 Db
Elburz Mts., Persia 89 Fb
El Callao, Venezuela 48 Eb
El Cardon, Venezuela 48 Ca
El Centro, California 45 Fj
Elche, Spain 67 Ec
El Chorro, Argentina 50 Db
El Cuy, Argentina 50 Ce
El Dab, Somalia 93 Kc
El Diwân, Egypt 95 Md
El Donfar, Somalia 93 Kb
El Dorado, Kansas 42 Gd
El Dorado, Mexico 46 Cc
El Dorado, Venezuela 48 Eb
Eldoret, Kenya 93 Hd
El Encanto, Colombia 48 Cd
Elephant I., Antarctica 100 Tc
Elephant Butte Res., New Me. 42 Ee
El Ergh, Libya 95 Kc
Eleşkirt, Turkey 88 Db
Eleuthera I., Bahama Is. 47 Da
Elewyt, Belgium 60 Cd
El Faiyum, Egypt 95 Mc
El Fasher, Sudan 95 Lf
El Ferrol del Caudillo, Spain 66 Aa
El Fuwara, Arabia 88 Dd
Elgena, Eritrea 93 Ha
El Geteina, Sudan 95 Mf
Elgg, Switzerland 61 Da
El Ghobbe, Arabia 88 Ce
Elgin, Illinois 40 Bd
Elgin, Scotland 58 Ec
El Giof. See Al Jawf
El Giza, Egypt 95 Mb
El Golea, Algeria 94 Fb
Elgon, Mt., Uganda 93 Gd
El Hamra, Syria 90 Fb
El Hamrat, Syria 90 Ec
El-Harrach, Algeria 94 Fa
El-Hayath, Arabia 88 Dd
El Hijane, Syria 90 Ed
El Hilla, Sudan 95 Lf
Elisabethville. See Lubumbashi
Elista, Russia 74 Dd
Elizabeth, New Jersey 44 Cb
Elizabeth, West Virginia 40 Ff
Elizabeth City, N. Carolina 43 Ld
Elizabeth I., Massachusetts 44 Eb
Elizabeth, Mt., Argentina 50 Cg
Elizavetgrad. See Kirovograd
Elizondo, Spain 67 Ea
El Jafr, Jordan 90 Eg
El Jauf, Libya 95 Kd
Elk, Poland 65 Kb
El Kharga, Egypt 95 Mc
Elkhart, Indiana 40 De
Elkhorn, Mt., Idaho 45 Gd
El Khushniye, Syria 90 Dd
Elkins, West Virginia 40 Gf
Elko, Nevada 45 Fe
Elkton, Maryland 44 Cc
El Lādhiqīya. See Latakia
Ellas, Greece 73 De
Ellenabad, India 86 Df
Ellensburg, Washington 45 Cb
Ellesmere, L., New Zealand 51 De
Ellezelles, Belgium 60 Bd
Ellice Is., Pacific Ocean 98 Gh
Ellichpur, India 84 Ed
Ellicott City, Maryland 44 Bc
Elliot, Cape Province 91 Df
Elliot, N. Terr., Aust. 53 Fc
Elliot Group, China 80 Lc
Ellora, India 84 Ed
Elm, Switzerland 61 Eb
El Ma'arra, Syria 90 Ea
Elma Dagh, Turkey 88 Bb
El Madhiq, Arabia 88 Ce
El Mansura, Egypt 95 Mb
El Mazar, Jordan 90 Df
El Mazra'a, Jordan 90 Df
El Meget, Somalia 93 Kd
El Menzil, Jordan 90 Ef
Elmira, New York 44 Ba
El Minya, Egypt 95 Mc
El Molar, Spain 66 Db
El Muwaqqar, Jordan 90 Ef
El Negro, Venezuela 48 Eb
El Obeid, Sudan 95 Mf
El Odaiya, Sudan 95 Lf
El Pardo, Spain 66 Db
El Paso, Illinois 40 Be
El Paso, Texas 42 Ee
Elphinstone I., Burma 85 Jf
El Pintado, Argentina 50 Db
El Portugues, Peru 48 Bc
El Puente del Arzobispo, Sp. 66 Cc
El Qadmus, Syria 90 Eb
El Qanawat, Syria 90 Ee
El Qaryatein, Syria 90 Fc
El Qathma, Arabia 88 De
El Qatrana, Jordan 90 Ef
El Qatrun, Libya 95 Hd
El Quds esh Sherif. See Jerusalem
El Quneitra, Syria 90 Dd
El Quseir, Syria 90 Ec
El Quweira Jordan 90 Dh
Elroy, Wisconsin 40 Ad
El Sadi. See Wajer
El Salvador, Cent. America 47 Bd
Elsenborn, Belgium 60 Ed
Elsloo, Netherlands 60 Dd
Elspeet, Netherlands 60 Db
Elst, Netherlands 60 Dc
Elsterwerda, Germany 64 Ec
Eltham, New Zealand 51 Ec
El Tigre, Venezuela 48 Eb
El Toro, Spain 67 Eb
El Transito, Chile 50 Bc
Eluru, India 84 Fe
El Valle, Colombia 48 Bb
Elvas, Portugal 66 Bc
El Vigia, Venezuela 48 Cb
Ely, England 59 Hh
Ely, Nevada 45 Ff
Ely, Isle of, England 59 Hh
Emangulova, Russia 77 Md
Emba R., Kazakh. 74 Ed
Embarcación, Argentina 50 Db
Embóna, Greece 73 Ff
Embrun, France 69 Gd
Emden, Germany 64 Bb
Emerald, Queensland 53 Jd
Emilia-Romagna, reg., Italy 70 Cc
Eminabad, W. Pakistan 86 Dd
Emmaste, Estonia 63 Kg
Emmen, Netherlands 60 Eb
Empalme, Mexico 46 Bb
Empedrado, Argentina 50 Ec
Empire, Michigan 40 Dc
Emporia, Kansas 42 Gd
Emporium, Pennsylvania 44 Ab
Emptinne, Belgium 60 Dd
Ems, Germany 64 Bc
Enard B., Scotland 58 Db
Encantada, Cerro de, Mexico 46 Aa
Encarnación, Paraguay 50 Ec
Encontrados, Venezuela 48 Cb
Encounter B., S. Australia 53 Gg
Encruzilhada, Brazil 50 Fd

Garonne, R., *France* **69** De
Garoua, *Cameroon* **95** Hg
Garraway, *Liberia* **94** Dh
Garrison Res., *N. Dakota* **42** Fb
Garrovillas, *Spain* **66** Bc
Garsen, *Kenya* **95** Je
Gartok, *Tibet* **84** Fb
Gary, *Indiana* **40** Ce
Garza, *Argentina* **50** Dc
Garzon, *Colombia* **48** Bc
Gasan Kuli, *Turkman* **74** Ee
Gascogne, G. de, *Fr.-Sp.* **69** Be
Gascogne, prov., *France* **69** De
Gascoyne, R., *W. Australia* **52** Ce
Gasherbrum, Mt., *Kashmir* **86** Ec
Gasht, *Persia* **89** Hd
Gasselte, *Netherlands* **60** Eb
Gastonia, *N. Carolina* **43** Kd
Gastre, *Argentina* **50** Cf
Gat (Ghat), *Libya* **95** Hd
Gata, *Spain* **66** Bb
Gata, C., *Cyprus* **90** Bc
Gateshead, *England* **58** Ff
Gatineau R., *Quebec* **40** Jb
Gatooma, *Rhodesia* **91** Dc
Gatun L., *Panama* **47** Ce
Gaud-i-Zirreh, *Afghanistan* **89** Hd
Gauhati, *India* **85** Hc
Gaurihar, *India* **87** Cc
Gāvbandī, *Persia* **89** Fd
Gavdhos, I., *Crete* **73** Eg
Gavião, *Portugal* **66** Bc
Gāv Koshi, *Persia* **89** Gd
Gävle, *Sweden* **63** Gf
Gävle Bukten, *Sweden* **63** Gf
Gavur D., *Turkey* **88** Cb
Gawler Ra., *S. Australia* **53** Gf
Gaya, *India* **87** Ec
Gaya, *Niger* **94** Ff
Gayaza, *Uganda* **93** Ge
Gaylord, *Michigan* **40** Dc
Gaza, *Cent. Afr. Rep.* **95** Jh
Gaza, *Egypt* **90** Cf
Gazi Antep, *Turkey* **88** Cb
Gazik, *Persia* **89** Hc
Gdansk, *Poland* **65** Ha
Gdynia, *Poland* **65** Ha
Gebeit, *Sudan* **95** Ne
Gedaref, *Sudan* **95** Nf
Gedinne, *Belgium* **60** Ce
Geelong, *Victoria* **53** Hg
Geelvink B., *W. Irian* **79** Ll
Geeraardsbergen. See Grammont
Gela, *Sicily* **71** Eg
Gelderland, *Netherlands* **60** Db
Geldrop, *Netherlands* **60** Dc
Gelib, *Somalia* **93** Jd
Gelibolu, *Turkey* **88** Aa
Gelinden, *Belgium* **60** Dd
Gelsenkirchen, *Germany* **64** Bc
Gemas, *W. Malaysia* **83** Cf
Gembloux, *Belgium* **60** Cd
Gemena, *Congo* **92** Dd
Gemert, *Netherlands* **60** Dc
Gemmenich, *Belgium* **60** Dd
Gemmi Pass, *Switzerland* **61** Cb
Genappe, *Belgium* **60** Cd
Gendringen, *Netherlands* **60** Ec
Geneina, *Sudan* **95** Kf
Genemuiden, *Netherlands* **60** Eb
General Acha, *Argentina* **50** De
General Alvarado, *Arg.* **50** Ee
General Alvear, *Argentina* **50** De
General Capdevila, *Argent.* **50** Dc
General Carneiro, *Brazil* **49** Gg
General Guido, *Argentina* **50** Ee
General José de San Martin, *Argentina* **50** Ec
General La Madrid, *Argent.* **50** De
General Lavalle, *Argentina* **50** Ee
General Madariaga, *Argent.* **50** Ee
General Pico, *Argentina* **50** De
General Pinto, *Argentina* **50** Dd
General Roca, *Argentina* **50** Ce
General Viamonte, *Argent.* **50** De
General Villegas, *Argentina* **50** De
Geneseo, *New York* **44** Ba
Geneva, *New York* **44** Ba
Geneva, L. of. See Léman, Lac
Génève (Geneva), *Switz.* **61** Bb
Genkai Nada, *Japan* **82** Ah
Gennargentu, Mte. del, *Sard.* **71** Be
Gennep, *Netherlands* **60** Dc
Genoa. See Genova
Genova, *Italy* **70** Bc
Genova, G. di, *Italy* **70** Bc
Gent. See Gand
Geographe B., *W. Australia* **52** Cf
Geographe Chan., *W. Aust.* **52** Bd
Georga Zemlya, *Arctic Oc.* **74** Da
George L., *New York* **44** Da
George L., *New S. Wales* **53** Jg
Georgetown, *Guyana* **48** Fb
Georgetown, *Delaware* **40** Jf
Georgetown, *Virginia* **44** Bc
George Town, *Gr. Cayman, West Indies* **47** Cc
George Town, *Penang I., W. Malaysia* **83** Ce
Georgetown, *Qnsld.* **53** Hc
Georgia, state, *U.S.A.* **43** Ke
Georgia. See Gruzinskaya rep.
Georgian B., *Ontario* **40** Fc
Georgian B. Is. Nat. Pk., *Ont.* **40** Fc
Georgina, R., *Queensland* **53** Gd
Georgiyevsk, *Russia* **74** Dd
Gera, *Germany* **64** Ec
Geraardsbergen, *Belgium* **60** Bd
Geraldine, *New Zealand* **51** Cf
Geraldton, *W. Australia* **52** Be
Gérgal, *Spain* **67** Dd
Gerlach, *Nevada* **45** De
Germania, *Argentina* **50** Dd
Germany, *Central Europe* **56** Kf
Gerona, *Spain* **67** Ga
Gers, dep., *France* **69** De
Gerze, *Turkey* **88** Ca
Getafe, *Spain* **66** Db
Gettysburg, *Pennsylvania* **44** Bc
Gevar. See Yuksekova
Gevgelija, *Yugoslavia* **72** Dd
Ghabaghib, *Syria* **90** Ed
Ghadames, *Libya* **95** Gb
Ghaghara, R., *India* **87** Db
Ghaida, *S. Yemen* **88** Eg
Ghail, *Arabia* **88** Ee
Ghana (Gold Coast), *W. Afr.* **94** Eg
Ghantur, *Syria* **90** Fc
Gharandal, *Jordan* **90** Dg
Ghardaia, *Algeria* **94** Fb
Gharian, *Libya* **95** Hb
Ghat, *Arabia* **88** Ed
Ghatal, *India* **87** Fd
Ghatampur, *India* **87** Cb
Ghatghat, *Arabia* **88** Ee
Ghats, Eastern, *India* **84** Fe
Ghats, Western, *India* **84** De
Ghauta, *Arabia* **88** Ee
Ghaziabad, *India* **86** Ef
Ghazipur, *India* **87** Dc
Ghazir, *Lebanon* **90** Dc
Ghazni, *Afghanistan* **89** Jc
Ghazouet, *Algeria* **94** Ea
Gheel, *Belgium* **60** Cc
Gheorgheni, *Rumania* **72** Ea
Ghislenghien, *Belgium* **60** Bd
Ghizao, *Afghanistan* **89** Jc
Ghorak, *Afghanistan* **89** Jc
Ghorian, *Afghanistan* **89** Hc
Ghotki, *W. Pakistan* **84** Cc
Ghubreh, *Muscat & Oman* **99** Ge
Giaour Dagh. See Gavur D.
Giarre, *Sicily* **71** Eg
Gibara, *Cuba* **47** Db
Gibeon, *S.-W. Africa* **91** Be
Gibraltar, *Spain* **66** Cd
Gibraltar, Str. of, *Spain* **66** Ce
Gibson Desert, *W. Aust.* **52** Dd
Gien, *France* **68** Ec
Giessen, *Germany* **64** Cc
Gifhorn, *Germany* **64** Db
Gifu, *Japan* **82** Eg
Giganta, La, *Mexico* **46** Bb
Gijon, *Spain* **66** Ca
Gila Des., *Arizona* **42** De
Gila R., *Arizona* **42** De
Gilau, *Rumania* **72** Da
Gilbert Is., *Pacific Ocean* **98** Gh
Gilbert, R., *Queensland* **53** Hc
Gilberton, *Qnsld.* **53** Hc
Gilbués, *Brazil* **49** Je
Gilgit & R., *Kashmir* **86** Dc
Gimel, *Switzerland* **61** Bb
Ginir, *Ethiopia* **93** Jc
Ginzo, *Spain* **66** Ba
Gioia, G. di, *Italy* **71** Ef
Giornico, *Switzerland* **61** Db
Girardot, *Colombia* **48** Cc
Girdle Ness, *Scotland* **58** Fc
Giresun, *Turkey* **88** Ca
Girga, *Egypt* **95** Mc
Giridih, *India* **87** Fc
Girishk, *Afghanistan* **89** Hc
Gironde, dep., *France* **69** Cd
Gironde, R., *France* **68** Cd
Girvan & R., *Scotland* **58** De
Gisborne, *New Zealand* **51** Gc
Gisenyi, *Rwanda* **93** Fe
Gisors, *France* **68** Db
Giswil, *Switzerland* **61** Db
Gitch, Mt., *Ethiopia* **93** Hb
Giurgiu, *Rumania* **72** Ec
Givry, *Belgium* **60** Cd
Gizhiga, *Russia* **75** Rb
Giżycko, *Poland* **65** Ja
Gjinokaster, *Albania* **73** Cd
Gjövik, *Norway* **63** Df
Glabbeek, *Belgium* **60** Cd
Gladstone, *Michigan* **40** Cc
Gladstone, *Queensland* **53** Kd
Gladwin, *Michigan* **40** Dd
Glamoc, *Yugoslavia* **70** Fc
Glamorgan, *Wales* **59** Ej
Glärnisch, Mt., *Switzerland* **61** Db
Glarus & canton., *Switz.* **61** Ea
Glasgow, *Kentucky* **43** Jd
Glasgow, *Scotland* **58** Ee
Glassboro, *New Jersey* **44** Cc
Glauchau, *Germany* **64** Ec
Glazov, *Russia* **77** La
Glen, *New Hampshire* **40** Lc
Glen Affric, *Scotland* **58** Dc
Glen Afton, *N.Z.* **51** Eb
Glendale, *California* **45** Dh
Glendive, *Montana* **42** Fb
Glen Falls, *New York* **40** Kd
Glen Garry, *Scotland* **58** Ed
Glenhope, *New Zealand* **51** Dd
Glen Innes, *New S. Wales* **53** Ke
Glenties, *Eire* **59** Bf
Glenville, *West Virginia* **40** Ff
Gletsch, *Switzerland* **61** Db
Glittertind, Mt., *Norway* **63** Cf
Gliwice, *Poland* **65** Hc
Globe, *Arizona* **42** De
Glogau. See Glogów
Glogów, *Poland* **65** Gc
Gloppen, *Norway* **62** Bf
Gloria, *Brazil* **49** Ke
Gloucester, *Massachusetts* **44** Ea
Gloucester, *New Jersey* **44** Cc
Gloucester & co., *England* **59** Fj
Gloversville, *New York* **44** Ca
Glukhov, *Ukraine* **76** Hf
Gmünd, *Austria* **64** Ee
Gmünd, *Germany* **64** Cd
Gmunden, *Austria* **64** Ee
Gniezno, *Poland* **65** Gb
Goa, *India* **84** De
Goalpara, *India* **85** Hc
Goalundo, *E. Pakistan* **87** Gd
Gobabis, *S.-W. Africa* **91** Bd
Gobi, The, *E. Asia* **75** Kd
Gobindpur, *India* **87** Fd
Godavari, R., *India* **84** Ee
Godda, *India* **87** Fc
Godech, *Bulgaria* **72** Dc
Goderich, *Ontario* **40** Fd
Godhra, *India* **84** Db
Godthaab, *Greenland* **41** Pc
Goes, *Netherlands* **60** Bc
Goesi, *New Guinea* **79** Kl
Gogama, *Ontario* **40** Fb
Gog Magog Hills, *England* **59** Hh
Gogra R., *India* **87** Db
Gogrial, *Sudan* **95** Lg
Gohana, *India* **86** Ef
Goiânia, *Brazil* **49** Hg
Goias, *Brazil* **49** Hf
Gökçeağac, *Turkey* **88** Ba
Goksun, *Turkey* **88** Cb
Golaghat, *India* **85** Hc
Gol'chikha, *Russia* **74** Ha
Golconda, *India* **84** Ee
Goldap, *Poland* **65** Ka
Golden B., *New Zealand* **51** Dd
Golden Lake, *Ontario* **40** Hc
Goldfield, *Nevada* **45** Eg
Goleniow, *Poland* **64** Fb
Golmo, *China* **78** Cc
Goltva, *Ukraine* **76** Hg
Gomal Pass, *W. Pakistan* **86** Bd
Gombe, *Nigeria* **95** Hf
Gomel', *Belorussia* **76** Ge
Gomera, I., *Canary Is.* **94** Bc
Gómez Farias, *Mexico* **46** Dc
Gómez Palacio, *Mexico* **46** Db
Gonaïves, *Haiti* **47** Ec
Gonave, I. de la, *Haiti* **47** Ec
Gonbad-e-Kavus, *Persia* **89** Gb
Gonda, *India* **87** Db
Gondal, *India* **84** Dd
Gondo, *Switzerland* **61** Db
Gönen, *Turkey* **73** Fd
Gongka Ling, *China* **78** De
Goniądz, *Poland* **65** Kb
Goodenough I., *New Guinea* **53** Ka
Gooderham, *Ontario* **40** Gc
Good Hope, C. of, *Cape Prov.* **91** Bf
Goodland, *Kansas* **42** Fd
Goodrich, *Wisconsin* **40** Ac
Goole, *England* **59** Gg
Goomalling, *W. Australia* **52** Cf
Goor, *Netherlands* **60** Eb
Goorle, *Netherlands* **60** Dc
Goose L., *Oregon-California* **45** Ce
Gopalpur, *India* **85** Fe
Göppingen, *Germany* **64** Cd
Gor, *Spain* **66** Dd
Gora, *China* **78** Ce
Gorakhpur, *India* **87** Db
Gordola, *Switzerland* **61** Db
Gordonvale, *Qnsld.* **53** Jc
Gore, *Ethiopia* **93** Hc
Goré, *Chad* **95** Jg
Gore, *New Zealand* **51** Bg
Gore Bay, *Ontario* **40** Ec
Gorey, *Eire* **59** Ch
Gorgan, *Persia* **89** Fb
Gorgona, I., *Italy* **70** Bd
Gorinchem, *Netherlands* **60** Cc
Gorizia, *Italy* **70** Dc
Gor'kiy, *Russia* **77** Gb
Gorlice, *Poland* **65** Jd
Gorlitz, *Germany* **64** Fc
Gorlovka, *Ukraine* **76** Lg
Gorodetz, *Russia* **77** Fb
Gorodishche, *Russia* **77** Gd
Gorodnitsa, *Ukraine* **76** Ef
Gorontalo, *Celebes* **79** Hk
Gorrahei, *Ethiopia* **93** Jc
Gorsel, *Netherlands* **60** Eb
Gorzów (Wielkopolski), *Poland* **64** Fb
Gosaint han, Mt., *Nepal-Tibet* **85** Gc
Göschenen, *Switzerland* **61** Db
Goshanak, *W. Pakistan* **84** Bc
Goshen, *New York* **44** Cb
Gospić, *Yugoslavia* **70** Ec
Gosport, *England* **59** Gk
Gossau, *Switzerland* **61** Ea
Gosselies, *Belgium* **60** Cd
Gossen, *Norway* **62** Be
Gostivar, *Yugoslavia* **72** Cd
Göta Älv, *Sweden* **63** Eg
Göteborg, *Sweden* **63** Dh
Gotha, *Germany* **64** Dc
Gothenburg. See Göteborg
Gotland, I., *Sweden* **63** Hh
Goto Retto, *Japan* **82** Ah
Gotska Sandön, *Sweden* **63** Hg
Göttingen, *Germany* **64** Cc
Gottwaldov, *Czechoslovakia* **65** Gd
Gouda, *Netherlands* **60** Cb
Goudswaard, *Netherlands* **60** Cc
Gough I., *Atlantic Ocean* **97** Kn
Goulburn, *New South Wales* **53** Jf
Goundam, *Mali* **94** Ee
Gouré, *Niger* **95** Hf
Gournay, *France* **68** Db
Gouverneur, *New York* **40** Jc
Gowanda, *New York* **40** Gd
Gowna L., *Eire* **59** Bg
Goya, *Argentina* **50** Ec
Gozo, I. (Brit.), *Malta* **71** Eg
Graaf Reinet, *Cape Province* **91** Cf
Grabow, *Poland* **65** Hc
Gračac, *Yugoslavia* **70** Ec
Gracefield, *Quebec* **40** Hb
Gracias, *Honduras* **47** Bd
Gracias a Dios, *Nicaragua* **47** Cd
Gradets, *Bulgaria* **72** Fc
Grado, *Spain* **66** Ba
Grafton, *New South Wales* **53** Ke
Grafton, *W. Virginia* **40** Ff
Grafton, Is., *Chile* **50** Bh
Graham Ld., *Antarctica* **100** Sc
Graham Bell, Os., *Arctic Oc.* **74** Fa
Grahamstown, *Cape Province* **91** Df
Grajewo, *Poland* **65** Kb
Grammont, *Belgium* **60** Be
Grampian Mts., *Scotland* **58** Dd
Gramsbergen, *Netherlands* **60** Eb
Granada, *Nicaragua* **47** Bd
Granada, *Spain* **66** Dd
Granby, *Quebec* **40** Kc
Gran Canaria, I., *Canary Is.* **94** Bc
Gran Chaco, *Argentina* **50** Dc
Grand Can., *China* **78** Gc
Grand I., *Michigan* **40** Cb
Grand I., *New York* **44** Aa
Grand R., *Michigan* **40** Dd
Grand R., *S. Dakota* **42** Fb
Grand Bassa. See Buchanan
Grand Bassam, *Ivory Coast* **94** Eg
Grand Canyon, *Arizona* **42** Dd
Grand Canyon Nat. Park, *Arizona* **42** Dd
Grand Cayman, I., *W.I.* **47** Cc
Grand Coulee Dam, *Wash.* **42** Cb
Grande, B., *Argentina* **50** Ch
Grande, Rio, *Brazil* **49** Gg
Grande Sa. See Sa. da Ibiapaba
Grande Comore, I., *Comores, Archipel des* **93** Jg
Grande de Santiago, R., *Me.* **46** Dc
Grand Forks, *N. Dakota* **42** Gb
Grand Haven, *Michigan* **40** Cd
Grand Island, *Nebraska* **42** Gc
Grand Junction, *Colorado* **42** Ed
Grand Lahou, *Ivory Coast* **94** Dg
Grand Ledge, *Michigan* **40** Dd
Grand Marais, *Minnesota* **40** Ab
Grand Mère, *Quebec* **40** Kb
Grandola, *Portugal* **66** Ac
Grand Piles, *Quebec* **40** Kb
Grand Rapids, *Michigan* **40** Dd
Grandrieu, *Belgium* **60** Cd
Grandson, *Switzerland* **61** Bb
Grand Teton Mt. & Nat. Park, *Wyoming* **42** Dc
Grane, *Norway* **62** Ed
Granity, *New Zealand* **51** Cd
Granja, *Brazil* **49** Jd
Grankulla, *Finland* **63** Lf
Granollers, *Spain* **67** Gb
Granön, *Sweden* **62** Hd
Grant Ld., *Arctic Ocean* **41** Qa
Grant Ra., *Nevada* **45** Ff
Grantham, *England* **59** Gh
Grantown-on-Spey, *Scotland* **58** Ec
Grants Pass, *Oregon* **45** Bd
Granville, *New York* **44** Da
Graskop, *Transvaal* **91** Ed
Gräsö, *Sweden* **63** Hf
Grassano, *Italy* **71** Fe
Grasse, *France* **69** Ge
Grassett, *Ontario* **40** Da
Grassier, *Switzerland* **61** Bb
Graubünden, canton, *Switz.* **61** Eb
Graus, *Spain* **67** Fa
Gravarne, *Sweden* **63** Dg
Grave, *Netherlands* **60** Dc
's Gravenhage, *Netherlands* **60** Cb
Gravenhurst, *Ontario* **40** Gc
's Gravenzande, *Netherlands* **60** Cb
Gray, *France* **68** Fc
Grayling, *Michigan* **40** Dc
Graz, *Austria* **65** Fe
Great Australian Bight, *Aust.* **52** Ef
Great Barrier Reef, *Aust.* **53** Jc
Great Barrington, *Mass.* **44** Da
Great Basin, *Nevada* **42** Cc
Great Blasket I., *Eire* **59** Ah
Great Dividing Ra., *Aust.* **53** Jd
Great Falls, *Montana* **45** Hb
Great Geysir, *Iceland* **62** Vm
Great Lake. See Tonle Sap
Great N. Mts., *W.Va., etc.* **44** Ac
Great Pt., *Massachusetts* **44** Eb
Great Salt L., *Utah* **45** Ge
Great Salt Lake Des., *Utah* **45** Ge
Great Sandy Des., *W. Aust.* **52** Dd
Great Sandy I. (Fraser I.) *Queensland* **53** Ke
Great Smoky Mts., Nat. Park, *Tenn./N. Car.* **43** Kd
Great South B., *New York* **44** Db
Great Torrington, *England* **59** Ek
Great Victoria Des., *W. Aust.* **52** Ee
Great Yarmouth, *England* **59** Jk
Grebbestad, *Sweden* **63** Dg
Greco, C., *Cyprus* **90** Cc
Greece, *S. Europe* **57** Nj
Greeley, *Colorado* **42** Fc
Green B., *Wisconsin* **40** Cc
Green Mts., *Vermont* **40** Kd
Green R., *Utah* **42** Ed
Green Bay, *Wisconsin* **40** Cc
Greenfield, *Indiana* **40** Df
Greenfield, *Massachusetts* **40** Kd
Greenland, *N. America* **41** Pb
Greenland Sea, *Greenland* **41** Mb
Greenock, *Scotland* **58** De
Greenport, *New York* **40** Ke
Greensboro, *N. Carolina* **43** Ld
Greensburg, *Pennsylvania* **44** Ab
Greenville, *Alabama* **43** Je
Greenville, *Liberia* **94** Dg
Greenville, *Michigan* **40** Dd
Greenville, *Mississippi* **43** He
Greenville, *S. Carolina* **43** Ke
Greenville, *Texas* **42** Ge
Greenwich, *Connecticut* **44** Db
Greenwich, *England* **59** Hj
Greenwich, *Rhode Island* **44** Eb
Greenwood, *Mississippi* **43** He
Greenwood, *S. Carolina* **43** Ke
Greenwood, *Wisconsin* **40** Ac
Greenwood L., *N.Y.-N.J.* **44** Cb
Gregory Ra., *Queensland* **53** Hc
Greifen See, *Switzerland* **61** Da
Greifswald, *Germany* **64** Ea
Grein, *Austria* **64** Fd
Greiz, *Germany* **64** Ec
Grenaa, *Denmark* **63** Dh
Grenada, I., *Windward Is.* **47** Gd
Grenadines, Is., *Windward Is.* **47** Gd
Grenchen, *Switzerland* **61** Ca
Grenoble, *France* **69** Fd
Grenville, C., *Queensland* **53** Hb
Gretna, *Louisiana* **43** Hf
Grevelingen, *Netherlands* **60** Cc
Grevená, *Greece* **73** Cd
Grey Ra., *Qnsld.-N.S.W.* **53** He
Greylock Mt., *Massachusetts* **44** Da
Greymouth, *New Zealand* **51** Ce
Greys Butte. See Juniper Mt.
Greystones, *Eire* **59** Cg
Greytown, *New Zealand* **51** Ed
Greytown. See San Juan del Norte
Griesalp, *Switzerland* **61** Cb
Griffin, *Georgia* **43** Ke
Griffith, *N.S.W.* **53** Jf
Grim C., *Tasmania* **53** Hh
Grimstad, *Norway* **63** Cg
Grimsby, *Lincs., Eng.* **59** Gg
Grindelwald, *Switzerland* **61** Db
Grindstone, *Michigan* **40** Ec
Grinnell Ld., *Arctic Ocean* **41** Qa
Griquatown, *Cape Province* **91** Ce
Grīva, *Latvia* **63** Mj
Grobiņa, *Latvia* **63** Jh
Gröbming, *Austria* **64** Ee
Grodno, *Belorussia* **76** Ce
Grodzisk, *Poland* **65** Gb
Groenlo, *Netherlands* **60** Eb
Groix, I. de, *France* **68** Bc
Groningen & prov., *Netherlands* **60** Ea
Grono, *Switzerland* **61** Eb
Groote Eylandt, *N. Territory, Australia* **53** Gb
Grootfontein, *S.-W. Africa* **91** Be
Grootfontein, *S.-W. Africa* **91** Bc
Groot Natuna I. See Bunguran Kep.
Grossevichi, *Russia* **75** Nd
Gross Glockner, *Austria* **64** Ee
Grosswardein. See Oradea
Groton, *New York* **44** Ba
Groznyy, *Russia* **74** Dd
Grudziądz, *Poland* **65** Hb
Grüsch, *Switzerland* **61** Eb
Gruz, *Yugoslavia* **72** Bc
Gruzinskaya, rep., *U.S.S.R.* **74** Dd
Grybów, *Poland* **65** Jd
Gsteig, *Switzerland* **61** Cb
Guabito, *Panama* **47** Ce
Guacanayabo, G. de, *Cuba* **47** Db
Guachipas, *Argentina* **50** Cc
Guadalajara, *Spain* **66** Db
Guadalajara, *Mexico* **46** Dc
Guadalcanal, *Spain* **66** Cc
Guadalcanal, I., *Solomon Is.* **98** Eh
Guadalcazar, *Mexico* **46** Dc
Guadalquivir, R., *Spain* **66** Cd
Guadalupe, *Mexico* **46** Dc
Guadalupe I., *Mexico* **46** Ab
Guadalupe Mts., *New Mexico-Texas* **42** Ee
Guadalupe R., *Texas* **42** Gf
Guadalupe-y-Calvo, *Mexico* **46** Cb
Guadarrama, *Spain* **66** Cb
Guadarrama, Sa. de, *Spain* **66** Db
Guadeloupe, I., *Leeward Is.* **47** Gc
Guadiana, R., *Spain* **66** Bc
Guadix, *Spain* **66** Dd
Guafo & G. de, *Chile* **50** Bf
Guaitecas, Is., *Chile* **50** Bf
Guajar-á-Mirim, *Brazil* **48** Df
Guajaratuba, *Brazil* **48** Ee
Gualeguaychu, *Argentina* **50** Ed
Guam, I., *Pacific Ocean* **98** Df
Guamá, *Brazil* **49** Hd
Guamini, *Argentina* **50** De
Guamo, *Colombia* **48** Cc
Guanabaçoa, *Cuba* **47** Cb
Guanacevi, *Mexico* **46** Cb
Guanahani. See San Salvador
Guanajuato, *Mexico* **46** Dc
Guanare, *Venezuela* **48** Db
Guanarito, *Venezuela* **48** Db
Guandacol, *Argentina* **50** Cc
Guane, *Cuba* **47** Cb
Guanica, *Puerto Rico* **47** Fc
Guanta. See Puerto La Cruz
Guantanamo, *Cuba* **47** Db
Guapi, *Colombia* **48** Bc
Guapiles, *Costa Rica* **47** Cd
Guapore, *Brazil* **50** Fc
Guapore (Rondonia), *Brazil* **48** Ef
Guapore, R., *Brazil-Bolivia* **48** Ef
Guaqui, *Bolivia* **48** Dg
Guarapuava, *Brazil* **50** Fc
Guarda, *Portugal* **66** Bb
Guasdualito, *Venezuela* **48** Cb
Guasipati, *Venezuela* **48** Eb
Guatemala, *Guatemala* **46** Fe
Guatemala, rep., *C. America* **46** Fe
Guatrache, *Argentina* **50** De
Guaviare, R., *Colombia* **48** Dc
Guaxupe, *Brazil* **49** Hh
Guayabal, *Venezuela* **48** Db
Guayama, *Puerto Rico* **47** Fc
Guayaquil, *Ecuador* **48** Bd
Guaymas, *Mexico* **46** Bb
Guben, *Germany* **64** Fc
Gubin. See Guben
Gudiyatam, *India* **84** Ef
Guelma, *Algeria* **94** Ga
Guelph, *Ontario* **40** Fd
Guemes, *Argentina* **50** Cb
Guéret, *France* **68** Dc
Guernsey, I., *Channel Is.* **68** Bb
Guernsey Res., *Wyoming* **42** Fc
Guerrero, *Mexico* **46** Cb
Guerrero, *Tamaulipas, Mex.* **46** Eb
Guerrero, state, *Mexico* **46** Dd
Gugera, *W. Pakistan* **86** Ce
Guiana Highlands, *S. America* **48** Ec
Guija, *Moçambique* **91** Ed
Guildford, *England* **59** Gj
Guillaumes, *France* **69** Gd
Guimaraes, *Brazil* **49** Jd
Guimarães, *Portugal* **66** Ab
Guinea, *West Africa* **94** Cf
Guinea, G. of, *N.-W. Africa* **92** Ad
Guines, *Cuba* **47** Cb
Guingamp, *France* **68** Bb
Guiria, *Venezuela* **48** Ea
Guisanbourg, *Fr. Guiana* **49** Gc
Guise, *France* **68** Eb
Guisisil, Vol., *Nicaragua* **47** Bd
Gujar Khan, *W. Pakistan* **86** Cd
Gujranwala, *W. Pakistan* **86** Dd
Gujrat, *W. Pakistan* **86** Dd
Gulbarga, *India* **84** Ee
Gulbene, *Latvia* **63** Mh
Gulfport, *Mississippi* **43** Je
Gulistan, *W. Pakistan* **84** Cb
Gul Koh, *Afghanistan* **89** Jc
Gulpen, *Netherlands* **60** Dd
Gulran, *Afghanistan* **89** Hb
Gulu, *Uganda* **93** Gd
Gumel, *Nigeria* **95** Gf
Gummersbach, *Germany* **64** Bc
Gümüljina. See Komotini
Gümüsane, *Turkey* **88** Ca
Guna, *India* **87** Ac
Gunchu, *Japan* **82** Ch
Gunnedah, *N.S.W.* **53** Kf
Guntakal, *India* **84** Ee
Guntur, *India* **84** Fe
Gurais, *Kashmir* **86** Dc
Gurdaspur, *India* **86** Dd
Gurgaon, *India* **86** Ef
Gurgl, *Austria* **64** De
Gurha, *India* **84** Dc
Gurkha, *Nepal* **87** Eb
Gurla Mandhata, Mt., *Tibet* **84** Fb
Gurnigel, *Switzerland* **61** Cb
Gurskoy, *Norway* **62** Ae
Guru, *Tibet* **85** Gc
Gurupa, *Brazil* **49** Gd
Gurupa, I., *Brazil* **49** Gd
Guru Sikhar, *India* **84** Dd
Guryev, *Kazakh.* **74** Ed
Gusev, *Lithuania* **63** Kj
Guspini, *Sardinia* **71** Bf
Güstrow, *Germany* **64** Eb
Guthrie, *Oklahoma* **42** Gd
Guttannen, *Switzerland* **61** Db
Guyana, *S. America* **48** Fc
Guyenne, prov., *France* **69** Dd
Guzman, *Mexico* **46** Dd
Gwa, *Burma* **85** He
Gwadar, *Persia* **89** He
Gwadar, *W. Pakistan* **84** Bc
Gwalior, *India* **87** Bb
Gwanda, *Rhodesia* **91** Dd
Gweebarra B., *Eire* **59** Bf
Gwelo, *Rhodesia* **91** Dc
Gyangtse, *Tibet* **85** Gc
Gydanskiy Pol., *Russia* **74** Ga
Gympie, *Queensland* **53** Ke
Györ, *Hungary* **65** Ge
Gyula, *Hungary* **65** Je
Gzhatsk, *Russia* **76** Jd
Haag, *Switzerland* **61** Ea
Haaksbergen, *Netherlands* **60** Eb
Haarlem, *Netherlands* **60** Cb
Habana, *Cuba* **47** Cb
Habban, *S. Yemen* **88** Eg
Habbaniyah, *Iraq* **88** Dc
Habigang, *E. Pakistan* **85** Hd
Haboro, *Japan* **82** Gb
Hachinohe, *Japan* **82** Gd
Hachuman, *Japan* **82** Eg
Hadason, *Mongolia* **78** Da
Hadda, *Arabia* **88** Ce
Haddington, *Scotland* **58** Fe
Hadera, *Israel* **90** Ce
Haderslev, *Denmark* **63** Cj
Hadjin. See Saimbeyli
Haecht, *Belgium* **60** Cd
Haeju, *Korea* **78** Jc
Haelen, *Belgium* **60** Dd
Hafar, *Arabia* **88** Ed
Hafar al Ats, *Arabia* **88** Ed
Haffe. See Babenna
Hafnarfjördhur, *Iceland* **62** Vm
Hagen, *Germany* **64** Bc
Hageri, *Estonia* **63** Lg
Hagerstown, *Maryland* **44** Bc
Hagi, *Japan* **82** Bg
Hague, C. de la, *France* **68** Cb
Hague, The. See 's Gravenhage
Haibak, *Afghanistan* **89** Jb
Hai cheng, *China* **80** Lb
Haichow. See Tunghai
Haidar Pasha. See Kadiköy
Haifa, *Israel* **90** Ce
Haig, *W. Australia* **52** Ef
Hail, *Arabia* **88** Dd
Hailar, *China* **78** Ga
Haileybury, *Ontario* **40** Gb
Hailun, *China* **78** Ja
Hailuoto, *Finland* **62** Ld
Hainan I., *China* **81** En
Hainan Str., *China* **81** Dm
Hainaut, prov., *Belgium* **60** Bd
Haiphong, *N. Vietnam* **83** Db
Hair, *Arabia* **88** Ee
Haiten I., *China* **81** Jk
Haiti, rep., *West Indies* **47** Ec
Hajdúböszörmény, *Hungary* **65** Je
Hajima, Jebel, *Arabia* **88** Ce
Hajipur, *India* **87** Ec
Hajjar, *China* **78** Bc
Haka, *Burma* **85** Hd
Hakkâri, *Turkey* **88** Db
Hakodate, *Japan* **82** Gd
Hal, *Belgium* **60** Cd
Hala, *W. Pakistan* **84** Cc
Halacho, *Mexico* **46** Fc
Halaib, *Sudan* **88** Ce
Halba, *Lebanon* **90** Ec
Halbe, *Arabia* **88** Df
Halberstadt, *Germany* **64** Dc
Halden, *Norway* **63** Dg
Haleb. See Aleppo
Halebiye, *Syria* **88** Cb
Hali, *Arabia* **88** Df
Halia, *India* **87** Dc
Haliburton, *Ontario* **40** Gc
Halifax, *England* **59** Fg
Halifax B., *Queensland* **53** Jc
Halkett C., *Alaska* **43** Xk
Hall, *Germany* **64** Cd
Hall Is., *Caroline Is.* **98** Eg
Hall Ld., *Greenland* **41** Pa
Halle, *Germany* **64** Ec
Halle. See Hal
Hallein, *Austria* **64** Ee
Halley, B., *Antarctica* **100** Ab
Hälliste, *Estonia* **63** Lg
Hällnäss, *Sweden* **62** Hd
Halls Creek, *W. Australia* **52** Ec
Hallstavik, *Sweden* **63** Hf
Hallviken, *Sweden* **62** Fe
Halmahera, I., *Indonesia* **79** Jk
Halmstad, *Sweden* **63** Eh
Halsa, *Norway* **62** Ce
Hälsingborg, *Sweden* **63** Eh
Halys, C. See Bafra Br.
Hama, *Syria* **90** Eb
Hamada, *Japan* **82** Cg
Hamadan, *Persia* **88** Ec
Hamam, *Arabia* **88** Ee
Hamamatsu, *Japan* **82** Eg
Hamar, *Arabia* **88** Ee
Hamar, *Norway* **63** Df
Hambantota, *Ceylon* **84** Fg
Hamburg, *Germany* **64** Db
Hamburg, *New York* **44** Aa
Hamburg, *Pennsylvania* **44** Cb
Hamdanīya, *Syria* **90** Eb
Hämeenlinna, *Finland* **63** Lf
Hameln, *Germany* **64** Cb
Hamersley Ra., *W. Aust.* **52** Cd
Hami, *S. Yemen* **88** Eg
Hamidan, *Arabia* **89** Fe
Hamidiya, *Syria* **90** Dc
Hamilton, *New York* **44** Ca
Hamilton, *New Zealand* **51** Eb
Hamilton, *Ohio* **40** Df
Hamilton, *Ontario* **40** Gd
Hamilton, *Scotland* **58** Ee
Hamilton, *Victoria* **53** Hg
Hamina, *Finland* **63** Mf
Hamirpur, *India* **87** Cc
Hamm, *Germany* **64** Bc
Hammān, *Iraq* **88** Dc
Hamme, *Belgium* **60** Cc
Hammerdal, *Sweden* **62** Fe
Hammerfest, *Norway* **62** Ka
Hammond, *Indiana* **40** Ce
Hammonton, *New Jersey* **44** Cc
Hamont, *Belgium* **60** Dc
Hampden, *New Zealand* **51** Cf
Hampshire, co., *England* **59** Gj
Hamun-i-Helmand, *Persia-Afghanistan* **89** Hc
Hamun-i-Puzak, *Afghanistan* **89** Hc
Han, *Belgium* **60** Dd
Hanakiya, *Arabia* **88** Dd
Hanau, *Germany* **64** Cc
Hanchung, *China* **80** Cf
Hancock, *Michigan* **43** Jb
Hancock, *New York* **44** Cb
Handegg, *Switzerland* **61** Db
Handeni, *Tanzania* **93** Hi
Hanford, *California* **45** Dg
Hanford, *Washington* **45** Db
Hangchow, *China* **81** Kg
Hangchow B., *China* **80** Kg
Hangu, *W. Pakistan* **86** Bd
Han Kiang, *China* **78** Ed
Hankö & Fd., *Finland* **63** Kg
Hankow (Wuhan), *China* **80** Gg
Hanle, *Kashmir* **84** Eb
Hanmer, *New Zealand* **51** De
Hannibal, *Missouri* **43** Hd
Hannover, *Germany* **64** Cb
Hannut, *Belgium* **60** Dd
Hanö Bukten, *Sweden* **63** Fj

Hanoi, *N. Vietnam* 83 Db
Hanover, *Ontario* 40 Fc
Hanover, *Pennsylvania* 44 Bc
Hanover, I., *Chile* 50 Bh
Hansi, *India* 86 Ef
Hansweert, *Netherlands* 60 Cc
Hanumangarh. See Bhatnair
Hanyang, *China* 81 Gg
Hanyin, *China* 80 Df
Hao, I., *Tuamotu Arch.* 99 Lj
Haparanda, *Sweden* 62 Ld
Hapur, *India* 86 Ef
Haqal, *Arabia* 88 Bd
Haraiya, *India* 87 Db
Harak, *Arabia* 88 Cd
Harar, *Ethiopia* 93 Jc
Harardera, *Somalia* 93 Kd
Hara Usu Nur, *Mongolia* 78 Ba
Harbin. See Pinkiang
Harbor Beach, *Michigan* 40 Ed
Harbor Spring, *Michigan* 40 Dc
Harburg Wilhelmsburg, *Ger.* 64 Cb
Harda, *India* 84 Ed
Hardanger Fjell, *Norway* 63 Bf
Hardanger Fd., *Norway* 63 Bf
Hardenberg, *Netherlands* 60 Eb
Harderwijk, *Netherlands* 60 Db
Harding, *Natal* 91 Ef
Hardoi, *India* 87 Cb
Hardwar, *India* 86 Ff
Hardy, Pen., *Chile* 50 Cj
Hare I. See I. aux Lievres
Hareidland, *Norway* 62 Ae
Hargeisa, *Somalia* 93 Jc
Hari, R., *Sumatra* 79 Dl
Harian, *Persia* 89 Fb
Harib, *Arabia* 88 Ef
Harihar, *India* 84 Ef
Harim, *Syria* 90 Ea
Haripur, *W. Pakistan* 86 Cd
Hariq, *Arabia* 88 Ee
Harishpur, *India* 85 Gd
Harlan, *Kentucky* 43 Kd
Harlebeke, *Belgium* 60 Bd
Harlequin Hills, *Nevada* 45 De
Harlingen, *Netherlands* 60 Da
Harmanli. See Kharmanli
Harney, L., *Oregon* 45 Dd
Harney Basin, *Oregon* 42 Bc
Harnösand, *Sweden* 62 Ge
Harper, *Liberia* 94 Dh
Harran, *Turkey* 88 Cb
Harris, & Sd. of, *Scotland* 58 Cc
Harrisburg, *Pennsylvania* 44 Bb
Harrison, *Michigan* 40 Dc
Harrisonburg, *Virginia* 43 Ld
Harrisville, *Michigan* 40 Ec
Harrogate, *England* 59 Fg
Har Sagi, *Israel* 90 Cg
Hârşova, *Rumania* 72 Fb
Harsprânget, *Sweden* 62 Jc
Harstad, *Norway* 62 Gb
Hart, *Michigan* 40 Cd
Hartford, *Connecticut* 44 Db
Hartlepool, *England* 59 Gf
Harvard, *Illinois* 40 Bd
Harvard Mt., *Colorado* 42 Ed
Harwich, *England* 59 Hj
Haryana, state, *India* 86 Dd
Harz, Mts., *Germany* 64 Dc
Hasā, *Jordan* 90 Dg
Hasan D., *Turkey* 88 Bb
Hasanpur, *India* 87 Ba
Hasbaya, *Lebanon* 90 Dd
Hassan, *India* 84 Ef
Hasselt, *Belgium* 60 Dd
Hasselt, *Netherlands* 60 Eb
Hastiere, *Belgium* 60 Cd
Hastings, *England* 59 Hk
Hastings, *Michigan* 40 Dd
Hastings, *Minnesota* 43 Hc
Hastings, *Nebraska* 42 Gc
Hastings, *New Zealand* 51 Fc
Hatay, *Turkey* 88 Cb
Hateg, *Rumania* 72 Db
Hatha, *Arabia* 88 De
Hathras, *India* 87 Bb
Ha-tinh, *N. Vietnam* 83 Dc
Hatteras, C., *N. Carolina* 43 Ld
Hattiesburg, *Mississippi* 43 Je
Hatvan, *Hungary* 65 He
Hat Yai, *Siam* 79 Dj
Haudères, les, *Switzerland* 61 Cb
Haugesund, *Norway* 63 Ag
Haukipudas, *Finland* 62 Ld
Hauki vesi, *Finland* 62 Ne
Haura, *S. Yemen* 88 Eg
Hauraki Gulf, *New Zealand* 51 Eb
Hauroko, L., *New Zealand* 51 Af
Hausa, *Jordan* 90 Fh
Hausstock, Mt., *Switzerland* 61 Eb
Hauta, *S. Yemen* 88 Eg
Hauta, *Arabia* 88 Ee
Haut Atlas, Mts., *Morocco* 94 Db
Haut-Garonne, dep., *France* 69 De
Haut-Loire, dep., *France* 69 Ed
Haut-Marne, dep., *France* 68 Fb
Hautes, Alpes, dep., *France* 69 Gd
Haut-Saône, dep., *France* 68 Gc
Haute-Savoie, dep., *France* 68 Gc
Hautes-Pyrénées, dep., *Fr.* 69 De
Haute Vienne, dep., *France* 68 Dd
Haute Volta, *W. Africa* 94 Ef
Haut-Rhin., dep., *France* 68 Gc
Havana. See Habana
Havasu L., *Cal.-Ariz.* 45 Fh
Havelange, *Belgium* 60 Dd
Havelland, *Germany* 64 Eb
Havelock I., *Andaman Is.* 85 Hf
Havelock North, *N.Z.* 51 Fc
Haverfordwest, *Wales* 59 Dj
Haverhill, *Massachusetts* 44 Ea
Haverstraw, *New York* 44 Cb
Havre, *Belgium* 60 Cd
Havre, *Montana* 42 Eb
Havre de Grace, *Maryland* 44 Bc
Hawaii, I., *Hawaiian Is.* 99 Kf
Hawaiian Is., *Pacific Ocean* 98 Je
Hawea Flat, *New Zealand* 51 Bf
Hawera, *New Zealand* 51 Ec
Hawick, *Scotland* 58 Fe
Hawke B., *New Zealand* 51 Fc
Hawkesbury, *Ontario* 40 Jc
Hawr al Hammar, *Iraq* 88 Ec
Hawr Saniya, *Iraq* 88 Ec
Hay, *New South Wales* 53 Hf
Hayatpur, *India* 87 Fc
Hayes Pen., *Greenland* 41 Qb
Hazara Highlands, *Afghan.* 89 Hc
Hazard, *Kentucky* 43 Kd
Hazaribagh, *India* 87 Ed
Hazaribagh Ra., *India* 87 Dd
Hazarjuft, *Afghanistan* 89 Hc
Haẓawẓa, *Arabia* 88 Cc
Hazeva, *Israel* 90 Dg
Hazil, *Arabia* 88 Dd
Hazleton, *Pennsylvania* 44 Cb
Hazro, *W. Pakistan* 86 Cd
Heard I., *Indian Ocean* 96 Fk
Hebrides, Outer, *Scotland* 58 Bc
Hebron, *Jordan* 90 Df
Hecelchakan, *Mexico* 46 Fc
Hechingen, *Germany* 64 Cd
Hechtel, *Belgium* 60 Dc
Hector, Mt., *New Zealand* 51 Ed
Hede, *Sweden* 62 Ee
Hedemora, *Sweden* 63 Ff
Heemstede, *Netherlands* 60 Cb
Heer, *Netherlands* 60 Dd
Heerenveen, *Netherlands* 60 Db
Heerlen, *Netherlands* 60 Dd
Hegemann, C., *Greenland* 41 Nc
Heide, *Germany* 64 Ca
Heidelberg, *Germany* 64 Cd
Heidelburg, *Transvaal* 91 De
Heiden, *Switzerland* 61 Ea
Heijen, *Netherlands* 60 Dc
Heilbronn, *Germany* 64 Cd
Heinola, *Finland* 63 Mf
Heist, *Belgium* 60 Bc
Hejaz, *Arabia* 88 Ce
Hekla, Mt., *Iceland* 62 Wn
Helchteren, *Belgium* 60 Dc
Helder, Den, *Netherlands* 60 Cb
Helena, *Arkansas* 43 He
Helena, *Montana* 45 Gb
Helensburgh, *Scotland* 58 Dd
Helensville, *New Zealand* 51 Eb
Helgoland, I., *Germany* 64 Ba
Helgoländer Bucht, *Germany* 64 Ba
Hellin, *Spain* 67 Ec
Helmand Des., *Afghanistan* 89 Hc
Helmand R., *Afghanistan* 89 Hc
Helme, *Estonia* 63 Lh
Helmond, *Netherlands* 60 Dc
Helmsdale, *Scotland* 58 Eb
Helsingfors. See Helsinki
Helsingör, *Denmark* 63 Eh
Helsinki, *Finland* 63 Lf
Helston, *England* 59 Dk
Hemelum, *Netherlands* 60 Db
Hemnes, *Norway* 62 Ec
Hemse, *Sweden* 63 Hh
Henchow. See Hengyan
Hendaye, *France* 69 Ce
Henderson, *Kentucky* 43 Jd
Henderson, *New York* 40 Hd
Henderson I., *Pacific Ocean* 99 Nk
Hengam, I., *Persia* 89 Gd
Hengelo, *Netherlands* 60 Eb
Henghsien, *China* 81 Dl
Hengshan, *China* 81 Fj
Hengyang, *China* 81 Fj
Henley-on-Thames, *England* 59 Gj
Henlopen, C., *New Jersey* 44 Cc
Hennebont, *France* 68 Bc
Henrique de Carvalho, *Angola* 92 Ef
Henzada, *Burma* 85 Je
Heran, *Yemen* 88 Df
Herat, *Afghanistan* 89 Hc
Herau. See Herowabad
Herault, dep., *France* 69 Ee
Herbert, *N.Z.* 51 Cf
Herbertville, *New Zealand* 51 Fd
Herbesthal, *Belgium* 60 Ed
Herceg Novi, *Yugoslavia* 72 Bc
Heredia, *Costa Rica* 47 Cd
Hereford & co., *England* 59 Fh
Hereheretue, I., *Pacific Oc.* 99 Lj
Herford, *Germany* 64 Cb
Herinnes, *Belgium* 60 Cd
Heriot. See Edievale
Herisau, *Switzerland* 61 Ea
Herkimer, *New York* 44 Ca
Herma Ness, *Zetland* 58 Ja
Hermil, *Lebanon* 90 Ec
Hermite, Is., *Chile* 50 Cj
Hermon, Mt., See Sheikh
Hermosillo, *Mexico* 46 Bb
Herning, *Denmark* 63 Ch
Héron, *Belgium* 60 Dd
Heron I., *Qnsld.* 53 Kd
Herowabad, *Persia* 88 Eb
Herräng, *Sweden* 63 Hf
Herrera, *Argentina* 50 Dc
Herrera di Pisuerga, *Spain* 66 Ca
Hersey, *Michigan* 40 Dd
Hersselt, *Belgium* 60 Cc
Hertford & co., *England* 59 Gj
's Hertogenbosch, *Neth.* 60 Dc
Herval. See Joacaba
Hervas, *Spain* 66 Cb
Hervé, *Belgium* 60 Dd
Hervey, B., *Queensland* 53 Kd
Hervey Is., *Cook Is.* 98 Jj
Herzberg, *Germany* 64 Ec
Herzliya, *Israel* 90 Ce
Herzogenbuchsee, *Switz.* 61 Ca
Hesdin, *France* 68 Ea
Heught, Mt., *N. Terr., Aust.* 52 Fd
Heusden, *Netherlands* 60 Dc
Hève, C. de la, *France* 68 Db
Hexham, *England* 58 Ff
Hiakiang, *China* 81 Dk
Hibbing, *Minnesota* 43 Hb
Hicks Bay, *N.Z.* 51 Gb
Hidalgo, *Mexico* 46 Eb
Hidalgo, state, *Mexico* 46 Ec
Hieflau, *Austria* 64 Fe
Hierro, I., *Canary Is.* 94 Bc
Highland Park, *Illinois* 40 Cd
High Point, *N. Carolina* 43 Ld
Hiimeji, *Japan* 82 Dg
Hiiumaa, *Estonia* 63 Kg
Hijar, *Spain* 67 Eb
Hikone, *Japan* 82 Eg
Hildesheim, *Germany* 64 Cb
Hillah, al, *Iraq* 88 Dc
Hillman, *Michigan* 40 Ec
Hillsdale, *Michigan* 40 De
Hillston, *N.S.W.* 53 Jf
Hilversum, *Netherlands* 60 Db
Hilyan, *Arabia* 88 De
Himachal Pradesh, *India* 86 Ee
Himalaya Mts., *India, etc.* 84 Eb
Himanka, *Finland* 62 Kd
Himare, *Albania* 73 Bd
Hindeloopen, *Netherlands* 60 Db
Hindubagh, *W. Pakistan* 84 Cb
Hindu Kush, Mts., *Afghanistan-W. Pakistan* 84 Da
Hindupur, *India* 84 Ef
Hingan. See Ankang
Hingan, *China* 78 Ha
Hinganghat, *India* 84 Ed
Hingho, *China* 80 Fb
Hinghwa, *China* 80 Jf
Hinghwa. See Putien
Hingi, *China* 81 Bk
Hinglaj, *W. Pakistan* 84 Cc
Hingol R., *W. Pakistan* 84 Cc
Hingoli, *India* 84 Ee
Hinis, *Turkey* 88 Db
Hinnöy, *Norway* 62 Fb
Hinsdale, *New Hampshire* 44 Da
Hiro. See Birao
Hirosaki, *Japan* 82 Gd
Hiroshima, *Japan* 82 Cg
Hisaronu, *Turkey* 88 Ba
Hisban, *Jordan* 90 Df
Hispaniola, I., *West Indies* 47 Ec
Hissar, *India* 86 Df
Hissmofors, *Sweden* 62 Fe
Hisua, *India* 87 Ec
Hisya, *Syria* 90 Ec
Hit, *Iraq* 88 Dc
Hitra, *Norway* 62 Ce
Hivaoa, I., *Marquesas Is.* 99 Mh
Hiwasa, *Japan* 82 Dh
Hjälmaren, L., *Sweden* 63 Fg
Hjörring, *Denmark* 63 Ch
Hkamti, *Burma* 85 Jc
Hobart, *Tasmania* 53 Jh
Hoboken, *Belgium* 60 Cc
Hobro, *Denmark* 63 Ch
Hobsogol, *Mongolia* 75 Kc
Hochwan, *China* 81 Cg
Hodal, *India* 86 Eg
Hodeida, *Yemen* 88 Dg
Hódmezövásárhely, *Hungary* 65 Je
Hoek van Holland, *Neth.* 60 Cc
Hof, *Germany* 64 Dc
Hofei, *China* 80 Hg
Höfs Jökull, *Iceland* 62 Wm
Hofuf, *Arabia* 88 Ed
Hoganäs, *Sweden* 63 Eh
Hohe Tauern, *Austria* 64 Ee
Hohsien, *China* 81 Ek
Hoihong, *China* 81 Em
Hoihow, *Hai-Nan I.* 81 Em
Hokianga Harb., *N.Z.* 51 Da
Ho-kien-fu, *China* 80 Hc
Hokitika, *New Zealand* 51 Ce
Hokkaido I., *Japan* 82 Hc
Holbæk, *Denmark* 63 Dj
Holguin, *Cuba* 47 Db
Holinkoerh, *China* 80 Eb
Holland, *Michigan* 40 Cd
Holland, *New York* 44 Aa
Holland, Noord, prov., *Netherlands* 60 Cb
Holland, Parts of, *Lincs., Eng.* 59 Gh
Holland, Zuid, prov., *Netherlands* 60 Cb
Hollange, *Belgium* 60 De
Hollidaysburg, *Pennsylvania* 44 Ab
Hollogne, *Belgium* 60 Dd
Holly, *Michigan* 40 Ed
Hollywood, *California* 45 Dh
Holmestrand, *Norway* 63 Dg
Holmsund, *Sweden* 62 Je
Holstebro, *Denmark* 63 Ch
Holstein, *Germany* 64 Cb
Holsteinsborg, *Greenland* 41 Pc
Holten, *Netherlands* 60 Eb
Holwerd, *Netherlands* 60 Da
Holy I., *England* 58 Fe
Holy I., *Wales* 59 Dg
Holy Cross, *Alaska* 43 Wl
Holy Cross, Mt. of the, *Col.* 42 Ed
Holyhead, *Wales* 59 Dg
Holyoke, *Massachusetts* 40 Kd
Homer, *Alaska* 43 Xm
Homer, *New York* 40 Hd
Homestead, *Pennsylvania* 40 Ge
Homfray Str., *Andaman Is.* 85 Hf
Hommelvik, *Norway* 62 De
Homs, *Libya* 95 Hb
Homs, *Syria* 90 Ec
Honan. See Loyang
Honan, prov., *China* 80 Fe
Honda, *Colombia* 48 Cb
Honda, B., *Cuba* 47 Cb
Hondo, *Mexico* 46 Db
Honduras, rep., *C. America* 47 Bd
Honduras, C., *Honduras* 47 Bc
Honduras, G. of, *Brit. Hon.* 47 Bc
Hönefoss, *Norway* 63 Df
Honesdale, *Pennsylvania* 44 Cb
Honfleur, *France* 68 Db
Honghai B., *China* 81 Gl
Hong Kong (Gt. Br.), *China* 81 Gl
Honolulu, I., *Hawaiian Is.* 99 Ke
Honor, *Michigan* 40 Cc
Honshu I., *Japan* 82 Cg
Hood, Mt., *Oregon* 45 Cc
Hoofdplaat, *Netherlands* 60 Cc
Hooger Smilde, *Netherlands* 60 Eb
Hoogeveen, *Netherlands* 60 Eb
Hoogezand, *Netherlands* 60 Ea
Hooghalen, *Netherlands* 60 Eb
Hooghly, *India* 87 Gd
Hooghly R., *India* 87 Ge
Hook Hd., *Eire* 59 Ch
Hoopeston, *Illinois* 40 Ce
Hoorn, *Netherlands* 60 Db
Hoosick Falls, *New York* 40 Kd
Hoover Dam, *Arizona* 45 Fh
Hopeh, prov., *China* 80 Gc
Hopen, I., *Barents Sea* 74 Ba
Hopetoun, *W. Australia* 52 Df
Hope Town, *Andaman Is.* 85 Hf
Hopetown, *Cape Province* 91 Ce
Hopkinsville, *Kentucky* 43 Jd
Hoppo, *China* 81 Dm
Hoquiam, *Washington* 45 Bb
Horaždovice, *Czechoslovakia* 64 Ed
Horcasitas, *Mexico* 46 Bb
Horgen, *Switzerland* 61 Da
Horka, *Germany* 64 Fc
Hormoz, *Persia* 89 Fd
Hormoz I., *Persia* 89 Gd
Hormuz, Str. of, *Arabia-Persia* 89 Gd
Horn, *Austria* 65 Fd
Horn, *Iceland* 62 Ul
Horn, C. See Hornos, C. de
Hornavan, *Sweden* 62 Gc
Hornby, *N.Z.* 51 De
Hörnefors, *Sweden* 62 He
Hornell, *New York* 44 Ba
Hornopiren, Mt., *Chile* 50 Bf
Hornos, C. de, *Chile* 50 Cj
Hornsea, *England* 59 Gg
Horo, *Netherlands* 60 Dc
Horonobe, *Japan* 82 Hb
Horqueta, *Paraguay* 50 Eb
Horseheads, *New York* 44 Ba
Horsens, *Denmark* 63 Cj
Horse Shoe, *W. Australia* 52 Ce
Horsham, *England* 59 Gj
Horsham, *Victoria* 53 Hg
Horšovsky Tyn, *Czech.* 64 Ed
Horst, *Netherlands* 60 Ec
Horten, *Norway* 63 Dg
Hoşap, *Turkey* 88 Db
Hose Ra., *Sarawak* 79 Fk
Hoshangabad, *India* 87 Ad
Hoshiarpur, *India* 86 De
Hospel, *India* 84 Ee
Hospenthal, *Switzerland* 61 Db
Hossegor, *France* 69 Ce
Hoste, I., *Chile* 50 Cj
Hosur, *India* 84 Ef
Hotagen, *Sweden* 62 Ee
Hotseh, *China* 80 Ge
Hot Springs, *S. Dakota* 42 Fc
Hot Springs Nat. Park, *Ark.* 43 He
Hotton, *Belgium* 60 Dd
Houdelaincourt, *France* 68 Fb
Houffalize, *Belgium* 60 Dd
Houghton L., *Michigan* 40 Dc
Hourn L., *Scotland* 58 Dc
Housatonic, R., *Connecticut* 44 Db
Houston, *Texas* 42 Gf
Houten, *Netherlands* 60 Db
Houtman Abrolhos, *W. Aust.* 52 Be
Howard, *Michigan* 40 Dd
Howard, *Pennsylvania* 44 Bb
Howell, *Michigan* 40 Ed
Howick, *Natal* 91 Ee
Howland I., *Pacific Ocean* 98 Hg
Howrah, *India* 87 Gd
Hoy I., *Orkney* 58 Eb
Hoyes, *Spain* 66 Bb
Hoyun, *China* 78 Ff
Hozat, *Turkey* 88 Cb
Hrubieszów, *Poland* 65 Kc
Hsawnghsup. See Thaungdut
Hsenwi, *Burma* 85 Jd
Hsiachwan Shan, *China* 81 Fm
Hsi-an. See Sian
Hsi-ch'ang. See Sichang
Hsinchu, *Taiwan* 81 Kk
Hsi-ning. See Sining
Hsinking. See Changchun
Hsipaw, *Burma* 85 Jd
Hsüchang, *China* 80 Ff
Hsuchow. See Hsüchang
Huachi, *Bolivia* 48 Dg
Huacho, *Peru* 48 Bf
Huacrachuco, *Peru* 48 Be
Hualgayoc, *Peru* 48 Be
Hualien, *Taiwan* 81 Kl
Huanay, *Bolivia* 48 Dg
Huancabamba, *Peru* 48 Be
Huancane, *Peru* 48 Dg
Huancavelica, *Peru* 48 Bf
Huancayo, *Peru* 48 Bf
Huanchaca, *Bolivia* 48 Dh
Huanchaco, *Peru* 48 Be
Huanta, *Peru* 48 Cf
Huanuco, *Peru* 48 Be
Huaonta, *Nicaragua* 47 Cd
Huara, *Chile* 50 Ca
Huaras, *Peru* 48 Be
Huariaca, *Peru* 48 Bf
Huario, *Peru* 48 Bf
Huarmey, *Peru* 48 Bf
Huasco, *Chile* 50 Bc
Huatusco. See Coatepec
Huaylas, *Peru* 48 Be
Hubli, *India* 84 Ee
Huchow, *China* 80 Kg
Huddersfield, *England* 59 Fg
Hudiksvall, *Sweden* 63 Gf
Hudson, *New York* 44 Da
Hudson R., *New York* 44 Da
Hudson Falls, *New York* 40 Kd
Hue, *S. Vietnam* 83 Dc
Huedin, *Rumania* 72 Da
Huehuetenango, *Guatemala* 46 Fd
Huejutla, *Mexico* 46 Ec
Huelva, *Spain* 66 Bd
Huereal Overa, *Spain* 67 Ed
Huete, *Spain* 67 Db
Hughenden, *Queensland* 53 Hd
Huhehot, *China* 80 Eb
Huiarau Ra., *New Zealand* 51 Fc
Hüichŏn, *Korea* 78 Jb
Hukawng Valley, *Burma* 85 Jc
Hukow, *China* 78 Ge
Hukuntsi, *Botswana* 91 Cd
Hula L., *Israel* 90 Dd
Hulin. See Linkiang
Hull, *England* 59 Gg
Hull, *Quebec* 40 Jc
Hulst, *Netherlands* 60 Cc
Hulun. See Hailar
Hulun Chih, *China* 78 Ga
Hulutao, *China* 78 Hb
Huma, *China* 75 Mc
Humacao, *Puerto Rico* 47 Fc
Humaita, *Brazil* 48 Ee
Humaita, *Paraguay* 50 Ec
Humansdorp, *Cape Prov.* 91 Cf
Humay, *Peru* 48 Bf
Humbe. See Mutano
Humber R., *England* 59 Hg
Humboldt B., *California* 42 Bc
Humboldt Glacier, *Greenl'd.* 41 Qb
Humboldt R., *Nevada* 45 De
Hume Res., *New S. Wales* 53 Jg
Humenne, *Czechoslovakia* 65 Jd
Humphreys, Mt., *California* 45 Dg
Hun, *Libya* 95 Jc
Hunafloi, *Iceland* 62 Vm
Hunan, prov., *China* 81 Ej
Hungary, *Cent. Europe* 57 Mg
Hungnam, *Korea* 78 Jc
Hungtze Hu, *China* 80 Jf
Hunsrück, Mts., *Germany* 64 Bd
Hunter Is., *Tasmania* 53 Hh
Huntingdon & Peterborough, co., *Eng.* 59 Gh
Huntingdon, *Pennsylvania* 44 Ab
Huntington, *Indiana* 40 De
Huntington, *New York* 44 Db
Huntington, *W. Virginia* 43 Kd
Huntly, *New Zealand* 51 Eb
Huntly, *Scotland* 58 Fc
Huntsville, *Alabama* 43 Je
Huntsville, *Ontario* 40 Gc
Hunucma, *Mexico* 46 Fc
Hun-yüan-chow, *China* 80 Fc
Hunza, *Kashmir* 86 Db
Huon Is., *Pacific Ocean* 98 Fj
Huon Pen., *New Guinea* 53 Ja
Hupeh, prov., *China* 80 Fg
Hurd, C., *Ontario* 40 Fc
Hurghada, *Egypt* 95 Mc
Huron, *S. Dakota* 42 Gc
Huron, L., *U.S.A.-Canada* 43 Kc
Huskvarna, *Sweden* 63 Fh
Husum, *Germany* 64 Ca
Hutchinson, *Kansas* 42 Gd
Hüttenberg, *Austria* 64 Fe
Huttwil, *Switzerland* 61 Ca
Huy, *Belgium* 60 Dd
Hvar, I., *Yugoslavia* 70 Fd
Hwahsien, *China* 81 Fl
Hwaian, *China* 80 Jf
Hwaijen, *China* 80 Fc
Hwaiking. See Tsinyang
Hwaining, *China* 81 Hg
Hwaiyang, *China* 80 Gf
Hwaiyn. See Tsingkiang
Hwangchow. See Hwangkang
Hwang-Hai. See Yellow Sea
Hwang Ho, *China* 78 Gc
Hwang Ho, Mouth of, *China* 80 Jc
Hwanghsien, *China* 80 Kd
Hwangkang, *China* 80 Gg
Hweichow. See Sihsien
Hweimin, *China* 80 Hd
Hweinan, *China* 78 Jb
Hweitseh, *China* 81 Aj
Hwohsien, *China* 80 Ed
Hyden, *Kentucky* 44 Fb
Hyden, *W. Australia* 52 Cf
Hyde Park, *Vermont* 40 Kc
Hyderabad, *India* 84 Ee
Hyderabad, *W. Pakistan* 84 Cc
Hyères, *France* 69 Ge
Hyères, Is d', *France* 69 Ge
Hyndman Pk., *Idaho* 42 Dc
Hyogo, *Japan* 82 Dg
Hyrynsalmi, *Finland* 62 Nd
Hythe, *England* 59 Hj
Iasi, *Rumania* 76 Eh
Iauarete, *Colombia* 48 Dc
I. aux Lievres, *Quebec* 40 Lb
Ibadan, *Nigeria* 94 Fg
Ibague, *Colombia* 48 Bc
Ibarra, *Ecuador* 48 Bc
Ibb, *Yemen* 88 Dg
Ibembo, *Congo* 92 Ed
Ibicui, *Brazil* 50 Ec
Ibiza I., *Balearic Is.* 67 Fc
Ibresi, *Russia* 77 Hc
Ibri, *Muscat & Oman* 89 Ge
Ibwe Munyama, *Zambia* 91 Dc
Ica, *Peru* 48 Bf
Iça, R., *Brazil* 48 Dd
Içana, *Brazil* 48 Dc
Içel, *Turkey* 88 Bb
Iceland, I., *N. Atlantic Oc.* 56 Cb
Ichak, *India* 87 Ec
Ichang, *China* 80 Eg
Icheng, *China* 80 Fg
Ichow. See Lini
Ichun, *China* 81 Gj
Idah, *Nigeria* 94 Gg
Idaho, state, *U.S.A.* 42 Cc
Idaho Falls, *Idaho* 45 Gd
Ideles, *Algeria* 94 Gd
Idfu, *Egypt* 95 Md
Ídhra, I., *Greece* 73 Df
Idirtu, *China* 78 Cc
Idlib, *Syria* 90 Eb
Idutywa, *Cape Province* 91 Df
Ieper, *Belgium* 60 Ad
Ierissós, G. of, *Greece* 73 Dd
Ifakara, *Tanzania* 93 Hf
Iférouane, *Niger* 94 Ge
Ifni, terr., *N.-W. Africa* 94 Cc
Igan, *Sarawak* 79 Fk
Igarapé Miri, *Brazil* 49 Hd
Igarka, *Russia* 74 Hb
Ighil-Izane, *Algeria* 94 Fa
Iglesias, *Sardinia* 71 Bf
Igli, *Algeria* 94 Eb
Igoma, *Tanzania* 93 Gf
Igra, *Russia* 77 Lb
Iguaçú & R., *Brazil* 50 Fc
Iguala, *Mexico* 46 Ed
Iguapé, *Brazil* 50 Gb
Iguatu, *Brazil* 49 Ke
Igumira, *Tanzania* 93 Gf
Ihosy, *Madagascar* 93 Nl
Ihtiman, *Bulgaria* 72 Dc
Iida, *Japan* 82 Eg
Iisalmi, *Finland* 62 Me
Ijebu-Ode, *Nigeria* 94 Fg
Ijselmonde, *Netherlands* 60 Cc
Ijselmuiden, *Netherlands* 60 Db
Ijselstein, *Netherlands* 60 Db
Ijssel Meer, *Netherlands* 60 Db
Ijssel R., *Netherlands* 60 Eb
Ijui, *Brazil* 50 Fc
Ijzendijke, *Netherlands* 60 Bc
Ikaria, I., *Greece* 73 Ff
Ikisu, *Tanzania* 93 Ge
Ikla, *Estonia* 63 Lh
Ikushumbet, *Japan* 82 Gc
Ilagan, *Philippines* 79 Hg
Ilam, *Nepal* 87 Fb
Ilam, *Persia* 88 Ec
Ilanz, *Switzerland* 61 Eb
Ilawa, *Poland* 65 Hb
Ilawka, *Poland* 65 Ja
Ilbunga, *S. Aust.* 53 Ge
Ile-de-France, prov., *France* 68 Eb
Ile Mayotte, I., *Archipel. des Comores* 93 Kg
Ilfracombe, *England* 59 Ej
Ilhavo, *Portugal* 66 Ab
Ilhéus, *Brazil* 49 Kf
Ili, *Kazakh.* 74 Gd
Ilia, *Greece* 73 Cf
Ilic, *Turkey* 88 Cb
Ilich, *Kazakh.* 74 Fd
Iliktou (Hingan), *China* 78 Ha
Ilimsk, *Russia* 75 Kc
Iliodhrómia, I., *Greece* 73 De
Ilion, *New York* 44 Ca
Illapel, *Chile* 50 Bd
Ille-et-Vilaine, dep., *France* 68 Cb
Illescas, *Spain* 66 Db
Illimani, Mt., *Bolivia* 48 Dg
Illinois, state, *U.S.A.* 43 Hd
Illora, *Spain* 66 Dd
Il'men', Oz., *Russia* 76 Gb
Ilo, *Peru* 48 Cg
Iloilo, *Philippines* 79 Hh
Ilorin, *Nigeria* 94 Fg
Ilpi, *Russia* 75 Sb
Imabari, *Japan* 82 Cg
Iman, *Russia* 75 Nd
Imandra, Oz., *Russia* 74 Cb
Imerimandroso, *Madagascar* 93 Nk
Imi, *Ethiopia* 93 Jc
Immendingen, *Germany* 64 Ce
Imperatriz, *Brazil* 48 De
Imperatriz, *Brazil* 49 He
Imperia, *Italy* 70 Bd
Imperial Dam, *Arizona* 42 De
Imphal, *India* 85 Hd
Imroz, I., *Turkey* 88 Aa
Imtan, *Syria* 90 Ee
Inagua, I. Gt., *Bahama Is.* 47 Eb
Inagua, I. Lit., *Bahama Is.* 47 Eb
Inari & L., *Finland* 62 Mb
Inchkeith, *Scotland* 58 Ed
Inchŏn, *Korea* 78 Jc
Incourt, *Belgium* 60 Cd
Indaal, L., *Scotland* 58 Ce
Indals Älv, *Sweden* 62 Ge
Indaw, *Burma* 85 Jd
Indawgyi L., *Burma* 85 Jc
Independence, *Kansas* 42 Gd
Independencia, *Argentina* 50 Cd
India, rep., *S. Asia* 84-85
Indian Des. See Thar
Indiana, *Pennsylvania* 44 Ab
Indiana, state, *U.S.A.* 43 Jc
Indianapolis, *Indiana* 40 Cf
Indian L., *New York* 44 Ca
Indiga, *Russia* 74 Db
Indigirka, R., *Russia* 75 Pb
Indonesia, *S.-E. Asia* 79 Fl
Indore, *India* 84 Ed
Indre, dep., *France* 68 Dc
Indre-et-Loire, dep., *France* 68 Dc
Indur (Nizamabad), *India* 84 Ee
Indus, R., *W. Pakistan, etc.* 84 Cd
Inebolu, *Turkey* 88 Ba
Ingelmunster, *Belgium* 60 Bd
Ingersoll, *Ontario* 40 Fd
Ingham, *Queensland* 53 Jc
Inglefield Inlet, *Greenland* 41 Qb
Inglefield Ld., *Greenland* 41 Qb
Inglewood, *New Zealand* 51 Ec
Ing Luiggi, *Argentina* 50 De
Ingolstadt, *Germany* 64 Dd
Ingrid Christensen Coast, *Antarctica* 100 Fb
Inhambane, *Mozambique* 91 Fd
Inishark I., *Eire* 59 Ag
Inishbofin, I., *Eire* 59 Ag
Inishkea I., *Eire* 59 Af
Inishman, I., *Eire* 59 Ag
Inishmore, I., *Eire* 59 Ag
Inishmurray, I., *Eire* 59 Bf
Inishtrahull, *Eire* 58 Ce
Inishturk, I., *Eire* 59 Ag
Injune, *Queensland* 53 Je
Innertkirchen, *Switzerland* 61 Db
Innisfail, *Queensland* 53 Jc
Innsbruck, *Austria* 64 De
Inowrocław, *Poland* 65 Hb
Inquisivi, *Bolivia* 48 Dg
Ins, *Switzerland* 61 Ca
In Salah, *Algeria* 94 Fc
Insar, *Russia* 77 Gd
Insein, *Burma* 85 Je
In Shan. See Yin Shan
Insterburg. See Chernyakhovsk
Intelewa, *Surinam* 49 Fc
Interlaken, *Switzerland* 61 Cb
Interview I., *Andaman Is.* 85 Hf
Intragna, *Switzerland* 61 Db
Inutil, B., *Chile* 50 Ch
Inveraray, *Scotland* 58 Dd
Invercargill, *New Zealand* 51 Bg
Inverell, *N.S.W.* 53 Ke
Inverness & co., *Scotland* 58 Ec
Inverurie, *Scotland* 58 Fc
Investigator Str., *S. Aus.* 53 Gg
Inyati, *Rhodesia* 91 Dc
Inza, *Russia* 77 Hd
Inzer, *Russia* 77 Nc
Ioannina, *Greece* 73 Ce
Iola, *Kansas* 42 Gd
Iona I., *Scotland* 58 Cd
Ionia, *Michigan* 40 Dd
Ionian Is., *Greece* 73 Be
Ionian Sea, *Italy, etc.* 57 Mj
Ionishkis, *Lithuania* 63 Kh
Ios, I., *Greece* 73 Ef
Iowa, state, *U.S.A.* 43 Hc
Ipala, *Mexico* 46 Cc
Ipameri, *Brazil* 49 Hg
Ipen. See Ypres
Ipiales, *Colombia* 48 Bc
Ipin, *China* 81 Bh
Ipiros, *Greece* 73 Ce
Ipoh, *W. Malaysia* 83 Cf
Ippy, *Cent. Afr. Rep.* 95 Kg
Ipswich, *England* 59 Hh
Ipswich, *Queensland* 53 Ke
Ipu, *Brazil* 49 Jd
Iquique, *Chile* 50 Bb
Iquitos, *Peru* 48 Cd
Iracoubo, *French Guiana* 49 Gb
Iráklia, I., *Greece* 73 Ef
Iráklion, *Crete* 73 Eg
Iran (Persia), *Asia* 89 Fc
Irapa, *Venezuela* 48 Ea
Irapuato, *Mexico* 46 Dc
Iraq, *Asia* 88 Dc
Irazu, Vol., *Costa Rica* 47 Cd
Irbid, *Jordan* 90 De
Irbit, *Russia* 77 Rb
Ireland, Rep. of, (Eire), *British Isles* 59 Bg
Irendyk Khr., *Russia* 77 Ne
Irgiz, *Kazakh.* 74 Fd
Irian Barat, *Indonesia* 55 Nj
Irikinskiy, *Russia* 77 Pe
Iringa, *Tanzania* 93 Hf
Irish Sea, *British Isles* 59 Dg
Irkutsk, *Russia* 75 Kc
Irondale, *Ontario* 40 Gc
Iron Knob, *S. Australia* 53 Gf
Iron Mountain, *Michigan* 40 Cc
Iron River, *Michigan* 40 Bb
Ironton, *Ohio* 43 Kd
Ironwood, *Michigan* 40 Ab
Iroquois, *Ontario* 40 Jc
Iroquois Chute, *Quebec* 40 Kb
Irrawaddy, *Burma* 85 He
Irrawaddy, R., *Burma* 85 He
Irtysh, R., *Russia* 74 Fc
Irumu, *Congo* 93 Fd

Kurume, Japan 82 Bh
Kurunegala, Ceylon 84 Fg
Kusa, Russia 77 Pc
Kusaie, I., Caroline Is. 98 Fg
Kushersk, Russia 77 Ma
Kushiro, Japan 82 Jc
Kushk, Afghanistan 89 Hc
Kushka, Turkmen 74 Fe
Kushtia, E. Pakistan 87 Gd
Kushva, Russia 77 Pa
Kuskokwim B., Alaska 43 Wm
Kusma, Nepal 87 Da
Kustanay, Kazakh. 74 Fc
Kütahya, Turkey 88 Ab
Kutai R., Borneo 79 Gk
Kut-al-Hai. See Al Hayy
Kutaradja, Sumatra 79 Cj
Kutch, Gt. Rann of, India 84 Cd
Kutch & Gulf of, India 84 Cd
Kutchian, Japan 82 Gc
Kutina, Yugoslavia 70 Fc
Kutno, Poland 65 Hb
Kutsing, China 81 Ak
Kutu, Ethiopia 93 Gc
Kutum, Sudan 95 Kf
Kuusamo, Finland 62 Nd
Kuusjärvi, Finland 62 Ne
Kuwait & state, Persian Gulf 88 Ed
Kuyang, China 80 Eb
Kuybyshev, Russia 77 Kd
Kuybyshev, Russia 74 Gc
Kuybyshevskoye Vdkhr., Russia 77 Jc
Kuytan, Russia 75 Kc
Kuzhbal, Russia 77 Ga
Kuzino, Russia 77 Pb
Kuzmin, Yugoslavia 72 Bb
Kuznetsk, Russia 77 Hd
Kuzovatovo, Russia 77 Hd
Kvalöy, N., Norway 62 Ha
Kvalöy, S., Norway 62 Hb
Kvarken, Ostra, Sweden 62 Je
Kvarner, G. of, Yugoslavia 70 Ec
Kvarnerolo, G. of, Yugosl. 70 Ec
Kvesmenes, Norway 62 Jb
Kwaialein, Is., Marshall Is. 98 Fg
Kwakhanai, Botswana 91 Cd
Kwakoegron, Surinam 49 Fb
Kwangchang, China 81 Hj
Kwangchow Wan, China 81 Em
Kwangnan, China 81 Bk
Kwangping. See Yungnien
Kwangshun, China 81 Cj
Kwangsi, prov., China 81 Cl
Kwangsin. See Shangjao
Kwangtung, prov., China 81 Fl
Kwang-Tung (Luta) Pen., China 80 Kc
Kwania L., Uganda 93 Gd
Kweichih, China 81 Hg
Kweichow. See Fengkieh
Kweichow, prov., China 81 Bj
Kweihwa. See Kweisui
Kweihwa. See Tzeyum
Kweiki, China 81 Hh
Kweilin, China 81 Ek
Kweiping, China 81 El
Kweisui. See Huhehot
Kweiteh. See Shangkiu
Kweiyang, China 81 Cj
Kweiyang, China 81 Fk
Kwi-chu. See Phu Qui
Kwidzyn, Poland 65 Hb
Kwitao, Burma 85 Jc
Kwoka, Mt., W. Irian 79 Kl
Kyakhta, Russia 75 Kc
Kyancutta, S. Aust. 53 Gf
Kyangin, Burma 85 Je
Kyaukpadating, Burma 85 Jd
Kyaukpyu, Burma 85 He
Kyaukse, Burma 85 Jd
Kyauktaw, Burma 85 Hd
Kyelang, India 86 Ed
Kyi R., Tibet 85 Hc
Kymi, Finland 63 Mf
Kynšperk, Czechoslovakia 64 Ec
Kynuna, Qnsld. 53 Hd
Kyoga L., Uganda 93 Gd
Kyoto, Japan 82 Dg
Kyrenia, Cyprus 90 Bb
Kyshtym, Russia 77 Qc
Kythrea, Cyprus 90 Bb
Kyushu, I., Japan 82 Bh
Kyustendil, Bulgaria 72 Dc
Kyusyur, Russia 75 Ma
Kyzyl, Russia 75 Jc
Kyzyl Kum, Uzbek. etc. 74 Fd
Kyzylsk, Russia 77 Pd
Kzyl Orda, Kazakh. 74 Fd
Laanila, Finland 62 Mb
La Ascencion, Mexico 46 Ca
La Asuncion, Margarita I., Venezuela 48 Ea
Laban, Jordan 90 Dg
La Banda, Argentina 50 Dc
Labang, Sarawak 79 Fk
Labé, Guinea 94 Cf
Labelle, Quebec 40 Jb
Labouheyre, France 69 Cd
Laboulaye, Argentina 50 Dd
Labrea, Brazil 48 Ee
La Brea, Trinidad 48 Ea
Labuan, I., N.-W. Borneo 79 Gj
Labuk B., N. Borneo 79 Gj
La Canoa, Venezuela 48 Eb
La Carlota, Argentina 50 Dd
La Carolina, Spain 66 Dc
Laccadive Is., Indian Ocean 84 Df
La Ceiba, Venezuela 48 Cb
Lachen, Switzerland 61 Da
Lachine, Quebec 40 Kc
Lachlan R., New S. Wales 53 Jf
Lachmangarh, India 86 Dg
Lachute, Quebec 40 Jc
Lackawanna, New York 44 Aa
Lackawaxen, Pennsylvania 44 Cb
La Cocha, Argentina 50 Cc
Laconia, New Hampshire 44 Ea
La Copelina, Argentina 50 Ce
La Coruña, Spain 66 Aa
Lac-Rémi, Quebec 40 Jb
La Crosse, Wisconsin 43 Hc
La Cruz, Colombia 48 Bc
La Cruz, Mexico 46 Cb
Ladakh Ra., Tibet-Kashmir 84 Eb
Ladiz, Persia 89 Hd
Ladoga L. See Ladozhskoye Oz.
La Dorado, Colombia 48 Cb
Ladozhskoye Oz., Russia 76 Ga
Ladwa, India 86 Ef
Lady Neunes B., Antarctica 100 Lb
Ladysmith, Natal 91 De
Lae, New Guinea 53 Ja
Laeken, Belgium 60 Cd
Læsö, I., Denmark 63 Dh
La Esperanza, Honduras 47 Bd
La Estrada, Spain 66 Aa
La Fayette, Indiana 40 Ce
Lafayette, Louisiana 43 He
Lages, Brazil 49 Ke
Laggan L., Scotland 58 Ed
Laghouat, Algeria 94 Fb
Lagonegro, Italy 71 Ee
Lagos, Mexico 46 Dc
Lagos, Nigeria 94 Fg
Lagos, Portugal 66 Ad
La Grande, Oregon 45 Dc
La Grange, Georgia 43 Ke
Lagrange, Indiana 40 De
La Grange, W. Australia 52 Dc
La Granja, Spain 66 Cb
La Guaira, Venezuela 48 Da
La Guardia, Argentina 50 Cc
La Guardia, Spain 66 Ab
Laguna, Brazil 50 Gc
Lagunas, Peru 48 Be
Lagunillas, Bolivia 48 Eg
Laharpur, India 87 Cb
Lahej, S. Yemen 88 Dg
Lahijan, Persia 89 Fb
Laholm, Sweden 63 Eh
Lahore, W. Pakistan 86 De
Lahti, Finland 63 Lf
Laibach. See Ljubljana
Lai-chau, N. Vietnam 83 Cb
Laichow. See Yehsien
Laigle, France 68 Db
Laila, Arabia 88 Ee
Laingsburg, Cape Province 91 Cf
Lairg, Scotland 58 Eb
Laisamis, Kenya 93 Hd
Laishev, Russia 77 Jc
Laives, Italy 61 Gb
Laja, L., Chile 50 Be
La Japonesa, Argentina 50 Ce
Lajes, Brazil 50 Fc
La Junquera, Spain 67 Ga
La Junta, Colorado 42 Fd
Lakaträsk, Sweden 62 Jc
Lake Charles, Louisiana 43 Hf
Lake City, Michigan 40 Dc
Lake Edward, Quebec 40 Kb
Lakefield, Ontario 40 Gc
Lake Geneva, Wisconsin 40 Bd
Lake George, New York 44 Da
Lake Grace, W. Australia 52 Cf
Lake King, W. Aust. 52 Cf
Lakeland, Florida 43 Kf
Lake Majella, California 45 Cg
Lake Nash, N. Terr., Aust. 53 Gd
Lake Pleasant, New York 44 Ca
Lake Pukaki, N.Z. 51 Cf
Lake Victoria Res., Quebec 40 Hb
Lakeview, Oregon 45 Cd
Lakewood, New Jersey 44 Cb
Lakewood, New York 44 Aa
Lakewood, Ohio 40 Fe
Lakhimpur, India 87 Cb
Lakhimpur, India 85 Hc
Lakki, W. Pakistan 86 Bd
Lakkor Tso, Tibet 85 Fb
Lakonía, Greece 73 Df
Lakonía, G. of, Greece 73 Df
Lakota, Ivory Coast 94 Dg
Lakse Fd., Norway 62 Ma
Lakselv, Norway 62 La
Laktsang, Tibet 85 Fb
Lala Musa, W. Pakistan 86 Dd
Lalbagh, India 87 Gc
Lalganj, India 87 Ec
La Libertad, Ecuador 48 Ad
La Libertad, Guatemala 46 Fd
La Libertad, Nicaragua 47 Bd
La Ligua, Chile 50 Bd
Lalin, Spain 66 Aa
Lalitpur, India 87 Bc
La Maddalena, I., Sardinia 71 Be
La Malbaie, Quebec 40 Lb
Lamastre, France 69 Fd
Lambach, Austria 64 Ed
Lamballe, France 68 Bb
Lambayeque, Peru 48 Be
Lambert's Ld., Greenland 41 Mb
Lambertville, New Jersey 44 Cb
Lámbia, Greece 73 Cf
Lamé, Chad 95 Hg
Lamego, Portugal 66 Bb
Lamía, Greece 73 De
Lammermuir Hills, Scotland 58 Fe
Lamotrek Is., Caroline Is. 98 Dg
Lampazos, Mexico 46 Db
Lampedusa, I., Medit. Sea 95 Ha
Lampeter, Wales 59 Eh
Lamphun, Siam 83 Bc
Lampi, I., Burma 85 Jf
Lamu, Kenya 93 Je
Lamud, Peru 48 Be
Lanark & co., Scotland 58 Ee
Lancashire, co., England 59 Fg
Lancaster, England 59 Ff
Lancaster, New Hampshire 40 Lc
Lancaster, New York 44 Aa
Lancaster, Pennsylvania 44 Bb
Lancaster, Wisconsin 40 Ad
Lanchow, China 80 Dc
Landeck, Austria 64 De
Landen, Belgium 60 Dd
Landerneau, France 68 Ab
Landes, dep., France 69 Cd
Landfall, I. See Recalada
Landi Khana. See Tor Khama
Landi Kotal, W. Pakistan 86 Bc
Landon, Sweden 62 Ee
Landsberg, Germany 64 Dd
Landsberg. See Gorzów
Land's End, England 59 Dk
Landshut, Germany 64 Ed
Landskrona, Sweden 63 Ej
Langaa, Denmark 63 Ch
Langadhas, Greece 73 Dd
Langana L., Ethiopia 93 Hc
Langchung, China 80 Cg
Langeac, France 69 Ed
Langeland, I., Denmark 63 Dj
Längelmavesi, Finland 63 Lf
Langenthal, Switzerland 61 Ca
Langholm, Scotland 58 Fe
Lang Jökull, Iceland 62 Vm
Langkawi, I., W. Malaysia 83 Be
Langlade, Quebec 40 Ja
Langogne, France 69 Ed
Langon, France 69 Cd
Langöy, Norway 62 Fb
Langres, France 68 Fc
Langsa, Sumatra 79 Ck
Långsele, Sweden 62 Ge
Lang-Son, N. Vietnam 83 Db
Långträsk, Sweden 62 Jd
Languedoc, prov., France 69 Ee
Lanklaer, Belgium 60 Dc
Lankor Tso, Tibet 85 Fb
Lannion, France 68 Bb
Lansdale, Pennsylvania 44 Cb
Lansing, Michigan 40 Dd
Lanusei, Sardinia 71 Bf
Lanzarote, I., Canary Is. 94 Cc
Laoag, Philippines 79 Hg
Lao Bao, Laos 83 Dc
Lao-chang-Ho R., China 80 Hd
Lao Kay, N. Vietnam 83 Cb
Laon, France 68 Eb
La Oroya, Peru 48 Bf
Laos, Indo-China 83 Cc
Lao shan, China 80 Kd
Lapalisse, France 68 Ec
La Paragua, Venezuela 48 Eb
La Paz, Argentina 50 Ed
La Paz, Argentina 50 Cd
La Paz, Bolivia 48 Dg
La Paz, Honduras 47 Bd
La Paz, Mexico 46 Bc
Lapchung L., Tibet 85 Gb
Lapeer, Michigan 40 Ed
La Pelada, Argentina 50 Dd
La Pérouse, str., U.S.S.R.-Japan 82 Gb
Lapinlahti, Finland 62 Me
Lapithos, Cyprus 90 Bb
La Plata, Argentina 50 Ed
La Porte, Indiana 40 Ce
Laporte, Pennsylvania 44 Bb
Lapovo, Yugoslavia 72 Cb
Lappa Järvi, Finland 62 Ke
Lappeenranta, Finland 63 Nf
Lappland, N. Europe 41 Kc
Lapptrask, Sweden 62 Kc
Laprida, Argentina 50 De
Laptevykh Sea, Russia 75 La
Lăpuşul Românesc. See Tirgu Lăpus
Łapy, Poland 65 Kb
La Quiaca, Argentina 50 Cb
Lar, Persia 89 Fd
Larache, Morocco 94 Da
Laragne, France 69 Fd
Laramate, Peru 48 Cf
Laramie, Wyoming 42 Ec
Laramie Mts., Wyoming 42 Ec
Laranjeiras, Brazil 49 Kf
La Rasse, Switzerland 61 Ba
Larchwood, Ontario 40 Fb
Laredo, Texas 42 Gf
Largeau (Faya), Chad 92 Da
Largs, Scotland 58 De
Larino, Italy 71 Ee
La Rioja, Argentina 50 Cc
Larisa, Greece 73 De
Larkana, W. Pakistan 84 Cc
Larnaca & B., Cyprus 90 Bc
Larne, N. Ireland 59 Df
La Robla, Spain 66 Ca
Laroche, Belgium 60 Dd
La Rochelle, France 68 Cc
La Roda, Spain 67 Dc
Larrimah, N. Terr., Aust. 52 Fc
Lars Christensen Coast, Antarctica 100 Fc
Laruns, France 69 Ce
Larvik, Norway 63 Dg
Laryak, Russia 74 Gb
La Salle, Illinois 40 Be
Las Anod, Somalia 93 Kc
Las Cejas, Argentina 50 Dc
Las Colorados, Argentina 50 Be
Las Cruces, Mexico 46 Cb
Las Cruces, New Mexico 42 Ee
La Serena, Chile 50 Bc
Las Flores, Argentina 50 Ee
Lash. See Khash
Las Heras, Argentina 50 Cg
Lashio, Burma 85 Jd
Lashkar, India 87 Bb
Lashkar Gah, Afghanistan 84 Bb
Lasíthi, Crete 73 Eg
Las Khoreh, Somalia 93 Kb
Lasjerd, Persia 89 Fb
Las Lajas, Argentina 50 Be
Las Lomitas, Argentina 50 Db
Las Palmas, Canary Is. 94 Bc
Las Plumas, Argentina 50 Cf
Lassen Pk., California 45 Ce
Lassen Vol. Nat. Park, Cal. 45 Ce
Las Tablas, Panama 47 Ce
Lastovo, I., Yugoslavia 70 Fd
Las Vegas, Nevada 45 Fg
Las Vegas, New Mexico 42 Ed
Latacunga, Ecuador 48 Bd
Latakia, Syria 90 Db
Latina, Italy 71 De
Latrobe, Pennsylvania 44 Ab
Latrun, Jordan 90 Df
La Tuque, Quebec 40 Kb
Latvia, rep., U.S.S.R. 63 Kh
Laufen, Switzerland 61 Ca
Lauhkaung. See Launggyang
Launceston, England 59 Ek
Launceston, Tasmania 53 Jh
Launggyang, Burma 85 Jc
La Unión, Chile 50 Bf
La Unión, Mexico 46 Dd
La Unión, Salvador 47 Bd
La Unión, Spain 67 Ed
Laura, Queensland 53 Hc
La Urbana, Venezuela 48 Db
Laurel, Maryland 44 Bc
Laurel, Mississippi 43 Je
Laurel Hill, Pennsylvania 44 Ab
Laurent, Quebec 40 Kb
Lauria, Italy 71 Ee
Laurie, I., South Orkneys 100 Tc
Lausanne, Switzerland 61 Bb
Lautaro, Chile 50 Be
Lautem. See Vila Nova de Malaca
Lauzon, Quebec 40 Lb
Lavacherie, Belgium 60 Dd
Laval, France 68 Cb
Lavalle, Argentina 50 Cd
Lavalleja. See Minas
Lavamünd, Austria 64 Fe
Lavardac, France 69 Dd
La Vega, Rep. Dominicana 47 Ec
La Vela, Venezuela 48 Da
Laverton, W. Australia 52 De
Lavongai. See New Hanover
Lavos, Portugal 66 Ab
Lavras, Brazil 49 Hh
Lavras, Brazil 50 Fd
Lavras, Brazil 49 Ke
Lavrentiya, Russia 75 Tb
Lávrion, Greece 73 Ef
Lawk Sawk, Burma 85 Jd
Lawlers, W. Australia 52 De
Lawra, Ghana 94 Ef
Lawrence, Massachusetts 44 Ea
Lawrence, New Zealand 51 Bf
Lawton, Oklahoma 42 Ge
Lay, C., N. Vietnam 83 Dc
Laysan I., Hawaiian Is. 98 He
Lazarevac, Yugoslavia 72 Cb
Lazio, reg., Italy 71 Dd
Lead, S. Dakota 42 Fc
Leadville, Colorado 42 Ed
Leamington, England 59 Fh
Leamington, Ontario 40 Ed
Learmonth, W. Aust. 52 Bd
Leavenworth, Kansas 42 Gd
Łeba, Poland 65 Ga
Lebanon, New Hampshire 44 Da
Lebanon, Pennsylvania 44 Bb
Lebanon, W. Asia 88 Cc
Lebesby, Norway 62 Ma
Lebombo Mts., S. Africa 91 Ee
Lebork, Poland 65 Ga
Lebu, Chile 50 Be
Lebwa, Lebanon 90 Ec
Lecce, Italy 71 Ge
Lecco, Italy 70 Bc
Lectoure, France 69 De
Ledbury, England 59 Fh
Ledesma, Argentina 50 Db
Ledesma, Spain 66 Cb
Ledo, India 85 Jc
Lee R., Eire 59 Bj
Leeds, England 59 Fg
Leende, Netherlands 60 De
Leerbeek, Belgium 60 Cd
Leerdam, Netherlands 60 Dc
Leesburg, Virginia 44 Bc
Leeuwarden, Netherlands 60 Da
Leeuwin, C., W. Australia 52 Bf
Leeward Is., West Indies 47 Gc
Lefka, Cyprus 90 Ab
Lefkara, Cyprus 90 Bc
Lefkoniko, Cyprus 90 Bb
Lefroy, L., W. Australia 52 Df
Legaspi, Philippines 79 Hh
Legge Pk., Tasmania 53 Jh
Leghorn. See Livorno
Legnica, Poland 65 Gc
Leh, Kashmir 86 Ec
Le Havre, France 68 Db
Lehi, Utah 42 Dc
Lehututu, Botswana 91 Cd
Leiah, W. Pakistan 86 Be
Leicester & co., England 59 Gh
Leichhardt, R., Queensland 53 Gc
Leiden, Netherlands 60 Cb
Leigh Creek, S. Australia 53 Gf
Leighton Buzzard, England 59 Gj
Leignon, Belgium 60 Dd
Leimuiden, Netherlands 60 Cb
Leinster, prov., Eire 59 Cg
Leipzig, Germany 64 Ec
Leith, Scotland 58 Ee
Leitrim, co., Eire 59 Bf
Leix (Laoighis), co., Eire 59 Ch
Leiyang, China 81 Fj
Leka, Norway 62 Dd
Le Kef, Tunisia 95 Ga
Leksands Noret, Sweden 63 Ff
Leksvik, Norway 62 De
Leland, Michigan 40 Dc
Leleque, Argentina 50 Bf
Le Maire, Estrecho de, Argentina 50 Dh
Léman, Lac, Switzerland 61 Bb
Le Mans, France 68 Db
Lemberg. See Lvov
Lemnos. See Limnos, I.
Lemyethna, Burma 85 Je
Lena, R., Russia 75 Mb
Lenina, Pk., Kirgiz. 74 Ge
Leninabad, Uzbek. 74 Fd
Leninakan, Armyanskaya 74 Dd
Leningrad, Russia 76 Gb
Leninka, Russia 75 Sb
Leninogorsk, Kazakh. 74 Hc
Leninsk Kuznetskiy, Russia 74 Hc
Lenk, Switzerland 61 Cb
Lennox, I., Chile & Argent. 50 Cj
Lens, France 68 Ea
Lent, Netherlands 60 Dc
Lentiira, Finland 62 Nd
Lenvik, Norway 62 Hb
Lenya, Burma 85 Jf
Lenz, Switzerland 61 Eb
Lenzerheide, Switzerland 61 Eb
Leoben, Austria 64 Fe
Leominster, England 59 Fh
Leominster, Massachusetts 44 Ea
Léon, France 69 Ce
León, Mexico 46 Dc
León, Nicaragua 47 Bd
León, Spain 66 Ca
León, Monts de, Spain 66 Ba
Leonforte, Sicily 71 Eg
Leonidhion, Greece 73 Df
Leonora, W. Australia 52 De
Leontevo, Russia 76 Kb
Léopold II L., Congo 92 De
Léopoldville. See Kinshasa
Lephepe, Botswana 91 Dd
Lepontine, Alpi, Switz.-Italy 61 Db
Lercara Friddi, Sicily 71 Dg
Lerdo, Mexico 46 Db
Lerida, Spain 67 Fb
Lerma, Argentina 50 Cb
Lerma, Spain 66 Da
Lermoos, Austria 64 De
Léros, I., Greece 73 Ff
Le Roy, New York 44 Aa
Lerwick, Scotland 58 Ja
Lesbos. See Lesvos I.
Leskovac, Yugoslavia 72 Cc
Lesnoy, Russia 74 Cb
Lesotho, S. Africa 91 Ee
Lesozavodsk, Russia 75 Nd
Lesparre, France 69 Cd
Lessines, Belgium 60 Bd
Lestijärvi, Finland 62 Le
Lesvos, I., Greece 73 Ee
Leszno, Poland 65 Gc
Letea I., Rumania 72 Gb
Leti Kep., Indonesia 79 Jm
Leticia, Colombia 48 Dd
Letpadan, Burma 85 Jc
Letterkenny, Eire 58 Bf
Letur, Spain 67 Dc
Leucate, France 69 Ee
Leuk, Switzerland 61 Cb
Leuser, Mt., Sumatra 79 Ck
Leuven. See Louvain
Leuze, Belgium 60 Bd
Levádhia, Greece 73 De
Levanger, Norway 62 De
Leven L., Scotland 58 Ed
Levêque, C., W. Australia 52 Dc
Leviče, Czechoslovakia 65 Hd
Levick, Mt., Antarctica 100 Lb
Levin, New Zealand 51 Ed
Levis, Quebec 40 Lb
Levítha, I., Greece 73 Ff
Levkás, I., Greece 73 Ce
Levoča, Czechoslovakia 65 Jd
Lewes, England 59 Hk
Lewis, Butt of, Scotland 58 Cb
Lewis, I., Scotland 58 Cb
Lewis Ra., Montana 42 Db
Lewisburg, Pennsylvania 40 He
Lewiston, Idaho 45 Eb
Lewiston, Michigan 40 Dc
Lewistown, Illinois 40 Ae
Lewistown, Montana 42 Eb
Lewistown, Pennsylvania 44 Bb
Lexington, Kentucky 43 Kd
Leydsdorp, Transvaal 91 Ed
Leysele, Belgium 60 Ad
Leyte, I., Philippines 79 Hh
Lezajsk, Poland 65 Kc
Lha-kang Dzong, Tibet 85 Hc
Lhasa, Tibet 85 Hc
Lha-tse Dzong, Tibet 85 Gc
Lhontse Dzong, Tibet 85 Hc
Liangchow. See Wuwei
Liangshan, China 80 Hc
Liant, C., Siam 83 Cd
Liao R., China 78 Hb
Liaocheng, China 80 Hd
Liaohsien, China 80 Fd
Liao-tung, G. of, China 80 Kc
Liaoyang, China 80 Lb
Liari, W. Pakistan 84 Cc
Liberec, Czechoslovakia 64 Fc
Liberia, Costa Rica 47 Bd
Liberia, W. Africa 94 Cg
Libertad, Mexico 46 Bb
Libnan, Jebel, Lebanon 90 Dc
Libourne, France 69 Cd
Libreville, Gabon 92 Bd
Libya, N. Africa 95 Hc
Licata, Sicily 71 Dg
Licheng. See Tsinan
Lichfield, England 59 Fh
Lida, White Russia 76 De
Lida-di-Roma, Italy 71 De
Liddes, Switzerland 61 Cc
Lidköping, Sweden 63 Eg
Lidzbark, Poland 65 Ja
Liechtenstein, Europe 61 Ea
Liège & prov., Belgium 60 Dd
Liegnitz. See Legnica
Lieksa, Finland 62 Pe
Lienkong, China 81 Jj
Lienyunkang, China 80 Je
Lienz, Austria 64 Ee
Liepāja, Latvia 63 Jh
Lier, Belgium 60 Cc
Lierneux, Belgium 60 Dd
Liestal, Switzerland 61 Ca
Lievre R. du, Quebec 40 Jb
Lifu, I., Loyalty Is. 98 Fk
Ligure, Appennino, Italy 70 Bc
Liguria, reg., Italy 70 Bc
Ligurian Sea, Italy 70 Bc
Lihsien, China 81 Eh
Likiang, China 78 De
Likimi, Congo 92 Ed
Liling, China 81 Fj
Lilla Edet, Sweden 63 Eg
Lille, Belgium 60 Cc
Lille, France 68 Ea
Lillehammer, Norway 63 Df
Lillesand, Norway 63 Cg
Lillo, Belgium 60 Cc
Lillo, Spain 66 Dc
Lilongwe, Malawi 93 Gg
Lim Fd., Denmark 63 Ch
Lima, Ohio 40 De
Lima, Peru 48 Bf
Limache, Chile 50 Bd
Limassol, Cyprus 90 Bc
Limay, R., Argentina 50 Ce
Limay Mahuida, Argentina 50 Ce
Limbazi, Latvia 63 Lh
Limbourg, Belgium 60 Dd
Limburg, Germany 64 Cc
Limburg, prov., Belgium 60 Dd
Limchow. See Hoppo
Limeira, Brazil 49 Hh
Limerick (Luimneach), Eire 59 Bh
Limes, Belgium 60 De
Limmavady, N. Ireland 58 Ce
Limmen, Netherlands 60 Cb
Limmen Bight, N. Terr., Aust. 53 Gb
Limni, Greece 73 De
Limnos, I., Greece 73 Ee
Limoges, France 68 Dd
Limon, Costa Rica 47 Cd
Limousin, prov., France 68 Dd
Limoux, France 69 Ee
Limpopo R., Moçamb., etc. 91 Ed
Linares, Chile 50 Be
Linares, Mexico 46 Ec
Linares, Spain 66 Dc
Lincheng, China 80 He
Linchwan, China 81 Hj
Lincoln, Argentina 50 Dd
Lincoln, England 59 Gg
Lincoln, Michigan 40 Ec
Lincoln, Nebraska 42 Gc
Lincoln, New Zealand 51 De
Lincoln, & co., England 59 Gg
Lincoln Sea, Arctic Ocean 41 Qa
Lincoln Wolds, England 59 Gg
Lindau, Germany 64 Ce
Lindesay, Mt., Queensland 53 Ke
Lindesnes, Norway 63 Bh
Lindi, Tanzania 93 Hf
Lindley, Orange Free State 91 Dd
Lindos, Greece 73 Gf
Lindsay, Ontario 40 Gc
Lindsey, Lincs., England 59 Gg
Line Is., Pacific Ocean 99 Kg
Linfen, China 78 Fc
Lingchwan, China 81 Ek
Lingen, Germany 64 Bb
Lingga, I., Riouw Arch., Indon. 79 Ej
Lingling, China 78 Fe
Linguéré, Senegal 94 Be
Lingyun, China 81 Ck
Linhai, China 79 He
Linhares, Brazil 49 Jg
Linho, China 80 Cb
Linhsien, China 81 Fk
Lini, China 78 Gc
Linkiang, China 78 Jb
Linkiang, China 78 Ka
Linkiang. See Tsingkiang
Linköping, Sweden 63 Fg
Linkuva, Lithuania 63 Kh
Linnhe L., Scotland 58 Dd
Linosa, I., Medit. Sea 71 Dh
Linping, China 81 Gk
Lins, Brazil 50 Gb
Linsi, China 78 Gb
Lintan. See Kadiger
Linth, R., Switzerland 61 Eb
Linthal, Switzerland 61 Db
Linton, Quebec 40 Kb
Linyu, China 80 Jb
Linz, Austria 64 Fd
Lion, G. du, France 69 Fe
Lio Porgyul, Tibet 84 Eb
Liouesso, Fr. Congo 92 Dd
Lipa, Yugoslavia 70 Fc
Lipari Is. (Eolie, Isole), Italy 71 Ef
Lipetsk, Russia 76 Le
Liping, China 81 Dj
Lipovets, Ukraine 76 Fg
Lippstadt, Germany 64 Cc
Lipsói, I., Greece 73 Ff
Lira, Uganda 93 Gd
Lircay, Peru 48 Cf
Liria, Spain 67 Ec
Lisala, Congo 92 Ed
Lisboa, Portugal 66 Ac
Lisbon. See Lisboa
Lisburn, N. Ireland 59 Cf
Lisburne C., Alaska 43 Wl
Liscannor B., Eire 59 Ah
Lisdoonvarna, Eire 59 Ag
Lishih, China 80 Ed
Lishui, China 81 Jh
Lisianski, I., Hawaiian Is. 98 He
Lisieux, France 68 Db
Liski, Russia 77 De
L'Isle, Switzerland 61 Bb
L'Islet, Quebec 40 Lb
Lismore, Eire 59 Bh
Lismore, New South Wales 53 Ke
Listowel, Eire 59 Ah
Listowel, Ontario 40 Fd
Lith, Al, Arabia 88 De
Lithgow, New South Wales 53 Kf
Lithinon, C., Crete 73 Eg
Lithuania (Litovskaya S.S.R.), U.S.S.R. 63 Kj
Litoměrice, Czechoslovakia 64 Fc
Litovskaya S.S.R. See Lithuania
Little America, Antarctica 100 Mb
Little Belt Mts., Montana 42 Db
Little Current, Ontario 40 Fc
Little Falls, Minnesota 43 Hb
Little Falls, New York 44 Ca
Little Horn Mts., Arizona 45 Gj
Little River, New Zealand 51 De
Little Rock, Arkansas 43 He
Little Valley, New York 44 Aa
Littleton, New Hampshire 40 Lc
Liuan, China 78 Gd
Liuchow, China 78 Ef
Liupan Shan, China 80 Be
Liusvaara, Russia 62 Pe
Liverpool, New South Wales 53 Kf
Liverpool & B., England 59 Eg
Liverpool Coast, Greenland 41 Nb
Liverpool Ra., New S. Wales 53 Jf
Livingston, Guatemala 47 Bc
Livingston, Montana 42 Db
Livingston, I., S. Shetlands 100 Sc
Livingstone, Zambia 91 Dc
Livingstonia, Malawi 91 Eb
Livno, Yugoslavia 70 Fd
Livny, Russia 76 Ke
Livo Joki, Finland 62 Md
Livorno, Italy 70 Cd
Livramento, Brazil 50 Ed
Liwa, Muscat & Oman 89 Ge
Liwale, Tanzania 93 Hf
Liyepaya, Latvia 63 Jh
Lizard Pt., England 59 Dl
Ljubljana, Yugoslavia 70 Eb
Ljubuški, Yugoslavia 70 Fd
Ljungdalen, Sweden 62 Ee
Ljusdal, Sweden 63 Gf
Llandovery, Wales 59 Ej
Llandrindod Wells, Wales 59 Eh
Llandudno, Wales 59 Eg
Llanelli, Wales 59 Ej
Llanes, Spain 66 Ca
Llangollen, Wales 59 Eh
Llanguihue, L., Chile 50 Bf
Llano Estacado, New Mexico-Texas 42 Fe
Llano Grande, Mexico 46 Cc
Llerena, Spain 66 Bc
Llico, Chile 50 Bd
Lluchmayor, Balearic Is. 67 Gc
Loango, Fr. Congo 92 Ce
Lobbes, Belgium 60 Cd
Loberia, Argentina 50 Ee
Lobito, Angola 92 Cg
Lobos, Argentina 50 Ee
Locarno, Switzerland 61 Db
Lochalsh, Ontario 40 Da
Lochalsh, Kyle of, Scotland 58 Dc
Lochem, Netherlands 60 Eb
Lochinver, Scotland 58 Db
Lochnagar, Scotland 58 Ed
Lochy L., Scotland 58 Dd
Lock Haven, Pennsylvania 44 Bb
Lockerbie, Scotland 58 Ee
Lockport, New York 44 Aa
Locle, le, Switzerland 61 Ba
Loc Ninh, S. Vietnam 79 Eh
Lodeynoye Pole, Russia 76 Ha
Lodhran, W. Pakistan 86 Bf
Lodi, Wisconsin 40 Bd
Lödingen, Norway 62 Fb
Lodwar, Kenya 93 Hd
Łódź, Poland 65 Hc
Loenen, Netherlands 60 Db
Loewoek (Luwuk), Celebes 79 Hl
Lofer, Austria 64 Ee
Lofoten Is., Norway 62 Ec
Logan, Utah 42 Dc

Logansport, *Indiana* 40 Ce
Logone R., *Cameroon-Chad* 92 Cb
Logrono, *Spain* 67 Da
Lohardaga, *India* 87 Ed
Loharu, *India* 86 Df
Loikaw, *Burma* 85 Je
Loir, R., *France* 68 Cc
Loire, dep., *France* 68 Ed
Loire, R., *France* 68 Dc
Loire-Atlantique, dep., *Fr.* 68 Cc
Loiret, dep., *France* 68 Ec
Loir-et-Cher, dep., *France* 68 Dc
Loja, *Ecuador* 48 Bd
Loja, *Spain* 66 Cd
Loka, *Sudan* 95 Mh
Lokeren, *Belgium* 60 Cc
Lokka, *Finland* 62 Mc
Lökken, *Denmark* 63 Ch
Lökken, *Norway* 62 Ce
Loko, *Nigeria* 94 Gg
Lola, *Angola* 92 Cg
Lolland, *Denmark* 63 Dj
Lom, *Bulgaria* 72 Dc
Lomas, *Argentina* 50 Ed
Lomas, *Peru* 48 Cg
Lombardia, reg., *Italy* 70 Bc
Lomblem, I., *Indonesia* 79 Hm
Lombok, I. & Str., *Indonesia* 79 Gm
Lomé, *Togo* 94 Fg
Lomela, *Congo* 92 Ee
Lomié, *Cameroun* 95 Hh
Lommel, *Belgium* 60 Dc
Lomond, L., *Scotland* 58 Dd
Łomza, *Poland* 65 Kb
Loncoche, *Chile* 50 Be
Loncopue, *Argentina* 50 Be
Londiani, *Kenya* 93 He
London, *England* 59 Gj
London, *Ontario* 40 Fd
Londonderry & co., *N. Ire.* 58 Cf
Londonderry, C., *W. Aust.* 52 Eb
Londonderry, I., *Chile* 50 Bj
Long B., *S. Carolina* 43 Le
Long I., *Bahama Is.* 47 Db
Long I., *New York* 44 Db
Long, L., *Scotland* 58 Dd
Longa, *Brazil* 49 Je
Long Beach, *California* 45 Dj
Long Beach, *New Jersey* 44 Cc
Long Branch, *New Jersey* 44 Cb
Longchamps, *Belgium* 60 Dd
Longford & co., *Eire* 59 Bg
Long Island City, *New York* 44 Db
Long Island Sd., *N.Y., etc.* 44 Db
Long Point, *Ontario* 40 Fd
Longreach, *Queensland* 53 Hd
Longs Pk., *Colorado* 42 Ec
Longtown, *England* 58 Fe
Longué, *France* 68 Cc
Longueuil, *Quebec* 40 Kc
Longuyon, *France* 68 Fb
Longview, *Washington* 45 Bb
Longwy, *France* 68 Fb
Long-Xuyen, *S. Vietnam* 83 Dd
Lonneker, *Netherlands* 60 Eb
Lons-le-Saunier, *France* 68 Fc
Looc, *Philippines* 79 Hh
Loochristi, *Belgium* 60 Bc
Looe, *England* 59 Ek
Lookout, C., *N. Carolina* 43 Le
Loolmalasin, Mt., *Tanzania* 95 He
Loop Hd., *Eire* 59 Ah
Lopez C., *Gabon* 92 Be
Lopik, *Netherlands* 60 Cc
Lop Nor, *China* 78 Bb
Lopphavet, *Norway* 62 Ja
Lora Hamun, *W. Pakistan* 84 Bc
Lorain, *Ohio* 40 Ee
Loralai, *W. Pakistan* 84 Cb
Lorca, *Spain* 67 Ed
Lord Howe I., *Pacific Ocean* 98 El
Lordsburg, *New Mexico* 42 Ee
Lorena, *Brazil* 49 Jh
Loreto, *Brazil* 49 He
Loreto, *Mexico* 46 Be
Lorica, *Colombia* 48 Bb
Lorient, *France* 68 Bc
Lorn, Firth of, *Scotland* 58 Dd
Lorrach, *Germany* 64 Be
Lorraine, prov., *France* 68 Fb
Los Andes, *Chile* 50 Bd
Los Angeles, *California* 45 Dh
Los Angeles, *Chile* 50 Be
Los Blancos, *Argentina* 50 Db
Loshan, *China* 81 Ah
Lošinj, I., *Yugoslavia* 70 Ec
Los Lamentos. See Felix U Gomez
Los Menucos, *Argentina* 50 Cf
Los Pozos, *Chile* 50 Bc
Los Santos, *Panama* 47 Ce
Los Santos de Maimona, *Sp.* 66 Bc
Lossiemouth, *Scotland* 58 Ec
Los Teques, *Venezuela* 48 Da
Los Tigres, *Argentina* 50 Dc
Los Vilos, *Chile* 50 Bd
Lot, dep., *France* 69 Dd
Lot, R., *France* 69 Dd
Lota, *Chile* 50 Be
Lotbinière, *Quebec* 40 Lb
Lot-et-Garonne, dep. *Fr.* 69 Dd
Lottigna, *Switzerland* 61 Db
Loubet Coast, *Antarctica* 100 Sc
Loudéac, *France* 68 Bb
Loudima, *Fr. Congo* 92 Ce
Loudon, *Malawi* 93 Gg
Loudun, *France* 68 Dc
Louga, *Senegal* 94 Be
Loughborough, *England* 59 Gh
Loughborough's I., *Burma* 85 Jf
Loughrea, *Eire* 59 Bg
Louhans, *France* 68 Fc
Louiseville, *Quebec* 40 Kb
Louisiade Arch., *Papua* 53 Kb
Louisiana, state, *U.S.A.* 43 He
Louis Philippe Ld., *Antarc.* 100 Tc
Louis Trichardt, *Transvaal* 91 Dd
Louisville, *Kentucky* 43 Jd
Loulé, *Portugal* 66 Ad
Lourdes, *France* 69 Ce
Lourenço Marques, *Moçamb.* 91 Ee
Louriçal, *Portugal* 66 Ab
Lourinhã, *Portugal* 66 Ac
Louth, *England* 59 Hg
Louth, *N.S.W.* 53 Jf
Louth, co., *Eire* 59 Cg
Louvain, *Belgium* 60 Cd
Louveigne, *Belgium* 60 Dd
Louviers, *France* 68 Db
Lövånger, *Sweden* 62 Jd
Loviisa, *Finland* 63 Mf
Lövlid, *Sweden* 62 Gd
Lowa, *Congo* 92 Fe
Lowell, *Massachusetts* 40 Ld
Lowell, *Michigan* 40 Dd
Lowestoft, *England* 59 Jh
Łowicz, *Poland* 65 Hb
Lowville, *New York* 40 Jd
Loyalty Is., *Pacific Ocean* 98 Fk
Loyang, *China* 80 Fe
Loyung, *China* 81 Dk
Lozère, dep., *France* 69 Ed
Loznica, *Yugoslavia* 72 Bb
Luan. See Changchih
Luang Prabang, *Laos* 83 Cc
Luarca, *Spain* 66 Ba
Luashi, *Congo* 92 Eg
Lubaczów, *Poland* 65 Kc
Lubana, *Latvia* 63 Mh
Lubartów, *Poland* 65 Kc
Lübben, *Germany* 64 Ec
Lubbock, *Texas* 42 Fe
Lübeck, *Germany* 64 Db
Lübecker B., *Germany* 64 Da
Lubefu, *Congo* 92 Ee
Lubin, *Poland* 65 Gc
Lublin, *Poland* 65 Kc
Lubliniec, *Poland* 65 Hc
Lubuklinggau, *Sumatra* 79 Dl
Lubumbashi (Elisabethville), *Congo* 93 Eg
Luc, le, *France* 69 Ge
Lucala, *Angola* 92 Df
Lucania. See Basilicata
Lucca, *Italy* 70 Cd
Luce B., *Scotland* 59 Df
Lucea, *Jamaica* 47 Dc
Lucena, *Spain* 66 Cd
Lučenec, *Czechoslovakia* 65 Hd
Lucera, *Italy* 71 Ee
Lucerne (Luzern), *Switz.* 61 Da
Luch, *Russia* 77 Fb
Luchenya, *Malawi* 93 Hh
Luchow, *China* 81 Bh
Luchow (Hofei), *China* 80 Hg
Lucinda, *Pennsylvania* 44 Ab
Luckau, *Germany* 64 Ec
Luckenwalde, *Germany* 64 Eb
Lucknow, *India* 87 Cb
Lucknow, *Ontario* 40 Fd
Luçon, *France* 68 Cc
Luderitz, *S.-W. Africa* 91 Ae
Ludhiana, *India* 86 De
Ludington, *Michigan* 40 Cc
Ludlow, *England* 59 Fh
Ludvika, *Sweden* 63 Ff
Ludwigshafen, *Germany* 64 Cd
Ludwigslust, *Germany* 64 Db
Ludza, *Latvia* 63 Mh
Luebo, *Congo* 92 Ef
Luga, *Russia* 76 Fb
Lugano & L. di, *Switz.* 61 Db
Lugansk, *Ukraine* 76 Lg
Lugh Ferrandi, *Somalia* 93 Jd
Lugo, *Spain* 66 Ba
Lugoj, *Rumania* 72 Cb
Lugovay, *Kazakh.* 74 Gd
Luhit R., *India* 85 Jc
Luhsien. See Luchow
Luhwang Shan, I., *China* 81 Lh
Luichow. See Hoihong
Luichow Pen., *China* 78 Ef
Luime, *Angola* 92 Dg
Luitpold Cst., *Antarctica* 100 Ab
Luján, *Argentina* 50 Ed
Luján, *Argentina* 50 Cd
Lukachek, *Russia* 91 Nc
Lukala, *Congo* 92 Cf
Lukovit, *Bulgaria* 72 Ec
Lukoyanov, *Russia* 77 Gc
Lukula, *Congo* 92 Cf
Lule Älv, *Sweden* 62 Jc
Luleå, *Sweden* 62 Kd
Luluabourg, *Congo* 92 Ef
Lulung, *China* 80 Jc
Lumbres, *France* 68 Ea
Lummen, *Belgium* 60 Dd
Lumsden, *New Zealand* 51 Bf
Lund, *Sweden* 63 Ej
Lundy I., *England* 59 Dj
Lüneburg, *Germany* 64 Db
Lunel, *France* 69 Fe
Lunéville, *France* 68 Gb
Lungan. See Pingwu
Lungki, *China* 81 Hk
Lungnan, *China* 81 Gk
Lungsi, *China* 80 Be
Lungyen, *China* 81 Hk
Luni, *India* 84 Dc
Lunino, *Russia* 77 Gd
Lunz, *Austria* 64 Fe
Lupeh, *China* 78 Hb
Lupiro, *Tanzania* 93 Hf
Lupkow, *Poland* 65 Kd
Luputa, *Congo* 92 Ef
Luque, *Paraguay* 50 Ec
Luray, *Virginia* 40 Gf
Lurgan, *N. Ireland* 59 Cf
Luribay, *Bolivia* 48 Dg
Luröy, *Norway* 62 Ec
Lusaka, *Zambia* 91 Dc
Lusambo, *Congo* 92 Ee
Lusambo, *Congo* 92 Ef
Lushai Hills. See Mizo Hills
Lushnjë, *Albania* 73 Bd
Lushun, *China* 80 Kc
Lussanvira, *Brazil* 49 Gh
Lut Des., *Persia* 89 Gc
Lutembo, *Angola* 92 Eg
Luther, *Michigan* 40 Dc
Luton, *England* 59 Gj
Lutsen, *Minnesota* 40 Ab
Lutsk, *Ukraine* 76 Df
Luttre, *Belgium* 60 Cd
Luvia, *Finland* 63 Jf
Luwuk (Loewoek) *Celebes* 79 Hl
Luxembourg, and Grand-duchy, *N.-W. Europe* 68 Gb
Luxembourg, prov., *Belg.* 68 Fb
Luxeuil, *France* 68 Gc
Luxor, *Egypt* 95 Mc
Luzern & canton, *Switz.* 61 Da
Luziânia, *Brazil* 49 Hg
Luzilândia, *Brazil* 49 Jd
Luzon, I., *Philippines* 79 Hg
Luzon Str., *Philippines* 78 Hf
Luzy, *France* 68 Ec
Lvov, *Ukraine* 76 Dg
Lwanhsien, *China* 80 Jc
Lwan-ping, *China* 80 Hb
Lyallpur, *W. Pakistan* 86 Ce
Lybster, *Scotland* 58 Eb
Lycksele, *Sweden* 62 Hd
Lydavénai, *Lithuania* 63 Kj
Lydda, *Israel* 90 Cf
Lydenburg, *Transvaal* 91 Ee
Lyell, Mt., *California* 45 Dg
Lyell Ra., *New Zealand* 51 Dd
Lykens, *Pennsylvania* 44 Bb
Lyme B., *England* 59 Fk
Lyme Regis, *England* 59 Fk
Lynchburg, *Virginia* 43 Ld
Lynn, *Massachusetts* 44 Ea
Lynton, *England* 59 Ej
Lyon, *France* 68 Fd
Lyonnais, prov., *France* 68 Ed
Lyons, *New York* 44 Ba
Lyons, R., *W. Australia* 52 Cd
Lys, R., *Belgium, etc.* 60 Bd
Lyse, *Poland* 65 Jb
Lysekil, *Sweden* 63 Dg
Lyss, *Switzerland* 61 Ca
Lyster, *Quebec* 40 Lb
Lysva, *Russia* 77 Na
Lyttelton, *New Zealand* 51 De
Ma'an, *Jordan* 90 Dg
Maarheeze, *Netherlands* 60 Dc
Maarianhamina. See Mariehamn
Ma'arret en Numan, *Syria* 90 Eb
Maas, R., *Netherlands* 60 Ec
Maasbree, *Netherlands* 60 Ec
Maaseik, *Belgium* 60 Dc
Ma'asir. See Hazawza
Maassluis, *Netherlands* 60 Cc
Maastricht, *Netherlands* 60 Dd
Mabote, *Moçambique* 91 Ed
Mabrouk, *Mali* 94 Ee
Mabuki, *Tanzania* 93 Ge
Macaé, *Brazil* 49 Jh
Macaíba, *Brazil* 49 Ke
McAlester, *Oklahoma* 42 Ge
Macao (Port.), *China* 81 Fl
Macapá, *Brazil* 49 Gc
Macás, *Ecuador* 48 Bd
Macau, *Brazil* 49 Ke
Macauba, *Brazil* 49 Gf
Macclesfield, *England* 59 Fg
McCluer G., *New Guinea* 79 Kl
McComb, *Mississippi* 43 He
McConnellsburg, *Pa.* 44 Ac
Macdonald, L., *W. Australia* 52 Ed
Macdonnell Ra., *N.T., Aust.* 52 Fd
McDougall Ra., *N. Terr., Aust.* 53 Fc
Maceió, *Brazil* 49 Ke
Macerata, *Italy* 70 Dd
McGill, *Nevada* 45 Ff
Macgillycuddy's Reeks, *Eire* 59 Aj
McGregor Ra., *Queensland* 53 He
Mach, *W. Pakistan* 84 Cc
Machala, *Ecuador* 48 Bd
Machareti, *Bolivia* 48 Eh
Machicha, *Moçambique* 91 Fd
Machiques, *Venezuela* 48 Ca
Machiwara, *India* 86 Ee
Măcin, *Rumania* 72 Gb
Mackay, *Queensland* 53 Jd
Mackay, L., *W. Australia* 52 Ed
McKeesport, *Pennsylvania* 44 Ab
Mackenna, *Argentina* 50 Dd
Mackenzie, *Guyana* 48 Fb
Mackenzie Sea, *Antarctica* 100 Fc
Mackinac I. & Str. of, *Mich.* 40 Dc
Mackinaw, *Michigan* 40 Dc
McKinley, Mt., *Alaska* 43 Xl
Macloutsie, *Botswana* 91 Dd
Mac-Mahon, Fort, *Algeria* 94 Fc
McMillan, L., *New Mexico* 42 Fe
McMurdo Sd., *Antarctica* 100 Lb
Macomer, *Sardinia* 71 Be
Macon, *Belgium* 60 Cd
Mâcon, *France* 68 Fc
Macon, *Georgia* 43 Ke
Macouria, *Fr. Guiana* 49 Gc
McPherson, *Kansas* 42 Gd
Macpherson Ra., *Queensland* 53 Ke
Macquarie Harb., *Tasmania* 53 Jh
Macquarie I., *Pacific Ocean* 98 En
Macquarie, R., *N.S.W.* 53 Jf
Mac-Robertson Ld., *Antarc.* 100 Fb
Macroom, *Eire* 59 Bj
Macuje, *Colombia* 48 Cc
Macusani, *Peru* 48 Cf
Madaba, *Jordan* 90 Df
Madadi, *Chad* 95 Ke
Madagascar I., *Indian Ocean* 93 Nl
Madain Salih, *Arabia* 88 Cd
Madan, *Persia* 89 Gb
Madaripur, *E. Pakistan* 85 Hd
Madawaska, *Ontario* 40 Gc
Madeira, Is., *Atlantic Ocean* 94 Bb
Madeira, R., *Brazil* 48 Ee
Madhepur, *India* 87 Fb
Madhipura, *India* 87 Fc
Madhopur, *India* 84 Ec
Madhopur, *India* 86 Dd
Madhubani, *India* 87 Fb
Madhupur, *India* 87 Fc
Madhya Pradesh, *India* 84 Ed
Madison, *New Jersey* 44 Cb
Madison, *S. Dakota* 42 Gc
Madison, *Wisconsin* 40 Bd
Madisonville, *Kentucky* 43 Jd
Madoc, *Ontario* 40 Hc
Madona, *Latvia* 63 Mh
Madras, *India* 84 Ff
Madre, Sa., *Mexico* 46 Cb
Madre Austral, Lag. de la, *Mexico* 46 Ec
Madre de Dios, I., *Chile* 50 Ah
Madre de Dios, R., *Peru-Bolivia* 48 Df
Madre del Sur, Sa., *Mexico* 46 Dd
Madrid, *Spain* 66 Db
Madridejos, *Spain* 66 Dc
Madura, I., *Indonesia* 79 Fm
Madurai, *India* 84 Eg
Maebashi, *Japan* 82 Ff
Maestra, Sa., *Cuba* 47 Db
Mafeking, *Cape Province* 91 De
Mafia I., *Tanzania* 93 Hf
Mafra, *Portugal* 66 Ac
Mafraq, *Jordan* 90 Ee
Magad Plat. See Jol Plat.
Magadan, *Russia* 75 Qc
Magadi & L., *Kenya* 93 He
Magadino, *Switzerland* 61 Db
Magallanes, & Estrecho de, *Chile* 50 Bh
Magangué, *Colombia* 48 Cb
Magas. See Panāh
Magaz, *Spain* 66 Cb
Magburaka, *Sierra Leone* 94 Cg
Magdagachi, *Russia* 75 Mc
Magdala, *Ethiopia* 93 Hb
Magdalena, *Bolivia* 48 Ef
Magdalena, *Mexico* 46 Ba
Magdalena, B., *Mexico* 46 Bc
Magdalena, I., *Chile* 50 Bf
Magdalena, R., *Colombia* 48 Cb
Magdeburg, *Germany* 64 Db
Magellan, Str. of, *Chile* 50 Ch
Mageröya, *Norway* 62 Ma
Maggia, *Switzerland* 61 Db
Maggiore, L., *Italy* 70 Bb
Maghang Tsangpo R., *Tibet* 85 Gc
Maghara, Geb., *Egypt* 90 Bg
Magherafelt, *N. Ireland* 59 Cf
Maglaj, *Yugoslavia* 72 Bb
Maglie, *Italy* 71 Ge
Magnetic I., *Qnsld.* 53 Jc
Magnitogorsk, *Russia* 77 Pd
Magog, *Quebec* 40 Kc
Magwe, *Burma* 85 Jd
Mahabad, *Persia* 88 Eb
Mahabaleshwar, *India* 84 De
Mahaban, *India* 86 Eg
Mahabharat Ra., *Nepal* 87 Eb
Mahaddei Uen, *Somalia* 93 Kd
Mahadeo Hills, *India* 87 Ad
Mahail, *Arabia* 88 Df
Mahajamba, B. de, *Madag.* 93 Nk
Mahaian, *India* 86 Cf
Mahalapye, *Botswana* 91 Dd
Mahallat, *Persia* 89 Fc
Maham, *India* 86 Ef
Mahanadi R., *India* 85 Fd
Mahanoro, *Madagascar* 93 Nk
Mahanoy City, *Pennsylvania* 44 Bb
Mahbubnagar, *India* 84 Ee
Mahdia, *Tunisia* 95 Ha
Mahé, *India* 84 Ef
Mahendragiri, Mt., *India* 85 Fe
Mahia Pen., *New Zealand* 51 Fc
Mahmed-Hussein-magala. See Shahsavar
Mahmudabad, *India* 87 Cb
Mahmudabad, *Persia* 87 Fb
Mahua, *Mozambique* 93 Hg
Mahuva, *India* 84 Dd
Maida, *Yemen* 88 Df
Maidan, *Afghanistan* 89 Jc
Maidstone, *England* 59 Hj
Maiduguri, *Nigeria* 95 Hf
Maienfeld, *Switzerland* 61 Ea
Maihar, *India* 87 Cc
Maikal Ra., *India* 87 Cd
Maikop, *Russia* 74 Dd
Maimana, *Afghanistan* 89 Hb
Main R., *Germany* 64 Cd
Main Barrier Ra., *N.S.W.* 53 Hf
Maine, prov., *France* 68 Cb
Maine, state, *U.S.A.* 43 Nb
Maine-et-Loire, dep., *France* 68 Cc
Maing Kaing, *Burma* 85 Jd
Maingkwan, *Burma* 85 Jc
Mainpuri, *India* 84 Ec
Mainz, *Germany* 64 Cd
Maipo, Mt., *Argentina* 50 Cd
Maipu, *Argentina* 50 Ee
Maissin, *Belgium* 60 De
Mait & I., *Somalia* 93 Kb
Maitland, *New South Wales* 53 Kf
Maitland, L., *W. Australia* 52 De
Maiz, *Mexico* 46 Ec
Maizuru, *Japan* 82 Dg
Maja, I., *Indonesia* 79 El
Majagual, *Colombia* 48 Cb
Majitha, *India* 86 De
Majmaa, *Arabia* 88 Ed
Majorca, *Balearic Is.* 67 Gc
Majunga, *Madagascar* 93 Nk
Majuro, Is., *Marshall Is.* 98 Gg
Makale, *Ethiopia* 93 Hb
Makania, *Tanzania* 93 He
Makariev, *Russia* 77 Fb
Makarvey, *Russia* 77 Gb
Makassar, *Celebes* 79 Gm
Makassar Str., *Indonesia* 79 Gl
Makatea, I., *Tuamotu Arch.* 99 Lj
Makedhonia, *Greece* 73 Cd
Makemo, I., *Tuamotu Arch.* 99 Lj
Makeyevka, *Ukraine* 76 Kg
Makhach Kala, *Russia* 74 Dd
Makhai, *China* 78 Bc
Makikihi, *New Zealand* 51 Cf
Makindu, *Kenya* 93 He
Makkinga, *Netherlands* 60 Eb
Makla, Jebel el, *Arabia* 88 Cd
Makó, *Hungary* 72 Ca
Makongolosi, *Tanzania* 93 Gf
Makorako, Mt., *N.Z.* 51 Fc
Makram, *Arabia* 88 Ce
Makri, *India* 84 Fe
Makri. See Fethiye
Maksamaa, *Finland* 62 Ke
Maksmo. See Maksamaa
Maku, *Persia* 88 Db
Makum, *India* 85 Jc
Makurdi, *Nigeria* 94 Gg
Makwiro, *Rhodesia* 91 Ec
Malá, *Peru* 48 Bf
Malabang, *Philippines* 79 Hj
Malabar Coast, *India* 84 Df
Malabu, *Nigeria* 95 Hg
Malacca, *W. Malaysia* 79 Dk
Malacca, Str. of, *Sumatra-W. Malaysia* 79 Dk
Malad City, *Idaho* 42 Dc
Maladeta, Mt., *Spain* 67 Fa
Málaga, *Spain* 66 Cd
Malagasy Rep., *Indian Oc.* 93 Nl
Malaita, *Solomon Is.* 98 Fh
Malakal, *Sudan* 95 Mg
Malakand & Pass, *W. Pakistan* 86 Bc
Malån, *Sweden* 62 Hd
Malang, *Java* 79 Fm
Malanje, *Angola* 92 Df
Mälaren, L., *Sweden* 63 Gg
Malargue, *Argentina* 50 Ce
Malathia, *Kenya* 93 Hd
Malatya, *Turkey* 92 Cb
Malaut, *India* 86 De
Malawi (Nyasaland), *Cent. Africa* 93 Gg
Malaya. See West Malaysia
Malayer, *Persia* 88 Ec
Malaysia, *S.E. Asia* 83 De
Malazgirt, *Turkey* 88 Db
Malbork, *Poland* 65 Ha
Malchow, *Germany* 64 Eb
Malda, *India* 87 Gc
Maldegem, *Belgium* 60 Bc
Malden, *Massachusetts* 44 Ea
Malden, I., *Pacific Ocean* 99 Kh
Maldive Is., *Indian Ocean* 54 Gh
Maldon, *England* 59 Hj
Maldonado, *Uruguay* 50 Fd
Maléa, C., *Greece* 73 Df
Malé Karpaty, *Czech.* 65 Gd
Malekula, I., *New Hebrides* 98 Fj
Máleme, *Crete* 73 Dg
Maler Kotla, *India* 86 De
Malesherbes, *France* 68 Eb
Malgache, Rep., *Indian Oc.* 93 Pl
Malheur L., *Oregon* 45 Dd
Mali, *W. Africa* 94 Ee
Malihabad, *India* 87 Cb
Malin Hd., *Eire* 58 Ce
Malinau, *Borneo* 79 Gk
Malindi, *Kenya* 93 Je
Malines, *Belgium* 60 Cc
Malkangiri, *India* 85 Fe
Malko Türnovo, *Bulgaria* 72 Fd
Mallaig, *Scotland* 58 Dc
Mállia G., *Crete* 73 Eg
Mallorca I., *Balearic Is.* 67 Gc
Mallow, *Eire* 59 Bh
Malmberget, *Sweden* 62 Jc
Malmédy, *Belgium* 60 Ed
Malmesbury, *England* 59 Fj
Malmö, *Sweden* 63 Ej
Malmyzh, *Russia* 77 Kb
Maloggia, *Switzerland* 61 Eb
Malombe L., *Malawi* 93 Hg
Malone, *New York* 40 Jc
Malonga, *Congo* 92 Eg
Malta, *Montana* 42 Eb
Malta Chan., *Medit. Sea* 71 Eg
Malta I., *Mediterranean Sea* 71 Eh
Malters, *Switzerland* 61 Da
Malton, *England* 59 Gf
Malung, *Sweden* 63 Ef
Malvaglia, *Switzerland* 61 Db
Malvan, *India* 84 De
Malvern Hills, *England* 59 Fh
Malvina, *Quebec* 40 Lc
Malvinas, Isles. See Falkland Is.
Mama, *Russia* 75 Lc
Mamantel, *Mexico* 46 Fd
Mambasa, *Congo* 93 Fd
Mamonal, *Colombia* 48 Ba
Mamou, *Guinea* 94 Cf
Mampoko, *Congo* 92 Dd
Mamu, *Afghanistan* 89 Hd
Mamudju, *Celebes* 79 Gl
Man, *Ivory Coast* 94 Dg
Man, I. of, *Irish Sea* 59 Ef
Manacapuru, *Brazil* 48 Ed
Manacor, *Balearic Is.* 67 Gc
Manado, *Celebes* 79 Hk
Managua, *Nicaragua* 47 Bd
Managua L., *Nicaragua* 47 Bd
Manakha, *Yemen* 88 Df
Manamah, *Bahrein I.* 89 Fd
Mananjary, *Madagascar* 93 Nl
Manantenina, *Madagascar* 93 Nl
Manapouri L., *New Zealand* 51 Af
Manasarowar, L., *Tibet* 84 Fb
Manasquan, *New Jersey* 40 Je
Manassas, *Virginia* 40 Hf
Manaus, *Brazil* 48 Ed
Mancelona, *Michigan* 40 Dc
Manche, dep., *France* 68 Cb
Manchester, *England* 59 Fg
Manchester, *New Hampshire* 40 Ld
Manchouli, *China* 78 Ga
Manchuria, *China* 78 Ha
Mancora, *Peru* 48 Ad
Manda, *Tanzania* 93 Gg
Mandal, *Norway* 63 Bg
Mandalay, *Burma* 85 Jd
Mandal Gobi, *Mongolia* 78 Ea
Mandan, *N. Dakota* 42 Fb
Mandarin B., *China* 81 Em
Mander, *Netherlands* 60 Eb
Mandera, *Kenya* 93 Jd
Mandi, *India* 86 Ee
Mandih, *Philippines* 79 Hj
Mandla, *India* 87 Cd
Mandritsara, *Madagascar* 93 Nk
Mandvi, *India* 84 Cd
Manfredonia, G. di, *Italy* 71 Fe
Manfuha, *Arabia* 88 Ee
Mangaia, I., *Cook Is.* 99 Kk
Mangaldai, *India* 85 Hc
Mangalme, *Chad* 95 Jf
Mangalore, *India* 84 Df
Mangareva, I., *Tuamotu Arch.* 99 Mk
Mangaweka, *New Zealand* 51 Ec
Mangfall Geb., *Germany* 64 De
Manglaralto, *Ecuador* 48 Ad
Mangonui, *New Zealand* 51 Da
Mangrol, *India* 84 Dd
Mangualde, *Portugal* 66 Bb
Mangueira, L. da, *Brazil* 50 Fd
Manhattan, *Kansas* 42 Gd
Manhay, *Belgium* 60 Dd
Manhuaça, *Brazil* 49 Jh
Manicoré, *Brazil* 48 Ee
Manifold, C., *Queensland* 53 Kd
Manihi, *India* 87 Ec
Manihiki, I., *Pacific Ocean* 98 Jj
Manikarchar, *India* 87 Gc
Manikganj. See Dasara
Manikpur, *E. Pakistan* 85 Hd
Manila, *Philippines* 79 Hh
Manipur (Imphal), *India* 85 Hc
Manisa, *Turkey* 88 Ab
Manistee, *Michigan* 40 Cc
Manistee R., *Michigan* 40 Dc
Manistique, *Michigan* 40 Cb
Manitou Is., *Michigan* 40 Cc
Manitoulin I., *Ontario* 40 Ec
Manitowaning, *Ontario* 40 Fc
Manitowoc, *Wisconsin* 40 Cc
Maniwaki, *Quebec* 40 Hb
Maniyah, *Iraq* 88 Dc
Manizales, *Colombia* 48 Bb
Manja, *Madagascar* 93 Ml
Manjimup, *W. Australia* 52 Cf
Manka, *Taiwan* 81 Kk
Mankato, *Minnesota* 43 Hc
Mankheri, *India* 87 Ed
Manlleu, *Spain* 67 Ga
Manmad, *India* 84 Dd
Mannar, *Ceylon* 84 Eg
Mannar, G. of, *India* 84 Eg
Mannargudi, *India* 84 E
Mannheim, *Germany* 64 Cd
Manoa, *Bolivia* 48 De
Manokwari, *W. Irian* 79 Kl
Manono, *Congo* 92 Ff
Manosque, *France* 69 Fe
Manresa, *Spain* 67 Fb
Mansa, *Zambia* 91 Db
Mansehra, *W. Pakistan* 86 Cc
Mansfield, *England* 59 Gg
Mansfield, *Massachusetts* 40 Ld
Mansfield, *Ohio* 40 Ee
Mansfield, *Pennsylvania* 44 Bb
Mansfield, Mt., *Vermont* 40 Kc
Mansi, *Burma* 85 Jd
Mansilla de Las Mulas, *Spain* 66 Ca
Manta, *Ecuador* 48 Ad
Mantova, *Italy* 70 Cc
Mantua. See Mantova
Manú, *Peru* 48 Cf
Manua, I., *Samoa Is.* 98 Jj
Manuel Rodriguez, I., *Chile* 50 Bh
Manujan, *Persia* 89 Gd
Manus I., *Admiralty Is.* 98 Dh
Manyoni, *Tanzania* 93 Gf
Manzala L., *Egypt* 95 Mb
Manzanares, *Spain* 66 Dc
Manzanillo, *Cuba* 47 Db
Manzanillo, *Mexico* 46 Dd
Manzanillo, Pta., *Panama* 47 De
Mao, *Chad* 95 Jf
Mapia Is., *Pacific Ocean* 98 Cg
Mapimí, *Mexico* 46 Db
Mapinga. See Linchow
Mapire, *Venezuela* 48 Eb
Maqainama, *Arabia* 88 Ee
Maqatin, *S. Yemen* 88 Eg
Maqna, *Arabia* 88 Bd
Maquela do Zombo, *Angola* 92 Df
Maquinchao, *Argentina* 50 Cf
Mara, *Transvaal* 91 Dd
Maraã, *Brazil* 48 Dd
Marabá, *Brazil* 49 He
Maracá, I. de, *Brazil* 49 Gc
Maracaibo, *Venezuela* 48 Ca
Maracaibo, L. de, *Venezuela* 48 Cb
Maracanã, *Brazil* 49 Hd
Maracaçume, *Brazil* 49 Hd
Maracay, *Venezuela* 48 Da
Marada, *Libya* 95 Jc
Maradi, *Niger* 94 Gf
Maragheh, *Persia* 88 Eb
Maragogi, *Brazil* 49 Ke
Marakei, I., *Gilbert Is.* 98 Gg
Marakwet, *Kenya* 93 Hd
Maralinga, *S. Austr.* 52 Ff
Maramures, *Rumania* 65 Ke
Marand, *Persia* 88 Eb
Maranguape, *Brazil* 49 Kd
Marañón, R., *Peru* 48 Bd
Maras, *Turkey* 88 Cb
Maraú, *Brazil* 49 Kf
Maravilha, *Brazil* 48 De
Marbella, *Spain* 66 Cd
Marble Bar, *W. Australia* 52 Cd
Marblehead, *Massachusetts* 44 Ea
Marcelino, *Brazil* 48 Dc
Marche, *Belgium* 60 Dd
Marche, reg., *Italy* 70 Dd
Marchena, *Spain* 66 Cd
Marchin, *Belgium* 60 Dd
Mar Chiquita, *Argentina* 50 Dd
Marcus I., *Pacific Ocean* 98 Ee
Marcy, Mt., *New York* 40 Jc
Mardan, *W. Pakistan* 86 Cc
Mar del Plata, *Argentina* 50 Ee
Mardin, *Turkey* 88 Db
Mare, I., *Loyalty Is.* 98 Fk
Marechal Deodoro. See Alagoas
Maree, L., *Scotland* 58 Dc
Mareeba, *Qnsld.* 53 Jc
Marengo, *Wisconsin* 40 Ab
Margarita, I., *Venezuela* 48 Ea
Margarites, *Crete* 73 Eg
Margate, *England* 59 Hj
Marianao, *Cuba* 47 Cb
Marianas, Is., *Pacific Ocean* 98 Df
Marianna, *Arkansas* 43 He
Mariánské Lázně, *Czech.* 64 Ed
Marias, R., *Montana* 42 Db
Marib, *Yemen* 88 Df
Maribor, *Yugoslavia* 70 Eb
Maridi, *Sudan* 95 Lh
Marie Byrd Ld., *Antarctica* 100 Pb
Mariefred, *Sweden* 63 Gg
Marie Galante, I., *Leeward Is.* 47 Gc
Mariehamn, *Finland* 63 Hf
Marienbad. See Mariánské L.
Marienberg, *Netherlands* 60 Eb
Marienbourg, *Belgium* 60 Cd
Marienburg. See Malbork
Mariental, *S.-W. Africa* 91 Bd
Marienthal, *Russia* 77 Kc
Marienville, *Pennsylvania* 44 Ab
Mariestad, *Sweden* 63 Eg
Marietta, *Ohio* 40 Ff
Mari Indus, *W. Pakistan* 86 Bd
Marina Fall, *Guyana* 48 Fb
Marine City, *Michigan* 40 Ed
Marinette, *Wisconsin* 40 Cc
Marinha Grande, *Portugal* 66 Ac
Marion, *Indiana* 40 De
Marion, *Ohio* 40 Ee
Maritsa R., *Bulgaria, etc.* 72 Ed
Mariyampole. See Kapsukas
Mariyskaya A.S.S.R., *Russia* 74 Dc
Marj, el, *Libya* 95 Kb
Marjamaa, *Estonia* 63 Lg
Markala, *Mali* 94 Df
Markapur, *India* 84 Ee
Markelo, *Netherlands* 60 Eb
Marken, I., *Netherlands* 60 Db
Market Drayton, *England* 59 Fh
Market Harborough, *Eng.* 59 Gh
Markham, L., *Tibet* 85 Fa
Markham, Mt., *Antarctica* 100 Ka
Markovo, *Russia* 75 Sb
Marks, *Russia* 77 He
Markstay, *Ontario* 40 Fb
Marlboro, *Massachusetts* 44 Ea
Marlborough, *Guyana* 48 Fb
Marlette, *Michigan* 40 Ed
Marmagão, *Goa* 84 De
Marmande, *France* 69 Dd
Marmara, Sea of, *Turkey* 88 Aa
Marmaris, *Turkey* 88 Ab
Marne, dep., *France* 68 Fb
Maroua, *Cameroon* 95 Hf
Marouini, R., *Fr. Guiana* 49 Gc
Marquesas Is., *Pacific Ocean* 99 Mh
Marquette, *Michigan* 40 Cb
Marquina, *Spain* 67 Da
Marrakech (Marrakesh), *Morocco* 94 Db
Marree, *S. Australia* 53 Ge
Marsabit, *Kenya* 93 Hd
Marsa Hali, *Arabia* 88 Df
Marsala, *Sicily* 71 Dg
Marseille, *France* 69 Fe

Mont Laurier, Quebec 40 Jb
Montluçon, France 68 Ec
Montmédy, France 68 Fb
Montmirail, France 68 Eb
Montmorency, Quebec 40 Lb
Montoro, Spain 66 Cc
Montoursville, Pennsylvania 44 Bb
Montpelier, Idaho 42 Dc
Montpelier, Vermont 40 Kc
Montpellier, France 69 Ee
Montreal, Quebec 40 Kc
Montrejeau, France 69 De
Montreuil, France 68 Da
Montreuil Bellay, France 68 Cc
Montreux, Switzerland 61 Bb
Montrose, Pennsylvania 44 Bb
Montrose, Scotland 58 Fd
Mont-St-Jean, Belgium 60 Cd
Mont-St-Michel & B., Fr. 68 Cb
Montserrat, I., Leeward Is. 47 Gc
Monywa, Burma 85 Jd
Monza, Italy 70 Bc
Monze, Zambia 91 Dc
Monzon, Spain 67 Fb
Moora, W. Australia 52 Cf
Moore, L., W. Australia 52 Ce
Moorefield, W. Virginia 44 Ac
Moorfoot Hills, Scotland 58 Ee
Moorhead, Minnesota 42 Gb
Moorsel, Belgium 60 Cd
Moorslede, Belgium 60 Bd
Moosic Mts., Pennsylvania 44 Cb
Mopti, Mali 94 Ef
Moquegua, Peru 48 Cg
Mora, Ethiopia 93 Hb
Mora, Cameroon 95 Hf
Mora, Portugal 66 Ac
Mora, Spain 66 Dc
Mora, Sweden 62 Ff
Moradabad, India 87 Ba
Mora de Rubielos, Spain 67 Eb
Moramanga, Madagascar 93 Nk
Morano Calabro, Italy 71 Ff
Morar, India 87 Bb
Morar L., Scotland 58 Dd
Morat. See Murten
Moratalla, Spain 67 Ec
Morava, Czechoslovakia 65 Gd
Morava R., Yugoslavia 72 Cb
Moravska Trebova, Czech. 65 Gd
Morawhanna, Guyana 48 Fb
Moray, co., Scotland 58 Ec
Moray Firth, Scotland 58 Ec
Morbihan, dep., France 68 Bc
Mordova, Russia 77 Ed
Mordovskaya, aut. rep., Russia 74 Dc
Moreau R., S. Dakota 42 Fb
Morecambe & B., England 59 Ff
Moreda, Spain 66 Dd
Moree, New South Wales 53 Je
Moreira, Brazil 48 Ed
Mörel, Switzerland 61 Db
Morelia, Mexico 46 Dd
Morella, Spain 67 Eb
Morelos, Mexico 46 Db
Morelos, Mexico 46 Cb
Morelos, state, Mexico 46 Ed
Morena, Sa., Spain 66 Cc
Morere, New Zealand 51 Fc
Moreton B., Queensland 53 Ke
Morez, France 68 Gc
Morgan, S. Australia 53 Gf
Morgan City, Louisiana 43 Hb
Morgat, France 68 Ab
Morges, Switzerland 61 Bb
Morgins, Switzerland 61 Bb
Moriani, India 85 Hc
Morioka, Japan 82 Ge
Morlaix, France 68 Bb
Mornington, I., Chile 50 Ag
Moro G., Philippines 79 Hj
Morobe, New Guinea 53 Ja
Morocco, N.-W. Africa 94 Db
Morogoro, Tanzania 93 Hf
Morokwen, Cape Province 91 Ce
Moron, Cuba 47 Db
Morona, Ecuador 48 Bd
Morondava, Madagascar 93 Ml
Morón de la Frontera, Spain 66 Cd
Morotai, I., Indonesia 79 Jk
Moroto, Uganda 93 Gd
Morpeth, England 58 Fe
Morphou & B., Cyprus 90 Ab
Morrinhos, Brazil 49 Hg
Morrinsville, New Zealand 51 Eb
Morrisburg, Ontario 40 Jc
Morris Jesup C., Arctic Oc. 41 Na
Morrison, Illinois 40 Be
Morristown, New Jersey 44 Cb
Morristown, Tennessee 43 Kd
Morrisville, New York 40 Jd
Morrosquillo, G. de, Colomb. 48 Bb
Mors, Denmark 63 Ch
Morshansk, Russia 77 Ed
Mortagne, France 68 Db
Mortagua, Portugal 66 Ab
Mortain, France 68 Cb
Morven, New Zealand 51 Cf
Morven, Queensland 53 Je
Morvi, India 84 Dd
Moscow, Idaho 45 Eb
Moscow. See Moskva
Moselle, dep., France 68 Gb
Moselle, R., France 68 Gb
Mosera, I. See Masira I.
Mosgiel, New Zealand 51 Cf
Moshupa, Botswana 91 Dd
Mosjöen, Norway 62 Ed
Moskenesöy, Norway 62 Ec
Moskva, Russia 76 Kd
Mosonmagyarovar, Hungary 65 Ge
Mosqueiro, Brazil 49 Hd
Mosquera, Colombia 48 Bc
Moss, Norway 63 Dg
Mossamedes, Angola 91 Ac
Mossburn, New Zealand 51 Bf
Mosselbaai, Cape Province 91 Cf
Mossendjo, Fr. Congo 92 Ce
Mossoro, Brazil 49 Ke
Mossuma, Angola 92 Eg
Mossurize, Moçambique 91 Ed
Most, Czechoslovakia 64 Ec
Mostaganem, Algeria 94 Fa
Mostar, Yugoslavia 72 Ac
Mostardas, Brazil 50 Fd
Mosul, Iraq 88 Db
Mota del Marques, Spain 66 Cb
Motala, Sweden 63 Fg
Motatan, Venezuela 48 Cb
Motherwell, Scotland 58 Ee
Môtier, Switzerland 61 Cb
Môtiers, Switzerland 61 Bb
Motihari, India 87 Eb
Motôt, Switzerland 61 Cb
Motril, Spain 66 Dd
Motueka, New Zealand 51 Dd
Motul, Mexico 46 Gc
Moudhros, Greece 73 Ee
Moudon, Switzerland 61 Bb
Mouila, Gabon 92 Ce
Moukden. See Shenyang
Moulins, France 68 Ec
Moulmein, Burma 85 Je
Moulouya R., Morocco 94 Eb
Mount Bellew, Eire 59 Bg
Mount Carmel, Pennsylvania 44 Bb
Mount Carroll, Illinois 40 Bd
Mount Clemens, Michigan 40 Ed
Mount Dutton, S. Aust. 53 Ge
Mount Forest, Ontario 40 Fc
Mount Gambier, S. Aust. 53 Hg
Mount Holly, New Jersey 44 Cc
Mount Jewett, Pennsylvania 44 Ab
Mount Lofty Ra., S. Aust. 53 Gf
Mount Magnet, W. Aust. 52 Ce
Mount Morgan, Queensland 53 Kd
Mount Morris, New York 44 Ba
Mount Pleasant, Michigan 40 Dd
Mount Pleasant, Pa. 44 Ab
Mounts B., England 59 Dk
Mount Union, Pennsylvania 44 Bb
Mount Vernon, Virginia 40 Hf
Mount Vernon, W. Australia 52 Cd
Moura, Brazil 48 Ed
Moura, Portugal 66 Bc
Mourão, Portugal 66 Bc
Mourne Mts., N. Ireland 59 Cf
Moussoro, Chad 95 Jf
Moutier, Switzerland 61 Ca
Moutohora, New Zealand 51 Fc
Mowming, China 81 Em
Mowping, China 80 Kd
Moyale, Kenya 93 Hd
Moyobamba, Peru 48 Be
Mozambique. See Moçambique
Mozhga, Russia 77 Lb
Mozyr, Belorussia 76 Fe
Mpanda, Tanzania 93 Gf
Mporokoso, Zambia 93 Gf
Mstislavl, White Russia 76 Gd
Mtakuja, Tanzania 93 Gf
Mtito Andei, Kenya 93 He
Mtoko, Rhodesia 91 Ec
Mtsensk, Russia 76 Ke
Mu, R., Burma 85 Jd
Muádhdham, el, Arabia 88 Cd
Muang Chaiya, Siam 83 Be
Muang Chana, Siam 83 Ce
Muang Langsuan, Siam 83 Be
Muang Nan, Siam 83 Cc
Muang Palien, Siam 83 Be
Mubarraz, Arabia 88 Ed
Mubende, Uganda 93 Gd
Muchinga Mts., Zambia 93 Gg
Mucuri, Brazil 49 Kg
Mudanya, Turkey 88 Aa
Mudawwara, Jordan 90 Dh
Muddus Järvi, Finland 62 Mb
Mudgee, New S. Wales 53 Jf
Mudhnib, Arabia 88 Dd
Mueda, Moçambique 93 Hg
Muggendorf, Germany 64 Dd
Mugia, Spain 66 Aa
Muğla, Turkey 88 Ab
Muglad, Sudan 95 Lf
Muhamdi, India 87 Cb
Muhammadabad. See Darreh Gaz
Muhammadgarh, India 87 Bd
Muharraq, Persian Gulf 89 Fd
Mühldorf, Germany 64 Ed
Mühlehorn,, Switzerland 61 Ea
Muhu, Estonia 63 Kg
Muinak, Uzbek. 74 Ed
Muine Bheag, Eire 59 Ch
Mukalla, Aden Prot. 88 Eg
Mukdahan, Siam 83 Cc
Mukden. See Shenyang
Mukhtuya, Russia 75 Lb
Mukhu Väin, Estonia 62 Kg
Muktinath, Nepal 87 Da
Muktsar, India 86 De
Mula, Spain 67 Ec
Mulchen, Chile 50 Be
Mulege, Mexico 46 Bb
Mülhausen, Germany 64 Dc
Mülheim, Germany 64 Bc
Mülheim, Germany 64 Bc
Mulhouse, France 68 Gc
Mulki, India 84 Df
Mull I., Scotland 58 Dd
Mullaittivu, Ceylon 84 Fg
Muller Geb., Borneo 79 Fk
Mullet L., Michigan 40 Dc
Mullewa, W. Australia 52 Ce
Müllheim, Switzerland 61 Ea
Mullingar, Eire 59 Cg
Multan, W. Pakistan 86 Be
Multia, Finland 62 Le
Mumbondo, Angola 92 Cg
Mumbwa, Zambia 92 Fg
Muna, I., Indonesia 79 Hm
München, Germany 64 Dd
München Gladbach, Ger. 64 Bc
Muncie, Indiana 40 De
Mundiwindi, W. Aust. 52 Dd
Mundo Novo, Brazil 49 Jf
Mundrabilla, W. Aust. 52 Ef
Mungari, Moçambique 91 Ec
Munich. See München
Muniesa, Spain 67 Eb
Munising, Michigan 40 Cb
Munkfors, Sweden 63 Eg
Munnerstadt, Germany 64 Dc
Muñoz Gamero, Pen., Chile 50 Bh
Münster, Germany 64 Bc
Munster, Switzerland 61 Fb
Münster, Switzerland 61 Db
Münster, Switzerland 61 Da
Munster, prov., Eire 59 Ah
Muntok, Bangka I., Indon. 79 El
Muong Attopeu, Laos 83 Dd
Muong Borikone, Laos 83 Cc
Muong Saravane, Laos 83 Dd
Muonio, R., Swed.-Fin. 62 Kc
Muonionalusta, Sweden 62 Kc
Muotathal, Switzerland 61 Db
Mur, Yemen 88 Df
Murang'a, Kenya 93 He
Murakami, Japan 82 Fe
Murat, R., Turkey 88 Db
Murat Dagh, Turkey 88 Ab
Murca, Portugal 66 Bb
Murcheh Khur, Persia 89 Fc
Murchison, N.Z. 51 Dd
Murchison Falls, Uganda 93 Gd
Murchison Mts., N.Z. 51 Af
Murchison, R., W. Aust. 52 Ce
Murcia, Spain 67 Ed
Muresul (Maros), R., Rum. 72 Ca
Murfeesboro, Tennessee 43 Jd
Murgon, Qnsld. 53 Ke
Muri, Switzerland 61 Da
Muriae, Brazil 49 Jh
Murias de Paredes, Spain 66 Ba
Müritz See, Germany 64 Eb
Murjo, Mt., Java 79 Fm
Murmansk, Russia 74 Cb
Murom, Russia 77 Fc
Muroran, Japan 82 Gc
Muros, Spain 66 Aa
Murray, Utah 42 Dc
Murray, R., N.S.W., etc. 53 Jg
Murray Bridge, S. Australia 53 Gg
Murree, W. Pakistan 86 Cd
Mürren, Switzerland 61 Cb
Murrumbidgee, R., N.S.W. 53 Jf
Mursan, India 86 Eg
Murshidabad, India 87 Gc
Mursir. See Ash
Murten & See, Switzerland 61 Cb
Muroroa I., Tuamotu Arch. 99 Mk
Murwara, India 87 Cd
Murzuq, Libya 95 Hc
Muş, Turkey 88 Db
Musa Kala, Afghanistan 89 Hc
Musalamiya, Arabia 88 Ed
Muscat, Muscat & Oman 89 Ge
Muscat & Oman, Arabian Pen. 89 Ge
Muscatine, Iowa 43 Hc
Musemir, S. Yemen 88 Dg
Musgrave, Qnsld. 53 Hb
Musgrave Ra., S. Aust., etc. 52 Fe
Mushie, Congo 92 De
Muskeget Chan., Mass. 44 Eb
Muskegon, Michigan 40 Cd
Muskegon R., Michigan 40 Dd
Muskogee, Oklahoma 42 Gd
Musmar, Sudan 95 Ne
Musoma, Tanzania 93 Ge
Mussau, I., Pacific Ocean 98 Dh
Mussidan, France 69 Dd
Mustahil, Ethiopia 93 Jc
Mustajidda, Arabia 88 Dd
Mustang, Nepal 87 Da
Mustang I., Texas 42 Gf
Musters, L., Argentina 50 Cg
Muswellbrook, N.S.W. 53 Kf
Mut, Egypt 95 Lc
Mut, Turkey 88 Bb
Mutanda, Zambia 93 Fg
Mutano, Angola 91 Ac
Mutoray, Russia 75 Kb
Mutsu B., Japan 82 Gd
Mutton I., Eire 59 Ah
Mutumbo, Angola 92 Dg
Mutupet, India 84 Ef
Muwale, Tanzania 93 Gf
Muy, le, France 69 Ge
Muya, Japan 82 Dg
Muya, Russia 75 Lc
Muy Muy, Nicaragua 47 Bd
Muzaffarabad, Kashmir 86 Cc
Muzaffargarh, W. Pakistan 86 Be
Muzaffarnagar, India 86 Ef
Muzaffarpur, India 87 Eb
Muzhi, Russia 74 Fb
Muzquiz, Mexico 46 Db
Muztagh Ata, Mt., China 86 Da
Mwanza, Tanzania 93 Ge
Mweelrea, Eire 59 Ag
Mweru L., Congo 93 Ff
Mwinilunga, Zambia 92 Eg
Myadaung, Burma 85 Jd
Myanaung, Burma 85 Je
Myaungmya, Burma 85 Je
Myebon, Burma 85 Hd
Myingyan, Burma 85 Jd
Myinmolettkat, Mt., Burma 85 Jf
Myitkyina, Burma 85 Jc
Myjava, Czechoslovakia 65 Gd
Mymensingh, East Pakistan 85 Hd
Myohaung, Burma 85 Hd
Myrdal, Norway 63 Bf
Myslowice, Poland 65 Hc
Mysore, India 84 Ef
My Tho, S. Vietnam 79 Eh
Myzakyula, Estonia 63 Lg
Mziha, Tanzania 93 Hf
Mzimba, Malawi 93 Gg
Naantali, Finland 63 Kf
Naarden, Netherlands 60 Db
Nass, Eire 59 Cg
Nabadwip, India 87 Gd
Nabatiya, Lebanon 90 Dd
Nabberu, L., W. Australia 52 De
Nabha, India 86 Ee
Nablus, Jordan 90 De
Nacaome, Honduras 47 Bd
Nacimiento, Mexico 46 Db
Nacozari de Garcia, Mexico 46 Ca
Nadia. See Nabadwip
Nadiad, India 84 Dd
Nærøy, Norway 62 Dd
Næstved, Denmark 63 Dj
Nafels, Switzerland 61 Ea
Naft, Persia 88 Ee
Nafud Des., Arabia 88 Cd
Naga, S. Yemen 88 Eg
Naga, Philippines 79 Hh
Naga Hills, India 85 Hc
Nagalama, Uganda 93 Gd
Nagaland, India 83 Aa
Nagano, Japan 82 Ff
Nagaoka, Japan 82 Ff
Nagapattinam, India 84 Ef
Nagar, India 86 Ee
Nagar, Kashmir 86 Db
Nagar Karnul, India 84 Ee
Nagar Parkar, India 84 Dd
Nagasaki, Japan 82 Ah
Nagaur, India 84 Dc
Nagda, India 84 Ed
Nagercoil, India 84 Eg
Nagha Kalat, W. Pakistan 84 Cc
Nagina, India 87 Ba
Nagoya, Japan 82 Eg
Nagpur, India 84 Ed
Nagu, Finland 63 Jf
Nagykanizsa, Hungary 65 Ge
Naha, Japan 82 Mp
Nahael Niyeu, Argentina 50 Cf
Nahan, India 86 Ee
Nahariya, Israel 90 Dd
Nahavendi, Persia 88 Ee
Naifar, Iraq 88 Ec
Naihati, India 87 Gd
Nain, Persia 89 Fc
Naini Tal, India 87 Ba
Nain Sing Ra., Tibet 84 Fb
Nairn & co., Scotland 58 Ec
Nairobi, Kenya 93 He
Naisecho, Kenya 93 Hd
Naivasha & L., Kenya 93 He
Najd, Arabia 88 Dd
Najera, Spain 67 Da
Najibabad, India 87 Ba
Najin, Korea 78 Kb
Najira, Arabia 88 Ed
Nakajo, Japan 82 Fe
Nakatsu, Japan 82 Bh
Nakfa, Eritrea 93 Ha
Nakhichevan, Russia 74 De
Nakhla, Arabia 89 Fe
Nakhon Pathom, Siam 83 Cd
Nakhon Phanom, Siam 83 Cc
Nakhon Ratchasima, Siam 83 Cd
Nakhon Sawan, Siam 83 Cc
Nakhon Si Thammarat, Siam 83 Be
Nakl Mubarak, Arabia 88 Ce
Nakodar, India 86 De
Nakuru, Kenya 93 He
Nalagarh, India 86 Ee
Nalgonda, India 84 Ee
Nallamalai Hills, India 84 Ee
Nalusa, Zambia 92 Eg
Nalut, Libya 95 Hb
Namangan, Uzbek. 74 Gd
Namasagali, Uganda 93 Gd
Namatail, Moçambique 93 Hh
Nambala, Zambia 92 Fh
Namcha Barwa, China 78 Ce
Nam-dinh, N. Vietnam 83 Db
Namhoi, China 81 Fl
Namib Desert, S.-W. Africa 91 Ad
Namlea, I., Indonesia 79 Jl
Namling Dzong, Tibet 85 Gc
Nam Mao R. See Shweli R.
Namonuito, Is., Caroline Is. 98 Eg
Namorona, Madagascar 93 Nl
Nampa, Idaho 45 Ed
Nampula, Moçambique 93 Hh
Nams Vatn, Norway 62 Ed
Namsen R., Norway 62 Ed
Namsos, Norway 62 Dd
Namtsy, Russia 75 Mb
Namtu, Burma 85 Jd
Namur & prov., Belgium 60 Cd
Namutoni, S.-W. Africa 91 Bc
Namwala, Zambia 91 Dc
Namyang, China 81 Gk
Nana Kru, Liberia 94 Dh
Nanan. See Tayü
Nanao, Japan 82 Ef
Nanchang, China 81 Gh
Nancheng. See Hanchung
Nancheng, China 81 Hj
Nan-ching. See Nanking
Nanchung, China 80 Cg
Nancy, France 68 Gb
Nanda Devi, Mt., India 84 Eb
Nanded, India 84 Ee
Nanga Parbat, Kashmir 86 Dc
Nanjangud, India 84 Ef
Nankang. See Tsingtze
Nanking, China 80 Jg
Nannine, W. Australia 52 Ce
Nanning, China 81 Dl
Nanortalik, Greenland 41 Pd
Nanpara, India 87 Cb
Nanping, China 81 Jj
Nanripo, Moçambique 93 Hg
Nan Shan, China 78 Cc
Nantan, China 81 Ck
Nantes, France 68 Cc
Nanticoke, Pennsylvania 44 Bb
Nantucket, Massachusetts 44 Eb
Nantucket I., Massachusetts 44 Eb
Nantucket Sd., Mass 44 Eb
Nantung, China 80 Kf
Nanuque, Brazil 49 Jg
Nanyang, China 80 Ff
Nanyuki, Kenya 93 Hd
Naoetsu, Japan 82 Ff
Naoshera, Kashmir 86 Dd
Napa, California 45 Bf
Napanee, Ontario 40 Hc
Napas, Russia 74 Hc
Napier, New Zealand 51 Fc
Naples. See Napoli
Napoli, Italy 71 De
Napoli, G. di, Italy 71 De
Naqb Ashtar, Jordan 90 Dg
Nara, Mali 94 De
Nara, Japan 82 Dg
Naracoorte, S. Australia 53 Hg
Narathiwat, Siam 83 Ce
Narayanganj, E. Pakistan 85 Hd
Narbonne, France 69 Ee
Nares Ld., Greenland 41 Pa
Nari R., W. Pakistan 84 Cc
Narino, Colombia 48 Bc
Narken, Sweden 62 Kc
Narmada R., India 84 Dd
Narnaul, India 86 Df
Narok, Kenya 93 He
Narovchat, Russia 77 Fd
Narowal, W. Pakistan 86 Dd
Narrabri, New South Wales 53 Jf
Narragansett B., Rhode I. 44 Eb
Narranderra, New S. Wales 53 Jf
Narrogin, W. Australia 52 Cf
Narsimhapur, India 87 Bd
Narsinghgarh, India 87 Bc
Narva, Estonia 63 Ng
Narva Laht, Estonia 63 Mg
Narvik, Norway 62 Gb
Narwar, India 86 Ac
Naryan Mar, Russia 74 Eb
Narykary, Russia 74 Fb
Narym, Russia 74 Hc
Naryn, Kirgiz. 74 Hc
Naseby, New Zealand 51 Cf
Nashua & R., New Hamps. 44 Ea
Nashville, Tennessee 43 Jd
Nasi Järvi, Finland 63 Kf
Nasian, Ghana 94 Eg
Nasik, India 84 Dd
Nasirabad, India 84 Dc
Nassau, B. de, Chile 50 Cj
Nassau, Bahama Is. 47 Da
Nassau, I., Pacific Ocean 98 Jj
Nasser, L., Egypt 95 Md
Nässjö, Sweden 63 Fh
Nata, Panama 47 Ce
Natal, Brazil 49 Ke
Natal, Brazil 48 Ee
Natal, South Africa 91 Ee
Natal, Sumatra 79 Ck
Natchez, Mississippi 43 He
National City, California 45 Ej
Natividade, Brazil 49 Hf
Natron L., Tanzania 93 He
Nattavaara, Sweden 62 Jc
Naturaliste, C., W. Aust. 52 Bf
Naujoji Vilnia, Lithuania 63 Lj
Naukhas, S.-W. Africa 91 Bd
Naumburg, Germany 64 Dc
Nauplia. See Navplion
Naur, Jordan 90 Df
Nauru, I., Pacific Ocean 98 Fh
Naushahra. See Nowshera
Naushahro, W. Pakistan 84 Cc
Naushki, Russia 75 Kc
Nauta, Peru 48 Cd
Nautla, Mexico 46 Ec
Nava del Rey, Spain 66 Cb
Navalcarnero, Spain 66 Cb
Navalmoral, Spain 66 Cc
Navan, Eire 59 Cg
Navarino, I., Chile 50 Cj
Navarre, prov., France 69 Ce
Navarro, Argentina 50 Ee
Navojoa, Mexico 46 Cb
Navplion, Greece 73 Df
Navrongo, Ghana 94 Ef
Navsari, India 84 Dd
Nawa, Syria 90 Ee
Nawab Basoda, India 87 Bd
Nawabganj, India 87 Db
Nawabganj, India 87 Cb
Nawada, India 87 Ec
Nawahganj, India 87 Ba
Nawai, India 84 Ec
Nawalgarh, India 86 Dg
Náxos, I., Greece 73 Ef
Nayakhan, Russia 75 Qb
Nayarit, state, Mexico 46 Cc
Nayarit, Sa. de, Mexico 46 Dc
Nay Band, Persia 89 Fd
Nayfah, Arabia 89 Ff
Nayoro, Japan 82 Hb
Nazaré da Mata, Brazil 49 Ke
Nazareth, Israel 90 De
Nazas, Mexico 46 Db
Nazca, Peru 48 Cf
Naze, The. See Lindesnes
Nazilli, Turkey 88 Ab
Nazimovo, Russia 75 Jc
Ncheu, Malawi 93 Gg
Ndala, Tanzania 93 Ge
Ndeni, I., Santa Cruz Is. 98 Fj
Ndjolé, Gabon 92 Ce
Ndola, Zambia 93 Fg
Neagh L., N. Ireland 59 Cf
Neápolis, Crete 73 Eg
Near Is., Aleutian Islands 43 Um
Neath, Wales 59 Ej
Nebikon, Switzerland 61 Ca
Nebit-Dag, Turkmen 74 Ee
Nebo, Mt., Utah 45 Gf
Nebraska, state, U.S.A. 42 Fc
Necedah, Wisconsin 40 Ac
Neckar, R., Germany 64 Cd
Necochea, Argentina 50 Ee
Nederweert, Netherlands 60 Dc
Neede, Netherlands 60 Eb
Needles, California 45 Fh
Needles, The, Arizona 45 Fh
Needles, The, England 59 Fk
Neemuch, India 84 Dd
Neenah, Wisconsin 40 Bc
Neerpelt, Belgium 60 Dc
Negaunee, Michigan 40 Cb
Negombo, Ceylon 84 Eg
Negra Pt., Philippines 79 Hg
Negrais, C., Burma 85 He
Negritos, Peru 48 Ad
Negro, R., Argentina 50 De
Negro, R., Brazil 48 Ed
Negro, R., Uruguay 50 Ed
Negros, I., Philippines 79 Hj
Negru Vodă, Rumania 72 Gc
Nehbandān, Persia 89 Hc
Neilsville, Wisconsin 40 Ac
Neisse. See Nysa
Neiva, Colombia 48 Bc
Neksö, Bornholm I., Den. 63 Fj
Nelkan, Russia 75 Nc
Nellore, India 84 Ff
Nelma, Russia 75 Nd
Nelson, New Zealand 51 Dd
Néma, Mauritania 94 De
Neman, Russia 63 Kj
Nemikachi, L., Quebec 40 Jb
Nemours, Algeria. See Jhazaouet
Nemours, France 68 Eb
Nemunas, R., Lithuania 63 Kj
Nemuro, Japan 82 Jc
Nemuro B., Japan 82 Jc
Nenagh, Eire 59 Bh
Nendeln, Liechtenstein 61 Ea
Nene R., England 59 Gh
Neopolis, Brazil 49 Kf
Nepa, Russia 75 Kc
Nepal, Asia 85 Fc
Nepalganj, Nepal 87 Ca
Nérac, France 69 Dd
Nerchinsk, Russia 75 Lc
Neringa, Russia 76 Bd
Nerpio, Spain 67 Dc
Nes, Russia 74 Db
Nesna, Norway 62 Ec
Ness L., Scotland 58 Ec
Nesset, Norway 62 Ce
Nesslau, Switzerland 61 Ea
Nesthorn, Mt., Switzerland 61 Cb
Nesttun, Norway 63 Af
Netanya, Israel 90 Ce
Netherlands, W. Europe 56 Je
Nettuno, Italy 71 De
Neubrandenburg, Germany 64 Eb
Neuburg, Germany 64 Dd
Neuchâtel & canton, Switz. 61 Ba
Neuchâtel, L. de, Switz. 61 Bb
Neufchâteau, Belgium 60 De
Neufchâteau, France 68 Fb
Neufchâtel, France 68 Db
Neufelden, Austria 64 Ed
Neuhausen, Switzerland 61 Da
Neumünster, Germany 64 Ca
Neunkirch, Switzerland 61 Da
Neuquen, Argentina 50 Ce
Neusiedler See, Austria 65 Ge
Neuss, Germany 64 Bc
Neustadt, Germany 64 Da
Neustettin. See Szczecinek
Neustrelitz, Germany 64 Eb
Neu Ulm, Germany 64 Dd
Neuve Eglise. See Nieuwkerke
Neuveville, Switzerland 61 Ca
Neuvitas, Cuba 47 Db
Nevada, Missouri 43 Hd
Nevada, state, U.S.A. 42 Cd
Nevada, Sa., California 42 Bd
Nevada, Sa., Spain 66 Dd
Nevel, Russia 76 Fc
Nevel'sk, Russia 75 Pd
Nevers, France 68 Ec
Nevesinje, Yugoslavia 72 Bc
Neveyezhkino, Russia 77 Ge
Nevis, I., Leeward Islands 47 Gc
Nevşehir, Turkey 88 Bb
Nevyansk, Russia 77 Qb
New Albany, Indiana 43 Jd
New Amsterdam, Guyana 49 Fb
Newark, England 59 Gg
Newark, Delaware 44 Cc
Newark, New Jersey 44 Cb
Newark, Ohio 40 Ee
Newaygo, Michigan 40 Dd
New Bedford, Massachusetts 44 Eb
New Bern, N. Carolina 43 Ld
Newberry, Michigan 40 Db
New Bloomfield, Pa. 44 Bb
New Britain, Bismarck Arch. 98 Dh
New Britain, Connecticut 44 Db
New Brunswick, New Jersey 44 Cb
Newburgh, New York 44 Cb
Newbury, England 59 Gj
Newburyport, Mass. 44 Ea
New Caledonia, Pacific Oc. 98 Fk
Newcastle, Delaware 40 Jf
Newcastle, Natal 91 De
Newcastle, New S. Wales 53 Kf
Newcastle, N. Ireland 59 Cf
New Castle, New Jersey 44 Cc
New Castle, Pennsylvania 40 Fe
Newcastle Emlyn, Wales 59 Dh
Newcastle-under-Lyme, Eng. 59 Fg
Newcastle-upon-Tyne, Eng. 58 Fe
Newcastle Waters, N.T., Australia 53 Fc
Newchwang. See Yingkow
New City, New York 44 Cb
New Cumberland, W. Va. 40 Fe
New England Ra., N.S.W. 53 Kf
Newfane, Vermont 44 Da
New Forest, England 59 Fk
New Galloway, Scotland 58 Ee
New Georgia, I., Solomon Is. 98 Eh
New Guinea, Pacific Ocean 55 Pj
New Hampshire, state, U.S.A. 43 Mc
New Hanover, Bismarck Arch. 98 Dh
New Haven, Connecticut 40 Ke
Newhaven, England 59 Hk
New Hebrides, Is., Pac. Oc. 98 Fj
New Iberia, Louisiana 43 Hf
New Ireland, Bismarck Arch. 98 Eh
New Jersey, state, U.S.A. 43 Mc
New Liskeard, Ontario 40 Gb
New Lisbon, Wisconsin 40 Ad
New London, Connecticut 44 Db
New London, Wisconsin 40 Bc
Newmarket, Eire 59 Bh
Newmarket, England 59 Hh
Newmarket, Ontario 40 Gc
New Mexico, state, U.S.A. 42 Ee
New Norfolk, Tasmania 53 Jh
New Orleans, Louisiana 43 Jf
New Plymouth, N.Z. 51 Ec
Newport, Britain 59 Fj
Newport, I. of W., England 59 Gk
Newport, Kentucky 40 Df
Newport, New Hampshire 44 Da
Newport, Rhode Island 40 Le
Newport, Vermont 40 Kc
Newport News, Virginia 43 Ld
New Providence, I., Bahama Islands 47 Db
Newquay, England 59 Dk
New Rochelle, New York 44 Db
New Ross, Eire 59 Ch
Newry, N. Ireland 59 Cf
New Siberian Islands. See Novosibirskiye Ostrova
New South Wales, state, Australia 53 Jf
Newton, Massachusetts 44 Ea
Newton, New Jersey 44 Cb
Newton Abbot, England 59 Ek
Newton Stewart, Scotland 59 Ef
Newtown, Wales 59 Eh
Newtownards, N. Ireland 59 Df
New York, New York 40 Ke
New York, state, U.S.A. 43 Lc
New Zealand 51
Nexö. See Neksö
Neya, Russia 77 Ha
Neyriz, Persia 89 Fd
Neyshābūr, Persia 89 Gb
Nezhin, Ukraine 76 Gf
Nganglaring Tso, Tibet 85 Fb
N'Gaoundéré, Cameroon 95 Hg
Ngapara, New Zealand 51 Cf
Ngaruawahia, New Zealand 51 Eb
Ngatik, I., Caroline Islands 98 Eg
Ngauruhoe, Mt., N.Z. 51 Ec
Ngeuni, Sudan 95 Lg
Ngong, Kenya 93 He
Ngoring Nor, China 78 Cd
Nguigmi, Niger 95 Hf
Ngulu, I., Pacific Ocean 98 Cg
Ngwasi, Tanzania 93 Hf
Nha-Trang, S. Vietnam 83 Dd
Nhill, Victoria 53 Hg
Niafounké, Mali 94 Ee
Niagara, Ontario 40 Gd
Niagara Falls, New York 40 Gd
Niagara Falls, Ontario 40 Gd
Niah, Sarawak 79 Fk
Niamey, Niger 94 Ff
Nia Nia, Congo 93 Fd
Niapa, Mt., Borneo 79 Gk
Nias, I., Indonesia 79 Ck
Nicaragua, rep., Cent. Amer. 47 Bd
Nicaragua L., Nicaragua 47 Bd
Nicastro, Italy 71 Ff
Nice, France 69 Ge
Nicholson, Ontario 40 Ea
Nicobar Is., Indian Ocean 85 Hg
Nicolet, Quebec 40 Kb
Nicosia, Cyprus 90 Bb
Nicoya & Pen., Costa Rica 47 Bd

Nidau, *Switzerland* 61 Ca
Nidzica, *Poland* 65 Jb
Niedere Tauern, *Austria* 64 Ee
Niedersachsen, *Germany* 64 Cb
Nielle, *Ivory Coast* 94 Df
Niére, *Chad* 95 Kf
Nieuw Amsterdam, *Surinam* 49 Fb
Nieuwendijk, *Netherlands* 60 Cc
Nieuwersluis, *Netherlands* 60 Cb
Nieuwkerke, *Belgium* 60 Ad
Nieuwkoop, *Netherlands* 60 Cb
Nieuw Nickerie, *Surinam* 49 Fb
Nieuwpoort, *Belgium* 60 Cc
Nieuwpoort, *Netherlands* 60 Cc
Nieves, *Mexico* 46 Dc
Nièvre, dep., *France* 68 Ec
Nigde, *Turkey* 88 Bb
Niger, *W. Africa* 94 Ge
Niger R., *W. Africa* 94 Ff
Nigeria, *W. Africa* 94 Gg
Nighasan, *India* 87 Ca
Nigula, *Estonia* 63 Mg
Niigata, *Japan* 82 Ff
Niihau, I., *Hawaiian Is.* 98 Je
Niitaka Chain, *Taiwan* 81 Kl
Nijil, *Jordan* 90 Dg
Nijkerk, *Netherlands* 60 Db
Nijmegen, *Netherlands* 60 Dj
Nikaría. See Ikaría, I.
Nikiforos, *Greece* 72 Ed
Nikki, *Dahomey* 94 Fg
Nikko Nat. Park, *Japan* 82 Ff
Nikolayev, *Ukraine* 76 Gh
Nikolayevsk-na-Amure, *Russ.* 75 Pc
Nikolayevskiy, *Russia* 77 Ge
Nikolo-Berezovka, *Russia* 77 Mb
Nikolo-Kozel'sk, *Ukraine* 76 Hh
Nikol'sk, *Russia* 77 Ne
Nikol'skaya Pestrovka, *Russ.* 77 Gd
Nikopol, *Ukraine* 76 Jh
Niksar, *Turkey* 88 Ca
Nikšić, *Yugoslavia* 72 Bc
Nila, I., *Indonesia* 79 Jm
Nile, R., *N. Africa* 95 Me
Niles, *Michigan* 40 Ce
Nilgiri, *India* 85 Gd
Nilgiri Hills, *India* 84 Ef
Nilphamari, *E. Pakistan* 87 Gc
Nimach (Neemuch), *India* 84 Dd
Nîmes, *France* 69 Fe
Nimgiri, Mt., *India* 85 Fe
Nine de Julio, *Argentina* 50 De
Nineveh, *Iraq* 88 Db
Ningan, *China* 78 Jb
Ninganpao, *China* 80 Bd
Ningerh. See Puerh
Ninghai, *China* 81 Kh
Ninghsien, *China* 81 Fj
Ninghsien (Ningpo) *China* 81 Kh
Ningkwo. See Suancheng
Ninglingting. See Kinki
Ningpo, *China* 81 Kh
Ning-sia, *China* 80 Cc
Ningsiang, *China* 81 Fh
Ningteh. See Yinchwan
Ning-wu-fu, *China* 80 Fc
Ning-yüan chow, *China* 80 Kb
Ning-yüan-ting, *China* 80 Fb
Ninh-binh, *N. Vietnam* 83 Db
Ninh Hoa. See Nha Trang
Ninove, *Belgium* 60 Cd
Niobrara R., *Nebraska* 42 Fc
Nioro, *Mali* 94 De
Niort, *France* 68 Cc
Nios. See Íos, I.
Nipe, B. de, *Cuba* 47 Db
Nipissing, L., *Ontario* 40 Gb
Niquelandia, *Brazil* 49 Hf
Nirmal, *India* 84 Ee
Nis, *Yugoslavia* 72 Cc
Nischu, *Kashmir* 84 Eb
Nish. See Nis
Nishapur. See Neyshābūr
Nishio, *Japan* 82 Eg
Nisiros, I., *Greece* 73 Ff
Nissan, *Solomon Islands* 98 Eh
Nissi, *Estonia* 63 Lg
Niterói, *Brazil* 49 Jh
Nith R., *Scotland* 58 Ee
Nitra, *Czechoslovakia* 65 Hd
Nitrianske Pravno, *Czech.* 65 Hd
Niue, I., *Cook Islands* 98 Jj
Niut, Mt., *Borneo* 79 Ek
Nivala, *Finland* 62 Le
Nivelles, *Belgium* 60 Cd
Nivernais, prov., *France* 68 Ec
Nizamabad, *India* 84 Ee
Nizampatam, *India* 84 Fe
Nizana, *Israel* 90 Cg
Nizhne Udinsk, *Russia* 75 Jc
Nizhnie Lomov, *Russia* 77 Fd
Nizhniye Kresty, *Russia* 75 Rb
Nizhniy Tagil, *Russia* 77 Pb
Nizhnyaya Pesha, *Russia* 74 Db
Nizke Tatry, *Czech.* 65 Hd
Njombe, *Tanzania* 93 Gf
Nkonde, *Tanzania* 93 Gf
N'Kongsamba, *Cameroon* 95 Gh
Nmai R., *Burma* 85 Jc
Noagarh, *India* 85 Fd
Noakhali. See Sudharam
Noanama, *Colombia* 48 Bc
Noatak R., *Alaska* 43 Wl
Nocera, *Italy* 71 Ee
Nochistlan, *Mexico* 46 Ed
Noemfoor, I., *New Guinea* 79 Kl
Nœrbö, *Norway* 63 Ag
Nogales, *Arizona* 42 Ee
Nogaro, *France* 69 Ce
Nogent-le-Rotrou, *France* 68 Db
Nogent-sur-Seine, *France* 68 Eb
Noginsk, *Russia* 76 Ld
Nohar, *India* 86 Df
Noirmoutier, I. de, *France* 68 Bc
Nokhtuysk, *Russia* 75 Lc
Nola, *Cent. Afr. Rep.* 92 Dd
Nola, *Italy* 71 Ee
Nome, *Alaska* 43 Wl
Nominingue Ls., *Quebec* 40 Jb
Nomoi, Is., *Caroline Is.* 98 Eg
Nonancourt, *France* 68 Db
Nong-han, *Siam* 83 Cc
Nong Khai, *Siam* 83 Cc
Nongoma, *Natal* 91 Ee
Nonni, R. (Nun), *China* 78 Ha
Nonno, *Ethiopia* 93 Hc
Nonoava, *Mexico* 46 Cb
Nonouti, I., *Gilbert Islands* 98 Gh
Nōo, *Estonia* 63 Mg
Noonkanbah, *W. Aust.* 52 Dc
Noordeloos, *Netherlands* 60 Cc
Noordwolde, *Netherlands* 60 Eb
Nora, *Sweden* 63 Fg
Noranda, *Quebec* 40 Ga
Nord, dep., *France* 68 Ea
Nord Cap. See Horn, C.
Norddal, *Norway* 62 Be
Nordenshelda, Arkh., *Russia* 75 Ja
Nordhausen, *Germany* 64 Dc
Nordkapp, *Norway* 62 La
Nordkinn Halvöya, *Norway* 62 Ma
Nördlingen, *Germany* 64 Dd
Nordreisa, *Norway* 62 Jb
Nordrhein-Westfalen, *Ger.* 64 Bc
Nord Slesvig. See Jylland. S.
Nordstrand I., *Germany* 64 Ca
Nordvik, *Russia* 75 La
Nore, *Norway* 63 Cf
Nore R., *Eire* 59 Ch
Norfolk, *Nebraska* 42 Gc
Norfolk, *Virginia* 43 Ld
Norfolk, co., *England* 59 Hh
Norfolk I., *Pacific Ocean* 98 Fk
Norgama, *W. Pakistan* 84 Cc
Norheimsund, *Norway* 63 Bf
Norily, *Russia* 74 Hb
Normandie, prov., *France* 68 Cb
Normanby I., *Papua* 53 Ka
Normanton, *Queensland* 53 Hc
Norquiñ, *Argentina* 50 Be
Norquiñco, *Argentina* 50 Bf
Norris L., *Tennessee* 43 Kd
Norristown, *Pennsylvania* 44 Cb
Norrköping, *Sweden* 63 Gg
Norrsundet, *Sweden* 63 Gf
Norrtalje, *Sweden* 63 Hg
Norseman, *W. Australia* 52 Df
Norsholm, *Sweden* 63 Fg
North C., *Antarctica* 100 Lb
North C., *New Zealand* 51 Da
North Chan., *Ontario* 40 Eb
North Chan., *Scot.-N. Ire.* 58 De
North Downs, *England* 59 Hj
North I., *New Zealand* 51 Dc
North Sea, *W. Europe* 56 Gd
North Adams, *Massachusetts* 44 Da
Northallerton, *England* 59 Gf
Northam, *W. Australia* 52 Cf
Nilphamari...
Northampton, *Mass.* 44 Da
Northampton, *W. Aust.* 52 Be
Northampton & co., *Eng.* 59 Gh
North Bay, *Ontario* 40 Gb
North Bend, *Oregon* 45 Ad
North Berwick, *Scotland* 58 Fd
North Borneo. See Sabah
Northbridge, *Massachusetts* 44 Ea
North Carolina, state, *U.S.A.* 43 Kd
North Creek, *New York* 40 Jd
North Dakota, state, *U.S.A.* 42 Fb
North-East Foreland, *Greenland* 41 Ma
Northern Circars, *India* 84 Fe
Northern Ireland, *Brit. Isles* 59 Cf
Northern Rhodesia. See Zambia
Northern Territory, *Aust.* 52 Fc
North Land, See Severnaya Zemlya
North Little Rock, *Ark.* 43 He
North Platte & R., *Neb.* 42 Fc
North Pole, *Arctic Ocean* 41 a
North Riding, *Yorks., Eng.* 59 Ff
North Ronaldsay, I., *Orkney* 58 Fa
North Tonawanda, *N.Y.* 44 Aa
Northumberland, co., *Eng.* 58 Fe
Northumberland, *Pa.* 44 Bb
North Vietnam, *S.E. Asia* 81 Bm
Northville, *New York* 40 Jd
North West C., *W. Aust.* 52 Bd
Norton Sd., *Alaska* 43 Wl
Norwalk, *Connecticut* 44 Db
Norwalk, *Ohio* 40 Ee
Norwalk, *Michigan* 40 Cc
Norway, kingdom, *North-West Europe* 56 Kc
Norwich, *Connecticut* 44 Db
Norwich, *England* 59 Hh
Norwich, *New York* 44 Ca
Norwood, *Massachusetts* 44 Ea
Norwood, *New York* 40 Jc
Noshiro, *Japan* 82 Fd
Nosseghem, *Belgium* 60 Cd
Nossi Bé, I., *Madagascar* 93 Nj
Noto, *Sicily* 71 Eg
Noto Pen., *Japan* 82 Ef
Notodden, *Norway* 63 Cg
Nottawasaga B., *Ontario* 40 Fc
Nottingham & co., *England* 59 Gh
Nouakchott, *Mauritania* 94 Be
Nova Becej, *Yugoslavia* 72 Cb
Nova Chaves, *Angola* 92 Dg
Nova Cruz, *Brazil* 49 Ke
Nova Freixo, *Moçambique* 91 Gb
Nova Gaia, *Angola* 92 Dg
Nova Goa, *Goa* 84 Dg
Nova Iorque, *Brazil* 49 Je
Nova Lisboa, *Angola* 92 Dg
Novara, *Italy* 70 Bc
Nova Sofala, *Moçambique* 91 Ed
Nova Venecia, *Brazil* 49 Jg
Novaya Sibir, Ostrov, *Russ.* 75 Qa
Novaya Zemlya, *Russia* 74 Ea
Nové Zámky, *Czech.* 65 Hd
Novgorod, *Russia* 76 Gb
Novi, *Yugoslavia* 70 Ec
Novi Pazar, *Bulgaria* 72 Fc
Novi Pazar, *Yugoslavia* 72 Cc
Novi Sad, *Yugoslavia* 72 Bb
Novocherkassk, *Russia* 77 Eg
Novokuznetsk, *Russia* 74 Hc
Novo Mesto, *Yugoslavia* 70 Ec
Novomoskovsk, *Russia* 76 Ld
Novomoskovsk, *Ukraine* 76 Jg
Novo Redondo, *Angola* 92 Cg
Novorossiysk, *Russia* 74 Cd
Novoshakhtinsk, *Russia* 77 Dg
Novosibirsk, *Russia* 74 Hc
Novosibirskiye Ostrova, *Russia* 75 Na
Novourgench. See Urgench
Novska, *Yugoslavia* 70 Fc
Novy Jičin, *Czechoslovakia* 65 Hd
Novyy Port, *Russia* 74 Gb
Nowa Wilejka. See Naujoji Vilnia
Nowgong, *India* 85 Hc
Nowra, *New South Wales* 53 Kf
Nowshera, *W. Pakistan* 86 Cc
Nowy Sacz, *Poland* 65 Jd
Nowy Targ, *Poland* 65 Jd
Nowy Tomysl, *Poland* 65 Gb
Noya, *Spain* 66 Aa
Nozay, *France* 68 Cc
Nsanje, *Malawi* 91 Fc
Ntungamo, *Uganda* 93 Ge
Nuanetsi, *Rhodesia* 91 Ed
Nuassuak Pen., *Greenland* 41 Pb
Nueces R., *Texas* 42 Gf
Nueva, I., *Chile & Argent.* 50 Cj
Nueva Imperial, *Chile* 50 Be
Nueva Lubeca, *Argentina* 50 Bf
Nuevo, G., *Argentina* 50 Df
Nuevo Laredo, *Mexico* 46 Eb
Nuevo Leon, state, *Mexico* 46 Db
Nuits St Georges, *France* 68 Fc
Nukuhiva, I., *Marquesas, I.* 99 Lh
Nukuoro, I., *Caroline Is.* 98 Eg
Nukus, *Uzbek.* 74 Ed
Nules, *Spain* 67 Ec
Nullagine, *W. Australia* 52 Dd
Nullarbor, *S. Australia* 52 Ff
Nullarbor Plain, *W. Aust.* 52 Ef
Numata, *Japan* 82 Ff
Numazu, *Japan* 82 Fg
Nunchia, *Colombia* 48 Cb
Nunivak I., *Alaska* 43 Wl
Nunkiang, *China* 78 Ja
Nuoro, *Sardinia* 71 Be
Nuquí, *Colombia* 48 Bb
Nuri, *Mexico* 46 Cb
Nurmes, *Finland* 62 Ne
Nürnberg, *Germany* 64 Dd
Nurpur, *India* 86 Dd
Nurri, *Sardinia* 71 Bf
Nusaybin, *Turkey* 88 Db
Nushki, *W. Pakistan* 84 Cc
Nutrias, *Venezuela* 48 Cb
Nuwara Eliya, *Ceylon* 84 Fg
Nyada, *Sweden* 62 Ge
Nyåker, *Sweden* 62 He
Nyala, *Sudan* 95 Kf
Nyalikungu, *Tanzania* 93 Ge
Nyamlell, *Sudan* 95 Lg
Nyandoma, *Russia* 74 Db
Nyantakara, *Tanzania* 93 Ge
Nyanza, *Rwanda* 93 Fe
Nyasa, L., *Malawi* 93 Gg
Nyasaland. See Malawi
Nyazepetrovsk, *Russia* 77 Pb
Nyda, *Russia* 74 Gb
Nyeri, *Kenya* 93 He
Nyhammar, *Sweden* 63 Ff
Nyiregyháza, *Hungary* 65 Je
Nyköbing, *Denmark* 63 Dj
Nyköbing, *Denmark* 63 Ch
Nyköbing, I., *Denmark* 56 Le
Nyköping, *Sweden* 63 Gg
Nylstroom, *Transvaal* 91 Dd
Nymagee, *N.S.W.* 53 Jf
Nyngan, *New South Wales* 53 Jf
Nyon, *Switzerland* 61 Bb
Nyonga, *Tanzania* 93 Gf
Nyons, *France* 69 Fd
Nysa, *Poland* 65 Gc
Nysted, *Denmark* 63 Dj
Nyurba, *Russia* 75 Lb
Nyuya, *Russia* 75 Lb
Nzega, *Tanzania* 93 Ge
Oahu, I., *Hawaiian Islands* 99 Ke
Oak Ridge, *Tennessee* 43 Kd
Oakan, *Japan* 82 Jc
Oakham, *England* 59 Gh
Oakland, *California* 45 Bg
Oakland, *Maryland* 40 Gf
Oakville, *Ontario* 40 Gd
Oamaru, *New Zealand* 51 Cf
Oates Ld., *Antarctica* 100 Kc
Oaxaca & state, *Mexico* 46 Ed
Ob, R., *Russia* 74 Fb
Obama, *Japan* 82 Dg
Oban, *New Zealand* 51 Bg
Oban, *Scotland* 58 Dd
Obbia, *Somalia* 93 Kc
Obeh, *Afghanistan* 89 Hc
Oberammergau, *Germany* 64 De
Oberhausen, *Germany* 64 Bc
Oberriet, *Switzerland* 61 Ea
Oberwald, *Switzerland* 61 Db
Obi, I., *Indonesia* 79 Jl
Obidos, *Brazil* 49 Fd
Obidos, *Portugal* 66 Ac
Obihiro, *Japan* 82 Hc
Obo, *Cent. Afr. Rep.* 95 Lg
Obo, *Mongolia* 78 Db
Obock, *Fr. Somaliland* 93 Jb
Oborona, *Russia* 77 Ed
Obrayera, *Nicaragua* 47 Cd
Obskaya Guba, *Russia* 74 Gb
Ocampo, *Mexico* 46 Ec
Ocana, *Colombia* 48 Cb
Ocana, *Spain* 66 Dc
Occidental, Cord., *Colombia* 48 Bc
Ocean I., *Pacific Ocean* 98 Fh
Ocean City, *New Jersey* 44 Cc
Ochil Hills, *Scotland* 58 Ed
Ocland, *Rumania* 72 Ea
Ocoa, B. de, *Rep. Dom.* 47 Ec
Ocona, *Peru* 48 Cg
Oconto, *Wisconsin* 40 Bc
Ocos, *Guatemala* 46 Fe
Ocotal, *Nicaragua* 47 Bd
Ocumare, *Venezuela* 48 Da
Ocussi Ambeno, *Port. Timor* 79 Hm
Oda, *Ghana* 94 Eg
Odaka, *Japan* 82 Gf
Odate, *Japan* 82 Gd
Odawara, *Japan* 82 Fg
Odemira, *Portugal* 66 Ad
Odemiş, *Turkey* 88 Ab
Odense, *Denmark* 63 Dj
Oder R., *Germany* 64 Fb
Odessa, *Ukraine* 76 Gh
Odienné, *Ivory Coast* 94 Dg
Odoorn, *Netherlands* 60 Eb
Odorhei, *Rumania* 72 Ea
Odra R., *Poland* 64 Fb
Odzala, *Fr. Congo* 92 Cd
Oedelem, *Belgium* 60 Bc
Oeiras, *Brazil* 49 Je
Of, *Turkey* 88 Da
Offaly (Ui Failghe), co., *Eire* 59 Bg
Offenbach, *Germany* 64 Cc
Ogaki, *Japan* 82 Eg
Ogden, *Utah* 45 He
Ogdensburg, *New York* 40 Jc
Ogoja, *Nigeria* 94 Gg
Ogr, *Sudan* 95 Lf
Ogulin, *Yugoslavia* 70 Ec
Ohakune, *New Zealand* 51 Ec
Ohau, L., *New Zealand* 51 Bf
Ohey, *Belgium* 60 Dd
O'Higgins, Mt., *Chile* 50 Bg
Ohio, state, *U.S.A.* 43 Kc
Ohio R., *U.S.A.* 43 Jd
Ohrid, *Yugoslavia* 72 Cd
Ohridsko Jezero, *Yugoslavia* 72 Cd
Ohura, *New Zealand* 51 Ec
Oiapoque, R., *Brazil, etc.* 49 Gc
Oignies, *Belgium* 60 Cd
Oil City, *Pennsylvania* 44 Ab
Oil Springs, *Ontario* 40 Ed
Oirschot, *Netherlands* 60 Dc
Oise, dep., *France* 68 Eb
Oita, *Japan* 82 Bh
Oiticica, *Brazil* 49 Je
Ojinaga, *Mexico* 46 Db
Ojiya, *Japan* 82 Ff
Ojacaliente, *Mexico* 46 Dc
Ojo de Agua, *Argentina* 50 Dc
Ojo del Toro, Pico, *Cuba* 47 Dc
Oka R., *Russia* 77 Fc
Okahandja, *S.-W. Africa* 91 Bd
Okanogan R., *Washington* 42 Cb
Okaukuejo, *S.-W. Africa* 91 Bc
Okavango, R., *Angola* 91 Bc
Okayama, *Japan* 82 Cg
Okeechobee, L., *Florida* 43 Kf
Okehampton, *England* 59 Ek
Okha, *Russia* 75 Pc
Okhansk, *Russia* 77 Mb
Okhotsk, *Russia* 75 Pc
Okhotsk, Sea of, *Russia* 75 Pc
Okinawa Gunto, *Japan* 82 Mp
Oki gunto, *Japan* 82 Cf
Oklahoma, state, *U.S.A.* 42 Gd
Oklahoma City, *Oklahoma* 42 Gd
Okmulgee, *Oklahoma* 42 Gd
Oktyabrskoy Revolyutsiy, Os., *Russia* 75 Ja
Okućani, *Yugoslavia* 70 Fc
Okuru, *New Zealand* 51 Be
Okushiri I., *Japan* 82 Fc
Olaine, *Latvia* 63 Kh
Olanchito, *Honduras* 47 Bc
Öland, I., *Sweden* 63 Gh
Olasan, *Ethiopia* 93 Kc
Olavarria, *Argentina* 50 De
Olawa, *Poland* 65 Gc
Olbia, *Sardinia* 71 Be
Olcott, *New York* 44 Aa
Oldcastle, *Eire* 59 Cg
Oldenburg, *Germany* 64 Da
Oldenburg, *Germany* 64 Cb
Oldenzaal, *Netherlands* 60 Eb
Old Forge, *Pennsylvania* 44 Cb
Oldham, *England* 59 Fg
Old Orchard Beach, *Maine* 44 Ea
Olean, *New York* 44 Aa
Olecko, *Poland* 65 Ka
Olekminsk, *Russia* 75 Mb
Olenek, *Russia* 75 Lb
Olenek, R., *Russia* 75 Ma
Olenekskiy Zaliv, *Russia* 75 Ma
Oléron, I. d', *France* 68 Cd
Olga, *Russia* 75 Nd
Olifants Kloof, *Botswana* 91 Cd
Olimbos, Mts., *Greece* 73 Dd
Oliva de Jerez, *Spain* 66 Bc
Olivares, *Spain* 67 Dc
Olivares, Cerro de, *Argent.* 50 Cd
Oliveira, *Brazil* 49 Jf
Olivenza, *Spain* 66 Bc
Olivone, *Switzerland* 61 Db
Ollague, *Chile* 48 Dh
Ollague, Mt., *Bolivia* 48 Dh
Olmedo, *Spain* 66 Cb
Olney, *Illinois* 40 Bf
Olomouc, *Czechoslovakia* 65 Gd
Olot, *Spain* 67 Ga
Olovyannaya, *Russia* 75 Lc
Olpe, *Germany* 64 Bc
Olst, *Netherlands* 60 Eb
Olsztyn, *Poland* 65 Jb
Olten, *Switzerland* 61 Ca
Oltu, *Turkey* 88 Da
Oltul R., *Rumania* 72 Eb
Olvera, *Spain* 66 Cd
Olympia, *Greece* 73 Cf
Olympia, *Washington* 45 Bb
Olympic Nat. Park, *Wash.* 42 Bb
Olympus. See Olimbos
Olympus, Mt., *Washington* 42 Bb
Olyutorskiy Zaliv, *Russia* 75 Rb
Omagh, *N. Ireland* 59 Cf
Omaguas, *Peru* 48 Cd
Omaha, *Nebraska* 42 Gc
Oman, *Arabia* 89 Ge
Oman, G. of, *Arabia-Persia* 89 Ge
Omarama, *N.Z.* 51 Cf
Omaruru, *S.-W. Africa* 91 Bd
Ombombo, *S.-W. Africa* 91 Ac
Omdurman, *Sudan* 95 Me
Omer, *Michigan* 40 Ec
Ometepec, *Mexico* 46 Ed
Ommen, *Netherlands* 60 Eb
Omoa, *Honduras* 47 Bc
Omsk, *Russia* 74 Gc
Omuta, *Japan* 82 Bh
Omutninsk, *Russia* 77 La
Onaway, *Michigan* 40 Dc
Öndör Hän, *Mongolia* 78 Fa
Onega & R., *Russia* 74 Cb
Onehunga, *New Zealand* 51 Eb
Oneida, *New York* 44 Ca
Oneida L., *New York* 44 Ca
Oneonta, *New York* 44 Ca
Onezhskoye Oz., *Russia* 74 Cb
Ongole, *India* 84 Fe
Ongudai, *Russia* 74 Hc
Oniiba, *S.-W. Africa* 91 Bc
Onitsha, *Nigeria* 94 Gg
Onjül, *Mongolia* 78 Ea
Onoto, *Venezuela* 48 Db
Onotoa I., *Gilbert Islands* 98 Gh
Onslow, *W. Australia* 52 Bd
Onslow B., *N. Carolina* 43 Le
Ontario, L., *U.S.A.-Canada* 43 Lc
Onteniente, *Spain* 67 Ec
Ontiñena, *Spain* 67 Fb
Oodnadatta, *S. Australia* 53 Ge
Ooldea, *S. Australia* 52 Ef
Oostburg, *Netherlands* 60 Bc
Oostcamp, *Belgium* 60 Bc
Oostende. See Ostende
Ooster Schelde, *Netherlands* 60 Bc
Oosterwolde, *Netherlands* 60 Eb
Oosthuizen, *Netherlands* 60 Cb
Oostmalle, *Belgium* 60 Cc
Oostvoorne, *Netherlands* 60 Cc
Ootacamund, *India* 84 Ef
Opala, *Russia* 75 Qc
Opari, *Sudan* 95 Mh
Opatija, *Yugoslavia* 70 Ec
Opava, *Czechoslovakia* 65 Gd
Ophir, Mt., *W. Malaysia* 83 Cf
Ophoven, *Belgium* 60 Dc
Opochka, *Russia* 76 Fc
Opodepe, *Mexico* 46 Ba
Opole, *Poland* 65 Gc
Oporto. See Porto
Opotiki, *New Zealand* 51 Fc
Oppa B., *Japan* 82 Ge
Oppein. See Opole
Opunake, *New Zealand* 51 Dc
Oputo, *Mexico* 46 Ca
Oqair. See Uqair
Oradea, *Rumania* 72 Ca
Orai, *India* 87 Bc
Oran, *Algeria* 94 Ea
Orange, *France* 69 Fd
Orange, *Massachusetts* 44 Da
Orange, *Texas* 43 He
Orange R., *S. Africa* 91 Be
Orange Free State, *S. Africa* 91 De
Orangeburg, *S. Carolina* 43 Ke
Orangeville, *Ontario* 40 Fd
Oranje Geb., *Surinam* 49 Fc
Oras, *Philippines* 79 Jh
Orăştie, *Rumania* 72 Db
Orasul Stalin. See Brasov
Oravita, *Rumania* 72 Cb
Oravská Magura, *Czech.* 65 Hd
Orbe, *Switzerland* 61 Bb
Orcera, *Spain* 67 Dc
Orchha, *India* 87 Bc
Ord, Mt., *W. Australia* 52 Ec
Ordenes, *Spain* 66 Aa
Ord River, *W. Australia* 52 Ec
Ordu, *Turkey* 88 Ca
Ordzhonikidze, *Russia* 74 Dd
Ordzhonikidzegrad. See Bezhitsa
Örebro, *Sweden* 63 Fg
Oregon, *Illinois* 40 Bd
Oregon, state, *U.S.A.* 42 Bc
Oregon City, *Oregon* 45 Bc
Öregrund, *Sweden* 63 Hf
Orekhovo Zuyevo, *Russia* 76 Ld
Orel, *Russia* 76 Ke
Orellana, *Peru* 48 Be
Orellana, *Spain* 66 Cc
Orenburg, *Russia* 77 Me
Orense, *Spain* 66 Ba
Orepuki, *New Zealand* 51 Ag
Oresund, *Denmark-Sweden* 63 Ej
Orgaña, *Spain* 67 Fa
Orgaz, *Spain* 66 Dc
Orhon R., *Mongolia* 78 Da
Oriental, Cord., *Colombia* 48 Cb
Oriental, Cord., *Peru* 48 Be
Orihuela, *Spain* 67 Ec
Orillia, *Ontario* 40 Gc
Orinoco, R., *Venezuela* 48 Eb
Orissa, state, *India* 85 Fd
Oristano & G. di., *Sardinia* 71 Bf
Orivesi, *Finland* 62 Ne
Oriximiná, *Brazil* 49 Fd
Orizaba, *Mexico* 46 Ed
Orizare, *Bulgaria* 72 Fc
Orizona, *Brazil* 49 Hg
Orkanger, *Norway* 62 Ce
Orkney, *Scotland* 58 Fb
Örland, *Norway* 62 Ce
Orlando, *Florida* 43 Kf
Orléanais, prov., *France* 68 Dc
Orléans, *France* 68 Dc
Orleans, I. of, *Quebec* 40 Lb
Orléansville. See El-Asnam
Orman, *Syria* 90 Ee
Ormara, *W. Pakistan* 84 Bc
Ormondville, *New Zealand* 51 Fd
Ornach, *W. Pakistan* 84 Cc
Orne, dep., *France* 68 Cb
Örnsköldsvik, *Sweden* 62 He
Orochen, *Russia* 75 Mc
Orocue, *Colombia* 48 Cc
Oroluk, I., *Caroline Islands* 98 Eg
Oron. See Kochumdek
Orontes, R., *Syria* 88 Cb
Orosei, G. di, *Sardinia* 71 Be
Orosi, Vol., *Costa Rica* 47 Bd
Orsa, *Sweden* 63 Ff
Orsha, *White Russia* 76 Gd
Orsières, *Switzerland* 61 Cb
Orsk, *Russia* 77 Pe
Orsova, *Rumania* 72 Db
Ortegal, C., *Spain* 66 Ba
Orthez, *France* 69 Ce
Ortiz, *Mexico* 46 Cb
Ortiz, *Venezuela* 48 Db
Orugueira, *Spain* 66 Ba
Orulgan, Khrebet, *Russia* 75 Mb
Oruro, *Bolivia* 48 Dg
Orust, *Sweden* 63 Dg
Oryekhovo, *Russia* 77 Ge
Osa, *Russia* 77 Ge
Osa, *Russia* 77 Mb
Osaka, *Japan* 82 Dg
Oschiri, *Sardinia* 71 Be
Oscoda, *Michigan* 40 Ec
Osen, *Norway* 62 Dd
Osh, *Kirgiz.* 74 Gd
Oshawa, *Ontario* 40 Gd
O Shima, *Japan* 82 Fg
Oshkosh, *Wisconsin* 40 Bc
Oshnoviyeh, *Persia* 88 Eb
Osijek, *Yugoslavia* 72 Bb
Osilo, *Sardinia* 71 Be
Osipenko, *Russia* 75 Nc
Osipovichi, *Belorussia* 76 Fe
Osire Sud, *S.-W. Africa* 91 Bd
Oskarshamn, *Sweden* 63 Gh
Oslo, *Norway* 63 Dg
Oslo Fd., *Norway* 63 Dg
Osmanabad, *India* 84 Ee
Osmancik, *Turkey* 88 Ba
Osnabrück, *Germany* 64 Cb
Osorio, *Brazil* 50 Fc
Osorno, *Chile* 50 Bf
Osorno, *Spain* 66 Ca
Osowiec, *Poland* 65 Kb
Oss, *Netherlands* 60 Dc
Ossining, *New York* 44 Db
Ostavall, *Sweden* 62 Fe
Ostende, *Belgium* 60 Ac
Österreich, Nieder, prov., *Austria* 65 Fd
Österreich, Ober, prov., *Austria* 64 Fd
Östersund, *Sweden* 62 Fe
Östhammar, *Sweden* 63 Hf
Ostrava, *Czechoslovakia* 65 Hd
Ostroda, *Poland* 65 Hb
Ostrołeka, *Poland* 65 Jb
Ostrov, *Rumania* 72 Gb
Ostrov, *Russia* 76 Fc
Ostrovno, *Russia* 75 Rb
Ostrowiec, *Poland* 65 Jc
Ostrów Mazowiecka, *Poland* 65 Jb
Ostuni, *Italy* 71 Fe
Östvagöy, *Norway* 62 Fb
Osumikaikyō, *Japan* 82 Bj
Osuna, *Spain* 66 Cd
Oswego & R., *New York* 44 Ba
Oswestry, *England* 59 Eh
Ota, *Japan* 82 Cg
Otago Peninsula, *N.Z.* 51 Cf
Otaki, *New Zealand* 51 Ed
Otaru & B., *Japan* 82 Gc
Otasuts, *Japan* 82 Gc
Otavalo, *Ecuador* 48 Bc
Otepaa, *Estonia* 63 Mg
Othris, Mts., *Greece* 73 De
Otira, *New Zealand* 51 Ce
Otjiwarongo, *S.-W. Africa* 91 Bd
Otoçac, *Yugoslavia* 70 Ec
Otoineppu, *Japan* 82 Hb
Otorohanga, *New Zealand* 51 Ec
Otradnyy, *Russia* 77 Kd
Otranto, Str. of, *It.-Albania* 73 Bd
Otsego, L., *New York* 44 Ca
Otsu, *Japan* 82 Dg
Ottawa, *Illinois* 40 Be
Ottawa, *Kansas* 43 Gd
Ottawa, *Ontario* 40 Jc
Ottawa R., *Quebec, etc.* 40 Hb
Otterlo, *Netherlands* 60 Db
Otteröy, *Norway* 62 Be
Ottignies, *Belgium* 60 Cd
Otting, *Germany* 64 Ed
Ottumwa, *Iowa* 43 Hc
Otus, *Russia* 76 Jj
Otway, B., *Chile* 50 Bh
Otway, C., *Victoria* 53 Hg
Otwock, *Poland* 65 Jb
Ötz, *Austria* 64 De
Ötztaler Alpen, *Italy-Austria* 70 Cb
Ouachita Mts., *Arkansas, etc.* 43 He
Ouachita R., *Arkansas* 43 He
Ouagadougou, *Volta* 94 Ef
Ouahigouya, *Volta* 94 Ef
Ouangolodougou, *Iv. Cst.* 94 Dg
Ouargla, *Algeria* 94 Gb
Oubangui R., *Congo* 92 Dd
Ouddorp, *Netherlands* 60 Bc
Oudecappelle, *Belgium* 60 Bc
Oudenaarde. See Audenarde
Oudenbosch, *Netherlands* 60 Cc
Oudtshoorn, *Cape Province* 91 Cf
Ouessant, I. d', *France* 68 Ab
Ouezzane, *Morocco* 94 Db
Ouidah, *Dahomey* 94 Fg
Oulu, *Finland* 62 Ld
Oulu Järvi, *Finland* 62 Md
Oulu Joki, *Finland* 62 Md
Oum Chalouba, *Chad* 95 Ke
Ounas Joki, *Finland* 62 Lc
Ouricuri, *Brazil* 49 Je
Ourinhos, *Brazil* 49 Hh
Ouro Preto, *Brazil* 49 Jh
Ouse, R., *England* 59 Gf
Ouse, R., *England* 59 Hh
Outjo, *S.-W. Africa* 91 Bd
Ouyen, *Victoria* 53 Hg
Ovalle, *Chile* 50 Bd
Ovar, *Portugal* 66 Ab
Over Flakkee I., *Netherlands* 60 Cc
Overijssel, prov., *Nether.* 60 Eb
Överkalix, *Sweden* 62 Kc
Övermark, *Finland* 62 Je
Overpelt, *Belgium* 60 Dc
Övertornea, *Sweden* 62 Kc
Oviedo, *Spain* 66 Ca
Ovruch, *Ukraine* 76 Ff
Owaka, *New Zealand* 51 Bg
Owasco L., *New York* 44 Ba
Owatonna, *Minnesota* 43 Hc
Owego, *New York* 44 Ba
Owen, *Wisconsin* 40 Ac
Owen I., *Burma* 85 Jf
Owensboro, *Kentucky* 43 Jd
Owens L., *California* 45 Eg
Owen Sound, *Ontario* 40 Fc
Owen Stanley Ra., *Papua* 53 Ja
Owerri, *Nigeria* 94 Gg
Owo, *Nigeria* 94 Gg
Owosso, *Michigan* 40 Dd
Owyhee R., *Oregon* 45 Ed
Oxford, *Maryland* 40 Hf
Oxford, *New York* 40 Jd
Oxford & co., *England* 59 Gj
Oxley's Pk., *New S. Wales* 53 Jf
Oyem, *Gabon* 92 Cd
Oymyakon, *Russia* 75 Pb
Oyo, *Nigeria* 94 Fg
Oyster B., *Tasmania* 53 Jh
Ozark Plat., *Missouri, etc.* 43 Hd
Ozarks, L. of the, *Missouri* 43 Hd
Ozd, *Hungary* 65 Jd
Ozerki, *Russia* 77 Gd
Ozhogino, *Russia* 75 Pb
Ozieri, *Sardinia* 71 Be
Ozun, *Rumania* 72 Eb
Paan, *Burma* 85 Je
Paan, *China* 78 Ce
Paarl, *Cape Province* 91 Bf
Pabaži, *Latvia* 63 Lh
Pabianice, *Poland* 65 Hc
Pabna, *E. Pakistan* 87 Gd
Pacaraima, Sa., *Brazil, etc.* 48 Ec
Pacasmayo, *Peru* 48 Be
Pachbhadra, *India* 84 Dc
Pachen, *Tibet* 78 Bd
Pachow. See Pachung
Pachuca, *Mexico* 46 Ec
Pachung, *China* 80 Cg
Paços, *Portugal* 66 Ab
Padam, *Kashmir* 86 Ed
Padang, *Sumatra* 79 Dl
Paderborn, *Germany* 64 Cc
Padilla, *Bolivia* 48 Eg
Padova, *Italy* 70 Cc
Padrauna, *India* 87 Eb
Padre I., *Texas* 42 Gf
Padstow, *England* 59 Dk
Padua. See Padova
Paducah, *Kentucky* 43 Jd
Padul, *Spain* 66 Dd
Paeroa, *New Zealand* 51 Eb
Pafuri, *Moçambique* 91 Ed
Pagai Is., *Indonesia* 79 Dl
Pagan, *Burma* 85 Hd
Pagan I., *Mariana Is.* 98 Df
Pagasaí, G. of, *Greece* 73 De
Pago, I., *Yugoslavia* 70 Ec
Pagong L., *Kashmir-Tibet* 84 Eb
Paharpur, *W. Pakistan* 86 Bd
Pahiatua, *New Zealand* 51 Ed

Pahlavi Dezh, Persia 89 Fb
Pahsien, China 80 Hc
Pahsien. See Chungking
Paignton, England 59 Ek
Paiho, China 80 Ef
Paijanne, L., Finland 63 Lf
Pai-Khoi Khrebet, Russia 74 Fb
Pailingmiao, China 78 Fb
Pailani, India 87 Cc
Paimpol, France 68 Bb
Painted Des., Arizona 42 Dd
Paisley, Ontario 40 Fc
Paisley, Scotland 58 Ee
Paita, Peru 48 Ae
Pai Tu Hu, China 80 Hg
Pajakumbuh, Sumatra 79 Dl
Pajala, Sweden 62 Kc
Pajares, Spain 66 Ca
Pajde, Estonia 63 Lg
Pakanbaru, Sumatra 79 Dk
Pakaur, India 87 Fc
Pakchan, Burma 85 Jf
Pak-hoi, China 81 Dm
Pakistan, S. Asia 84 Cc
Pak-lay, Laos 83 Cc
Pakokku, Burma 85 Jd
Pakpattan, W. Pakistan 86 Ce
Pakrac, Yugoslavia 70 Fc
Paks, Hungary 65 He
Pakse, Laos 83 Dc
Pakwach, Uganda 93 Gd
Palafrugell, Spain 67 Gb
Palaiokhóra, Crete 73 Dg
Palamau, India 87 Ed
Palamcottah, India 84 Eg
Palamós, Spain 67 Gb
Palamuse, Estonia 63 Mg
Palana, Russia 75 Rc
Palanpur, India 84 Dd
Palapye Road., Botswana 91 Dd
Palau Is., Pacific Ocean 79 Kj
Palaw, Burma 83 Bd
Palawan, I., Philippines 79 Gj
Paldiski, Estonia 63 Lg
Palembang, Sumatra 79 Dl
Palena, Chile 50 Bf
Palencia, Spain 66 Ca
Palenque, Mexico 46 Fd
Paleokhorio, Cyprus 90 Bc
Palermo, Argentina 50 Db
Palermo, Sicily 71 Df
Palestina, Chile 50 Cb
Palestine, Texas 42 Ge
Palestine, W. Asia 88 Cc
Paletwa, Burma 85 Hd
Palghat, India 84 Ef
Palgrave Pt., S.-W. Africa 91 Ad
Palgu Tso, Tibet 85 Gc
Palhoça, Brazil 50 Gc
Pali, India 84 Dc
Palimé, Togo 94 Fg
Palisade, Nevada 45 Ee
Paliseul, Belgium 60 De
Palizada, Mexico 46 Fd
Palk Str., India 84 Eg
Palkot, India 87 Ed
Palliser B., New Zealand 51 Ed
Palm I., Qnsld. 53 Jc
Palma, Balearic Is. 67 Gc
Palma, Moçambique 93 Jg
Palma, I., Canary Is. 94 Bc
Palmares, Brazil 50 Fd
Palmas, Brazil 50 Fc
Palmas, B., Mexico 46 Cc
Palmas C., Liberia 94 Dh
Palmas, G. of, Sardinia 71 Bf
Palma Sola, Venezuela 48 Da
Palm Beach, West, Florida 43 Kf
Palmeira, Brazil 50 Fc
Palmer Arch., Antarctica 100 Sc
Palmerston, Ontario 40 Fd
Palmerston I., Cook Islands 99 Jj
Palmerston North, N.Z. 51 Ed
Palmerston South, N.Z. 51 Cf
Palmira, Colombia 48 Bc
Palms, Michigan 40 Ed
Palmyra, Syria 88 Cc
Palmyra I., Pacific Ocean 98 Jg
Palni Hills, India 84 Ef
Paloh, Borneo 79 Ek
Paloich, Sudan 95 Mf
Palo Santo, Argentina 50 Ec
Palpa, Nepal 87 Db
Palu, Turkey 88 Db
Palwal, India 86 Ef
Palz do Vinho, Portugal 66 Bb
Pamban Chan., India 84 Eg
Pamekasan, Indonesia 79 Fm
Pamiers, France 69 De
Pamir, Mts., Russia 74 Ge
Pamlico Sd., N. Carolina 43 Ld
Pampas, Peru 48 Cf
Pamplona, Columbia 48 Cb
Pamplona, Spain 67 Ea
Panache L., Ontario 40 Fb
Panagyurishte, Bulgaria 72 Ec
Panāh, Persia 89 Hd
Panama & rep., Cent. Amer. 47 De
Panama, G. of, Panama 47 De
Panama Canal, Cent. Amer. 47 Gb
Panama City, Florida 43 Je
Panarea, I., Italy 71 Ef
Panay, I., Philippines 79 Hh
Pančevo, Yugoslavia 72 Cb
Panciu, Rumania 72 Fb
Pandan, Philippines 79 Hh
Pan de Azucar, Chile 50 Bc
Pandharpur, India 84 Ee
Pando, Uruguay 50 Ed
Pandora, Costa Rica 47 Ce
Panevezis, Lithuania 63 Lj
Panfilov, Kazakh. 74 Hd
Panfilovo, Russia 77 Fe
Pangala, Fr. Congo 92 Ce
Pangkiang, China 78 Fb
Panguitch, Utah 42 Dd
Pania Mutombo, Congo 92 Ef
Panipat, India 86 Ef
Panja, China 78 Bc
Panjim. See Nova Goa
Panjnad R., W. Pakistan 86 Bf
Pannerden, Netherlands 60 Ec
Panruti, India 84 Ef
Pantanaw, Burma 85 Je
Pantar, I., Indonesia 79 Hm
Pantelleria, I., Medit. Sea 71 Dg
Pao-an-chow, China 80 Gb
Paochang, China 80 Ga
Paochi. See Paoki
Pão de Açúcar, Brazil 49 Ke
Paoki, China 80 Ce
Paoking. See Shaoyang
Paola, Italy 71 Ff
Paoning. See Langchung
Paosham, China 78 Ce
Paoting, China 80 Gc
Pao-tow, China 80 Db
Papakura, New Zealand 51 Eb
Papantla, Mexico 46 Ec
Papa Stour I., Scotland 58 Ha
Papa Westray, I., Orkney Is. 58 Fa
Papenburg, Germany 64 Bb
Papendrecht, Netherlands 60 Cc
Paphos, Cyprus 90 Ac
Paposo, Chile 50 Bc
Papua, prov., New Guinea 53 Ha
Papua, G. of, Papua 53 Ha
Papun, Burma 85 Je
Pará, Brazil 49 Hd
Para, R., Brazil 49 Hd
Paracatu, Brazil 49 Hg
Paracel Is. & Reefs,
S. China Sea 83 Ec
Parachinar, W. Pakistan 86 Bd
Paracin, Yugoslavia 72 Cc
Paracurú, Brazil 49 Kd
Parag. See Park
Paragould, Arkansas 43 Hd
Paraguari, Paraguay 50 Ec
Paraguay, rep., S. America 50 Eb
Paraguay, R., Argent., etc. 50 Ec
Parah, Afghanistan 89 Hc
Parakes, Botswana 91 Cc
Parakou, Dahomey 94 Fg
Paramaribo, Surinam 49 Fb
Paramonga, Peru 48 Bf
Paramoshir, Russia 75 Qc
Parana, Argentina 50 Dd
Paranã, Brazil 49 Hf
Parana, R., Argentina 50 Ec
Paranagua, Brazil 50 Gc
Paranáiba & R., Brazil 49 Gg
Parang, Philippines 79 Hj
Paranga, Uganda 93 Gd
Parapóla, I., Greece 73 Df
Paratinga, Brazil 49 Jf
Parbati R., India 84 Ed
Parbhani, India 84 Ee
Parchim, Germany 64 Db
Pardubice, Czechoslovakia 65 Fc
Parecis, Sa. dos, Brazil 48 Ef
Pareora, New Zealand 51 Cf
Pariaguan, Venezuela 48 Eb
Parika, Guyana 48 Fb
Parinari, Peru 48 Cd
Parintins, Brazil 49 Fd
Paris, France 68 Eb
Paris, Illinois 40 Cf
Paris, Ontario 40 Fd
Paris, Texas 42 Ge
Parita, B. de, Panama 47 Ce
Pariz, Persia 89 Gd
Park, Persia 89 Hd
Park Ra., Wyoming 42 Ec
Parker Dam, Arizona 42 De
Parkersburg, W. Virginia 40 Ff
Parkes, New South Wales 53 Jf
Park Falls, Wisconsin 40 Ac
Parma, Italy 70 Cc
Parnagua, Brazil 49 Jf
Parnaiba, Brazil 49 Jd
Parnaiba, R., Brazil 49 Jd
Parnu & G., Estonia 63 Lg
Paro, Bhutan 87 Gb
Paron, India 84 Ed
Parowan, Utah 45 Gg
Parral, Chile 50 Be
Parral, Mexico 46 Cb
Parramatta, New S. Wales 53 Kf
Parras, Mexico 46 Db
Parry I., Ontario 40 Fc
Parry Sound, Ontario 40 Fc
Parsa, India 87 Ec
Parsons, Kansas 42 Gd
Parsons, W. Virginia 44 Ac
Partabgarh, India 84 Dd
Partabgarh. See Pratapgarth
Partabpur, India 87 Dd
Parthenay, France 68 Cc
Partinico, Sicily 71 Df
Pasadena, California 45 Dh
Pasargadae, Persia 89 Fc
Pasawng, Burma 85 Je
Pas-de-Calais, dep., France 68 Ea
Paskuh, Persia 89 Hd
Pasley, C., W. Australia 52 Df
Pasni, W. Pakistan 84 Bc
Paso de Indios, Argentina 50 Cf
Paso de los Libres, Argentina 50 Ec
Paso de los Toros, Uruguay 50 Ed
Paso Limay, Argentina 50 Bf
Paso Robles, California 45 Ch
Pasrur, W. Pakistan 86 Dd
Passaic, New Jersey 44 Cb
Passau, Germany 64 Ed
Passchendaele, Belgium 60 Bd
Passero C., Sicily 71 Eg
Passo Fundo, Brazil 50 Fc
Passos, Brazil 49 Hh
Pasto, Colombia 48 Bc
Pastrana, Spain 66 Db
Pasvik Elv, Norway 62 Nb
Pásztó, Hungary 65 He
Patan, India 84 Dd
Patan, India 84 De
Patan, Nepal 87 Eb
Pataudi, India 86 Ef
Pataz, Peru 48 Be
Patchogue, New York 44 Db
Patea, New Zealand 51 Ec
Paterno, Sicily 71 Eg
Paterson, New Jersey 44 Cb
Pathankot, India 86 Dd
Pathari, India 87 Bd
Pathfinder Res., Wyoming 42 Ec
Patiala, India 86 Ee
Patkai Hills, Burma 85 Jc
Pátmos, I., Greece 73 Ff
Patna, India 85 Fd
Patna, India 87 Ec
Patos, Brazil 49 Ke
Patos, L. dos, Brazil 50 Fd
Patos de Minas, Brazil 49 Hg
Patquia, Argentina 50 Cd
Pátrai, Greece 73 Ce
Pátrai, G. of, Greece 73 Ce
Patras. See Pátrai
Patrasayar, India 87 Fd
Patricio Lynch, I., Chile 50 Ag
Partocinio, Brazil 49 Hg
Pattani, Siam 83 Ce
Patti, Sicily 71 Ef
Patutahi, New Zealand 51 Fc
Patzcuaro, Mexico 46 Dd
Pau, France 69 Ce
Pau d'Arco, Brazil 49 He
Pau dos Ferros, Brazil 49 Ke
Paulistana, Brazil 49 Je
Paungde, Burma 85 Je
Pauni, India 84 Ed
Pautrask, Sweden 62 Gd
Pavia, Italy 70 Bc
Pāvilosta, Latvia 63 Jh
Pavlodar, Kazakh. 74 Gc
Pavlograd, Ukraine 76 Jg
Pavlovka, Russia 77 Fe
Pavlovo, Russia 77 Fc
Pavlovsk, Russia 77 Ee
Pavlovski, Russia 76 Ld
Paw Paw, Michigan 40 Dd
Pawtucket, Rhode Island 44 Eb
Paxoi, I., Greece 73 Ce
Payerne, Switzerland 61 Bb
Paynes Find, W. Aust. 52 Ce
Paysandu, Uruguay 50 Ed
Paz, R., Salvador 47 Ad
Pazardzhik, Bulgaria 72 Ec
Peak, The, England 59 Fg
Peak Hill, W. Australia 52 Cd
Pearl Harbour, Hawaiian Is. 99 Ke
Peary Ld., Greenland 41 Na
Pebane, Moçambique 93 Hh
Pebas, Peru 48 Cd
Pebble I., Falkland Islands 50 Eh
Pébo, Cent. Afr. Rep. 95 Jg
Peć, Yugoslavia 72 Cc
Pechenga, Russia 74 Cb
Pechora, R., Russia 74 Eb
Pecos, Texas 42 Fe
Pecos R., Texas 42 Fe
Pécs, Hungary 72 Ba
Pedernales, Venezuela 48 Eb
Pedhoulas, Cyprus 90 Ac
Pedregal, Panama 47 Ce
Pedreiras, Brazil 49 Jd
Pedro Afonso, Brazil 49 He
Pedro Azul, Brazil 49 Jg
Pedro Juan Caballero, Para. 50 Eb
Pedroll, Brazil 49 Jd
Pedro Luro, Argentina 50 De
Pedro Pt., Ceylon 84 Fg
Peebles & co., Scotland 58 Ee
Peekskill, New York 44 Db
Peenemünde, Germany 64 Ea
Peetri, Estonia 63 Lg
Pegasus B., New Zealand 51 De
Pegu, Burma 85 Je
Pegu Yoma, Burma 85 Je
Pehan, China 78 Ja
Pehchen, China 80 Kb
Pehowa, India 86 Ef
Pehuajó, Argentina 50 De
Pei-ching. See Peking
Peineta, Mt., Chile 50 Bh
Peiping. See Peking
Peipus, L. See Chudskoye Oz
Peixe, Brazil 49 Hf
Pekan, W. Malaysia 83 Cf
Pekin, Illinois 40 Be
Peking, China 80 Hb
Pelagie Is., Medit. Sea 95 Ha
Pélagos, I., Greece 73 De
Peleduy, Russia 75 Lc
Pelèe I., Ontario 40 Ee
Peleng, I., Indonesia 79 Hl
Peljesac Pen., Yugoslavia 70 Fd
Pelkosenniemi, Finland 62 Mc
Pella, Greece 73 Cd
Pellegrini, Argentina 50 De
Pellworm I., Germany 64 Ca
Peloponnisos, Greece 73 Cf
Pelotas, Brazil 50 Fd
Pemba I., E. Africa 93 Hf
Pembroke, Ontario 40 Hc
Pembroke & co., Wales 59 Dj
Pembroke, C., Falkland Is. 50 Eh
Penafiel, Portugal 66 Ab
Peñafiel, Spain 66 Cb
Penalva, Brazil 49 Jd
Penambo Ra., Sarawak 79 Fk
Peña Negra, Sa. de, Spain 66 Ba
Penang, I., W. Malaysia 83 Ce
Penápolis, Brazil 49 Gh
Peñaranda de Bracamonte,
Spain 66 Cb
Peñarroya, Spain 66 Cc
Penas, G. de, Chile 50 Bg
Pendembu, Sierra Leone 94 Cg
Pendleton, Oregon 45 Dc
Pend Oreille, L., Idaho 42 Cb
Penedo, Brazil 49 Kf
Penedono, Portugal 66 Bb
Penggaram, W. Malaysia 83 Cf
Penghu Is., China 81 Jl
Penglai, China 80 Kd
Pengpu, China 78 Gd
Penhalonga, Rhodesia 91 Ec
Peniche, Portugal 66 Ac
Peñiscola, Spain 67 Fb
Pennine, Alpi, Switzerland 61 Cb
Pennine Chain, England 59 Ff
Penns Grove, New Jersey 44 Cc
Pennsylvania, state, U.S.A. 43 Lc
Penn Yan, New York 44 Ba
Penong, S. Australia 52 Ff
Penonome, Panama 47 Ce
Penrith, England 59 Ff
Pensacola, Florida 43 Je
Pentland Firth, Scotland 58 Eb
Pentland Hills, Scotland 58 Ee
Pentwater, Michigan 40 Cd
Penza, Russia 77 Gd
Penzance, England 59 Dk
Penzhino, Russia 75 Rb
Penzhinskaya Guba, Russia 75 Rb
Peoria, Illinois 40 Be
Peperga, Netherlands 60 Eb
Pepinster, Belgium 60 Dd
Peqin, Albania 72 Bd
Peralta, Spain 67 Ea
Perdido, Mte., Spain 67 Fa
Pereira, Colombia 48 Bc
Perello, Spain 67 Fb
Perez, Chile 50 Cc
Pergamino, Argentina 50 Dd
Perho, Finland 62 Le
Perico, Argentina 50 Cb
Perigueux, France 69 Dd
Perija, Sa. de, Venezuela 48 Ca
Perim I., Red Sea 88 Dg
Peristéra I., Greece 73 Ee
Perlas & Lag. de las, Nic. 47 Cd
Perlas, Arch. de las, Pan. 47 De
Perm, Russia 77 Nb
Pernambuco. See Recife
Péronne, France 68 Eb
Péronnes, Belgium 60 Cd
Perpignan, France 69 Ee
Perrot I., Quebec 40 Jc
Perry, New York 44 Aa
Persepolis, Persia 89 Fd
Persia (Iran), Asia 89 Fc
Persian Gulf, Arabia, etc. 88 Ed
Perth, Ontario 40 Hc
Perth, W. Australia 52 Cf
Perth & co., Scotland 58 Ed
Perth Amboy, New Jersey 44 Cb
Peru, Indiana 40 Ce
Peru, rep., S. America 48 Cf
Perufune, Japan 82 Hc
Perugia, Italy 70 Dd
Peruibe, Brazil 49 Hh
Peruwelz, Belgium 60 Bd
Pervijze, Belgium 60 Ac
Pervomaysk, Ukraine 76 Gg
Perwez, Belgium 60 Cd
Pesaro, Italy 70 Dd
Pescadores, Is. See Penghu Is.
Pescara, Italy 70 Ed
Peschici, Italy 71 Fe
Peshawar, W. Pakistan 86 Bc
Peshtigo R., Wisconsin 40 Bc
Pêso do Régua, Portugal 66 Bb
Pesqueira, Brazil 49 Ke
Pestravka, Russia 77 Jd
Petah Tiqva, Israel 90 Ce
Petalioí, G. of, Greece 73 Ef
Petalioí, I., Greece 73 Ef
Petaluma, California 45 Bf
Peterborough, England 59 Gh
Peterborough, Ontario 40 Gc
Peterborough, S. Australia 53 Gf
Peter I, I., Antarctica 100 Rc
Peterhead, Scotland 58 Fc
Petermann Fd., Greenland 41 Pa
Petermann Pk., Greenland 41 Nb
Petermann Ra., W. Aust. 52 Ee
Petersburg, Alaska 43 Zm
Petersburg, Virginia 43 Ld
Peto, Mexico 46 Gc
Petone, New Zealand 51 Ed
Petorca, Chile 50 Bd
Petoskey, Michigan 40 Dc
Petra, Jordan 90 Dg
Petra Velikogo Zaliv, Russia 75 Nd
Petrich, Bulgaria 72 Dd
Petrinja, Yugoslavia 70 Fc
Petriu. See Chachnengsao
Petrodvorets, Russia 76 Fb
Petrolandia, Brazil 49 Ke
Petrolia, Ontario 40 Ed
Petrolina, Brazil 49 Je
Petropavlovsk, Kazakh. 74 Fc
Petropavlovsk, Russia 75 Qc
Petropolis, Brazil 49 Jh
Petrovac, Yugoslavia 72 Cb
Petrovsk, Russia 77 Nd
Petrovsk, Russia 75 Kc
Petrovsk, Russia 77 Gd
Petrozavodsk, Russia 74 Cb
Petsamo. See Pechenga
Pevek, Russia 75 Sb
Pézenas, France 69 Ee
Pforzheim, Germany 64 Cd
Phagwara, India 86 De
Phalodi, India 84 Dc
Phanom Dang Raek, Siam 83 Cd
Phan Rang, S. Vietnam 83 Dd
Phan-Thiet & B. of, S. Viet. 83 Dd
Phaphund, India 87 Bb
Phatthalung, Siam 83 Be
Phet Buri, Siam 83 Bd
Philadelphia, Pennsylvania 40 Je
Philippeville, Belgium 60 Cd
Philippeville, Algeria. See Skikda
Philippi, W. Virginia 40 Ff
Philippi, L., Queensland 53 Gd
Philippines, East Indies 79 Hh
Philippopolis. See Plovdiv
Phillaur, India 86 De
Phillip Edward I., Ontario 40 Fc
Phillips, Wisconsin 40 Ac
Phillipsburg, New Jersey 44 Cb
Phitsanulok Muang, Siam 83 Cc
Phnom-Penh, Cambodia 83 Cd
Phoenix, Arizona 42 De
Phoenix I., Phoenix Is. 98 Hh
Phoenix Is., Pacific Ocean 98 Hh
Phoenixville, Pennsylvania 44 Cb
Pho-mo-chang-thang Tso,
Tibet 85 Hc
Phou San, Mt., Laos 83 Cc
Phu-dien, N. Vietnam 83 Dc
Phuket, Siam 79 Cj
Phulji, W. Pakistan 84 Cc
Phulpur, India 87 Dc
Phu Qui, N. Vietnam 83 Dc
Phu-Quoc, I., S. Vietnam 83 Cd
Piacenza, Italy 70 Bc
Pianosa, I., Italy 70 Cd
Pias, Portugal 66 Bc
Piatra Neamt, Rumania 72 Fa
Piazza Armerina, Sicily 71 Eg
Piazzi, I., Chile 50 Bh
Pibor Post, Sudan 95 Mg
Piceno. See Ascoli
Pichanal, Argentina 50 Db
Picher, Oklahoma 43 Hd
Pichilemu, Chile 50 Bd
Pickering, England 59 Gf
Picos. See Colinas
Picton, New South Wales 53 Kf
Picton, New Zealand 51 Dd
Picton, Ontario 40 Hd
Picun Leufu, Argentina 50 Ce
Pidark, W. Pakistan 84 Bc
Piedad, La, Mexico 46 Dc
Piedrahita, Spain 66 Cb
Piedras Negras, Mexico 46 Db
Piedra Sola, Uruguay 50 Ed
Pieksämäki, Finland 62 Me
Pielinen, Finland 62 Ne
Piemonte, region, Italy 70 Ac
Pierre, S. Dakota 42 Fc
Pietarsaari, Finland 62 Ke
Pietermaritzburg, Natal 91 Ee
Pietersburg, Transvaal 91 Dd
Pigue, Argentina 50 De
Pihtipudas, Finland 62 Le
Pikes Pk., Colorado 42 Ed
Pila, Argentina 50 Ee
Pila, Poland 65 Gb
Pilao Arcado, Brazil 49 Jf
Pilar, Argentina 50 Dd
Pilar, Paraguay 50 Ec
Pilar, C., Chile 50 Bh
Pilcaniyeu, Argentina 50 Bf
Pilibhit, India 87 Ba
Pilos, Greece 73 Cf
Pilsen. See Plzeň
Piltene, Latvia 63 Jh
Pi Mai, Siam 83 Cc
Pimentel, Peru 48 Be
Pina, Spain 67 Eb
Pinaki I., Tuamotu Arch. 99 Mj
Pinarbasi, Turkey 88 Cb
Pinar del Rio, Cuba 47 Cb
Pind Dadan Khan,
W. Pakistan 86 Cd
Pindhos, Mts., Greece 73 Ce
Pindi Gheb, W. Pakistan 86 Cd
Pine Bluff, Arkansas 43 He
Pine Creek, N. Terr., Aust. 52 Fb
Pinetown, Natal 91 Ee
Ping-chüan-chow, China 80 Jb
Pingelap, I., Caroline Is. 98 Fg
Pingelly, W. Australia 52 Cf
Pingkiang, China 81 Fh
Pingliang, China 80 Ce
Pinglo, China 81 Ek
Pingrup, W. Australia 52 Cf
Ping-ting-chow, China 80 Fd
Pingwu, China 80 Bf
Pingyang. See Linfen
Pingyüan, China 80 Hd
Pinhel, Portugal 66 Bb
Pini, I., Indonesia 79 Ck
Pinjarra, W. Australia 52 Bf
Pinkiang, China 78 Ja
Pinnaroo, S. Australia 53 Hg
Pinos, Mexico 46 Dc
Pinos, I. de, Cuba 47 Cb
Pinos, Mt., California 45 Dh
Pinrang, Celebes 79 Gl
Pinsk, Belorussia 76 Ee
Pintados, Chile 50 Cb
Pinto, Argentina 50 Dc
Pioneer, Os., Russia 75 Ja
Piotrkow, Poland 65 Hc
Pipar, India 84 Dc
Pipestone, Minnesota 42 Gc
Pipinas, Argentina 50 Ee
Pippli, India 85 Gd
Piqua, Ohio 40 De
Piracuruca, Brazil 49 Jd
Piraeus. See Piraievs
Piraievs, Greece 73 Df
Piramide, Mt., Chile 50 Bg
Piranhaquara, Brazil 49 Gd
Piranhas, Brazil 49 Ke
Pirapora, Brazil 49 Jg
Piratini, Brazil 50 Fd
Piray, Argentina 50 Fc
Pirgos, Greece 73 Df
Pirgos, Greece 73 Cf
Pirgos, Crete 73 Eg
Pirin Planina, Bulgaria 72 Dd
Piripiri, Brazil 49 Jd
Piritu, Venezuela 48 Ea
Pirmasens, Germany 64 Bd
Pirna, Germany 64 Ec
Pirot, Yugoslavia 72 Dc
Pir Panjal Ra., Kashmir 86 Dd
Pisa, Italy 70 Cd
Pisagua, Chile 50 Ba
Pisco, Peru 48 Bf
Pisek, Czechoslovakia 64 Fd
Pishin, W. Pakistan 84 Cb
Pishin, Persia 89 Hd
Pisticci, Italy 71 Fe
Pitangui, Brazil 49 Jg
Pitcairn I., Pacific Ocean 99 Mk
Pite Älv, Sweden 62 Hd
Piteå, Sweden 62 Jd
Piterka, Russia 77 He
Piteşti, Rumania 72 Eb
Pithiviers, France 68 Eb
Pithoria, India 87 Bc
Pitlochry, Scotland 58 Ed
Pitt, Mt., Oregon 45 Bd
Pitt R., California 45 Ce
Pittsburg, Kansas 43 Hd
Pittsburgh, Pennsylvania 40 Ge
Pittsfield, Massachusetts 40 Kd
Pittston, Pennsylvania 44 Cb
Piua-Petri, Rumania 72 Fb
Piura, Peru 48 Ae
Piza, Latvia 63 Jh
Piz Sardona, Switzerland 61 Eb
Placer Guadalupe, Mexico 46 Cb
Plainfield, New Jersey 40 Je
Plainwell, Michigan 40 Dd
Pláka B., Crete 73 Eg
Plakoti C., Cyprus 90 Cb
Plana, Czechoslovakia 64 Ed
Planaltina, Brazil 49 Hg
Planina, Yugoslavia 70 Ec
Plasencia, Spain 66 Bb
Plaški, Yugoslavia 70 Ec
Plassen, Norway 63 Ff
Plastun, Russia 75 Nd
Plata, R. de la, Argentina 50 Ed
Platamón, Greece 73 Dd
Platí, Greece 73 Dd
Platres, Cyprus 90 Ac
Platt Nat. Park, Oklahoma 42 Ge
Platte R., N. & S., Nebraska 42 Fc
Plattsburg, New York 40 Kc
Plauen, Germany 64 Ec
Plav, Yugoslavia 72 Bc
Plavnica, Yugoslavia 72 Bc
Playas, Ecuador 48 Ad
Playas L., New Mexico 42 Ee
Plaza Huincul, Argentina 50 Ce
Pleasantville, New Jersey 44 Cc
Pleiku, S. Vietnam 79 Eh
Plenty, B. of, New Zealand 51 Fb
Plessisville, Quebec 40 Lb
Plettenberg B., Cape Prov. 91 Cf
Pleven, Bulgaria 72 Ec
Pljevlja, Yugoslavia 72 Bc
Płock, Poland 65 Hb
Ploeşti, Rumania 72 Fb
Plomarion, Greece 73 Fe
Plomosa Mts., Arizona 45 Gj
Plon, Germany 64 Da
Płońsk, Poland 65 Jb
Plovdiv, Bulgaria 72 Ec
Plumtree, Rhodesia 91 Dd
Plymouth, Indiana 40 Ce
Plymouth, Massachusetts 40 Le
Plymouth, New Hampshire 40 Ld
Plymouth, Pennsylvania 44 Cb
Plymouth, Wisconsin 40 Bd
Plymouth & Sd., England 59 Ek
Plynlimmon, Wales 59 Eh
Plzeň, Czechoslovakia 64 Ed
Poai, China 80 Fe
Pobedy Peak, Kirgiz 74 Hd
Pobla de Segur, Spain 67 Fa
Pocatello, Idaho 45 Gd
Pochinki, Russia 77 Gc
Pochutla, Mexico 46 Ed
Podkagernaya, Russia 75 Rb
Podkamennaya Tunguska,
Russia 74 Hb
Podlubovo, Russia 77 Mc
Podolsk, Russia 76 Kd
Pogamasing, Ontario 40 Fb
Pohai, G. of, China 80 Jc
Pohai, Str. of, China 80 Kc
Point à Pitreê, Leeward Is. 47 Gc
Poitiers, France 68 Dc
Poitoumarche, prov., Fr. 68 Cc
Poix, Belgium 60 Dd
Poix, France 68 Db
Pokaakku, I., Pacific Ocean 98 Ff
Pokhara, Nepal 87 Da
Pokka, Finland 62 Lb
Pokrovsk, Russia 77 Fd
Pokrovsk, Russia 77 Dg
Pokrovsk (Engels), Russia 77 He
Pokrovskoe, Russia 75 Mb
Pola. See Pula
Pola de Laviana, Spain 66 Ca
Poland, Central Europe 56 Mf
Polesk, U.S.S.R. 63 Jj
Polevskoi, Russia 77 Qb
Polgahawela, Ceylon 84 Fg
Polgar, Hungary 65 Je
Poli, Cameroon 95 Hg
Pollaigos, I., Greece 73 Ef
Policastro, G. di, Italy 71 Ef
Poligny, France 68 Fc
Polillo Is., Philippines 79 Hh
Pólinos. See Políaigos, I.
Polis, Cyprus 90 Ab
Pollensa, Balearic Islands 67 Gc
Polotsk, Belorussia 76 Fd
Polson, Montana 45 Fb
Poltava, Ukraine 76 Jg
Põltsamaa, Estonia 63 Mg
Poluostrov Buzachi, Kazakh. 74 Ed
Põlva, Estonia 63 Mg
Polynesia, Pacific Ocean 98 Jk
Poman, Argentina 50 Cc
Pombal, Brazil 49 Ke
Pombal, Portugal 66 Ac
Pombetsu, Japan 82 Hc
Pomene, Moçambique 91 Fd
Pommersche B., Germany 64 Fa
Pomorie, Bulgaria 72 Fc
Pomos, Pt., Cyprus 90 Ab
Ponape, I., Caroline Islands 98 Eg
Ponca City, Oklahoma 42 Gd
Ponce, Puerto Rico 47 Fc
Pondicherry, India 84 Ef
Ponente, Riviera di, Italy 70 Ad
Ponferrada, Spain 66 Ba
Ponoy, Russia 74 Db
Pons, France 68 Cd
Pons, Spain 67 Fb
Ponta Grossa, Brazil 50 Fc
Pont-Audemer, France 68 Db
Pontchartrain, L., Louisiana 43 Hf
Pont Chateau, France 68 Bc
Pont d'Ain, France 68 Fc
Ponte, Switzerland 61 Eb
Ponte da Barca, Portugal 66 Ab
Ponte de Sôr, Portugal 66 Ac
Ponte Nova, Brazil 49 Jh
Pontevedra, Spain 66 Aa
Pontiac, Illinois 40 Be
Pontiac, Michigan 40 Ed
Pontianak, Borneo 79 El
Pontivy, France 68 Bb
Pontoise, France 68 Eb
Pontresina, Switzerland 61 Eb
Ponts, les, Switzerland 61 Bb
Pontypool, Britain 59 Ej
Pontypool, Ontario 40 Gc
Pontypridd, Wales 59 Ej
Ponza, I., Italy 71 De
Poole, England 59 Fk
Poona, India 84 De
Pooncarie, N.S.W. 53 Hf
Poopo, Bolivia 48 Dg
Poopo, L., Bolivia 48 Dg
Popa Mt., Burma 85 Jd
Popayan, Colombia 48 Bc
Poperinge, Belgium 60 Ad
Poplar Bluff, Missouri 43 Hd
Popocatapetl, Mt., Mexico 46 Ed
Popokabaka, Congo 92 Df
Popovača, Yugoslavia 70 Fc
Poppel, Belgium 60 Dc
Porahat, India 87 Ed
Porbandar, India 84 Cd
Poreč, Yugoslavia 70 Dc
Pori, Finland 63 Jf
Porjus, Sweden 62 Hc
Porkhov, Russia 76 Fc
Porkkala, Finland 63 Lg
Porlamar, Margarita I.,
Venezuela 48 Ea
Pornic, France 68 Bc
Poronaysk, Russia 75 Pd
Póros I., Greece 73 Df
Porsanger Fd., Norway 62 La
Porsanger Halvöy, Norway 62 La
Porsgrund, Norway 63 Cg
Portachuelo, Bolivia 48 Eg
Port Adelaide, S. Australia 53 Gf
Portadown, N. Ireland 59 Cf
Portage, Wisconsin 40 Bd
Portageville, New York 44 Aa
Portalegre, Portugal 66 Bc
Port Antonio, Jamaica 47 Dc
Portarlington, Eire 59 Cg
Port Arthur (Lushun), China 78 Hc
Port Arthur, Texas 43 Hf
Port Augusta, S. Australia 53 Gf
Port au Prince, Haiti 47 Ec
Port Blair, Andaman Islands 85 Hf
Port Chalmers, N.Z. 51 Cf
Port Chester, New York 44 Db
Port Clinton, Ohio 40 Ee
Port Cornwallis, Andaman I. 85 Hf
Port Dalhousie, Ontario 40 Gd
Port Darwin, Falkland Is. 50 Eh
Port de Paix, Haiti 47 Eb
Port Dickson, W. Malaysia 83 Cf
Port Douglas, Queensland 53 Jc
Port Dover, Ontario 40 Fd
Portel, Brazil 49 Gd
Port Elgin, Ontario 40 Fc

Port Elizabeth, *Cape Prov.* 91 Df
Port Ellen, *Scotland* 58 Ce
Port Etienne, *Mauritania* 94 Bd
Port Harcourt, *Nigeria* 94 Gh
Port Hedland, *W. Australia* 52 Cd
Port Hope, *Michigan* 40 Ed
Port Hope, *Ontario* 40 Gd
Port Huron, *Michigan* 40 Ed
Portimão, *Portugal* 66 Ad
Port Jackson, *New S. Wales* 53 Kf
Port Jervis, *New York* 44 Cb
Port Kembla, *New S. Wales* 53 Kf
Portland, *Oregon* 45 Bc
Portland, *Victoria* 53 Hg
Portland Bill, *England* 59 Fk
Portland Point, *Jamaica* 47 Dc
Portlaoise, *Eire* 59 Cg
Port Lincoln, *S. Australia* 53 Gf
Port Loko, *Sierra Leone* 94 Cg
Port Lyautey, *Morocco* 94 Db
Port M'Nicoll, *Ontario* 40 Gc
Port Macquarie, *N.S.W.* 53 Kf
Portmadoc, *Wales* 59 Eh
Port Moresby, *Papua* 53 Ja
Portneuf, *Quebec* 40 Kb
Port Nolloth, *Cape Prov.* 91 Be
Port Norris, *New Jersey* 40 Jf
Porto, *Portugal* 66 Ab
Porto Acre, *Brazil* 48 De
Porto Alegre, *Brazil* 50 Fd
Porto Alexandre, *Angola* 91 Ac
Porto Amelia, *Moçambique* 93 Jg
Portobelo, *Panama* 47 De
Porto Botte, *Sardinia* 71 Bf
Porto Camargo, *Brazil* 49 Gh
Porto d'Ascoli, *Italy* 70 Dd
Porto de Mos, *Brazil* 49 Gd
Porto de Moz, *Portugal* 66 Ac
Porto Empedocle, *Sicily* 71 Dg
Porto Esperanca, *Brazil* 49 Fg
Porto Espiridião, *Brazil* 48 Fg
Porto Franco, *Brazil* 49 He
Port of Spain, *Trinidad* 48 Ea
Porto Guaira, *Brazil* 49 Gh
Port Okha, *India* 84 Cd
Portola, *California* 45 Cf
Porto Lucena, *Brazil* 50 Fc
Porto Mendes, *Brazil* 49 Gh
Porto Nacional, *Brazil* 49 Hf
Porto Novo, *Dahomey* 94 Fg
Porto Novo, *India* 84 Ef
Port Ontario, *New York* 44 Ba
Porto Seguro, *Brazil* 49 Kg
Porto Torres, *Sardinia* 71 Be
Porto Vecchio, *Corsica* 71 Be
Porto Vêlho, *Brazil* 48 Ee
Portoviejo, *Ecuador* 48 Ad
Portpatrick, *Scotland* 59 Df
Port Pegasus, *New Zealand* 40 Ke
Port Phillip B., *Victoria* 53 Hg
Port Pirie, *S. Australia* 53 Gf
Port Pleasant, *New Jersey* 40 Je
Portree, *Scotland* 58 Cc
Port Rowan, *Ontario* 40 Fd
Port Royal, *Jamaica* 47 Dc
Portrush, *N. Ireland* 58 Ce
Port Safaga, *Egypt* 95 Mc
Port Said, *Egypt* 95 Mb
Port St John's, *Cape Prov.* 91 Df
Port Shepstone, *Natal* 91 Ef
Portsmouth, *England* 59 Gk
Portsmouth, *Ohio* 40 Ef
Portsmouth, *Virginia* 43 Ld
Port Stanley, *Ontario* 40 Fd
Port Sudan, *Sudan* 95 Ne
Port Swettenham, *W. Malaysia* 83 Cf
Port Taufiq, *Egypt* 95 Mc
Portugal, *W. Europe* 57 Ej
Portugalia, *Angola* 92 Ef
Portuguese Guinea, *N.-W. Africa* 94 Bf
Portumna, *Eire* 59 Bg
Port Vendres, *France* 69 Ee
Port Victoria, *Kenya* 93 Gd
Port Washington, *Wisconsin* 40 Cd
Port Weller, *Ontario* 40 Gd
Poru Tso, *Tibet* 85 Fb
Porvenir, *Chile* 50 Bh
Porvoo, *Finland* 63 Lf
Posadas, *Argentina* 50 Ec
Posadowsky, B., *Antarctica* 100 Gc
Poschiavo, *Switzerland* 61 Fb
Poseh, *China* 81 Cl
Posen. See Poznan
Poshan, *China* 80 Hd
Posht-e-Badam, *Persia* 89 Gc
Poso, *Celebes* 79 Hl
Poso Danau, *Celebes* 79 Gl
Possession I., *Antarctica* 100 Lb
Poste M. Cortier, *Algeria* 94 Fd
Poste Weygand, *Algeria* 94 Fd
Posušje, *Yugoslavia* 70 Fd
Potapovo, *Russia* 74 Hb
Potchefstroom, *Transvaal* 91 De
Potemkino, *Russia* 77 Ge
Potenza, *Italy* 71 Ee
Poti, *Gruzinskaya, Russia* 74 Dd
Potiskum, *Nigeria* 95 Hf
Potomac R., *Maryland, etc.* 44 Ac
Potosi, *Bolivia* 48 Dg
Potrerillos, *Chile* 50 Cc
Potsdam, *Germany* 64 Eb
Pottstown, *Pennsylvania* 40 Je
Pottsville, *Pennsylvania* 40 He
Poughkeepsie, *New York* 40 Ke
Pouso Alegre, *Brazil* 49 Ff
Pouso Alegre, *Brazil* 49 Hh
Povenets, *Russia* 74 Cb
Poverty B., *New Zealand* 51 Gc
Povoa de Varzim, *Portugal* 66 Ab
Povorino, *Russia* 77 Fe
Powder R., *Montana* 42 Eb
Powell Creek, *N.T., Aust.* 53 Fc
Poyang, *China* 81 Hh
Poyang Hu, *China* 81 Hh
Poza de la sal, *Spain* 66 Da
Požarevac, *Yugoslavia* 72 Cb
Požega, *Yugoslavia* 72 Ab
Poznan, *Poland* 65 Gb
Pozo Almonte, *Chile* 50 Cb
Pozoblanco, *Spain* 66 Cc
Prachin Buri, *Siam* 83 Cd
Prado, *Brazil* 49 Kg
Praga, *Poland* 65 Jb
Prague. See Praha
Praha, *Czechoslovakia* 64 Fc
Prai, *W. Malaysia* 83 Ce
Praid, *Rumania* 72 Ea
Prainha, *Brazil* 48 Ee
Prainha, *Brazil* 49 Gd
Prairie, *Queensland* 53 Hd
Prairie du Chien, *Wisconsin* 43 Hc
Prairie du Sac, *Wisconsin* 40 Bd
Prang, *Ghana* 94 Eg
Pratapgarth, *India* 87 Cc
Prato, *Italy* 70 Cd
Pravia, *Spain* 66 Ba
Pregolya, R., *Russia* 63 Jj
Prenay, *Lithuania* 63 Kj
Prentice, *Wisconsin* 40 Ac
Přerov, *Czechoslovakia* 65 Gd
Prescott, *Arizona* 45 Gh
Prescott, *Ontario* 40 Jc
President R. Sáenz-Pena, *Argentina* 50 Dc
Presidente Hermes, *Brazil* 48 Ef
Prešov, *Czechoslovakia* 65 Jd
Prespansko, Jezero, *Albania, etc.* 73 Cd
Pressburg. See Bratislava
Přeštice, *Czechoslovakia* 64 Ed
Preston, *England* 59 Fg
Prestwick, *Scotland* 58 De
Pretoria, *Transvaal* 91 De
Pretty Boy L., *Maryland* 44 Bc
Préveza, *Greece* 73 Ce
Pribilof Is., *Bering Sea* 43 Vm
Příbram, *Czechoslovakia* 64 Fd
Priego, *Spain* 66 Cd
Prieska, *Cape Province* 91 Ce
Prignitz, *Germany* 64 Db
Prijedor, *Yugoslavia* 70 Fc
Prijepolje, *Yugoslavia* 72 Bc
Prilep, *Yugoslavia* 72 Cd
Priluki, *Ukraine* 76 Hf
Prince Albert, *Cape Prov.* 91 Cf
Prince Albert Mts., *Antarc.* 100 Lb
Prince Edward Is., *Indian Oc.* 96 Bj
Prince Edward Pen., *Ont.* 40 Hd
Prince Harald Ld., *Antarc.* 100 Db
Prince of Wales, C., *Alaska* 43 Wl
Prince of Wales I., *Qnsld.* 53 Hb
Princes Lake, *Ontario* 40 Gc
Princess Astrid Ld., *Antarc.* 100 Cb
Princess Charlotte B., *Queensland* 53 Hb
Princess Elizabeth Ld., *Antarctica* 100 Fb
Princess Ragnhild Ld., *Antarctica* 100 Db
Princeton, *Illinois* 40 Be
Princeton, *Kentucky* 43 Jd
Princeton, *Wisconsin* 40 Bd
Prince William Sd., *Alaska* 43 Yl
Príncipe I., *G. of, Guinea* 92 Bd
Principe da Beira, *Brazil* 48 Ef
Pringles, *Argentina* 50 Df
Prins Karls Forland, *Arctic Ocean* 74 Aa
Prinzapolca, *Nicaragua* 47 Cd
Pripyat (Pripet) Marshes, *White Russia* 76 Ee
Pripyat (Pripet), R., *White Russia* 76 Ff
Pristina, *Yugoslavia* 72 Cc
Pritzwalk, *Germany* 64 Eb
Privolnoye, *Russia* 77 He
Prizren, *Yugoslavia* 72 Cc
Prizzi, *Sicily* 71 Dg
Progreso, *Mexico* 46 Gc
Prokop'yevsk, *Russia* 74 Hc
Prokuplje, *Yugoslavia* 72 Cc
Prome, *Burma* 85 Je
Propria, *Brazil* 49 Kf
Prosperine, *Qnsld.* 53 Jd
Provence, *prov., France* 69 Fe
Providence, *Rhode Island* 40 Le
Providence I., *Indian Ocean* 96 De
Provins, *France* 68 Eb
Provo, *Utah* 42 Dc
Prozor, *Yugoslavia* 70 Fd
Prudentopolis, *Brazil* 50 Fc
Prudhoe Ld., *Greenland* 41 Qb
Prüm, *Germany* 64 Bc
Prut, R., *Russia, etc.* 76 Fj
Przasnysz, *Poland* 65 Jb
Przemyśl, *Poland* 65 Kd
Przhevalsk, *Kirgizskaya. S.S.R.* 74 Gd
Psará, I., *Greece* 73 Ee
Pskov, *Russia* 76 Fc
Pskovskoye Oz., *Russia* 76 Fb
Ptuj, *Yugoslavia* 70 Eb
Puan, *Argentina* 50 De
Pucacuro, *Peru* 48 Bd
Pucallpa, *Peru* 48 Ce
Puchezh, *Russia* 77 Fb
Puchow. See Yungtsi
Puck, *Poland* 65 Ha
Pudasjärvi, *Finland* 62 Md
Pudukkottai, *India* 84 Ef
Puebla & state, *Mexico* 46 Ed
Puebla Bonito, *New Mexico* 42 Ed
Puebla de Alcocer, *Spain* 66 Cc
Puebla de Sanabria, *Spain* 66 Ba
Puebla de Trives, *Spain* 66 Ba
Pueblo, *Colorado* 42 Fd
Pueblo Hundido, *Chile* 50 Cc
Puelches, *Argentina* 50 Ce
Puenteareas, *Spain* 66 Aa
Puente Caldelas, *Spain* 66 Aa
Puentedeume, *Spain* 66 Aa
Puerh, *China* 78 Df
Puerhken, *Mongolia* 75 Jd
Puerto Aisen, *Chile* 50 Bg
Puerto Armuelles, *Panama* 47 Ce
Puerto Asis, *Colombia* 48 Bc
Puerto Ayacucho, *Venezuela* 48 Db
Puerto Barrios, *Guatemala* 46 Gd
Puerto Bermudez, *Peru* 48 Cf
Puerto Berrio, *Colombia* 48 Cb
Puerto Cabello, *Venezuela* 48 Da
Puerto Cabezas, *Nicaragua* 47 Cd
Puerto Carreno, *Colombia* 48 Db
Puerto Casado, *Paraguay* 50 Eb
Puerto Chicama, *Peru* 48 Be
Puerto Colombia, *Colombia* 48 Ca
Puerto Córdoba, *Colombia* 48 Cd
Puerto Cortes, *Honduras* 46 Gd
Puerto Coyle, *Argentina* 50 Ch
Puerto Cumarebo, *Venez.* 48 Da
Puerto de Carrizal, *Chile* 50 Bc
Puerto de Chanaral, *Chile* 50 Bc
Puerto de Santa Maria, *Sp.* 66 Bd
Puerto Deseado, *Argentina* 50 Cg
Puerto Gaiba. See Puerto Quijarro
Puerto Grether, *Bolivia* 48 Eg
Puerto Harberton, *Argent.* 50 Ch
Puerto Heath, *Bolivia* 48 Df
Puerto La Cruz, *Venezuela* 48 Ea
Puerto Leguizamo, *Colombia* 48 Cd
Puerto Libertad, *Salvador* 47 Bd
Puertollano, *Spain* 66 Cc
Puerto Lobos, *Argentina* 50 Cf
Puerto Madryn, *Argentina* 50 Cf
Puerto Maldonado, *Peru* 48 Df
Puerto Montt, *Chile* 50 Bf
Puerto Morelos, *Mexico* 46 Gc
Puerto Natales, *Chile* 50 Ch
Puerto Nuevo, *Colombia* 48 Db
Puerto Pirámides, *Argentina* 50 Df
Puerto Plata, *Rep. Domin.* 47 Ec
Puerto Princesa, *Phil.* 79 Gj
Puerto Quellen, *Chile* 50 Bf
Puerto Quijarro, *Bolivia* 48 Fg
Puerto Rico, I., *W. Indies* 47 Fc
Puerto Suarez, *Bolivia* 49 Fg
Puerto Sucre, *Bolivia* 48 Df
Puerto Varas, *Chile* 50 Bf
Puerto Victoria, *Peru* 48 Ce
Puerto Villamizar, *Colombia* 48 Cb
Puerto Visser, *Argentina* 50 Cg
Puerto Wilches, *Colombia* 48 Cb
Pueyrredón, L., *Argentina* 50 Bg
Pugachev, *Russia* 77 Jd
Pugal, *India* 86 Cf
Puget, *France* 69 Ge
Puget Sd., *Washington* 42 Bb
Puglia, *dep., Italy* 71 Fe
Pühalepa, *Estonia* 63 Kg
Puigcerdá, *Spain* 67 Fa
Puimro, *Brazil* 49 Gc
Pukaki, L., *New Zealand* 51 Cf
Pukapuka I., *Pacific Ocean* 98 Jj
Pukapuka I., *Tuamotu Arch.* 99 Mj
Pukchong, *Korea* 78 Jb
Pukekohe, *New Zealand* 51 Eb
Pukow, *China* 80 Jf
Pula, *Yugoslavia* 70 Dc
Pulacayo, *Bolivia* 50 Cb
Pulap, I., *Caroline Islands* 98 Dg
Pulaski, *New York* 40 Hd
Pulicat I., *India* 84 Ff
Pulkkila, *Finland* 62 Ld
Pulo Condore, I., *Indo-China* 83 De
Pultneyville, *New York* 44 Ba
Puma, *Tanzania* 93 Ge
Puna, I., *Ecuador* 48 Ad
Punakha, *Bhutan* 87 Gb
Punch, *Kashmir* 86 Dd
Pundri, *India* 86 Ef
Punjab, *India* 86 De
Puno, *Peru* 48 Cg
Punta Alta, *Argentina* 50 De
Punta Arenas, *Chile* 50 Bh
Punta Colorado, *Chile* 50 Bc
Punta del Faro, *Sicily* 71 Ef
Punta de Pedras, *Brazil* 49 Hd
Punta Gorda, *Brit. Hond.* 47 Bc
Puntarenas, *Costa Rica* 47 Ce
Punta Salinas, *Venezuela* 48 Ca
Punxsutawney, *Pennsylvania* 44 Ab
Punyu. See Canton
Puolanka, *Finland* 62 Md
Puquio, *Peru* 48 Cf
Purang Chaka, *Tibet* 85 Fb
Puri, *India* 85 Ge
Purificacion, *Colombia* 48 Cc
Purna, *India* 84 Ee
Purnea, *India* 87 Fc
Pursat, *Cambodia* 83 Cd
Purulia, *India* 87 Fd
Purus, R., *Brazil, etc.* 48 De
Purwa, *India* 87 Cb
Pusan, *Korea* 78 Jc
Pushchino, *Russia* 75 Kc
Pusht-e-Kuh, Mts., *Persia* 88 Ec
Putao. See Fort Hertz
Putaruru, *N.Z.* 51 Ec
Putbus, *Germany* 64 Ea
Putien, *China* 81 Jk
Putignano, *Italy* 71 Fe
Putnam, *Connecticut* 44 Eb
Putnok, *Hungary* 65 Jd
Putorana, Gory, *Russia* 75 Jb
Puttalam, *Ceylon* 84 Eg
Putte, *Belgium* 60 Cc
Putte, *Belgium* 60 Cc
Putten, *Netherlands* 60 Db
Putumayo, R., *Colombia, etc.* 48 Cd
Putussibau, *Borneo* 79 Fk
Puula Vesi, *Finland* 63 Mf
Puurs, *Belgium* 60 Cc
Puy, le, *France* 69 Ed
Puyallup, *Washington* 45 Bb
Puy-de-Dôme, *dep., France* 68 Ed
Pyapon, *Burma* 85 Je
Pyatistennoye, *Russia* 75 Rb
Pyhä Järvi, *Finland* 62 Le
Pyhä Järvi, *Finland* 63 Kf
Pyhäntä, *Finland* 62 Md
Pyinmana, *Burma* 85 Je
Pyŏngyang, *Korea* 78 Jc
Pyramid L., *Nevada* 45 De
Pyramid Pk., *California* 45 Cf
Pyrénées, Mts., *France-Sp.* 67 Ea
Pyrénées-Orientales, *dep., France* 69 Ee
Pyrzyce, *Poland* 64 Fb
Pyu, *Burma* 85 Je
Pyzdry, *Poland* 65 Gb
Qabatiya, *Israel* 90 De
Qafar, *Arabia* 88 Dd
Qaiya, *Arabia* 88 Ee
Qala Mashiz, *Persia* 89 Gd
Qal'at al Akhdhar, *Arabia* 88 Cd
Qal'at Dar al Hamra, *Arabia* 88 Cd
Qal'at de Dab'a, *Jordan* 90 Ef
Qal'at el Marqah, *Syria* 90 Db
Qal'at el Mudiq. See Ma'arret en Numan
Qal'at Uneiza, *Jordan* 90 Dg
Qalqiliya, *Jordan* 90 Ce
Qamr, B., *S. Yemen* 89 Ff
Qara, *Egypt* 95 Lc
Qardaha, *Syria* 90 Eb
Qartaba, *Lebanon* 90 Dc
Qasab, *Trucial States* 89 Gd
Qasim, *Arabia* 88 Dd
Qasr Amij, *Iraq* 88 Dc
Qasr el Azraq, *Jordan* 90 Ef
Qasr e Qand, *Persia* 89 Hd
Qasr Haiyaniya, *Arabia* 88 Dd
Qasr ibn Aliya, *Arabia* 88 Dd
Qasr-i-Shirin, *Persia* 88 Ec
Qa'taba, *Yemen* 88 Dg
Qatana, *Syria* 90 Ed
Qatar, *Persian Gulf* 89 Fd
Qatif, *Arabia* 88 Ed
Qayen, *Persia* 89 Gc
Qazvin, *Persia* 89 Fb
Qena, *Egypt* 95 Mc
Qeshm I., *Persia* 89 Gd
Qeys I., *Persia* 89 Fd
Qishn, *S. Yemen* 89 Ff
Qishran I., *Arabia* 88 Ce
Qohoud, *Persia* 89 Fc
Qom, *Persia* 89 Fc
Qotur, *Persia* 88 Db
Qoz Bal 'Air, *Arabia* 88 Df
Quabbin Res., *Massachusetts* 44 Da
Quakenbrück, *Germany* 64 Bb
Quang Tri., *S. Vietnam* 79 Eg
Quarai, *Brazil* 50 Ed
Quatre Bras, *Belgium* 60 Cd
Qubeiyat, *Lebanon* 90 Ec
Quchan, *Persia* 89 Gb
Queen Alexandra Ra., *Antarctica* 100 Ka
Queen Anne, *Maryland* 44 Cc
Queen Charlotte B., *Falkland Islands* 50 Dh
Queen Mary Ld., *Antarctica* 100 Gc
Queen Maud Ld., *Antarc.* 100 Cb
Queen Maud Ra., *Antarc.* 100 Pa
Queen's Chan., *N. Terr., Australia* 52 Eb
Queensland, *state, Australia* 53 Hd
Queenstown, *Cape Province* 91 Df
Queenstown, *New Zealand* 51 Bf
Queenstown. See Cobh
Queenstown, *Tasmania* 53 Jh
Queimadas, *Brazil* 49 Kf
Quelimane, *Moçambique* 91 Fc
Quemu Quemú, *Argentina* 50 De
Quequen, *Argentina* 50 Ee
Queretaro, *Mexico* 46 Dc
Quetta, *W. Pakistan* 84 Cb
Quezaltenango, *Guatemala* 46 Fe
Quezon City, *Philippines* 79 Hh
Quibdo, *Colombia* 48 Bb
Quiberon, B. de., *France* 68 Bc
Quievrain, *Belgium* 60 Bd
Quila, *Mexico* 46 Cc
Quilca, *Peru* 48 Cg
Quilino, *Argentina* 50 Dd
Quillabamba, *Peru* 48 Cf
Quillan, *France* 69 Ee
Quillota, *Chile* 50 Bd
Quilon (Kollam), *India* 84 Eg
Quilpie, *Queensland* 53 He
Quimper, *France* 68 Ab
Quimperle, *France* 68 Bc
Quince Mil, *Peru* 48 Cf
Quincy, *Illinois* 43 Hd
Quincy, *Massachusetts* 40 Ld
Quines, *Argentina* 50 Cd
Quiney, *Michigan* 40 De
Quintana de la Serena, *Sp.* 66 Cc
Quintanar de la Orden, *Sp.* 66 Dc
Quintana Roo, *state, Mexico* 46 Gd
Quipapa, *Brazil* 49 Ke
Quiriquire, *Venezuela* 48 Ea
Quiroga, *Spain* 66 Ba
Quissanga, *Moçambique* 93 Jg
Quissico, *Moçambique* 91 Ed
Quitapa, *Angola* 92 Dg
Quito, *Ecuador* 48 Bd
Quixada, *Brazil* 49 Kd
Quixeramobim, *Brazil* 49 Ke
Qunsulye, *Arabia* 88 De
Quorn, *S. Australia* 53 Gf
Quryat, *Muscat & Oman* 89 Ge
Qus, *Egypt* 95 Mc
Qusaiba, *Arabia* 88 De
Qusayar, *S. Yemen* 89 Fg
Quseir, *Egypt* 95 Mc
Qusuriya, *Arabia* 88 Dd
Quteifa, *Syria* 90 Ed
Quyon, *Quebec* 40 Hc
Raahe, *Finland* 62 Ld
Raasay & Sd of, *Scotland* 58 Cc
Rab, I., *Yugoslavia* 70 Ec
Raba, *Sumbawa I., Indon.* 79 Gm
Rabat, *Morocco* 94 Db
Rabat Kerim, *Persia* 89 Fb
Rabigh, *Arabia* 88 Ce
Rabkob. See Dharmjaygarh
Rabkor, *Russia* 76 Fe
Race, The, *Conn.-New York* 44 Db
Rach-Gia, *S. Vietnam* 83 Dd
Raciborz, *Poland* 65 Hc
Racine, *Wisconsin* 40 Cd
Rada, *Yemen* 88 Dg
Radak Chain, *Marshall Is.* 98 Gf
Rădăuti, *Rumania* 76 Dh
Radhanpur, *India* 84 Dd
Radhwa, Jebel, *Arabia* 88 Ce
Radnevo, *Bulgaria* 72 Ec
Radnor, *co., Wales* 59 Eh
Radom, *Poland* 65 Jc
Radomir, *Bulgaria* 72 Dc
Radomsko, *Poland* 65 Hc
Radstadt, *Austria* 64 Ee
Radviliskis, *Lithuania* 63 Kj
Radzyn, *Poland* 65 Kc
Rae Bareli, *India* 87 Cb
Raeside, L., *W. Australia* 52 De
Raetihi, *New Zealand* 51 Ec
Rafaela, *Argentina* 50 Dd
Rafah, *Egypt* 90 Cf
Rafsanjan, *Persia* 89 Gc
Raga, *Sudan* 95 Lg
Ragaz, Bad, *Switzerland* 61 Ea
Raghugarh, *India* 87 Ac
Raghunathpur, *India* 87 Fd
Raglan, *New Zealand* 51 Eb
Raglan Ra., *New Zealand* 51 Dd
Ragunda, *Sweden* 62 Ge
Ragusa (Dubrovnik), *Yugosl.* 70 Gd
Ragusa, *Sicily* 71 Eg
Rahaeng. See Tak
Raheita, *Eritrea* 93 Jb
Rahhyut, *Muscat & Oman* 89 Ff
Raiatea, I., *Society Islands* 99 Kj
Raichur, *India* 84 Ee
Raida, *S. Yemen* 88 Eg
Raiganj, *India* 87 Gc
Raikot, *India* 86 Ee
Raingarh, *India* 86 Ee
Rainier, Mt., *Washington* 45 Bb
Raipur, *India* 84 Fd
Raivavae, I., *Austral Is.* 99 Lk
Raiwind, *W. Pakistan* 86 De
Raja, Mt., *Borneo* 79 Fl
Rajahmundry, *India* 84 Fe
Rajakhera, *India* 87 Bb
Rajang, R., *Sarawak* 79 Fk
Rajanpur, *W. Pakistan* 86 Bf
Rajapalaiyam, *India* 84 Eg
Rajasthan, *state, India* 84 Dc
Rajgarh, *India* 86 Df
Rajkot, *India* 84 Dd
Rajmahal, *India* 87 Fc
Rajmahal Hills, *India* 87 Ec
Rajura, *India* 84 Ee
Rakahanga, I., *Pacific Oc.* 98 Jh
Rakaposhi, Mt., *Kashmir* 86 Db
Raka Tsangpo, R., *Tibet* 85 Gc
Rakvere, *Estonia* 63 Mg
Raleigh, *N. Carolina* 43 Ld
Raleigh B., *N. Carolina* 43 Le
Ralik Chain, *Marshall Is.* 98 Fg
Ram, *Jordan* 90 Dh
Rama, *Ethiopia* 93 Jb
Rama, *Israel* 90 De
Ramadi, *Iraq* 88 Dc
Ramallah, *Jordan* 90 Df
Ramallo, *Argentina* 50 Dd
Ramanthapuran, *India* 84 Eg
Rambouillet, *France* 68 Db
Rameswaram, *India* 84 Eg
Ramgarh, *India* 86 Df
Ramgarh, *India* 87 Cd
Ramgarh, *India* 87 Ed
Ram Hormuz, *Persia* 88 Ec
Ramkola, *India* 87 Dd
Ramla, *Israel* 90 Cf
Ramnagar, *India* 87 Cd
Ramnagar, *Kashmir* 86 Dd
Ramnagar, *W. Pakistan* 86 Cd
Râmnicul Sărat, *Rumania* 72 Fb
Râmnicu Valcea, *Rumania* 72 Eb
Ramore, *Ontario* 40 Fa
Ramoutsa, *Botswana* 91 Dd
Rampur, *India* 84 Fd
Rampur, *India* 86 Ee
Rampur, *India* 87 Ba
Rampur Boalia, *E. Pakistan* 87 Gc
Ramree, *Burma* 85 He
Ramscappelle, *Belgium* 60 Ac
Ramsele, *Sweden* 62 Ge
Ramsey, *Isle of Man* 59 Ef
Ramsey, I., *Wales* 59 Dj
Ramsey, *Ontario* 40 Eb
Ramsgate, *England* 59 Hj
Ramsjö, *Sweden* 63 Fe
Ramtha, *Jordan* 90 Ee
Ramtok, *India* 84 Ed
Ran Fd., *Norway* 62 Ec
Ranaghat, *India* 87 Gd
Rancagua, *Chile* 50 Bd
Rance, *Belgium* 60 Cd
Ranchi, *India* 87 Ed
Randazzo, *Sicily* 71 Eg
Randers, *Denmark* 63 Dh
Randolph, *Vermont* 40 Kd
Randsfjord, *Norway* 62 Df
Ranenburg, *Russia* 77 Ed
Ranfurly, *New Zealand* 51 Cf
Rangamati, *E. Pakistan* 85 Hd
Ranger, *Texas* 42 Ge
Rangiora, *New Zealand* 51 De
Rangitaiki, R., *New Zealand* 51 Fc
Rangitikei, R., *New Zealand* 51 Ed
Rangitoto Ra., *New Zealand* 51 Ec
Rangoon & R., *Burma* 85 Je
Rangpur, *E. Pakistan* 87 Gc
Rania, *India* 86 Df
Ranibennur, *India* 84 Ef
Raniganj, *India* 87 Fc
Raniganj, *India* 87 Fd
Ranikhet, *India* 87 Ba
Rannoch L., *Scotland* 58 Ed
Rantauparapat, *Sumatra* 79 Ck
Rantekombola, Mt., *Celebes* 79 Gh
Rantsila, *Finland* 62 Ld
Ranua, *Finland* 62 Md
Rapa, I., *Austral Islands* 99 Lk
Rapadama, *Volta* 94 Ef
Rapid City, *S. Dakota* 42 Fc
Rapla, *Estonia* 63 Lg
Rapperswil, *Switzerland* 61 Da
Raqqa, *Syria* 88 Cb
Rarotonga, I., *Cook Island* 99 Kk
Ras al Had, *Muscat & Oman* 89 Ge
Ras al Khaymah, *Trucial St.* 89 Gd
Ras Dashan, Mt., *Ethiopia* 93 Hb
Rashad, *Sudan* 95 Mf
Rashadiya, *Jordan* 90 Dg
Rasheiya, *Lebanon* 90 Dd
Rashm, *Persia* 89 Fb
Rasht, *Persia* 88 Eb
Raška, *Yugoslavia* 72 Cc
Rason, L., *W. Australia* 52 De
Rasova, *Rumania* 72 Fb
Rasskazovo, *Russia* 77 Ed
Ratangarh, *India* 86 Df
Rat Buri, *Siam* 83 Bd
Rathlin I., *N. Ireland* 58 Ce
Ratibor. See Raciborz
Ratikon, Mts., *Switz.-Austria* 61 Ea
Ratnagiri, *India* 84 De
Rättvik, *Sweden* 63 Ff
Raton, *New Mexico* 42 Fd
Rauch, *Argentina* 50 Ee
Raudha, *Yemen* 88 Df
Raukumara Ra., *N.Z.* 51 Fc
Rauma, *Finland* 63 Jf
Rautas, *Sweden* 62 Hb
Rautavaara, *Finland* 62 Ne
Rautio, *Finland* 62 Ld
Ravar, *Persia* 89 Gc
Ravenna, *Italy* 70 Dc
Ravi R., *W. Pakistan* 86 De
Rawaidha, *Arabia* 88 De
Rawalpindi, *W. Pakistan* 86 Cd
Rawandiz, *Iraq* 88 Db
Rawatsar, *India* 86 Df
Rawene, *New Zealand* 51 Da
Rawlinna, *W. Australia* 52 Ef
Rawlins, *Wyoming* 42 Ec
Rawson, *Argentina* 50 Cf
Rays Hill, *Pennsylvania* 44 Ac
Rayadrug, *India* 84 Ef
Rayon. See Cardenas
Rayon, *Mexico* 46 Bb
Razelm L., *Rumania* 72 Gb
Razan, *Persia* 88 Eb
Razgrad, *Bulgaria* 72 Fc
Razmak, *W. Pakistan* 86 Ad
Ré, I. de, *France* 68 Cc
Reading, *England* 59 Gj
Reading, *Pennsylvania* 40 Je
Real, Cord., *Bolivia* 48 Dg
Real, Cord., *Ecuador, etc.* 48 Bd
Real Castillo, *Mexico* 46 Aa
Realico, *Argentina* 50 De
Realp, *Switzerland* 61 Db
Reata, *Mexico* 46 Db
Rebun, I., *Japan* 82 Gb
Recalada, *Chile* 50 Ah
Recalde, *Argentina* 50 De
Recherche Arch., *W. Aust.* 52 Df
Rechna Doab, *W. Pakistan* 86 Ce
Recht, *Belgium* 60 Ed
Recife, *Brazil* 49 Le
Reconquista, *Argentina* 50 Ec
Recreio, *Brazil* 49 Fe
Red L., *Minnesota* 43 Hb
Red R., *Louisiana, etc.* 43 He
Red R., *Minnesota, etc.* 42 Gb
Red R. See Song-koi
Red Sea, *Africa-Arabia* 54 Cf
Redbank, *New Jersey* 44 Cb
Redding, *California* 45 Be
Redfield, *S. Dakota* 42 Gc
Redlands, *California* 45 Eh
Red Lodge, *Montana* 42 Eb
Redon, *France* 68 Bc
Redondela, *Spain* 66 Aa
Redruth, *Michigan* 40 Bb
Ree L., *Eire* 59 Bg
Reed City, *Michigan* 40 Dd
Reedsburg, *Wisconsin* 40 Ad
Reefton, *New Zealand* 51 Ce
Refresco, *Chile* 50 Cc
Regencia, *Brazil* 49 Kg
Regensburg, *Germany* 64 Ed
Reggan, *Algeria* 94 Fc
Reggio Calabria, *Italy* 71 Ef
Reggio nell'Emilia, *Italy* 70 Cc
Reghin, *Rumania* 72 Ea
Registro do Araguaia, *Brazil* 49 Gg
Rehoboth, *S.-W. Africa* 91 Bd
Rehovot, *Jordan* 90 Cf
Reichenbach, *Germany* 64 Ec
Reigate, *England* 59 Gj
Reigi, *Estonia* 63 Kg
Reims, *France* 68 Fb
Reina Adelaide, Arch. de la, *Chile* 50 Bh
Reinosa, *Mexico* 46 Eb
Reinosa, *Spain* 66 Ca
Reitan, *Norway* 62 De
Reitz, *Orange Free State* 91 De
Rekinniki, *Russia* 75 Rb
Remansão, *Brazil* 49 Hd
Remanso, *Brazil* 49 Je
Rembang, *Java* 79 Fm
Remedios, *Cuba* 47 Db
Remedios, *Panama* 47 Ce
Remeshk, *Persia* 89 Gd
Remiremont, *France* 68 Gb
Remoulins, *France* 69 Fe
Remscheid, *Germany* 64 Bc
Remüs, *Switzerland* 61 Fb
Rena, *Norway* 63 Df
Renaix. See Ronse
Renca, *Argentina* 50 Cd
Rendsburg, *Germany* 64 Ca
Renfrew, *Ontario* 40 Hc
Renfrew, *co., Scotland* 58 Ee
Rengat, *Sumatra* 79 Dl
Reni (Taranagar), *India* 86 Df
Renigunta, *India* 84 Ef
Renk, *Sudan* 95 Mf
Renkum, *Netherlands* 60 Dc
Renmark, *S. Australia* 53 Hf
Rennell, I., *Solomon Islands* 98 Fj
Rennes, *France* 68 Cb
Reno, *Nevada* 45 Df
Renovo, *Pennsylvania* 40 He
Rensselaer, *New York* 40 Kd
Renswoude, *Netherlands* 60 Db
Reo, *Flores I., Indonesia* 79 Hm
Réole la, *France* 69 Cd
Republica Dominicana, *W.I.* 47 Ec
Republican, R., *Nebraska* 42 Gc
Republic of South Africa, *Africa* 91 Ce
Repulse B., *Queensland* 53 Jd
Requena, *Peru* 49 Cd
Requena, *Spain* 67 Ec
Resita, *Rumania* 72 Cb
Resistencia, *Argentina* 50 Ec
Resolution I., *New Zealand* 51 Af
Rethel, *France* 68 Fb
Réthimnon, *Crete* 73 Eg
Rethy, *Belgium* 60 Dc
Réunion, I., *Indian Ocean* 96 Dg
Reusel, *Netherlands* 60 Dc
Reutlingen, *Germany* 64 Cd
Reutte, *Austria* 64 De
Revda, *Russia* 77 Qb
Revel. See Tallinn
Revilla Gigedo Is., *Mexico* 46 Bd
Revivim, *Israel* 90 Cf
Rewa, *India* 87 Cc
Rewari, *India* 86 Ef
Rey, I. del, *Panama* 47 De
Reydharfjord, *Iceland* 62 Zm
Reyes, *Mexico* 46 Dd
Reykjavik, *Iceland* 62 Um
Rezā'iyeh, *Persia* 88 Db
Rēzekne, *Latvia* 63 Mh
Rheden, *Netherlands* 60 Eb
Rhein R., *Germany* 64 Bc
Rheine, *Germany* 64 Bb
Rheinland-Pfalz, *Germany* 64 Bc
Rhenen, *Netherlands* 60 Dc
Rheydt, *Germany* 64 Bc
Rhine R. See Rhein R.
Rhinelander, *Wisconsin* 40 Bc
Rhode Island, *state, U.S.A.* 44 Eb
Rhodes (Rodhos) I., *Gr.* 73 Gf
Rhodesia, N. See Zambia
Rhodesia, *Cent. Africa* 91 Dc
Rhön Geb., *Germany* 64 Cc
Rhondda, *Wales* 59 Ej
Rhône, *dep., France* 68 Fd
Rhône, R., *France, etc.* 69 Fd
Rhyl, *Wales* 59 Eg
Riaño, *Spain* 66 Ca
Riau Arch., *Indonesia* 79 Dk
Riaza, *Spain* 66 Db
Ribadeo, *Spain* 66 Ba
Ribadesella, *Spain* 66 Ca
Ribble, R., *England* 59 Fg
Ribe, *Denmark* 63 Cj
Ribeirão Preto, *Brazil* 49 Hh
Ribera, *Sicily* 71 Dg
Riberalta, *Bolivia* 48 Df
Richards C., *Arctic Ocean* 41 Ra
Richardson Mts., *N.Z.* 51 Bf
Richfield, *Utah* 42 Dd
Richland, *Washington* 45 Db
Richland Center, *Wisconsin* 40 Ad
Richmond, *California* 45 Bg
Richmond, *Cape Province* 91 Cf
Richmond, *Indiana* 40 Df
Richmond, *New York* 40 Je
Richmond, *New Zealand* 51 Dd
Richmond, *Quebec* 40 Kc
Richmond, *Queensland* 53 Hd

Richmond, *Virginia* **43** Ld
Ricla, *Spain* **67** Eb
Riddes, *Switzerland* **61** Cb
Ridgetown, *Ontario* **40** Fd
Ridgway, *Pennsylvania* **40** Ge
Ridi, *Nepal* **87** Db
Ridout, *Ontario* **40** Eb
Riesa, *Germany* **64** Ec
Rietavas, *Lithuania* **63** Jj
Rieti, *Italy* **70** Dd
Riga, *Latvia* **63** Lh
Riga, G. of, *Latvia* **63** Kh
Rigan, *Persia* **89** Gd
Rigmati, *Persia* **89** Gd
Rignasco, *Switzerland* **61** Db
Rig-Rig, *Chad* **95** Hf
Rijeka, *Yugoslavia* **70** Ec
Rijswijk, *Netherlands* **60** Cb
Rimatara, I., *Austral Is.* **99** Kk
Rimini, *Italy* **70** Dc
Rincon, *Cuba* **47** Cb
Rincón, *New Mexico* **42** Ee
Rindal, *Norway* **62** Ce
Ringelspitz, Mt., *Switz.* **61** Eb
Ringköbing, *Denmark* **63** Ch
Ringvassöy, I., *Norway* **62** Hb
Rinihue, *Chile* **50** Be
Riobamba, *Ecuador* **48** Bd
Rio Bonito, *Brazil* **49** Jh
Rio Branco, *Brazil* **50** Gc
Rio Branco, *Brazil* **48** De
Rio Branco, *Uruguay* **50** Fd
Rio Bueno, *Chile* **50** Bf
Rio Chico, *Argentina* **50** Cg
Rio Chico, *Venezuela* **48** Da
Rio Colorado, *Argentina* **50** De
Rio Cuarto, *Argentina* **50** Dd
Rio de Janeiro, *Brazil* **49** Jh
Rio de Oro. *See* Convención
Rio-de-Oro (*Sp. W. Africa*) **94** Bd
Rio do Sul, *Brazil* **50** Gc
Rio Gallegos & R., *Argent.* **50** Ch
Rio Grande, *Brazil* **50** Fd
Rio Grande, *Mexico* **46** Dc
Rio Grande del Norte, *Mexico-U.S.A.* **46** Db
Riohacha, *Colombia* **48** Ca
Rio Hondo, *Argentina* **50** Dc
Rio Muerto, *Argentina* **50** Dc
Rio Mulato, *Bolivia* **48** Dg
Rio Muni, *W. Africa* **92** Cd
Rio Negro, *Brazil* **50** Gc
Rionero in Vulture, *Italy* **71** Ee
Rio Pardo, *Brazil* **49** Gh
Rio Verde, *Brazil* **49** Gg
Rio Verde, *Ecuador* **48** Bc
Rio Verde, *Mexico* **46** Ec
Rioz, *France* **68** Gc
Ripats, *Sweden* **62** Jc
Ripley, *California* **45** Fj
Ripley, *New York* **44** Aa
Ripley, *W. Virginia* **40** Ff
Ripon, *England* **59** Ff
Ripon, *Quebec* **40** Jc
Ripon, *Wisconsin* **40** Bd
Risafe, *Syria* **88** Cb
Risalpur, *W. Pakistan* **86** Cc
Risbäck, *Sweden* **62** Jc
Rishiri, I., *Japan* **82** Gb
Rishon-le-Zion, *Israel* **90** Cf
Risör, *Norway* **63** Cg
Ristijärvi, *Finland* **62** Nd
Ritchie's Arch., *Andaman Is.* **85** Hf
Rivadavia, *Argentina* **50** Db
Rivas, *Nicaragua* **47** Bd
Rivera, *Argentina* **50** De
Rivera, *Uruguay* **50** Ed
Riverhead, *New York* **40** Ke
Rivero, I., *Chile* **50** Bg
Riversdale, *New Zealand* **51** Bf
Riverside, *California* **45** Ej
Riverside Mt., *California* **45** Fh
Riverton, *New Zealand* **51** Bg
Riviera di Levante, *Italy* **70** Bc
Riviera di Ponente, *Italy* **70** Ad
Rivière à Pierre, *Quebec* **40** Kb
Riyadh (Ar Riyadh), *Arabia* **88** Ee
Riyaq, *Lebanon* **90** Ed
Rizaiyeh. *See* Rezā'iyeh
Rize, *Turkey* **88** Da
Rizokarpaso, *Cyprus* **90** Cb
Rizzuto C., *Italy* **71** Ff
Roa, *Spain* **66** Db
Roanne, *France* **68** Fc
Roanoke, *Virginia* **43** Ld
Roaringwater B., *Eire* **59** Aj
Roatan I., *Honduras* **47** Bc
Robat Thana, *W. Pakistan* **84** Bc
Robertsfors, *Sweden* **62** Jd
Robertsganj, *India* **87** Dc
Robertsport, *Liberia* **94** Cg
Robeson Ch., *Arctic Ocean* **41** Qa
Robore, *Bolivia* **48** Fg
Roca, la, *Spain* **66** Bc
Rocafuerte, *Ecuador* **48** Bd
Rocha, *Uruguay* **50** Bd
Rochdale, *England* **59** Fg
Rochefort, *Belgium* **60** Dd
Rochefort, *France* **68** Cd
Rochester, *England* **59** Hj
Rochester, *Michigan* **40** Ed
Rochester, *Minnesota* **43** Hc
Rochester, *New Hampshire* **40** Ld
Rochester, *New York* **40** Hd
Roche-sur-Yon, la, *France* **68** Cc
Rockall, I., *Atlantic Ocean* **54** Fb
Rockefeller Plateau, *Antarc.* **100** Pb
Rockford, *Illinois* **40** Bd
Rockhampton, *Queensland* **53** Kd
Rock Hill, *S. Carolina* **43** Ke
Rock Island, *Illinois* **40** Ae
Rockland, *Massachusetts* **44** Ea
Rockland, *Ontario* **40** Jc
Rock Pt., *New Zealand* **51** Dd
Rock Springs, *Wyoming* **42** Ec
Rockstone, *Guyana* **48** Fb
Rockville, *Maryland* **44** Bc
Rocky Mount, *N. Carolina* **43** Ld
Rocky Mts., *N. America* **42** Db
Rocky Mountain Nat. Park, *Colorado* **42** Ec
Rocroi, *France* **68** Fb
Rödby, *Denmark* **63** Dj
Rodchevo, *Russia* **75** Qb
Rodez, *France* **69** Ed
Rodhopi, *Greece* **72** Ed
Rodhos & I., *Greece* **73** Gf
Rodkhan, *W. Pakistan* **84** Bc
Rodopi Planina, *Bulg.-Greece* **72** Dd
Rodosto. *See* Tekirdag
Rodriquez, I., *Indian Ocean* **96** Ef
Roebourne, *W. Australia* **52** Cd
Roermond, *Netherlands* **60** Dc
Roeselare (Roulers), *Belg.* **60** Bd
Rœulx, *Belgium* **60** Cd
Rogachev, *White Russia* **76** Ge
Rogers City, *Michigan* **40** Ec
Rogliano, *Corsica* **69** Kh
Rohri, *W. Pakistan* **84** Cc
Rohtak, *India* **86** Ef
Roi Et, *Siam* **83** Cc
Roisin, *Belgium* **60** Bd
Rojas, *Argentina* **50** Dd
Rokiškis, *Lithuania* **63** Lj
Rolde, *Netherlands* **60** Eb
Rolle, *Switzerland* **61** Bb
Rolvsöy, *Norway* **62** Ka
Roma, *Queensland* **53** Je
Roma, *Sweden* **63** Hh
Roma, *Italy* **71** De
Roma, I., *Indonesia* **79** Jm
Roman, *Rumania* **72** Fa
Romans, *France* **69** Fd
Romanshorn, *Switzerland* **61** Ea
Romanzof, C., *Alaska* **43** Wl
Rome, *Georgia* **43** Je
Rome, *New York* **40** Jd
Rome (Roma), *Italy* **71** De
Romerée, *Belgium* **60** Cd
Romford, *England* **59** Hj
Romney, *W. Virginia* **40** Gf
Romny, *Ukraine* **76** Hf
Römö, I., *Denmark* **63** Cj
Romont, *Switzerland* **61** Bb
Romsdalshorn, *Norway* **62** Be
Ron, *N. Vietnam* **83** Dc
Ronda, *Kashmir* **86** Dc
Ronda, *Spain* **66** Cd
Rondeau, *Ontario* **40** Fd
Rondônia, *Brazil* **48** Ef
Ronehamn, *Sweden* **63** Hh
Rönne, *Bornholm, I., Den.* **63** Fj
Ronne B., *Antarctica* **100** Sb
Ronneby, *Sweden* **63** Fh
Ronse. *See* Renaix
Ronse's Point, *New York* **40** Kc
Roosendaal, *Netherlands* **60** Cc
Roosevelt, I., *Antarctica* **100** Mb
Roosevelt Res., *Arizona* **42** De
Rooseveltown, *New York* **40** Jc
Roper, R., *N. Terr., Aust.* **53** Fb
Roquefort, *France* **69** Cd
Rori, *India* **86** Df
Röros, *Norway* **62** De
Rorschach, *Switzerland* **61** Ea
Rös Vatn, *Norway* **62** Fd
Rosa, la, *Switzerland* **61** Fb
Rosa, Monte, *Switz.-Italy* **61** Cc
Rosablanche, Mt., *Switz.* **61** Cb
Rosarinho. *See* Axinim
Rosario, *Argentina* **50** Dd
Rosario, *Brazil* **49** Jd
Rosario, *Chile* **50** Bb
Rosario, *Mexico* **46** Aa
Rosario, *Mexico* **46** Cc
Rosario de la Frontera, *Argentina* **50** Dc
Rosario Oeste, *Brazil* **49** Ff
Rosario Tala, *Argentina* **50** Ed
Rosas, *Spain* **67** Ga
Rosas, G. of, *Spain* **67** Ga
Roscommon, *Michigan* **40** Dc
Roscommon & co., *Eire* **59** Bg
Roscrea, *Eire* **59** Bh
Rose, I., *Samoa* **98** Jj
Roseburg, *Oregon* **45** Bd
Roseires, *Sudan* **95** Mf
Rosenheim, *Germany* **64** Ee
Rosetta (Rashid), *Egypt* **95** Mb
Rosignano Marittamo, *Italy* **70** Cd
Rosignol, *Guyana* **48** Fb
Roslavl, *Russia* **76** He
Rosport, *Luxembourg* **60** Ee
Ross, *England* **59** Fj
Ross, *New Zealand* **51** Ce
Ross Ice Shelf, *Antarctica* **100** Ma
Ross, I., *Antarctica* **100** Lb
Ross I., *Burma* **85** Jf
Ross Sea, *Antarctica* **100** Mb
Rossa, *Switzerland* **61** Eb
Ross & Cromarty, co., *Scot.* **58** Dc
Rossano, *Italy* **71** Ff
Rosseau L., *Ontario* **40** Gc
Rossel I., *Papua* **53** Kb
Rossignol, *Belgium* **60** Dc
Rosslare Harb., *Eire* **59** Ch
Rosslyn, *Virginia* **44** Bc
Rosta, *Norway* **62** Hb
Rostock, *Germany* **64** Ea
Rostov, *Russia* **77** Dg
Rostov, *Russia* **76** Lc
Roswell, *New Mexico* **42** Fe
Rota, I., *Mariana Islands* **98** Df
Rothenburg, *Germany* **64** Dd
Rotherham, *England* **59** Gg
Rothesay, *Scotland* **58** De
Roti, I., *Indonesia* **79** Hn
Rotorua, *New Zealand* **51** Fc
Rotterdam, *Netherlands* **60** Cc
Rotuma, I., *Fiji* **98** Gj
Roubaix, *France* **68** Ea
Rouen, *France* **68** Db
Rõuge, *Estonia* **63** Mh
Roulers, *Belgium* **60** Bd
Roundup, *Montana* **42** Eb
Roura, *Fr. Guiana* **49** Gc
Rous, Pen., *Chile* **50** Cj
Rousay I., *Orkney, Scotland* **58** Ea
Rousbrugge, *Belgium* **60** Ad
Roussillon, prov., *France* **69** Ee
Rouveen, *Netherlands* **60** Eb
Rouyn, *Quebec* **40** Ga
Rovaniemi, *Finland* **62** Lc
Roveredo, *Switzerland* **61** Eb
Rovigo, *Italy* **70** Cc
Rovinari, *Rumania* **72** Db
Rovno, *Ukraine* **76** Ef
Roxas, *Philippines* **79** Hh
Roxburgh, *New Zealand* **51** Bf
Roxburgh, co., *Scotland* **58** Fe
Roxbury, *New York* **44** Ca
Royal Canal, *Eire* **59** Cg
Royale, I., *Michigan* **40** Bb
Royan, *France* **68** Cd
Rožňava, *Czechoslovakia* **65** Jd
Rtishchevo, *Russia* **77** Fd
Ruahine Ra., *New Zealand* **51** Fc
Ruapehu, Mt., *New Zealand* **51** Ec
Ruawai, *N.Z.* **51** Eb
Rubtsovsk, *Russia* **74** Hc
Ruby, *Alaska* **43** Xl
Rudauli, *India* **87** Cb
Rudbar, *Afghanistan* **89** Hc
Ruddervoorde, *Belgium* **60** Bc
Rudkōbing, *Denmark* **63** Dj
Rudok, *Tibet* **84** Eb
Rudolf L., *Kenya* **93** Hd
Ruel, *Ontario* **40** Fb
Ruffec, *France* **68** Dc
Rufino, *Argentina* **50** Dd
Rugby, *England* **59** Gh
Rügen, I., *Germany* **64** Ea
Rui Barbosa, *Brazil* **49** Jf
Rujiena, *Latvia* **63** Lh
Ruk, *W. Pakistan* **84** Cc
Rukumkot, *Nepal* **87** Da
Rukwa L., *Tanzania* **93** Gf
Rum Cay, *Bahama Islands* **47** Eb
Rum, I., *Scotland* **58** Cd
Rumania, *Central Europe* **57** Pg
Rumbek, *Sudan* **95** Lg
Rumburk, *Czechoslovakia* **64** Fc
Rumegies, *France* **60** Bd
Rumigny, *France* **60** Ce
Rumillies, *Belgium* **60** Bd
Rum Jungle, *N. Terr., Aust.* **52** Fb
Rumoi, *Japan* **82** Gc
Rumuruti, *Kenya* **93** Hd
Runanga, *New Zealand* **51** Ce
Rungwa, *Tanzania* **93** Gf
Rungwe Mt., *Tanzania* **93** Gf
Rupar, *India* **86** Ee
Rupbas, *India* **87** Ab
Rurrenabaque, *Bolivia* **48** Df
Rurutu, I., *Austral Islands* **99** Kk
Rusape, *Rhodesia* **91** Ec
Ruse (Ruschuk), *Bulgaria* **72** Ec
Ruseifa, *Jordan* **90** Ee
Rusele, *Sweden* **62** Hd
Rusne, R., *Lithuania* **63** Jj
Russas, *Brazil* **49** Kd
Russelkonda, *India* **85** Fe
Russell, *New Zealand* **51** Ea
Russian Socialist Federated Soviet Reps. (Russia) **74-75**
Russkoye Ust'ye, *Russia* **75** Pa
Russo, *Switzerland* **61** Db
Rustak, *Afghanistan* **89** Jb
Rutbah, *Iraq* **88** Dc
Ruthi, *Switzerland* **61** Ea
Ruthin, *Wales* **59** Eg
Rutland, *Vermont* **40** Kd
Rutland, co., *England* **59** Gh
Rutland I., *Andaman Is.* **85** Hf
Ruurlo, *Netherlands* **60** Eb
Ruvuma R., *Moçambique* **93** Hg
Ruweiba, *Sudan* **95** Le
Ruwenzori, Mt., *Uganda* **93** Gd
Ružomberok, *Czechoslovakia* **65** Hd
Rvazhsk, *Russia* **76** Me
Rwanda, *Cent. Afr.* **93** Fe
Ryan, L., *Scotland* **58** Df
Ryazan, *Russia* **76** Ld
Rybachiy, Pol., *Russia* **74** Cb
Rybinsk, *Russia* **76** Lb
Rybinskoye Res., *Russia* **76** Lb
Rybnoye, *Russia* **75** Ka
Ryde, *I. of W., England* **59** Gk
Rye, *England* **59** Hk
Rye Patch Res., *Nevada* **45** De
Rymarov, *Czechoslovakia* **65** Gd
Rypin, *Poland* **65** Hb
Ryukyu Retto, *Japan* **78** Hf
Rzeszów, *Poland* **65** Jc
Rzhev, *Russia* **76** Jc
Saalfeld, *Germany* **64** Dc
Saanen, *Switzerland* **61** Cb
Saarbrucken, *W. Germany* **64** Bd
Saaremaa, Os., *Lithuania* **63** Kg
Saari Selkä, *Finland* **62** Nb
Saarland, *Europe* **64** Bd
Saarlouis, *W. Germany* **64** Bd
Saas Grund, *Switzerland* **61** Cb
Saavedra, *Argentina* **50** De
Saavedra, *Chile* **50** Be
Sabac, *Yugoslavia* **72** Bb
Sabadell, *Spain* **67** Gb
Sabah (North Borneo), *Malaysia* **63** Gj
Sabalan, Mt., *Persia* **88** Eb
Sabalgarh, *India* **84** Ec
Sabana, Arch. de, *Cuba* **47** Cb
Sabanalarga, *Colombia* **48** Ca
Sabancuy, *Mexico* **46** Fd
Sab Biyar, *Syria* **90** Fd
Sabha, *Jordan* **90** Ee
Sabile, *Latvia* **63** Kh
Sabiñanigo, *Spain* **67** Ea
Sabinas, *Mexico* **46** Db
Sabine, *Texas* **43** Hf
Sabine R., *Louisiana/Texas* **43** He
Sabine Mt., *Antarctica* **100** Lb
Sable, *France* **68** Cc
Sable, C., *Florida* **43** Kf
Sables d'Olonne, les, *France* **68** Cc
Sabrina Coast, *Antarctica* **100** Hc
Sabzevar (Shindand), *Afghanistan* **89** Hc
Sabzawar, *Persia* **89** Gb
Sacaca, *Bolivia* **48** Dg
Sacandaga Res., *New York* **44** Ca
Sacedon, *Spain* **67** Db
Sackets Harbor, *New York* **40** Hd
Sacramento, *Brazil* **49** Hg
Sacramento, *California* **45** Cf
Sacramento R., *California* **45** Cf
Sada, *Yemen* **88** Df
Sádaba, *Spain* **67** Ea
Sadabad, *India* **87** Bb
Sa da Bandeira, *Angola* **92** Cg
Sadad, *Syria* **90** Ec
Sa. da Ibiapaba, *Brazil* **49** Jd
Sadaich. *See* Sadij
Sadhaura, *India* **86** Ee
Sadij, *Persia* **89** Gd
Sadiya, *India* **85** Jc
Sa 'diya, Jebel, *Arabia* **88** De
Sadmarda, *Afghanistan* **89** Hb
Sado, I., *Japan* **82** Fe
Sadra, *India* **84** Dd
Saeki, *Japan* **82** Bh
Safad, *Israel* **90** Ed
Safed Koh Ra., *Afghanistan-W. Pakistan* **86** Bc
Safi, *Morocco* **94** Db
Safi, *Syria* **90** Df
Safidabeh, *Persia* **89** Hc
Safita, *Syria* **90** Ec
Safranbolu, *Turkey* **88** Ba
Saga, *Japan* **82** Bh
Sagaing, *Burma* **85** Jd
Sagami, B., *Japan* **82** Fg
Sagar, *India* **87** Bd
Sagar I., *India* **87** Gd
Sagauli, *India* **87** Eb
Saginaw, *Michigan* **40** Dd
Saginaw B., *Michigan* **40** Ed
Sagone, G. de, *Corsica* **70** Bd
Sagres, *Portugal* **66** Ad
Sagua la Grande, *Cuba* **47** Cb
Sagunto, *Spain* **67** Ec
Saham, *Muscat & Oman* **89** Ge
Sahand, Mt., *Persia* **88** Eb
Sahara, *N. Africa* **94** Ec
Sahara Des., *Africa* **94–95** Dd
Saharanpur, *India* **86** Ef
Saharien Atlas, Mts., *Algeria* **94** Fb
Sahaswan, *India* **87** Ba
Sahiadriparvat Ra., *India* **84** Ed
Sahibganj, *India* **87** Fc
Sahiwal, *W. Pakistan* **86** Ce
Sahuayo, *Mexico* **46** Dc
Sahuaripa, *Mexico* **46** Cb
Sahugun, *Spain* **66** Ca
Sahun, *S. Yemen* **88** Eg
Sahy, *Czechoslovakia* **65** Hd
Sahyadri Mts., *India* **84** De
Saibai, I., *Torres Str., Qnsld.* **53** Ha
Saida. *See* Sidon
Saidabad, *Persia* **89** Gd
Saidapet, *India* **84** Ff
Said Bundas, *Sudan* **95** Kg
Saidpur, *India* **87** Dc
Saignelégier, *Switzerland* **61** Ba
Saigon, *S. Vietnam* **83** Dd
Sailana, *India* **84** Dd
Saimaa Kanal, *Fin.-Russ.* **63** Nf
Saimaa, L., *Finland* **63** Mf
Saimbeyli, *Turkey* **88** Bc
St Abbs Hd., *Scotland* **58** Fe
St Affrique, *France* **69** Ee
St Agrève, *France* **69** Fd
St Albans, *England* **59** Gj
St Albans, *Vermont* **40** Kc
St Amour, *France* **68** Fc
St André C., *Madagascar* **93** Mk
St Andrews, *New Zealand* **51** Cf
St Andrews, *Scotland* **58** Fd
Ste Anne de Beaupré, *Que.* **40** Lb
Ste Anne de la Pérade, *Que.* **40** Kb
St Anns Bay, *Jamaica* **47** Dc
St Anthony, *Idaho* **42** Dc
St Antönien, *Switzerland* **61** Eb
St Antonis, *Netherlands* **60** Dc
St Augustin, C. de., *Madag.* **93** Ml
St Augustine, *Florida* **43** Kf
St Austell, *England* **59** Dk
Ste Barbara, *Venezuela* **48** Eb
St Barthélemy, I., *Leeward I.* **47** Gc
St Béat, *France* **69** De
St Bernard Pass, Gd., *Switzerland-Italy* **70** Ac
St Bride's B., *Wales* **59** Dj
St Brieuc, *France* **68** Bb
St Calais, *France* **68** Dc
St Catherines, *Ontario* **40** Gd
Ste Cécile, *Quebec* **40** Lc
St Chamond, *France* **68** Fd
St Charles, *Michigan* **40** Dd
St Chély d'Apcher, *France* **69** Ed
St Christopher, I. (St Kitts), *Leeward Islands* **47** Gc
St Clair, *Michigan* **40** Ed
St Clair, L., *Mich.-Ont.* **40** Ed
St Cloud, *Minnesota* **43** Hb
Ste Croix, *Switzerland* **61** Bb
St Croix, *West Indies* **47** Gc
St Croix, R., *Wisconsin* **43** Hb
St David's Hd., *Wales* **59** Dj
St Denis, *France* **68** Eb
St di Nova Siri, *Sicily* **71** Fe
St Dizier, *France* **68** Fb
St Elias Mt., *Alaska* **43** Yl
Saintes, *France* **68** Cd
St Étienne, *France* **68** Fd
St Eustatius, I., *Leeward Is.* **47** Gc
St Fargeau, *France* **68** Ec
St Filipsland, *Netherlands* **60** Cc
St Florent & G. de, *Corsica* **70** Bd
St Florentin, *France* **68** Eb
St Flour, *France* **68** Ed
St Francis B., *S.-W. Africa* **91** Ae
St Francis, L., *Quebec* **40** Jc
St Francis R., *Quebec* **40** Kc
St François, L., *Quebec* **40** Lc
St Fulgent, *France* **68** Cc
St Gabriel de Brandon, *Que.* **40** Kb
St Gallen & canton, *Switz.* **61** Ea
St Gaudens, *France* **69** De
St George I., *Bering Sea* **43** Vm
St Georges, *Fr. Guiana* **49** Gc
St George's Chan., *Ireland-Wales* **59** Cj
St Gérard, *Belgium* **60** Cd
St Germain, *France* **68** Eb
St German, *Puerto Rico* **47** Fc
St Gheorghe I., *Rumania* **72** Gb
St Ghislain, *Belgium* **60** Bd
St Gilgen, *Austria* **64** Ee
St Gilles, *Belgium* **60** Cc
St Gilles, *France* **69** Fe
St Gillis-Waas, *Belgium* **60** Cc
St Gingolph, *Switzerland* **61** Bb
St Girons, *France* **69** De
St Gotthard, pass, *Switz.* **61** Db
St Guenolé, *France* **68** Ac
St Helena, *Atlantic Ocean* **97** Kk
St Helena B., *Cape Province* **91** Bf
St Helens, *England* **59** Eg
St Helens, Mt., *Washington* **45** Bb
St Hubert, *Belgium* **60** Dd
St Hyacinthe, *Quebec* **40** Kc
St Ignace, *Michigan* **40** Dc
St Imier, *Switzerland* **61** Ba
St Irénée, *Quebec* **40** Lb
St Ives, *England* **59** Dk
St Jean, *Belgium* **60** Ad
St Jean, *France* **68** Gd
St Jean, *Quebec* **40** Kc
St Jean d'Angély, *France* **68** Cd
St Jean de Luz, *France* **69** Ce
St Jérôme, *Quebec* **40** Kc
St Joachim, *Quebec* **40** Lb
St John's, *Michigan* **40** Dd
St Johnsbury, *Vermont* **40** Kc
St John's I., *Red Sea* **88** Ce
St Joseph, *Michigan* **40** Cd
St Joseph, *Missouri* **43** Hd
St Joseph I., *Ontario* **40** Eb
Ste Justine, *Quebec* **40** Lb
St Kilda, I., *Scotland* **58** Bc
St Laurent, *Fr. Guiana* **49** Gb
St Lawrence, *Queensland* **53** Jd
St Lawrence I., *Alaska* **43** Vl
St Lawrence Seaway, *N. America* **40** Jc
St Leger, *Belgium* **60** De
St Leonard, *Belgium* **60** Cc
St Léonard, *France* **68** Dd
St Lin, *Quebec* **40** Kc
St Lô, *France* **68** Cb
St Louis, *Mauritania* **94** Be
St Louis, *Michigan* **40** Dd
St Louis, *Missouri* **43** Hd
St Louis, L., *Quebec* **40** Kc
St Lucia C., *Natal* **91** Ee
St Lucia, I., *Windward Is.* **47** Gd
St Lucia L., *Natal* **91** Ee
St Luke's I., *Burma* **85** Jf
St Maartensdijk, *Netherlands* **60** Cc
St Magnus B., *Shetland* **58** Ha
St Maixent, *France* **68** Cc
St Malo & Gulf, *France* **68** Bb
St Marc, *Haiti* **47** Ec
St Mard, *Belgium* **60** De
Ste Marie C., *Madagascar* **93** Nm
Ste Marie I., *Madagascar* **93** Nk
St Martin, I., *Leeward Is.* **47** Gc
St Mary Is., *India* **84** Df
St Mary's, *Ontario* **40** Fd
St Mary's, *Pennsylvania* **44** Ab
St Mary's, *Tasmania* **53** Jh
St Mary's L., *Scotland* **58** Ee
St Mary's Pk., *S. Australia* **53** Gf
St Matthew I., *Alaska* **43** Vl
St Matthew's I., *Burma* **85** Jg
St Maurice, *Switzerland* **61** Bb
St Maurice R., *Quebec* **40** Kb
St Maximin, *France* **69** Fe
St Meen, *France* **68** Bb
St Michael, *Alaska* **43** Wl
St Michaels, *Maryland* **40** Hf
St Moritz, *Switzerland* **61** Eb
St Nazaire, *France* **68** Bc
St Nicolaasga, *Netherlands* **60** Db
St Nicolas. *See* St Niklaas
St Niklaas, *Belgium* **60** Cc
St Niklau, *Switzerland* **61** Cb
St Odilienberg, *Netherlands* **60** Ec
St Omer, *France* **68** Ea
Saintonge, prov., *France* **68** Cd
St Paul, *Minnesota* **43** Hc
St Paul I., *Bering Sea* **43** Vm
St Paul, I., *Indian Ocean* **96** Fh
St Paul de Fenouillet, *France* **69** Ee
St Peter, L., *Quebec* **40** Kb
St Petersburg, *Florida* **43** Kf
St Petersburg, *Pennsylvania* **44** Ab
St Pierre, *Martinique, W.I.* **47** Gd
St Pierre, *Quebec* **40** Lb
St Pol, *France* **68** Ea
St Polten, *Austria* **65** Fd
St Pons, *France* **69** Ee
St Pourçain, *France* **68** Ec
St Quentin, *France* **68** Eb
St Raymond, *Quebec* **40** Kb
St Rémi d'Amherst. *See* Lac-Rémi
St Sébastien C., *Madagascar* **93** Nj
St Sernin-sur-Rance, *France* **69** Ee
St Servan, *France* **68** Bb
St Sever, *France* **69** Ce
St Simeon, *Quebec* **40** Lb
St Thecle, *Quebec* **40** Kb
St Thomas, *Ontario* **40** Fd
St Thomas, I., *Virgin Is.* **47** Gc
St Trond. *See* St Truiden
St Tropez, *France* **69** Ge
St Truiden, *Belgium* **60** Dd
St Valery, *France* **68** Da
St Valery-en-Caux, *France* **68** Db
St Veit, *Austria* **64** Fe
St Vincent, *Windward Is.* **47** Gd
St Vincent, C., *Madagascar* **93** Ml
St Vincent, G., *S. Australia* **53** Gg
St Vith, *Belgium* **60** Ed
Saipan, I., *Mariana Is.* **98** Df
Saiping. *See* Sinyang
Saiun (Saywūn), *S. Yemen* **88** Ef
Saivomuotka, *Sweden* **62** Kb
Saiyidwala, *W. Pakistan* **86** Ce
Saka Dzong, *Tibet* **85** Gc
Sakai, *Japan* **82** Dg
Sakakah, *Arabia* **88** Dd
Saka Kalat, *W. Pakistan* **84** Cc
Sakania, *Congo* **93** Fg
Sakarya, R., *Turkey* **88** Bb
Sakata, *Japan* **82** Fe
Sakesar, *W. Pakistan* **86** Cd
Sakha, *Arabia* **88** De
Sakhalin, *Russia* **75** Pc
Sakhalinskiy Zaliv, *Russia* **75** Pc
Saki, *Russia* **76** Hj
Sakiai, *Lithuania* **63** Kj
Sakishima Gunto, Is., *Japan* **82** Kk
Sakti, *India* **87** Dd
Sakylä, *Finland* **63** Kf
Sala, *Czechoslovakia* **65** Gd
Sala, *Sweden* **63** Gg
Salacgriva, *Latvia* **63** Lh
Sala Consilina, *Italy* **71** Ee
Salada, L., *Mexico* **46** Aa
Salado, R., *Argentina* **50** Dc
Salaga, *Ghana* **94** Eg
Salahiya, *Syria* **88** Dc
Salajar, I., *Indonesia* **79** Hm
Salala, *Muscat & Oman* **89** Ff
Salama, *Guatemala* **46** Fd
Salamanca, *Mexico* **46** Dc
Salamanca, *New York* **40** Gd
Salamanca, *Spain* **66** Cb
Salamaua, *New Guinea* **53** Ja
Salamina, *Colombia* **48** Bb
Salamís & I., *Greece* **73** Df
Salangen, *Norway* **62** Gb
Salas, *Spain* **66** Ba
Salas de los Infantes, *Spain* **66** Da
Salatsgriva. *See* Salacgriva
Salaverry, *Peru* **48** Be
Sala-y-Gomez I., *Pacific Oc.* **99** Qk
Salbris, *France* **68** Ec
Saldana, *Spain* **66** Ca
Saldus, *Latvia* **63** Kh
Sale, *Victoria* **53** Jg
Salekhard, *Russia* **74** Fb
Salem, *India* **84** Ef
Salem, *Massachusetts* **40** Ld
Salem, *New Jersey* **40** Jf
Salem, *Oregon* **45** Bc
Salemi, *Sicily* **71** Dg
Sälen, *Sweden* **63** Ef
Salerno, *Italy* **71** Ee
Salerno, G. di, *Italy* **71** Ee
Salford, *England* **59** Fg
Salgueiro, *Brazil* **49** Ke
Salida, *Colorado* **42** Ed
Salina, *Kansas* **42** Gd
Salina, I., *Italy* **71** Ef
Salina Cruz, *Mexico* **46** Ed
Salinas. *See* Salinópolis
Salinas, *California* **45** Cg
Salinas, *Ecuador* **48** Ad
Salinas, *Mexico* **46** Dc
Salinas, *Mexico* **46** Db
Salinas R., *California* **45** Cg
Saline R., *Kansas* **42** Gd
Salinitas, *Chile* **50** Bb
Salinópolis, *Brazil* **49** Hd
Salisbury, *England* **59** Fj
Salisbury, *Maryland* **43** Kd
Salisbury, *N. Carolina* **43** Kd
Salisbury, *Rhodesia* **91** Ec
Salisbury, L., *Uganda* **93** Gd
Salisbury Plain, *England* **59** Fj
Salkhad, *Syria* **90** Ee
Sallyana, *Nepal* **87** Da
Salmon R., *Idaho* **45** Fc
Salmon Gums, *W. Australia* **52** Df
Salmon River Mts., *Idaho* **45** Ec
Salo, *Finland* **63** Kf
Salon, *France* **69** Fe
Salon, *India* **87** Cb
Salonica. *See* Thessaloníki
Salonta, *Rumania* **72** Ca
Salqin, *Syria* **90** Ea
Salsette I., *India* **84** De
Salt Fd., *Norway* **62** Fc
Salt L., *W. Australia* **52** Bd
Salt Ls., *W. Australia* **52** Ee
Salt Ra., *W. Pakistan* **84** Db
Salt R., *Arizona* **42** De
Salta, *Argentina* **50** Cb
Saltdal, *Norway* **62** Fc
Saltee, Is., *Eire* **59** Ch
Saltillo, *Mexico* **46** Db
Salt Lake City, *Utah* **45** He
Salto, *Argentina* **50** Dd
Salto, *Uruguay* **50** Ed
Salto da Divisa, *Brazil* **49** Kg
Salton Sea, *California* **45** Fj
Saltrou, *Haiti* **47** Ec
Salum & G. of, *Egypt* **95** Lb
Salur, *India* **85** Fe
Salut, Is. du, *Fr. Guiana* **49** Gb
Saluzzo, *Italy* **70** Ac
Salvador (Bahia), *Brazil* **49** Kf
Salvador, El, rep., *C. Amer.* **47** Bd
Salvaterra, *Portugal* **66** Ac
Salvatierra, *Mexico* **46** Dc
Salzburg, *Austria* **64** Ee
Salzwedel, *Germany* **64** Db
Salzgitter, *Germany* **64** Db
Samahala, *Botswana* **91** Cc
Samalut, *Egypt* **95** Mc
Samana & B. de, *Rep. Dom.* **47** Fc
Samar, I., *Philippines* **79** Jh
Samarai, *Papua* **53** Kb
Samarinda, *Borneo* **79** Gl
Samarkand, *Uzbek.* **74** Fe
Samarra Balad, *Iraq* **88** Dc
Samastipur, *India* **87** Ec
Samāwa, *Iraq* **88** Ec
Sambalpur, *India* **85** Fd
Sambava, *Madagascar* **93** Pj
Sambeek, *Netherlands* **60** Dc
Sambhal, *India* **87** Ba
Sambhar, *India* **86** Dg
Sambor, *Ukraine* **76** Cg
Samborombón, B., *Argent.* **50** Ee
Sambre, R., *Belgium* **60** Cd
Samedan, *Switzerland* **61** Eb
Sameminato, *Japan* **82** Gd
Sami, *W. Pakistan* **84** Bc
Samira, *Arabia* **88** Dd
Sam Ka, *Burma* **85** Jd
Sam-nua, *Laos* **83** Cb
Samoa, Is., *Pacific Ocean* **98** Hj
Samokov, *Bulgaria* **72** Dc
Samorogouan, *Upper Volta* **94** Ef
Samos, I., *Greece* **73** Ff
Samothrace. *See* Samothráki I.
Samothráki I., *Greece* **73** Ed
Sampacho, *Argentina* **50** Dd
Sampit, *Borneo* **79** Fl
Samrée, *Belgium* **60** Dd
Samsat, *Turkey* **88** Cb
Samshui, *China* **81** Fl
Samsö, I., *Denmark* **63** Dj
Samsu, *Korea* **78** Jb
Samsun, *Turkey* **88** Ca
Samthar, *India* **87** Bc
San, *Mali* **94** Ef
San'a, *Yemen* **88** Df
Sanam, *Jebel, Iraq* **88** Ec
San Ambrosio I., *Pacific Oc.* **99** Tk
Sanana, *Moluccas* **47** Jl
Sanandaj, *Persia* **88** Eb
San Angelo, *Texas* **42** Fe
San Antioco, I., *Sardinia* **71** Bf
San Antonio, *Chile* **50** Cb
San Antonio, *Chile* **50** Bd
San Antonio, *Mexico* **46** Cc
San Antonio, *Texas* **42** Gf
San Antonio, C., *Argentina* **50** Ee
San Antonio, C., *Cuba* **47** Cb
San Antonio R., *Texas* **42** Gf
San Antonio Oeste, *Argent.* **50** Df
Sanaraipo, *Venezuela* **48** Db
San Bartolomeu de Messines, *Portugal* **66** Ad
San Benedetto del Tronto, *It.* **70** Dd
San Benito Is., *Mexico* **46** Ab
San Bernardino, *California* **45** Eh
San Bernardino Ra., *Cal.* **45** Eh
San Bernardo, *Chile* **50** Bd
San Blas, *Argentina* **50** Df
San Blas, *Mexico* **46** Cc
San Blas, *Mexico* **46** Cb
San Blas, C., *Florida* **43** Jf
San Blas, G. de, *Panama* **47** De
San Borja, *Mexico* **46** Bb
San Carlos, *Argentina* **50** Cc
San Carlos, *Argentina* **50** Cd
San Carlos, *Argentina* **50** Cd
San Carlos, *Chile* **50** Be
San Carlos, *Mexico* **46** Ec
San Carlos, *Nicaragua* **47** Cd
San Carlos, *Amazonas, Ven.* **48** Dc
San Carlos, *Cojedes, Venez.* **48** Db
San Carlos L., *Arizona* **42** De
San Carlos de Bariloche, *Argentina* **50** Bf
San Carlos del Zulia, *Venez.* **48** Cb
Sanchez, *Rep. Dominica* **47** Fc
San Clemente, *Spain* **67** Dc

San Cosme, Paraguay 50 Ec
San Cristobal, Argentina 50 Dd
San Cristobal, Mexico 46 Fd
San Cristobal, Venezuela 48 Cb
San Cristobal I., Galapagos I. 99 Sh
San Cristobal, I., Solomon Is. 98 Fj
Sancti Spiritus, Cuba 47 Db
Sand, Norway 63 Bg
Sandakan, N. Borneo 79 Gj
Sanday I., Orkney 58 Fa
Sandefjord, Norway 63 Dg
Sandgate, Queensland 53 Ke
Sandhornöy, Norway 62 Ec
Sandia, Peru 48 Df
San Diego, California 45 Ej
San Diego, C., Argentina 50 Ch
San Diego de Cabrutica, Venezuela 48 Eb
Sandikli, Turkey 88 Bb
Sandila, India 87 Cb
San Dimas, Mexico 46 Cc
Sandnes, Norway 63 Ag
Sandoa, Congo 92 Ef
San Domingos, Portugal 66 Bd
Sandoway, Burma 85 He
Sandpoint, Idaho 42 Cb
Sandstone, W. Australia 52 Ce
Sandträsk, Sweden 62 Jc
Sandusky, Michigan 40 Ed
Sandusky, Ohio 40 Ee
Sandvig, Bornholm, I., Den. 63 Fj
Sandwich, Ontario 40 Ed
Sandy C., Queensland 53 Kd
San Esteban de Gormaz, Sp. 66 Db
San Felipe, Chile 50 Bd
San Felipe, Guatemala 46 Fe
San Felipe, Mexico 46 Fd
San Felipe, Mexico 46 Dc
San Felipe, Venezuela 48 Ba
San Feliu de Guixols, Spain 67 Gb
San Feliu de Llobregat, Sp. 67 Fb
San Félix, Venezuela 48 Eb
San Felix I., Pacific Ocean 99 Sk
San Fernando, Chile 50 Bd
San Fernando, Mexico 46 Ec
San Fernando, Mexico 46 Ab
San Fernando, Philippines 79 Hg
San Fernando, Trinidad 48 Ea
San Fernando de Apure, Venezuela 48 Db
San Fernando de Atabapo, Venezuela 48 Dc
Sanford, Mt., Alaska 43 Yl
San Francisco, Argentina 50 Dd
San Francisco, California 45 Bg
San Francisco Pk., Arizona 42 Dd
Sanga, Angola 92 Dg
Sangareddipet, India 84 Ee
Sanggau, Borneo 79 Fk
Sangihe Kep., Indonesia 79 Jk
San Giovanni in Fiore, Italy 71 Ff
Sangkulirang, Borneo 79 Gk
Sangla Hill, W. Pakistan 86 Ce
Sangre de Cristo Mts., Colo. 42 Ed
Sangre Grande Town, Trinidad 48 Ea
Sangrur, India 86 De
Sanguin, Liberia 94 Dg
San Ignacio, Bolivia 48 Df
San Ignacio, Bolivia 48 Eg
San Ignacio, Mexico 46 Cc
San Ignacio, Mexico 46 Bb
San Ignacio, Paraguay 50 Ec
San Javier, Argentina 50 Ed
San Javier, Bolivia 48 Eg
San Javier, Chile 50 Be
San João, Portugal 66 Bb
San Joaquim, Bolivia 48 Ef
San Jorge, G., Argentina 50 Cg
San José, Bolivia 48 Eg
San José, California 45 Cg
San José, Colombia 48 Cc
San José, Costa Rica 47 Ce
San José, Guatemala 46 Fe
San José, Uruguay 50 Ed
San José, G., Argentina 50 Df
San José, I., Mexico 46 Bb
San José Carpizo, Mexico 46 Fd
San José de Amacuro, Venez. 48 Eb
San José de Feliciano, Argent. 50 Ed
San José del Cabo, Mexico 46 Cc
San José de Ocune, Colo. 48 Cc
San José Pimas, Mexico 46 Cb
San Juan, Bolivia 48 Fg
San Juan, Puerto Rico 47 Fc
San Juan, Peru 48 Bg
San Juan, Venezuela 48 Da
San Juan & R., Argentina 50 Cd
San Juan, C., Argentina 50 Dh
San Juan Mts., Colorado 42 Ed
San Juan, R., Mexico 46 Ec
San Juan, R., Nicaragua 47 Bd
San Juan R., Utah, etc. 42 Dd
San Juan de Camarones, Mexico 46 Cb
San Juan de Guadalupe, Me. 46 Dc
San Juan del Norta, Nic. 47 Cd
San Juan de los Lagos, Me. 46 Dc
San Juan del Rio, Mexico 46 Ec
San Juan del Sur, Nicaragua 47 Bd
San Julian, Argentina 50 Cg
San Justo, Argentina 50 Dd
Sankuri Post, Kenya 93 He
San Lazaro, C., Mexico 46 Bc
San Leandro, California 45 Cg
San Lorenzo, Argentina 50 Dd
San Lorenzo, Ecuador 48 Bc
San Lorenzo, Honduras 47 Bd
San Lorenzo, Mexico 46 Cb
San Lorenzo, Peru 48 Df
San Lorenzo Is., Mexico 46 Bb
San Lorenzo del Escorial, Sp. 66 Cb
Sanlucar la Mayor, Spain 66 Bd
San Lucas, Bolivia 48 Dh
San Lucas, C., Mexico 46 Cc
San Luis, Argentina 50 Ec
San Luis, Argentina 50 Cd
San Luis, Cuba 47 Db
San Luis de la Paz, Mexico 46 Dc
San Luis Obispo, California 45 Ch
San Luis Potosi & state, Mexico 46 Dc
Sanluri, Sardinia 71 Bf
San Marcos, Colombia 48 Bb
San Marino, rep., Italy 70 Dd
San Martin, Argentina 50 Bf
San Martin, Colombia 48 Cc
San Martin, L., Chile-Argent. 50 Bg
San Martin de los Andes, Argentina 50 Bf
San Martin de Valdeiglesais, Spain 66 Cb
San Martinho, Portugal 66 Ac
San Mateo, Spain 67 Fb
San Matias, Bolivia 48 Fg
San Matias, G., Argentina 50 Df
San Maura. See Levkás I.
Sanmenhsia, China 80 Ee
San Miguel, Bolivia 48 Eg
San Miguel, Mexico 46 Dc
San Miguel, Peru 48 Cf
San Miguel, Salvador 47 Bd
San Miguel. See Rey, I. del
San Miguel, B. de, Panama 47 De
San Miguel I., California 45 Ch
San Miguel, R., Bolivia 48 Eg
San Miguel de Tucuman, Argentina 50 Cc
San Nicolás, Argentina 50 Dd
San Pablo, Bolivia 48 Dh
San Pablo, C., Argentina 50 Ch
San Pedro, Argentina 50 Ed
San Pedro, Brit. Honduras 47 Bc
San Pedro, California 45 Dj
San Pedro, Ivory Coast 94 Dh
San Pedro, Mexico 46 Db
San Pedro, Paraguay 50 Eb
San Pedro Chan., California 45 Dj
San Pedro de Arimena, Colombia 48 Cc
San Pedro del Gallo, Mexico 46 Db
San Pedro de Lloc, Peru 48 Be
San Pedro de Macoris, Rep. Dominicana 47 Fc
San Pedro do Sul, Portugal 66 Ab
San Pedro Sula, Honduras 47 Bc
San Pietro I., Sardinia 71 Bf
San Quintin & B., Mexico 46 Ca
San Rafael, Argentina 50 Cd
San Rafael, California 45 Bg
San Rafael, New Mexico 42 Ed
San Ramon, Peru 48 Bf
San Remo, Italy 70 Ad
San Roque, Argentina 50 Ec
San Salvador, Angola 92 Cf
San Salvador, Bahama Is. 47 Eb
San Salvador, Salvador 47 Bd
Sansanne Mango, Togo 94 Ff
San Sebastian, Spain 67 Da
San Sebastian & B. de, Argentina 50 Ch
San Severo, Italy 71 Ee
Sans Souci, Ontario 40 Fc
Santa, Peru 48 Be
Santa Ana, Bolivia 48 Df
Santa Ana, Bolivia 48 Fg
Santa Ana, California 45 Ej
Santa Ana, Ecuador 48 Ad
Santa Ana, Mexico 46 Ba
Santa Ana, Salvador 47 Bd
Santa Anna (do Bananal) I. de, Brazil 49 Gf
Santa Antonio da Gloria. See Gloria
Santa Barbara, California 45 Dh
Santa Barbara, Honduras 47 Bd
Santa Barbara Chan., Cal. 45 Ch
Santa Catalina, Chile 50 Cc
Santa Catalina I., California 45 Dj
Santa Catalina, I., Mexico 46 Bb
Santa Catalina, Mt. See Encantada, Cerro de
Santa Catarina, Mexico 46 Cc
Santa Catarina, I., Brazil 50 Gc
Santa Clara, Brazil 48 Df
Santa Clara, Cuba 47 Cb
Santa Clara, Sa., Mexico 46 Bb
Santa Coloma de Farnes, Sp. 67 Gb
Santa Cruz, Argentina 50 Ch
Santa Cruz, Bolivia 48 Eg
Santa Cruz, California 45 Bg
Santa Cruz, Chile 50 Bd
Santa Cruz, Mexico 46 Ba
Santa Cruz, Peru 48 Be
Santa Cruz, Philippines 79 Hh
Santa Cruz Chan. & I., Cal. 45 Dj
Santa Cruz. I. See St Croise
Santa Cruz Is., Pacific Ocean 98 Fj
Santa Cruz, R., Argentina 50 Bh
Santa Cruz de la Zarza, Sp. 66 Dc
Santa Cruz del Sur, Cuba 47 Db
Santa Cruz de Tenerife, Canary Is. 94 Bc
Santa Elena, Ecuador 48 Ad
Santa Eufemia, G. di, Italy 71 Ff
Santa Fé, Argentina 50 Dd
Santa Fé, Cuba 47 Cb
Santa Fé, New Mexico 42 Ed
Santa Filomena, Brazil 49 He
Santa Helena, Brazil 50 Fb
Santa Helena, Brazil 49 Hd
Santa Helena, Brazil 49 Fe
Santai, China 80 Bg
Santa Innes, B., Mexico 46 Bb
Santa Isabel, Argentina 50 Ce
Santa Isabel, Fernando Poo 94 Gh
Sta Isabel, Solomon Islands 98 Eh
Santalnes, I., Chile 50 Bh
Santa Lucia, Cuba 47 Db
Santa Margarita, I., Mexico 46 Bc
Santa Maria, Argentina 50 Cc
Santa Maria, Brazil 50 Fc
Santa Maria, California 45 Ch
Santa Maria, Mexico 46 Cb
Santa Maria, I., Atlantic Oc. 94 Bb
Santa Maria, I., Chile 50 Be
Santa Maria, Mt., Argentina 50 Ce
Santa Maria del Rio, Mex. 46 Dc
Santa Maria di Leuca C., It. 71 Gf
Santa Maria la Real de Nieva, Spain 66 Cb
Santa Marta, Colombia 48 Ca
Santa Monica, California 45 Dh
Santa Monica B., California 45 Dj
Santander, Colombia 48 Bc
Santander, Spain 66 Da
Santa Paula, California 45 Dh
Santa Quiteria, Brazil 49 Jd
Santarem, Brazil 49 Gd
Santarem, Portugal 66 Ac
Santa Rita, Brazil 49 Fe
Santa Rita, Venezuela 48 Ca
Santa Rosa, Argentina 50 Cd
Santa Rosa, Argentina 50 Cd
Santa Rosa, Bolivia 48 Eg
Santa Rosa, Brazil 50 Fc
Santa Rosa, California 45 Bf
Santa Rosa, Honduras 47 Bd
Santa Rosa I., California 45 Cj
Santa Rosa de Toay, Argent. 50 De
Santa Rosalia, Mexico 46 Bb
Santa Sylvina, Argentina 50 Dc
Santa Vitoria do Palmar, Brazil 50 Fd
Santee R., S. Carolina 43 Ke
Santiago, Brazil 50 Fc
Santiago, Chile 50 Bd
Santiago, Mexico 46 Cc
Santiago, Mexico 46 Cc
Santiago, Panama 47 Ce
Santiago, Rep. Dominicana 47 Ec
Santiago de Compostela, Sp. 66 Aa
Santiago, Cerro, Panama 47 Ce
Santiago, Sa. de, Bolivia 48 Fg
Santiago de Cuba, Cuba 47 Dc
Santiago del Estero, Argent. 50 Dc
Santiago Papasquiaro, Me. 46 Cc
Santillana, Spain 66 Ca
Santipur, India 87 Gd
Santis, Mt., Switzerland 61 Ea
Santo Angelo, Brazil 50 Fc
Santo Antonio, Brazil 48 Ef
Santo Antonio, Brazil 49 Gd
Santo Antonio do Zaire, Angola 92 Cf
Santo Corazon, Bolivia 48 Fg
Santo Domingo, Cuba 47 Cb
Santo Domingo, Rep. Dominicana 47 Fc
Santo Domingo, Mexico 46 Aa
Santo Thome, Argentina 50 Ec
San Tomé, Venezuela 48 Eb
Santorini. See Thíra, I.
Santos, Brazil 49 Hh
Santo Tomas, Mexico 46 Aa
Santo Tomas, Peru 48 Cf
Santvliet, Belgium 60 Cc
San Urbano, Argentina 50 Dd
San Vicente, Salvador 47 Bd
San Vicente del Caguan, Colombia 48 Cc
San Vito C., Italy 71 Fe
São Antonio do Ica, Brazil 48 Dd
São Bento do Norte, Brazil 49 Ke
São Borja, Brazil 50 Ec
São Carlos, Brazil 49 Hh
São Cristovão, Brazil 49 Kf
São Domingos, Brazil 49 Hf
São Felix, Brazil 49 Ge
São Francisco, Brazil 49 Je
São Francisco, Brazil 49 Jg
São Francisco, R., Brazil 49 Ke
São Francisco do Sul & I. de, Brazil 50 Gc
Sao Hill, Tanzania 93 Hf
São Jeronimo, Brazil 49 Gh
São Jeronimo, Brazil 50 Fc
São Joao da Barra, Brazil 49 Jh
São Joao da Boa Vista, Brazil 49 Hh
São Joao del Rei, Brazil 49 Jh
São João do Araguaya, Brazil 49 He
São João do Piaul, Brazil 49 Je
São Joaquim, Brazil 48 Dc
São José, Brazil 50 Fd
São José, Brazil 50 Gc
São José, Brazil 48 Dd
São José do Mipibu, Brazil 49 Ke
São José do Rio Prêto, Brazil 49 Hh
São Lourenço & R., Brazil 49 Fg
São Luis, Brazil 49 Jd
São Luis, I. de, Brazil 49 Jd
São Luiz Gonzaga, Brazil 50 Fc
São Mateus, Brazil 49 Kg
São Mateus do Sul, Brazil 50 Fc
São Miguel, I., Atlantic Oc. 94 Ba
Saona, I., Rep. Dominicana 47 Fc
Saône, R., France 68 Fc
Saône-et-Loire, dep. France 68 Fc
São Paulo, Brazil 49 Hh
São Paulo de Luanda, Angola 92 Cf
São Paulo de Olivença, Brazil 48 Dd
São Raimundo Nonato, Brazil 49 Je
São Romão, Brazil 48 De
São Sebastião, Brazil 48 Ee
São Sebastião & I. da, Brazil 49 Hh
São Simão, Brazil 49 Hh
São Tomé I., G. of Guinea 92 Bd
São Vicente, Brazil 49 Hh
Sapiéntza I., Greece 73 Cf
Saposoa, Peru 48 Be
Sapotnica, Yugoslavia 72 Cd
Sapporo, Japan 82 Gc
Sapri, Italy 71 Ee
Sapulpa, Oklahoma 42 Gd
Saqqez, Persia 88 Db
Saragossa (Zaragoza), Sp. 67 Eb
Saraguro, Ecuador 48 Bd
Saraikela, India 87 Ed
Sarajevo, Yugoslavia 72 Bc
Sarala, Russia 74 Hc
Saranac Lake, New York 40 Jc
Sarandi del Yi, Uruguay 50 Ed
Sarangarh, India 85 Fd
Saransk, Russia 77 Gc
Sarapul, Russia 77 Lb
Sarasota, Florida 43 Kf
Saratoga L., New York 44 Da
Saratoga Springs, New York 44 Da
Saratov, Russia 77 Ge
Saratsi-ting, China 80 Eb
Sarawak, Borneo 79 Fk
Sarbaz, Persia 89 Hd
Sárbogárd, Hungary 65 He
Sarco, Chile 50 Bc
Sardarshahr, India 86 Df
Sardasht, Persia 88 Eb
Sardegna, I., Italy 71 Be
Sardhana, India 86 Ef
Sardinia (Sardegna), Italy 71 Be
Sardoal, Portugal 66 Ac
Sareks Nat. Park, Sweden 62 Gc
Sargans, Switzerland 61 Ea
Sari, Persia 89 Fb
Sarikamis, Turkey 88 Da
Sarina, Queensland 53 Jd
Sariñena, Spain 67 Eb
Sar-i-Pul, Afghanistan 89 Jb
Sar-i-pul, Persia 88 Ec
Sark, I., Channel Islands 68 Bb
Sarkad, Hungary 65 Je
Sarlat, France 69 Dd
Sarmi, W. Irian 79 Ll
Sarmiento, Mt., Chile 50 Bh
Sarna, Sweden 63 Ef
Sarnen, Switzerland 61 Db
Sarnia, Ontario 40 Ed
Sarno, Italy 71 Ee
Saronic G., Greece 73 Df
Saronno, Italy 70 Bc
Sarpsborg, Norway 63 Dg
Sarpul. See Shahsavar
Sarrebourg, France 68 Gb
Sarreguemines, France 68 Gb
Sarre Union, France 68 Gb
Sarria, Spain 66 Ba
Sart, Belgium 60 Dd
Sartene, Corsica 71 Be
Sarthe R. & dep., France 68 Dc
Sarufutsu, Japan 82 Hb
Saruru, Japan 82 Hc
Sarvar, Hungary 65 Ge
Sasa Baneh, Ethiopia 93 Jc
Sasaram, India 87 Ec
Sasebo, Japan 82 Ah
Saskylakh, Russia 75 La
Sasovo, Russia 77 Ec
Sassandra & R., Ivory Coast 94 Dh
Sassari, Sardinia 71 Be
Sassnitz, Germany 64 Ea
Sastre, Argentina 50 Dd
Sas-van-Gent, Netherlands 60 Bc
Satadougou, Mali 94 Cf
Satara, India 84 De
Säter, Sweden 63 Ff
Satevo, Mexico 46 Cb
Satins, France 68 Fc
Satka, Russia 77 Pc
Satkhira, E. Pakistan 87 Gd
Satoraljaujhely, Hungary 65 Jd
Satpura Ra., India 84 Dd
Satu Mare, Rumania 65 Ke
Satun, Siam 83 Ce
Sauda, Norway 63 Bg
Saudhárkrókur, Iceland 62 Wm
Saudi Arabia, S.W. Asia 88 De
Saugeen Pen., Ontario 40 Fc
Saugerties, New York 40 Kd
Saulieu, France 68 Fc
Sault Ste Marie, Michigan 40 Db
Sault Ste Marie, Ontario 40 Db
Saumur, France 68 Cc
Saunders, I., S. Sandwich Is. 100 Ad
Saurashtra. See Kathiawar
Sava, R., Yugoslavia 72 Bb
Savai'i, I., Samoa 98 Hj
Savanna, Illinois 40 Ad
Savannah, Georgia 43 Ke
Savannah R., Georgia/S. Carolina 43 Ke
Savannakhet, Laos 83 Cc
Savanna la Mar, Jamaica 47 Dc
Savantvadi, India 84 De
Savanur, India 84 Ef
Save, Dahomey 94 Fg
Save R., Moçambique 91 Ed
Saveh, Persia 89 Fb
Savenay, France 68 Cc
Savoie, dep., France 68 Gd
Savoie, prov., France 68 Gd
Savona, Italy 70 Bc
Savonlinna, Finland 62 Nf
Savu Sea, Indonesia 79 Hm
Savukoski, Finland 62 Nc
Sawa, S. Yemen 88 Ef
Sawqirah B., Muscat & Oman 89 Gf
Saxnäs, Sweden 62 Fd
Saxton, Pennsylvania 86 Ab
Saya, Syria 90 Db
Saya Buri. See Pak-lay
Sayan, Peru 48 Bf
Sayan, Vostochnyy, Russia 75 Jc
Sayan, Zapadnyy, Russia 75 Jc
Sayhut, S. Yemen 89 Ff
Sayre, Pennsylvania 44 Bb
Sayula, Mexico 46 Dd
Scafell Pike, England 59 Ef
Scalea, Italy 71 Ef
Scânteia, Rumania 72 Fa
Scanzano, Italy 71 Fe
Scapa Flow, Orkney, Scot. 58 Eb
Scarborough, England 59 Gf
Scărisoara, Rumania 72 Da
Schaffhausen & canton, Switz. 61 Da
Schelde, Ooster & Wester, Netherlands 60 Bc
Schenectady, New York 40 Jd
Scheveningen, Netherlands 60 Cb
Schiedam, Netherlands 60 Cc
Schiermonnikoog I., Nether. 60 Ea
Schiphol, Netherlands 60 Cb
Schleins, Switzerland 61 Fb
Schleswig, Germany 64 Ca
Schleswig-Holstein, Germany 64 Ca
Schneidemühl. See Pila
Schoharie, New York 44 Ca
Schönbuhl, Switzerland 61 Ca
Schönebeck, Germany 64 Dc
Schongau, Germany 64 De
Schoonhoven, Netherlands 60 Cc
Schötz, Switzerland 61 Da
Schouwen I., Netherlands 60 Bc
Schuchinsk, Kazakh. 74 Gc
Schull, Eire 59 Aj
Schuls, Switzerland 61 Fb
Schüpfheim, Switzerland 61 Db
Schwabach, Germany 64 Dd
Schwägalp, Switzerland 61 Ea
Schwandorf, Germany 64 Ed
Schwaner Geb., Borneo 79 Fl
Schwarzhorn, Mt., Switz. 61 Cb
Schwarzwald, Germany 64 Cd
Schwedt, Germany 64 Fb
Schweidnitz. See Swidnica
Schweinfurt, Germany 64 Dc
Schwerin, Germany 64 Db
Schwyz & canton, Switz. 61 Da
Sciacca, Sicily 71 Dg
Scilly, Is. of, England 59 Cl
Scituate, Massachusetts 44 Ea
Scoresby Ld., Greenland 41 Nb
Scoresby Sd., Greenland 41 Nb
Scotia, Ontario 40 Gc
Scotia Sea, Antarctica 100 Td
Scotland, Great Britain 58 Fb
Scott I., Antarctica 100 Mc
Scott, Mt., Oregon 42 Bc
Scottsbluff, Nebraska 42 Fc
Scottsdale, Tasmania 53 Jh
Scranton, Pennsylvania 40 Je
Scugog L., Ontario 40 Gc
Scutari. See Shkodër
Scutari. See Uskudar
Seaford, Delaware 40 Jf
Sea Isle City, New Jersey 40 Jf
Sea Lion Is., Falkland Is. 50 Eh
Searchmont, Ontario 40 Db
Seattle, Washington 45 Bb
Sebastián Vizcaino, B. de, Mexico 46 Bb
Sebenico. See Sibenik
Sebewaing, Michigan 40 Ed
Sebha, Libya 95 Hc
Sebin Karahisar, Turkey 88 Ca
Sečovce, Czechoslovakia 65 Jd
Secretary I., New Zealand 51 Af
Secunderabad, India 84 Ee
Seda, Lithuania 63 Kh
Sedalia, Missouri 43 Hd
Sedan, France 68 Fb
Sedano, Spain 66 Da
Seddon, New Zealand 51 Ed
Seddonville, New Zealand 51 Cd
Sedhiou, Senegal 94 Bf
Sedom, Israel 90 Df
Sedrun, Switzerland 61 Db
Seeheim, S.-W. Africa 91 Be
Seelisberg, Switzerland 61 Db
Sées, France 68 Db
Seewis, Switzerland 61 Eb
Sefrou, Morocco 94 Eb
Sefton, New Zealand 51 De
Sefton, Mt., New Zealand 51 Ce
Segorbe, Spain 67 Ec
Ségou, Mali 94 Df
Segovia, Spain 66 Cb
Segovia, R., Nicaragua 47 Cd
Séguela, Ivory Coast 94 Dg
Sehe. See Cha Thing Phra
Sehkuheh, Persia 89 Hc
Sehwan, W. Pakistan 84 Cc
Seibo, Rep. Dominicana 47 Fc
Seiland, Norway 62 Ka
Seine, R., France 68 Db
Seine-et-Marne, dep., France 68 Eb
Seine-et-Oise, dep., France 68 Db
Seine Maritime, dep., France 68 Db
Seitler, Russia 76 Jj
Seiyala, Egypt 95 Md
Sekenke, Tanzania 93 Ge
Seki, Japan 82 Eg
Sekieshan I., China 81 Lg
Sekondi, Ghana 94 Eg
Sektyakh, Russia 75 Ma
Selby, England 59 Gg
Selemiya, Syria 90 Fb
Selenge, R., Mong.-Russia 75 Kd
Selima Oasis, Sudan 95 Ld
Selinsgrove, Pennsylvania 44 Bb
Selkirk & co., Scotland 58 Fe
Selle, Sa. de la, Haiti 47 Ec
Selles, France 68 Dc
Selma, Alabama 43 Je
Selva, Argentina 50 Dc
Selwyn, Queensland 53 Hd
Selwyn Ra., Queensland 53 Gd
Sem, Norway 63 Dg
Semarang, Java 79 Fm
Semawe, Jeb. See Har Sagi
Seminoe Res., Wyoming 42 Ec
Semipalatinsk, Kazakh. 74 Hc
Semnan, Persia 89 Fb
Senador Pompeu, Brazil 49 Ke
Sena Madureira, Brazil 48 De
Sendai, Japan 82 Ge
Seneca L., New York 40 Hd
Seneca Falls, New York 44 Ba
Sénégal, W. Africa 94 Bf
Sénégal R., W. Africa 94 Ce
Senev, Michigan 40 Cb
Senga Hill, Zambia 93 Gf
Sengilei, Russia 77 Jd
Senhor do Bonfim, Brazil 49 Jf
Senise, Italy 71 Fe
Senj, Yugoslavia 70 Ec
Senja, Norway 62 Gb
Senneterre, Quebec 40 Ha
Sens, France 68 Eb
Senta, Yugoslavia 72 Cb
Sentinel Ra., Antarctica 100 Rb
Seondha, India 87 Bb
Seoni, India 87 Bd
Seoni-Malwa, India 87 Ad
Seoul. See Sŏul
Separation Pt., New Zealand 51 Dd
Sepólno, Poland 65 Gb
Sepulveda, Spain 66 Db
Sequeros, Spain 66 Bb
Sequoia Nat. Park., Cal. 45 Dg
Serai, Syria 90 Db
Serakhs, Turkmen 74 Fe
Seram I., Indonesia 79 Jl
Serampore, India 87 Gd
Serbia, Yugoslavia 72 Cc
Serdeles, Libya 95 Hc
Serdobsk, Russia 77 Gd
Sergach, Russia 77 Gc
Sergiyevsk, Russia 77 Kc
Serifos, I., Greece 73 Ef
Sermata, I., Indonesia 79 Jm
Serov, Russia 74 Fc
Serowe, Botswana 91 Dd
Serpa, Portugal 66 Bd
Serpins, Portugal 66 Ab
Serpukhov, Russia 76 Kd
Sérrai, Greece 72 Dd
Serre San Bruno, Italy 71 Ff
Serrezuela, Argentina 50 Cd
Sertã, Portugal 66 Ac
Sertãnia, Brazil 49 Ke
Sertig, Switzerland 61 Eb
Sérvia, Greece 73 Dd
Sesheke, Zambia 91 Cc
Sete, France 69 Ee
Sete Lagoas, Brazil 49 Jg
Setif, Algeria 94 Ga
Setubal, Portugal 66 Ac
Sevan, Oz., Armyanskaya 74 Dd
Sevastopol, Russia 76 Hj
Sevelen, Switzerland 61 Ea
Severac-le-Château, France 69 Ed
Severn, Cape Province 91 Ce
Severn, R., England 59 Fj
Severnaya Dvina, Russia 74 Db
Severnaya Zemlya, Russia 75 Ka
Sevier L., Utah 45 Gf
Sevilla, Spain 66 Cd
Seville. See Sevilla
Seward, Alaska 43 Ym
Seward Pen., Alaska 43 Wl
Seybaplaya, Mexico 46 Fd
Seychelles, Is., Indian Ocean 96 De
Seydhisfjördhur, Iceland 62 Za
Seyhan, Turkey 88 Cb
Seymchan, Russia 75 Qb
Seymour, Indiana 40 Df
Seyne, France 69 Gd
Sezanne, France 68 Eb
Sfakiá. See Khóra Sfakion
Sfântu Gheorghe, Rumania 72 Eb
Sfax, Tunisia 95 Hb
Sfira, Syria 90 Fa
Shaam, Trucial States 89 Gd
Shackleton, Antarctica 100 Ab
Shadegan, Persia 88 Ec
Shadrinsk, Russia 77 Rb
Shadwan, I., Egypt 95 Mc
Shaftesbury, England 59 Fj
Shag Rocks, Atlantic Ocean 100 Td
Shahabad, India 86 Ee
Shahabad, India 87 Cb
Shahba, Syria 90 Ee
Shahbandar, W. Pakistan 84 Cd
Shahdād, Persia 89 Gc
Shahdadkot, W. Pakistan 84 Cc
Shahdadpur, W. Pakistan 84 Cc
Shahdara, India 86 Ef
Shahdheri, W. Pakistan 86 Cd
Shahdol, India 87 Cd
Shahganj, India 87 Db
Shahhat, Libya 95 Kb
Shahin, Persia 88 Eb
Shahjahanpur, India 87 Bb
Shahjui, Afghanistan 89 Jc
Shahpur, W. Pakistan 86 Cd
Shāhpūr, Persia 88 Db
Shahpura, India 84 Dc
Shahrakht, Persia 89 Hc
Shahr-e-Babak, Persia 89 Gc
Shahreza, Persia 89 Fc
Shahr-i-Zabul. See Zabol
Shahrud, Persia 89 Gb
Shahsavar, Persia 89 Fb
Shahsien, China 81 Hj
Shaiba, Arabia 88 Dd
Shajara, Arabia 88 Ee
Shakhty, Russia 77 Eg
Shakpets. See Shakubetsueki
Shakubetsueki, Japan 82 Hc
Shala L., Ethiopia 93 Hc
Shalasha, Sudan 95 Lf
Shamil, Persia 89 Gd
Shammar, Jabal, Arabia 88 Dd
Shamokin, Pennsylvania 40 He
Shanghai, China 80 Kg
Shangjao, China 81 Hh
Shangkiu, China 80 Ge
Shangtu, China 80 Fb
Shangtung, prov., China 80 Hd
Shangyiu, China 81 Gk
Shan-hai-kwan. See Linyu
Shanhsien. See Sanmenhsia
Shannah, Arabia 89 Ff
Shannon, Eire 59 Bh
Shannon, New Zealand 51 Ed
Shannon, I., Greenland 41 Mb
Shannon R., Eire 59 Bg
Shansi, prov., China 80 Ec
Shantarskiye Os., Russia 75 Nc
Shantung Pen., China 78 Hc
Shaohing, China 81 Kg
Shaowu, China 81 Hj
Shaoyang, China 81 Ej
Shapinsay, I., Orkney Is. 58 Fa
Shaqa, Arabia 88 Df
Shaqra, Arabia 88 Ed
Sharakpur, W. Pakistan 86 De
Sharjah, Trucial Oman 89 Gd
Shark B., W. Australia 52 Be
Sharon, Pennsylvania 40 Fe
Sharqi, Jeb. esh, Leb.-Syria 90 Ec
Sharr, Jebel el, Arabia 88 Cd
Sharya, Russia 77 Ga
Shasi, China 81 Fg
Shasta, California 45 Be
Shasta, Mt., California 45 Be
Shasta Res., California 45 Ce
Shatra, Iraq 88 Ec
Shatt-al-Arab, Iraq 88 Ec
Shaubek, Jordan 90 Dg
Shawano, Wisconsin 40 Bc
Shawinigan, Quebec 40 Kb
Shawnee, Oklahoma 42 Gd
Shchors, Ukraine 76 Gf
Sheboygan, Wisconsin 40 Cd
Sheelin L., Eire 59 Cg
Sheep Haven, Eire 58 Be
Sheerness, England 59 Hj
Sheffield, England 59 Gg
Sheffield, New Zealand 51 Ce
Sheikh, Jeb. esh, Syria 90 Dd
Sheikh 'Abd er Rahman. See Arka
Sheikh Miskin, Syria 90 Ee
Sheikh 'Othman, S. Yemen 88 Eg
Sheik Seraq, Syria 90 Fd
Shekha, S. Yemen 88 Ef
Shekhupura, W. Pakistan 86 Ce
Sheklung, China 81 Fl
Shelburne, Ontario 40 Fc
Shelby, Michigan 40 Cd
Shelby, Montana 42 Db
Shelikhova, Zaliv, Russia 75 Qc
Shelter I., New York 44 Db
Shenandoah, Pennsylvania 44 Bb
Shenandoah Junct., W. Va. 44 Bc
Shenandoah Nat. Park, Virginia 43 Ld
Shenandoah R., Virginia 44 Bc
Shenchow. See Yüanling
Shendam, Nigeria 95 Gg
Shendi, Sudan 95 Me
Shëngjin, Albania 72 Bd
Shenkursk, Russia 74 Db
Shensi, prov., China 80 De
Shenyang, China 80 Lb
Sheopur, India 84 Ec
Shepetovka, Ukraine 76 Ef
Shepparton, Victoria 53 Jg
Sherada, Ethiopia 93 Hc
Sherard Osborn Fd., Greenland 41 Pa
Sherbro I., Sierra Leone 94 Cg
Sherbrooke, Quebec 40 Lc
Sheridan, Wyoming 42 Ec
Sherman, Texas 42 Ge
Sherpur, E. Pakistan 87 Gc
Shetland (Zetland), Scotland 58 Ja
Shevaroy Hills, India 84 Ef
Shiant Is., Scotland 58 Cc
Shibam, S. Yemen 88 Ef
Shibarghan, Afghanistan 89 Jb
Shibata, Japan 82 Ff
Shibetsi, Japan 82 Jc
Shibin el Kom, Egypt 95 Mb
Shiel, L., Scotland 58 Dd
Shigatse, Tibet 85 Gc
Shihnan. See Enshih
Shih Pao Shan, China 78 Ee
Shihshow, China 81 Fh
Shihtao, China 80 Ld
Shihtsien, China 81 Dj
Shikarpur, W. Pakistan 84 Cc
Shikohabad, India 87 Bb
Shikoku, I., Japan 82 Ch
Shilka & R., Russia 75 Lc

Shillelagh, Eire 59 Ch
Shillong, India 85 Hc
Shilongol. See Silinhot
Shimoga, India 84 Ef
Shimo Jima, Japan 82 Ah
Shimoni, Kenya 93 He
Shimonoseki, Japan 82 Bg
Shin, L., Scotland 58 Eb
Shinas, Muscat & Oman 89 Ge
Shinghar, W. Pakistan 86 Ae
Shingshal & Pass, Kashmir 86 Db
Shingu, Japan 82 Dh
Shinjo, Japan 82 Ge
Shinshar, Syria 90 Ec
Shinyanga, Tanzania 93 Ge
Shipets. See Shibetsi
Shiraishi, Japan 82 Gf
Shiraz, Persia 89 Fd
Shireza, W. Pakistan 84 Cc
Shisur, Arabia 89 Ff
Shiuchow. See Kukong
Shiuhing. See Koyiu
Shivpuri, India 87 Ac
Shizugawa, Japan 82 Ge
Shizuoka, Japan 82 Fg
Shklov, Belorussia 76 Gd
Shkodër, Albania 72 Bc
Shoka. See Changhua
Sholapur, India 84 Ee
Shonai. See Tsuruoka
Shorkot, W. Pakistan 86 Ce
Short Mts., W. Virginia 44 Ac
Shoshone Falls, Idaho 42 Dc
Shoshone Res., Wyoming 42 Ec
Shovo Tso, Tibet 85 Fb
Shreveport, Louisiana 43 He
Shrewsbury, England 59 Fh
Shropshire (Salop), co., Eng. 59 Fh
Shtora, Lebanon 90 Dd
Shuikow, China 81 Jj
Shujaabad, W. Pakistan 86 Bf
Shumagin Is., Alaska 43 Xm
Shumaisa, Arabia 88 Ee
Shumen. See Kolarovgrad
Shumerlya, Russia 77 Hc
Shunking. See Nanchung
Shunteh. See Singtai
Shuqra, S. Yemen 88 Eg
Shurab, Persia 89 Gc
Shurma, Arabia 88 De
Shuru Tso, Tibet 85 Gb
Shushal, Kashmir 84 Eb
Shushtar, Persia 88 Ec
Shusf, Persia 89 Hc
Shuya, Russia 77 Eb
Shuyang, China 80 Je
Shwebo, Burma 85 Jd
Shwedaung, Burma 85 Je
Shwegyin, Burma 85 Je
Shweli R., Burma 85 Jd
Sialkot, W. Pakistan 86 Dd
Siam. See Thailand
Siam, G. of. See Thailand, G. of
Sian, China 80 De
Siangtan, China 81 Fj
Siangyang, China 80 Ff
Siangyin, China 81 Fh
Siapu, China 81 Jj
Siargao, I., Philippines 79 Jj
Siaton, Philippines 79 Hj
Šiauliai, Lithuania 63 Kj
Sib, Muscat & Oman 89 Ge
Sibenik, Yugoslavia 70 Ed
Siberut, I., Indonesia 79 Cl
Sibi, W. Pakistan 84 Cc
Sibiu, Rumania 72 Eb
Sibolga, Sumatra 79 Ck
Sibsagar, India 85 Hc
Sibu, Sarawak 79 Fk
Sicasica, Bolivia 48 Dg
Sichang, China 78 De
Sicie C., France 69 Fe
Sicilia. I. See Sicily
Sicilian Chan., Medit. Sea 71 Cg
Sicily (Sicilia), I., Italy 71 Dg
Sicuani, Peru 48 Cf
Sid, Yugoslavia 72 Bb
Sideby, Finland 63 Je
Siderno Marina, Italy 71 Ff
Sidhout, India 84 Ef
Sidi Barrani, Egypt 95 Lb
Sidi-bel-Abbès, Algeria 94 Ea
Sidi Ifni, Ifni, N.-W. Africa 94 Cc
Sidlaw Hills, Scotland 58 Ed
Sidnaw, Michigan 40 Bb
Sidney, New York 40 Jd
Sidon, Lebanon 90 Dd
Sidri, Gulf of, Libya 95 Jb
Siedlce, Poland 65 Kb
Siegen, Germany 64 Cc
Siem-Reap, Cambodia 83 Cd
Siena, Italy 70 Cd
Sieradz, Poland 65 Hc
Siero, Spain 66 Ca
Sierra Colorada, Argentina 50 Cf
Sierra Grande, Argentina 50 Cf
Sierra Leone, W. Africa 94 Cg
Sierra Madre, Mexico 46 Cb
Sierra Mojada, Mexico 46 Db
Sierra Rosaria, Argentina 50 Cf
Sífnos, I., Greece 73 Ef
Sigean, France 69 Ee
Sighet, Rumania 65 Ke
Sighisoara, Rumania 72 Ea
Siglufjördhur, Iceland 62 Wl
Sigmaringen, Germany 64 Cd
Sigsig, Ecuador 48 Bd
Sigüenza, Spain 66 Db
Siguiri, Guinea 94 Df
Sigulda, Latvia 63 Lh
Sihanoukville, Cambodia 79 Dh
Sihl See, Switzerland 61 Da
Sihsien, China 81 Jh
Siilinjärvi, Finland 62 Me
Sikandarabad, India 86 Ef
Sikandra Rao, India 87 Bb
Sikar, India 86 Dg
Sikasso, Mali 94 Df
Si Kiang, R., China 78 Ff
Siking. See Sian
Sikinos, I., Greece 73 Ef
Sikkim, India 87 Gb
Sila, La, Italy 71 Ff
Silairsk, Russia 77 Nd
Silao, Mexico 46 Dc
Silchar, India 85 Hd
Silenen, Switzerland 61 Db
Silenrieux, Belgium 60 Cd
Sil Garhi, Nepal 87 Ca
Silifke, Turkey 88 Bb
Silinhot, China 78 Gb
Silistra, Bulgaria 72 Fb
Siljan, L., Sweden 63 Ff
Silkeborg, Denmark 63 Ch
Silloth, England 58 Ef
Sils, Switzerland 61 Eb
Silvânia, Brazil 49 Hg
Silvaplana, Switzerland 61 Eb
Silva Porto, Angola 92 Dg
Silver L., Oregon 45 Cd
Silvercreek, New York 40 Gd
Silves, Brazil 48 Fd
Silves, Portugal 66 Ad
Silvretta, Mts., Austria-Switz. 64 Ce
Simard, L., Quebec 40 Gb
Simcoe, Ontario 40 Fd
Simcoe, L., Ontario 40 Gc
Simeulue, I., Indonesia 79 Ck
Simferopol, Russia 76 Jj
Simi, I., Greece 73 Ff
Simla, India 86 Ee
Simleul Silvaniei, Rumania 65 Ke
Simo, Finland 62 Ld
Simola, Finland 63 Nf
Simon, L., Quebec 40 Jc
Simpelveld, Netherlands 60 Dd
Simplon and Pass, Switz. 61 Db
Simpson Des., Australia 53 Ge
Simpson, I., Chile 50 Bg
Simuna, Estonia 63 Mg
Sinai, pen., Egypt 95 Mc
Sinaloa, state, Mexico 46 Cb
Sinaloa & R., Mexico 46 Cb
Sinamaica, Venezuela 48 Ca
Sinbo, Burma 85 Jd
Sinchang, China 81 Kh
Sin-chow, China 80 Fd
Sindel, Bulgaria 72 Fc
Sindhuli Garhi, Nepal 87 Eb
Sind Sagar Doab, W. Pakistan 86 Be
Sines, Portugal 66 Ad
Singa, Sudan 95 Mf
Singapore, & Str., S. E. Asia 83 Cf
Singaradja, Bali I., Indon. 79 Gm
Singen, Germany 64 Ce
Singhana, India 86 Df
Singida, Tanzania 93 Ge
Singitic G., Greece 73 Dd
Singkawang, Borneo 79 Ek
Singkep, I., Riouw Arch., Indon. 79 Dl
Singora. See Songkhla
Singsingsia, China 78 Bb
Singtai, China 80 Gd
Singtze, China 81 Hh
Sinho, China 80 Gd
Sinhsien, China 78 Fc
Sinhwa, China 81 Ej
Sining, China 78 Dc
Siniscola, Sardegna 71 Be
Sinj, Yugoslavia 70 Fd
Sinjar, & Jebel, Iraq 88 Db
Sinjil, Palestine 90 De
Sinkiang, China 54 Hd
Sin-min-fu, China 80 Lb
Sinnamary, Fr. Guiana 49 Gb
Sinning, China 81 Ej
Sinoe L., Rumania 72 Gb
Sinoia, Rhodesia 91 Ec
Sinop, Turkey 88 Ca
Sintra, Portugal 66 Ac
Sinuiju, Korea 78 Hb
Sinyang, China 80 Ff
Sion, Switzerland 61 Cb
Sioux City, Iowa 42 Gc
Sioux Falls, S. Dakota 42 Gc
Siparia, Trinidad 48 Ea
Sipolilo, Rhodesia 91 Ec
Sipora, I., Indonesia 79 Cl
Siquisique, Venezuela 48 Da
Sira, India 84 Ef
Sira. See Siros, I.
Siracusa, Sicilia 71 Eg
Sirajganj, E. Pakistan 87 Gc
Sir Edward Pellew Group, N. Territory, Australia 53 Gc
Siretul, R., Rumania 72 Fa
Sirhind, India 86 Ee
Siri, Ethiopia 93 Hc
Sirjan, Persia 89 Gd
Sirna, I., Greece 73 Ff
Sironcha, India 84 Ee
Sironj, India 84 Ed
Siros, I., Greece 73 Ef
Sirsa, India 86 Df
Sirsi, India 87 Ba
Sirsi, India 84 Df
Sirte & G. of, Libya 95 Jb
Sisak, Yugoslavia 70 Fc
Sisaket, Siam 83 Cc
Sisal, Mexico 46 Fc
Sisi, Botswana 91 Dd
Sisopon, Cambodia 83 Cd
Sisteron, France 69 Fd
Sitamarhi, India 87 Eb
Sitamau, India 84 Ed
Sitapur, India 87 Cb
Sitara, Arabia 88 Ee
Sithonia, Greece 73 Dd
Sitia, Crete 73 Fg
Sitka, Alaska 43 Zm
Sitpur, W. Pakistan 86 Bf
Sittang, Burma 85 Je
Sittang, R., Burma 85 Je
Sittard, Netherlands 60 Dd
Sitten. See Sion
Sivand, Persia 89 Fc
Sivas, Turkey 88 Cb
Siverek, Turkey 88 Cb
Sivrihisar, Turkey 88 Bb
Sivry, Belgium 60 Cd
Siwa, Egypt 95 Lc
Siwalik Hills, India 84 Eb
Siwan, India 87 Eb
Sjælland, Denmark 63 Dj
Sjötorp, Sweden 63 Eg
Skadarsko Jezero, Yugosl.-Alb. 72 Bc
Skagafjord, Iceland 62 Wl
Skagens, Denmark 63 Dh
Skagerrak, Norway-Denmark 63 Bh
Skagway, Alaska 43 Zm
Skaneateles, L., New York 44 Ba
Skara, Sweden 63 Eg
Skardu, Kashmir 86 Dc
Skarnes, Norway 63 Df
Skegness, England 59 Hg
Skellefte Älv, Sweden 62 Hd
Skellefteå, Sweden 62 Jd
Skiathos, I., Greece 73 De
Skibbereen, Eire 59 Aj
Skien, Norway 63 Cg
Skierniewice, Poland 65 Jc
Skiftet Kihti, Finland 63 Jf
Skikda (Philippeville), Algeria 69 Qh
Skipton, England 59 Fg
Skíros, I., Greece 73 Ee
Skive, Denmark 63 Ch
Skofja Loka, Yugoslavia 70 Eb
Skópelos, I., Greece 73 De
Skopin, Russia 76 Le
Skopje, Yugoslavia 72 Cc
Skövde, Sweden 63 Eg
Skovorodino, Russia 75 Mc
Skradin, Yugoslavia 70 Ed
Skrunda, Latvia 63 Kh
Skudeneshavn, Norway 63 Ag
Skuodas, Lithuania 63 Jh
Skye, I., Scotland 58 Cc
Slagelse, Denmark 63 Dj
Slamet, Mt., Java 79 Em
Slaney R., Eire 59 Ch
Slatina, Yugoslavia 72 Ab
Slatina, Rumania 72 Eb
Slatington, Pennsylvania 44 Cb
Slăveni, Rumania 72 Eb
Slavgorod, Russia 74 Gc
Slavonia, Yugoslavia 72 Ab
Slavyansk, Ukraine 76 Kg
Slea Hd., Eire 59 Ah
Sleat, Sd. of, Scotland 58 Dc
Sleydinge, Belgium 60 Bc
Slide Mt., New York 40 Jd
Sliedrecht, Netherlands 60 Cc
Slieve Aughty, Mts., Eire 59 Bg
Slieve Bloom Mts., Eire 59 Bg
Slieve Mish, Mts., Eire 59 Ah
Sligo & co., Eire 59 Bf
Sligo B., Eire 59 Bf
Slite, Sweden 63 Hh
Sliven, Bulgaria 72 Fc
Slobodskoy, Russia 77 Ka
Sloka, Latvia 76 Cc
Slonim, Belorussia 76 De
Sloten, Netherlands 60 Db
Slough, England 59 Gj
Slovakia, Czechoslovakia 65 Hd
Slovenija, Yugoslavia 70 Ec
Slovensko, Czechoslovakia 65 Hd
Sluis, Netherlands 60 Bc
Sluiskil, Netherlands 60 Bc
Slunj, Yugoslavia 70 Ec
Słupsk, Poland 65 Ga
Slussfors, Sweden 62 Gd
Slutsk, Belorussia 76 Ee
Slyne Hd., Eire 59 Ag
Slyudyanka, Russia 75 Kc
Smethport, Pennsylvania 44 Ab
Smilde, Netherlands 60 Eb
Smiltene, Latvia 63 Lh
Smith, I., South Shetlands 100 Sc
Smith Falls, Ontario 40 Hc
Smithton, Tasmania 53 Hh
Smoky Hill R., Kansas 42 Fd
Smöla, Norway 62 Be
Smolensk, Russia 76 Hd
Smyrna (Izmir), Turkey 88 Ab
Snaefell, Isle of Man 59 Df
Snake, R. & Canyon, Washington, etc. 45 Db
Snares Is., New Zealand 51 Ah
Snåsa, Norway 62 Ed
Snåsa Vatn, Norway 62 Dd
Sneek, Netherlands 60 Da
Sneen, Eire 59 Aj
Sneeuw Gebergte, W. Irian 79 Ll
Snizort L., Scotland 58 Cc
Snöhetta, Mt., Norway 62 Ce
Snow Pk. See Medicine Bow Pk.
Snowdon, Wales 59 Eg
Snow Water L., Nevada 42 Dc
Snowy Mts., Vict.- N.S.W. 53 Jg
Soasin, Moluccas 79 Jk
Soazza, Switzerland 61 Eb
Sobakin, Russia 77 Jd
Sobrado, Brazil 49 Ge
Sobral, Brazil 49 Jd
Sobrance, Czechoslovakia 65 Kd
Sobraon, India 86 Dd
Society Is., Pacific Ocean 99 Kj
Socorro, Colombia 48 Cb
Socorro, New Mexico 42 Ee
Socorro I., Mexico 46 Bd
Socotra I., Indian Ocean 93 Lb
Soc-trang, S. Vietnam 83 De
Sodankylä, Finland 62 Mc
Söderfors, Sweden 63 Gf
Söderhamn, Sweden 63 Gf
Söderköping, Sweden 63 Gg
Södertälje, Sweden 63 Gg
Sodiri, Sudan 95 Lf
Sodus, New York 44 Ba
Sodus Pt., New York 44 Ba
Soepiori, I., W. Irian 79 Ll
Soest, Germany 64 Cc
Soest, Netherlands 60 Db
Sofiya (Sofia), Bulgaria 72 Dc
Sogamosa, Colombia 48 Cb
Sognadal, Norway 63 Bg
Sogne Fd., Norway 63 Af
Sögut, Turkey 88 Ba
Sohag, Egypt 95 Mc
Sohagpur, India 87 Cd
Sohan R., W. Pakistan 86 Cd
Sohar, Muscat & Oman 89 Ge
Sohawal, India 87 Cc
Soheb, S. Yemen 88 Eg
Sohna, India 86 Ef
Soignies, Belgium 60 Cd
Soissons, France 68 Eb
Soke, Turkey 88 Ab
Sok Gomba. See Pachen
Sok Karmalinsk, Russia 77 Lc
Sokode, Togo 94 Eg
Sokol, Russia 76 Lb
Sokolo, Mali 94 Df
Sokota, Ethiopia 93 Hb
Sokoto, Nigeria 94 Ff
Solai, Kenya 93 Hd
Solbad Hall, Austria 64 De
Soledad, Venezuela 48 Eb
Soledade, Brazil 49 Ge
Solent, The, England 59 Gk
Solenzara, Corsica 71 Be
Sol Iletsk, Russia 74 Ec
Solimoes, R. See Amazonas
Solingen, Germany 64 Bc
Sollefteå, Sweden 62 Ge
Sollum. See Salûm
Solok, Sumatra 79 Dl
Solomon Is., Pacific Ocean 98 Eh
Solomon R., Kansas 42 Gd
Solon, India 86 Ee
Solothurn & canton, Switz. 61 Ca
Solsona, Spain 67 Fa
Solstad, Norway 62 Dd
Soltau, Germany 64 Cb
Solund, I., Norway 63 Af
Solway Firth, Eng.-Scot. 58 Ef
Solwezi, Zambia 92 Fg
Soma, Turkey 88 Ab
Somalia, Somali Republic 93 Jd
Sombor, Yugoslavia 72 Bb
Sombreiro Chan., Nicobar I. 85 Hg
Sombrerete, Mexico 46 Dc
Sombrero I., Leeward Is. 47 Gc
Somcuța Mare, Rumania 65 Ke
Someren, Netherlands 60 Dc
Somerset, Pennsylvania 40 Ge
Somerset, Queensland 53 Hb
Somerset, co., England 59 Ej
Somerset Res., Vermont 44 Ab
Somerville, New Jersey 44 Cb
Somme, Belgium 60 Dd
Somme, dep., France 68 Eb
Somme, R., France 68 Da
Sommieres, France 69 Fe
Somoto, Nicaragua 47 Bd
Somovit, Bulgaria 72 Ec
Somzee, Belgium 60 Cd
Son R., India 87 Ec
Sonamukhi, India 87 Fd
Sonbarsa, India 87 Fc
Sönderborg, Denmark 63 Cj
Sonepat, India 86 Ef
Song-Cau, S. Vietnam 83 Dd
Songea, Tanzania 93 Hg
Songkhla, Siam 83 Ce
Song-koi, R., N. Vietnam 83 Cb
Sonhat, India 87 Dd
Sonkajärvi, Finland 62 Me
Sonkovo, Russia 76 Kc
Sonmiani, W. Pakistan 84 Cc
Sonneberg, Germany 64 Dc
Sonogno, Switzerland 61 Db
Sonora, state & R., Mexico 46 Bb
Sonoyta, Mexico 46 Ba
Sonpur, India 87 Dd
Sonpur, India 87 Ec
Sonson, Colombia 48 Bb
Soochow, China 80 Kg
Soping. See Yuyu
Soppero, Sweden 62 Jb
Sopron, Hungary 70 Fb
Sopur, Kashmir 86 Dc
Sora, Italy 71 De
Sorata, Bolivia 48 Dg
Sorbas, Spain 67 Dd
Sorell, Tasmania 53 Jh
Sörenberg, Switzerland 61 Db
Sörfold, Norway 62 Fc
Sorgono, Sardinia 71 Be
Soria, Spain 67 Db
Soriano, Uruguay 50 Ed
Sornico, Switzerland 61 Db
Sorocaba, Brazil 49 Hh
Soroka, Russia 77 Ld
Soroki, Moldavia 76 Fg
Sorol, I., Caroline Is. 98 Cg
Soromesis, Botswana 91 Cc
Soron, India 87 Bb
Sorong, New Guinea 79 Kl
Sororoca, Brazil 48 Ec
Soroti, Uganda 93 Gd
Söröy, I., Norway 62 Ka
Sorrento, Italy 71 Ee
Sorsele, Sweden 62 Gd
Sortavala, Karelia 62 Pf
Sosnovka, Russia 77 Ed
Sosnovo, Ozerskoye, Russia 75 Lc
Sosnowiec, Poland 65 Hc
Sosva, Russia 74 Fc
Soto la Marina, Mexico 46 Ec
Sotra, I., Norway 63 Af
Sotuta, Mexico 46 Gc
Souanke, Fr. Congo 92 Cd
Soudan, W. Africa 94 De
Soudan, N. Terr., Aust. 53 Gd
Souflion, Greece 72 Fd
Souillac, France 69 Dd
Sŏul, Korea 78 Jc
Soure, Brazil 49 Hd
Soure, Portugal 66 Ab
Sour El Ghozlane, Algeria 94 Fa
Sousel, Brazil 49 Gd
Sousse, Tunisia 95 Ha
Souterraine, la, France 68 Dc
South Downs, England 59 Gk
South I., New Zealand 51 Be
South Africa, Rep. of, Africa 91 Ce
Southampton, England 59 Fk
Southampton, New York 40 Ke
Southampton, Ontario 40 Fc
South Arabia, Federation & Prot. 88 Eg
South Australia, state, Aust. 52 Fe
South Bend, Indiana 40 Ce
South Bend, Washington 45 Bb
Southbridge, Massachusetts 44 Da
Southbridge, New Zealand 51 Ce
South Carolina, state, U.S.A. 43 Ke
South China Sea, Asia 55 Kh
South Dakota, state, U.S.A. 42 Fc
South-East C., Tasmania 53 Jh
Southend, England 59 Hj
Southern Alps, New Zealand 51 Bf
Southern Cross, W. Aust. 52 Cf
Southern Ocean, Antarctica 100 Cc
Southern Rhodesia. See Rhodesia
Southern Yemen, Republic of, S.W. Asia 88 Dg
South Georgia, I., Atlantic Ocean 100 Ad
South Hadley Falls, Mass. 44 Da
South Haven, Michigan 40 Cd
South Magnetic Pole 100 Jc
South Milwaukee, Wisconsin 40 Cd
South Orkneys, Is., Atl. Oc. 100 Sc
South Polar Plateau, Antarc. 100 Ma
South Pole, Antarctica 100 a
Southport, England 59 Eg
Southport, Queensland 53 Ke
South River, New Jersey 44 Cb
South Ronaldsay I., Orkney 58 Fb
South Sandwich, Is., Atl. Oc. 100 Ad
South Shetland Is., Antarc. 100 Tc
South Shields, England 58 Gf
South Thule, I., South Sandwich Is. 100 Ad
South-West C., Tasmania 53 Jh
South-West Africa, S. Africa 91 Bd
Southwold, England 59 Jh
Souza, Brazil 49 Ke
Souzel, Portugal 66 Bc
Sovetsk, Russia 63 Jj
Sovetskaya Gavan, Russia 75 Pd
Sovietsk, Russia 77 Jb
Soy, Kenya 93 Hd
Soya & B., Japan 82 Gb
Soya Str., Japan 82 Gb
Soya Misaki, Japan 82 Hb
Soyopa, Mexico 46 Cb
Spa, Belgium 60 Dd
Spain, W. Europe 57 Fh
Spalato. See Split
Spalding, England 59 Gh
Spandau, Germany 64 Eb
Spanish, Ontario 40 Eb
Spanish Fork, Utah 42 Dd
Spanish Guinea, Cent. Afr. 92 Bd
Spanish Sahara, W. Africa 94 Cc
Spanish Town, Jamaica 47 Dc
Sparks, Nevada 45 Df
Sparta. See Sparti
Sparta, Wisconsin 40 Ad
Spartanburg, S. Carolina 43 Ke
Sparti, Greece 73 Df
Spartivento C., Italy 71 Fg
Spassk, Russia 77 Fd
Spassk Dalniy, Russia 78 Kb
Spassk-Ryszanskiy, Russia 77 Ec
Spencer G., S. Australia 53 Gf
Spenser Mts., New Zealand 51 De
Sperrin Mts., N. Ireland 59 Cf
Spétsai I., Greece 73 Df
Spey R., Scotland 58 Ec
Speyer, Germany 64 Cd
Spezand, W. Pakistan 84 Cb
Spezia, La, Italy 70 Bc
Spinazzola, Italy 71 Fe
Spiringen, Switzerland 61 Db
Spitsbergen, Arctic Ocean 74 Aa
Spitsbergen, Vest, Arctic Oc. 74 Aa
Spittal, Austria 64 Ee
Split, Yugoslavia 70 Fd
Splügen, Switzerland 61 Eb
Splügen Pass, Switz.-Italy 61 Eb
Spokane, Washington 45 Eb
Spoleto, Italy 70 Dd
Spontin, Belgium 60 Cd
Sporadhes, Aegean Sea 73 Ff
Sporadhes, Voriai, Agean Sea 73 Ee
Spree R., Germany 64 Eb
Spremberg, Germany 64 Fc
Sprimont, Belgium 60 Dd
Springbok, Cape Province 91 Be
Springburn, N.Z. 51 Ce
Springfield, Illinois 40 Bf
Springfield, Massachusetts 40 Kd
Springfield, Missouri 43 Hd
Springfield, Ohio 40 Ef
Springfield, Vermont 44 Da
Springfontein, O.F.S. 91 Df
Springsure, Queensland 53 Jd
Springville, New York 40 Gd
Springville, Utah 42 Dc
Spruce Knob, W. Virginia 44 Ac
Spruga, Switzerland 61 Db
Squillace, G. di, Italy 71 Ff
Srbija (Serbia) Yugoslavia 72 Cc
Srebrenica, Yugoslavia 72 Bb
Sredinnyy, Khrebet, Mts., Russia 75 Rc
Sredne Kamchatsk, Russia 75 Rc
Sredne Kolymak, Russia 75 Qb
Sredne Vilyuysk, Russia 75 Mb
Śrem, Poland 65 Gb
Srepok, Cambodia 83 Dd
Sretensk, Russia 75 Lc
Srikakulam, India 85 Fe
Sri Madnopur, India 86 Dg
Srinagar, Kashmir 86 Dc
Srirangapatnar, India 84 Ef
Srivilliputtur, India 84 Eg
Srnetica, Yugoslavia 70 Fc
Środa, Poland 65 Gb
Stackpool, Ontario 40 Fb
Stadacona, Quebec 40 Kb
Staden, Belgium 60 Ad
Staffa I., Scotland 58 Cd
Stafford & co., England 59 Fh
Stalingrad. See Volgograd
Stalino, Russia 75 Jb
Stalino, Ukraine 76 Kh
Stambaugh, Michigan 40 Bb
Stamford, Connecticut 40 Ke
Stamproi, Netherlands 60 Dc
Stanchik, Russia 75 Qa
Standerton, Transvaal 91 De
Standish, Michigan 40 Dd
Stanislav. See Ivano-Frankovsk
Stanley, Falkland Is. 50 Eh
Stanley Falls, Congo 92 Fd
Stanleyville. See Kisangani
Stann Creek, Brit. Honduras 47 Bc
Stanovoy Khrebet, Mts., Russia 75 Mc
Stans, Switzerland 61 Db
Stansmore Ra., W. Australia 52 Ed
Stanthorpe, Queensland 53 Ke
Stanton, Michigan 40 Dd
Staphorst, Netherlands 60 Eb
Starachowice, Poland 65 Jc
Stara Planina, Bulgaria 72 Ec
Staraya Russa, Russia 76 Gc
Stara Zagora, Bulgaria 72 Ec
Starbuck, I., Pacific Ocean 99 Kh
Stargard, Poland 64 Fb
Star'obelsk, Ukraine 76 Lg
Starodub, Russia 76 He
Starogard, Poland 65 Hb
Staro Konstantinov, Ukraine 76 Eg
Staryy Oskol, Russia 76 Kf
Staten I., New York 44 Cb
Staten I. See Estados I.
Stattlandet, Norway 62 Ae
Staunton, Virginia 43 Ld
Stavanger, Norway 63 Ag
Stavelot, Belgium 60 Dd
Stavenisse, Netherlands 60 Cc
Stavern, Norway 63 Dg
Staveren, Netherlands 60 Db
Stavropol, Russia 74 Dd
Steckborn, Switzerland 61 Da
Steelton, Pennsylvania 44 Bb
Steenbergen, Netherlands 60 Cc
Steenkool, W. Irian 79 Kl
Steensel, Netherlands 60 Dc
Steenwijk, Netherlands 60 Eb
Stefanie L., Ethiopia 93 Hd
Steiermark, prov., Austria 64 Fe
Stein, Switzerland 61 Da
Steinkjer, Norway 62 De
Stekene, Belgium 60 Cc
Stenay, France 68 Fb
Stendal, Germany 64 Db
Stenträsk, Sweden 62 Hc
Stephenson, Michigan 40 Cc
Stepnoy. See Elista
Stepnyak, Kazakh. 74 Gc
Sterea, Greece 73 Ce
Sterling, Colorado 42 Fc
Sterling, Illinois 40 Be
Sterlitamak, Russia 77 Md
Sternberk, Czechoslovakia 65 Gd
Sterrebeek, Belgium 60 Cd
Stettin (Szczecin), Poland 64 Fb
Steubenville, Ohio 40 Fe
Stevens Point, Wisconsin 40 Bc
Stewart I., Chile 50 Bh
Stewart Is., New Zealand 51 Ag
Stewart Sd., Andaman Is. 85 Hf
Steyr, Austria 64 Fd
Stia, Italy 70 Cd
Stillwater, Minnesota 43 Hb
Stimlje, Yugoslavia 72 Cc
Stip, Yugoslavia 72 Dd
Stirling & co., Scotland 58 Ed
Stirling Ra., W. Australia 52 Cf
Stjernöy, Norway 62 Ka
Stockholm, Sweden 63 Hg
Stockport, England 59 Fg
Stockton, California 45 Cg
Stockton-on-Tees, England 59 Gf
Stoke-on-Trent, England 59 Fg
Stolbovaya, Russia 75 Qb
Stolp. See Słupsk
Ston, Yugoslavia 70 Fd
Stonehaven, Scotland 58 Fd
Stony L., Ontario 40 Gc
Stor Sjön, Sweden 62 Fe
Stora Lulevatten, Sweden 62 Hc
Stora Sjöfallets Nat. Park, Sweden 62 Gc
Storavan, Sweden 62 Hd
Stord, I., Norway 63 Ag
Stören, Norway 62 De
Storforshei, Norway 62 Fc
Storlien, Sweden 62 De
Stornoway, Scotland 58 Cb
Storsund, Sweden 62 Jd
Storuman, Sweden 62 Gd
Storvik, Sweden 63 Gf
Stowmarket, England 59 Hh
Strabane, N. Ireland 58 Cf
Strachan, Quebec 40 Ja
Strachan I., Papua 53 Ha
Strahan, Tasmania 53 Hh
Stralsund, Germany 64 Ea
Strand, Norway 63 Bg
Stranda, Norway 62 Be
Strange, Norway 63 Df
Strangford L., N. Ireland 58 Df
Strangways Springs, S. Aust. 53 Ge
Stranraer, Scotland 58 Df
Strasbourg, France 68 Gb
Strasburg, Virginia 44 Ac
Strässa, Sweden 63 Fg
Stratford, Connecticut 44 Db
Stratford, Michigan 40 Dc
Stratford, New Zealand 51 Ec
Stratford, Ontario 40 Fd
Stratford-on-Avon, England 59 Fh
Strathroy, Ontario 40 Fd
Straubing, Germany 64 Ed
Strbské Pleso, Czech. 65 Jd
Streaky B., S. Australia 53 Ff
Streator, Illinois 40 Be
Strelka, Russia 75 Qb
Strelka, Russia 75 Kb
Strelka, Russia 75 Jc
Strenči, Latvia 63 Lh
Stribro, Czechoslovakia 64 Ed
Strijbeek, Netherlands 60 Cc
Strijen, Netherlands 60 Cc
Strimón, G. of, Greece 73 Ed
Stromboli, I., Italy 71 Ef
Stromeferry, Scotland 58 Dc
Stromness, Orkney 58 Eb
Strömsberg, Sweden 63 Gf
Strömsbruk, Sweden 63 Gf
Strömstad, Sweden 63 Dg
Strömsund, Sweden 62 Fe
Ströms Vattudal, Sweden 62 Fd
Strömtorp, Sweden 63 Fg
Strongoli, Italy 71 Ff
Stronsay I., Orkney 58 Fa
Stroud, England 59 Fj
Stroudsburg, Pennsylvania 44 Cb
Struga, Yugoslavia 72 Cd
Struma, R., Bulg.-Greece 72 Dd
Strumica, Yugoslavia 72 Dd
Stryy, Ukraine 76 Cg
Strzelin, Poland 65 Gc
Stuart Ra., S. Australia 53 Fe
Stuart Highway, N.T., Aust. 53 Fc
Stugun, Sweden 62 Fe
Stung-Treng, Cambodia 83 Dd
Sturgeon Bay, Wisconsin 40 Cc
Sturgeon Falls, Ontario 40 Gb
Sturt Des., S. Aust., etc. 53 He
Stuttgart, Germany 64 Cd
Suakin, Sudan 95 Ne
Suancheng, China 80 Jg
Süan-hwa, China 80 Gb
Suaqui, Mexico 46 Cb
Subeimanieh. See Karaj
Subh, Jebel, Arabia 88 Ce
Subotica, Yugoslavia 72 Ba
Sucha, Poland 65 Hd
Suchan, Russia 75 Nd
Süchow. See Tungshan
Sucre, Bolivia 48 Dg
Sudan, Africa 95 Lf
Sudbury, England 59 Hh
Sudbury, Ontario 40 Fb
Suddie, Guyana 48 Fb
Sudety, Mts., Czech., etc. 65 Fc
Sudharam, E. Pakistan 85 Hd
Suez, Egypt 95 Mc
Suez Canal, Egypt 95 Mb
Suez, Gulf of, Egypt 95 Mc
Sufeina, Arabia 88 Dd
Suffolk, Virginia 43 Ld
Suffolk, co., England 59 Hh
Suhl, Germany 64 Dc
Suifu. See Ipin
Suihwa, China 78 Ja
Suining, China 80 Hf
Suipacha, Bolivia 48 Dh
Suiteh, China 80 Ed
Sujangarh, India 86 Dg
Sujanpur, India 87 Eb
Sujanpur, India 86 Ee
Sujica, Yugoslavia 70 Fd

Sukadana, Borneo 79 Fl
Sukhothai, Siam 83 Bc
Sukhumi, Gruzinskaya 74 Dd
Sukkur, W. Pakistan 84 Cc
Sukow, China 80 Fd
Sukumo, Japan 82 Ch
Sulaiman Ra., W. Pakistan 84 Db
Sulaimiya, Arabia 88 Ee
Sulaiyil, Arabia 88 Ee
Sulawesi, Celebes 79 Gl
Sulaymānīya, Iraq 88 Eb
Sulęcin, Poland 64 Fb
Sulgen, Switzerland 61 Ea
Sulina, Rumania 72 Gb
Sulitelma, Mt., Norway 62 Gc
Sullana, Peru 48 Ad
Sulmona, Italy 71 Dd
Sultan Bulak. See Razan
Sultan Dagh, Turkey 88 Bb
Sultan Hamud, Kenya 93 He
Sultaniyeh, Persia 88 Eb
Sultanpur, India 87 Db
Sultanpur, India 86 De
Sulu Arch., Philippines 79 Hj
Sulu Kep., Indonesia 79 Jl
Sulu Sea, Philippines 79 Gj
Sumagawa, Japan 82 Hc
Sumatra, I., Indonesia 79 Ck
Sumba, I., Indonesia 79 Gm
Sumbawa, I., Indonesia 79 Gm
Sumbur, Mongolia 78 Ea
Sumburgh Hd., Shetland 58 Jb
Sümeg, Hungary 65 Ge
Sumiswald, Switzerland 61 Ca
Sumperk, Czechoslovakia 65 Gd
Sumprabum, Burma 85 Jc
Sumter, S. Carolina 43 Ke
Sumy, Ukraine 76 Jf
Suna, Tanzania 93 Gf
Sunapee, L., New Hampshire 44 Da
Sunart L., Scotland 58 Dd
Sunbury, Pennsylvania 40 He
Suncho Corral, Argentina 50 Dc
Sunchow. See Kweiping
Suncook, New Hampshire 40 Ld
Sunda Str., Indonesia 79 Dm
Sundargarh, India 87 Ed
Sunderland, England 58 Gf
Sundridge, Ontario 40 Gc
Sundsvall, Sweden 62 Ge
Sungari Res., China 78 Jb
Sungari R., China 78 Ha
Sungkiang, China 80 Kg
Sunndal, Norway 62 Ce
Suntar, Russia 75 Lb
Sunyani, Ghana 94 Eg
Suonenjoki, Finland 62 Me
Supaul, India 87 Fb
Superior, Wisconsin 43 Hb
Superior, L., U.S.A.-Canada 43 Jb
Suq ash Shuyukh, Iraq 88 Ec
Sur, Muscat & Oman 89 Ge
Sur (Tyre), Lebanon 90 Dd
Sura R., Russia 77 Hc
Surab, W. Pakistan 84 Cc
Surabajo, Java 79 Fm
Surajgarh, India 86 Df
Surakarta, Java 79 Fm
Suran, Syria 90 Eb
Surapur, India 84 Ee
Surapur, India 84 Ee
Surat, India 84 Dd
Suratgarh, India 86 Df
Surat Thani, Siam 83 Be
Surendranagar, India 84 Dd
Surgères, France 68 Cc
Surgut, Russia 74 Gb
Suri, India 87 Fd
Surigao Str., Philippines 79 Jj
Surin, Siam 83 Cd
Surinam, rep., S. America 49 Fc
Suriname, R., Surinam 49 Fc
Suriya, S. Yemen 88 Eg
Surling, Mt. See Bonom Mhai, Mts.
Surrey, co., England 59 Gj
Sursee, Switzerland 61 Da
Sursk, Ukraine 76 Jg
Surtsey, I., Iceland 62 Vu
Süs, Switzerland 61 Fb
Susa, Persia 88 Ec
Susak, Yugoslavia 70 Ec
Susquehanna R., Pa., etc. 40 Hf
Sussex, co., England 59 Gk
Susteren, Netherlands 60 Dc
Sutherland, Cape Province 91 Cf
Sutherland, co., Scotland 58 Db
Suting. See Tahsien
Sutlej R., W. Pakistan 86 Ce
Sutsien, China 80 Jf
Sutton, Ontario 40 Gc
Suure Jaani, Estonia 63 Lg
Suvavesi, Finland 62 Ne
Suvorov, I., Pacific Ocean 98 Jj
Suwair, Arabia 88 Dc
Suwalki, Poland 65 Ka
Suwayh, Muscat & Oman 89 Ge
Suwayq, Muscat & Oman 89 Ge
Suweilih, Jordan 90 De
Suwo Nada, Japan 82 Bh
Svalbard, Arctic Ocean 74 Aa
Svanstein, Sweden 62 Kc
Svappavaara, Sweden 62 Jc
Svärholt, Halvöy, Norway 62 La
Svartenhuk Pen., Greenland 41 Pb
Svartisen, Norway 62 Fc
Svartvik, Sweden 62 Ge
Švekšna, Lithuania 63 Jj
Svendborg, Denmark 63 Dj
Sverdlovsk, Russia 77 Qb
Sverdrup, Os., Russia 74 Ga
Svetogorsk, Russia 63 Nf
Svetozarevo, Yugoslavia 72 Cc
Svishtov, Bulgaria 72 Ec
Svitavy, Czechoslovakia 65 Gd
Svlyazhsk, Russia 77 Jc
Svobodny, Russia 75 Mc
Svolvær, Norway 62 Fb
Swabi, W. Pakistan 86 Cb
Swakopmund, S.-W. Africa 91 Ad
Swale R., England 59 Ff
Swan, R., W. Australia 52 Cf
Swan Hill, Victoria 53 Hg
Swansea, Tasmania 53 Jh
Swansea & B., Wales 59 Ej
Swanton, Vermont 40 Kc
Swarzewo, Poland 65 Ha
Swastika, Ontario 40 Fb
Swat & R., W. Pakistan 86 Cc
Swatow, China 81 Hl
Swaziland, S. Africa 91 Ee
Sweden, N.-W. Europe 56 Lc
Swellendam, Cape Province 91 Cf
Swidnica, Poland 65 Gc
Swietochlowice, Poland 65 Hc
Swilly L., Eire 58 Be
Swindon, England 59 Fj
Swinemünde. See Swinoujście
Swinoujście, Poland 64 Fa
Switzerland, Central Europe 57 Jg
Swords, Eire 59 Cg
Syas'stroy, Russia 76 Ha
Sycamore, Illinois 40 Bd
Sydney, New South Wales 53 Kf
Sydproven, Greenland 41 Pd
Syeti Vrach, Bulgaria 72 Dd
Syktyvkar, Russia 74 Eb
Sylhet, E. Pakistan 85 Hd
Sylt, I., Germany 63 Cj
Sylte, Norway 62 Be
Syracuse, New York 44 Ba
Syracuse (Siracusa), Sicily 71 Eg
Syr Darya, Kazakh. 74 Fd
Syria, W. Asia 88 Cb
Syrian Des., Iraq, etc. 88 Cc
Sysert, Russia 77 Qb
Syurkum, Russia 75 Pc
Syzran, Russia 77 Jd
Szarvas, Hungary 65 Je
Szczecin, Poland 64 Fb
Szczecinek, Poland 65 Gb
Szczecinski, Zal., Ger.-Pol. 64 Fb
Szczytno, Poland 65 Jb
Szechwan, prov., China 80 Ag
Szeged, Hungary 72 Ca
Székesféhervar, Hungary 65 He
Szekszard, Hungary 72 Ba
Szemao, China 78 Df
Szeming. See Amoy
Szenan, China 81 Dj
Szengen, China 81 Dl
Szentes, Hungary 65 Je
Szolnok, Hungary 65 Je
Szombathely, Hungary 70 Fb
Szreńsk, Poland 65 Jb
Szprotawa, Poland 65 Fc
Taba, Arabia 88 Dd
Tabala, Arabia 88 Df
Tabas, Persia 89 Gc
Tabasara, Sierra de, Panama 47 Ce
Tabasco, state, Mexico 46 Fd
Tabas Sunnikhane, Persia 89 Hc
Tabatinga, Brazil 48 Dd
Tabelbala, Algeria 94 Ec
Table Mt., Cape Province 91 Bf
Taboieiro, Brazil 48 Fe
Tábor, Czechoslovakia 64 Fd
Tabora, Tanzania 93 Ge
Tabora, Tanzania 93 Gf
Tabriz, Persia 88 Eb
Tabu, Ivory Coast 94 Dh
Tabut, S. Yemen 89 Ff
Tabuk, Arabia 88 Cd
Tacambaro, Mexico 46 Dd
Tacloban, Philippines 79 Hh
Tacna, Peru 48 Cg
Taco, Argentina 50 Dc
Tacoma, Washington 45 Bb
Taconic Mts., N.Y.-Mass. 44 Da
Tacuarembo, Uruguay 50 Ed
Tadjoura & G. of, Fr. Som. 93 Jb
Tadzhikskaya, rep., U.S.S.R. 74 Fe
Taegu, Korea 78 Jc
Taejŏn, Korea 78 Jc
Tafalla, Spain 67 Ea
Taff R., Wales 59 Ej
Tafila, Jordan 90 Dg
Taft, Persia 89 Fc
Taftville, Connecticut 44 Db
Taganrog & G., Russia 76 Lh
Taga Zong, Bhutan 85 Hc
Tagdempt, Algeria 94 Fa
Taguá, Brazil 49 Jf
Tagula, I., Papua 53 Kb
Tagus R. (Tajo R.) Sp.-Port. 66 Bc
Tahakopa, New Zealand 51 Bg
Ta Hao, China 81 Fl
Tahat Mt., Algeria 94 Gd
Tahcheng, China 75 Hd
Ta Hingan Ling, China 78 Ha
Tahiti, I., Society Islands 99 Kj
Tahoe, L., California 45 Cf
Tahora, New Zealand 51 Ec
Tahoua, Niger 94 Gf
Tahsien, China 80 Cg
Tahta, Egypt 95 Mc
Tahuna, Indonesia 79 Jk
Tai-an, China 80 Hd
Taichow. See Linhai
Taichung, Taiwan 81 Kk
Taieri, R., New Zealand 51 Cf
Taïf, Arabia 88 De
Tai-hang-shan, China 80 Fd
Taihape, New Zealand 51 Ec
Taihsien, China 80 Kf
Taihsien, China 81 Gj
Tai Hu, China 80 Jg
Taiku, China 80 Fd
Taima, Arabia 88 Cd
Tainan, Taiwan 81 Kl
Taipale, Finland 62 Ne
Taipei, Taiwan 81 Kk
Taiping. See Tsungshan
Taiping, W. Malaysia 83 Cf
Taiping. See Tangtu
Taipingchwan, China 78 Hb
Taipinght. See Wanyuan
Taira, Japan 82 Gf
Tairadate Str., Japan 82 Gd
Taishan I., China 81 Lg
Taishet, Russia 75 Jc
Taishun, China 81 Jj
Taitao, Pen. de, Chile 50 Bg
Taiwan, I., China 78 Hf
Taiwan Kaikyo, China 78 Gf
Taiwara, Afghanistan 89 Hc
Taiyetos, Mts., Greece 73 Df
Taiyiba, Jordan 90 Dg
Taiyuan, China 80 Fd
Ta'izz, Yemen 88 Dg
Tajan, Borneo 79 Fl
Tajo, R., Spain-Portugal 66 Bc
Tajrish, Persia 89 Fb
Tajumulco, Mt., Guatemala 46 Fd
Tak, Siam 83 Bc
Takada, Japan 82 Ff
Takahashi, Japan 82 Cg
Takaka, New Zealand 51 Dd
Takamatsu, Japan 82 Dg
Takao. See Kaohsiung
Takaoka, Japan 82 Ef
Takapuna, New Zealand 51 Eb
Takasaki, Japan 82 Ff
Takaungu, Kenya 93 He
Takayama, Japan 82 Ef
Takefu, Japan 82 Eg
Takhta Bazar, Turkmen 74 Fe
Takht-i-Sulaiman, W. Pakistan 86 Be
Takingeun, Sumatra 79 Ck
Takla Makan, des., China 74 He
Takoradi, Ghana 94 Eh
Ta-ku, China 80 Hc
Takuapa, Siam 83 Be
Talagang, W. Pakistan 86 Cd
Talaimanar, Ceylon 84 Eg
Talar Ra., W. Pakistan 84 Bc
Talara, Peru 48 Ad
Talasski Ala Tau, Kirgizskaya S.S.R. 74 Gd
Talavera de la Reina, Spain 66 Cc
Talca, Chile 50 Be
Talcahuano, Chile 50 Be
Taldy Kurgan, Kazakh. 74 Gd
Tali, China 80 De
Tali, China 78 Ce
Taliabu, I., Indonesia 79 Hl
Talien, China 80 Kc
Taliwang, Sumbawa I., Indon. 79 Gm
Tallahessee, Florida 43 Ke
Tallata-Mafara, Nigeria 94 Gf
Tallinn, Estonia 63 Lg
Talmenka, Russia 74 Hc
Talou Shan, China 78 Ee
Talsi, Latvia 63 Kh
Taltal, Chile 50 Bc
Tamale, Ghana 94 Eg
Tamanrasset, Algeria 94 Gd
Tamaqua, Pennsylvania 44 Cb
Tamarite de Litera, Spain 67 Fb
Tamási, Hungary 65 He
Tamatave, Madagascar 93 Nk
Tamaulipas, state, Mexico 46 Ec
Tamaya, Chile 50 Bd
Tamba, Rhodesia 91 Dd
Tambach, Kenya 93 Hd
Tambacounda, Senegal 94 Cf
Tambo, Queensland 53 Jd
Tambo de Mora, Peru 48 Bf
Tambohorano, Madagascar 93 Mk
Tamboril, Brazil 49 Jd
Tambov, Russia 77 Ed
Tambura, Sudan 95 Lg
Tame, Colombia 48 Cb
Tamel Aiken, Argentina 50 Bg
Tamiahua & L., Mexico 46 Ec
Ta-ming, China 80 Gd
Tamins, Switzerland 61 Eb
Tamise, Belgium 60 Cc
Tamluk, India 87 Fd
Tammisaari, Finland 63 Kg
Tammu, Burma 85 Hd
Tampa and B., Florida 43 Kf
Tampere, Finland 63 Kf
Tampico, Mexico 46 Ec
Tamra, Arabia 88 Ee
Tamsalu, Estonia 63 Mg
Tamtsak Bulak, Mongolia 78 Ga
Tamworth, New S. Wales 53 Kf
Tana Fd., Norway 62 Na
Tana, I., New Hebrides 98 Fj
Tana, L., Ethiopia 93 Hb
Tana, R., Norway 62 Mb
Tanabe, Japan 82 Dh
Tanabu, Japan 82 Gd
Tanaga I., Aleutian Is. 43 Vm
Tanah Merah, W. Malaysia 83 Ce
Tanami, N. Terr., Australia 52 Ec
Tanana, Alaska 43 Xl
Tanana, R., Alaska 43 Yl
Tananarive, Madagascar 93 Nk
Tancheng, China 80 Je
Tanda, India 87 Db
Tanda Urmar, India 86 De
Tandil, Argentina 50 Ee
Tandjung, Java, Indonesia 79 Em
Tandjungpandan, Indonesia 79 El
Tandjungredeb, Borneo 79 Gk
Tandjungselor, Borneo 79 Gk
Taneatua, New Zealand 51 Fc
Tanegashima, Japan 82 Bj
Tanegashima Kaikyo, Japan 82 Bj
Tanen-taung-gyi Mts., Siam-Burma 83 Bc
Tanga, Tanzania 93 Hf
Tanganyika. See Tanzania
Tanganyika, L., Congo, etc. 93 Ff
Tangen, Norway 63 Df
Tanger (Tangier), Morocco 94 Da
Tangermünde, Germany 64 Eb
Tangier. See Tanger
Tang-shan, China 80 Jc
Tangshan, China 80 He
Tangtu, China 80 Jg
Tangui, Russia 75 Kc
Tanimbar Kep., Indonesia 79 Km
Tank, W. Pakistan 84 Db
Tankapirtti, Finland 62 Mb
Tankse, Kashmir 84 Eb
Tännäs, Sweden 62 Ee
Tannenberg, Poland 65 Jb
Tanta, Egypt 95 Mb
Tanzania, E. Africa 93 Gf
Tao, Burma 85 Hd
Taoan, China 78 Ha
Taochow. See Lintan
Taofu, China 78 Dd
Taormina, Sicily 71 Eg
Tapa, Estonia 63 Lg
Tapachula, Mexico 46 Fe
Tapah, W. Malaysia 83 Cf
Tapajos, R., Brazil 49 Fd
Tapalque, Argentina 50 De
Tapan, Sumatra 79 Dl
Tapanui, New Zealand 51 Bf
Tapa Shan, China 80 Df
Tapauá, Brazil 48 Ee
Taplang Dzong, Nepal 87 Fb
Tapti R., India 84 Ed
Tapuaenuku, Mt., N.Z. 51 Dd
Taqa, Muscat & Oman 89 Ff
Taquara, Brazil 50 Fc
Taquaritinga, Brazil 49 Ke
Tara, Russia 74 Gc
Tārābulus esh Shām. See Tripoli
Taradale, New Zealand 51 Fc
Tarahumare, Sa., Mexico 46 Cb
Tarakan, Borneo 79 Gk
Tarakli, Turkey 88 Ba
Taranaki Bight, N., N.Z. 51 Dc
Taranaki Bight, S., N.Z. 51 Dc
Tarancón, Spain 66 Db
Taranto, Italy 71 Fe
Taranto, G. di, Italy 71 Ff
Tarapoto, Peru 48 Be
Taraqua, Brazil 48 Dd
Tararua Ra., New Zealand 51 Ed
Tarascon, France 69 De
Tarasp, Switzerland 61 Fb
Tarata, Peru 48 Cg
Tarauaca, Brazil 48 Ce
Tarawa, I., Gilbert Is. 98 Gg
Tarawera, New Zealand 51 Fc
Tarazona, Spain 67 Eb
Tarazona de la Mancha, Sp. 67 Ec
Tarbagatai Khrebet, Kazakh. 74 Hd
Tarbat Ness, Scotland 58 Ec
Tarbert, Scotland 58 De
Tarbert, Scotland 58 Cc
Tarbes, France 69 De
Tarchan, Tibet 84 Fb
Tarcoola, S. Australia 53 Ff
Taree, N.S.W. 53 Kf
Tärendö, Sweden 62 Kc
Târgoviste, Rumania 72 Eb
Tarija, Bolivia 48 Eh
Tarim, Arabia 88 Ef
Tarlac, Philippines 79 Hh
Tarma, Peru 48 Bf
Tarn, dep. & R., France 69 Ee
Tärna, Sweden 62 Fd
Tarn-et-Garonne, dep., Fr. 69 Dd
Tarnobrzeg, Poland 65 Jc
Tarnów, Poland 65 Jc
Tarnowskie Gory, Poland 65 Hc
Tarn Taran, India 86 De
Tarnu Măgurele, Rumania 72 Ec
Taroom, Qnsld. 53 Je
Taroudant, Morocco 94 Db
Tarragona, Spain 67 Fb
Tarrega, Spain 67 Fb
Tarsale, Russia 74 Gb
Tarso Muri, Mt. See Kegueur Tedi
Tarsus, Turkey 88 Bb
Tartagal, Argentina 48 Eh
Tartas, France 69 Ce
Tartu, Estonia 63 Mg
Tartus, Syria 90 Dc
Tarum, Persia 89 Gd
Taseevo, Russia 75 Jc
Tashi Bhup Tso, Tibet 85 Fb
Tashihto, China 78 Bb
Tashkent, Uzbek. 74 Fd
Tashkurghan, Afghanistan 89 Jb
Tash Kurghan, China 86 Db
Tashmalik, China 86 Da
Tasil, Syria 90 Ee
Taskan, Russia 75 Qb
Tasköprü. See Gökçeağac
Tasman B., New Zealand 51 Dd
Tasman, Mt., New Zealand 51 Ce
Tasman Mts., New Zealand 51 Dd
Tasmania I. & state, Aust. 53 Jh
Tassgong, Bhutan 85 Hc
Tata, Hungary 65 He
Tatakoto, Tuamotu Arch. 99 Mj
Tatarsk, Russia 74 Gc
Tatarskaya, aut. rep., Russia 74 Ec
Tatarskiy Proliv, Russia 75 Pd
Tating, China 81 Bj
Tatranská Lomnica, Czech. 65 Jd
Tatry, Mts., Poland-Czech. 65 Hd
Tatta, W. Pakistan 84 Cd
Tatu, R., China 78 Dd
Tatuhí, Brazil 49 Hh
Tatung, China 80 Fb
Tatung Ho, R., China 78 Dc
Taua, Brazil 49 Je
Tuapeçaçú, Brazil 48 Ed
Taubate, Brazil 49 Hh
Taumarunui, New Zealand 51 Ec
Taungdwingyi, Burma 85 Jd
Taung-gyi, Burma 85 Jd
Taungup, Burma 85 He
Taunton, England 59 Ek
Taunton, Massachusetts 40 Le
Taunus, Mts., Germany 64 Cc
Taupo & L., New Zealand 51 Fc
Tauragé, Lithuania 63 Kj
Tauranga & Harb., N.Z. 51 Fb
Tauste, Spain 67 Eb
Tauysk, Russia 75 Pc
Tavda, Russia 74 Fc
Taverne, Switzerland 61 Db
Tavistock, England 59 Ek
Tavolara, I., Sardinia 71 Be
Tavoy & R., Burma 85 Jf
Tavoy I., Burma 85 Jf
Tavsanli, Turkey 88 Ab
Tawang, India 85 Hc
Tawas City, Michigan 40 Ec
Tawau, N. Borneo 79 Gk
Tawitawi, I., Philippines 79 Hj
Taxco, Mexico 46 Ed
Tay, Firth of & R., Scotland 58 Ed
Tay L., Scotland 58 Ed
Tayga, Russia 74 Hc
Taymyr, Ozero, Russia 75 Ka
Taytay, Philippines 79 Gh
Tayü, China 81 Gk
Tayung, China 81 Eh
Taza, Morocco 94 Eb
Tazovskaya G., Russia 74 Gb
Tazovskoye, Russia 74 Gb
Tbilisi, Gruzinskaya 74 Dd
Tchad. See Chad, rep.
Tchad, L. See Chad, L.
Tchaourou, Dahomey 94 Fg
Tczew, Poland 65 Ha
Te Anau, L., New Zealand 51 Af
Teano Ra., W. Australia 52 Cd
Teapa, Mexico 46 Fd
Te Aroha, New Zealand 51 Eb
Tea Tree, N. Terr., Aust. 53 Ed
Te Awamutu, New Zealand 51 Ec
Teboursouk, Tunisia 95 Ga
Tebyulyakh, Russia 75 Pb
Tecamachalco, Mexico 46 Ed
Tecka & R., Argentina 50 Bf
Tecolutla, Mexico 46 Ec
Tecpan, Mexico 46 Dd
Tecumseh, Michigan 40 Ed
Tedzhen, Turkmen 74 Fe
Tees, R., England 59 Gf
Tegerhi, Libya 95 Hd
Tegucigalpa, Honduras 47 Bd
Tehchow, China 80 Hd
Tehran, Persia 89 Fb
Tehri, India 84 Eb
Tehsien. See Tehchow
Tehuacan, Mexico 46 Ed
Tehuantepec, Mexico 46 Ed
Tehuantepec, G. of, Mexico 46 Ed
Tehuantepec, Isthmus of, Mexico 46 Ed
Teian. See Anlu
Teifi R., Wales 59 Eh
Teign R., England 59 Ek
Tejo R., Portugal 66 Bc
Tejo (Tagus) R., Spain/Portugal 66 Bc
Tekapo, L., New Zealand 51 Ce
Te Karaka, New Zealand 51 Fc
Tekari, India 87 Ec
Tekirdag, Turkey 88 Aa
Te Kuiti, New Zealand 51 Ec
Tela, Honduras 47 Bc
Tel Aviv-Yafo, Israel 90 Ce
Telen, Argentina 50 Ce
Telkalakh, Syria 90 Ec
Tell Bise, Syria 90 Ec
Tellicherry, India 84 Ef
Telok Anson, W. Malaysia 83 Cf
Teloloapan, Mexico 46 Ed
Telpos-iz, Russia 74 Eb
Telsen, Argentina 50 Cf
Telshyay, Lithuania 63 Kj
Telukbetung, Sumatra 79 Em
Tembeling, W. Malaysia 83 Cf
Temblador, Venezuela 48 Eb
Temesvar. See Timisoara
Temir, Kazakh. 74 Ed
Temir Tau, Russia 74 Hc
Temnikov, Russia 77 Fc
Temosachic, Mexico 46 Cb
Tempio, Sardinia 71 Be
Temple, Texas 42 Ge
Temta, Russia 77 Gb
Temuco, Chile 50 Be
Temuka, New Zealand 51 Cf
Tenanzingo, Mexico 46 Ed
Tenasique, Mexico 46 Fd
Tenasserim, Burma 85 Jf
Tenasserim R., Burma 85 Jf
Tenby, Wales 59 Dj
Ten Degrees Chan., Andaman Islands 85 Hg
Tenerife, I., Canary Is. 94 Bc
Ténès, Algeria 94 Fa
Tengchow. See Penglai
Tengiz, Oz., Kazakh. 74 Fc
Tenke, Congo 92 Fg
Tennant's Creek, N. Territory, Australia 53 Fc
Tennessee, state, U.S.A. 43 Jd
Tennessee Pass, Colorado 42 Ed
Tennessee, R.,Tennessee etc. 43 Jd
Tenterfield, New S. Wales 53 Ke
Ten Thousand Is., Florida 43 Kf
Ten Thousand Smokes, Val. of, Alaska 43 Xm
Teocaltiche, Mexico 46 Dc
Téophilo Otoni, Brazil 49 Jg
Tepatitlan, Mexico 46 Dc
Tepehuanes, Mexico 46 Cb
Tepelene, Albania 73 Cd
Tepic, Mexico 46 Dc
Teramo, Italy 70 Dd
Ter Apel, Netherlands 60 Eb
Terban Jebel, Arabia 88 Df
Terborg, Netherlands 60 Ec
Teresina, Brazil 49 Je
Teressa I., Nicobar Is. 85 Hg
Terezin, Czechoslovakia 64 Fc
Teri, W. Pakistan 86 Bd
Teri Nam Tso, Tibet 85 Gb
Termez, Uzbek. 74 Fe
Termini Imerese, Sicily 71 Df
Termoli, Italy 71 Ee
Termonde, Belgium 60 Cc
Ternate, Halmahera I. 79 Jk
Terneuzen, Netherlands 60 Bc
Terni, Italy 70 Dd
Ternopol, Ukraine 76 Dg
Terpeniya, Zal, Russia 75 Pd
Terracina, Italy 71 De
Terralba, Sardinia 71 Bf
Terra Santa, Brazil 49 Fd
Terre Adélie, Antarctica 100 Kc
Terre Haute, Indiana 40 Cf
Terror Mt., Antarctica 100 Lb
Terschelling I., Netherlands 60 Da
Teruel, Spain 67 Eb
Tervola, Finland 62 Lc
Tervueren, Belgium 60 Cd
Teshio, Japan 82 Hb
Tessaoua, Niger 94 Gf
Tessenderloo, Belgium 60 Dc
Tetas, Pta., Chile 50 Bb
Tete, Moçambique 91 Ec
Tetuan, Morocco 94 Da
Tetyukhe, Russia 75 Nd
Tetyushi, Russia 77 Jc
Teulada, Sardinia 71 Bf
Teulada C., Sardinia 71 Bf
Teutoburger Wald, Germany 64 Bb
Tevere. See Tiber
Teviot R., Scotland 58 Fe
Tevriz, Russia 74 Gc
Te Waewae B., N.Z. 51 Ag
Texarkana, Arkansas 43 He
Texas, state, U.S.A. 42 Fe
Texcoco, Mexico 46 Ed
Texel I., Netherlands 60 Ca
Tezpur, India 85 Hc
Thachap Kangri, Tibet 84 Fb
Thadiq, Arabia 88 Ed
Thailand (Siam), S.E. Asia 83 Cc
Thailand, G. of, S.E. Asia 79 Dh
Thakhek, Laos 83 Cc
Thal, W. Pakistan 86 Bd
Thale Sap, L., Siam 83 Cd
Thalkirch, Switzerland 61 Eb
Thames, New Zealand 51 Eb
Thames, Firth of, N.Z. 51 Eb
Thames R., Connecticut 44 Db
Thames R., England 59 Hj
Thana, India 84 De
Thanesar, India 86 Ef
Thanh-hoa, N. Vietnam 83 Dc
Thanjavur, India 84 Ef
Thann, France 68 Gc
Thar Des., India 86 Cf
Thargomindah, Qnsld. 53 Ge
Tharrawaddy, Burma 85 Je
Tharsis, Spain 66 Bd
Thásos I., Greece 73 Ed
Thásos Str., Greece 73 Ed
Thaton, Burma 85 Je
Thaungdut, Burma 85 Hd
Thayetmyo, Burma 85 He
Thazi, Burma 85 Jd
Theodore, Queensland 53 Ke
Thérmai, G. of, Greece 73 Dd
Thermiá. See Kithnos, I.
Thesprotia, Greece 73 Ce
Thessalía, Greece 73 De
Thessaloníki, Greece 73 Dd
Thetford, England 59 Hh
Thetford Mines, Quebec 40 Lb
Theux, Belgium 60 Dd
Thief River Falls, Minnesota 42 Gb
Thielsen, Mt., Oregon 45 Cd
Thielt, Belgium 60 Bc
Thiers, France 68 Ed
Thies, Senegal 94 Bf
Thimbu, Assam 85 Gc
Thingvalla vatn, Iceland 62 Vm
Thio, Eritrea 93 Jb
Thionville, France 68 Gb
Thíra, I., Greece 73 Ef
Thirsk, England 59 Gf
Thirtyone Mile L., Quebec 40 Jb
Thisted, Denmark 63 Ch
Thistilfjord, Iceland 62 Yl
Thityabin, Burma 85 Jd
Thiviers, France 68 Dd
Thjórsá, R., Iceland 62 Wm
Thok Jalung, Tibet 84 Fb
Thomastown, Eire 59 Ch
Thomasville, Georgia 43 Ke
Thomson, R., Queensland 53 Hd
Thomson Ville, Michigan 40 Cc
Thompsonville, Connecticut 44 Db
Thongwa, Burma 85 Je
Thorn. See Torun
Thornhill, Scotland 58 Ee
Thorshavn, Færøe Is. 56 Fc
Thórshöfn, Iceland 62 Yl
Thouars, France 68 Cc
Thourout, Belgium 60 Bc
Thousand Isles, New York 40 Jc
Thraki, Dhitiki, Greece 72 Ed
Three Kings Is., N.Z. 51 Da
Three Points C., Ghana 94 Eh
Three Rivers, Michigan 40 Cd
Throssel Ra., W. Australia 52 Dd
Thueyts, France 69 Fd
Thuin, Belgium 60 Cd
Thun, Switzerland 61 Cb
Thunder B., Michigan 40 Ec
Thuner See, Switzerland 61 Cb
Thur, R., Switzerland 61 Da
Thurgau, canton, Switz. 61 Da
Thüringer Wald, Germany 64 Dc
Thurles, Eire 59 Bh
Thursday I., Queensland 53 Hb
Thurso, Scotland 58 Eb
Thusis, Switzerland 61 Eb
Tiassale, Ivory Coast 94 Dg
Tibati, Cameroon 95 Hg
Tiber, R., Italy 70 Dd
Tiberias & L., Israel 90 De
Tibet, S. Asia 54 He
Tiburon, Haiti 47 Ec
Tiburon I., Mexico 46 Bb
Ticino, canton, Switzerland 61 Db
Ticonderoga, New York 40 Kd
Ticul, Mexico 46 Gc
Tidjikja, Mauritania 94 Ce
Tiebissou, Ivory Coast 94 Dg
Tiefencastel, Switzerland 61 Eb
Tieh-ling, China 80 La
Tiel, Netherlands 60 Dc
Tielt, Belgium 60 Bc
Tien Chih, China 78 Df
Tien-ching. See Tientsin
Tien-chwang-tai, China 80 Kb
Tienen. See Tirlemont
Tienpao, China 81 Cl
Tienpaoshan, China 80 Hb
Tiensha Pass, China 80 Ce
Tienshai, China 80 Be
Tien Shan, Central Asia 74 Gd
Tienshui, China 78 Ed
Tientsin, China 80 Hc
Tiermas, Spain 67 Ea
Tierra del Fuego, Chile-Argentina 50 Ch
Tiffin, Ohio 40 Ee
Tigănesti, Rumania 72 Fb
Tighina. See Bendery
Tigil, Russia 75 Qc
Tigris, R., Iraq 88 Ec
Tijoca, Brazil 49 Hd
Tijuana, Mexico 42 Ce
Tikhvin, Russia 76 Hb
Tikrit, Iraq 88 Dc
Tiksi, Russia 75 Ma
Tilburg, Netherlands 60 Dc
Tilbury, England 59 Hj
Tilcara, Argentina 50 Cb
Tilichiki, Russia 75 Rb
Tillamook, Oregon 45 Ac
Tillangchong I., Nicobar Is. 85 Hg
Tillsonburg, Ontario 40 Fd
Tilos, I., Greece 73 Ff
Tilsit. See Sovetsk
Timanski Kryazh, Russia 74 Eb
Timaru, New Zealand 51 Cf
Timbuktu. See Tombouctou
Timiskaming, Quebec 40 Gb
Timisoara, Rumania 72 Cb
Timmins, Ontario 40 Fa
Timor, I. & Sea, Indonesia 79 Hn
Timote, Argentina 50 De
Tinaca Pt., Philippines 79 Jj
Tindouf, Algeria 94 Dc
Tineo, Spain 66 Ba
Tingchow. See Changting
Tinghsien, China 80 Gc
Tingnan, China 81 Gk
Tingo Maria, Peru 48 Be
Tingri Dzong, Tibet 85 Gc
Tinian, I., Mariana Is. 98 Df
Tinkhannock, Pennsylvania 44 Cb
Tinnevelly. See Tirunelvelei
Tinogasta, Argentina 50 Cc
Tinos, I., Greece 73 Ef
Tinsukia, India 85 Jc
Tintigny, Belgium 60 Dd
Tintina, Argentina 50 Dc
Tinwald, New Zealand 51 Ce
Tioman, Pulau, I., W. Malaysia 83 Cf
Tionesta, Pennsylvania 44 Ab
Tipperary & co., Eire 59 Bh
Tiracumba, Sa. de, Brazil 49 Hd
Tiran, Arabia 88 Bd
Tirana. See Tiranë
Tiranë, Albania 72 Bd
Tiraspol, Moldavia 76 Fh
Tire, Turkey 88 Ab
Tireboli, Turkey 88 Ca
Tiree I., Scotland 58 Cd
Tirgu Jiu, Rumania 72 Db
Tirgu Mures, Rumania 72 Ea

Tîrgu Lâpus, Rumania 65 Ke
Tirgu Ocua, Rumania 72 Fa
Tirich Mir, W. Pakistan 86 Bb
Tirlemont, Belgium 60 Cd
Tirlyanskii, Russia 77 Pc
Tirnavos, Greece 73 De
Tirol, Austria 64 De
Tiruchendur, India 84 Eg
Tiruchirappalli, India 84 Ef
Tiru Kona Malai. See Trincomalee
Tirunelveli, India 84 Eg
Tirupati, India 84 Ef
Tiruvannamalai, India 84 Ef
Tisa. R., Yugoslavia 72 Cb
Tisiye, Syria 90 Ee
Tissa, Nigeria 95 Hg
Tisza R., Hungary 65 Je
Titalyah, E. Pakistan 87 Gb
Titicaca, L., Bolivia-Peru 48 Dg
Titisee, Germany 64 Ce
Titograd, Yugoslavia 72 Bc
Titov-Veles, Yugoslavia 72 Cd
Titovo Uzice, Yugoslavia 72 Bc
Titu, Rumania 72 Eb
Titusville, Pennsylvania 40 Ge
Tiverton, England 59 Ek
Tiwi, Muscat & Oman 89 Ge
Tixkokob, Mexico 46 Gc
Tixtla, Mexico 46 Ed
Tizimin, Mexico 46 Gc
Tizi Ouzou, Algeria 94 Fa
Tjalang, Sumatra 79 Ck
Tjilatjap, Java 79 Em
Tjirebon, Java 79 Em
Tjörn, I., Sweden 63 Dg
Tlacotalpan, Mexico 46 Ed
Tlaltenango, Mexico 46 Dc
Tlapa, Mexico 46 Ed
Tlaxcala, Mexico 46 Ed
Tlaxiaco, Mexico 46 Ed
Tlemcen, Algeria 94 Eb
Tméssa, Libya 95 Jc
Toay, Argentina 50 De
Toba, Japan 82 Eg
Tobago, I., Windward Is. 47 Gd
Toba, Donau, Sumatra 79 Ck
Tobarro, Spain 67 Ec
Tobel, Switzerland 61 Ea
Tobelo, Halmahera I. 79 Jk
Tobermory, Ontario 40 Fc
Tobermory, Scotland 58 Cd
Toboali, Bangka I., Indonesia 79 El
Tobol, Russia 77 Rd
Toboli, Celebes 79 Hl
Tobolsk, Russia 74 Fc
Tobruk, Libya 95 Kb
Tocantinópolis, Brazil 49 He
Tocina, Spain 66 Cd
Toco, Chile 50 Cb
Tocopilla, Chile 50 Bb
Tocuyo, Venezuela 48 Cb
Todenyang, Kenya 93 Hd
Todos Santos, Mexico 46 Bc
Todos Santos, B., Mexico 46 Aa
Togarakaikyo, Japan 82 Aj
Toghraqbulaq, China 78 Bb
Togo, West Africa 94 Fg
To Huping Tso, Tibet 85 Fb
Tojo, Japan 82 Cg
Tokachi Dake, Japan 82 Hc
Tokanga, Russia 74 Db
Tokanui, New Zealand 51 Bg
Tokar, Sudan 93 Ha
Tokara Retto, Japan 82 Nn
Tokat, Turkey 88 Ca
Tokelau Is., Pacific Ocean 98 Hh
Tokmak, Kirgizskaya S.S.R. 74 Gd
Toko, New Zealand 51 Ec
Tokomaru, New Zealand 51 Gc
Tokoto, China 80 Eb
Tokushima, Japan 82 Dh
Tokuyama, Japan 82 Bg
Tokyo & B., Japan 82 Fg
Tolaga Bay, New Zealand 51 Gc
Tolbukhin, Bulgaria 72 Fc
Toledo, Chile 50 Bc
Toledo, Ohio 40 Ee
Toledo, Spain 66 Cc
Toledo, Mtes. de, Spain 66 Cc
Tolen & I., Netherlands 60 Cc
Tolmin, Yugoslavia 70 Db
Tolo, G. of, Celebes 79 Hd
Toluca, Mexico 46 El
Tolun, China 80 Ha
Tölz, Bad, Germany 64 De
Tomah, Wisconsin 40 Ac
Tomahawk, Wisconsin 40 Bc
Tomar, Portugal 66 Ac
Tomari, Russia 75 Pd
Tomaszów Mazowiecki, Pol. 65 Jc
Tomatumari, Guyana 48 Fb
Tombigbee R., Alabama 43 Je
Tombouctou, Mali 94 Ee
Tome, Chile 50 Be
Tomiko, Ontario 40 Gb
Tomini, G. of, Celebes 79 Hl
Tomkinson Ra., W. Aust. 52 Ee
Tommot, Russia 75 Mc
Tomsk, Russia 75 Hc
Tom's River, New Jersey 40 Jf
Tonala, Mexico 46 Fd
Tonawanda, New York 44 Aa
Tönder, Denmark 63 Cj
Tondi, India 84 Eg
Tonga, Sudan 95 Mg
Tonga, Is., Pacific Ocean 98 Hk
Tongareva, I., Pacific Ocean 99 Kh
Tongeren, Belgium 60 Dd
Tongobory, Madagascar 93 Ml
Tongoy, Chile 50 Bd
Tongres. See Tongeren
Tongue, Scotland 58 Eb
Tongue R., Montana 42 Eb
Tonichi, Mexico 46 Cb
Tonk, India 84 Ec
Tonkin, N. Vietnam 83 Cb
Tonkin, G. of, Indo-China 83 Db
Tonkhil, Mongolia 78 Ba
Tonkova, Russia 74 Hb
Tonle Sap, Cambodia 83 Cd
Tonneins, France 69 Dd
Tonnerre, France 68 Fc
Tonopah, Nevada 45 Ef
Tönsberg, Norway 63 Dg
Tooele, Utah 45 Ge
Toowoomba, Queensland 53 Ke
Top Oz, Karel.-Fin. 74 Cb
Topeka, Kansas 42 Gd
Topolčany, Czechoslovakia 65 Hd
Topolobampo & B., Mexico 46 Cb
Torbat-e-Heydariyeh, Persia 89 Gb
Torbat-e-Jam, Persia 89 Hb
Torhout. See Thourout
Tori, India 87 Ed
Torino. See Turin
Toriñana, Spain 66 Aa
Torit, Sudan 95 Mh
Tor Khama, W. Pakistan 86 Bc
Torma, Estonia 63 Mg
Torne Älv, Sweden 62 Kc
Torne Träsk, Sweden 62 Hb
Torneträsk, Sweden 62 Hb
Tornio, Finland 62 Ld
Tornquist, Argentina 50 De
Törökszentmiklós, Hungary 65 Je
Toroni, G. of, Greece 73 Dd
Toronto, Ontario 40 Gd
Tororo, Uganda 93 Gd
Toros Dağlari, Mts., Turkey 88 Bb
Torquay, England 59 Ek
Torre Annunziata, Italy 71 Ee
Torreblanca, Spain 67 Fb
Torre del Greco, Italy 71 Ee
Torrelaguna, Spain 66 Db
Torrelapaja, Spain 67 Eb
Torrelavega, Spain 66 Da
Torrens, L., S. Australia 53 Gf
Torrente, Spain 67 Ec
Torreon, Mexico 46 Db
Torres, Mexico 46 Bb
Torres Is., Pacific Ocean 98 Fj
Torres Str., Queensland 53 Hb
Torres Novas, Portugal 66 Ac
Torres Vedras, Portugal 66 Ac
Torrevieja, Spain 67 Ed
Torridon, L., Scotland 58 Dc
Torrijos, Spain 66 Cc
Torrington, Connecticut 44 Db
Torrox, Spain 66 Dd
Torsby, Sweden 63 Ef
Tortola, I., Virgin Is. 47 Gc
Tortorici, Sicily 71 Ef
Tortosa, Spain 67 Fb
Tortue, I., Haiti 47 Eb
Tortuga I., Mexico 46 Bb
Torud, Persia 89 Gb
Torun, Poland 65 Hb
Tõrva, Estonia 63 Mh
Tory, I., Eire 58 Be
Torzhok, Russia 76 Jc
Tosa B., Japan 82 Ch
Toscana, dep., Italy 70 Cd
Tosco-Emiliano, Appennino, Mts., Italy 70 Cc
Tossa, Spain 67 Gb
Tostado, Argentina 50 Dc
Totana, Spain 67 Ed
Totling, Tibet 84 Eb
Totma, Russia 74 Dc
Totnes, England 59 Ek
Totonicapam, Guatemala 46 Fd
Totsk, Russia 77 Ld
Tottori, Japan 82 Dg
Touba, Ivory Coast 94 Dg
Toubkal, Mt., Morocco 94 Db
Touggourt, Algeria 94 Gb
Toul, France 68 Fb
Toulon, France 68 Fe
Toulouse, France 69 De
Toungoo, Burma 85 Je
Touquet, le, France 68 Da
Touraine, prov., France 68 Dc
Tourakom, Laos 85 Ke
Tourbis L., Quebec 40 Jb
Tourcoing, France 68 Ea
Tour-du-Pin, la, France 68 Fd
Tournai, Belgium 60 Bd
Tournon, France 69 Fd
Tournus, France 68 Fc
Tours, France 68 Dc
Touwsrivier, Cape Province 91 Cf
Towanda, Pennsylvania 44 Bb
Towari, Celebes 79 Hl
Townsville, Queensland 53 Jc
Towson, Maryland 44 Cc
Towuti Danau, Celebes 79 Hl
Towy R., Wales 59 Ej
Towyn, Wales 59 Eh
Toyama & B., Japan 82 Ef
Tozeur, Tunisia 95 Gb
Trabzon, Turkey 88 Ca
Tradom, Tibet 85 Fc
Trairi, Brazil 49 Kd
Traiguen, Chile 50 Be
Traiguen, I., Chile 50 Bg
Traipú, Brazil 49 Ke
Tralee & B., Eire 59 Ah
Tramore, Eire 59 Ch
Tranås, Sweden 63 Fg
Trancas, Argentina 50 Cc
Trancoso, Portugal 66 Bb
Trang, Siam 83 Be
Trangan, I., Indonesia 79 Km
Tranquebar, India 84 Ef
Transvaal, S. Africa 91 Dd
Transylvania, Rumania 72 Da
Transylvanian Alps, Rumania 72 Db
Trapani, Sicily 71 Df
Traralgon, Victoria 53 Jg
Trasimeno, L., Italy 70 Dd
Trasparga, Spain 66 Ba
Traunstein, Germany 64 Ee
Traverse, B., Michigan 40 Dc
Traverse Is., Atlantic Ocean 100 Ad
Traverse City, Michigan 40 Dc
Třebič, Czechoslovakia 65 Fd
Trebinje, Yugoslavia 72 Bc
Trebizond (Trabzon), Turkey 88 Ca
Treinta-y-Tres, Uruguay 50 Fd
Trelew, Argentina 50 Cf
Trelleborg, Sweden 63 Ej
Tremadoc B., Wales 59 Eh
Trembling Mt., Quebec 40 Jb
Tremiti Is., Italy 70 Ed
Tremp, Spain 67 Fa
Trencin, Czechoslovakia 65 Hd
Trenel, Argentina 50 De
Trenque Lauquen, Argentina 50 De
Trent. See Trento
Trent Canal, Ontario 40 Gc
Trent, R., England 59 Gg
Trentino-Alto Adige, reg., It. 70 Cb
Trento, Italy 70 Cb
Trenton, Michigan 40 Ed
Trenton, Missouri 43 Hc
Trenton, New Jersey 44 Cb
Trenton, Ontario 40 Hc
Tréport, le, France 68 Da
Tres Arroyos, Argentina 50 De
Tres Lomas, Argentina 50 De
Tres Marias, Is., Mexico 46 Cc
Tres Montes, Pen., Chile 50 Ag
Três Rio, Brazil 49 Jh
Tres Virgenes, Las, Mexico 46 Bb
Treves. See Trier
Treviso, Italy 70 Dc
Trevna, Bulgaria 72 Ec
Triana, Spain 66 Bd
Tricase, Italy 71 Gf
Trichinopoly. See Tiruchirappalli
Trichur, India 84 Ef
Trier, Germany 64 Bd
Trieste, Italy 70 Dc
Trikeri Str., Greece 73 De
Trikkala, Greece 73 Ce
Trikomo, Cyprus 90 Bb
Trim, Eire 59 Cg
Trincomalee, Ceylon 84 Fg
Trinidad, Bolivia 48 Ef
Trinidad, Colorado 42 Fd
Trinidad, Cuba 47 Db
Trinidad, Uruguay 50 Ed
Trinidad, I., Argentina 50 De
Trinidad, I., Atlantic Ocean 97 Hl
Trinidad I., West Indies 48 Ea
Trinity R., Texas 42 Ge
Trionto C., Italy 71 Ff
Tripoli, Lebanon 90 Dc
Tripoli, Libya 95 Hb
Tripolis, Greece 73 Df
Tripolitania, Libya 95 Hc
Tripura, India 85 Hd
Tristan da Cunha, Atl. Oc. 97 Jm
Triunfo, Mexico 46 Bc
Trivandrum, India 84 Eg
Trn, Bulgaria 72 Dc
Trnava, Czechoslovakia 65 Gd
Trobriand Is., Papua 53 Ka
Trogir, Yugoslavia 70 Fd
Trois Ponts, Belgium 60 Dd
Troitsk, Russia 77 Qc
Troitsk, Russia 77 Fc
Troitsko Pechorsk, Russia 74 Eb
Trollhättan, Sweden 63 Eg
Trollheimen, Norway 62 Ce
Tromen, Mt., Argentina 50 Be
Tromsö, Norway 62 Hb
Tronchiennes, Belgium 60 Bc
Trondheim & Fd., Norway 62 De
Troödos, Cyprus 90 Ac
Troon, Scotland 58 De
Tropea, Italy 71 Ef
Troppau. See Opava
Trosa, Sweden 63 Gg
Trout Lake, Michigan 40 Db
Troy, New York 40 Kd
Troy, Turkey 88 Ab
Troyes, France 68 Fb
Truba, Arabia 88 Dd
Trubia, Spain 66 Ba
Trucial States, Persian Gulf 89 Fe
Truer Ra., N. Terr., Aust. 52 Fd
Trujillo, Honduras 47 Bc
Trujillo, Peru 48 Be
Trujillo, Rep. Dominicana 47 Ec
Trujillo, Spain 66 Cc
Trujillo, Venezuela 48 Cb
Truk I., Caroline Is. 98 Eg
Truksum, Tibet 85 Fb
Trumbull, Mt., Arizona 45 Gg
Truns, Switzerland 61 Db
Truro, England 59 Dk
Trutnov, Czechoslovakia 65 Fc
Trzebnica, Poland 65 Gc
Tržič, Yugoslavia 70 Eb
Tsabong, Botswana 91 Ce
Tsagan Olom, Mongolia 78 Ca
Tsahura, S. Yemen 88 Eg
Tsamkong, China 83 Eb
Tsangbe, Bhutan 87 Gb
Tsanghsien, China 80 Hc
Tsangwu. See Wuchow
Tsaochow. See Hotseh
Tsaoking, China 80 Gd
Tsaritsyn. See Volgograd
Tschenstochau. See Czestochowa
Tschiertschen, Switzerland 61 Eb
Tsehchow. See Tsincheng
Tsengshing, China 81 Fl
Tses, S.-W. Africa 91 Be
Tsesis. See Cesis
Tshikapa, Congo 92 Ef
Tsho Mirari L., Kashmir 86 Fd
Tsimlyanskoye Vdkhr., Russia 77 Ff
Tsinan, China 80 Hd
Tsincheng, China 80 Fe
Tsinchow. See Tienshui
Tsin-chow, China 80 Gc
Tsingchow. See Yitu
Tsing Hai. See Ching Hai
Tsingkiang, China 81 Gh
Tsingkiang, China 80 Jf
Tsingkow, China 80 Je
Tsingtao, China 80 Kd
Tsingyüan. See Paoting
Tsingyün, China 81 Fl
Tsining, China 78 Gc
Tsinkiang, China 81 Jk
Tsinyang, China 80 Fe
Tsitsihar, China 78 Ha
Tsivory, Madagascar 93 Nl
Tsivylsk, Russia 77 Hc
Tso-motre-tung, L., Tibet 85 Gc
Tsu, Japan 82 Eg
Tsugaru Str., Japan 82 Gd
Tsugitaka, Mt. See Tsukao Shan
Tsukao Shan, Taiwan 78 Hf
Tsungfa, China 81 Fl
Tsungming, China 80 Kg
Tsungtso, China 78 Ef
Tsunhwa, China 80 Hb
Tsunyi, China 81 Cj
Tsuruga, Japan 82 Eg
Tsuruoka, Japan 82 Fe
Tsuyama, Japan 82 Dg
Tsuyung, China 78 De
Tua, Congo 92 De
Tua, Portugal 66 Bb
Tuakau, New Zealand 51 Eb
Tuamarino, New Zealand 51 Dd
Tuamotu Arch., Pacific Oc. 99 Mj
Tuao, Philippines 79 Hg
Tuapse, Russia 74 Cd
Tuatapere, New Zealand 51 Ag
Tuba, R., Russia 75 Jc
Tubai, I., Society Islands 99 Lj
Tubarão, Brazil 50 Gc
Tubeiq Jeb. el, Jordan 90 Fh
Tubas, Jordan 90 Dе
Tübingen, Germany 64 Cd
Tubize, Belgium 60 Cd
Tubuai, I., Austral Islands 99 Lk
Tubutama, Mexico 46 Ba
Tucacas, Venezuela 48 Da
Tuckernuck I., Mass. 44 Eb
Tuckerton, New Jersey 40 Jf
Tucson, Arizona 42 De
Tucumcari, New Mexico 42 Fd
Tucupare, Brazil 49 Fe
Tucupita, Venezuela 48 Eb
Tucurui, Brazil 49 Hd
Tudela, Spain 67 Ea
Tufi, Papua 53 Ja
Tug, Turkey 88 Db
Tuguegarao, Philippines 79 Hg
Tugur, Russia 75 Nc
Tukums, Latvia 63 Kh
Tula, Mexico 46 Ec
Tula, Mexico 46 Ec
Tula, Russia 76 Kd
Tulagi, I., Solomon Islands 98 Eh
Tulan. See Dulan
Tulancingo, Mexico 46 Ec
Tularosa, New Mexico 42 Ee
Tulcan, Ecuador 48 Bc
Tulcea, Rumania 72 Gb
Tulchin, Ukraine 76 Fg
Tulear, Madagascar 93 Ml
Tuli, Rhodesia 91 Dd
Tulkarm, Jordan 90 De
Tullamore, Eire 59 Cg
Tulle, France 69 Dd
Tulsa, Oklahoma 42 Gd
Tulua, Colombia 48 Bc
Tulun, Russia 75 Kc
Tumaco & Rada de, Colomb. 48 Bc
Tumany, Russia 75 Qb
Tumbes, Peru 48 Ad
Tumkur, India 84 Ef
Tumlong, India 87 Gb
Tummel R., Scotland 58 Ed
Tummo, Libya 95 Hd
Tump, W. Pakistan 84 Bc
Tumu, Ghana 94 Ef
Tumucumaque, Sa., Brazil 49 Gc
Tumupasa, Bolivia 48 Df
Tunas de Zaza, Cuba 47 Db
Tunbridge Wells, England 59 Hj
Tundla, India 84 Ec
Tundubai, Sudan 95 Kf
Tunduru, Tanzania 93 Hg
Tüngan, China 81 Ej
Tungchang. See Liaocheng
Tungchow, China 80 De
Tungchwan. See Hweitseh
Tungchwan. See Santai
Tunghai, China 80 Je
Tungho, China 78 Ja
Tunghsien, China 80 Hc
Tunghwa, China 78 Jb
Tungjen, China 81 Dj
Tungkun, China 81 Fl
Tungkwan, China 80 Ee
Tungkwan, China 80 De
Tungliao, China 78 Hb
Tungshan (Suchow), China 80 He
Tungtai, China 80 Kf
Tung Ting Hu, China 81 Fh
Tunguska, R., Russia 75 Jb
Tunhwang, China 78 Bb
Tuni, India 85 Fe
Tunis, Tunisia 95 Ha
Tunisia, N. Africa 95 Gb
Tunja, Colombia 48 Cb
Tunnsjö, Norway 62 Ed
Tunuyan & R., Argentina 50 Cd
Tuoy Khaya, Russia 75 Lb
Tuparoa, New Zealand 51 Gb
Tupelo, Mississippi 43 Je
Tupilco, Mexico 46 Fd
Tupinambaranas, I., Brazil 48 Fd
Tupiza, Bolivia 48 Dh
Tupper Lake, New York 40 Jc
Tuquerres, Colombia 48 Bc
Tura, India 85 Hc
Tura, Russia 75 Jb
Turabah, Arabia 88 Dе
Turan, Persia 89 Gb
Turbo, Colombia 48 Bb
Turda, Rumania 72 Da
Tureia I., Tuamotu Arch. 99 Mk
Turfan & Depression, China 78 Ab
Turgay, Kazakh. 74 Fd
Turgutlu, Turkey 88 Ab
Türi, Estonia 63 Lg
Turiaçu, Brazil 49 Hd
Turiamo, Venezuela 48 Da
Turin (Torino), Italy 70 Ac
Turkestan, Kazakh., etc. 74 Fd
Turkey, Europe-Asia 88 Cb
Turkmenskaya, rep., U.S.S.R. 74 Ed
Turks Is., Bahamas Is. 47 Eb
Turku, Finland 63 Kf
Turneffe Is., Brit. Honduras 47 Bc
Turnhout, Belgium 60 Cc
Tŭrnovo, Bulgaria 72 Ec
Turnu Severin, Rumania 72 Db
Turquino, Pico de, Cuba 47 Dc
Turrialba, Costa Rica 47 Ce
Turshiz. See Käshmar
Turtkul, Uzbek. 74 Fd
Turukta, Russia 75 Lb
Turukhansk, Russia 74 Hb
Turzovka, Czechoslovakia 65 Hd
Tus, Persia 89 Gb
Tuscaloosa, Alabama 43 Je
Tuscarora Mts., Pa. 44 Bb
Tuscola, Illinois 40 Bf
Tuticorin, India 84 Eg
Tuttlingen, Germany 64 Ce
Tutuila, I., Samoa 98 Hj
Tuwairifa, Arabia 88 Ee
Tuxpan, Mexico 46 Ec
Tuxpan, Mexico 46 Cc
Tuxtepec, Mexico 46 Ed
Tuxtla & Vol. de, Mexico 46 Ed
Tuxtla Gutierrez, Mexico 46 Fd
Tuy, Spain 66 Aa
Tuyen-Quang, N. Vietnam 83 Db
Tuy-hoa, S. Vietnam 83 Dd
Tuyun, China 81 Cj
Tuz Golu, Turkey 88 Bb
Tuzla, Yugoslavia 72 Bb
Tvärån, Sweden 62 Jd
Tvurditsa, Bulgaria 72 Ec
Twante, Burma 85 Je
Tweed, Ontario 40 Hc
Tweed R., Scotland 58 Fe
Tweedsmuir Hills, Scotland 58 Ee
Twenty-five de Mayo, Argent. 50 Ce
Twenty-five de Mayo, Argent. 50 De
Twin Falls, Idaho 45 Fd
Two Harbors, Minnesota 43 Hb
Two Mountains, L. of, Que. 40 Jc
Two Rivers, Wisconsin 40 Cc
Tyler, Texas 42 Ge
Tygda, Russia 75 Mc
Tyndinskiy, Russia 75 Mc
Tyndall, Mt., New Zealand 51 Ce
Tyne R., England 58 Ff
Tynemouth, England 58 Ge
Tynset, Norway 62 De
Tyre (Sur), Lebanon 90 Dd
Tyrone, Pennsylvania 44 Ab
Tyrone, co., N. Ireland 59 Cf
Tyrrhenian Sea, Italy 71 Ce
Tyumen, Russia 74 Fc
Tzechung, China 80 Gd
Tzeli, China 81 Eh
Tzeya Ho, China 78 Gc
Tzeyang, China 80 Gd
Tzeyun, China 81 Ck
Uau el Chebir. See Wau el Kebir
Uaupés & R., Brazil 48 Dc
Uba, Brazil 49 Jh
Ubait, Arabia 88 Cd
Ubari, Libya 95 Hc
Uberaba, Brazil 49 Hg
Uberlandia, Brazil 49 Hg
Überlingen, Germany 64 Ce
Ubon, Muang, Siam 83 Cc
Ubsa Nur, Mongolia 75 Jc
Ucayali, R., Peru 48 Ce
Uch, W. Pakistan 86 Bf
Uchiura-wan, Japan 82 Gc
Uchiza, Peru 48 Be
Udain, Yemen 88 Dg
Udaipur, India 84 Dd
Uddevalla, Sweden 63 Dg
Udd Jaur, Sweden 62 Gd
Uden, Netherlands 60 Dc
Udine, Italy 70 Db
Udon Thani, Siam 83 Cc
Udskaya Guba, Russia 75 Nc
Udzha. See Bor Yuryakh
Uelen, Russia 75 Tb
Ueno, Japan 82 Eg
Ufa, Russia 77 Mc
Uganda, E. Africa 93 Gd
Ugwashi-Uku, Nigeria 92 Bc
Uherske Hradiště, Czech. 65 Gd
Uí Failghe, co., Eire 59 Bg
Uinta Mts., Utah 42 Dc
Uist, North, I., Scotland 58 Cc
Uist, South, I., Scotland 58 Cc
Uitenhage, Cape Province 91 Df
Uitgeest, Netherlands 60 Cb
Ujhani, India 87 Bb
Ujpest, Hungary 65 He
Ukerewe Is., Tanzania 93 Ge
Ukermark, Germany 64 Eb
Ukhta, Russia 74 Cb
Ukiah, California 45 Bf
Ukmerge, Lithuania 63 Jj
Ukraine, rep., U.S.S.R. 76 Eg
Ulan, Mongolia 75 Jd
Ulan Bator, Mongolia 78 Ea
Ulanhot, China 78 Ha
Ulan Ude, Russia 75 Kc
Ulcinj, Yugoslavia 72 Bd
Ulithi, I., Pacific Ocean 98 Cf
Ullapool, Scotland 58 Dc
Ullared, Sweden 63 Eh
Ulldecona, Spain 67 Fb
Ullswater, L., England 59 Ff
Ullung Do, Sea of Japan 82 Bf
Ulm, Germany 64 Cd
Ulster, prov., Eire-N. Ire. 58 Bf
Ulua, R., Honduras 47 Bc
Ulukişla, Turkey 88 Bb
Ulverston, England 59 Ef
Ulyanovsk, Russia 77 Jc
Ulzen, Germany 64 Db
Uman, Ukraine 76 Gg
Umanak Fd., Greenland 41 Pb
Umarkot, W. Pakistan 84 Cc
Umbria, dep., Italy 70 Dd
Umea, Sweden 62 Je
Umm ar Rusuys, Muscat & Oman 89 Ge
Umm el Qulban, Arabia 88 Dd
Umm Kuteira, Sudan 95 Lf
Umm Lej, Arabia 88 Cd
Umm Qasr, Iraq 88 Ec
Umm Rasas. See Umm ar Rusuys
Umm Ruwaba, Sudan 95 Mf
Umnak I., Aleutian Is. 43 Wm
Umtali, Rhodesia 91 Ec
Umtata, Cape Province 91 Df
Umvuma, Rhodesia 91 Ec
Una, India 86 Ee
Una R., Yugoslavia 70 Fc
Unadilla, New York 44 Ca
Unalakleet, Alaska 43 Wl
Unalaska, Aleutian Is. 43 Wm
Unayzah, Arabia 88 Dd
Uncastillo, Spain 67 Ea
Uncia, Bolivia 48 Dg
Undzhul. See Onjül
União, Brazil 49 Jd
União da Vitoria, Brazil 50 Fc
Uniejów, Poland 65 Hc
Unimak I., Aleutian Is. 43 Wm
Unini, Peru 48 Cf
Union, Argentina 50 Ce
Union, Argentina 50 Cc
Union, S. Carolina 43 Ke
Union of Soviet Socialist Republics, Europe-Asia 54-55
Uniontown, Pennsylvania 44 Ac
Unionville, Nevada 45 De
United Arab Rep. See Egypt
United Kingdom of Gt. Britain & N. Ireland 58
United States of America 42-43
Unnao, India 87 Cb
Unst I., Shetland, Scotland 58 Ja
Unterwalden, canton, Switz. 61 Db
Unzha, Russia 77 Ga
Uozu, Japan 82 Ef
Upata, Venezuela 48 Eb
Upemba L., Congo 92 Ff
Upernivik, Greenland 41 Pb
Upington, Cape Province 91 Ce
Upolu, I., Samoa 98 Hj
Upper Marlboro, Maryland 44 Bc
Upper Sandusky, Ohio 40 Ee
Upper Volta, W. Africa 94 Ef
Uppsala, Sweden 63 Gg
Uqair, Arabia 88 Ed
Ur, Iraq 88 Ec
Uracoa, Venezuela 48 Eb
Urakawa, Japan 82 Hc
Ural, R., Kazakh., etc. 74 Ec
Uralsk, Kazakh. 74 Ec
Uralskiye Khrebet, Russia 74 Ec
Urapunga, N. Terr., Aust. 53 Fb
Ura Tyube, Tadzhik. 74 Fe
Urawa, Japan 82 Fg
Urbakh, Russia 77 He
Urcos, Peru 48 Cf
Urda, Kazakh. 74 Dd
Urdzhar, Kazakh. 74 Hd
Ure R., England 59 Ff
Ures, Mexico 46 Bb
Urfa, Turkey 88 Cb
Urga. See Ulan Bator
Urgench, Uzbek. 74 Ed
Urgun, Afghanistan 89 Jc
Uri, canton, Switzerland 61 Db
Uribe, Colombia 48 Cc
Uribia, Colombia 48 Ca
Urnäsch, Switzerland 61 Ea
Urtazymsk, Russia 77 Pd
Urtein, Mongolia 78 Ga
Uruapan, Mexico 46 Dd
Urubamba & R., Peru 48 Cf
Urucará, Brazil 48 Fd
Uruçui, Brazil 49 Je
Urucuia, Brazil 49 Hg
Urudangi, Qnsld. 53 Gd
Uruguaiana, Brazil 50 Ec
Uruguay, rep., S. America 50 Ed
Uruguay, R., Uruguay, etc. 50 Ed
Urumchi, China 74 Hd
Urumes Sughra, Syria 90 Ea
Urussanga, Brazil 50 Gc
Urville, T. d', W. Irian 79 Ll
Uryupinsk, Russia 77 Fe
Urzhum, Russia 77 Kb
Urziceni, Rumania 72 Fb
Usak, Turkey 88 Ab
Usakos, S.-W. Africa 91 Bd
Usborne, Mt., Falkland Is. 50 Eh
Usedom, Germany 64 Ea
Ushant I. See Ouessant, I.d'
Ushirombo, Tanzania 93 Ge
Ush Tobe, Kazakh. 74 Gd
Ushuaia, Argentina 50 Ch
Uska, India 87 Db
Uskedal, Norway 63 Ag
Uskub. See Skoplje
Uskudar, Turkey 88 Aa
Usole Siberskoye, Russia 75 Kc
Uspenskiy, Kazakh. 74 Gd
Usquil, Peru 48 Be
Ussel, France 68 Ed
Ussuri, R., Russia-China 75 Nd
Ussuriysk, Russia 75 Nd
Ust' Aldan, Russia 75 Mb
Ust' Amginskoye, Russia 75 Nb
Ust' Apuka, Russia 75 Rb
Ust' Belaya, Russia 75 Sb
Ust' Bolsheretsk, Russia 75 Qc
Ust' Chaun, Russia 75 Sb
Uster, Switzerland 61 Da
Usti nad Labem, Czech. 64 Fc
Ust' Ishim, Russia 74 Gc
Ust' Kamenogorsk, Kazakh. 74 Hc
Ust' Khayryuzovo, Russia 75 Qc
Ust' Kut, Russia 75 Kc
Ust' Maya, Russia 75 Nb
Ust' Port, Russia 74 Hb
Ust' Sopochnoye, Russia 75 Qc
Ust' Tsilma, Russia 74 Eb
Ust' Uda, Russia 75 Kc
Ust' Usa, Russia 74 Eb
Ust' Uyskoye, Russia 77 Rc
Ust' Yenisey, port, Russia 74 Hb
Ustyurt, plat, Kazakh. 74 Ed
Ustyuzhna, Russia 76 Jb
Usu. See Abuta
Usumacinta, R., Mexico 46 Fd
Utah, state, U.S.A. 42 Dd
Utah L., Utah 42 Dc
Utajarvi, Finland 62 Md
Utena, Lithuania 63 Lj
Utete, Tanzania 93 Hf
Uthal, W. Pakistan 84 Cc
Utiariti, Brazil 48 Ff
Utica, New York 40 Jd
Utiel, Spain 67 Ec
Utraula, India 87 Db
Utrecht, Natal 91 Ee
Utrecht & prov., Neth. 60 Db
Utrera, Spain 66 Cd
Utsjoki, Finland 62 Mb
Utsunomiya, Japan 82 Ff
Uttar Pradesh, India 84 Ec
Uttaradit, Siam 83 Cc
Uusikaarlepyy, Finland 62 Ke
Uusikaupunki, Finland 63 Jf
Uvac, Yugoslavia 72 Bc
Uvat, Russia 74 Fc
Uvea, I., Loyalty Islands 98 Fk
Uvira, Congo 93 Fe
Uwajima, Japan 82 Ch
Uxbridge, Massachusetts 44 Ea
Uxbridge, Ontario 40 Gc
Uxmal, Mexico 46 Gc
Uyu Chaung R., Burma 85 Jc
Uyuni, Bolivia 48 Dh
Uzbekskaya, rep., Russia 74 Fd
Uzdin, Yugoslavia 72 Cb
Uzgen, Kirgizskaya S.S.R. 74 Gd
Uzhgorod, Ukraine 76 Cg
Uzyansk, Russia 77 Nd
Vaal R., S. Africa 91 De
Vaalwater, Transvaal 91 Dd
Vaasä, Finland 62 Je
Vac, Hungary 65 He
Vache, I. La, Haiti 47 Ec
Vadsö, Norway 62 Na
Vaduz, Liechtenstein 61 Ea
Væröy, Norway 62 Ec
Vags Fd., Norway 62 Gb
Vah, R., Czechoslovakia 65 Gd
Vaila I., Shetland, Scotland 58 Ha
Vairowal, India 86 De
Valais, canton, Switzerland 61 Cb
Valcheta, Argentina 50 Cf
Valday, Russia 76 Hc
Valday Hills, Russia 76 Hc
Valdepeñas, Spain 66 Dc
Valderredible, Spain 66 Da
Valderrobres, Spain 67 Fb
Valdez, Alaska 43 Yl
Valdez, Pen., Argentina 50 Df
Valdivia, Chile 50 Be
Valdosta, Georgia 43 Ke
Valea-lui-Mihai, Rumania 65 Ke
Valença, Brazil 49 Je
Valença, Brazil 49 Kf
Valençay, France 68 Dc

Valence, France 69 Fd
Valencia, Spain 67 Ec
Valencia, Venezuela 48 Da
Valencia, Gulf of, Spain 67 Fc
Valencia de Alcantara, Spain 66 Bc
Valencia de Don Juan, Spain 66 Ca
Valenciennes, France 68 Ea
Văleni de Munte, Rumania 72 Fb
Valentia I., Eire 59 Aj
Valentin, Mt., Chile 50 Bg
Valera, Venezuela 48 Cb
Valga, Estonia 63 Mh
Valjala, Estonia 63 Kg
Valjevo, Yugoslavia 72 Bb
Valkeakoski, Finland 63 Lf
Valkenburg, Netherlands 60 Dd
Valladolid, Mexico 46 Gc
Valladolid, Spain 66 Cb
Valldemosa, Balearic Is. 67 Gc
Valle-D'Aosta, reg., Italy 70 Ac
Valle de La Pascua, Venez. 48 Db
Valle de Santiago, Mexico 46 Dc
Valledupar, Colombia 48 Ca
Vallejo, California 45 Bf
Vallenar, Chile 50 Bc
Valletta, Malta 71 Eh
Valley City, N. Dakota 42 Gb
Valleyfield, Quebec 40 Jc
Vallgrund, Finland 62 Je
Vallorbe, Switzerland 61 Ab
Valmaseda, Spain 66 Da
Valmiera, Latvia 63 Lh
Valognes, France 68 Cb
Valona (Vlone), Albania 73 Bd
Valona B., Albania 73 Bd
Valoria la Buena, Spain 66 Cb
Valparaiso, Chile 50 Bd
Valparaiso, Mexico 46 Dc
Vals Platz, Switzerland 61 Eb
Valtimo, Finland 62 Ne
Valverde de Júcar, Spain 67 Dc
Valverde del Camino, Spain 66 Bd
Van & Gölu, Turkey 88 Db
Vana Vändra, Estonia 63 Lg
Vanavara, Russia 75 Kb
Van Buren, Arkansas 43 Hd
Vancouver, Washington 45 Bc
Van Diemen, C., N.T., Aust. 52 Fb
Van Diemen G., N.T., Aust. 52 Fb
Vanegas, Mexico 46 Dc
Vänern, L., Sweden 63 Eg
Vänersborg, Sweden 63 Eg
Vangaindrano, Madagascar 93 Nl
Vankarem, Russia 75 Tb
Vannes, France 68 Bc
Vannöy, Norway 62 Ha
Van Rhyns Dorp, Cape Prov. 91 Bf
Vanua Levu, I., Fiji 98 Gj
Var, dep., France 69 Ge
Varanasi, India 87 Dc
Varanger Fd., Norway 62 Pb
Varanger Halvöya, Norway 62 Na
Varaždin, Yugoslavia 70 Fb
Varberg, Sweden 63 Eh
Vardar R., Greece, etc. 72 Dd
Vardö, Norway 62 Pa
Vares, C. de, Spain 66 Ba
Varese, Italy 70 Bc
Varkaus, Finland 62 Me
Varna, Bulgaria 72 Fc
Varnavin, Russia 77 Gb
Värtsilä, Finland 62 Pe
Vasht. See Gasht
Vasknarva, Estonia 63 Mg
Vassar, Michigan 40 Ed
Vastanfors, Sweden 63 Fg
Västerås, Sweden 63 Gg
Väster Dal Älv, Sweden 63 Ef
Västervik, Sweden 63 Gh
Vasvar, Hungary 65 Ge
Vatican City, Italy 71 De
Vaticano C., Italy 71 Ef
Vatna Jökull, Iceland 62 Xm
Vatomandry, Madagascar 93 Nk
Vättern, L., Sweden 63 Fg
Vättis, Switzerland 61 Eb
Vaucluse, dep., France 69 Fd
Vaud, canton, Switzerland 61 Bb
Vaxjö, Sweden 63 Fh
Vaygach Ostrov, Russia 74 Fa
Vechel, Netherlands 60 Dc
Vedia, Argentina 50 Dd
Vedrin, Belgium 60 Cd
Veere, Netherlands 60 Bc
Vega & Fd., Norway 62 Dd
Vegorritis, L., Greece 73 Cd
Vejle, Denmark 63 Cj
Vela, Argentina 50 Ee
Velaines, Belgium 60 Bd
Velebit Planina, Yugoslavia 70 Ec
Velestinon, Greece 73 De
Velez Rubio, Spain 67 Dd
Velikiy Ustyug, Russia 74 Db
Velikiye Luki, Russia 76 Gc
Velizh, Russia 76 Gd
Velletri, Italy 71 De
Vellore, India 84 Ef
Velp, Netherlands 60 Db
Velsen, Netherlands 60 Cb
Velsk, Russia 76 Na
Venado, Mexico 46 Dc
Venado Tuerto, Argentina 50 Dd
Vendee, dep., France 68 Cc
Vendôme, France 68 Dc
Venendaal, Netherlands 60 Db
Veneto, reg., Italy 70 Cc
Venezia, & G. di, Italy 70 Dc
Venezuela, rep., S. America 48 Db
Venezuela, G. de, Venezuela 48 Ca
Vengurla, India 84 De
Venice (Venezia), Italy 70 Dc
Venlo, Netherlands 60 Ec
Venraij, Netherlands 60 Dc
Ventotene, I., Italy 71 De
Ventspils, Latvia 63 Jh
Ventura, California 45 Dh
Vera. See Jobson
Vera, Spain 67 Ed
Veracruz and state, Mexico 46 Ed
Veramin, Persia 89 Fb
Veraval, India 84 Dd
Verbania, Switzerland 61 Dc
Vercelli, Italy 70 Bc
Verde C. (Vert C.), Senegal 94 Bf
Verdun, France 68 Fb
Verdun, Quebec 40 Kc
Vereshchagino, Russia 74 Hb
Vereshchagino, Russia 77 Ma
Vereya, Russia 77 Cc
Verga C., Guinea 94 Cf
Vergara, Uruguay 50 Fd
Vergennes, Vermont 40 Kc
Verin, Spain 66 Bb
Verkhne Imbatskoye, Russia 74 Hb
Verkhne Uralsk, Russia 77 Pd
Verkhne Vilyuysk, Russia 75 Mb
Verkhoturye, Russia 74 Fc
Verkhoyansk, Russia 75 Nb
Verkhoyanskiy Khr., Russia 75 Mb
Vermillion, S. Dakota 42 Gc
Vermont, state, U.S.A. 43 Mc
Verneuil, France 68 Db
Veroia, Greece 73 Dd
Verona, Italy 70 Cc
Verrieres, les, Switzerland 61 Bb
Versailles, France 68 Eb
Versam, Switzerland 61 Eb
Vert C, Senegal 94 Bf
Vertryck, Belgium 60 Cd
Verviers, Belgium 60 Dd
Vervins, France 68 Eb
Vesanto, Finland 62 Me
Vesoul, France 68 Gc
Vessem, Netherlands 60 Dc
Vest Fd., Norway 62 Ec
Vesta. See Pandora
Vesterålen, Is., Norway 62 Fb
Vest Spitsbergen, Arctic Oc. 74 Aa
Vest Vågöy, Norway 62 Eb
Vesyegonsk, Russia 76 Kb
Veszprem, Hungary 65 Ge
Vetluga & R., Russia 77 Gb
Veurne, Belgium 60 Ac
Vevey, Switzerland 61 Bb
Vex, Switzerland 61 Cb
Veys, Persia 88 Ec
Viacha, Bolivia 48 Dg
Viana, Brazil 49 Jd
Viborg, Denmark 63 Ch
Vibo Valentia, Italy 71 Ff
Vicente de la Barquera, S., Spain 66 Ca
Vicenza, Italy 70 Cc
Vich, Spain 67 Gb
Vichuquen, Chile 50 Bd
Vichy, France 68 Ec
Vicksburg, Mississippi 43 He
Vicosa, Brazil 49 Jd
Victor Harbour, S. Australia 53 Gg
Victoria, Argentina 50 Dd
Victoria, Hong Kong 78 Ff
Victoria, state, Australia 53 Hg
Victoria Falls, Rhodesia 91 Dc
Victoria L., Uganda, etc. 93 Ge
Victoria Ld., Antarctica 100 Lb
Victoria Mt., Burma 85 Hd
Victoria Mt., Papua 53 Ja
Victoria, R., N. Terr., Aust. 52 Fc
Victoria Point, Burma 85 Jf
Victoria River Downs, N. Territory, Australia 52 Ec
Victoriaville, Quebec 40 Kb
Victoria West, Cape Province 91 Cf
Victorica, Argentina 50 Ce
Vicuna, Chile 50 Bd
Vidago, Portugal 66 Bb
Vidin, Bulgaria 72 Db
Viedma, Argentina 50 Df
Viedma, L., Argentina 50 Cg
Vienna (Wien), Austria 65 Gd
Vienne, France 68 Fd
Vienne, dep., France 68 Dc
Vienne R., France 68 Dc
Vientiane, Laos 83 Cc
Vieques, I. de, West Indies 47 Fc
Vierlingsbeek, Netherlands 60 Ec
Vierwaldstatter See, Switz. 61 Da
Vierzon Ville, France 68 Ec
Viesïte, Latvia 63 Lh
Vietnam, Indo-China 83 Dc
Vif, France 69 Fd
Vigan, Philippines 79 Hg
Vigan, le, France 69 Ee
Vigia, Brazil 49 Hd
Vigia Chico, Mexico 46 Gd
Vigo & R., Spain 66 Aa
Vigrestad, Norway 63 Ag
Vihanti, Finland 62 Ld
Vijayanagar, India 84 Ee
Vijayavada, India 84 Fe
Vijosë R., Albania 73 Bd
Vikaviskis, Lithuania 63 Kj
Vikna, Norway 62 Dd
Vila Arriaga, Angola 92 Cg
Vila de Cangombe, Angola 92 Dg
Vila de João Belo, Moçamb. 91 Ee
Vila Lugela. See Mocuba
Vila Luso, Angola 92 Dg
Vila Machado, Moçambique 91 Ec
Vila Manica, Moçambique 91 Ec
Vilanculos, Moçambique 91 Fd
Vilāne, Latvia 63 Mh
Vila Nova de Cerveira, Portugal 66 Ab
Vila Nova de Famalicão, Portugal 66 Ab
Vila Nova de Malaca, Timor I., Indonesia 79 Jm
Vila Pery, Moçambique 91 Ec
Vila Real, Portugal 66 Bb
Vilar Formoso, Portugal 66 Bb
Vila Serpa Pinto, Angola 92 Dg
Vila Velha de Rodao, Port. 66 Bc
Vila Verissimo, Angola 92 Ef
Vila Viçosa, Portugal 66 Bc
Vilcheka, Os., Arctic Ocean 78 Fa
Vilhelmina, Sweden 62 Gd
Vilhena, Brazil 48 Ef
Viljandi, Estonia 63 Lg
Villa Angela. See Santa Sylvina
Villa Bella, Bolivia 48 Df
Villa Bens, Sp. Sahara 94 Cc
Villablino, Spain 66 Ba
Villacañas, Spain 66 Dc
Villacarriedo, Spain 66 Da
Villach, Austria 64 Ee
Villa Cisneros, Sp. Sahara 94 Bd
Villa Constitución, Argentina 48 Dd
Villa del Rosario, Paraguay 50 Eb
Villa de Rosario, Argentina 50 Dd
Villa Dolores, Argentina 50 Cd
Villafranca, Spain 66 Ba
Villafranca del Cid, Spain 67 Eb
Villafranca del Panadés, Sp. 67 Fb
Villaggio-Duca-Abruzzi, Somalia 93 Kd
Villaguay, Argentina 50 Ed
Villa Guillermina, Argentina 50 Ec
Villa Hermosa, Mexico 46 Fd
Villa Hidalgo, Mexico 46 Db
Villa Ingavi, Bolivia 48 Eh
Villa Iris, Argentina 50 De
Villajoyosa, Spain 67 Ec
Villalba, Spain 66 Ba
Villaldama, Mexico 46 Db
Villalón de Campos, Spain 66 Ca
Villalonga, Argentina 50 De
Villalpando, Spain 66 Cb
Villa Maria, Argentina 50 Dd
Villa Mercedes, Argentina 50 Cd
Villa Montes, Bolivia 48 Eh
Villa Murtinho, Brazil 48 Df
Villanueva de Córdoba, Sp. 66 Cc
Villanueva-de-la-Serena, Sp. 66 Cc
Villanueva -y Geltrú, Spain 67 Fb
Villaodrid, Spain 66 Ba
Villaputzu, Sardinia 71 Bf
Villarcayo, Spain 66 Da
Villareal, Spain 67 Ec
Villarrica, Chile 50 Be
Villarrica, Paraguay 50 Ec
Villarrobledo, Spain 67 Dc
Villavicencio, Colombia 48 Cc
Villaviciosa, Spain 66 Ca
Villa Viejo, Colombia 48 Bc
Villazon, Bolivia 48 Dh
Villefort, France 69 Ed
Villefranche-de-Rouergue, France 69 Dd
Ville Marie, Quebec 40 Gb
Villena, Spain 67 Ec
Villeneuve-sur-Lot, France 69 Dd
Villeurbanne, France 68 Fd
Villingen, Germany 64 Cd
Villupuram, India 84 Ef
Vilna. See Vilnius
Vilnyus, Lithuania 63 Lj
Vilvorde, Belgium 60 Cd
Vilyuysk, Russia 75 Mb
Vimioso, Portugal 66 Bb
Vimperk, Czechoslovakia 64 Ed
Viña del Mar, Chile 50 Bd
Vinaroz, Spain 67 Fb
Vincennes, Indiana 40 Cf
Vinchiaturo, Italy 71 Ee
Vindel Älv, Sweden 62 Hd
Vindhya Ra., India 84 Ed
Vineland, New Jersey 44 Cc
Vineyard Sd., Mass. 44 Eb
Vinga, Rumania 72 Cb
Vinh, N. Vietnam 83 Dc
Vinkovci, Yugoslavia 72 Bb
Vinnitsa, Ukraine 76 Fg
Vintes, Ecuador 48 Bd
Viranşehir, Turkey 88 Cb
Virgin Is., West Indies 47 Gc
Virginia, Minnesota 43 Hb
Virginia, state, U.S.A. 43 Ld
Viroqua, Wisconsin 40 Ad
Virovitica, Yugoslavia 72 Ab
Virpazar, Yugoslavia 72 Bc
Virtasalmi, Finland 62 Me
Virton, Belgium 60 De
Virtsu, Estonia 63 Kg
Viru, Peru 48 Be
Vis, I., Yugoslavia 70 Fd
Visalia, California 45 Dg
Visby, Gotland, Sweden 63 Hh
Visé, Belgium 60 Dd
Viseu, Brazil 49 Hd
Viseu, Portugal 66 Bb
Vishakhapatnam, India 85 Fe
Viški, Latvia 63 Mh
Viso, Mte., Italy 70 Ac
Visoko, Yugoslavia 72 Bc
Visp, Switzerland 61 Cb
Vista Alegre, Brazil 48 Ec
Vistula (Wisła), R., Poland 65 Jc
Vitebsk, Belorussia 76 Gd
Viterbo, Italy 70 Dd
Vitigudino, Spain 66 Bb
Viti Levu, I., Fiji 98 Gj
Vitim, R., Russia 75 Lc
Vitoria, Brazil 49 Jh
Vitoria, Spain 67 Da
Vitoria do Mearim, Brazil 49 Jd
Vitry-le-François, France 68 Fb
Vittangi, Sweden 62 Jc
Vitteaux, France 68 Fc
Vittoria, Sicily 71 Eg
Viver, Spain 67 Ec
Vivero, Spain 66 Ba
Vivi, Russia 75 Jb
Vivorata, Argentina 50 Ee
Vizianagram, India 85 Fe
Vizirul, Rumania 72 Fb
Vizovice, Czechoslovakia 65 Gd
Vizzini, Sicily 71 Eg
Vlaanderen, Oost, Belgium 60 Bd
Vlaanderen, West, Belgium 60 Bd
Vlaardingen, Netherlands 60 Cc
Vladimir, Russia 76 Mc
Vladimirovka, Russia 77 Hf
Vladivostok, Russia 75 Nd
Vlieland I., Netherlands 60 Ca
Vlissingen, Netherlands 60 Bc
Vlone, Albania 73 Bd
Vltava R., Czechoslovakia 64 Fc
Voghera, Italy 70 Bc
Vohemar, Madagascar 93 Pj
Võhma, Estonia 63 Lg
Voi, Kenya 93 He
Voiotía, Greece 73 De
Voiron, France 68 Fd
Voitsberg, Austria 64 Fe
Voiviis, L., Greece 73 De
Vojvodina, Yugoslavia 72 Bb
Volcano B. See Uchiura wan
Volga, R., Russia 74 Dd
Volgograd, Russia 77 Gf
Volissos, Greece 73 Ee
Volkhov, R., Russia 76 Gb
Vollenhove, Netherlands 60 Db
Volochanka, Russia 75 Ja
Volochisk, Ukraine 76 Eg
Vologda, Russia 76 Lb
Volokolamsk, Russia 76 Jc
Vólos, Greece 73 De
Volovets, Ukraine 76 Cg
Volozhin, Belorussia 76 Ed
Volsk, Russia 77 Hd
Volta. See Upper Volta
Volta, L., Ghana 94 Eg
Volta, White, R., Ghana 94 Fg
Voltveti, Estonia 63 Lg
Vonêche, Belgium 60 Cd
Voorburg, Netherlands 60 Cb
Voorschoten, Netherlands 60 Cb
Voorst, Netherlands 60 Eb
Voorthuizen, Netherlands 60 Db
Vopnafjordhur, Iceland 62 Ym
Vorab, Mt., Switzerland 61 Eb
Vorarlberg, Austria 64 Ce
Vorauen, Switzerland 61 Da
Vorkuta, Russia 74 Fb
Vormsi, I., Estonia 63 Kg
Voronezh, Russia 76 Lf
Vosges, dep. & mts., France 68 Gb
Voss, Norway 63 Bf
Vostok I., Pacific Ocean 99 Kj
Votkinsk, Russia 77 Lb
Vouvry, Switzerland 61 Bb
Vouziers, France 68 Fb
Voxna, Sweden 63 Ff
Voyampolka, Russia 75 Qc
Voznesensk, Ukraine 76 Gh
Vrancv, Czechoslovakia 65 Jd
Vrangelya Ostrov, Russia 75 Sa
Vranje, Yugoslavia 72 Cc
Vratsa, Bulgaria 72 Dc
Vrbas, Yugoslavia 72 Bb
Vrchovina Českomoravska, Czechoslovakia 65 Fd
Vredefort, O.F.S. 91 De
Vrin, Switzerland 61 Eb
Vrindavan, India 87 Ab
Vroomshoop, Netherlands 60 Eb
Vršac, Yugoslavia 72 Cb
Vrútky, Czechoslovakia 65 Hd
Vryburg, Cape Province 91 Ce
Vučitrn, Yugoslavia 72 Cc
Vukovar, Yugoslavia 72 Bb
Vulcano, I., Italy 71 Ef
Vulpera, Switzerland 61 Fb
Vuolijoki, Finland 62 Md
Vurbitsa, Bulgaria 72 Fc
Vyatka (Kirov), Russia 77 Ja
Vyatka, R., Russia 74 Dc
Vyazemskiy, Russia 75 Nd
Vyazma, Russia 76 Jd
Vyazniki, Russia 77 Fb
Vyborg, Russia 76 Fa
Vyrtsyarv Oz., Estonia 63 Mg
Vyru, Estonia 63 Mh
Vyshniy Volochek, Russia 76 Jc
Vyskov, Czechoslovakia 65 Gd
Vytegra, Russia 76 Ka
Wa, Ghana 94 Ef
Waalhaven, Netherlands 60 Cc
Waalwijk, Netherlands 60 Dc
Wabash & R., Indiana 40 De
Wabos. See Searchmont
Wabra, Arabia 88 Ed
Wabuda, I., New Guinea 53 Ha
Waco, Texas 42 Ge
Wad, W. Pakistan 84 Cc
Wadden Zee, Netherlands 60 Da
Wad Hamid, Sudan 95 Me
Wadi-es-Sir, Jordan 90 Df
Wadi Gemal I., Egypt 95 Nd
Wadi Halfa, Sudan 95 Md
Wadi Musa, Jordan 90 Dg
Wad Medani, Sudan 95 Mf
Wafi, Arabia 88 De
Wageningen, Netherlands 60 Dc
Wagga Wagga, N.S.W. 53 Jg
Wagin, W. Australia 52 Cf
Wahla, Arabia 88 Df
Waiau, New Zealand 51 De
Waichow. See Waiyeung
Waigeo, I., W. Irian 79 Kl
Waiheke I., New Zealand 51 Eb
Waihi, New Zealand 51 Eb
Waikaia, New Zealand 51 Bf
Waikare, Moana, N.Z. 51 Fc
Waikari, New Zealand 51 De
Waikato, R., New Zealand 51 Ec
Waikouaiti, New Zealand 51 Cf
Waimakariri, R., N.Z. 51 De
Waimate, New Zealand 51 Cf
Waimes, Belgium 60 Ed
Wainganga R., India 84 Ed
Waingapu, Sumba I., Indon. 79 Hm
Wainwright, Alaska 43 Xk
Waipara, New Zealand 51 De
Waipawa, New Zealand 51 Fc
Waipukurau, New Zealand 51 Fc
Wairarapa, L., New Zealand 51 Ed
Wairau, R., New Zealand 51 Dd
Wairoa, New Zealand 51 Fc
Waitara, New Zealand 51 Ec
Waitomo, New Zealand 51 Ec
Waiku, New Zealand 51 Eb
Waiyeung, China 81 Gl
Wajir, Kenya 93 Jd
Wakamatsu, Japan 82 Ff
Wakasa B., Japan 82 Dg
Wakatipu, L., N. Zealand 51 Bf
Wakayama, Japan 82 Dg
Wakba. See El Jafr
Wake I., Pacific Ocean 98 Ff
Wakefield, England 59 Gg
Wakrah, Qatar 89 Fe
Wakuan Hu. China 80 Hf
Walachia, Rumania 72 Eb
Walbrzych, Poland 65 Gc
Walcheren I., Netherlands 60 Bc
Wald, Switzerland 61 Da
Waldia, Ethiopia 93 Hb
Waldport, Oregon 45 Ac
Walen See, Switzerland 61 Ea
Walenstadt, Switzerland 61 Ea
Wales, Great Britain 59 Eh
Walgett, N.S.W. 53 Jf
Walgreen Coast, Antarctica 100 Qb
Walker L., Nevada 45 Df
Walkerton, Ontario 40 Fc
Walkerville, Ontario 40 Ed
Wallace, Idaho 45 Fb
Wallaceburg, Ontario 40 Ed
Wallaroo, S. Australia 53 Gf
Wallaston, Mt., N.T., Aust. 52 Fc
Walla-Walla, Washington 45 Db
Wallenpaupack, L., Pa. 44 Cb
Wallowa Mts., Oregon 45 Dc
Walsall, England 59 Fh
Walsh, Qnsld. 53 Hc
Walsoorden, Netherlands 60 Cc
Waltham, Massachusetts 44 Ea
Waltham, Quebec 40 Hc
Walton, New York 44 Ca
Walvis Bay, S.-W. Africa 91 Ad
Walwale, Ghana 94 Ef
Wamba, Congo 93 Fd
Wamel, Netherlands 60 Dc
Wampsville, New York 40 Jd
Wana, W. Pakistan 86 Ad
Waqaaring, N.S.W. 53 He
Wanaka & L., New Zealand 51 Bf
Wandiwash, India 84 Ff
Wandoan, Qnsld. 53 Je
Wandre, Belgium 60 Dd
Wandsbek, Germany 64 Db
Wan Fou Shan, China 81 Gh
Wanganui & R., N.Z. 51 Ec
Wangaratta, Victoria 53 Jg
Wanhsien, China 78 Ed
Wankie, Rhodesia 91 Dc
Wanning, Hainan 81 En
Wanping, China 80 Hc
Wanyuan, China 80 Df
Warandab, Ethiopia 93 Jc
Warangal, India 84 Ee
Wardair, Ethiopia 93 Kc
Wardha & R., India 84 Ed
Ware, England 41 Pe
Waremme, Belgium 60 Dd
Warka, Poland 65 Jc
Warmbad, S.-W. Africa 91 Be
Warmbaths, Transvaal 91 Dd
Warnemünde, Germany 64 Ea
Warner Valley, Oregon 45 Dd
Warner's Ra., Oregon 45 Cd
Warneton, Belgium 60 Ad
Warora, India 84 Ed
Warragul, Victoria 53 Jg
Warren, Illinois 40 Bd
Warren, Ohio 40 Fe
Warren, Pennsylvania 44 Ab
Warrenpoint, N. Ireland 59 Cf
Warrenton, Virginia 44 Bc
Warri, Nigeria 94 Gg
Warrington, England 59 Fg
Warrnambool, Victoria 53 Hg
Warsaw, Indiana 40 De
Warsaw, New York 44 Aa
Warsaw. See Warszawa
Warszawa, Poland 65 Jb
Warta, Poland 65 Hc
Warta R., Poland 65 Hb
Warwick, Queensland 53 Ke
Warwick, Rhode Island 44 Eb
Warwick & co., England 59 Fh
Wasatch Mts., Utah 42 Dd
Wasen, Switzerland 61 Ca
Wash, The, England 59 Hh
Washakie Needles, Wyoming 42 Ec
Washington, District of Columbia 40 Hf
Washington, New Jersey 44 Cb
Washington, Ohio 40 Ef
Washington, Pennsylvania 40 Fe
Washington, Virginia 44 Ac
Washington, state, U.S.A. 42 Bb
Washington I., Pacific Ocean 98 Jg
Washington Ld., Greenland 41 Qa
Washir, Afghanistan 89 Hc
Washuk, W. Pakistan 84 Bc
Wasmes, Belgium 60 Bd
Wassen, Switzerland 61 Db
Waterbury, Connecticut 44 Db
Waterford (Port Láirge), Eire 59 Ch
Waterford Harb., Eire 59 Ch
Waterloo, Belgium 60 Cd
Waterloo, Iowa 43 Hc
Waterloo, Ontario 40 Fd
Waterloo, Quebec 40 Kc
Watertown, New York 40 Jd
Watertown, S. Dakota 42 Gc
Watertown, Wisconsin 40 Bd
Watervliet, New York 44 Da
Watford, England 59 Gj
Watkins Glen, New York 44 Ba
Watlings I., Bahamas Is. 47 Eb
Watou, Belgium 60 Ad
Watsa, Congo 93 Fd
Watsonville, California 45 Cg
Wau, New Guinea 53 Ja
Wau, Sudan 95 Lg
Wauchope, N. Terr., Aust. 53 Fd
Wau el Kebir, Libya 95 Jc
Waukegan, Illinois 40 Cd
Waukesha, Wisconsin 40 Bd
Waupaca, Wisconsin 40 Bc
Waupun, Wisconsin 40 Bd
Wasau, Wisconsin 40 Bc
Wautoma, Wisconsin 40 Bc
Wauwatosa, Wisconsin 40 Bd
Wave Hill, N. Terr., Aust. 52 Fc
Waveney R., England 59 Hh
Waverly, New York 44 Ba
Waverly, Ohio 40 Ef
Wavre, Belgium 60 Cd
Waycross, Georgia 43 Ke
Wayland. See Nicholson
Waynesboro, Pennsylvania 44 Bc
Waynesburg, Pennsylvania 40 Ff
Wazirabad, W. Pakistan 86 Dd
Waziristan, N. & S. Pakistan 86 Ad
Weald, The, England 59 Hj
Wear R., England 59 Ff
Weatherly, Pennsylvania 44 Cb
Webbwood, Ontario 40 Fb
Wechelderzande, Belgium 60 Cc
Weda B., Halmahera, Indon. 79 Jk
Weddell I., Falkland Islands 50 Dh
Weddell Sea, Antarctica 100 Ac
Weed, California 45 Be
Weedon, Quebec 40 Lc
Weedsport, New York 44 Ba
Weert, Netherlands 60 Dc
Weesen, Switzerland 61 Ea
Weesp, Netherlands 60 Db
Weichang, China 80 Jb
Weiden, Germany 64 Ed
Weifang, China 80 Jd
Wei-hai, China 80 Ld
Wei Ho, R., China 78 Ed
Weihwei. See Chihsien
Weimar, Germany 64 Dc
Weinfelden, Switzerland 61 Ea
Weiser, Idaho 45 Ec
Wei Shan Hu, China 80 He
Weissenfels, Germany 64 Dc
Weisshorn, Mt., Switzerland 61 Cb
Weissmies, Mt., Switzerland 61 Db
Weisstannen, Switzerland 61 Ea
Wejh. See Al Wajh
Welford, Queensland 53 He
Welland, Ontario 40 Gd
Wellesley Is., Queensland 53 Gc
Wellin, Belgium 60 Dd
Wellingborough, England 59 Gh
Wellington, New Zealand 51 Ed
Wellington, I., Chile 50 Bg
Wells, England 59 Hh
Wells, England 59 Fj
Wells, Nevada 45 Fe
Wellsboro, Pennsylvania 44 Bb
Wellsville, New York 44 Ba
Wels, Austria 64 Ed
Welshpool, Wales 59 Eh
Wema, Congo 92 Ee
Wembo Niama, Congo 92 Ee
Wenatchee, Washington 45 Cb
Wenchow, China 81 Kh
Wenshan, China 81 Bl
Wensi, China 80 Ee
Wernhout, Netherlands 60 Cc
Wervershoof, Netherlands 60 Db
Wervica, Belgium 60 Bd
Wesel, Germany 64 Bc
Wesenberg, Germany 64 Eb
Weser R., Germany 64 Cb
Wessel Is., N. Terr., Aust. 53 Gb
West Allis, Wisconsin 40 Bd
West Barra, Shetland 58 Ja
West Bend, Wisconsin 40 Bd
West Bengal, India 85 Gd
West Branch, Michigan 40 Dc
West Bromwich, England 59 Fh
West Chester, Pennsylvania 44 Cc
Westende, Belgium 60 Ac
Westerloo, Belgium 60 Cc
Westerly, Rhode Island 44 Eb
Western Australia, state, Australia 52 Dd
Wester Schelde, Netherlands 60 Bc
Westfalen, Germany 64 Cc
Westfield, Massachusetts 40 Kd
Westfield, New York 44 Aa
Westfield, Pennsylvania 44 Bb
West Hartlepool, England 59 Gf
West Indies, Caribbean Sea 97 Cg
West Irian, prov., N. Guinea 79 Kl
Westkapelle, Netherlands 60 Bc
West Lothian, co., Scotland 58 Ee
West Malaysia (Malaya), S.E. Asia 79 Dk
Westmeath, co., Eire 59 Cg
Westminster, Maryland 44 Bc
Westmorland, co., England 59 Ff
West Nicholson, Rhodesia 91 Dd
Weston, N. Borneo 79 Gj
Weston, West Virginia 40 Ff
Weston-super-Mare, England 59 Fj
West Pakistan, S. Asia 84 Cc
West Palm Beach, Florida 43 Lf
West Point, New York 44 Db
Westport, Eire 59 Ag
Westport, New Zealand 51 Cd
Westport, Ontario 40 Hc
Westray I., Orkney 59 Ea
West Riding, Yorks., Eng. 59 Fg
West Virginia, state, U.S.A. 43 Kd
Westwood, Netherlands 60 Db
Wetar, I. & Str., Indonesia 79 Jm
Wetterhorn, Mt., Switzerland 61 Db
Wexford & co., Eire 59 Ch
Weymont, Quebec 40 Kb
Weymouth, England 59 Fk
Whakataki, New Zealand 51 Fd
Whakatane, New Zealand 51 Fb
Whales, B. of, Antarctica 100 Mb
Whalsey I., Shetland 58 Ja
Whangarei, New Zealand 51 Ea
Wharanui, New Zealand 51 Ed
Whataroa, New Zealand 51 Ce
Wheeler Pk., Nevada 45 Ff
Wheeling, W. Virginia 40 Fe
Whitby, England 59 Gf
Whitby, Ontario 40 Gd
White Mts., New Hampshire 40 Lc
White R., Arkansas 43 Hd
White R., S. Dakota 42 Fc
Whitefish, Montana 42 Db
Whitefish B., Michigan 40 Db
Whitehall, Michigan 40 Cd
Whitehall, New York 40 Kd
Whitehaven, England 59 Ef
White Oil Springs. See Naft
White Plains, New York 44 Db
White River Junction, Vt. 43 Mc
White Russia, rep. See Belorussia
White Volta, R., Ghana 94 Eg
Whiting, New Jersey 40 Jf
Whitney, Ontario 40 Gc
Whitney, Mt., California 45 Dg
Whittier, California 45 Dj
Wiarton, Ontario 40 Fc
Wichita, Kansas 42 Gd
Wichita Falls, Texas 42 Ge
Wick, Scotland 58 Eb
Wicklow & co., Eire 59 Ch
Wicklow Head, Eire 59 Ch
Wicklow Mts., Eire 59 Cg
Wielbark, Poland 65 Jb
Wielen, Poland 65 Gb
Wieliczka, Poland 65 Jd
Wielun, Poland 65 Hc
Wien, Austria 65 Gd
Wiener Neustadt, Austria 65 Ge
Wiesbaden, Germany 64 Cc
Wiesen, Switzerland 61 Eb
Wigan, England 59 Fg
Wight, I. of, England 59 Gk
Wigtown & co., Scotland 59 Ef
Wigtown B., Scotland 59 Ef
Wijhe, Netherlands 60 Eb
Wijk, Netherlands 60 Dd
Wijk, Netherlands 60 Dc
Wil, Switzerland 61 Ea
Wilcannia, New S. Wales 53 Hf
Wildhorn, Mt., Switzerland 61 Cb
Wildstrubel, Mt., Switzerland 61 Cb
Wildwood, New Jersey 40 Jf
Wilhelmshaven, Germany 64 Cb
Wilkes Coast, Antarctica 100 Jc
Wilkes Ld., Antarctica 100 Hb
Wilkes Barre, Pennsylvania 44 Cb
Wilkin's Str., Antarctica 100 Sb
Wilkolaz, Poland 65 Kc
Willamette R., Oregon 45 Bc
Willemsdorp, Netherlands 60 Cc
Willemstad, Curaçao I. 48 Da
Willemstad, Netherlands 60 Cc
Williambury, W. Aust. 52 Bd
William Creek, S. Aust. 53 Ge
Williams, Arizona 42 Dd
Williamsport, Pennsylvania 44 Bb
Willimantic, Connecticut 44 Db
Williston, N. Dakota 42 Fb
Williston, Cape Province 91 Cf
Willmar, Minnesota 42 Gb
Willowmore, Cape Province 91 Cf
Wills Mt., Pennsylvania 44 Ac
Wilmette, Illinois 40 Cd
Wilmington, California 45 Dj
Wilmington, Delaware 44 Cc
Wilmington, N. Carolina 43 Le
Wilnis, Netherlands 60 Cb
Wilno, Ontario 40 Hc
Wilson, N. Carolina 43 Ld
Wiltshire (Wilts), co., Eng. 59 Fj
Wiluna, W. Australia 52 De

Winburg, Orange Free State 91 De
Winchendon, Massachusetts 40 Kd
Winchester, England 59 Gj
Winchester, Ontario 40 Jc
Winchester, Virginia 44 Ac
Wind Cave Nat. Park, S. Dakota 42 Fc
Windermere & L., England 59 Ff
Windhoek, S.-W. Africa 91 Bd
Windorah, Qnsld. 53 He
Wind River Pk.&Mts.,Wyo. 42 Ec
Windsor, Connecticut 44 Db
Windsor, England 59 Gj
Windsor, Ontario 40 Ed
Windsor Mills, Quebec 40 Lc
Windsor, Vermont 40 Kd
Windward Is., West Indies 47 Gd
Windward Pass, West Indies 47 Ec
Wingham, Ontario 40 Fd
Winghe-St Georges,Belgium 60 Cd
Winnebago L., Wisconsin 40 Bc
Winnemucca, Nevada 45 Ee
Winnemucca L., Nevada 45 De
Winner, S. Dakota 42 Gc
Winning Pool, W. Aust. 52 Bd
Winnipesaukee, L., N.H. 40 Ld
Winschoten, Netherlands 60 Ea
Winslow, Arizona 42 Dd
Winsted, Connecticut 44 Db
Winston-Salem, N. Carolina 43 Kd
Winter Ra. See Fremont Mts.
Winterhaven, California 45 Fj
Winterswijk, Netherlands 60 Ec
Winterthur, Switzerland 61 Da
Winton, New Zealand 51 Bg
Winton, Queensland 53 Hd
Wisbech, England 59 Hh
Wisconsin, state, U.S.A. 43 Hc
Wisconsin R., Wisconsin 40 Bc
Wisconsin Rapids,Wisconsin 40 Bc
Wisła R., Poland 65 Jc
Wismar, Germany 64 Db
Witham R., England 59 Gg
Withlacoochee B., Florida 43 Kf
Witputs, S.-W. Africa 91 Be
Witry, Belgium 60 De
Witten, Germany 64 Bc
Wittenberg, Germany 64 Ec
Wittenberge, Germany 64 Db
Wittenoom, Western Aust. 52 Cd
Wittingen, Germany 64 Db
Wittstock, Germany 64 Eb
Włocławek, Poland 65 Hb
Woerden, Netherlands 60 Cb
Wognum, Netherlands 60 Db
Wohlen, Switzerland 61 Da
Wokam, I., Indonesia 79 Km
Wolbrom, Poland 65 Hc
Woleai, I., Caroline Islands 98 Dg
Wolfe I., Ontario 40 Hc
Wolfeboro, New Hampshire 40 Ld
Wolfsberg, Austria 64 Fe
Wolgast, Germany 64 Ea
Wolhusen, Switzerland 61 Ca
Wollal, W. Australia 52 Dc
Wollaston Foreland, Greenland 41 Mb
Wollaston Is., Chile 50 Cj
Wollongong, New S. Wales 53 Kf
Wolvega, Netherlands 60 Eb
Wolverhampton, England 59 Fh
Wolverthem, Belgium 60 Cd
Wolverton, England 59 Gh
Woman River, Ontario 40 Eb
Wŏnsan, Korea 78 Jc
Wonthaggi, Victoria 53 Jg
Woodbury, New Jersey 44 Cc
Woodlark I., New Guinea 53 Ka
Woodroffe, Mt., S. Australia 52 Fe
Woods Hole, Massachusetts 44 Eb
Woods, L., N. Terr., Aust. 52 Fc
Woodside, Victoria 53 Jg
Woodstock, Illinois 40 Bd
Woodstock, Ontario 40 Fd
Woodstock, Vermont 44 Da
Woodstock, Virginia 44 Ac
Woodsville, New Hampshire 40 Kc
Woodville, New Zealand 51 Ed
Woomera, S. Australia 53 Gf
Woonsocket, Rhode Island 44 Eb
Wooramel, W. Aust. 52 Be
Worcester, Cape Province 91 Bf
Worcester, Massachusetts 40 Ld
Worcester & co., England 59 Fh
Workington, England 58 Ef
Workum, Netherlands 60 Db
Worms, Germany 64 Cd
Worthington, Minnesota 42 Gc
Worthington, Ontario 40 Fb
Wotho, I., Marshall Islands 98 Ff
Woudenberg, Netherlands 60 Db
Woudrichem, Netherlands 60 Cc
Wounta. See Huaonta
Wour, Chad 95 Jd
Wouw, Netherlands 60 Cc
Wowoni, I., Indonesia 79 Hl
Wrangel I. (Os. Vrangelya), Arctic Ocean 75 Sa
Wrangell, Alaska 43 Zm
Wrangell, Mt., Alaska 43 Yl
Wrath C., Scotland 58 Db
Wrexham, Wales 59 Fg
Wright, Philippines 79 Jh
Wrocław, Poland 65 Gc
Wubin, W. Aust. 52 Cf
Wuchang, China 78 Jb
Wuchang, China 81 Gg
Wuchih, Hainan Island 78 Eg
Wuchow, China 81 El
Wuchwan, China 80 Eb
Wudam, Muscat & Oman 89 Ge
Wuestwezel, Belgium 60 Cc
Wuhan, China 80 Gg
Wuhing. See Huchow
Wuhsien. See Soochow
Wuhu, China 80 Jg
Wukang, China 81 Ej
Wukari, Nigeria 95 Gg
Wukiang, China 80 Gd
Wu Kiang, R., China 78 Ee
Wular, L., Kashmir 86 Dc
Wuntho, Burma 85 Jd
Wuppertal, Germany 64 Bc
Wurttemberg, Germany 64 Cd
Wurung, Queensland 53 Hc
Wurzburg, Germany 64 Cd
Wurzen, Germany 64 Ec
Wusiang, China 80 Fd
Wusih, China 80 Kg
Wuti, China 80 Hd
Wutsin, China 80 Kg
Wuwei, China 80 Ad
Wu Yi Shan, China 81 Hj
Wuyüan, China 80 Db
Wuyun, China 78 Ja
Wyandotte, Michigan 40 Ed
Wyandra, Queensland 53 Je
Wye R., England 59 Fh
Wyk, Germany 64 Ca
Wyndham, New Zealand 51 Bg
Wyndham, W. Australia 52 Ec
Wynghene, Belgium 60 Bc
Wyoming, state, U.S.A. 42 Ec
Wyoming Pk., Wyoming 42 Dc
Wysokie Mazowieckie, Poland 65 Kb
Wyszkow, Poland 65 Jb
Xanthi, Greece 72 Ed
Xanxere, Brazil 50 Fc
Xapuri, Brazil 48 Df
Xeró. See Peristera I.
Xilókastron, Greece 73 De
Xingu, Brazil 48 De
Xique Xique, Brazil 49 Jf
Yaan, China 78 Dd
Yaate, Lebanon 90 Ec
Yablonovy Khrebet, Russia 75 Lc
Yabrud, Syria 90 Ed
Yagvildino, Russia 77 Nc
Yakhtul, Yemen 88 Dg
Yakima, Washington 45 Cb
Yako, Volta 94 Ef
Yakoma, Congo 92 Ed
Yaku Jima, Japan 82 Aj
Yaku Kaikyo. See Tanegashima Kaikyo
Yakutsk, Russia 75 Mb
Yale, Michigan 40 Ed
Yalgoo, W. Australia 52 Ce
Yalinga, Cent. Afr. Rep. 92 Ec
Yalouke, Cent. Afr. Rep. 92 Dc
Yalta, Russia 76 Jj
Yalu, China 78 Ha
Yalu R., China, etc. 78 Hb
Yalung R., China 78 Dd
Yalutorovsk, Russia 74 Fc
Yamada. See Ise
Yamagata, Japan 82 Fe
Yamaguchi, Japan 82 Bg
Yamal, Pol., Russia 74 Fa
Yambol, Bulgaria 72 Fc
Yamdok Tso, Tibet 85 Hc
Yamethin, Burma 85 Jd
Yampol, Ukraine 76 Fg
Yampol, Ukraine 76 Eg
Yamsk, Russia 75 Qc
Yamuna R., India 87 Aa
Yanam, India 85 Fe
Yanaoca, Peru 48 Cf
Yanbu 'al Bahr, Arabia 88 Ce
Yandoon, Burma 85 Je
Yangchow. See Kiangtu
Yangi Hissar, China 86 Ea
Yang-kao, China 80 Fb
Yangku. See Taiyuan
Yangtze Kiang, China 80 Eg
Yangyuan, China 80 Gb
Yankton, S. Dakota 42 Gc
Yannina. See Ioannina
Yaouiba, Bolivia 48 Eh
Yaoundé, Cameroon 95 Hh
Yap, I., Pacific Ocean 98 Cg
Yaraka, Queensland 53 Hd
Yarda, Chad 95 Je
Yarensk, Russia 74 Db
Yarim, Yemen 88 Dg
Yarkand, China 86 Ea
Yaroslavl, Russia 76 Lc
Yartsevo, Russia 75 Jb
Yarumal, Colombia 48 Bb
Yarylgach, Russia 76 Hj
Yasin, Kashmir 86 Cb
Yasothon, Siam 79 Dg
Yass, New S. Wales 53 Jf
Yatakala, Niger 94 Ff
Yatsushiro, Japan 82 Bh
Yatung, Tibet 85 Gc
Yauca, Peru 48 Cg
Yauri, Peru 48 Cf
Yautepec, Mexico 46 Ed
Yawata, Japan 82 Bh
Yazd, Persia 89 Fc
Yazdan, Persia 89 Hc
Yazd-e-Khrast, Persia 89 Fc
Ybbs, Austria 64 Fd
Ye, Burma 85 Je
Yecla, Spain 67 Ec
Yecora, Mexico 46 Cb
Yéfira, Greece 73 Dd
Yefremov, Russia 76 Le
Yehkiatsi, China 78 Gd
Yehpaishow, China 80 Jb
Yehsien, China 80 Jd
Yelabuga, Russia 77 Lc
Yelan, Russia 77 Fe
Yelatma, Russia 77 Ec
Yeldyak, Russia 77 Nc
Yelets, Russia 76 Le
Yelizarovo, Russia 74 Fb
Yell I. & Sd., Shetland 58 Ja
Yellandu, India 84 Fe
Yellow R. See Hwang Ho
Yellow Sea, China 80 Ke
Yellowstone, L., Wyoming 42 Dc
YellowstoneNat. Park, Wyo. 42 Dc
Yellowstone R., Montana 42 Eb
Yelwa, Nigeria 94 Ff
Yemanzhelinka, Russia 77 Qc
Yemen, S.-W. Asia 88 Df
Yenakiyevo, Ukraine 76 Lg
Yenan. See Fushih
Yenangyaung. See Kyaukpadating
Yen-Bay, N. Vietnam 83 Cb
Yenbo. See Yanbu 'al Bahr
Yencheng, China 80 Kf
Yenchih. See Mingshui
Yenchow. See Kienteh
Yenchow. See Tzeyang
Yenisey, R., Russia 74 Hb
Yeniseysk, Russia 75 Jc
Yeniseyskiy Zaliv, Russia 74 Ha
Yenkishih, China 78 Jb
Yenping. See Nanping
Yentai, China 80 Kd
Yeovil, England 59 Fk
Yeppoon, Qnsld. 53 Kd
Yeráki, Greece 73 Df
Yerbogachen, Russia 75 Kb
Yerevan, Armyanskaya 74 Dd
Yerofei Pavlovich, Russia 75 Mc
Yeropol, Russia 75 Rb
Yeshbum, S. Yemen 88 Eg
Yessey, Russia 75 Kb
Yeste, Spain 67 Dc
Yesud ha Ma'ala, Israel 90 Dd
Ye-u, Burma 85 Jd
Yeu, I. d', France 68 Bc
Yeungkong, China 78 Ff
Yeysk, Russia 74 Cd
Yhu, Paraguay 50 Ec
Yi, R., Uruguay 50 Ed
Yianisadhes Is., Crete 73 Fg
Yiannitsá, Greece 73 Dd
Yiáros. See Yioúra, I.
Yibna, Israel 90 Cf
Yidha, Greece 73 Dd
Yihsien, China 80 Gc
Yingchow. See Fowyang
Yingchwan, China 80 Cc
Yinghsien, China 80 Fc
Yingkisha. See Yangi Hissar
Yingkow, China 80 Lb
Yingtak, China 81 Fk
Yin Shan, China 80 Cb
Yioúra, I., Greece 73 Ef
Yithion, Greece 73 Df
Yitu, China 80 Jd
Yiyang, China 81 Fh
Yocalla, Bolivia 48 Dg
Yochow. See Yoyang
Yogovsk, Russia 77 Nb
Yokkaichi, Japan 82 Eg
Yoko, Cameroon 95 Hg
Yokohama, Japan 82 Fg
Yokosuku, Japan 82 Fg
Yokote, Japan 82 Ge
Yola, Nigeria 95 Hg
Yonago, Japan 82 Cg
Yone Zawa, Japan 82 Gf
Yonkers, New York 44 Db
Yonne, dep., France 68 Ec
York, England 59 Gg
York, Nebraska 42 Gc
York, Pennsylvania 44 Bc
York, W. Australia 52 Cf
York C., Greenland 41 Qb
York, C., Queensland 53 Hb
York Sd., W. Australia 52 Db
Yorke Pen., S. Australia 53 Gf
Yorkshire (Yorks), co., Eng. 59 Ff
Yorkshire Moors, England 59 Gf
Yorkshire Wolds, England 59 Gf
Yoro, Honduras 47 Bd
Yosemite Nat. Park, Cal. 45 Dg
Yoshkar Ola, Russia 77 Hb
Youghal & Harb., Eire 59 Bj
Youghiogheny River Res., Penn., etc. 44 Ac
Youkadouma, Cameroon 95 Jh
Young, N.S.W. 53 Jf
Young I., Balleny Islands 100 Lc
Youngstown, Ohio 40 Fe
Yoyang, China 81 Fh
Yozgat, Turkey 88 Bb
Ypres, Belgium 60 Ad
Ypsilanti, Michigan 40 Ed
Yreka, California 45 Be
Yssingeaux, France 69 Fd
Ystad, Sweden 63 Ej
Ytterhogdal, Sweden 62 Fe
Yüanchow. See Chihkiang
Yüanchow. See Ichun
Yüanling, China 81 Eh
Yubi C., Morocco 94 Cc
Yucamani, Mt., Peru 48 Cg
Yucatan, state, Mexico 46 Gc
Yucatan Chan., Mex.-Cuba 47 Bb
Yugoslavia, Cent. Europe 70 Fc
Yuhsien, China 80 Gc
Yuhwan, China 81 Kh
Yukhnov, Russia 76 Jd
Yukon, R., Alaska 43 Wl
Yuksekova, Turkey 88 Db
Yulin, China 80 Dc
Yulin, Hainan 81 Dn
Yuma, Arizona 42 De
Yumen, China 75 Jd
Yungchow. See Lingling
Yungfu, China 81 Ek
Yungki. See Kirin
Yungkia. See Wenchow
Yungnien, China 80 Gd
Yungning, China 81 Dl
Yungning, China 78 De
Yungping. See Lulung
Yungshun, China 81 Dh
Yungsin, China 81 Gj
Yungsui, China 81 Dh
Yungsui, China 81 Dh
Yungtsi, China 80 Ee
Yunhsien, China 80 Ef
Yunsi, China 80 Ef
Yurievets, Russia 77 Fb
Yurimaguas, Peru 48 Be
Yurlovka, Russia 77 Hd
Yurmysh, Russia 77 Rb
Yushu, China 78 Cd
Yuta, Jordan 90 Df
Yuti, Bolivia 48 Eg
Yütze, China 80 Fd
Yuyang, China 81 Dh
Yuyu, China 80 Fb
Yverdon, Switzerland 61 Bb
Zaachila, Mexico 46 Ed
Zaandam, Netherlands 60 Cb
Zabaykal'sk, Russia 75 Ld
Zabid, Yemen 88 Dg
Zabol, Persia 89 Hc
Zabrze, Poland 65 Hc
Zacapa, Guatemala 46 Ge
Zacapoaxtla, Mexico 46 Ed
Zacatecas & state, Mexico 46 Dc
Zader, Yugoslavia 70 Ec
Zadonsk, Russia 76 Le
Zafarwal, W. Pakistan 86 Dd
Zafra, Spain 66 Bc
Zagazig, Egypt 95 Mb
Zagreb, Yugoslavia 70 Ec
Zahedan, Persia 89 Hd
Zahle, Lebanon 90 Dd
Zahran, Arabia 88 Df
Zaidiya, Yemen 88 Df
Zainsk, Russia 77 Lc
Zaječar, Yugoslavia 72 Dc
Zakho, Iraq 88 Db
Zakin, Afghanistan 89 Hc
Zakinthos, I., Greece 73 Cf
Zakroczyn, Poland 65 Jb
Zákros, Crete 73 Fg
Zălău, Rumania 65 Ke
Zalew Wislany, Poland 65 Ha
Zalt Bommel, Netherlands 60 Dc
Zambezi R., S.-E. Africa 91 Ec
Zambia, Cent. Afr. 75 Db
Zamboanga, Philippines 79 Hj
Zamora, Ecuador 48 Bd
Zamora, Mexico 46 Dd
Zamora, Spain 66 Cb
Zandberg, Netherlands 60 Eb
Zandvoort, Netherlands 60 Cb
Zanesville, Ohio 40 Ef
Zangla, Kashmir 86 Ed
Zank, Muscat & Oman 89 Ge
Zante. See Zakinthos I.
Zanthus, W. Aust. 52 Df
Zanzibar & I., E. Africa 93 Hf
Zapala, Argentina 50 Be
Zapallar. See General José de San Martin
Zapata Pen., Cuba 47 Cb
Zaporozhye, Ukraine 76 Jh
Zara, Turkey 88 Cb
Zara. See Zader
Zaragoza, Colombia 48 Cb
Zaragoza, Mexico 46 Ec
Zaragoza, Spain 67 Eb
Zaragozo, Mexico 46 Db
Zarand, Persia 89 Gc
Zarasai, Lithuania 63 Mj
Zarauz, Spain 67 Da
Zaraza, Venezuela 48 Db
Zaria, Nigeria 94 Gf
Zarki, Poland 65 Hc
Zarnuqa, Arabia 88 Ed
Zarqa, Jordan 90 Ee
Zaruma, Ecuador 48 Bd
Zarzis, Tunisia 95 Hb
Zatec, Czechoslovakia 64 Ec
Zativinsk, Russia 75 Mc
Zawiercie, Poland 65 Hc
Zaysan, Kazakh. 74 Hd
Zaysan, Oz., Kazakh. 74 Hd
Zbaszyn, Poland 65 Fb
Zdúnska Wola, Poland 65 Hc
Zealand. See Sjælland
Zebak, Afghanistan 89 Kb
Zebdani, Syria 90 Ed
Zebid Qadhima, Arabia 88 Ce
Zeebrugge, Belgium 60 Bc
Zeeland, prov., Netherlands 60 Bc
Zeerust, Transvaal 91 De
Zegharta, Lebanon 90 Dc
Zeila, Somalia 93 Jb
Zeist, Netherlands 60 Db
Zeitz, Germany 64 Ec
Zele, Belgium 60 Cc
Zelenogradsk, Russia 63 Jj
Železná Ruda, Czech. 64 Ed
Zella, Libya 95 Jc
Zelman, Russia 77 Ge
Zelzate, Belgium 60 Bc
Zemio, Cent. Afr. Rep. 95 Lg
Zemun, Yugoslavia 72 Cb
Zenica, Yugoslavia 72 Ab
Zepce, Yugoslavia 72 Ab
Zermatt, Switzerland 61 Cb
Zernez, Switzerland 61 Fb
Zetland (Shetland), Scotland 58 Ja
Zevenbergen, Netherlands 60 Cc
Zeya, Russia 75 Mc
Zeyma, Arabia 88 De
Zgierz, Poland 65 Hc
Zgorzelec. See Görlitz
Zhdanov, Ukraine 76 Kh
Zhigansk, Russia 75 Mb
Zhitomir, Ukraine 76 Ff
Zhmerinka, Ukraine 76 Fg
Ziarat, W. Pakistan 84 Cb
Ziba. See Dhaba
Zidani Most, Yugoslavia 70 Eb
Zierikzee, Netherlands 60 Bc
Zijpe, Netherlands 60 Cc
Zikhron Ya'aqov, Israel 90 Ce
Zilaf, Syria 90 Fe
Zile, Turkey 88 Ca
Zilfi, Arabia 88 Dd
Zilina, Czechoslovakia 65 Hd
Zima, Russia 75 Kc
Zimapan, Mexico 46 Ec
Zindajan, Afghanistan 89 Hc
Zinder, Niger 95 Gf
Zingst, pen., Germany 64 Ea
Zion Nat. Park, Utah 45 Gg
Zipaquira, Colombia 48 Cb
Zira, India 86 De
Zirc, Hungary 65 Ge
Zitacuaro, Mexico 46 Dd
Zittau, Germany 64 Fc
Zizers, Switzerland 61 Eb
Zlatoust, Russia 77 Pc
Zmeinogorsk, Russia 74 Hc
Znin, Poland 65 Gb
Znojmo, Czechoslovakia 65 Gd
Zofingen, Switzerland 61 Ca
Zöhab, Persia 88 Ec
Zoisa, Tanzania 93 Hf
Zolder, Belgium 60 Dc
Zollino, Italy 71 Ge
Zomba, Malawi 93 Hh
Zonguldak, Turkey 88 Ba
Zorita, Spain 66 Cc
Zoute, le, Belgium 60 Bc
Zoutkamp, Netherlands 60 Ea
Zrenjanin, Yugoslavia 72 Cb
Zuara, Libya 95 Hb
Zuevka, Russia 77 Ka
Zug & canton, Switzerland 61 Da
Zuger See, Switzerland 61 Da
Zuid Beijerland, Netherlands 60 Cc
Zuider Zee. See Ijssel Meer
Zuidland, Netherlands 60 Cc
Zuidwolde, Netherlands 60 Eb
Zuila, Libya 95 Jc
Zukur, Jab., Yemen 88 Dg
Zula, Eritrea 93 Ha
Zulfikar, Afghanistan 89 Hb
Zumbo, Moçambique 91 Ec
Zumpango, Mexico 46 Ed
Zundert, Netherlands 60 Cc
Zungeru, Nigeria 94 Gg
Zürich & canton, Switz. 61 Da
Zürich See, Switzerland 61 Da
Zurzach, Switzerland 61 Da
Zutphen, Netherlands 60 Eb
Zwai L., Ethiopia 93 Hc
Zwartsluis, Netherlands 60 Eb
Zweelo, Netherlands 60 Eb
Zweibrucken, W. Germany 64 Bd
Zweisimmen, Switzerland 61 Cb
Zwickau, Germany 64 Ec
Zwoleń, Poland 65 Jc
Zwolle, Netherlands 60 Eb
Zyrardów, Poland 65 Jb
Zyryanka, Russia 75 Pb
Zyryanovsk, Kazakh. 74 Hd
Zyyi, Cyprus 90 Bc

TABLE OF DISTANCES

(STATUTE MILES)

	Vienna	Tokyo	Sydney	Singapore	San Francisco	Rome	Rio de Janeiro	Peking	Paris	Ottawa	Oslo	New York	Nairobi	Moscow	Madrid	London	Lisbon	Lagos	Johannesburg	Istanbul	Hong Kong	Hamburg	Geneva	Delhi	Darwin	Colombo	Cologne	Chicago	Cape Town	Canberra	Calcutta	Cairo	Buenos Aires	Brasilia	Bombay	Beirut	Bahamas (Nassau)	Baghdad
Athens	793	5,906	9,522	5,627	6,791	648	6,035	4,737	1,306	4,820	1,625	4,921	2,838	1,402	1,466	1,501	1,772	2,544	4,434	345	5,310	1,268	1,068	3,110	7,676	4,103	1,212	5,446	4,976	9,452	4,252	693	7,274	5,937	3,211	716	5,737	1,199
Baghdad	1,764	5,196	8,324	4,431	7,460	1,824	6,939	3,914	2,394	5,837	2,386	5,985	2,442	1,599	2,660	2,554	2,970	3,208	4,245	1,004	5,550	2,186	2,192	1,960	6,458	2,917	2,225	6,418	4,967	8,252	2,767	796	8,143	6,942	2,012	513	6,880	
Bahamas (Nassau)	5,126	7,596	9,477	10,613	2,761	5,072	4,025	7,868	4,486	1,404	4,670	1,096	7,779	5,673	4,301	4,335	4,102	5,454	7,879	5,879	9,070	4,740	4,692	8,364	10,399	9,783	4,666	1,297	7,492	9,590	9,037	6,418	4,318	3,457	8,792	6,449		
Beirut	1,390	5,594	8,813	4,934	7,299	1,361	6,481	4,336	1,981	5,483	2,123	5,604	2,430	1,533	2,180	2,163	2,484	2,786	4,173	614	5,752	1,849	1,761	2,470	6,998	3,388	1,847	6,090	4,811	8,739	3,279	350	7,700	6,458	2,698			
Bombay	3,703	4,183	6,312	2,432	8,392	3,831	8,339	2,945	4,353	7,569	4,129	7,786	2,819	3,139	4,671	4,481	4,981	4,737	4,327	2,995	2,672	4,057	4,173	709	4,508	949	4,151	8,042	5,116	6,246	1,035	2,698	9,287	8,546				
Brasilia	5,928	10,996	8,777	7,970	6,072	5,523	569	10,531	5,421	4,571	6,157	4,242	5,852	6,945	4,820	4,531	3,832	3,876	5,876	6,269	11,187	5,888	5,448	8,845	10,484	8,855	5,678	4,738	4,281	8,730	9,563	6,158	1,466					
Buenos Aires	7,358	11,403	7,311	9,863	6,465	6,945	1,213	12,001	6,878	5,639	7,624	5,303	6,473	8,388	6,266	6,919	5,985	4,933	5,044	7,616	11,467	7,348	6,892	9,815	9,117	9,167	7,135	5,624	4,279	7,272	10,279	7,366						
Cairo	1,470	5,939	8,950	5,129	7,458	1,321	6,153	4,678	1,992	5,508	2,271	5,602	2,203	1,809	2,080	2,195	2,365	2,443	3,893	763	5,048	1,946	1,755	2,736	7,206	3,513	1,900	6,137	4,507	8,863	3,533							
Calcutta	4,245	3,187	5,679	1,801	7,816	4,482	10,093	2,018	4,876	7,619	4,456	7,918	3,840	3,449	5,318	5,637	5,734	5,263	5,593	3,647	1,642	4,747	4,504	816	3,756	1,232	4,646	7,966	6,026	5,640								
Canberra	9,885	4,933	148	3,863	7,572	10,093	8,339	5,594	10,515	10,007	9,937	10,090	7,407	9,013	10,915	10,569	11,221	9,503	6,703	9,237	4,596	10,107	10,385	6,440	1,952	5,350	10,276	9,379	6,685									
Cape Town	5,673	9,147	6,830	6,001	10,252	5,251	3,784	8,040	5,803	8,026	6,503	7,804	2,548	6,313	5,339	6,010	5,333	2,974	790	5,224	7,372	6,074	5,597	5,769	6,962	4,890	5,903	8,520										
Chicago	4,701	6,307	9,233	9,355	1,851	4,826	5,309	6,585	4,140	651	4,044	723	8,022	4,956	4,192	3,945	3,997	5,980	8,712	5,476	7,788	4,249	4,385	7,472	9,345	8,977	4,248											
Cologne	463	5,809	10,292	6,441	5,600	677	5,942	4,860	247	3,072	639	3,765	4,008	1,284	883	331	1,149	3,069	5,475	1,239	5,729	227	323	3,862	8,334	5,102												
Colombo	4,658	4,261	5,430	1,698	9,047	4,739	8,508	3,208	5,295	8,530	5,098	8,755	3,019	4,106	5,569	5,416	5,247	4,141	3,916	2,523	5,019	5,105	1,513	3,746	4,571													
Darwin	8,008	3,365	1,960	2,079	7,652	8,238	9,970	3,727	8,583	9,683	7,990	9,983	6,466	7,062	9,070	8,619	8,847	7,404	6,602	2,656	2,833	8,151	8,480	4,571														
Delhi	3,448	3,640	6,483	2,580	7,692	3,669	8,740	2,352	4,091	7,055	3,724	7,304	3,366	2,702	4,509	4,183	4,828	4,980	5,019	2,833	2,344	3,732	3,946															
Geneva	507	6,094	10,425	6,523	5,823	444	5,680	5,104	245	3,754	962	3,852	3,782	1,498	627	468	929	2,745	5,189	1,190	5,918	540																
Hamburg	476	5,584	10,114	6,306	5,523	826	6,160	4,645	459	3,652	433	3,801	4,100	1,096	1,107	463	1,366	3,273	5,619	1,236	5,536																	
Hong Kong	5,418	1,787	4,585	1,606	6,900	5,764	10,998	1,213	5,986	8,055	5,441	8,054	4,444	6,540	5,993	5,986	6,847	7,357	6,661	4,989																		
Istanbul	779	5,575	9,297	5,383	6,709	843	6,377	4,394	1,393	4,872	1,522	5,003	2,966	1,106	1,686	1,562	2,003	2,849	4,637																			
Johannesburg	5,181	8,414	6,851	5,378	10,552	4,799	4,433	7,259	5,414	8,132	6,028	7,972	1,809	5,698	5,034	5,638	5,093	2,811																				
Lagos	2,971	8,380	9,647	6,935	7,801	2,494	3,745	7,119	2,913	5,363	3,704	5,249	2,381	3,886	2,380	3,109	2,359																					
Lisbon	1,432	6,931	11,294	7,385	5,669	1,161	4,794	6,009	894	3,345	1,694	3,441	4,023	2,419	319	972																						
London	791	5,959	10,575	6,760	5,354	908	5,750	5,077	215	3,323	723	3,441	4,250	1,565	774																							
Madrid	1,122	6,699	10,980	7,068	5,800	844	5,062	5,729	641	3,541	1,474	3,580	3,848	2,126																								
Moscow	1,033	4,656	9,020	5,249	5,862	1,491	7,169	3,607	1,542	4,437	1,012	4,660	3,944																									
Nairobi	3,624	6,992	7,541	4,631	9,600	3,346	5,553	5,719	4,026	7,369	4,456	7,352																										
New York	4,227	6,747	9,949	9,534	2,580	4,281	4,804	6,842	3,621	328	3,668																											
Oslo	848	5,237	9,918	6,251	5,189	1,253	6,486	4,374	822	3,480																												
Ottawa	4,095	6,427	9,863	9,213	2,440	4,176	5,131	6,509	3,518																													
Paris	648	6,037	10,534	6,666	5,578	689	5,688	5,116																														
Peking	4,636	1,308	5,558	2,770	5,922	5,068	10,764																															
Rio de Janeiro	6,136	11,538	8,403	9,781	6,612	5,713																																
Rome	477	6,135	10,137	6,224	6,250																																	
San Francisco	5,997	5,148	7,424	8,445																																		
Singapore	6,027	3,296	3,915																																			
Sydney	9,923	4,858																																				
Tokyo	5,681																																					

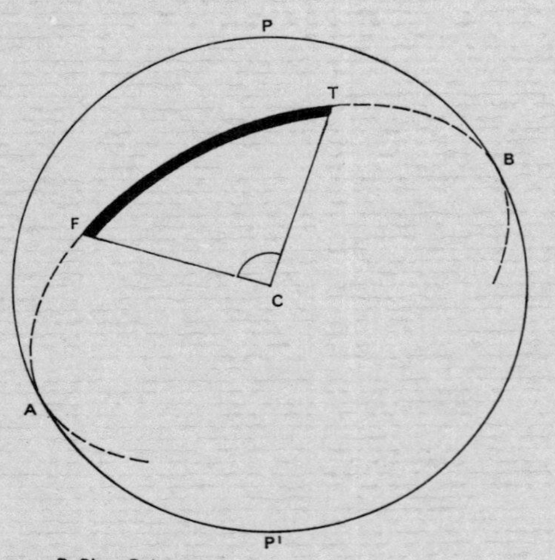

P, P' = Poles
C = Centre of Earth
AB = Great Circle
FT = Two points on Great Circle AB. Thick line is the shortest distance between F and T

GREAT CIRCLE DISTANCES

Our Chart shows the shortest distance between any two places, calculated by the "great circle" method.

A great circle described on the surface of a globe is a circle which divides the globe into two exactly equal parts. If two points are marked on the globe and a great circle is described so as to pass through both points (and only one great circle can do so), then the length of the shorter of the two arcs of this great circle which lie between the two points is the shortest distance that can be measured between them. By using this method, the shortest distance between any two places on the Earth can be calculated.

On the various map projections in this Atlas, the great circle will appear in different shapes: it is important to appreciate the properties of the particular map in use if a great circle distance is to be measured from it.

A close degree of accuracy in obtaining a great circle distance can be achieved by the solution of a spherical trigonometry problem, the sides and angles of the triangle being made up from the relevant values from the sphere.

A great circle is the path of the rays detected by radio direction finders. All meridians are great circles.

WEATHER CHART

HOW HOT IS IT? Average monthly temperatures — in degrees Fahrenheit at sea-level												Height in feet above sea-level		HOW WET IS IT? Average monthly rainfall — in inches												
JAN	FEB	MAR	APR	MAY	JUNE	JULY	AUG	SEP	OCT	NOV	DEC			JAN	FEB	MAR	APR	MAY	JUNE	JULY	AUG	SEP	OCT	NOV	DEC	Total for year
−18·0	−16·5	−8·5	8·5	31·0	49·0	56·5	50·0	38·0	20·0	−3·0	−16·0	30	Aklavik	·5	·5	·4	·5	·5	·8	1·4	1·4	·9	·9	·8	·4	9·0
83·5	82·0	76·5	67·5	59·5	54·0	53·0	58·0	65·0	73·0	78·5	82·0	1,901	Alice Springs	1·7	1·3	1·1	·4	·6	·5	·3	·3	·3	·7	1·2	1·5	9·9
48·0	49·0	53·0	59·5	68·5	76·0	81·0	81·0	74·5	67·0	58·0	51·5	351	Athens	2·2	1·6	1·4	·8	·8	·6	·2	·4	·6	1·7	2·8	2·8	15·9
49·5	53·0	59·5	71·0	82·0	89·0	93·0	93·0	87·0	76·5	64·0	53·0	111	Baghdad	·9	1·0	1·1	·5	·1	<·1	<·1	<·1	<·1	·1	·8	1·0	5·5
77·1	70·5	72·5	75·0	77·5	80·5	81·5	82·5	81·5	79·0	75·5	73·0	12	Bahamas (Nassau)	1·4	1·5	1·4	2·5	4·6	6·4	5·8	5·3	6·9	6·5	2·8	1·3	46·4
56·5	57·0	60·0	65·0	71·0	76·0	80·0	81·5	79·5	75·0	67·0	60·0	111	Beirut	7·5	6·2	3·7	2·2	·7	·1	<·1	<·1	·2	2·0	5·2	7·3	35·1
75·0	75·0	79·0	82·5	85·5	84·0	81·0	80·5	80·5	82·5	81·0	78·0	37	Bombay	·1	·1	·1	<·1	·7	19·1	24·3	13·4	10·4	2·5	·5	·1	71·2
74·0	73·0	69·5	62·5	55·5	49·0	49·5	51·5	55·0	59·5	66·0	71·5	89	Buenos Aires	3·1	2·8	4·3	3·5	3·0	2·4	2·2	2·4	3·1	3·4	3·3	3·9	37·4
56·0	58·5	63·5	70·0	77·0	81·5	83·0	83·0	79·0	75·5	68·0	59·0	381	Cairo	·2	·2	·2	·1	·1	<·1	0	0	<·1	<·1	·1	·2	1·1
67·5	71·5	81·0	86·0	86·5	85·5	84·0	83·5	84·0	81·5	74·0	67·0	21	Calcutta	·4	1·2	1·4	1·7	5·5	11·7	12·8	12·9	9·9	4·5	·8	·2	63·0
68·5	68·5	63·5	55·5	48·5	43·5	42·5	45·0	49·5	55·5	61·5	66·5	1,837	Canberra	1·9	1·7	2·2	1·6	1·8	2·1	1·8	2·2	1·6	2·2	1·9	2·0	23·0
69·0	69·5	67·5	62·5	58·0	55·5	54·0	55·0	57·0	61·0	64·0	67·0	56	Cape Town	·6	·3	·7	1·9	3·1	3·3	3·5	2·6	1·7	1·2	·7	·4	20·0
65·5	66·5	68·5	70·5	71·0	70·0	69·5	70·0	70·5	70·0	68·5	68·0	3,418	Caracas	·9	·4	·6	1·3	3·1	4·0	4·3	4·3	4·2	4·3	3·7	1·8	32·9
73·0	73·5	73·5	72·5	69·5	67·0	68·0	70·0	73·0	74·0	73·5	72·5	2,723	Catalão	11·8	10·2	8·8	3·8	1·1	·3	·5	·3	2·3	6·1	8·3	14·9	68·4
25·0	27·0	36·0	47·5	57·5	67·5	73·5	72·0	65·5	54·0	40·5	29·5	823	Chicago	2·0	2·0	2·6	2·8	3·4	3·5	3·3	3·2	3·1	2·6	2·4	2·0	32·9
61·5	61·0	58·0	53·5	48·0	43·5	42·5	44·0	48·5	53·0	56·5	60·0	32	Christchurch, N.Z.	2·2	1·7	1·9	1·9	2·6	2·6	2·7	1·9	1·8	1·7	1·9	2·2	25·1
36·0	38·0	43·0	49·5	57·5	62·5	65·5	64·5	59·0	51·0	43·0	38·0	184	Cologne	2·0	1·8	1·8	1·9	2·0	2·6	3·2	2·8	2·1	2·5	2·2	2·5	27·4
79·0	79·5	81·0	82·0	82·5	81·0	81·0	81·0	81·0	80·0	79·0	78·5	24	Colombo	3·5	3·5	5·8	9·1	14·6	8·8	5·3	4·3	6·3	13·7	12·4	5·8	93·1
83·5	83·5	84·0	84·0	82·0	78·5	77·0	79·5	82·5	85·0	86·0	85·0	97	Darwin	15·2	12·3	10·0	3·8	·6	·1	<·1	·1	·5	2·0	4·7	9·4	58·7
57·0	62·0	72·5	82·0	92·0	92·5	88·5	86·0	84·0	79·0	68·0	59·5	714	Delhi	·9	·7	·5	·3	·5	2·9	7·1	6·8	4·6	·4	·1	·4	25·2
61·0	60·5	61·0	62·5	64·5	67·5	70·5	71·5	71·5	69·5	66·0	62·5	82	Funchal, Madeira	2·5	2·9	3·1	1·3	·7	·2	<·1	<·1	1·0	3·0	3·5	3·3	21·5
34·0	36·5	43·0	49·5	57·0	64·0	67·5	66·5	60·5	51·0	42·0	35·5	1,329	Geneva	1·9	1·8	2·2	2·5	3·0	3·1	2·9	3·6	3·6	2·8	3·1	2·4	32·9
63·0	62·5	62·5	65·0	70·0	75·0	79·0	80·0	78·0	74·0	68·5	65·0	151	Hamilton, Bermuda	4·4	4·7	4·8	4·1	4·6	4·4	4·5	5·4	5·2	5·8	5·0	4·7	57·6
−5·5	−5·0	6·0	18·0	31·5	40·0	47·0	48·0	40·5	31·0	20·0	4·0	49	Hebron, Labrador	·9	·7	·9	1·1	1·6	2·1	2·7	2·7	3·3	1·6	1·1	·6	19·3
60·0	59·0	63·5	71·0	78·0	81·5	82·5	82·5	81·0	77·0	69·5	63·5	109	Hong Kong	1·3	1·8	2·9	5·4	11·5	15·5	15·0	14·2	10·1	4·5	1·7	1·2	85·1
40·5	42·0	45·5	53·0	60·5	68·5	73·0	73·5	68·0	60·5	53·5	46·0	59	Istanbul	3·7	2·3	2·6	1·9	1·4	1·3	1·7	1·5	2·3	3·8	4·1	4·9	31·5
48·0	49·0	55·5	61·5	69·0	72·5	75·0	75·5	73·5	70·0	61·5	52·0	2,485	Jerusalem	5·2	5·2	2·5	1·1	·1	<·1	0	0	<·1	·5	2·8	3·4	20·8
68·0	67·5	65·0	61·0	54·5	50·5	51·0	55·5	60·5	65·0	66·0	67·5	5,463	Johannesburg	4·5	4·3	3·5	1·5	1·0	·3	·3	·3	·9	2·2	4·2	4·9	27·9
81·0	83·0	83·5	83·0	81·5	79·5	78·5	77·5	78·5	79·5	81·5	81·5	10	Lagos	1·1	1·8	4·0	5·9	10·6	18·1	11·0	2·5	5·5	8·1	2·7	1·0	72·3
74·0	75·0	74·5	71·5	67·0	63·0	62·0	61·0	62·5	64·5	67·0	70·0	394	Lima	<·1	<·1	<·1	<·1	·2	·2	·3	·3	·3	·1	·1	<·1	1·6
75·5	75·5	74·5	72·5	66·5	61·0	61·0	66·0	74·5	80·5	79·0	76·5	3,161	Livingstone	5·7	6·0	4·3	1·0	·3	·1	0	<·1	·1	·9	2·9	5·2	26·5
39·5	40·0	44·0	48·0	54·0	60·0	64·0	63·0	59·0	51·0	44·0	40·5	149	London	2·0	1·5	1·4	1·8	1·8	1·6	2·0	2·2	1·8	2·3	2·5	2·0	22·9
55·5	56·5	57·5	60·0	62·5	66·0	70·5	71·0	69·5	65·0	61·5	51·0	312	Los Angeles	3·1	3·0	2·8	1·0	·4	·1	<·1	<·1	·2	·6	1·2	2·6	15·0
49·5	51·0	53·5	57·5	64·0	70·5	75·0	76·5	72·5	65·5	57·5	51·5	75	Majorca	1·4	1·6	1·5	1·3	1·3	1·0	·1	·8	2·5	2·8	2·8	2·2	19·4
54·0	56·0	61·0	64·0	66·0	65·5	63·0	63·5	63·5	60·0	57·0	54·5	7,575	Mexico City	·5	·2	·4	·8	2·1	4·7	6·7	6·0	5·1	2·0	·7	·3	29·5
67·5	68·0	71·0	73·5	77·5	80·0	82·0	82·0	81·0	77·5	72·0	69·0	25	Miami	2·8	2·1	2·5	3·2	6·8	7·0	6·1	6·3	8·0	9·2	2·8	2·0	58·8
81·0	81·5	82·5	81·0	78·5	77·5	76·0	76·0	77·0	79·0	80·0	80·5	52	Mombasa	1·0	·7	2·5	7·7	12·6	4·7	3·5	2·5	2·5	3·4	3·8	2·4	47·3
15·0	16·5	24·5	39·0	54·5	62·0	65·5	62·0	52·0	40·0	27·0	18·0	505	Moscow	1·5	1·4	1·1	1·9	2·2	2·9	3·0	2·9	1·9	2·7	1·7	1·6	24·8
65·5	67·0	67·0	66·5	64·0	61·5	60·0	61·0	63·5	65·5	65·0	64·5	5,971	Nairobi	1·5	2·5	4·9	8·3	6·2	1·8	·6	·9	1·2	2·1	4·3	3·4	37·7
54·5	57·5	63·0	69·0	75·5	81·0	83·0	83·0	79·5	71·5	62·5	56·0	8	New Orleans	4·6	4·2	4·7	4·8	4·5	5·5	6·6	5·8	4·8	3·5	3·8	4·6	57·4
30·5	31·0	37·5	49·5	60·5	68·5	74·0	73·0	69·5	59·0	44·0	35·0	314	New York	3·7	3·8	3·6	3·2	3·2	3·3	4·2	4·3	3·4	3·5	3·0	3·6	42·8
25·0	26·0	32·5	42·0	52·5	60·0	64·5	61·0	52·5	43·0	33·0	27·5	308	Oslo	1·7	1·3	1·4	1·6	1·8	2·4	2·9	3·8	2·5	2·9	2·3	2·3	26·9
12·0	12·5	25·5	41·0	55·0	65·0	69·5	66·0	58·0	45·5	32·5	16·5	339	Ottawa	2·9	2·2	2·8	2·7	2·5	3·5	3·4	2·6	3·2	2·9	3·0	2·6	34·3
37·0	39·0	44·0	50·5	57·0	62·5	65·5	65·0	59·5	51·5	43·5	38·0	164	Paris	1·5	1·3	1·5	1·7	2·0	2·1	2·1	2·0	2·0	2·2	2·0	1·9	22·3
74·0	74·0	71·0	66·5	61·0	57·0	55·5	56·0	58·5	61·5	66·5	71·0	197	Perth, W. Australia	·3	·4	·8	1·7	5·1	7·1	6·7	5·7	3·4	2·2	·8	·5	34·7
78·5	79·0	77·5	74·5	71·5	70·0	69·0	70·0	70·0	71·5	73·5	76·5	201	Rio de Janeiro	4·9	4·8	5·1	4·2	3·1	2·1	1·6	1·7	2·6	3·1	4·1	5·4	42·7
64·0	63·5	61·5	56·5	51·0	47·5	45·5	47·0	50·5	54·5	57·5	61·5	980	Rotorua	4·4	4·1	3·5	4·6	5·5	5·3	4·9	5·0	4·8	4·9	4·3	3·7	55·0
46·5	47·5	52·0	57·0	64·5	71·0	76·0	76·0	72·0	63·0	54·5	48·5	377	Rome	2·7	2·3	1·5	1·7	2·0	1·0	·6	·9	2·7	3·7	3·8	2·8	25·7
23·5	22·0	27·5	35·5	42·5	52·5	59·5	61·0	54·5	46·5	37·0	29·0	243	St. John's, Newfoundland	5·3	4·9	4·6	4·2	3·6	3·5	3·5	3·7	3·8	5·3	5·9	5·5	53·8
50·0	53·0	54·5	56·5	57·0	59·0	59·0	59·0	62·0	61·0	57·0	52·0	52	San Francisco	4·7	3·8	3·1	1·5	·7	·1	<·1	<·1	·3	1·0	2·5	4·4	22·1
34·5	37·0	40·5	48·5	58·5	67·0	72·0	71·5	64·0	56·5	44·5	39·0	75	Sevastopol	1·1	1·1	1·1	·9	·6	1·1	·8	·6	1·1	1·5	1·2	1·1	12·2
79·5	80·5	81·5	81·5	82·0	81·5	81·5	81·0	81·0	80·5	80·5	80·5	33	Singapore	9·9	6·8	7·6	7·4	6·8	6·8	6·7	7·7	7·0	8·2	10·0	10·1	95·0
71·5	71·5	69·5	64·5	59·0	54·5	53·0	55·5	59·0	63·5	67·0	70·0	138	Sydney	3·5	4·0	5·0	5·3	5·0	4·6	4·6	3·0	2·9	2·8	2·9	2·9	46·5
53·5	54·5	56·5	58·0	63·5	68·0	72·0	73·5	70·5	65·5	58·5	54·5	239	Tangier	4·5	4·2	4·8	3·5	1·7	·6	<·1	<·1	·9	3·9	5·8	5·4	35·3
24·5	30·0	41·5	56·5	68·5	77·5	81·5	79·5	70·5	58·0	41·0	28·5	13	Tientsin	·2	·1	·4	·5	1·1	2·4	7·4	6·0	1·7	·6	·4	·2	21·0
38·0	39·5	45·0	54·5	62·5	69·5	76·5	79·0	72·5	62·0	51·5	42·5	19	Tokyo	1·9	2·9	4·2	5·3	5·8	6·5	5·6	6·0	9·2	8·2	3·8	2·2	61·6
64·0	64·0	62·0	59·5	56·5	54·0	53·5	54·0	55·0	57·5	60·5	62·5	135	Valparaiso, Chile	·1	<·1	·3	·6	4·1	5·9	3·9	2·9	1·3	·4	·2	·2	19·9
36·5	39·0	43·5	49·0	55·0	60·5	64·0	63·5	57·0	50·5	43·5	39·0	45	Vancouver	8·6	5·8	5·0	3·3	2·8	2·5	1·2	1·7	3·6	5·8	·8·3	8·8	57·4
30·0	33·0	40·5	49·0	58·0	63·5	67·0	65·5	59·0	49·5	40·0	33·5	664	Vienna	1·5	1·4	1·8	2·0	2·8	2·7	3·0	2·7	2·0	2·0	1·9	1·8	25·6
−3·0	1·5	16·0	37·5	52·0	62·0	67·0	63·5	54·0	41·0	21·5	6·0	786	Winnipeg	·9	·9	1·2	1·4	2·3	3·1	3·1	2·5	2·3	1·5	1·1	·9	21·2

< = less than

THE READER'S DIGEST GREAT WORLD ATLAS

SECOND EDITION

Published by

THE READER'S DIGEST ASSOCIATION (CANADA) LIMITED
215 Redfern Avenue, Montreal 6, Quebec

THE READER'S DIGEST ASSOCIATION LIMITED
25 Berkeley Square, London, W.1, and Parkade, Strand Street, Cape Town

THE READER'S DIGEST ASSOCIATION PTY. LIMITED
Reader's Digest Building, 26-32 Waterloo Street, Surry Hills, Sydney

Printing and Binding by

JOHN BARTHOLOMEW & SON LTD., EDINBURGH   BROWN KNIGHT & TRUSCOTT LTD., TONBRIDGE

HAZELL WATSON & VINEY LTD., AYLESBURY   CURWEN PRESS LTD., LONDON   BEN JOHNSON & CO. LTD., YORK

Relief maps, pages 8-28, 114-115 © Geographical Projects Limited, London, 1961

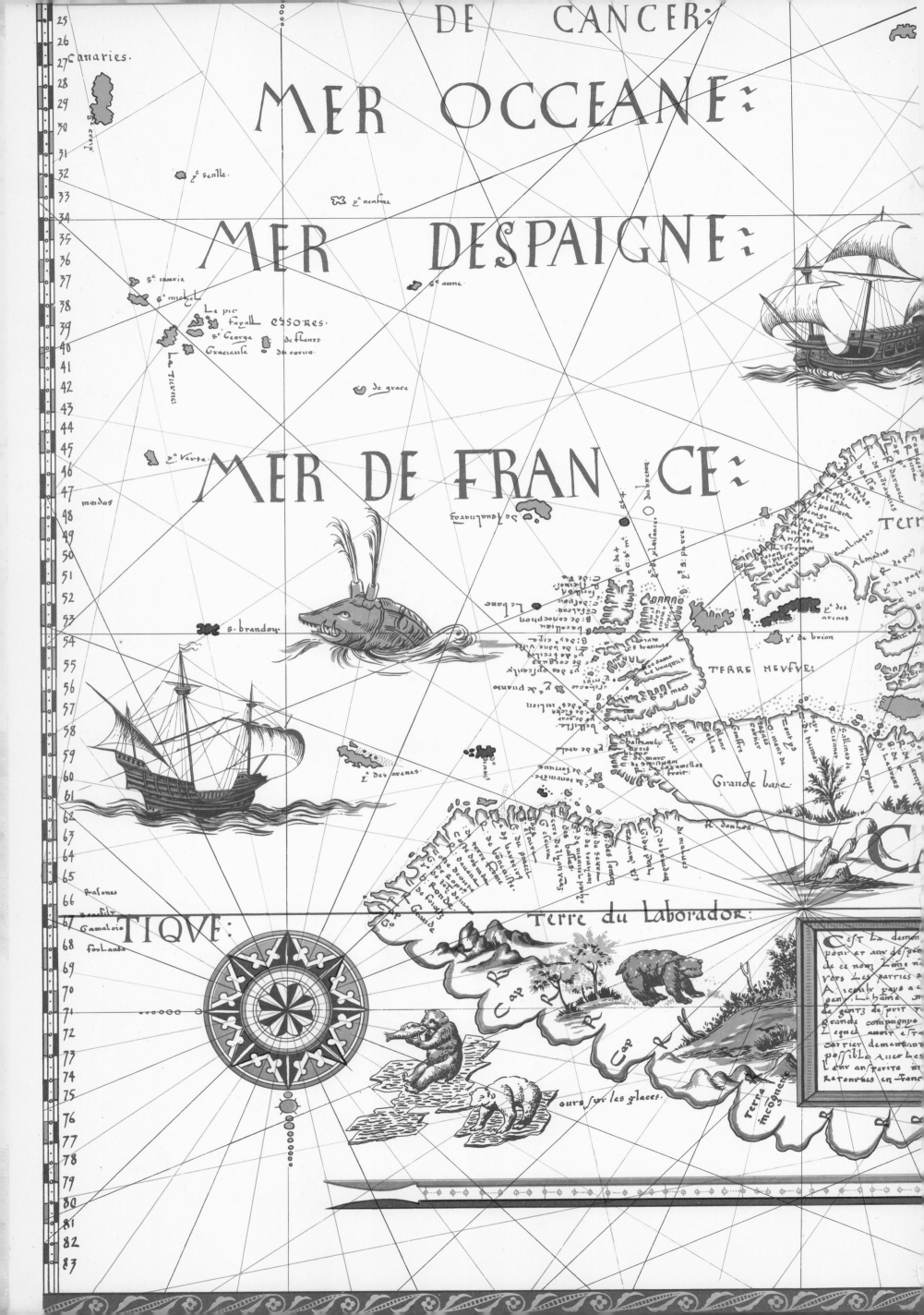

DE CANCER:

MER OCCEANE:

MER DESPAIGNE:

MER DE FRAN CE:

TERRE NEVFVE:

Grande bane.

Terre du Laborador:

TIQVE:

ours sur les glaces.